REUBEN DENTON NEVIUS

A GENTLEMAN OF THE OLD SCHOOL:

Reuben Denton Nevius

1827–1913

BOTANIST

BUILDER

TEACHER

CHURCHMAN

☩

by

DAVID W. POWERS III *and* GREGORY L. NELSON

To Julianne—
I hope you enjoy this
obscure bit of Northwest
history. Best wishes
Greg

Book design by Kathy Campbell

Cover photo of Reuben Denton Nevius courtesy of the Library of the Gray
Herbarium, Harvard University, Cambridge, Massachusetts, USA.

DEDICATED TO THE MEMORY OF

DAVID W. POWERS III

1942-1994

MAY IT BE A LASTING MEMORIAL TO HIM AS

SCHOLAR, HISTORIAN, SON, BROTHER AND FRIEND.

David W. Powers III

PREFACE

THIS BOOK IS ABOUT A REMARKABLE MAN, Reuben Nevius, who lived in a remarkable age. He started out as a priest in the Protestant Episcopal Church, and spent the first twenty years of his ministry serving various churches. It was then, at age 47, that he began his great missionary work. He went on to found at least thirty congregations, building churches or starting church building funds at each location. His impact on Oregon and Washington in their infancy was enormous, and he was almost single-handedly responsible for the penetration of the Episcopal church in Eastern Oregon, Western Idaho, and the State of Washington. When he arrived in the Northwest transportation was mainly by boat, horseback, or wagon (when roads were available).

Throughout his career Nevius maintained a dedicated interest in botany. He was in the forefront of the field in America, corresponding regularly with Asa Gray, the "Father of Botany in America." Nevius collected specimens wherever he went, sending many of them back to Gray at Harvard. As a result at least five plants were named for him, and he became well known throughout the botanical world. Wherever he went he carried with him his pocket microscope, slides and magic lantern, giving lectures whenever there was the slightest hint of a ready audience. He taught botany in schools and privately in homes. He amassed a large library of books, and, if he was not able to take them with him when he moved, would give them freely away to friends and fellow clergy.

The story of Nevius's career is necessarily also the story of the early church in the Northwest. Four of the bishops with whom he worked are highlighted here, three as pioneers and active encouragers of Nevius, and one as a fellow missionary and close friend. In addition, a brief history of those churches for which Nevius's connection could be documented are included. Wherever possible, pictures of the churches as they existed in Nevius's day are shown as well as modern views of the twenty-two churches that still stand today.

Nevius worked tirelessly throughout his life to further the church. He spent over 40 years in the Northwest, and for most of those years was actively conducting services and whenever possible starting congregations. His first missionary church was built when he was 47, and his last completed when he was 78. He was still traveling and "tending his flock" in his 86th year. He certainly was a man who deserves to be recognized today, as he was in his own day, as a builder, architect, scholar, teacher, priest and warm friend to thousands of early settlers in the Northwest.

ACKNOWLEDGEMENTS

DAVID W. POWERS III's untimely death interrupted his efforts to complete his book about Nevius. David was raised in the Episcopal Church in Ontario, Oregon, and from his youth was exposed to the Nevius churches. He attended youth camps at Cove, where Ascension Church became a lifelong favorite retreat. He gained his appreciation of the Gothic style wood churches probably long before he entered the University of Oregon School of Architecture and Allied Arts. His serious interest in Nevius and his churches must date from about 1976, when, as grants manager for the State Historic Preservation Office, he had a role in reviewing the federally assisted restoration of St. Thomas Church in Canyon City. He wrote a paper on the eastern Oregon Nevius churches, and became fascinated by the life of Nevius. After his death in San Francisco, his ashes were interred at Ascension Church, a return to his peaceful retreat and an eternal connection with his passion for the Nevius churches.

David began seriously working on this book over fifteen years ago, when he pursued the design of the "Nevius Churches" of eastern Oregon. He started out to discover whether Nevius had actually designed the churches attributed to him. In the course of his studies, he amassed boxes full of information on Nevius and his life work. David wrote in preface to a paper on the Oregon Nevius churches: "Two persons other than myself have contributed to the research for this paper. In the early 1950s Howland Atwood, then with the Huntington Library in San Marino, California, assembled a body of material about Reuben Nevius's early life and his scientific attainments. At the same time the Rev. Albert Allen, then rector of St. Thomas' Episcopal Church in Canyon City, Oregon, also collected material about Nevius and interviewed people who remembered him. Mr. Allen most graciously loaned me his notes and a copy of Mr. Atwood's material. I have supplemented this with information about Nevius's Oregon and Washington years as well as detail about his early life."

David also listed as people meriting a mention of thanks the following people: Marion Dean Ross; Philip Dole; Elisabeth Walton Potter; Ruth Farnham; Peggy Hansen; Louis Perkins; David Talbot—who has long awaited this work; Kenyon Chambers; OSU; The Rev. Chandler C. Jackson, Historiographer; and The Rev. Irene Martin (Cathlamet, Washington). He also received assistance and encouragement from Jean S. Eastman of Ovid, New York.

David worked hard on this book, and he may have had it almost complete when he resigned his position as Deputy Oregon State Historic Preservation Officer, and Manager, Oregon Historic Preservation Office, in 1990. He told me that one of his goals was to take the time to complete this book. When his life was tragically cut short in San Francisco in January of 1994, his laptop computer was stolen, and may have contained an almost final version. David and I were fraternity brothers and roommates at Willamette University, and he named me as his executor. After taking care of his worldly affairs, I determined to find someone to complete this book. Following over four years of searching, I decided to take on the challenge myself. I was ill-prepared to complete it, but have grown to a level of excitement that almost equals that which David had attained. Nevius was truly a fascinating "Renaissance Man" of the 19th and 20th centuries, and his accomplishments are remarkable.

In completing this work, I must thank first David's parents, David "Tip" and Betty Lou Powers. They have been an inspiration and a comfort to me since college days, and continue to be. The tragic loss of their son, David (the fifth of that name in the Powers family) was a mighty blow from which they are still recovering. I count it a small favor to complete this work as a comfort to them, and to share all of David's wonderful research with the rest of the world. I also thank David's sisters, Pamela Powers Looney, and Dianne Powers Winder. Without the encouragement and support of the family I would not attempt to complete this.

I have also found others who have been a great help in expanding and completing this book. I thank Diane Wells, Archivist of the Diocese of Olympia in Seattle for her tremendous help and support. I also thank Randy Burton from Holy Trinity in Juneau. He responded to my email with vigor and soon had compiled articles from the local papers of 1895 and 1896 that brought to light Nevius's activity there. John Larson, from the Polson Museum in Hoquiam was a great help on the churches of his area. Mary Redman of Bellingham, Carol Erickson of Blaine, and especially Martha Olson of the Foothills Historical Society Museum in Buckley were very helpful as well. Heather Heard reviewed the botany section for technical accuracy. Elisabeth Walton Potter was of invaluable help in looking over the rough draft and making excellent suggestions. Many people in local libraries, museums and churches were very kind and helpful in my research. Last but by far from least I thank my wife, Linda, whose tolerance of my many projects and abiding love give me the strength to take on things I have no business doing such as this book.

In writing the book I had the records David had stored in his older, desktop, computer, and most of his research materials. David had completed the first 23 pages of the biography of Nevius. He had done great work on the Oregon churches, and research on some of the Washington ones. Readers may find references in these sections which might normally call for a footnote. Where I have known David's source or where he has so capably footnoted his text you will find one. In some cases the reference is unknown to me. He had completed a rough draft of his "biographical notes," which contained a summation of all the sources he uncovered in his research. When I determined to include his writing on the Oregon churches, I also set out to find or create short histories on all the others. In writing about Nevius I found that his life was closely tied to that of four of his bishops, and I included them to round out the picture. I do not know what David's final publication would have looked like, but I feel that I have preserved the best of his writing on the subject and expanded it to be somewhat similar to the book he would have done. I hope the final product would have pleased him, but most of all I hope that it will further the knowledge of a wonderful man, Reuben Nevius, whose contribution to the Northwest has almost been lost with the passage of time.

—Gregory L. Nelson
Keizer, Oregon 2001

Table of Contents

CHAPTER I

BIOGRAPHICAL PORTRAIT

Reuben Denton Nevius was born on a farm in the Finger Lakes Region of central New York State on November 26, 1827. After graduating from Union College, Schenectady, in 1848, he went to Michigan for a year to teach school, and then to Georgia. While there he decided to enter the ministry of the Episcopal church. He was ordained a deacon in 1852 and a priest in 1853. He settled at Tuscaloosa, Alabama, in 1855, where he remained throughout the Civil War.

While at Tuscaloosa two motivating interests emerged which would distinguish Nevius's life. One was a special interest in missionary work, at first among the "slave population." The other was a passion for the newly popular science of botany. As the country was opening up to scientific travel new plants and species were being regularly discovered. He began a correspondence with pioneer botanist Dr. Asa Gray at Harvard University, which would continue over the next four decades.

After the Civil War Nevius married a longtime sweetheart and moved to Oil City, Pennsylvania. Then he went to Mobile, Alabama, where his wife and children died of yellow fever in the summer of 1870, a few months after he had been granted a Doctor of Divinity degree by the College of William and Mary.

In early 1872 Nevius accepted a call from Trinity Church in Portland, Oregon, but the following year he volunteered for "circuit rider" missionary duty in the new towns of Eastern Oregon. By 1876 he had established congregations and erected churches in La Grande, Baker City, Union, The Dalles, Cove and Canyon City, designing the buildings at Union, The Dalles and Canyon City himself.

Nevius moved to eastern Washington in 1879 and then to western Washington in 1884, continuing to establish congregations and to build churches into the 1890s. He died at Tacoma on December 14, 1913. Highly revered and widely loved for his wisdom, wit, and charm, his obituary was carried in the *New York Times.*

During his lifetime Nevius served more than 38 congregations and was involved with the building of at least 17 church buildings. Six plants and mosses were named after him, including *Chaenactis nevii*, a member of the sunflower family found only in the vicinity of Oregon's John Day Valley. In later years he became especially interested in the study of microscopic organisms and diatoms, delighting to call himself "a diatomaniac."

PARENTS

Benjamin Hageman Nevius (father), b. June 2, 1802 (some sources give 1803); m. Mary Denton, 1826; d. Ovid, N.Y., October 10, 1830 (age 28 yrs. 4 mos.).

Mary Denton Nevius (mother), b. September 11, 1805; m. Benjamin Hageman Nevius 1826; m. Chester D. Eastman (b. 1794, d. 1879) 1832; d. Ovid, N.Y., June 7, 1900 (age 94 yrs 9 mos.).

SIBLINGS

John Livingston Nevius (brother), b. Ovid, N.Y., March 4, 1829; m. Helen Coan June 15, 1853; d. Chefoo, China, October 19, 1893 (age 64 yrs. 6 mos.).

Mary Eastman (half-sister); b. Ovid, N.Y. January 22, 1833; d. Ovid, N.Y., June 1, 1835 (age 2 yrs. 4 mos.).

Hannah Eastman (half-sister), b. Ovid, N.Y., January 9, 1835; m. Dr. David Warner Birge (b. Manchester, Conn., December 6, 1822; d. 1901) November 5, 1856; d. Ovid, N.Y., July 10, 1866 (age 31 yrs. 5 mos.).

Benjamin N. Eastman (half-brother), b. Ovid N.Y., December 2, 1836; d. Ovid, N.Y., February 9, 1840 (age 3 yrs. 3 mos.).

William C. Eastman (half-brother), b. Ovid, N.Y., February 1, 1839; d. Ovid, N.Y., February 17, 1839 (age 16 days).

Benjamin Nevius Eastman (half-brother), b. Ovid, N.Y., January 28, 1840; m. Cornilia Post (b. vicinity Ovid, N.Y., April 16, 1844; d. March 23 1866) November 26, 1863; d. (Syracuse, N.Y.?) June 22, 1892 (age 52 yrs 5 mos.).

William Lyman Eastman (half-brother) b. Ovid, N.Y., April 22, 1842; m. Augusta Nash (b. Hadley, Mass., September 1, 1842; d. Ovid, N.Y., April 30 1912) June 6, 1866; d. Ovid, N.Y.(?), November 16, 1902 (age 60 yrs. 7 mos.).

Mary Denton Eastman (half sister), b. Ovid, N.Y., June 30, 1844; m. James Harris (b. vicinity Ovid, N.Y.; d. Cleveland, Ohio) 1867; d. Cleveland, Ohio, March 4, 1937 (age 92 yrs. 8 mos.).

Clinton D. Eastman (half-brother), b. Ovid, N.Y., September 15, 1846; d. Ovid, N.Y., April 12, 1901 (age 54 yrs. 7 mos.).

CHILDHOOD AND EDUCATION

Reuben Denton Nevius was born November 26, 1827, on a farm between Ovid and Lodi in New York State's Finger Lakes country, the first child of Benjamin Hageman and Mary Denton Nevius. A younger brother, John Livingston Nevius, was born in 1829. The Nevius family (pronounced Neé-vee-us and often found as "Nevins") was of Dutch descent, the founding ancestor of the American branch having migrated to New Amsterdam about 1650.[1] Benjamin and Mary Nevius were devout members of the Presbyterian Church: he became an ardent supporter of the temperance movement then gaining momentum, and she was widely acclaimed for her piety. Benjamin Nevius died of a fall shortly before

Reuben's third birthday. Two years later Mary Denton Nevius married John Eastman. They lived in New England for a year, taking Reuben with them, and then returned to the farm at Ovid.[2]

The Nevius boys were well educated. Beginning in 1838, when Reuben was nearly twelve, the brothers attended Ovid Academy together and then in 1845 they entered Union College, Schenectady, from which they graduated in 1848 with Bachelor of Arts Degrees.[3] Reuben seems to have spent some time in New York City[4] and then in late 1849, as he neared his twenty-second birthday, he went to Marshall, Michigan,[5] presumably to teach. Meanwhile John went to Columbus, Georgia, where he established a successful private school.

[6]Mary Denton Nevius Eastman had hoped that her sons would enter the ministry. Shortly after arriving in Georgia, John Nevius wrote his mother that he had been thinking a good deal about religion, and soon after he joined Columbus's Presbyterian Church. By mid-February, 1850, he said that he "seemed to be living in another world."[7] Meanwhile Reuben, in a break with his family's Calvinist tradition, joined the Episcopal Church[8] and the brothers, who corresponded throughout their lives, debated various points of theology and sectarian interpretation in their letters to each other. In May 1849 John wrote Reuben, "I rejoice that we differ so little in essentials; and I pray that our churches may never separate us in affection." He continued, "I have just received a letter from Mother, and she seems to be enjoying almost a heaven on earth in the realization of the answer to her prayers in the conversion of her sons."[9]

A year later, in November 1850, Reuben joined his brother John in Columbus, Georgia, and took charge of his school. John had decided to study for the Presbyterian ministry at Princeton, and left Columbus a few weeks later. Reuben Nevius too had decided to enter the ministry, apparently while he was in Michigan.[10] In the two years that he remained in Columbus, teaching and studying for the ministry, Nevius would have known the Rev. Thomas Fielding Scott, rector of Columbus's Trinity Church. Scott, like Nevius, had a Presbyterian background and he was widely respected for his fine preaching and his ecumenical views. In a biography written by Louis L. Perkins, Historiographer of the Diocese of Eastern Oregon, he states that Nevius lived and boarded with Scott. In 1853 Scott was elected the first Missionary Bishop of Oregon and Washington Territories. He was consecrated bishop in Christ Church, Savannah, on January 8, 1854, almost one year after Nevius was ordained a deacon in the same church.

Ordination—Savannah, Georgia

Nevius was ordained a deacon by Bishop Stephen Elliott, first Bishop of Georgia, on Sunday, January 9, 1853, at Christ Church, Savannah. "I regret to state," Elliott noted, "that I was unable to retain Mr. Nevius in the Diocese. He was at once transferred to the Diocese of Alabama."[11] A month later the Right Rev. Nicholas H. Cobbs, Bishop of Alabama, reported that Nevius had been put in charge of Christ Church, Wetumpka, "in connection with the Episcopal High School in Montgomery,"[12] a few miles away.

1. Reuben Denton Nevius

LIBERTY HILL, ALABAMA

Meanwhile, Nevius's brother John had decided to become a missionary to China. He was ordained a Presbyterian minister on May 23, 1853, married his childhood sweetheart, Helen Stanford Coan, in June of that year and with his bride sailed for China in September. In November Reuben Nevius moved from Wetumpka, Alabama, to Liberty Hill in Dallas County, where he took charge of St. David's Church.[13] On May 14, 1854, he was ordained a priest by Bishop Cobbs at Carlowville, in conjunction with the Annual Convention of the Diocese of Alabama.[14]

Nevius remained at Liberty Hill for a year and a half, resigning on May 15, 1855. "In leaving this field of labor," he commented, "I shall carry with me happy remembrances of a kind, zealous, and refined people, and a rich harvest of experiences and profit, drawn mostly from my connection with the slave population." He noted that services had been held on Sunday mornings for the whites and Sunday evenings for the slaves, and that the slaves had been instructed, "during most of the year, in a Sunday School held in the evening after the sermon."[15] He also had begun to hold evening services at nearby Athens, and had opened a mission station in the "lower part of Dallas County," where a new parish would "very soon be organized, and a neat country church erected from an ample subscription already raised."[16]

Nevius' school was probably an economic necessity. As a Bishop of Alabama later observed, "The ministerial salary, not over-large in prospect, was oftentimes even smaller in realization. Not a few of the clergy were compelled to eke out their salary by adding school-teaching to their clerical duties. Some of the clergy must have welcomed a bright Sunday morning and a large congregation with somewhat more than spiritual joy, for their whole support came from the unpledged Sunday offerings of the congregation."[17] Nevius's annual report for 1855[18] lists only fourteen white communicants and twenty-seven colored, though attendance at services was probably several times greater than that. Collections available for his use over the past year totaled $147.50. This may have been supplemented by a small grant from the Diocesan Missionary Society,[19] but his church-related income cannot have been much more than twelve to fifteen dollars a month. Even though that would compare to a monthly income of several hundred dollars in the late 1980s, it is clear that an additional income was absolutely necessary.[20] But Nevius

2. Postcard of Christ Church, Savannah

seems also to have taken a genuine interest in teaching for, as we shall see, he involved himself with schools, Sunday schools, lecturing and research all of his life. The evening Sunday school for slaves at Liberty Hill was a sizable undertaking with six teachers and 100 "scholars."[21] Unlike his parochial school it was, of course, free of charge and therefore provided no income.

TUSCALOOSA, ALABAMA

In May 1855 Nevius, then twenty-seven, left Liberty Hill to accept a call from Christ Church, Tuscaloosa, where he would remain for the next decade. This church maintained a parochial school and had built a separate chapel, St. Philip's, for its black communicants.[22]

Nevius took a special interest in natural history, especially botany, at least from the time he was in Michigan.[23] He had begun to assemble an herbarium, which, by the time he went to Tuscaloosa, contained several hundred specimens. Soon after his arrival there he became acquainted with Professor Michael Tuomey, Chair of Geology, Mineralogy and Agricultural Chemistry at the University of Alabama. Tuomey had been appointed State Geologist and had conducted a two-year survey of Alabama's geography and natural resources, which he was organizing and preparing to publish.[24] In 1856 Tuomey and Nevius began to collaborate on a "register of the Flora" of the Tuscaloosa area.[25] This project was interrupted, however, when Tuomey became ill and died at the age of fifty-one on March 30, 1857.[26]

A little over a year later on May 11, 1858, Nevius sent Prof. Asa Gray at Harvard University specimens of a shrub and a sedum that he couldn't identify, asking him to "do me the favor to give me the names."[27] In this "golden age" of botany[28] when many native plants remained unidentified and unclassified, Prof. Gray, like his colleagues and rivals, corresponded with professional and amateur botanists everywhere, in their efforts to assemble and publish comprehensive guides to the continent's flora.[29] Gray's reply does not survive, but Nevius's excited response to it of May 29, 1858, reveals that Gray considered the sedum to be a new species and the shrub to be a whole new genus. "I hasten to tell you of my very agreeable surprise at finding that I had made a discovery and to thank you for the kind notice you have taken of the same, "wrote Nevius, "and nothing will give me greater pleasure than to correspond with you if you will do me the favor to help me in my study regarding those plants with which I have found difficulty." Gray also asked Nevius to collect specimens of Croomia, a plant particular to the Tuscaloosa area, which Nevius was glad to do: "And my dear Sir let me add, I shall esteem myself fortunate in being able to do you any service, and you may command me in every respect in which I may be able to aid you in your invaluable researches. I will send you the specimens you desire as soon as I can go for them and prepare them for the mail." Nevius mentioned that he had just returned from a trip to Huntsville, nearly 200 miles north "over the Cumberland Mountains," where he had found "many new and interesting plants."

Nevius wrote again on June 21, repeating his thanks for help with his studies and thanking Gray for a copy of Torrey and Gray's *Flora of North America*, which Nevius had mentioned in his previous letter that he did not have. "I will direct Mr. Daniel Dana, of whom I order all my books, to call and get it for me and send it with some books I am now about to order." He provided additional detail about the new sedum and enclosed more specimens of the newly discovered shrub. " The shrub is a very beauty and well worth cultivation," he noted, and added that if it proved to be a new genus, he and his "friends and associates in the study, Prof. Wymand & Dr. Mallet of the University," hoped "to be permitted to name the Genus in complement to our old and lamented friend Prof. Tuomey—*Tuomeya*."

Nevius wrote again on July 12, thanking Gray for "cordial agreement" in the naming of the new genus. "Your disposition to do me the unmerited honor of giving it my name was pleasing to me," he said, "but far less so than my ability to honor the name of a most excellent and deserving man—my friend—in such an enduring monument…." Nevius agreed, however, that the new species of sedum might be named after himself, in order that he might "enter by enrollment, in a more modest way than you at first designed, the honorable and gentle guild of *Botanists.*" Merely to have a species named after himself was "a monument more lasting than brass." "I think, however, that you have mistaken my name," he added, "as indeed all people do to whom I do not particularly say it is **Nevius** not **Nevins**."[30] My name you will see is already latinized." He concluded with more information about Croomia and said that he would be glad to collect the orchids of the area, as asked.[31]

Nevius wrote Gray again on October 18, 1858, after returning from a "visit home" to thank Gray for letters he had received in New York and Ovid, and to ask "of the progress of Tuomeya etc."[32] He had met "a couple of very good botanists" in his "native town." "I made good use of the few plants I took on with me," he reported. "I got by exchange nearly 600 determined specimens, among them a good collection of mosses and ferns and a large and almost full suit of Carices."[33]

In his next letter to Gray of November 15, 1858, Nevius began, "You may know how greatly I have been disappointed by being anticipated by Prof. Harvey in choice of a name for my *new Genus.*" Harvey had named a genus of alga for Tuomey in a work just published[34] and, like Gray, had suggested naming the new shrub after Nevius. "Prof. Harvey's compliment has given me pleasure," wrote Nevius, "but I cannot help but wishing that he had been a few months later in publishing his book. I do not see what can be done but to accept your kind proposition to give the Genus the less honorable name Nevia, except it would be proper to call it *Toomara* and trust to the usual note to designate the person…. I will leave the whole matter entirely in your hands," he added, "and beg you will be godfather to the new Genus."

"I am delighted with your Botany for Beginners," Nevius continued, "and although I have my class (I am instructing a class in the School of Mrs. Tuomey)[35] pretty well on in the 'Manual' and do not *need* a more elementary book now, I shall order some for prizes, and gift books. Many girls will study it when they have left school, who will not study the Manual." Nevius said that he had never studied the carices "at all," but added, "with the advantage of the determined species I have procured by exchange, I hope I may be able to find the one you want," and he promised to "watch the Croomia."

"I must say," he said in closing, "that I find the New Genus makes *excellent pipe stems.* I will tell you how I found it out. A friend of mine brought me from Florida a pipe stem of a superior quality. I noticed one day that it closely, yet not exactly, resembled the New Genus, and on examination of the wood under the microscope, I am convinced that if it is not the *same plant,* it is the *same Genus,* and equally good for the purpose above mentioned. If you are a smoker I shall be glad to send you one."[36]

Asa Gray's article notifying the scientific community of the two newly identified plants appeared in the *Memoirs of the American Academy of Arts and Sciences* in early 1859.[37] He named the new sedum, "a small, white-flowered species, "*Sedum nevii*[38] and the new genus of shrub, also white flowering,[39] *Neviusia alabamensis*, providing a detailed description of it in Latin. Nevius, of course, was delighted. "Your article is quite an imposing one," he wrote, "and it surprised me by its fullness. I am glad to know that there is an importance in its discovery, aside from the discovery itself, in its bearing upon the affinities of other genera."[40]

Meanwhile Nevius penned an account of Prof. Michael Tuomey's life which was published anonymously in the January 1859 issue of the *Alabama Education Journal*.[41] Nevius's biography outlined the chronology of Tuomey's life and detailed Tuomey's contributions to the study of the natural sciences. Concurrent as it was with the publication of the evolutionist theories of Alfred Russel Wallace and Charles Darwin, which rocked the foundations of fundamental Biblical belief, Nevius's paean to Tuomey gives insight to the views of its author as well: "In his study of Natural Sciences," observed Nevius, "Prof. Tuomey opened the book of Nature with all the reverence with which he opened his Bible. To him it was the Book of God, filled with inspired and unequivocal revelation of His love to man—abounding in sublime themes suggestive of thought, in a true poetry of simplicity and harmonious adaptation of cause and effect, in a history fresh, after the lapse of untold ages, from the hand of God...."

Nevius was thirty-three when the Civil War broke out in 1861. He remained in Tuscaloosa, a native of New York in the Deep South, until it was over. No indication of his political views has come to hand. It may be that his views, as appears to be the case in other matters, generally reflected those of the Episcopal Church as a whole. With strong pro- and anti-slavery elements among its membership, the national Church endeavored to remain apolitical, as it traditionally had done, and tended to oppose the war as a struggle of brother against brother; views that did little to enhance its popularity with either side. After hostilities broke out, the Northern Church held that those dioceses in the secessionist states continued to be full members, and included them in roll calls at General Conventions. Noting that the Anglican Communion had always organized itself within political boundaries, diocese in the Southern states established a separate organization, the Protestant Episcopal Church in the Confederate States of America, with a constitution almost identical to its Northern counterpart. The two branches remained on good terms and quickly reunited when hostilities ceased. An example of the camaraderie that endured is that two old friends, Bishop McIlvanie of Ohio, an influential Northern Churchman, and Bishop Polk of Louisiana, who became a Confederate general, included each other in their public prayers—by name—throughout the War.

Available information indicates only that Nevius continued to concern himself with missionary work among the blacks, presenting twenty-one adults to Bishop Richard Hooker Wilmer for confirmation in 1864.[42] A later Bishop of Alabama observed, "That such work as this should have been conducted amidst the horrors of a war of which the Negro was the immediate occasion, is remarkable."[43]

The war orphaned many children, creating a need to provide for them. In 1864 Bishop Wilmer proposed three regional orphanages, including one at Tuscaloosa. Nevius and the vestry of Christ Church took special interest in this project, and $50,000 soon was raised in Tuscaloosa and adjacent parishes. Of this, $30,000 was spent on a building and grounds, $10,000 for care, and $10,000 was set aside for an endowment.[44] Eight orphans were soon taken in and the home was operated in conjunction with a parochial school of fifty pupils. The orphanage and school were committed to three deaconesses, whom Bishop Wilmer "set apart by prayer, but without imposition of hands," in Christ Church on December 20, 1864.[45]

The war did not directly affect Tuscaloosa until its very end. In April 1865 Federal troops occupied the city and burned the two buildings that housed the University of Alabama. Christ Church, a mile and a half away, was not harmed, but a situation of Constitutional proportions evolved which must have affected Nevius and his parishioners.[46] At issue was "A Prayer for the President of the United States, and all in Civil Authority," a routine part of the liturgy contained in the Book of Common Prayer. In 1862 Bishop Wilmer had advised his clergy that, should they find themselves occupied by Northern forces and were prevented from saying a prayer for the President of the Confederate States, or were required to say a prayer for the President of the United States, they should close their churches. He then advocated a change in the official form of the prayer in the Confederate Church, to make it a prayer for "all in Civil Authority" without specification of political allegiance. In May and June of 1865, with the War over, he issued Pastoral Letters urging submission by his clergy and laity to the authority of the United States, and himself took an oath of allegiance to it. But as long as military rule prevailed in his diocese, he also forbade the use of the Prayer for the President of the United States *and all in Civil Authority*, taking the view that military rule did not constitute civil authority, and that the prayer was there-

fore inappropriate. This worked for a while, but in late September 1865 the military authorities charged Wilmer with disloyalty and forbade him or his clergy to preach or to hold public services, except by permission requested and granted through military channels. Within a month civil government was re-established, which otherwise would have defused the issue, but the military order remained in force until January 1866, giving rise to charges that the Church's Constitutional rights had been violated.

Wilmer's position "greatly exasperated"[47] Churchmen in his own diocese, as well as Churchmen nationally who were trying to mend the breech of separation. Nevius's role in all this remains unknown, except that he resigned the rectorship of Christ Church, Tuscaloosa, sometime before February 2, 1866, when his successor took charge.[48] He seems to have remained on excellent terms with his parish-

3. The Nevius/Eastman brothers, circa 1866

ioners,[49] and would return to visit them many years later.

Nevius was listed as "on duty abroad" from the Diocese of Alabama at the time of its Annual Convention in May 1866, and his exact whereabouts are unknown until August. But it seems that some or all of this time was spent visiting his family in New York State. His brother John and sister-in-law Helen had returned home on a three-year leave from their mission in China, learning of the assassination of President Lincoln upon their arrival in New York harbor on April 15, 1865.[50] A post-War reunion of the family seems to have taken place in 1866, evidenced by a portrait in the Eastman family collection of the Reverends Reuben and John Nevius together with their half-brothers Benjamin, William and Clinton Eastman, a portrait which must have been taken about this time.[51]

OIL CITY, PENNSYLVANIA

In August 1866 Nevius accepted a call from Oil City in northwestern Pennsylvania, about 200 miles from Ovid. This call had been issued jointly by Christ Church, Oil City, and St. John's Church in nearby Rouseville, oil-country mission stations that had been opened several years earlier.[52] The congregations met in rented halls and Nevius was their first permanent clergyman.[53] Within a few months of his arrival Christ Church, Oil City, adopted a "perfected charter" and was recognized as a self-supporting parish.[54]

Nevius opposed the usual system for meeting parish expenses, the "subscription" or "rental" of pews. Instead, he advocated the "Free Church System" which relied on offerings at services, "he pledging himself and the Vestry that no subscription would be resorted to make up any deficiency."[55] At first an annual salary of $1,200 was stipulated but soon this was reduced to $600, "to be paid *through the offertory* weekly, monthly or quarterly, the margin of the excess of the offering being relied upon for the rest of his support." Meanwhile the Ladies Auxiliary Society raised funds to cover all other expenses. Feelings about these matters ran high: one vestryman resigned when the stipulated salary was reduced.[56] But, Nevius, commented, "The result of this scheme was perfectly satisfactory to the rector. The Church was kept free from debt, the support of the rector was not felt as a burden upon the parish, and the parish was self-sustaining from the first." He refused to accept permanent assignment, insisting that a new call be issued annually,[57] and in the face of an economic depression, he started a parochial school.[58]

About this time Reuben Denton Nevius married Margaret Mercer Toumey.[59] She was the daughter of his old mentor, Prof. Michael Tuomey, and his widow Sarah with whom Nevius had associated in teaching school. "Minnie" was in her mid-twenties.[60] Reuben celebrated his fortieth birthday in November, 1867. Many years later a relative mentioned that they "had twins who died,"[61] but this is not confirmed by other sources. It may or may not be true.

4. Minnie Nevius, circa 1868

MOBILE, ALABAMA

The Neviuses left Oil City in February, 1869, to accept a call from St. John's Church, Mobile, Alabama. Bishop Wilmer observed that Nevius would be "warmly welcomed" by his "numerous friends among the clergy and laity" in the diocese where he "in former years had been so closely identified."[62] Nevius's penchant for missionary work soon manifested itself again. By October of that year a new church had been built at a mission station he tended on the shores of the nearby West Fowl River.[63]

On February 22, 1870, Nevius was granted a Doctor of Divinity degree by the College of William and Mary, Williamsburg, Virginia.[64] But that summer an epidemic of Yellow Fever broke out in Mobile, and on October 17 Minnie Nevius died. She was buried the following day by the Rev. T. A. Massey.[65] Nevius also was ill at the time.[66] During this time Nevius may have performed special services in Ashville, Alabama. St. John's Church in Ashville was built of board and batten type. The chancel was in the north and the entrance in the south. There were thirteen stained glass windows. After the Civil War the church doors were closed. Occasionally a rector would come up from Mobile for a special service. In 1870 the building was sold. It was carefully dismantled, loaded on ox wagons and laboriously transported to Elyton, a distance of fifty miles. Then it was painstakingly rebuilt and the cornerstone was laid on April 19, 1871.[67] This church clearly resembles those in Union, The Dalles, and Canyon City.

PORTLAND, OREGON

Meanwhile the Vestry of Trinity Church, Portland, Oregon, voted to call Nevius as rector, and Judge Matthew P. Deady sent a telegram on February 22, 1872, to George R. Barker at Germantown, Pennsylvania, for Dr. Nevius of Mobile containing a call to the Rectorship of Trinity parish. Nevius responded that he would like to remain in his present parish until Easter morning, April 1. Deady sent a letter to Nevius at Ovid, New York, containing a draft for $215.63, and accepting his terms. Nevius was a passenger on the steamer Ajax sailing from San Francisco to Portland on Saturday, April 27, 1872.[68] Nevius arrived on April 30th, and became rector after a year in which Rev. George Burton conducted services during a search for a permanent rector. He called on Judge Deady on May 1, and made a good impression. Nevius was officially connected with the Jurisdiction of Oregon and Washington Territory on June 22, 1872.[69]

In his report to the annual convocation of the jurisdiction, Nevius reported on August 31, 1872, that Trinity had a congregation of 107 communicants. The Vestry, and particularly Judge Deady were not satisfied with Nevius, and communicated that to him in November. On December 3, 1872, the Vestry received his resignation to take effect on July 1.[70] It was accepted, and they agreed to pay him his usual stipend until that time. Trinity's new church was completed about this time, but it was not consecrated until August 31, 1873. Bishop Morris wrote to Nevius in May of 1873 suggesting that Nevius spend the next three months until Convocation in Eastern Oregon.

EASTERN OREGON

St. Stephen's Church, Baker ✠ *St. John's Church, Union*
Ascension Church, Cove ✠ *St. Paul's Church, The Dalles* ✠ *St. Thomas's Church, Canyon City*

On June 7, 1873, Nevius officially began work in Eastern Oregon. He preached his last sermon at Trinity on June 8, and the congregation raised $93 to assist with the Mission at La Grande. Nevius visited La Grande, Union, Cove and Baker, and reported that there was promise in all of them. He reported "[We] have one organized Parish [at La Grande], waiting only for the architect's plan to build their church, and the prospect of good congregations in two other places."[71] He began the membership with 47 communicants, according to his report of August 28, 1873.

On November 1, 1873, Karl Muller published in *Flora*, a German periodical, the naming of two mosses Mnium Neevii, and Grimmia Neevii, after Nevius. They had been collected while he was in Mobile.

The cornerstone for St. Peter's Church in La Grande was laid on November 8, 1873. The Baker City church cornerstone was laid on November 17; that of St. John's Church, Union, on November 18; and the church in Cove on November 19, 1873.[72] The *Baker City Herald* reported in late 1873, "The Rev. Dr. Nevius, of the Episcopal Church, preached a very appropriate Thanksgiving sermon at the Court House on Thanksgiving Eve. This gentleman is an earnest, zealous Christian worker, and is doing much good in this community. Nevius had completed the Vestry room of the church by January of 1874, and was occupying it as a study and rectory. The *Oregon Churchman* reported in early March, 1874, that the Baker church had adopted plans of Krumbein & Gilbert of Portland, for their new building. In May of 1874, while returning from a visit to Portland, Nevius preached at The Dalles and Canyon City. He then stopped at Eldorado on his way home. He asked for six more missionaries to serve these areas as well as Northern Idaho, which they were to visit in July.[73]

The *Oregon Churchman* reported in August of 1874 that Nevius' mission embraced the whole of Union and Baker counties, and extended into Grant

5. Reuben Denton Nevius, 1872. Oregon Historical Society neg. no. 74144

County. Bishop Morris held services at La Grande, Cove, Union, Baker City, Mormon Basin, Eldorado and Canyon City, all within Nevius' labors. He had confirmed 69 persons within the past 18 months, and three church buildings were under construction. In his report to the Annual Convocation of 1874, Nevius reported services held in his regular four places, and in addition Canyon City had been visited twice, and The Dalles three times. St. Peter's in La Grande had 34 communicants, services being held in the Methodist Church. Cove had 7 communicants, with an average attendance of 50. He reported that the church building was under contract, and hoped to occupy it by Christmas. St. John's Church, in Union, was near completion, and there were 8 communicants, with 18 attending services. The Baker church had 15 communicants, and 33 attending on Sundays.

The Bishop sent Rev. John W. Sellwood on a missionary tour in Eastern Oregon, stopping in The Dalles and Canyon City, then traveling to Baker City, Union and La Grande. He reported "The Dr. [Nevius] is doing a fine work through all this vast region of country, and has placed the Church as a true pioneer before this people. He is an itinerant missionary, in the truest sense, and is laying foundations for the Church far and wide, which can never be obliterated or destroyed. He feels very much encouraged in his work, and throws his whole heart into it with the deepest enthusiasm. When I left him he was just entering upon a long missionary trip which would take him from four to six weeks, reaching places where seldom if ever religious services are held. Thus he is doing the work of an evangelist, a tried and a blessed work."[74]

Nevius wrote to the Bishop on December 15, 1874, "We shall have service here [in Baker] on St. Stephen's Day [December 26], going into the church on the bare floor, everything extemporized save the stove and lamps. If you do not give us another name I shall call the church 'St. Stephen.'"

When Bishop Morris began his annual visitation to eastern Oregon in June of 1875, he visited first at The Dalles, finding the church building there in progress. He then went to Canyon City, where he met Nevius and conducted services on July 1 and July 4. Preparations were being made to build a church there, and funds were raised during the visit. The two then rode to Prairie City and held a service. After a two-day stage ride they arrived at Baker City, where Morris conducted two services.

St. John's Church in Union was consecrated on July 14 after a hasty raising of funds to lift the debt still owed. It was a memorial to Rev. Geo. Natt, a Pennsylvania priest whose wife had donated the first $500. "The church is novel in construction and appearance, and is thought to be a model for a cheap church when labor and material can be had at moderately low prices. The church has cost about $2,000.[75] After the service the Bishops (Morris and Tuttle, from Idaho) rode by moonlight to visit the church under construction at Cove to inspect it. At this time work had also begun on a church at Pendleton. The following day, July 15, 1875, they rode to La Grande to consecrate St. Peter's Church. It had been funded first by a donation of $500 from a lady in western New York. The congregation raised all the rest of the funds themselves.

Travel for the missionaries in these times was extremely difficult. Most trips were made by horse, exposed to the elements which could change quickly. Nevius early on had arranged free passage on the stage from Canyon City to Baker City which was generously donated by the stage owners. After pleas by the Bishop a small amount was donated in 1874 for a buggy which gave some protection. The Rev. George T. Kaye joined Nevius as an associate in 1875. In August Nevius started on a visitation to his district which covered over 700 miles and took over seven weeks. On the trip he visited The Dalles, where a church building had begun to be built in May. That church was named St. Paul's, and was being built like the Union church with improvements (probably by Nevius). The plan was developed with the design of getting the most Church for the money.

After waiting for windows to arrive from the East, St. Paul's in The Dalles was finally opened for services on Christmas Day in 1875. An article in the *Oregon Churchman* stated: "Whatever may be thought or said of the Episcopal denomination there is one fact which cannot be denied; which is, that their houses of worship are always a credit to their projectors and founders. They may be small; but they are always neat, cozy and inviting, pleasant to the eye—everything appropriate and in order. The new Episcopal church in this city is no exception to this rule. It is not only cozy, neat and tasteful in all its appointments; but in many respects it is beautiful, and reflects much credit on those who planned and those who executed." Nevius remained in The Dalles for two months holding frequent services, 63 in all with 57 sermons and lectures.[76] The church cost about $2,500. The altar design was taken from *Church Architecture* (New York: A. J. Bicknell & Co., 1873), and is by Frederick Clark Withers, a prominent and influential architect of the period. The Bishop reported, "This little church, capable of holding about one hundred persons, is after Trinity Church Portland altogether the most beautiful church we have."[77] He also stated, "Dr. Nevius will remain one Sunday more at The Dalles, when he will leave for Canyon City, the next nearest point in his field, distant however 280 (sic. 180) miles. To reach there at this season of the year he must make a circuit of nearly 350 (sic 250) miles, and cross the Blue Mountains twice over such roads and in such conveyances, as would terrify the ordinary traveler, but which are trifles to the hardy Oregon Missionary."

In a letter of March 22, 1876, Dr. Nevius wrote, "I am now waiting an opportunity to cross the mountains on my way home, after an absence of three months. Late rains have so softened the deep snow on the divides as to make the passage very difficult. There is still sleighing for 60 of the 90 miles between Canyon and Baker." He goes on to report, "My journey to this valley was unusually pleasant for a winter ride of 180 miles. the winter is far the best time for missionary work in interior towns. At that time the miners have come in from their mountain camps and the people have little to do."

On Easter, April 16, 1876, services were held for the first time in the Church of the Ascension at Cove. It was an improvement on the design of the church at Walla Walla, with uniquely beautiful windows. The west, circular window, was especially beautiful, being a triplet dedicated as memorials to the Robert French family, parents and brother

6. Reuben Denton Nevius, circa 1875

of S. G. French, a local supporter of the church, depicting in the center an angel receiving an aged saint, with St. John on the South, and Faith on the north side. The cost was $3,500, with $1,000 contributed from the east, mostly from contacts of the French family. The Grand Ronde Valley churches were presided over by the Rev. Mr. Kaye, and a parsonage at Cove was under construction.

On May 4, 1876, Nevius wrote to Dr. Asa Gray, commenting on his botanical research, and enclosing a photograph of himself. Nevius spoke of his planned travels, 300 miles round trip to The Dalles, and 250 miles east to Boise City, with several stops in mining camps not visited before. The trip was to take three months. While in The Dalles he and a companion were to leave their wagon there and take go by river to Portland and then to Seattle for the annual Convocation of the jurisdiction. [78] It was about this time that Nevius sent a sample of chaenactis nevii to Dr. Gray, a sunflower which grows only in the John Day Valley. It was not published until 1883. It is one of two yellow wildflowers that bloom on clay hillsides in the vicinity of the John Day Fossil Beds in late spring, withering and drying in late summer.[79]

Of course Nevius could not resist stopping along the way to open new missionary territory. He visited Heppner for the first time, and met with potential parishioners. He gave a full evening service, and all the people of the town (about 100) were present.

Nevius returned to Baker City by mid-August, and on August 22nd he and Bishop Morris set out for Canyon City. "Not having taken fully into account the roughness of an untried mountain road, night overtook them when they were some sixteen miles short of the hospitable miner's house where they were expected. Nothing was left but to stop at a deserted cabin, in the forest, long inhabited only by the wood rats, and to make themselves as comfortable as they could, with the remains of their lunch for supper, and a miner's board bunk for their bed. Their poor horses fared worse than this, in a hard snow storm which came up during the night, chilling them to their bones. The bright sun of the next morning cheered and inspired man and beast, and by noon the discouraged travelers were comfortably quartered, and most hospitably entertained for the night by a bachelor miner of the 'Olive Creek Diggins.'"[80] They proceeded on to Prairie City, where they held services and viewed a lot which had been given for a church. On August 26th they arrived in Canyon City, and laid the cornerstone for St. Thomas' Church there.

On July 15, 1877, Bishop Morris held the opening service in St. Thomas' Church in Canyon City, and was assisted by Nevius. Morris commented, "The building of a church at Canyon City was an undertaking of a good deal of boldness, and has been carried on by the Missionary in charge, with untir-

7. *Reuben Denton Nevius, May 4, 1876, courtesy of the Library of the Gray Herbarium, Harvard University, Cambridge, Massachusetts, USA.*

ing energy. …One of the peculiarities of its construction is that the Vestry room abuts against the mountainside, and extends over a beautiful and unfailing spring of cool and crystal water—symbolic I trust of the refreshing and purifying influences that are to flow out from this house of God for all time to come." On the 25th of July the Bishop consecrated the Church of the Ascension in Cove, assisted by Nevius, Revs. L. H. Wells, Geo. T. Kaye, and W. L. McEwan. Morris went on with Wells to Weston, where he consecrated All Saints Church, and to Pendleton, where the Church of the Redeemer was to be consecrated, but was postponed. St. Paul's Church in Walla Walla had been consecrated earlier that spring, in April of 1877.

In 1879 Allium nevii, a wild onion know known as Allium douglasii, var. nevii, was named for Nevius by Sereno Watson in *Proceedings of the American Academy*. Watson noted that it had been collected at Hood River, Oregon. Also in 1879 the Oregon Railway and Navigation Company began building a railroad on the south bank of the Columbia River.

EASTERN WASHINGTON

Good Samaritan, Colfax, W.T. ✠ *Church of the Nativity, Lewiston, I.T.* ✠ *St. Luke's Church, Coeur d'Alene, I.T.*
All Saints' Church, Spokane Falls ✠ *St. Peter's Church, Pomeroy* ✠ *St. Matthew's Church, Sprague*

An article in the *Oregon Churchman* on September 1, 1879, states that "On the first of October, the Rev. Dr. Nevius will take charge of the large Missionary district in Eastern Washington Territory and Northern Idaho." Nevius was to take charge of the "Umatilla" mission from the Rev. Lemuel H. Wells. Wells, headquartered in Walla Walla, was to be permanently stationed there as rector of St. Paul's Church, at the request of the congregation.

A key date for the Church of the Nativity in Lewiston was the appointment October 16, 1879, of the Rev. R. D. Nevius as a missionary in northeastern Washington with headquarters at Spokane Falls. Bishops Morris and Tuttle agreed that although Idaho was part of the missionary district of Montana, Idaho, and Utah, Dr. Nevius would serve the Lewiston church. Nevius wrote that he was granted an annual stipend by Bishop Morris of $600, and by Bishop Tuttle of $400. During the winter of 1879 meetings were held in the Red Cross building in Lewiston. Nevius settled his residence in Lewiston, while his canonical residence remained in Spokane Falls.

In his report to the Annual Convocation held in Portland in June of 1880, Nevius reported that he had visited and held services in Mt. Idaho and Grangeville, Idaho; Pataha, Pomeroy, Colfax, Spokane, Colville and Palouse City, Washington; and at Fort Coeur d'Alene and Farmington, Idaho.

In the summer of 1880 Mr. Sereno Watson, a botanist from Harvard and colleague of Asa Gray, visited the Pacific Northwest. Nevius seems to have met Watson at Colville, but not to have traveled with him. On December 15, 1880, John Adams Paddock was consecrated the first Bishop of Washington Territory in New York. His first service was to be Easter, April 17, 1881, in Vancouver.

Rev. Lemuel H. Wells in 1914 reminisced about the early church in eastern Washington: "About 1880, when the Northern Pacific Railway was building and the city of Spokane had about 600 inhabitants, Dr. Nevius, then living in Lewiston, began holding occasional services here, then moved here and built a little church at the edge of the town on the corner of Riverside and Lincoln, opposite the present post office. He soon opened a school for boys and girls in the church, and called it the Rodney Morris School." Although the church struggled, during a visit from Wells they decided upon a new tract of land for a school. Later, during the ministry of C. B. Crawford, a substantial frame church building was built in 1887.

On May 20, 1881, Bishop Paddock made his first visit to Walla Walla, and was joined by Bishops Morris and Tuttle, as well as Dr. Nevius, and Revs. Wells, McConkey and Wood. This was the first gathering of three Bishops at any one place west of the Rocky Mountains. Nevius also attended the first Convocation of the Washington Missionary Jurisdiction at St. Luke's in Vancouver, on August 24, 1881. Nevius was appointed to practically every committee, including being named registrar of the jurisdiction.

Rt. Rev. Wells recalled in his 1914 memoirs that about 1881 he and Nevius visited Dayton, about 30 miles from Walla Walla, and Nevius pushed on 30 miles farther to Pomeroy, where there was a young town, and there he gathered a congregation and built a church. It was also in 1882, in March, that Nevius wrote an obituary for his friend and supporter, S. G. French, who had been such a support in building of the Cove church. Also in 1882 the railroad was completed from The Dalles to Walla Walla, making travel much easier. In their travels to Eastern Oregon, Rev. R. L. Stevens wrote that he and Bishop Morris, after a hard trip from Pendleton to La Grande by wagon, visited the Cove church: "From La Grande we drove to the Cove fifteen miles distant. The Church here is a little gem. A gothic structure with stained glass windows, and with all the appointments for service complete excepting lamps or means of lighting. Close by is a pretty parsonage occupied by Mr. Smith.... At the close of the service the Bishop made a touching allusion to Mr. French by whose influence the Church at the Cove was built and sustained during his life, and who in his death, has left such noble monuments of his zeal for the Master's service...."[81]

Nevius attended the Second Convocation in Seattle in June of 1882. The Bishop reported on spending several months in the eastern part of the state with Dr. Nevius. Among other places they visited, Sprague was reported as an encouraging opening. The Bishop reported that a little church was under construction there. In his Registrar's report, Nevius asked for copies of historical addresses by the Clergy as well as information on new missions and parishes. He reported that All Saints Chapel in Spokane had 6 communicants and 22 children in the Parish School. Coeur d'Alene had been visited seven times, and services held at a Chapel of the Fort. Nevius reported five visits to Fort Colville where four or five families attended services, their children were baptized, and a Sunday School met regularly. He reported that Sprague had sprung into existence since the last report. Regular services had been maintained for the past three months, and a building had been erected where services now were held. There were five communicants at Colfax Mission.

Sprague was primarily a tent city. "The first service has held in one of the new buildings, which was a saloon, but some of the congregation were in undue haste to slake their thirst at the conclusion of the service, and the surroundings were not conducive to devotion, they decided to erect a church ready for the next monthly service." Dr. Nevius went to the railroad to get land, went to a lumber company and scrounged lumber to be delivered, gave them the plans, and said, "I'll be back in six months." At this next service, the Doctor arrived on Friday and found all the material on the ground, but not a stroke had been done upon the structure. So the whole town got out early on Saturday morning with hammers, axes, saws and any tool they happened to have, and by midnight the church was finished and ready for service the next day.[82] Sprague had been started at the end of the Northern Pacific Railroad line. According to an article by Mrs. B. Gard Ewing, when night came during construction they continued to work by torches and lanterns. As the building drew near to completion they one-by-one gathered up their tools and departed until, as midnight approached, one figure alone remained hard at work at the peak of the roof, and just as Saturday ended and Sunday began, the last hammer strokes rang upon the midnight air, and cap boards were fastened in place and crowned the finished structure. Dr. Nevius descended, stiff and exhausted, but happy in the completed tabernacle of his God—the church built in a day. It was named St. Matthew's Church. Nevius turned fifty-five that year.

On June 10, 1883, Bishop Paddock joined Nevius for the consecration of St. Peter's Church in Pomeroy. In addition the Bishop visited Spokane, Cheney, Sprague, Fort Coeur d'Alene, Walla Walla, Dayton and Waitsburgh. In his address to the Third Convocation of the Washington Missionary Jurisdiction, Bishop Paddock reported that he had been to Alaska to determine the missionary needs there. He also reported "The Rev. Dr. Nevius, who has been for several years engaged in active Missionary labor east of the mountains expects for a time to take charge of this important Parish [St. John's, Olympia] in the Capital of the Territory."

In the July 1, 1883 issue of *Columbia Churchman*, it was reported that the Bishop had secured resident clergy for Spokane Falls and Pomeroy, with the prospect of putting a third clergyman in the field for undeveloped stations. "Rev. Dr. Nevius, who has hitherto had charge of the field will thus be relieved to take charge of some new field as yet untried until it can be likewise divided and supplied. He goes first to the Yakima country to spy it out and report to the Bishop, when he will for a time have residence at Olympia, which is now without a rector."

OLYMPIA, WASHINGTON TERRITORY

St. Paul's Church, Whatcom [Bellingham] ✠ *St. John's Church, Olympia [second building]*
Church of the Epiphany, Chehalis

Nevius became rector of St. John's Church, Olympia, Washington Territory in July, 1883. He resigned in the fall of 1886, but did not depart until March 2, 1887.[83] On his way to Olympia, Nevius held services in Goldendale and in Yakima. At the time Yakima had about 500 inhabitants, with Congregational and Campbellite churches. He conducted four services there, and recommended further visits. Ellensburg had about 300 inhabitants, but no Episcopalians. There were no churches there at the time. He recommended further visits here as well.

Nevius wasted no time in missionary work in western Washington. He arrived in Olympia in June of 1883, and by September 12th he was visiting Whatcom and setting up a guild there. He held two services at Whatcom, a service at Bellingham, and obtained lots donated for a church in each place. On the same trip he held services in Anacortes, LaConner, Orcas Island, and San Juan Island. When he re-

8. Annie Wright Seminary circa 1910

turned to Olympia he urged and secured appointment of a committee to plan the erection of a new church there. He was present at the cornerstone ceremony for Annie Wright Seminary in Tacoma on August 22-23. In December Nevius was appointed to a Mission at Chehalis, where he was warmly received, picking up on work started by Rev. Henry S. Bonnell, who was stationed in Tacoma. On September 7, 1883, the transcontinental line from St. Paul to Portland and to Tacoma was completed.

On February 16, 1884, the congregation at Chehalis committed to building a church. In March of that year Rev. Bonnell of Tacoma died after traveling to California in hopes of improved health. Dr. Nevius assumed the position of rector of the Church of the Epiphany, Chehalis, a position he had shared with Bonnell. Nevius furnished plans for a church building in June, and a building committee was appointed. The building was completed by September, and the first service was held September 14th, with Bishop Paddock, Dr. Nevius, and Rev. Janvrin Vincent officiating.

In July of 1884 Bishop Paddock announced at the Annual Convocation that Rev. L. H. Wells had agreed to take the Tacoma position vacated by Bonnell's death. Nevius reported 49 communicants at St. John's Olympia. He reported that only half his time had been spent in Olympia, and the rest on Missionary duty. He reported 15 communicants at Chehalis, where a church was in the process of being built.

In August of 1884 Nevius visited the Bellingham Bay region again

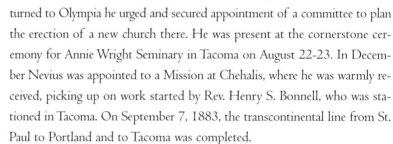

9. Reuben Denton Nevius, circa 1883

with Bishop Paddock. Services were held at LaConner, Whatcom, Bellingham, and Anacortes. At Whatcom subscriptions were raised for the erection of a church. In a September article in the *Columbia Churchman*, the faculty at Annie Wright Seminary in Tacoma included Rev. R. D. Nevius, botany instructor.

The first service was held on September 14th, 1884, at the Church of the Epiphany, Chehalis, officiated by Bishop Paddock, Dr. Nevius, and Rev. Janvrin Vincent. It was consecrated in June of 1886, although William West and others had freed it from debt by the first service. Nevius reported that he remained in charge at Chehalis until February 1, 1885, and at Whatcom for part of 1884.

Nevius and Bishop Paddock participated in organizing the Mission at Yakima in 1884. They visited in January before the city moved from Yakima City (Union Gap), to North Yakima, which had been platted by the Northern Pacific Railroad along their line to Puget Sound. Two lots had been donated by the railroad at the southeast corner of East Yakima and Naches Avenues.

Nevius continued his interest in botany, sending some samples of marine plants covered with diatoms to the *American Monthly Microscopical Journal* noted in their May 1885 issue on pages 97-98. In November he wrote Dr. Asa Gray at Harvard enclosing some slides, asking for identification of some specimen, and congratulating Dr. Gray on his seventy-fifth birthday.

Nevius visited Gray's Harbor country in the spring of 1886 and held services there. Elma and Montesano petitioned the Bishop in March to establish missions in their respective communities. In his report of June 1885, the Bishop stated: "St. John's Parish, Olympia, some time since erected a small building, for its Rector's use, on a portion of the Parsonage lot, and has recently, I rejoice to say, accepted plans and secured subscriptions, looking to the immediate erection of a new Church. By the Rector at Olympia, a Service has occasionally been given at Tumwater;...."

VISIT EAST

"In 1886 Dr. Nevius was elected the delegate to General Convention from the convocation of Washington, and on August 16 [sic, 15], he resigned as he did not plan to return west after the meeting of the General Convention in October. The vestry granted him leave of absence and tried to get him to return, but on March 2, 1887, he mailed his resignation from Utica, New York. Shortly afterward he returned [to Washington State]."[84] The Bishop and Nevius attended the General Convention meeting in October in Chicago. The Bishop continued east to Norwich, Connecti-

10. Nevius reading to Mother 1887

cut, and Dr. Nevius also visited his family in the east. Nevius wrote, "On the 13th of March, 1887, my six months leave of absence having expired, I found my duty constraining me to defer my return to W. T., and I accordingly resigned the charge of St. John's Church, Olympia, thereby surrendering a relation which I had found uniformly a pleasant one."[85] He continued his connection with the Jurisdiction, and indicated to the Bishop that he might return in the autumn.

Nevius reported that during his absence he officiated as minister in charge at Trinity Church, Utica, New York, for three months and in other places from Sunday to Sunday. He assisted in the services at St. Paul's Church, Chattanooga, Tennessee, on Christmas Day, 1887. In January of 1888 he was visiting in Tuskaloosa, Alabama. Nevius raised funds for missionary work, and returned west by May of 1888.

At the Convocation of May 23-25, 1888, Nevius was present, and was listed as "General Missionary." In the Bishop's address he reported: "The Rev. Dr. Nevius, a veteran missionary in these parts, is welcomed among us again, after an absence of more than a year. Since his return he has given most of his time to Ellensburg and North Yakima, in which thriving towns, churches will, it is hoped, be erected at an early day."

NORTH YAKIMA, WASHINGTON TERRITORY

St. Michael's Church, Yakima ✠ *Grace Church, Ellensburg* ✠ *Calvary Church, Roslyn/Cle Elum*

Nevius wasted no time in developing the congregations in Yakima and Ellensburg, with St. Michael's Church, Yakima begun about July 20, 1888, and completed for services on Christmas Day.[86] The church was built of native stone, and was 25 feet wide and 50 feet long.[87] It was built with the chancel area made of wood so that the building could be expanded. The cost of the building was $4,000. Bishop Morris visited Yakima and Ellensburg in December, 1888, on his way back from the Pan-Anglican Council in England. In March, 1889, the walls of the church were planted by the Sunday School children with ivy started from a cutting from the Trinity Church of Boston, Massachusetts. In 1889 lots were obtained for building a church in Ellensburg.

Nevius wrote to Sereno Watson at Harvard on March 14, 1889, asking about his latest book, and informing him that he was residing permanently at North Yakima. He wrote again in April 2, 1889, asking for updates and revisions since their last publication. He asked for identification of a specimen, and commented on a School of Botany he had heard might be started in the Olympia area.

In September of 1889 Nevius visited Elma, Montesano, Aberdeen and Hoquiam, in the Gray's Harbor area. On November 11, 1889, Washington became the 42nd state. On May 15, 1890, Nevius ended his relation with the Yakima Mission, moving on to Grays Harbor.

GRAYS HARBOR VICINITY, WASHINGTON

St. Luke's Church, Elma ✠ *St. Mark's Church, Montesano*
✠ *St. David's Church, Hoquiam* ✠ *St. Andrew's Church, Aberdeen*
✠ *St. Mark's Church, Ocosta* ✠ *St. John's Church, South Bend*

Dr. Nevius moved to Montesano in the Grays Harbor area just before June of 1890. In Nevius's report on Gray's Harbor to the June 1890 Convocation, meeting at St. John's Church, Olympia, he reported: "This Mission has been visited by me two to three times a year for five years, and having promised for so long a time that clerical services would be secured for it, I felt constrained, in the failure to secure a Missionary for it, to take it myself, though my action would leave Yakima and Ellensburgh without clergymen."

In November of 1890 Nevius reported on church activities at Elma, Montesano, Aberdeen, Hoquiam, and South Bend. The reception in South Bend was warm, and a mission was organized there under the name St. John's, South Bend. In a letter of May 12, 1891, Nevius gave his address as Hoquiam.

On July 19, 1891, the new St. John's Church at Olympia was opened for services. In August of 1891, the Rev. John N. Forrest Bell relieved Nevius in the Gray's Harbor Mission. At the time Dr. Nevius was living in Ocosta. Nevius evidently became dean of the district of Rev. L. H. Wells, which included Pierce, Mason and Thurston Counties. On June 5, 1892, Nevius spoke along with others at the dedication of the new Trinity Church, Seattle, the prior one having been destroyed by fire.

On June 22, 1892, Nevius's half-brother Benjamin Nevius Eastman died at the age of 52 in Syracuse, New York.

At the June, 1892, Convocation Nevius was referred to as in charge of St. John's Mission, South Bend, and St. Mark's Mission, Ocosta. Bishop Paddock reported that in 1892 the rector from Olympia left, and Nevius also served at St. John's Church there. In June of 1892 the State of Washington was divided into the Missionary District of Olympia (Western Washington) and the Missionary District of Spokane (Eastern Washington). The Rt. Rev. John Adams Paddock, became the first Bishop of Olympia.[88] Rev. Lemuel H. Wells was elected as Missionary Bishop of Spokane.

St. Mark's Church, Ocosta, was opened on August 31, 1892. "An interesting sermon was preached by Bishop Paddock, and the Rev. Mr. Bell in a few well chosen remarks alluded to the great work in church building which Dr. Nevius, the veteran missionary, has accomplished, he having built during the past seventeen years the total number of twenty churches in Washington and Oregon." He voiced the feeling of the citizens in expressing his regret that through illness the doctor was unable to be present. Nevius was hospitalized in March of 1892, in Tacoma. In November of 1892 Rev. Dr. Wells took his place as the first Bishop of Spokane. Nevius celebrated his sixty-fifth birthday on November 26, 1892, living in Tacoma.

11. Fannie Paddock Hospital c. 1908

Reminiscences of the Rev. Mark Jukes in about 1940, related to St. Paul's Church in Bellingham read as follows: "It was at this time that Dr. Nevius, whose name for near half a century has been a household word among Episcopalians in the states of Washington and Oregon, was lying very ill in the Hospital in Tacoma (Fannie Paddock). It will be remembered that he came to the North West from the state of Georgia after recovering from a severe attack of Yellow Fever: he was for some time unconscious, and during that time his wife and daughter [other sources say twins] both took the fever and died: as he recovered consciousness, he continually asked for his wife, but the doctors fearing a relapse put off telling him of his loss until later. After his recovery his great desire seemed to be to overcome his sorrow in eagerness for the Master's work & 30 years ago he was reputed to have had a hand in establishing most of the early churches in the dioceses of Oregon and Washington and at the time of my arrival was again laid low & his life despaired of & Bishop Wells before leaving for Spokane, went to the hospital to bid him farewell & speaking to him of the apparent impossibility of his recovery gently told him, that he had reserved a place for him beside his own two children who were laying in the cemetery there. Dr. Nevius, despite his weakness managed to raise himself on his elbow and thanked the Bishop for his thoughtful kindness, but told him with indomitable spirit, that he was not going to die just yet: this was the beginning of his recovery, shortly after this, he was carried on board a Trans Pacific Steamer on a mattress, and undertook the voyage to the Korea [China] where he spent a year [five months] with his brother, a Presbyterian Missionary in that country. After this rest he returned, and for some years [was] at Blaine and at a small Church in the outskirts of Tacoma."

12. Nevius with brother John in China

VISIT TO CHINA

"Gone to China.—The Rev. R. D. Nevius, D.D., formerly rector of Trinity Church, this city [Portland], and for many years a pioneer missionary to Oregon and Washington, left Tacoma for northern China on March 31st, to visit a brother who had been a missionary in that country nearly forty years. He goes to benefit his health, having been an inmate of the Fannie Paddock Hospital since last August. Dr. Nevius has many friends in Washington and it is through their kindness that he is able to make the trip."[89]

Nevius's brother John and his wife Helen had served in China as missionaries since 1853. They had returned home in 1890 for a visit, it is likely that they saw Reuben, as they visited the Puget Sound area, and John spoke at the Presbyterian Church in Olympia on August 12th. His topic was "China, Corea and Japan." Helen Nevius kept diaries of their times and wrote about them later. She writes, "In April of this year my husband's brother, Rev. R. D. Nevius, D.D., came to us in extreme ill health from the west [p. 462] coast of the United States, in hope that a sea-voyage and the change might restore him. This hope was realized, and at the end of five months [September?] he returned to America, and is now comparatively well. For more than forty years the brothers had seldom met, and it was a kind providence which brought them together again in the far-away home of the one, even though the flight of time and different environments had made them as unlike as brothers often are. Still they were alike in many things. Neither had changed at all in, for instance, his love of poetry; and many pleasant evenings were spent listening to 'Dr. Reuben' reading Tennyson or the Brownings, or to 'Dr. John' reading or reciting from Shakespeare or Byron, or his old favorite, 'Gertrude of Wyoming.' 'Dr. Reuben' liked also to interest his plodding brother in the marvels of nature [seen] through the microscope and to get his assistance in studying the flora or the geology of this new, strange land. Sometimes they would go off boating on the bay, crossing over to the bluffs for a picnic; but such outings were not frequent—time was too precious and work too pressing."

Meanwhile back in Washington population was booming due to the railroads. [Speaking of Bishop Paddock:] "During his thirteen year episcopate [1880-1894] the completion of the transcontinental lines of the Northern Pacific Railroad to Portland in 1883 and to Seattle in 1887 and the Great Northern Railroad to Seattle in 1893 brought a tremendous rush of new settlers. Population increased over 400 per cent in the state as a whole. In western Washington the Grays Harbor area and the region north of Seattle to the Canadian border were opened up extensively as the lumbering industry developed. Depressions in 1886-87 and 1892-93 failed to stop the advance."[90]

On October 19, 1893, shortly after Reuben Nevius's return, his brother, John Livingston Nevius, died in Chefoo, China. He was age 64 years, 6 months. Upon his return, Nevius wrote: " I am glad to announce my arrival at home after a few months' visit to my brother in China, and I owe the friends whose kindnesses made the visit possible for me this much—that I should make some of my impressions and observations common to them and myself. Writing for this month's issue, as I should have done for your last [in December 1893] had I not been still quite fatigued and unable at once to do the thousand things presenting themselves to me on my arrival; I must give my letter a sad coloring by announcing the very sudden death of the dear brother whom I visited and whom I left last October apparently in good health. He was known to only a few of those to whom your paper will come. They as well as all your readers who are known to me will be touched with a sympathetic pain for me in my bereavement." Nevius went on to say that John had lived in Chefoo, the most northern treaty port of China, and had retired from his ministry to the interior, where he and others had established some sixty missions and parishes served by native preachers and teachers, most of whom had

13. R. D. Nevius, circa 1894   14. John Livingston Nevius, 1829-1893

been trained by him. Nevius added that his brother's primary work while he was there was newly trans-lating the Bible into the native language. "Five months of my absence was spent in perfect rest at Chefoo. I did not go into the interior, but I had a fine opportunity to become acquainted with the missionary work and its trials, dangers and successes. ...I am glad to say to my many friends to whom I am so much beholden for their ready generous sympathy in my long illness, and although I am advised to have a longer period of rest, I am almost restored to health and have good hopes soon to engage in active work as before."[91]

BLAINE, WASHINGTON

Christ Church, Blaine

"The Rev. Dr. Nevius is at present in charge of the Mission at Blaine and is improved in health. Blaine is an important town on our northern border, and a veteran missionary like Dr. Nevius can accomplish much good for the church in that locality. We have received inquires concerning the school lately acquired by the church in Blaine and refer inquirers to the Rev. L. W. Applegate of Tacoma."[92] Even in his later years Nevius met with adversity and overcame it. Only a few days before the church school in Blaine was scheduled to open, on February 1, 1894, the building was completely destroyed by fire. The school was relocated in borrowed quarters, and opened as scheduled.

Rev. Mark Jukes, in his reminiscences, related: "On one occasion Dr. Nevius told me of an amus-ing incident in connection with his reluctance to identify himself professionally with the clergy of other denominations. The occasion was a union service held in connection with commemoration [of] Memo-rial day May 30th where he was present in the audience, he was pressed to take a seat on the platform which he declined with thanks. At the close of the service the leader on the Platform announced that Dr. Nevius would dismiss the congregation, thinking to force his hand. The Dr. was equal to the oc-casion. He looked round about him and said 'Ladies & Gentlemen, you have my permission to depart.' A Roman Catholic who was present, and with whom he was not altogether in sympathy religiously, seized his hand and giving it a hearty shake said 'That is the best thing I have heard in a long time.'"

Bishop Paddock died on March 4, 1894, while in California. His services were held at St. Luke's in Tacoma. The Rt. Rev. William M. Barker was appointed as successor, and arrived in Tacoma on April 18, 1894, by railroad from St. Paul. On May 6 the new bishop made a visit to Christ Church, Blaine. The House of Bishops elected him Bishop of the Missionary Jurisdiction of Olympia on October 17th. By November things were going well in Blaine, and the church was adjusting to new prayer books and hymnals.[93]

In his Bishop's report printed in the *Journal*, Jurisdiction of Olympia, June 26, 1895, Bishop Barker reported the consecration of St. Andrew's Church, Aberdeen, "the best of our Mission churches." He also reported the completion of the Ocosta church.

JUNEAU, ALASKA

Trinity Church, Juneau ✠ *St. Luke's Church, Douglas Island*

Bishop Barker had sent Rev. George Buzzelle as a deposition to Alaska in 1895, returning just before the June Convocation. The November edition of the *Washington Churchman* gave Juneau as the address for Dr. Nevius. Nevius apparently spent the winter of 1895-1896 in Juneau establishing a church there. Nevius had gathered several families for services, organized Sunday School classes, and a ladies guild. An announcement in the Juneau *Searchlight* of September 7 announced that he was conducting services. He held regular services there and on Douglas Island until at least March 21, 1896. An article in the February 1, issue of the *Searchlight* referred to a magic lantern show and lecture he gave on "Observations in Japan and China." It was so well received that he had to repeat it. The paper went on to say "Dr. Nevius during his five months stay in Juneau has made many warm friends outside his parish, and as the period for which he was appointed to this mission has expired, undoubtedly many people will avail themselves of this privilege of seeing and hearing this refined and scholarly gentleman. There is an especial fitness in making this coming entertainment a somewhat substantial testimonial of the regard of our people and with this end in view the gentlemen who have the management of it have wisely fixed upon a moderate charge for admission and placed tickets upon sale at the various prominent stores of the town. We need not say that we trust that as Juneau is lacking in intellectual pleasures our people may not miss the

opportunity now offered to enjoy one of such high character and to attest their appreciation of whatever is refining and instructive as well as entertaining." He returned to Washington by April of 1896. The Missionary District of Alaska had been established in 1892, and the first Bishop of Alaska, Peter Trimble Rowe, was elected in 1895. The Juneau *Searchlight* on July 25, 1896, announced that Holy Trinity Church was so far completed that it was being used for services.

15. Nevius circa 1905, Oregon Historical Society neg.n. 74142

TACOMA, WASHINGTON

St. John the Divine, Buckley

On June 13, 1896, Rev. George Herbert Watson, D.D., died. He had been rector of Trinity Church in Seattle for eighteen years. Nevius preached a memorial sermon on Sunday, June 21. The annual convocation met in Seattle and Tacoma a few days later. The September 20, 1896, *Washington Churchman* states that Nevius was officiating at the regular services at Trinity in Seattle on September 20th. His address was given at that time as Tacoma. The June 15, 1897 issue showed Nevius as being in charge of the Church of the Holy Communion in Tacoma. He was appointed one of three Examining Chaplains for new clergy, as he often served. He celebrated his seventieth birthday the following November.

In the minutes of the 1898 Convocation, Nevius's address was given as Fannie C. Paddock Hospital, Tacoma. He was listed as pastor at the Church of the Holy Communion, Tacoma, and St. Paul's mission, Buckley. He was again an active participant in the proceedings. The Buckley Church was dedicated on January 6, 1896, as St. John the Divine.

On June 7, 1900, Nevius's mother died in Ovid, New York. She was 94 years and 9 months of age. Nevius attended the annual convocation at Trinity Church, Seattle, the following October. He was again an Examining Chaplain, and was on the "Quiet Day" committee.

BLAINE, WASHINGTON

Christ Church, Blaine

Nevius apparently returned to Blaine by November, when his health allowed. On December 21, 1900, he noted in the Parish Register of St. Paul's, Whatcom, the sources of items donated to the church. "The curled maple alms basin was made by Rev. R. Nevius. It was the first one used by the mission and was carried for years by the first boy baptized. The only male member of the church [Leslie Knaggs]." The church was apparently enlarged about this time, with the nave extended and a tower built. The first services were led by Bishop Morris, with Rev. R. D. Nevius, D.D. attending. It was stated that he had overseen the planning and building of the church twenty-five years earlier. Nevius preached the sermon and Morris was the celebrant at communion.

On February 21, 1901, Bishop Barker died at age 46

16. Nevius with William West, Chehalis, c. 1898

of a heart condition. Nevius's half-brother, Clinton Denton Eastman, died in Ovid on April 12, aged 54 years, 7 months. On April 26, 1901, Bishop Wells reported on a visit to Blaine, "Dr. Nevius is not only ministering to his people in the ordinary way, but is also bringing in the young people, through the study of Nature, to the worship of Nature's God." Rt. Rev. Frederic W. Keator, D.D. was elected Bishop of Olympia at the General Assembly in San Francisco on October 19, 1901, and arrived in Tacoma on January 25, 1902.

Bishop Keator visited Christ Church, Blaine, in March, and again in July, assisting Dr. Nevius in services. Nevius attended the annual Convocation in Seattle, where Bishop Keator's address stressed unity within the district. On November 16, 1902, Nevius's half-brother, William Lyman Eastman, died at age 60 years and 7 months. November 26th was Nevius's seventy-fifth birthday.

The Convocation of 1903 met in May at St. Luke's Church, Tacoma. Nevius was present, and was reappointed as chair of the Committee on Christian Education. Sometime during the year Nevius retired. January 9, 1903, was the fiftieth anniversary of his ordination as deacon. On September 19, 1903, Bishop Keator gave his consent to the sale of the parish house at Blaine.[94] The Bishop was in Blaine on September 25th, and again on December 16th, to meet with the parish committee on plans for the new church, which Nevius undoubtedly helped to plan.

RETIREMENT

Nevius retired to Tacoma, to become priest in charge of old St. Peter's Church.[95] At the 1904 Convocation at Trinity Church in Tacoma, Bishop Keator reported that the old church and lots in Blaine had been sold, and a new church erected. "In 1905, the parish being vacant, (St. Peters, Tacoma) the Rev. R. D. Nevius, a retired clergyman, resident and serving in the diocese above mentioned since 1872, undertook to hold at least Sunday morning services, with holy eucharists, as priest in charge."[96] Nevius again attended the Convocation in 1905 at Epiphany Church, Chehalis.

At the 1906 Convocation, held at St. Luke's Church, Tacoma, Bishop Keator requested Dr. Nevius to memorialize Bishop Morris in a resolution noting his recent death. The Bishop's House in Tacoma was sold for $18,000. Nevius attended the Harvest Festival and Anniversary of the Parish at St. Michael's Church in Yakima in 1906, celebrating its 21st birthday, where he was recognized as the founder and preacher for the day.

Nevius attended once more the Convocation in June, 1907, at Bellingham. He celebrated his 80th birthday on November 26, 1907. An unidentified newspaper clipping from September, 1908, said "The picture of the rector was taken on the eightieth anniversary of his birth. He is still hale and active." Nevius lived in an upstairs room across from Fannie Paddock Hospital, and collected diatoms from tide flats whenever he got the chance, according to Mrs. Quinn Trott Neal, whose family knew him well.

In March of 1908 the cornerstone was laid for a Parish House at Baker City by Bishop Paddock, and it was named 'Nevius Hall'.[97] At the Convocation in May of 1908 at Vancouver, Nevius was elected as a delegate to the Eighth Missionary Council. In September Nevius attended the first Convocation of the new Missionary District of Eastern Oregon, at Pendleton. It had been separated from the Diocese of Oregon in October of 1907. In 1907 the bell tower for St. Peter's in Tacoma was declared too decayed to continue. It was an old growth fir, cut off at 50 feet, with the bell installed at the top. To replace it, a new tower was built around the old trunk, and at the same elevation and in the same place.

An article in the *Oregon Churchman* in March of 1909 stated, "Of the eleven Church buildings in Eastern Oregon, six are the result of the labors and consecrated efforts of Rev. R. D. Nevius, D.D., who in 1873 resigned the rectorship of Trinity Church, Portland, Oregon, in order to give himself as a pioneer missionary, seeking the places where no other missionary of the Church had been before, and working under the direction of the Bishop to start missions and build churches in new fields wherever possibilities of future development justified it. He was the first resident clergyman of the Church in Eastern Oregon, starting on June 7, 1873, in the Grande Ronde Valley, where churches at La Grande, the Cove and Union are evidences of his self-sacrificing labors. Crossing into the Powder River Valley, he gathered the congregation and built the Church at Baker City, and with that as a center, extended his ministry into the John Day River Valley and built the church in Canyon City, besides preaching at Connor Creek, Granite Creek, Heppner, Humboldt Basin, Lostine, Malheur (Eldorado), Mormon Basin, Sparta, North Powder, Rye Valley, Prairie City and many other points. During this same period he built the Church at The Dalles, residing there for several weeks at a time in ministering to the people....Since leaving Eastern Oregon in October, 1879, the same consecrated zeal has shown itself in his work in building churches at Spokane, Pomeroy, Sprague and Yakima, in Eastern Washington; and on Puget Sound at Chehalis and Whatcom; while he started the work which resulted in the building of churches by his successors at Lewiston, Idaho, Ellensburg and East Sound, in Washington, and Juneau in Alaska. Upon his completing the fiftieth year of his ministry, he retired from responsible work, although he is still as young in mind and as interested in all that affects the Church as he was half a century ago, and although 81 years old, drove by stage across the Blue Mountains last summer to revisit the scene of his former labors. He is now resident at Tacoma, being priest in charge of St. Peter's Church, whose famous steeple is the oldest in the United States."

On September 14, 1910, a Special Convocation was held at St. Mark's, Seattle, for the purpose of organization as a diocese. Nevius was present, and was elected fourth alternate Clerical Deputy to the General Convention. On September 29, 1910, Nevius preached the 25th anniversary sermon at Yakima. [98] Nevius celebrated his birthday on November 26th, and sent a picture to his sister-in-law, Augusta Eastman, of himself and his hostess taken that day.

Nevius participated as usual in the 1911 Convocation, held on May 30-31, in Seattle. On April 22, 1912, Augusta Nash Eastman died in Ovid, aged

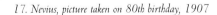

17. Nevius, picture taken on 80th birthday, 1907

60 years, 7 months. He again attended the Convocation at St. Luke's Church, Tacoma, in May. In a letter from Rowland M. Harper, Geographer, University of Alabama, to Howland Atwood, Huntington Library dated August 22, 1952, he stated, "Dr. Nevius was here [at the University of Alabama] for a brief visit in 1912 or 1913, but I saw him only a little while, and neglected to get more details about his work around here. I do not know that he ever published anything, in botanical literature at least."

Actually, Nevius took a sentimental trip in 1912. The *Tuscaloosa News* reported on March 31 that Nevius was expected there that spring, and that he had stopped in Los Angeles to visit an old school friend from Ovid, retired U.S. Senator Cole of California, whom he had not seen for 72 years. Nevius visited Cole at his "Colegrove" home before traveling to Tuscaloosa. Nevius visited in Tuscaloosa for some time. On April 19 the local paper reported that he would leave the next day for Mobile to visit friends there, returning to stay for another week in Tuscaloosa at the home of Mrs. Bryce. He preached at Christ Church, Tuscaloosa on April 28th. On May 1 he left on his return journey, stopping in Birmingham to visit his nephew, Mr. McLean (son of his wife's sister). He then planned to stop in Chattanooga to visit his sister-in-law, Nora Tuomey McLean. The paper stated:

"While the guest of Mrs. Bryce, his friends have enjoyed his genial and delightful company on many occasions, and his return to the scenes of early manhood has been a great pleasure to his companions and former pupils of those early days."

Nevius was again in attendance at the Convocation on May 27-28, 1913, at St. John's Church, Olympia. As usual he was an Examining Chaplain, but he was no longer listed as priest in charge of St. Peter's, but as a Non-Parochial clergy.

Nevius remained active until his death, although his eyesight failed in the final few months. When he could no longer read, he had someone read the service to him and memorized it so that he could still lead. In January of 1913 he was in Hoquiam at Holy Trinity to perform a baptism. In July of that year he presided over services in Buckley at St. John the Divine. He probably went to many other of his churches when he was asked.

On December 14, 1913, Nevius died suddenly while at the home of

18. Nevius with hostess on 80th birthday, age 83

19. Nevius circa 1913

Howard Taylor at Eagle Gorge near Tacoma. Taylor was Speaker of the House of Representatives for the Washington Legislature. The Portland *Oregonian* carried the following on December 15, 1913:

REUBEN D. NEVIUS DIES
Church Founder and Botanist Passes in Tacoma Aged 86

"Tacoma, Dec. 14.—Reuben D. Nevius, D.D., who founded more than 30 Episcopal Churches in the Pacific Northwest, died in this city today at the age of 86.

"He came to the Coast 41 years ago and settled at Portland as rector of Trinity Church, later becoming general missionary for Oregon, Washington, and Idaho. He was a botanist whose work was recognized throughout the world and a plant named in his honor, the 'Neviusia Alabamaensis,' is grown extensively in the conservatories of England."

Numerous articles were written about him in the places he knew best. The La Grande *Evening Observer*, on December 18, after reviewing his many accomplishments wrote:

"As instance of his virility of mind, only last week, the Rev. Upton H. Gibbs received a letter from him enclosing some Mss. [manuscripts], asking for his criticism and revision. The doctor wrote, 'I have dictated my thoughts in a compact and merely suggestive way, in a series of what I call theses, mere dogmatic statements, as compact as I could make them and brief. Having now no pulpit of my own I have imagined a congregation made up of my godchildren, young and old, to whom I have preached lying on my couch.'

"Full of years and labors and rich, not in this world's goods, but in the love of his friends and former parishioners, he is now gone to his reward.

" 'Life's work well done,

"Life's race well run

"Now cometh rest.'"

"With three bishops and nineteen clergymen officiating, the funeral of Rev. R. D. Nevius, the pioneer missionary of the Episcopal Church in the District of Oregon, Washington and Alaska, who died Sunday at the age of 86, was held yesterday in Trinity Church [now Christ Church, Tacoma]. The officiating bishops were Frederic W. Keator, of the Diocese of Olympia, Lemuel H. Wells, of the Diocese of Spokane, and Charles S. Scadding of Oregon.

"The full robed choir of Trinity church sang. The celebration of holy communion was direct in charge of the three bishops and Revs. Charles Y. Gromes of Trinity Church, Tacoma, and H. H. Gowen of Trinity Church, Seattle.

"The pall bearers were: Rev. E. M. Rogers, Rev. C. W. DeBois, Rev. Rodney Arney and Rev. Cameron Morrison.

"The only relative of Dr. Nevius present was Charles Dunlap of Puyallup, a cousin. The body was cremated."[99]

The *Seattle Churchman*, in the January, 1914, issue, wrote:

"When the history of the Church's work in the Pacific Northwest comes to be written it is certain that a distinguished place must be given to the life and labor of Dr. R. D. Nevius, who passed away from a long earthly ministry at Eagle Gorge on Sunday, Dec. 14. To few have been given to accomplish so much in so many and so varied fields and to hold high to the last the brimming cup of an enthusiasm greater and more precious than that of youth...."

In his annual address to the Convocation, at St. Marks in Seattle, on May 20, 1914, Bishop Keator spoke of Nevius's past and dedication. He also stated, "In recent years, when failing physical strength had unfitted him for the continuous care of a mission, I have found it hard to say him Nay when he has pleaded with me to let him take up the work in some place and build one more Church. When denied this privilege, he was, nevertheless, always ready to go wherever he might be sent for a single service, and even after his eyesight had so failed that he could no longer read the services in the Prayer Book, he found some one to read them to him over and over again until he could say them from memory, in order that he might be useful. While his physical powers waned with increasing years, his spiritual strength was unabated even to the moment when the call came which summoned him to the clearer vision of the Lord whom he loved and whom he had served so faithfully and well. With us through so many years, we miss him today, but who shall say he is not with us still? Who shall say that his prayers no longer go up with our prayers to the great Head of the Church for His blessing upon and His guidance of this Diocese which he loved so well."

In a letter to Professor Albert R. Sweetser of Eugene dated at The Dalles November 19, 1917, Elisabeth L. Lang wrote of Nevius:..."He was a man of delightful personality, of wonderful learning and the wisest botanist I have ever known. He loved the study of plant life above all else. Death had taken his entire family—wife, children, parents, brothers and sisters, and apparently had filled that terrible void in his life by devotion to the study of growing things. Children always loved him as dearly as he loved them and it was wonderful to find the numberless places in which he had sown the seeds of his craft. I know of many persons whose love of forestry and plants was begun in childhood through the marvels disclosed by Dr. Nevius' microscope. I wish I had the power to describe him to you properly; a gentleman of the highest breeding and refinement; a scholar of the most advanced class, and a most affectionate and kindly teacher of all who came under his ministrations."

20. Nevius in garden. Oregon Historical Society, neg.no.60578

INDEX TO CHURCHES

Indicates that church of Nevius's day still stands.

CHAPTER 2

THE NEVIUS CHURCHES

There are six Episcopal churches in Eastern Oregon traditionally called the "Nevius Churches." Nevius "built" over thirty churches in his lifetime. His efforts were part of a large Episcopal Church building campaign conducted in the 1870s. The Episcopal Church began building in Oregon with the arrival of Rt. Rev. Thomas Fielding Scott in 1854. He was the first missionary Bishop of Oregon, Washington and Idaho Territories. His work was financed by the Board of Domestic and Foreign Missions, who paid his salary, but expected him to raise the funds for building. Bishop Scott built "meetinghouse type" churches with little architectural pretension. Although Scott made trips east to raise funds for churches, he largely built and equipped St. Stephen's, Portland and St. Paul's, Oregon City, at his own expense. After his sudden death in 1867 in New York, Rt. Rev. Benjamin Wistar Morris II, D.D., became bishop in place of Scott. His son, Benjamin Wistar Morris III, was a leading New England architect during the period from 1900 to the 1930s. Bishop Morris was a patron of architecture, and had definite ideas about the proper and correct design of church buildings. In 1874 he had Good Samaritan Hospital built, along with a new rectory.

A publication which was much used in those days, and which shows similarities with building in the Northwest was George Woodward's *Rural Church Architecture*, published in 1870, and again in 1875. It was a reprint of a book commissioned by the Congregational Church in Albany, New York, in 1852, in which leading architects of the day were invited to submit designs for model churches.

Buildings such as St. Helen's Hall, a remodeled St. Stephen's Church, Bishop Scott Grammar School, St. David's Church in Portland, St. Andrew's Chapel in Kalama, Washington, St. Luke's Church in Vancouver, and Trinity Church, Portland, were already accomplished or well under way by the time Nevius ar-

21. Nevius, age about 85. Oregon Historical Society, neg.no.74143

rived in 1872. St. Luke's and Trinity were designed by Albert H. Jordan, a Portland architect.

Jordan had been born in Great Britain and emigrated to the US about 1840. He and his brother had practiced architecture in Hartford, Connecticut. About 1852 Jordan moved to Detroit, where he worked until 1861. He was in San Mateo, California, in 1865 when he participated in organizing St. Matthew's Episcopal Church there. By 1871 he was in Portland, where he designed the Vancouver church, and designed a house for Judge Matthew P. Deady in July of 1872. He also designed St. Paul's Church in Walla Walla, and the Bank of British Columbia Building in Portland. He died suddenly on October 23, 1872, of a cerebral hemorrhage at the age of 52. No doubt Nevius had met him, since he arrived in April of that year, and they are likely to have had discussions on church architecture. Jordan was actively working on the construction of the new Trinity Church, of which Nevius was to be rector, as well as an adjacent rectory.

Nevius's arrival in Portland was during the construction of Trinity Church, to which he was called as rector. He had left for Eastern Oregon as a missionary by the time it was consecrated. This chapter will document churches which either were built under Nevius's supervision or which Nevius served during his ministry in the Northwest.

The normal process during Nevius's time was for a missionary church to begin with the acquisition of a lot. At times one was given to the church as a way to start out. When it was determined that the community was ready, a cornerstone would be laid, usually with the Bishop contributing "seed" money either from his own purse or money raised in the East for the purpose. Local funds were raised by the missionary and through the efforts of the women's guilds. At some point a plan would be obtained, and a foundation laid. Construction would begin, usually by a hired contractor, and various phases would be celebrated. "Under cover" would mean that it was framed and the roof on. "Enclosed" would enable it to be used for services. "Finished" would mean that the insides were complete, and "Furnished" would mean that the furnishings were all acquired, including a stove, lamps, chancel furniture and a bell. The church would not be consecrated until it was free of debt.

Nevius appears to have been familiar with church construction, and may have participated in building a church in Alabama. He certainly would have been familiar with the construction of Trinity Church in Portland, which had barely been started when he arrived. When he became a missionary in eastern Oregon he was confronted with new challenges. Funds such as were expended on Trinity were not available there, and construction costs were much higher, as materials needed to be shipped to remote locations. As a scholar, Nevius became familiar with the resources available, mostly in design books of the day, and applied his own ideas to improving them. St. John's Church, Union, was likely built according to a design proposed by him, or by Bishop Morris and Nevius, as Morris was familiar with architecture and was the father of a successful architect of the day. Ascension in Cove and St. Paul's in The Dalles were improvements on that design. Nevius provided the design and did much of the actual work at St. Matthew's in Sprague. The Church of the Epiphany in Chehalis bears much resemblance to the

Union church, but with a larger tower. The church in Juneau appears to have a floor plan similar to one in Woodward's design book. It is likely that when Nevius knew he was going to raise funds for a church, he brought along his design books plus his personal experience in building economical and attractive churches. Where no architect was employed, he could speed things along by suggesting what had worked for him in the past. For further discussion see the section on St. John's, Union.

Churches Associated with Nevius

(churches known to be constructed under the direct supervision of Nevius are marked with an asterisk)

NAME	DATE	STARTED/BUILT
Christ Church, Wetumpka, Alabama	1853	
St. David's Church, Liberty Hill, Alabama	1853-55	
Mission station, Athens, Alabama	1855	1855
St. Mary's, lower Dallas Co., Alabama	1855	1855
Christ Church, Tuscaloosa, Alabama	1855-66	
St. Philip's Chapel (for blacks), Tuscaloosa		
Christ Church, Oil City, Pennsylvania	1866-69	
St. John's Church, Rouseville, Pennsylvania	1866	
St. John's Church, Mobile, Alabama	1869-72	
Chapel, West Fowl River*, Alabama	1869/70	
Elyton (now Birmingham), Alabama (*church moved from Ashville*)	1870/71	
Trinity Church, Portland, Oregon* (*2nd building*)	1872-73	1872
Eastern Oregon	1873-79	
St. Peter's Church, La Grande*	1873-75	1873
St. Stephen's Church, Baker City*	1873-79	1873
St. John's Church, Union*	1873-75	1873
Ascension Church, Cove*	1873-75	1873-76
St. Paul's Church, The Dalles*	1874-79	1874
St. Thomas' Church, Canyon City*	1874-79	1874
Mission, Prairie City	1875-79	1875
Services held in Sparta, 1874; Connor Creek, Heppner, Humboldt Basin (now Mormon Basin), Rye Valley, 1876; Granite Creek, 1877.		
Eastern Washington/Northern Idaho	1879-83	
Church of the Nativity, Lewiston, Idaho	1879-81	1890
St. Luke's Ft. Coeur d'Alene, Idaho	1879-83	1892
All Saints' Church, Spokane Falls*	1880-83	1880
Ft. Colville	1880	

Grace Church, Dayton	1880-83	1902
Good Samaritan, Colfax *(with Lemuel H. Wells)*	1881-82	1888
St. Matthew's Church, Sprague*	1882-83	1882
Mission, Cheney	1882-83	1882
St. Peter's Church, Pomeroy*	1883	1883

Services in Ellensburg, Goldendale & Yakima, 1883.

Western Washington/Alaska　　　　　　　1883-86

St. John's Church, Olympia	1883-87	*(2nd building)* 1884
Church of the Epiphany, Chehalis*	1883-85	1884
St. Paul's Church, Whatcom (now Bellingham)	1883-84	1884
"General Missionary" Western Washington	1887-92	
St. Michael's Church, North Yakima*	1887-90	1888
"Small cottage," North Yakima	1888	
Grace Church, Ellensburg	1887-90	1897
Parish House, Ellensburg	1890	
St. David's Church, Hoquiam	1890-91	1906
"Missionary house," Hoquiam	1890	
St. Andrew's Church, Aberdeen	1895	
St. Mark's Church, Ocosta*	1890-92	1892
St. John's Church, South Bend	1890-92	1914
St. Luke's Church, Elma	1890-92	1911
St. Mark's Church, Montesano	1890-92	1909

Services at Elma and Montesanto, 1887-92, Grays Harbor City, 1891.

Christ Church, Blaine *(see below)*	1894-97	1904
Trinity Church, Juneau, Alaska*	1895-96	1896
St. Luke's Church, Douglas Island, Alaska	1895-96	
Trinity Church, Seattle *(2nd building)*	1896	1891
Chaplain, Fannie Paddock Hospital		
Church of Holy Communion	1897-1900	1893
St. John the Divine Church, Buckley	1898-1900	1896
Christ Church, Blaine*	1900-04	1904
St. Peter's Church, Tacoma	1904-12	1874

Trinity Church

Portland, Oregon

Trinity Church, the first completely organized parish of the Episcopal Church in the Pacific Northwest, was consecrated by Bishop Thomas Fielding Scott on September 24, 1854. The second church building, designed by Albert H. Jordan, and built by Lauritz Therkleson, was located at SW 5th and Oak. The plans were made between August of 1871, and February of 1872. Judge Matthew Deady was the Senior Warden during that time, and must have taken a leading role in the process. The contract was given to Therkleson in March to build it for $17,000. The cornerstone was laid on April 25, just two days before Nevius arrived. The spire was raised on Friday, August 9, 1872, with a 2,000 lb bell which had been cast in New York from a 17th century Spanish canon from Vera Cruz, Mexico. The exterior was finished by December, 1872, but the church was not consecrated until August 31, 1873, two months and 24 days after Nevius left for Eastern Oregon. The stained glass windows were ordered from London. The cost including furniture and organ was $20,000. The church burned in 1902.

22. First Trinity Church 1854-1873. Oregon Historical Society, neg.no.60578

23. Second Trinity Church 1873. Oregon Historical Society, neg.no.30212

St. Peter's Church

La Grande, Oregon

Episcopal services had been held in La Grande in Eastern Oregon's fertile Grande Ronde valley and adjacent points as early as 1865. The Grande Ronde became an important center of agricultural production when gold strikes triggered a rush of population into adjacent regions of Idaho and Oregon in the early 1860s.

A tireless fundraising campaign conducted in the East by Bishop Morris had netted a gift of $500 from a lady in Niagara Falls, New York. This donation was accompanied by a request that a church be built "at some missionary point and called 'St. Peter's' after her own parish church," and by early 1873 Morris was considering a "small, neat, and comfortable church" at La Grande. During the 1873 spring tour of the eastern portion of his jurisdiction, Morris organized a congregation, received two lots as a site for a church, and raised a local subscription of $1,525. Confident that the total would reach $2,500 he reported, "A plan will be immediately obtained from the East, and a proper, churchly building erected." Nevius arrived in La Grande a month later to take charge of the project.

The source of this plan is unknown. It may have been supplied through the lady contributor from Niagara Falls. It has been suggested that it was supplied by the Episcopal Board of Domestic and Foreign Missions, but the author has found no evidence of this. It may have been supplied by a Portland builder or architect, possibly E. M. Burton or Warren H. Williams, both of whom had prior or subsequent involvement in Episcopal Church-sponsored projects. Or, it may have been obtained from one of the many contemporary suppliers of mail-order architectural plans. Whatever the source, the result was a simple, rectangular, steeply-gabled building with horizontal siding, a Gothic bell cote, and a small narthex or porch. It suggested little of the organic integrity which subsequent examples of the so-called "Nevius Churches" were to display.

In his annual Convocation address of late August, 1873, Bishop Morris noted that the people of La Grande were "waiting only for the architect's plan to build their church." Nevius reported in a letter to the Bishop of about the same time that "the ground was already staked out and the people were eager to get construction started."

With characteristic exuberance he added, "should we go on this way you will be more likely called to consecrate in

24. St. Peter's Church LaGrande 1875

November than to lay the corner stone." The cornerstone was duly laid by the Bishop on the afternoon of Saturday, November 8, 1873. Though construction had probably begun, it did not progress as rapidly as Nevius had hoped. It was not until August, 1874 that the *Oregon Churchman* reported that the church "is under roof and enclosed." It was first used for a wedding on Thursday, September 24, 1874, about a year after construction began. There were no seats (Nevius reported "they were not needed on this oc-

casion....") or other liturgical furnishings. But Nevius and members of the congregation quickly built temporary platforms, chancel rail, altar and seats so that services could begin the following Sunday.

Next summer, on Tuesday, July 15, 1875, the church was consecrated, signifying that it was free of debt, by Bishop Morris assisted by The Right Rev. Daniel Sylvester Tuttle of Utah, Idaho and Montana Territories; the Rev. Dr. Nevius, and Nevius's newly-arrived assistant, the Rev. George T. Kaye, stationed at Cove.

25. St. Peter's, LaGrande, 1924

Following the arrival of the railroad, the building was moved in 1887 from La Grande's upper "old town" to Fourth and "O" Streets. A later photograph shows that stepped buttresses had been added to the ends and middle of the nave, probably when the building was moved. It was demolished in 1924 to make way for the present church building on the site.

Union, Oregon

The cornerstone of St. John's Church in Union was laid Tuesday, November 18, 1873, the day after the cornerstone was laid for the church in Baker City, by Bishop Morris assisted by the Rev. Dr. Nevius. Morris received the deed to two lots from "Mr. Hannah" the same day. The *Oregon Churchman* of February 1, 1874, added that the church "...is to be a memorial to the Rev. G. W. Natt, of the Diocese of Pennsylvania, in which Mr. Natt began his ministry, and where he left so many memories of his devout and saintly life. Five hundred dollars of the cost will be provided by his widow, and by former friends and parishioners. The Bishop of the Missionary jurisdiction (Morris) received baptism at the hands of Mr. Natt, and was intimately associated with him in his ministerial work."

Construction work seems to have begun within the next several months and, unlike Baker, progressed smoothly. During his July, 1874, tour of eastern Oregon, Bishop Morris noted, "The Church buildings at La Grande, Union, and Baker City are progressing steadily, though not with the rapidity that we sometimes see on this side of the mountains." "Our Union Items" in the Baker City *Bedrock Democrat* of August 19 reported, "Work on the Episcopal Church is being rapidly pushed forward by S. Sisson, Esq." The first recorded service, though perhaps not the first time the building was used, was Easter, March 28, 1875.

St. John's was consecrated several months later on Wednesday, July 14, 1875, by Bishop Morris and visiting Bishop Daniel Sylvester Tuttle of Utah, Idaho and Montana, Nevius, and Nevius's newly arrived assistant, the Rev. George T. Kaye stationed at the Cove. St. Peter's, La Grande, was consecrated the following day. The consecration account contained in a letter published in the *Oregon Churchman* of July 22, 1875, unsigned but probably by Nevius or Kaye, continues:

"Chancel Carpets, Altar and Lectern covers, Bible and Prayer Books for Chancel, a Communion Service, Alms Basin and Font, make this beautiful church complete for Divine Service.

Other generous offerings chiefly from Portland have helped to speed the work. The church is novel in construction and appearance, and is thought to be a model for a cheap church when labor and material can be had at moderately low prices. The church has cost about $2,000. It is believed that the same building could be erected in Portland for $1,200 or $1,400. It is admirably built, Mr. Samuel Sisson the contractor having wrought upon it with unusual care and faithfulness under many difficulties and perplexities. It is built of undressed 1¼ inch plank placed on the inside of the buttressed frame with open timbered roof. The roof is of dressed tongued and

26. St. John's Union January 15, 1875

grooved sheeting, supported by heavy truss timbers all chamfered. The framing timbers are beautifully related to each other; they are dressed and chamfered. A wood cut of the church may be seen in *Home and Abroad* for February, 1875."

This "wood cut" or steel engraving labeled "Rockwood Photo Engraving Process" was probably made from a photograph now in the collection of the Oregon Historical Society. The original print is mounted on a small card measuring $2\frac{9}{16}$ by $4\frac{1}{8}$ inches. An unidentified hand wrote on the reverse side, "Horizon line is faintly marked. It (sic.) is a mountain ridge bare, save with scattered fir forests near the summit. It is one mile away, intervening country flat fenced fields. Fill angle of tower marked (a) with battened boards like front of church. Fill windows or not as you please. Take the painter and scaffolding down."

The engraver ignored the landscape instructions and failed to fill in the angle of the tower with boards (the carpenter must have failed to do this too because a later view shows the tower open), but he took the painter and scaffolding down and filled in the windows just as he pleased. The rose window in the engraving contains trefoil tracery, a feature that apparently never existed. The original photograph must have been taken sometime in late summer or early fall of 1874, prior to publication of the engraved view in early 1875. The church was obviously near completion when the photograph was taken and therefore should have been usable several months before the first recorded Easter service described above.

The Medieval architecture of northern Europe is often considered to be one of the most successfully integrated syntheses of structural necessity, economic use of material, and visual expression ever attained in the history of architecture. By the time of the American Revolution, most of these buildings had fallen into states of poor repair or ruin. Labeled "Gothic," a term of derision, they were considered relics of a dim and uncivilized past. Fashionable and knowledgeable persons looked to models from Greek and Roman civilization for inspiration in matters architectural and otherwise. For example, the architectural forms of the Roman Republic were quickly adopted as appropriate forms for state-houses and other public and private buildings, including churches, in the new American Republic. This enthusiasm for classical antiquity was fueled by the discovery of Pompeii about 1770 and other archaeological excavations of the time.

Doubts lingered, however, about the appropriateness of pagan temple-forms for houses of Christian worship. Around the turn of the nineteenth century scholars in England and France began to take a closer look at the medieval "Christian" buildings in their own back yards, and to argue that these were the most appropriate models for ecclesiastical architecture. Moreover, they noted that this architecture was better suited to the climactic conditions of northern Europe than the classical forms of the brighter and warmer south. The argument caught on and by the time the British Houses of Parliament were begun in 1836, the so-called "Gothic Revival" was well underway along with the "battle of the styles" that was to continue through the nineteenth century.

27. St. John's Union early 1875

It should be noted that some scholars have observed that medieval building traditions never really died out in rural areas of England, Europe, and even colonial America, where sizable buildings such as churches, barns, and mills continued to be built in the old, familiar ways. This phenomenon has been dubbed the "Gothic Survival."

Some of the stones of this architectural debate were cemented by an English political and religious controversy of the 1830s. In reaction to a Parliamentary proposal that certain articles of faith and ritual be discarded in the established Church of England to make the national church more appealing to divergent "nonconformist" groups, traditionalists seized upon the legacy of native heritage. Known as the "Oxford Movement" or "Ecclesiology," defenders of the old ways began a counter-movement that included an emphasis on "correct" or "pointed" Christian architecture. These so-called "high churchmen" also placed an emphasis on sacramental liturgy in contrast to the more evangelical "low churchmen" who placed greater emphasis on preaching.

Augustus Welby Northmore Pugin, a child prodigy, architect, and British high churchman who converted to Roman Catholicism, published an influential book in 1841 entitled *The True Principles of Pointed or Christian Architecture* in which he set forth the intellectual clarity of medieval buildings. His opening statement was, "the two great rules for design are these: First, that there should be no features about a building which are not necessary for convenience, construction, or propriety; Second that all ornament should consist of enrichment of the essential construction of the building."

American architectural thinkers of the time were dissatisfied with the limitations of the Classical or Greek Revival style of architecture. Though they were of widely divergent religious opinion, many quickly accepted the arguments of Pugin and other proponents of the Gothic. The climate of the northern United States is similar to that of northern Europe, and most Americans of that time were of North European descent. Pugin's *True Principles* offered direction in the search to find or develop an architecture that was appropriate to the people and conditions of the United States.

Two subsequent books by Andrew Jackson Downing, a horticulturist and a native of New York's Hudson River Valley, had widespread impact in America. They were: *Cottage Residences, Rural Architecture and Landscape Gardening* (1842), and *The Architecture of Country Houses* (1850). Much of the material in these books was also published in the *Horticulturist*, a quarterly publication edited by Downing. Downing thought that it was silly to squeeze the architectural requirements for daily living into rigid classical forms, and that Greek temples or Gothic castles built of wood were a sham. He also detested the use of white and red paint because these pigments were unnatural, glaring, and inharmonious in the landscape. Instead he favored the use of pastel tans, browns and greys that resembled the natural colors of stone. But Dawning's great contribution to the development of American architecture was that he presented Pugin's two "principles" in a format that could be readily understood by Americans. He stressed the importance of the "fitness" of architectural forms, materials and modes of construction to the intended purposes of buildings; and "truthfulness" in the expression of materials and employment of ornament. Downing endorsed the newly-developed "balloon" frame, the earliest form of the stud-wall framing system that is the standard way of constructing light wooden buildings today, and urged the use of vertical board-and-batten siding because it truthfully expressed the vertical stud frame within the walls. Neither an architect himself nor strictly confined to the Gothic Revival style as the only suitable expression of his concepts, Downing published the works of like-minded contemporary architects, many of whom designed in the Gothic mode. This cadre formed a society that later became the American Institute of Architects. Many also were involved in the Ecclesiological debate and its architectural manifestations which had surfaced in the Episcopal Church, the Church of England's American counterpart, about 1840. The American Ecclesiologists argued that the simple rural churches of the early English Gothic period were especially appropriate models for American churches because of their directness and simplicity of form and construction, as well as their durability and picturesque appearance. At this time there were no schools of architectural training in the United States nor an organized profession of architectural practice. Books such as Downing's were commonly known as "pattern books" and were an important means of disseminating architectural thought as well as specific designs. Downing's ideas were repeated in many later pattern books.

St. John's, Union epitomized Downing's principles of "fitness" and "truthfulness" in architectural design. Whether "Gothic Revival" or "Gothic Survival," it was thoroughly Gothic in form and spirit. Ackland[100] and others have postulated that north European principles of building in stone grew out of an understanding of building in hewn timber. St. John's, Union was a vigorous and handsome demonstration of Gothic construction principles translated to the requirements of building in milled timber. Ornament and structure were one and the same. Nothing was superfluous. It successfully attained the goal of enclosing a volume of space with a refinement of material. Both "cheap" and "churchlike," it was admirably fitted to the requirements of the frontier where labor skilled in the fitting of timber necessary for mining and mill and barn building was readily available, but where materials were expensive.

Like its Gothic predecessors, St. John's relied on a clearly expressed structural frame to carry a thin membrane of material that enclosed space. The membrane in this wooden example consisted of vertical boards mounted on the inside of the timber frame. They carried no structural loads but only enclosed space. On the exterior, the joints between the vertical boards that formed the walls were covered by battens of 2" by 2" stock cut on the diagonal so that the battens were triangular in section. On the interior the joints were covered by a beaded or molded batten. The interior surface was then oiled or varnished, and the exterior was painted. Like its Gothic predecessors, the building was organized in bays which were clearly expressed by exterior buttresses. These buttresses carried the loads from the roof trusses and provided the building's lateral support. Surviving parts of St. John's and inspection of photographs indicate the nave measured about 23' by 40'.

Nevius was responsible for this design. Contemporary sources are strangely silent about Nevius's design talent, perhaps because it was common knowledge and perhaps because of the sensitive nature of earlier events in Portland. But Bishop Morris, speaking of Nevius in his Convocation address of 1883 commented almost in passing: "One thing to be seen as worthy of special notice is the style and character of the church buildings designed and erected by him. St. John's, Union, St. Thomas, Canyon City, and St. Peter's, Dalles, are examples of a very admirable style of architecture, for small wooden churches of moderate cost, and their influence on the state of the people is already observable."

It is not known if Nevius had built churches in the South or in Pennsylvania before he came to Oregon, or if he borrowed this design from another source. If it was original, Nevius may have been assisted in its development by the contractor Samuel Sisson. Sisson seems to have played a special role of some kind because he is the only contractor mentioned in the *Oregon Churchman* between 1871 and 1876, during which time over fifteen Episcopal church-sponsored building projects were undertaken. Little is known of him other than he was born in New York State in the 1830s, may have known Nevius as a youth, came to the Grande Ronde valley in the 1860s, and lived in Oro Dell in 1870. Oro Dell was a small mill village located at the mouth of a creek, about where the west La Grande freeway interchange is located now. This suggests that Sisson may have had skills as a millwright. If indeed he was a builder of mills or barns, he could represent a counterpart "Gothic Revival" element. Nevius, a horticulturist, most probably was a reader of the *Horticulturist*, and therefore was exposed as a young man to Downing's ideas.

The early photograph of St. John's shows that it had a patterned roof like the other Oregon churches attributable to Nevius, (except possibly The Dalles). The bottom layer of limited paint scrapings taken from the surviving parts of the building indicates that the chamfered posts were a dark brown. A guess based on color schemes of the period is that the board-and-batten siding was a shade of "drab": a tan or yellowish tan color. The painting of the church appears to have been incomplete in the early photograph.

A later photograph, probably taken shortly before the church was dismantled and moved to Cove in 1927, shows that few alterations had been made. No record of structural failures or other needed repair has come to light, but the photograph shows that the stone buttress foundations had been replaced with brick foundations, and that a tower-like projection, detailed in keeping with the architecture of the church, possibly a chimney, had been added.

The crumbling of the original stone buttress foundations testifies to the functional nature of the buttresses, which concentrated the powerful forces of winds acting on the large roof area and transferred these loads to the buttress foundation directly. The December, 1910, Sanborn Insurance map for Union indicates that electricity had been installed, but that the church was still heated by a stove. In 1930 the parts of the dismantled building were reassembled with considerable alteration on the grounds of Ascension Summer School in Cove, where it was named Morris Hall and used for a kitchen and refectory. Two bays were added to the chancel end of the former nave and the pitch of the roof was reduced considerably. A partial second story was inserted beneath a shed-roofed dormer and the whole given simple Craftsman-style detail. The building was moved to another location on the same grounds in the 1960s and is used as a crafts hall today.

29. St. John's Union after 1928

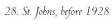

28. St. Johns, before 1928

30. St. John's Union, Cove 1993

St. Stephen's Church

Baker City, Oregon

St. Stephen's was under construction in November of 1873, when the Baker City *Bedrock Democrat* reported "...And now workmen are engaged upon the foundation of the Church, the enclosed fence and a small house which Dr. Nevius is putting up for an office or study, and which will be the vestry room of the future Church.... The contract for the new Church will be given out as soon as a plan shall have been adopted." The cornerstone was laid at 2:00 p.m. on Monday, November 17, 1873, by Morris and Nevius "during a great wind storm." Morris had held occasional services in Baker since 1870. In his May, 1873 tour of eastern Oregon he was offered two different building sites and began a subscription fund, offering $500 toward the construction of a church if an additional $1,500 could be raised locally. About $900 of that had been subscribed when Nevius arrived from Portland that summer.

The vestry room, measuring 12' x 20', was completed by February 1, 1874. Dubbed Nevius's "Prophet's Chamber," he did some of the work himself and began living in it at once, shifting his base of operations from La Grande to Baker City. An overall plan must have been adopted fairly quickly because a contract was let to build the church sometime during this period. But the contractors "threw up the contract" soon after because they had not received a scheduled payment. Their condition was that lumber, which had been delivered to the site, be paid for. When Bishop Morris visited the following July he found Nevius "nicely fixed in his vestry room, with the church lots fenced and trees planted, the stone foundation of the church and chancel built, the lumber for the building all on the ground and *all paid for* (emphasis original).

An early chronicler, the Rev. Octavius Parker, relates, "The plan for the Church which was substantially that of St. John Church Union was at the advice of the Bishop changed and a plan was adopted which was supposed to be cheaper." This must have been done during the Bishop's July, 1874 visit because construction was progressing again by August 15 under a new contract with different builders, with the hopes of completion by Christmas. Parker continues, "The Church was built chiefly during the absence of the Missionary (Nevius) and mistakes were made in choosing and placing the roof timbers. When too late the roof was found to be too weak to be self-supporting and much to the regret of the missionary the Church generally was but a pitiable piece of work."

As anticipated, the church was complete enough to be used for services by the end of the year. Nevius, writing to Bishop Mor-

31. St. Stephen's, Baker City

ris on December 15, 1874, reported, "...we shall have services here on St. Stephen's Day going into the church on the bare floor, everything extemporized save the stove and the lamps. If you do not give us another name, I shall call the church "St. Stephen." St. Stephen's Day is December 26, the day after Christmas. However, the Baker City *Bedrock Democrat* of December 30, probably on the basis of an announcement issued by Nevius, reported that "The Episcopal Church...will be used for Divine Service on New Year's Day, for the first time." Whatever the actual date of the first service in the building, "St. Stephen's" became the name of the new church.

The itinerary for the Bishop's tour of eastern Oregon planned for July, 1875, published in preceding issues of the *Oregon Churchman*, noted that he planned to consecrate St. Stephen's at that time as well as new churches in La Grande and Union. But the July 22 issue of the *Oregon Churchman* reported, "after examining the affairs of the churches in this place (Baker) and Union he determined...to lift the debt on St. John's Church, Union, that it might be consecrated." The "affairs" examined by the Bishop may have extended beyond financial matters, but the reason given by Morris in his opening address to the Convocation of 1875 was "a debt of a few hundred dollars which prevented its consecration." St. Stephen's was not to be consecrated until September 4, 1889.

The earliest view of this building was published in early 1876. It was a steel engraving showing an unbuttressed rectangular nave, a steeply-gabled roof with a broad band of patterned shingles, and a bell cote surmounted by a sizable cross with trefoil arms, triangular-headed door and window openings with shallow hood moldings reminiscent of the mitered arches common to Anglo-Saxon architecture, and no porch. An item of particular interest is that it clearly showed an extended chancel flanked by a small vestry transept or wing to the north. The chancel end of this church, like certain other Nevius churches, faced west. In the Rockwood view the nave roof met the roof of the transept awkwardly.

The bell cote and the chancel are both points of mystery. The bell cote does not appear in the earliest known photograph, which was taken after a porch was added about 1890 and probably before the church was moved to the adjacent lot north in 1902. This bell cote probably existed and was removed when a "new roof" was put on between 1884 and 1887. The posts to support it are still visible on the inside of the east wall, though they no longer carry their intended loads to the foundation due to intervention of an enlarged door frame that appears to date from a renovation of 1949-1953. There is no record of a bell ever having been installed in this church.

The nave appears originally to have had an unstudded three-bay post-and-beam frame with vertical board-and-batten siding, measuring 26' x 50' in all. The "new roof" project of 1884-1887 may have been a complete rebuilding of the roof and its supporting structure. A shingled roof should have lasted longer than ten to twelve years in Baker's climate, which is generally dry but inclined to heavy snow loading. Perhaps the original "pitiable piece of work" referred to by Octavius Parker had begun to fail completely. The buttresses are not mentioned until 1890 but probably were added in the mid-1880s along with the restructured roof. There was an almost continuous series of projects undertaken to improve the

Baker City church through the 1880s.

The Rev. Joshua N. T. Goss supervised a major rehabilitation costing about $3,000 in 1889 and 1890. The *Oregon Churchman* of July, 1889, reported that the "church is undergoing some very much needed repairs...." The October, 1890, issue reported a number of items of new chancel furniture and that, "The walls on the outside have been strengthened by new buttresses, and the large extent of the roof relieved with (dormer) hoods placed over the windows and about midway between eaves and ridge. A good sized vestry has been built on, and a commodious vestibule added in front." The nave's east gable was shingled about this time and parish records show that the rose window was added, as well as stained glass for this and various other windows, including the chancel window.

32. St. Stephen's Baker 1993

The matter of the chancel is also puzzling. The Rev. Octavius Parker recorded between 1882 and 1884 that he "...built four more rooms to the one erected by Dr. Nevius —the chancel being one of these rooms. The work cost between $1,200 and $1,300 making a good substantial home for the missionary." A later chronicler noted "chancel opened" during the Goss period (1888-1890) in his highly accurate notes made about 1910. Yet, Bishop Morris noted, "The stone foundation of the church and chancel (was) built" when he visited in July, 1874; and the earliest known view of the church, published in 1876, shows a volume that appears to be an extended chancel.

It may be that all of the written accounts are correct. The church may have been planned with an extended chancel and the foundation for it was built the winter of 1873-74 along with Nevius's "Prophet's Chamber." Then, when the "cheaper" plan was adopted at the Bishop's urging in the summer of 1874, it was decided to build the nave but not the chancel. The 1876 Rockwood view may have been enhanced to show features that did not exist at the time, as was done with the Rockwood view of the church at Union. The depiction of the cross on the chancel gable and the angle at which the chancel and vestry roofs meet are not entirely convincing in this view of the Baker City church. The vestry room, twenty feet long, would have extended about thirteen feet northward of the nave if the foundation for the planned chancel was twelve feet square, the same depth as the vestry; or fifteen feet northward if the chancel was fourteen feet square, the approximate dimension of a chancel built later at The Dalles. The 1876 view indicates that the vestry wing extended something on the order of twelve to fifteen feet north of the nave.

To continue with this possible scenario, the chancel may have been built by Parker in the early 1880s, either as a dwelling space that could be opened to the nave at some future time, or as the planned chancel for which a foundation already existed. The former possibility is problematical if there were an existing window in the chancel end of the nave because a dwelling room would have blocked the light to it.

Therefore it seems most likely that Parker built the chancel. There are no other references to chancel work other than installation of a "new window" in the accounts of the work done about 1890 under Goss. Barry's later note that the chancel was "opened" may be erroneous, based perhaps on an oral account that confused the work done in the early 1880s with the work done five or so years later. Or, it may mean only that a window was installed, thus "opening" an unlighted chancel. At any rate, this chancel was demolished in the renovation of 1949-53, when another bay was added to the nave and a new chancel larger than the original one was built.

The "new" chancel window of about 1890, which has been incorporated into the renovation of 1949-53, was a pointed arch subdivided by tracery into three lancet panels with three diamond-shaped panels above them. The original miter-headed door and window openings appear to have been converted to pointed arches at this time as well. Gas lighting was installed between 1892 and 1894. The battered buttresses installed about 1890 were con-

33. St. Stephen's, Baker City, 2001

verted sometime later to battered-and-stepped buttresses that appear in photographs taken in the 1920s. This was probably done when the building was moved to the adjacent lot to the north in 1902, at which time electric lights were installed. A basement was placed under the original nave during the renovation of 1949-53, which was completed by encasing the old stone nave and its various additions, including a new vestry wing, in brick. The building has been little changed since, and is in regular use today.

34 St. Stephen's, interior

35. St. Stephen's, interior

Ascension Church

Cove, Oregon

The cornerstone was laid for an unnamed church at Cove at 2:00 p.m., Wednesday, November 19, 1873, the day after the cornerstone was laid for St. John's church in Union. Samuel Gautier French, the first postmaster of "Forest Cove," had offered an annual stipend of $500 toward the support of a resident clergyman. French, member of a prominent Maryland and New Jersey family, had come to the area in the early 1860s for reasons of health. He acquired 100 acres of virgin land and became a gentleman farmer and orchardist. In addition to his horticultural interests, he established a grist mill with two partners from Missouri in 1866.

If construction of the church was planned or underway at the time of the laying of the cornerstone, it did not progress far because the following summer the *Oregon Churchman* reported, "At the Cove the work has been delayed from a necessary change in the architect's plan, the first plan being entirely too elaborate and costly." According to a later edition of the *Oregon Churchman* this "architect's plan" was Albert H. Jordan's plan for St. Paul's church in Walla Walla.

Jordan previously had designed St. Luke's church in Vancouver, Washington Territory, begun in the fall of 1871; and Trinity Church, Portland, begun in the spring of 1872. Construction of the Walla Walla church began October 1, 1872, several weeks before Jordan's death, and was completed six months later according to the Walla Walla *Statesman* of March 22, 1873. This remarkably detailed account reported that the erection of this new church promised "to mark an era in the architectural history" of the region and that ample provision had been made for ventilation, considered a great improvement upon similar structures in the area. It gave nave dimensions of 28' by 51' (the nave at Cove measures 25' by 50½'), and reported local fears that the imposing spire might not resist the heavy winds that are common to eastern Oregon and Washington. It also mentioned that the church had "three sets of truss rafters," was painted "in imitation of stone," and cost $5,000.

The plan that was finally used was a modified version of Jordan's original plan for the Walla Walla church, "the tower and the spire excepted" and with "the addition of a bell cote." Nevius probably was responsible for the revision to Jordan's plan. Samuel Sisson could have been involved as well. Construction of the magnificently-sited Cove church and a companion Gothic rectory began in earnest sometime in late 1874 or early 1875, just as the church at Union was being completed. Construction progressed fairly rapidly because a letter in the October 7, 1875, issue of the *Oregon Churchman*, probably Nevius's annual pre-Convocation report, noted that the church was "near completion," and that together with a parsonage "now building," should be ready for occupancy that winter. It continued, "The Church of the Ascension, at the Cove." Apparently a contribution from the Church of the Ascension in New York, reported later in the *Oregon Churchman* had just been

36. Ascension Church, Cove 1876/78

received unknown as yet to Nevius. The church was not completed until the following spring. The first service was held Easter Sunday, May 4, 1876. It was consecrated on Wednesday, July 25, 1877, complete with nave and chancel furniture "simply yet very neatly made by the carpenter from good and tasteful patterns." The cost was $3,500, which perhaps included the rectory.

Like the Union church, Ascension church at the Cove had a patterned roof consisting of a single broad band of scalloped shingles below the midline of the slopes. The source of this shingle pattern seems to have been Jordan's design for the Walla Walla church, shown in a steel engraving published in the January 15, 1875, issue of *Home and Abroad.*

Like Union, the Cove church was built with simple battered buttresses rather than the more elaborate stepped buttresses employed at Walla Walla. Like Walla Walla and unlike Union, the Cove church originally had buttresses only at the corners of the nave. Little is known of the framing system of the Cove church, except that during a replacement of interior wall surfaces in 1983 the carpenters observed four inch wall studs, and that the bell cote is supported by four-by-six inch posts in the west wall that straddle the rose window and nave door, long side in plane with the wall. Paint scrapings taken by the author (David Powers) in 1980 indicate that the church originally was painted a light pearl gray, which would have been harmonious with the blues and greens of the surrounding Blue Mountain landscape. Like the church at Walla Walla, the church at the Cove was built with ventilation dormers in the roof of the nave.

The intermediate buttresses which now bolster each bay of the Cove church and the iron tie rods now beneath the roof trusses were probably added in 1897 when the church was reroofed and a robing room or vestry was added to the chancel end, which faces east. A north wing and five rooms were added to the north side of the rectory at this time, as well as a two-story porch. The upper story was an enclosed sleeping porch, perhaps one of the five added "rooms." This porch was removed in the mid-1950s, at which time a smaller porch was added along with a new north wing to replace the 1897 wing which had been removed sometime previously.

A 300 pound bell manufactured by Meneely and Kimberly of Troy, New York, and costing about $140 was installed in the bell cote in 1878. Photographs of the chancel taken in the 1920s show that it was flanked by enclosures or vestries formed by free-standing partitions the same height as the chancel wainscoting. Whether or not these were original is not known. They were removed about 1940. An oval-shaped heating stove at the rear of the nave was removed in the 1960s and replaced by an oil stove, which in turn was re-

37. Ascension Church, Cove, 1890

moved after it nearly set the church afire and was replaced by an electric furnace in the summer of 1983. Electrical service had been installed by the mid-1920s. Today the building is used for the Ascension Summer School chapel and is well maintained.

38. Ascension Church, Cove, 2001

39. Ascension Church, Cove, circa 1990

40. Baptismal font, interior Ascension Church

St. Paul's Church

The Dalles, Oregon

Bishop Morris laid the cornerstone for a church at The Dalles at 4:00 p.m., Friday, May 28, 1875, several months after completion of the church at Union. Nevius was not present. Perhaps he was at the Cove getting the long-delayed work on the church there underway and planning the new rectory. Or perhaps he was in Portland to greet his new assistant, the elderly Rev. George T. Kaye, who arrived with his wife sometime in May to take up residence at the Cove and to assist Nevius on his large circuit.

Episcopal services had been held at The Dalles as early as 1855. The new church was to be called St. Paul's, the name having been suggested by a member of the newly-organized congregation whose early religious training had been at old St. Paul's in Baltimore. $500 had been given by General Joseph Eaton, a member of Trinity church, Portland, "to secure the erection of a church in some part of this wide field," and that amount had been matched by local citizens. The *Oregon Churchman* reported that the site "under the 'shadow of great rock'" had been chosen to be safe from the fires that had plagued The Dalles in recent years. The *Oregon Churchman* also reported that "the city has given land for general church purposes," but deed records indicate the lot was conveyed to Morris by a woodsawyer for $50 gold coin on February 17, 1875. Morris had signed a contract with Charles Kron to build the "unfinished" church for $989, a week before the cornerstone was laid, and work on the foundation had already begun. The *Oregon Churchman* reported that the new church "is being built after a very proper design." Nevius, in a later issue wrote, "It is built like the Church at Union, and is an improvement upon that Church. The plan has been developed with the design of getting the most church for the least money. It has been much admired."

As with the church at Union, construction progressed smoothly. On July 15 the *Oregon Churchman* reported, "The foundations are built, the lumber is on hand seasoning and the church will be completed during the summer or early fall," and on August 26: "The Church edifice is rapidly approaching completion: the roof is put on, and considerable of the funds necessary to the completion of the interior is in the hands of the building committee. Some kind of friend is needed to help with a bell." With characteristic enthusiasm Nevius wrote on September 28 that it was "only wanting for its windows from the East for completion and consecration." It may be that Nevius was a little ahead of himself and that some interior finishing was still in progress because it wasn't until November 25 that the *Oregon Churchman* reported: "The Church building is entirely completed with the exception of the chancel arrangements and the windows. The latter are ordered from the East, and are now on the way." Then on December 23 the *Oregon Churchman* reported: "The stained glass windows for this church arrived from the east on the last steamer from San Francisco, and have been for-

41. The Dalles Church, circa 1876

warded to their destination. The Church has been completed for some time and all (is) ready for the windows even to the inside painting and varnishing."

This last-minute arrival of the windows revived abandoned hopes that the church could be ready by Christmas. Nevius was alerted and he arrived from Baker City late on Christmas Eve. He found "the chancel window and the west window" in place, but the side windows were too large for the openings. "However," said Nevius, "we all went to work on Christmas morning, and the windows were put in place temporarily. The stove and chancel furniture were brought in, and as the workmen left the church at 11:00 a.m. a few persons, who had been hastily called, came in and one more new congregational voice was added to that of 'the church throughout all the world,' in her Christmas joy."

Nevius was especially pleased with the quality of workmanship in the new building. In addition he observed: "...My pet plan for a cheap and tasteful church is now realized beyond my expectation and my hopes.... The plan of the church is the same as that from which St. John's, Union, was built, in some important respects it is an improvement upon that much admired church, as might be expected, and is thought to furnish a model for a cheap church which cannot easily be excelled." Nevius continued with a detailed description of the windows, as he was to do five months later with the windows in Ascension Church at the Cove. He noted that the windows at The Dalles were manufactured by Slack and Booth of Orange, N. J., and explained the symbolism contained within the chancel window, given by General Joseph Eaton in memory of his son J. Horace Eaton who had died at Annapolis, and the "west" (liturgical west, geographic east) rose window given by Judge L. L. McArthur at The Dalles. The panels from the rose window, removed in a remodeling of 1900, are now fixed in a horizontal window cut into the geographic east end of the nave's south wall.

The chancel furniture that was brought in along with the stove on Christmas morning seems to have been already made and stored elsewhere until the church was ready. This furniture probably consisted at least of an altar and a pulpit. According to a local tradition the altar was designed or made by Nevius himself. The embossed emblems on its front were carved by Mrs. Mary Varney Lang, who also made a book rest designed by Nevius. This tradition enlarges the possibility that the "tasteful patterns" from which the nave and chancel furniture at the Cove were made were supplied by Nevius as well. Local tradition also ascribes the design of a handsome alms basin made from a tree root to him. Nevius seems to have taken the design for the altar from a pattern book published in 1873.

An early photograph of St. Paul's taken after 1880 and probably before 1883 shows that the church was very closely modeled on the design of St. John's, Union. The original bays of the extant nave suggest that it originally measured about 22' by 40', a foot narrower than reconstructed measurements of the church at Union. However, the nave of the church at The Dalles was divided into three bays instead of four, and the buttresses were stepped rather than battered. These buttresses appear to have been patterned after the Albert H. Jordan's design for St. Paul's Church at Walla Walla, after which the church at the Cove was modeled. It is unclear whether or not the church at The Dalles had a patterned roof, but it is clear that there was no bell tower as at Union. Otherwise the detailing of the narthex, rose window, and wall framing of the liturgical west end was very similar.

Unlike the lancet windows in the side walls of the nave at Union, the side windows at The Dalles are miter-arched with shallow hood moldings like the windows originally at the church in Baker City. The chancel window was also miter-arched (the shape of the chancel window at Union is not known). The handsome pediment or hood molding over the inside of the chancel window at St. Paul's may be original, but more likely dates from renovations made around the turn of the century. The nave was scissor trussed at each bay, as was most probably the nave at Union. The scissors truss was originally expressed on the outside of the chancel wall at The Dalles, as it was at a third church built from this same basic design which will be examined below.

Paint scrapings taken from St. Paul's indicate that it was originally painted a tan or buff color common to the period and known at the time as "fawn" or "drab." Downing advocated the use of these hues because they were neutral and harmonious with the landscape. Drab contains a small amount of red pigment and should have worked very well next to the outcropping of dark reddish brown rock adjacent to the church. The early photograph indicates that all body and trim elements were painted this color, and that the only trim color, perhaps a dark brown, was used on the rose window tracery and maybe on the window sash as well.

The completed church cost $2,500. It was consecrated Sunday, November 23, 1879. Like its Gothic predecessors, St. Paul's has been altered and added to over the years. The first addition, in 1880, was a small gabled wing west of the chancel end which extended north of the nave. This was used for a study, sleeping room, and vestry room like Nevius's "Prophet's Chamber" at Baker City, and probably was very similar to it in organization and arrangement except that there was no extended chancel or chancel foundation at The Dalles.

In 1883 a bell was acquired from the wreck of the *Queen of the Pacific*, which had "stuck" on the Columbia bar. This bell was placed in "mountings," but of what kind or exactly where is uncertain. The bell does not appear in early photographs, but the Vestry minutes of May 6, 1896, note that "the Bell tower had become loose and needed some attention." The adjacent lot to the south was purchased in 1883 as well for a rectory which was occupied April 2, 1885, and cost $1,200. An additional room and a bathroom were added to it in 1889. This rectory was demolished in 1928 and another erected on the site.

42. St. Paul's Church, circa 1900

Horizontal drop siding was added to the church sometime between 1880 and 1897, possibly in early 1890 when, according to the vestry minutes, the "Committee on Repairing Church reported progress" and it was decided "to have the Church primed at once." Also the porch steps were turned 90 degrees to the north about this time. Electricity may have been installed about then as well. The vestry had "decided to adopt the electric lights provided they do not cost more than the lamps" in 1888, and formed a "Committee on Electric Lights" in 1889 which reported "progress" in July and September. However, a $10.50 bill for "coal oil" was paid in 1893. Electricity had been installed by December 1897, when a $21 bill for seven months' service was paid. A "street Lamp," probably electric, was "presented to the church" by the city in 1890. Whatever the date, much of this very early knob-and-tube electric system as well as additions made to it, probably in the 1920s, survive intact and are still in regular service.

"Ventilation" was a topic discussed frequently by the vestry. An estimate of $160 "without excavating" to install a furnace was obtained in 1888, but $40 collected for the "Furnace Fund" was transferred to the General Fund in January, 1889. "Ventilating the church" was discussed again in 1893, but nothing was done except to clean the stovepipe and buy more cordwood. Finally, in 1897, a room was excavated under the church and "a flue built 30 feet high with a ventilator in (the) base." Though the accounts are unclear, it seems that a furnace was installed at this time as well.

The Rev. Joshua N. T. Goss, who had been at Baker City earlier and was responsible for renovation work there, was called to The Dalles in March of 1896. He remained through 1897. Soon After he arrived the "bell tower" was attended to and the church windows were repaired by Povey Brothers of Portland. The "ventilation" improvements were made before he left.

Several major changes were made from 1898 to 1900, apparently in piecemeal fashion. In 1898 the vestry decided to add a chancel costing $190. It was designed locally by J. C. Crandall and was completed by July 6. In 1899 the vestry decided not to build an organ chamber on the south side of the chancel, but a two manual Kimball pipe organ was not acquired until 1905.

Major alterations were made in 1900, the twenty-fifth anniversary of the building of the church. Barry notes in the church records that the church was "extended 14 feet," suggesting that the fourteen-foot square chancel added two years earlier was moved fourteen feet westward and a bay added to the nave. The small transepts flanking this bay, which measure fourteen feet, seem to be a later alteration but could have been added at this time. At any rate, the rose window and the porch were removed from the east end and the porch was moved to the east side of the 1880 vestry room. A rusticated stone porch surmounted by a frame bell tower was added to the east end of the north nave wall, and a rusticated stone base added to the nave. A fine arched window of Povey glass, known as the "lily window," was added to the east wall of the nave where the original porch and door had been. The present nave and chancel paneling was probably installed at this time as well. The alterations of 1900 cost about $2,000.

The round "chair window" or St. Cecilia window was added in 1912. A parish hall was added to the west end of the chancel and vestry room in 1931. It was named Remington Hall after the Bishop of eastern Oregon at the time. All the exterior wooden walls were stuccoed sometime before 1950, probably when Remington Hall was built in 1931. The building has been little changed since. After the parish built a new church at another location in 1961, the old church was used for a museum. It was extensively restored in 1990 under the advice of David W. Powers, architect, and State Historic Preservationist. Today it is used for the offices and chapel of the Episcopal Bishop of eastern Oregon.

43. St. Paul's The Dalles late 1890s

44. St. Paul's Church, c. 1928

45. St. Paul's Church, December 1990

46. St. Paul's Church Alms Basin, August 1983

47. St. Paul's Church, 1990

48. Altar, St. Paul's Church, August 1983

49. St. Paul's Church, August 2001

51. St. Paul's Church, August 1999

50. St. Paul's Church, August 1999

52. St. Paul's Church, November 1990

Church of the Redeemer

Pendleton, Oregon

Nevius did not apparently have anything to do with the building of this church, but it was built in 1875 while he was a missionary in the area. The cornerstone of the church was laid four days before the laying of the cornerstone at The Dalles. Pendleton was part of the "Umatilla mission," a circuit in charge of the Rev. Lemuel H. Wells based in Walla Walla. The *Oregon Churchman* of June 3, 1875, reported "Mr. Wells has secured a very beautiful plan for the church, from an officer of the Army at Walla Walla which is worthy of much commendation for its churchly character, simplicity, and avoidance of every unnecessary expense." The article continues, "It seems to have been the idea of the designer of this plan to produce a good effect, without the use of a single superfluous foot of lumber, the expenditure of one unnecessary cut of the saw or chisel, or a useless blow of the workman's hammer. If this common sense principle could by any possibility be communicated to some of our more accomplished and ambitious architects, it would be the securing of a great desideratum in our wide Missionary fields; where the erection of expensive churches is a simple impossibility, and yet where there is a true desire to have no share in increasing the monuments of ugliness and deformity, called churches, now scattered all over the land. This little church at Pendleton, owes its name, and its existence to the gift of $500 from a member of the Church of the Redeemer, Brooklyn, Long Island. The officer referred to was probably "Maj. Barnhardt," mentioned later in he article in connection with Pendleton and Weston. The original Pendleton church, affectionately known as the "Little Brown Jug," is the subject of several colorful legends. This building appears to have had a knee-braced post-and-beam frame with board-and-batten infill, and a bell tower with a truncated hip roof at the center of the liturgical west end.

Wells reported that when the church was built the congregation raised money to purchase a bell for the tower, and when the bell arrived the whole town turned out to help haul it up into its place as there was no machinery for that purpose. When the bell was hung the crowd, who by this time were pretty drunk, took turns in ringing the bell all night until sunrise and then the more sober ones helped to carry the others who had fallen asleep to their homes. Wells fitted up a sleeping room in the tower of the church, as much of the time he held evening service for them, holding the morning service at Walla Walla and riding over thirty miles in time for the evening service at Pendleton. It was demolished about 1897 when a new church was built.

53. Church of the Redeemer, Pendleton, circa 1880.
Oregon Historical Society, neg.no. 53445

All Saints Church

Weston, Oregon

The cornerstone was laid on July 16, 1875. This church is sometimes attributed to Nevius, but there is no evidence to support it. Bishop Morris described the setting. "The whole scene at this point was very beautiful and impressive. A calm and quiet evening just closing in, the full moon appearing in the East, the rolling hills in view on all sides, rich in the varied colors of the advancing harvest, the white robed Clergy, the gathered assembly, standing, sitting, and reclining on the hill-side, the little village nestled at the foot; with the sound of Prayer and Sacred Song—all together made a scene rarely equaled for picturesque beauty and impressiveness." The steeply gabled stud-framed nave with vertical tongue-and-groove siding measures about 20' by 36' and is divided into three bays by scissor trusses. The detailing of the trusses and their connections, however, is different than the detailing of surviving examples directly attributable to Nevius. The nave is unbuttressed. The chancel of All Saints' faced west. The east gable was surmounted by a small bell tower that appears in early photographs to have been capped by a truncated hip roof similar to the tower at Pendleton. All Saints' was moved to Milton Freewater in 1944 and re-named St. James' church. Little altered over the years, it is well-maintained and in regular use today.

54. St. James, Milton-Freewater, 2001

55. All Saints Church rectory, Weston, August 1983

57. *Wells window, All Saints/St. James Church*

56. *All Saints Church, Milton-Freewater, August 1983*

St. Thomas' Church

Canyon City, Oregon

The last Oregon church directly attributable to Nevius is St. Thomas' Church, Canyon City. Canyon City sprang up after gold was discovered in the area in the early 1860s. A fire in 1870, the first of several disastrous fires and floods, destroyed much of the business and residential districts. Nevius, Morris, and others started holding Episcopal services in Canyon City beginning in 1874, and the John Day Valley was added to Nevius's circuit. Nevius and Morris were enthusiastically received and both wrote warmly of their visits to Canyon City and the surrounding area. At the urging of local residents, a subscription was started and initial steps were taken toward building a church in the summer of 1875. The corner-stone was laid by Morris and Nevius on the afternoon of Saturday, August 26, 1876. The lot on which the church stands was donated by W. H. Clark, a prominent miner of the seventies.

There are no specific literary references to a plan or source of design for this building but the church was obviously built from Nevius's "pet plan," first employed at Union and then refined at The Dalles. Like The Dalles, the nave measured about 22' by 40' and was divided into three bays rather than four as at Union. The church at The Dalles had no provision for a bell. But at Canyon City the design for Union's bell tower was flattened to form a simple two dimensional bell cote. The sectional dimensions of timbers appear to have been reduced slightly as well. These factors along with open battered buttresses gave the church a more spindly appearance than the others. The arched doors and miter-headed windows were similar in design to those at The Dalles and Baker City. The chancel of Canyon City church faces east.

Nevius's design was intended to be inexpensive, but St. Thomas' clearly was the economy model of the three. The population of the John Day valley was not as large as the Grande Ronde or The Dalles, and the church seems to have been built more at the urging of the people than as a result of Bishop Morris's usual careful assessment of future potential. The *Oregon Churchman* of September 7, 1876, observe, "It will be an effort to complete the church..." Nonetheless, construction moved ahead quickly and all the funds seem to have come from local sources. No clear reference as to why the church was named St. Thomas' has come to light.

After the first service in the nearly completed building on July 15, 1877, Bishop Morris commented, almost with a sigh of relief, that the "building of this church was an undertaking of a good deal of boldness," and lamented that he could not help with funding to pay for the finishing details and furnishings. A contract for seats was not let until May, 1886, and the church was at last complete for consecration on June 20, 1889.

While in general the detailing of the Canyon City church demonstrated a tendency toward increased economy in the use of materials, the roof was an exception. Instead of the single broad band patterned shingles employed elsewhere, the nave and porch were covered with alternating bands of diamond-cut and square-butt shingles, and a cross pattern of diamond shingles was incorporated into the roof of the bell cote. A "Prophet's Chamber" vestry wing was added to the south side of the nave at an unknown early date. It was carefully detailed to match the architecture of the original building, and was framed in the same manner. Measuring about 13' by 14', it was smaller than the vestries at Baker or The Dalles but had a loft that seems to have been intended for a sleeping chamber.

About the turn of the century horizontal drop siding was nailed to the exterior battens of the nave an vestry. A photograph of the church with Nevius and Bishop Robert Lewis Paddock, probably taken just before or after the September 30, 1908, Convocation of the newly created Missionary District of Eastern Oregon in Pendleton at which Nevius was present, shows the church as it appeared at that time. The drop siding was probably added here, as at The Dalles, to solve one of the problems common to "plank" or "box" board-and-batten construction: excessive infiltration of outside air.

Even with the additional layer of siding, a member of the St. Thomas' congregation remarked to the author (David Powers) in 1976 that "the wind just whistled through the walls." Another potential problem that is frequently suggested is placement of the structural frame outside the walls where it is fully exposed to the weather. Surprisingly this seems not to have been a major problem, due perhaps to eastern Oregon's dry climate. With the exception of buttresses, which are more exposed to the weather than other structural elements and are also subject to heavy stresses, the fabric of these exposed-frame buildings

58. St. Thomas Canyon City, Nevius and R. L. Paddock, 1908

would seem to have suffered no more decay than would be expected of any wooden building, and have survived extended periods of little or no maintenance remarkably well. The ridge of St. Thomas' roof has acquired a permanent northward camber or "set" from prolonged loading by winds from the south. This can be viewed easily from the hill behind the church.

St. Thomas' escaped two fires that destroyed much of Canyon City, one in the late 1890s and another in April, 1937. It underwent a major rehabilitation in 1976 to celebrate the building's centennial. The horizontal drop siding was removed as well as the original triangular battens on all elements except the porch. Structural repairs were made and a layer of rigid insulation was applied to the exterior of the walls and new boards and battens matching the originals were installed. The result was a loss of about two inches of reveal of the framing timbers, but the infiltration problem was solved enabling the congregation to use the building year-round. Services had been held at another location during the cold and windy winter months. The final exterior appearance closely resembles the original appearance and the inside appearance remains unchanged. Restoration architect Alfred Staehli determined that the original paint colors were a shade of "drab" with reddish brown trim, and the building appears in these colors today. A unique feature of St. Thomas' is a small spring that flows out of the base of the hill behind the vestry wing. A segmental arched grotto-like niche over the spring was incorporated into the dry-stone retaining wall at the base of the hill at an early date, and baptisms are traditionally held here. A shed-roofed extension was made to the rear of the vestry wing so that the spring grotto is now under cover.

A September 23, 1939, article in the *Evening East Oregonian* (Pendleton) entitled "Church Survives All" states in part:

> "...The interior of the church was finished in knotty pine. The rafters are of hewn, beveled, crossed timbers, open to the roof. The pews are plank, whipsawed from the nearby forest. The windows, of diamond shaped stained glass were shipped by freight wagon. It has an ample vestry and quarters for a rector.

59. St. Thomas Canyon City

"Most of the present furniture of the chancel was presented in memorial of departed loved ones. The altar was donated in memory of Villa P. Sells and of Johanna Wood Chambers; the election set, in memory of Margaret Wood and Isaiah H. Wood; the candelabra in memory of William Otis Patterson, Mary Blake Patterson, and Mary Zoe Patterson; the cross on the altar in memory of Anna M. Lucas. The collection plate was presented by Lottie Mildred Sollinger, aged 7, and Fay Elizabeth Sollinger, aged 5. The font was presented by Oscar Schmidt.

"When the church first reared its belfry, Canyon City was a wild and woolly mining camp; throbbing with the lust of gold, and the tension of boom town life. It looked down on a straggling street, filled with pack trains, roughly dressed miners, black coated gamblers; upon the violence and lawlessness of a western mining camp. Many killings have taken place almost within the shadow of this histori[c]al little edifice.

"For over fifty years this church, steeped in history, has stood as a monument to the untiring labors of Doctor Nevius, offering its welcome hand to all seeking spiritual guidance. Many rectors have come and gone, but the little church goes on forever. It is known to every man, woman and child in Grant County, and to many hundreds throughout the state. It is a structure revered and loved by all: a shrine to the clergy of the Episcopal faith. And, like the cabin of Joaquin Miller, which stands on a nearby hillside, one of Oregon's historic structures."

60. St. Thomas Canyon City

Church of the Nativity

Lewiston, Idaho

Tradition has it that the first services in Lewiston were conducted by Rev. St. Michael Fackler, an early Oregon priest. This may be true, as Fackler traveled to Boise City during the summer of 1864, stopping at The Dalles, Umatilla, La Grande, Auburn, and perhaps Lewiston. Fackler was stationed in Boise City in 1865. He opened the church building there in September of 1866. Fackler died on board ship during a cholera epidemic on his way to the Atlantic coast to join his family in 1867. He was buried at Key West. Florida.

During the winter of 1879 services were held occasionally on Sundays in the Red Cross hall, furnished and rented by Nevius for $10 a month. "A very interesting Sunday School was gathered, which attained its largest growth, 50 boys and about 10 girls, in a few weeks. Most of the boys and one girl, Nellie Stainton, who was the organist for nearly a year in both church and school, were faithful and constant both at the service and also at Sunday school. Dr. Eli McClellan, U.S. Army, Lapwai Indian Agency, Mrs. Hudson, Mrs. Wiggins, Capt. Wibters of the U.S. Army and Mrs. John Stephens were the only communicants. Dr. McClellan was a warm personal friend and helper of the missionary. Nevius moved to Lewiston in 1880, making it his residence and headquarters in serving northern Idaho and eastern Washington.

In his address to the convocation in June of 1880, Bishop Morris reported that Dr. Nevius had removed from Baker City to Lewiston, Idaho, with charge of missionary work in both Washington and Idaho Territories. "While Dr. Nevius' actual residence is in Idaho, his canonical residence is still with us, and the larger part of his mission, geographically, is in this Jurisdiction. The Bishop of

61. Nativity, Lewiston, circa 1890

Idaho has taken a warm interest in the establishment of this joint Mission, and contributes generously to its support...."

In the summer of 1880, services were held in the Masonic Hall, the former place of worship being rented for business purposes. It was at this time that a guild was formed by which agency an organ was purchased, rents were paid and other expenses of the mission met.

In the spring of 1881, Bishop Daniel Sylvester Tuttle made his first visit and the missionary advised that Lewiston should be made into a separate mission with a resident clergyman, and recommended the Rev. J. D. McConkey in the place. McConkey succeeded Nevius in July of 1881. Services were held in the Universalist church during that time. In September of 1881 the church acquired a log cabin on D Street between 4th and 5th. It cost $1599, and served as a combination church and rectory for the next nine years. A permanent church was erected in 1890-91. Twice the congregation had reason to hope the building would be ready for the visit of the area bishop, once in 1888, and again in 1890. But it was not until 1891 that the last

62. Nativity, Lewiston, circa 1950. Courtesy Lewiston Morning Tribune

of the memorial windows from Munich and Switzerland reached New York on their way west.

The first of these windows, the nativity window in the east of the sanctuary, was dedicated to the memory of Evangeline Vollmer, oldest daughter of Mr. and Mrs. John P. Vollmer, who had died in 1881. The Good Shepherd window in the west was dedicated to the twin sons of Mr. and Mrs. J. D. Kester, who had died in 1882.

In 1919 and 1920 the nave of the church was moved from downtown up to the current site on Normal Hill. It was moved up hill with a steam winch and teams of horses. A new chancel was built from redwood to match the nave. The resulting church has perfect acoustics. In 1964 the Parish Hall and offices were constructed and the Parish Hall was named in honor of Rev. David Somerville, who served from 1904 to 1930.

On July 13, 1925, Lillian and Walter Disney were married at Nativity and their wedding records are among the documents and historic photographs that were displayed for the church's 1998 anniversary celebration.

In about 1950 the church was moved again on it's present site so that a basement could be built for a church hall, kitchen, and school classrooms.

63. Nativity, Lewiston, August 2001

St. Luke's Church

Coeur d'Alene, Idaho

Upon agreement between Bishops Tuttle and Morris, Dr. Nevius was to service northern Idaho even though it was part of the missionary district of Montana, Idaho and Utah. Nevius reported to the 1880 convention that he had visited and held services at Fort Coeur d'Alene. He reported, "Near Spokane, at the military post, Fort Coeur d'Alene (thirty miles), there are several zealous members of the Church among the officers. Among them service is held on Sundays, and the children of the post are taught in a Sunday School. " In June of 1881 Nevius reported that Fort Coeur d'Alene was still part of his charge, and services were given there, if possible, on every visit to Spokane Falls. Bishop Morris reported in 1882 that he had visited Fort Coeur d'Alene and confirmed two people, presented by the Rev. Dr. Nevius. He reported, "At the Military Post, we had the first services at the opening of the very neat and Churchly Building erected by the Government, for religious and other assemblings...." Nevius gave a report on the mission at the Convention that year. He stated that during the year ending June 15, 1882, he had visited there seven times. He reported 6 communicants. Nevius again held services at Fort Coeur d'Alene on Monday, June 4, 1883, with Bishop Paddock in attendance. In his report, Paddock stated, "...it was pleasant to note that about half the number were officers of the Post, and that it is the custom of the commanding officer to read morning prayer in his parlor, with a few assembled, each Sunday." In Nevius's report on the year ending June 25, 1883, he reported 11 communicants at Fort Coeur d'Alene. Nevius was replaced by the Rev. Mr. Burnett in July.

On September 16, 1891, the first service in town was held by Mr. Fred Sellick at the Odd Fellows Hall at the southwest corner of 4th and Sherman. Austin Carbin II deeded property to the church at 5th and Wallace. The first service was held in the new church on March 13, 1892. The altar, bishop's chair and baptismal font were made by soldiers at Fort Sherman. Rev. Herman Page was the first priest in charge. Early services were conducted by army officers and laymen. The cost of the new church was $2,000. A rectory was built in 1903, and the church was consecrated by Bishop Wells. The church was cut in two and a section added in the middle in 1911, bringing it to its present size.

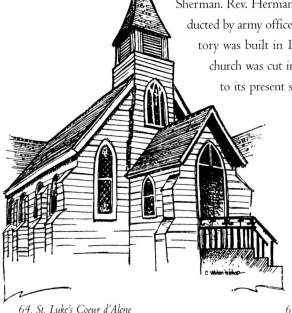

64. St. Luke's Coeur d'Alene   *65. St. Luke's 1892*

All Saints' Church

Spokane Falls, Washington

The first service of the Episcopal church in Spokane County was held by the Rev. R. D. Nevius, D.D., about 1880. A little church was built on the corner of Front and Howard, and a parish school for boys was held in the same building, which was afterwards moved to the present (Riverside and Lincoln, 1900) site of the cathedral and later burned down. The Rev. Dr. H. Compton Burnett succeeded Dr. Nevius as missionary, and the Rev. Charles B. Crawford succeeded him and was the first rector of All Saints' parish. About 1889 St. Mary's Hall was built in Cook's addition, and a girls' school carried on, first under Mrs. Summerville, and then under Mr. James Lyon. It was during Mr. Crawford's rectorship, in 1884, that the church of All Saints was built and was intended to be used ultimately as a parish house when the permanent structure should be erected. On Easter Sunday, April 21, 1889 the church building at First and Jefferson was consecrated. It had cost $8,000 to build. The bell for the church had been sent by Dr. Nevius, having been rescued from the church at Kalama when that church was abandoned due to a local recession. The bell now is displayed at Riverside Memorial Gardens. The church was of all wood construction but with fake buttresses imitating the stone churches of England, with two very shallow transepts and a stubby east end. Entrance to the narthex at the west end was through a tower projecting from the south wall, with a tall belfry and an even taller spire with four thin dormers in its base, the spire tapering to a needle point surmounted by the cross. The west gable had a large elaborately divided ogive window.

In 1891, besides the church and the little older church, now a school, there was a rectory on the northwest corner of the block, and a group of two-story frame buildings built this year filled the northeast quarter east of the school. In 1892 eastern Washington became a separate diocese under the name of the Missionary District of Spokane, and the Rt. Rev. Lemuel H. Wells, D.D., became its first bishop, with his residence in Spokane as his see city, and took All Saints church as his cathedral. Soon after this the rectory and the old church, then used as a chapel, and the chancel end of the present (1900) church, with a bishop's house partly built, and other buildings adjoining, were burned. Later St. Mary's hall was burned and the bishop secured a new site and building for the school on the corner of Pacific Avenue and Hemlock. Mrs. Henrietta B. Wells and Miss Julia P. Bailey became the principals. Probably at this time the church was enlarged, the south transept widened and extended to the property line, the east end considerably enlarged, and the north transept joined with a long two-story extension of the parish hall and classrooms. The Rev. J. Neilson Barry succeeded in 1899. In July 1897, a Protestant hospital was organized under the auspices of the Episcopal church in a building on the corner of Sprague and Madison streets, loaned by them. By 1905 the enlarged cathedral was alone on the west half of the block, with landscaping, trees and a stone wall at the sidewalk.

In 1925 three congregations joined to form the congregation of St. John the Evangelist, the sale of their properties providing some of the funds for the new construction. They were All Saints Cathedral, which stood at the corner of Jefferson Street and First Avenue, St. James' Church, and St. Peter's Church. The new cathedral was completed and the first service held on October 20, 1929. A newspaper article on November 10, 1929, stated as follows:

Rather than permit any part of the old frame structure to be desecrated as junk, trustees of All Saints' cathedral, Episcopal., First and Jefferson, have agreed to wreck the building and burn it. Bishop Cross recommended wrecking and removing the building to a safe spot where all of the timbers would be consigned in the flames and its life story ended with the abandonment of the cathedral as a house of worship. The property was occupied by a used car lot and a service station until in 1948 it was sold and occupied by the Greyhound bus depot.

The bell of All Saints' was removed from the tower when the first portion of the Cathedral of St. John was completed, and installed on the temporary wood office structure east of the church. When that was removed, it was stored, along with rows and rows of cut stone not yet built into the walls, in the back (north) yards of the church-owned houses immediately east, until the next building activity. The South Chapel, dedicated as All Saints' Chapel, has its own little bell tower at its southeast corner, built about 1950, and intended to have the All Saints' bell installed there.

66. *All Saints Spokane, circa 1905*

67. *All Saints Spokane, interior*

Grace Church

Dayton, Washington

Services were held in Dayton by Rev. Lemuel Wells as early as 1875. Nevius and Wells visited the area and conducted services in 1880. Bishop Wells recalled, "I remember how we heard that a town called Dayton had been started about thirty miles from Walla Walla, so we mounted our horses and rode up there. We found a large acreage surveyed, and laid out in city lots, but only one house, and the proprietor explained with some emotion that owing to the dearth of inhabitants, the city would be postponed for a year. He generously gave us a lot for a church, but it is still outside the center of population."

The Rev. William Fair was assigned to the Dayton mission in 1885. He established a kindergarten which was presided over by his sisters. Church services were held in the Kindergarten Building that year. Property was acquired in 1893 for a church for the sum of $1,000. It appears that a parish hall may have been built first, as the local paper reported that services were being held at Grace Hall in 1888. The church building was built about 1902, under the direction of Rev. Smith O. Dexter. There have been few resident priests in Dayton, with the minister coming from Walla Walla or Pomeroy most of its existence.

68. Grace Church, Dayton, August 2001

The Church of the Good Samaritan

Colfax. Washington

Colfax services were first held when Rev. R. D. Nevius of Baker City paid occasional visits during the pioneer days. He is likely to have visited about 1879, when he began his missionary work in Eastern Washington. Local tradition is that it may have been as early as 1873. The church was organized officially in 1888, and a regular minister was supplied. The first meetings of the church were held in the Opera Hall.

No sooner was the foundation of the first building completed than the ground on which it was built was condemned by the city for street purposes and the structure had to be torn down and rebuilt. Other misfortunes followed until the little congregation was overloaded with debts. This church was located on Golgotha Street, a little way east of Main, up on a hill.

In 1924 the large tower was removed from the building because it was considered unsafe. Also the wind moaned as it passed through it and disturbed the services. At that time the church was extensively remodeled.

As part of a five year plan of improvements, landscaping, remodeling, carpeting, and so forth had been completed in September of 1956 when a fire of unknown origin, though suspected arson, gutted the building. It was left standing but totally unfit for occupancy. In 1959 the congregation relocated and built a new church building.

69. Good Samaritan Colfax, circa 1895.
Washington State University Library

St. Matthew's Church

Sprague, Washington

The railroad was completed to Sprague in May of 1881. The city was incorporated November 28, 1883, with a population of about 500. By 1884 the town of Sprague was outdistancing its rival Davenport, some 40 miles north. Its future looked bright. A bitter contest by election determined Sprague to become the county seat and it held the honor for 12 years. In 1895 a devastating fire was followed by hard winters causing short crops, hard times, severe cold, deep snow and loss of herds of cattle in 1899-1900. The *Sprague Times* of November 21, 1902, reported, "During the afternoon of August 3, 1895, a destructive conflagration broke out in the heart of town and when the sun had slipped down behind the western horizon smoking ashes alone remained of property once valued at $1,000,000. All the business district save two stores was destroyed. The railroad shops and many dwellings were consumed. Then the shops were moved to Spokane and with a large voting population taken away, a fight was made to move the courthouse to Davenport and carried." The first church in Sprague had been built in a day, and was named St. Matthews*. The church did not survive the fire, and the congregation did not rebuild. For the story of the building of the church, see page 17, Chapter 1.

70. St. Matthews, Sprague, circa 1890

71. St. Matthews, interior. Christmas, 1887

St. Peter's Church

Pomeroy, Washington

Built by Nevius, probably started in 1882, it was consecrated by Bishop Paddock on June 10, 1883, with Nevius in attendance. St. Peter's was the second church built in Pomeroy, following the Catholic Church.

The first Episcopal services were held in the old Owsley school house by Bishop Lemuel H. Wells in 1873. The only member of the church there at the time was Clara Pomeroy (later Mrs. E. T. Wilson of Tacoma). Miss Pomeroy attended St. Paul's School in Walla Walla, and her tuition was paid to Mr. Wells with cattle raised on the Pomeroy ranch. At stated intervals Mr. Wells would come to the Pataha Creek to look over his flock, and always would hold services at the old Owsley school house. In 1881 Bishop Paddock donated $500.00 for an Episcopal church in Pomeroy. Rev. L. H. Wells raised $1000.00 more by donations, and the building was erected in 1882.

Other early records state the cost was $2000.00. A parish house was built later, in 1948, and for a number of years resident rectors held regular services there.

72. *Pomeroy Church, August 2001*

St. John's Church

Olympia, Washington

On January 7, 1864, the Legislative Assembly of the Territory of Washington passed "An Act to Incorporate Saint John's Church of Olympia." Section 1 of which reads as follows: "Be it enacted by the Legislative Assembly of the Territory of Washington, that Wm. Pickering, Richard Lane and S. W. Percival as trustees, and their successors in office, are hereby declared a body corporate and politic by law, by the name and style of the trustees of St. John's Church of Olympia; said church being under the control, direction and care of the Protestant Episcopal Church of the United States." The Act was signed by C. Crosby, Speaker of the House of Representatives, and O. B. McFadden, President of the Council.

On January 13, 1864, Lot 7 Block 7 of the town of Olympia, the corner of Seventh and Main (now Capitol Way), was purchased from Benjamin and Eliza P. Harned for the sum of Five Hundred Dollars. The Governor Hotel now stands partly on this property. In April the trustees met in the office of William Pickering and formally organized with William Pickering as President, Sam. W. Percival as Treasurer, and Richard Lane as Secretary.

In June 1865, came the Rev. Peter Edward Hyland from Portland, where he had been ministering at Trinity Church. An old frame carpenter shop on the church lot was converted into a church. The walls were upright boards, paneled and painted white. The ceiling was arched and plastered. Inside were green baize doors and the pews stretched across the middle of the building, There were two aisles with side pews on the sides. The center pews were divided down the middle by a board. Occupants carpeted and cushioned their own pews. The chancel was a platform built out into the church with a railing around three sides. A small melodeon provided the music and the choir sat in the front pews. Back of the sanctuary was a room used for the Sunday School which was supported on pilings over the bay into which it fell in 1872 when an earthquake shook the community. Miss Robie Willard was engaged as organist, although at times Mrs. Hyland played, and it is recorded that the Hyland children rode the chancel rail during service upon more than one occasion.

St. John's Church was regularly consecrated by the Rt. Rev. Thomas F. Scott on September 3, 1865, being the twelfth Sunday after Trinity, and two persons, Mrs. Robert Frost and Mrs. Charles (Martha) Grainger were confirmed. Mrs. Grainger had also been baptized the same day by Mr. Hyland.

In 1869 a bell was procured and forwarded to Olympia by the Right Reverend Benjamin Wistar Morris, who

73. St. John's, Olympia, circa 1939. Washington State Historical Society

had succeeded Bishop Scott in 1868. The Bishop paid half the cost of the bell and the parish the remainder of one hundred dollars, plus the cost of the addition of a belfry to the building. It rang for the first time on December 18, 1869.

Nevius was rector here from July, 1883, until March of 1887. He was undoubtedly the moving force behind a motion made at the annual meeting of April 14, 1884, to erect a new church on the property adjoining the rectory, and a committee was authorized to solicit and raise funds. Steadily and persistently this committee labored.

In 1886 Dr. Nevius was elected the delegate to General Convention from the Convocation of Washington, and on August 16, he resigned as he did not plan to return west after the meeting of General Convention in October. The vestry granted him leave of absence and tried to get him to return, but on March 2, 1887, he mailed his resignation from Utica, New York. Shortly afterwards he returned to eastern Washington where he did yeoman service in the establishment of the Church in that part of the state.

For nearly two years St. John's was without a regular rector. The Rev. William Gill supplied for a time in 1887, and the name of the Rev. B. E. Hatersham appears on the records in 1888 as officiating at a baptism. Dr. Nevius also returned for baptisms and burials. On April 23, 1888, the little old church building and its site was sold for fifteen hundred dollars to Elvira J. Silsby (Mrs. J. A. Silsby) by the wardens and vestrymen of St. John's and converted into a grocery and feed store.

Plans were drawn for the new church by C. N. Daniels, architect, of Tacoma. In May 1888, calls for bids were printed in the *Washington Standard*, Olympia, the *Post-Intelligencer*, Seattle, and the *Morning Oregonian*, Portland, Oregon, and on June 8 these were opened. At the annual meeting held in Tacoma Hall on April 22, 1889, the borrowing of fifteen hundred dollars was approved and it was secured from the American Church Building Fund Commission. The basement of the Church was built and converted into a chapel and services were held there beginning October 20, 1889.

Work on the Church proper was delayed for about a year and then, stimulated by a gift of $500.00 from Governor Ferry, work was resumed under the direction of Mr. Henry Lame, and was pushed as rapidly as the excellent craftsman would permit. Only the best lumber was used and workmanship was of the highest order. The cost of the building was $10,361.75. From the old church, the bell, the stained

glass window of St. John and St. Mary, and the Bishop's and Rector's chairs (which had come around the Horn in early days) were saved and incorporated into this building. The window had to be sent back to the Lamb's Studio in New York to have additions to the top and sides to make it suitable. The women paid for this.

One of the interesting features in connection

74. St. John's Olympia interior

with the finishing of the church was the plan adopted by the rector to equip the edifice. Rev. Horace Buck conceived the idea of writing to his friends in former parishes explaining that the church here in Olympia was constructing a new building and that all available funds had been expended on the structure leaving the matter of the necessary furniture a problem. The generous manner in which these friends responded indicated the high esteem in which he was held by his former associates.

The baptismal font of carved oak was contributed by the Sunday School of St. Thomas' Church, New Haven, Connecticut, where both Mr. and Mrs. Buck had attended as children. The brass altar cross was bought with thirty-two dollars sent for that purpose by St. John's, East Hartford, Connecticut, and bears the inscription "From St. John's in the East to St. John's in the West." The clergy stall was a gift of a college chum, and the money for the pulpit came from a parish of which he had formerly been rector, the pulpit itself being designed and carved in Olympia by Springer, White & Co., who also made the pews.

The handsome rose window, nine feet in diameter, was a gift of a group of young women, known as St. John's Church Workers, founded in 1882. The window was made in England at a cost of five hundred dollars. The eagle lectern was a gift of a former parishioner, Mrs. Fanny Mary Wilkinson, of Tacoma, daughter of Judge Elwood Evans, and was dedicated to her memory and that of her sister, Rachel Evans Zabriske. One side window, a gift from St. John's Workers and Mrs. John Leary, is a memorial to Julia P. Ferry, the daughter of Washington State's first Governor; and another side window is in memory of Lurana Curtis and Phoebe Lurana, infant children of Samuel W. and Lurana Percival.

The opening of the new house of worship, with the dedication of its memorial windows, pulpit and lectern, on July 19, 1891, was a great occasion. Rev. Nevius was in attendance. Carpet for the chancel and cushions for the pews were supplied by St. John's Guild. To raise money for these and other projects associated with the new Church, they made sheets and pillow slips and hemmed curtains for the first Olympian Hotel; bound blankets for the National Guard of Washington; had teas and garden parties; gave bazaars and excursions. The work was carried from house to house for the different meetings in a large wicker clothes basket.

In 1891, as a result of the labors for several years of a group known as St. John's Musical Society, a pipe organ was purchased from Pilcher and presented to the church. It cost $1500.00 and Mr. Pilcher himself came West to install it.

In addition to his duties at South Bend and Ocosta, Nevius covered the pastorate at St. John's in 1891 and 1892 while the Bishop located a replacement for Rev. H. H. Buck.

The church was sold in 1949, and a new one constructed with first a parish hall in 1950, and a church in 1957. It is currently used as a Baptist church.

75. St. John's Olympia, 2000

Church of the Epiphany

Chehalis, Washington

On the 15th of August, 1883, a meeting of the people was held and a petition was signed, asking the bishop for the services of a missionary for Lewis county and said petition was accompanied by a subscription list amounting to $400 for the payment of the missionary's salary.

No missionary could be sent at that time, so Rev. Mr. Henry S. Bonnell continued with his week night services during the summer and autumn. In the month of December, 1883, Dr. Nevius, who was stationed at Olympia, commenced giving alternate Sunday services and also through the week, staying a week at each place.

On December 22, 1883, a meeting was held for the purpose of organizing a mission, of which the following minutes are taken from the record:

"At a meeting called by Rev. Dr. Nevius, for the purpose of organizing a Protestant Episcopal church mission here, William West was elected chairman and William Burmingham, secretary. ...Resolved that the name of said mission shall be Chehalis Mission of Lewis County, Washington." These proceedings were accepted by the bishop, and the organization, ratified by the bishop, appointed William West warden and treasurer of the mission. The Rev. Nevius continued to give services on alternate weeks and during the Epiphany gave a series of services at the school house.

P. C. Beaufort, one of the original members, recalled at the 25th anniversary as follows:

"The first service of the Church I attended here was held in Chehalis sometime in the fall of 1882 by that servant of the Most High, the Saintly Bonnell, rector of St. Luke's Church of Tacoma, Washington who has long since passed to rest in Paradise. After him came that grand old soldier of the Cross, the Rev. Dr. Nevius, who obeying the Master's injunction gathered up the fragments and formed the Parish of Epiphany. Our first services were held in the old school-house on First Street, long since passed away. It was a building 16 x 24, long since useless. I will ever remember the evening services held there. It was a typical pioneer service. Mr. West bringing from home all the lamps and lanterns he could find and some of us younger men bringing the candles. Some of them were of the short order and many of these went out before the services were half over. The singing at that first service can never be duplicated. There could be none just exactly like this again. And never can be. There was little cord and much discord. All doing their best.

"The Rev. Doctor intimated it would be better to have lamps in the future in the back part of the building than candles, as the draft would not be quite so liable to blow them out. It seemed that the younger members of the congregation were not so careful to keep their candles burning.

"In the meantime our Presbyterian friends were building a church. The community being small at the time, and this city being mostly Town Site, covered with stumps, logs and brush, we all contributed liberally to the building fund of that church in hopes for the time at least to have a church home. We held Service there for a short time and during this time the Bishop, the Right Rev. Paddock of Blessed memory, held his first confirmation services here, consisting of a class of five. The parties being Miss Putney, Miss Smith, Mr. and Mrs. James T. Berry and myself. All have passed into Eternal Life excepting myself. There being some misunderstanding as to the time we could have service in the church and Mr. Nevius could be with us only certain times in the month, he being rector of St. John's of Olympia and his parish consisting of the whole Southwestern Washington Territory, his time was necessarily limited. The then resident [Presbyterian] minister, the Rev. Broulette whose desire was to have services at the same time that the Rev. Dr. Nevius was here. There was but two things for us to do, go back to the old school house or build a church of our own. We did both. Dr. Nevius held service in the School house. After the service we held a meeting, and then and there organized the parish, and concluded to build as soon as possible. Then the Rev. Dr. suggested the name of Epiphany for the parish and it was adopted. Thus another parish was planted by that pioneer apostle of the Church...."

The mission was so much encouraged by the success of the Epiphany services that on February 16, 1884, a meeting was called at which it was decided to build a church. The amount pledged was over $900 and an acre of land.

Plans were furnished for the church on the 7th of June, 1884 by Nevius, and a contract was made with M. T. Moore to build the church. The building was completed by September. The first service was held September 14, 1884, with Bishop Paddock, Nevius, and Rev. Janvrin Vincent officiating. (In 1866 or 1867 the Rev. P. E. Hyland had traveled from Olympia by horseback to hold the first Episcopal Service in Lewis County at the historic Claquato Church.) Meanwhile Dr. Nevius had been doing effective work for the church, organized a Women's Guild of eighteen members (not one of them having any previous knowledge of the church or her ways). He also baptized five and presented ten for confirmation and at the annual convocation held in Seattle in July, 1884, made a glowing report including the statement, "And from the first, it has

76. *Epiphany, Chehalis. Lewis County Historical Society photo*

not had one shock of opposition or any jar of needless friction and thus it has been a continued pleasure
to its missionary." Epiphany became a parish on April 23, 1885, and the newly completed church building was consecrated in June of 1886, when the convocation for that year was held there. It was free from
debt even though (according to William West, a warden at the time) some of the money provided was
used for drink by the contractor. A rectory was built in 1895. A parish house was built in 1904 as a
memorial to Jane A. Tighe. In 1963 a new church building was completed and the congregation moved
across town. The church buildings were sold, and later torn down by the new owners.

77. Epiphany, Chehalis, circa 1905

St. Paul's Church

Whatcom (Bellingham), Washington

Nevius first visited here in June of 1883, and funds were raised for erection of the church by August of 1884. Mrs. C. I. Roth reminisced:

"The history of St. Paul's Church begins shortly after the arrival of the Washington Colony in 1883. The colony had entered into settlement with the townsite proprietors, who consisted of H. Roeder, the Peabody heirs, and William Utter.

In the colony were two ladies who were to play an important part in the religious and social life on Bellingham Bay. They were Mrs. Cora M. Gardner and Mrs. William Powell. Together with one of our resident ladies, Mrs. W. L. Steinweg, they induced Bishop Paddock of Tacoma to send Rev. R. D. Nevius to this spot, to undertake the organization of a church."

Mrs. Roth had a clear remembrance of the first meeting which was held to organize the parish; how, in spite of the boggy going underfoot and timber which barred the way between homes in those days, the ladies got together, made their plans, and executed them.

Under the direction of Dr. Nevius, these women organized a Guild, on September 12, 1883. It was composed of 29 members. Not all of these were enthusiastic, however, and the onus of the work fell upon the willing shoulders of these two women. Through fairs and festivals organized by them, as well as entertainments of various kinds, the original funds for the building were collected. And at the time of the completion of the church but little debt remained.

The site was donated by Mr. Roeder and the Peabody heirs, who also donated sites for various other churches as well as The Revellie, when it was first organized.

Dr. Nevius, after continuing his ministry here, with occasional services for the people, as a missionary, finally succeeded in securing, in 1884, a truly good and noble man, the conscientious layman, Mr. J. H. Birkhead, who was later ordained. About this time the contract for the erection of the original church was let to the firm, Messrs. Tod & Richardson, who together with six others built the first Episcopal Church here....

It wasn't until 1903 that St. Paul's was incorporated as a parish, due to the hard economic times of that era. In 1900 the Rev. A. Whitfield Cheatham arrived and was pastor for thirteen years. During his ministry there St. Luke's hospital was begun, and St. Paul's church was enlarged by the addition of a transverse section between the chancel and the nave. Nevius wrote, "The Church was enlarged in 1900 under the direction of Mr. J. C. Crandall [sic C. J. Crandall], and was advised and undertaken by the Guild. The nave was extended to the front by the addition of ["14," crossed out] 16 ft and the tower was built. The church was opened for services on Sunday, the "belate?" of Christmas day by Rt. Rev. B. W. Morris D.D. attended by Rev. R. D. Nevius, D.D.—under the direction of whom—the latter—the mission was opened and the Church planned and built. It was the 25th anniversary of its first use for divine service [that it was] reopened after this enlargement On the occasion the sermon was preached by Rev. Dr. Nevius. The Bishop [Morris] was the celebrant at the Holy Eucharist." It is supposed that it was during this enlargement that the entry porch was moved from the south side to the front of the building. In 1925 the congregation decided to build a new church building. The original church building on Walnut Street is still owned by the church, and is now being used as a Jewish synagogue.

78. St. Paul's, Whatcom, 1884

79. St. Paul's, Whatcom, 1944

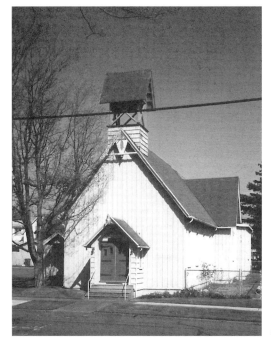

80. St. Paul's, Bellingham, 1944

81. St. Paul's, Bellingham, 2000

St. Michael's Church

Yakima, Washington

On September 29, 1885, during the first year of North Yakima's existence, Nevius established the parish of St. Michael's as a mission. The church had been originally organized by Nevius in late 1884 at Yakima City (Union Gap), and moved in January to the new site where the Northern Pacific Railroad company had donated two lots. Services were held in a commercial building and at the Moxee schoolhouse. In 1888 Dr. Nevius organized a building committee of Colonel William Ferrand Prosser, special agent of the General Land Office for Oregon and Washington, William Seinweg, cashier of the First National Bank of Yakima, and Henry Blatchford Scudder, a dairy farmer. Plans for the new church, drawn as a gift by Edward Tuckerman Potter, a church architect of New York and Newport, Rhode Island, were received by Mr. Scudder on June 5. The plans provided for a much larger church than was built, and were later used in additions to the original building.

"The new church, built of uncut basalt rock hauled from Garretson's Grade ('Painted Rocks') by horse-drawn wagons, was Gothic in style. The structure, seating 125 people, was 48 feet by 25 feet with 12 foot high walls and high pitched roof. The front gable of the church (west end) was carried up above the planes of the roof in three equal stages of six feet each, was surmounted by a large stone cross, and had three long narrow windows of cathedral glass from Coulter and Sons, Cincinnati.

"The first services in the new church were held on Christmas Day 1888 when Dr. Nevius used 'God With Us' as his text. Dr. Nevius reported that the building had cost about $4,000, with $450 provided by the Women's Guild of the mission. About $600 was given by personal (non resident) friends of the parishioners and of Dr. Nevius, including the Rev. Philips Brooks, Rector of Trinity Church, Boston, later Bishop of Massachusetts and writer of the Christmas hymn, 'O Little Town of Bethlehem.' The first communion service, later sent to Bishop Rowe in Alaska (probably at the suggestion of Nevius, who was in Alaska when Rowe arrived), was given by the Rev. Leonard K. Storrs of St. Paul's, Brookline, whom Mr. Scudder had previously served as senior warden. In March of 1889 the walls of the church were planted by the Sunday school children with ivy started from a cutting from the Trinity Church of Boston."[101] Nevius left the church for Montesano on May 15, 1889.

In 1891 the chancel end of the church, 18 feet long by 16 feet deep, including the sanctuary with three windows, was built of wood so that it could be removed as the church was expanded. The first pipe organ was acquired during the week of March 25, 1903.

On October 1, 1910, St. Michael's Parish held its twenty-fifth anniversary. Dr. Nevius preached the 10 a.m. Sermon and was a guest of honor at a reception in the Rectory and at a banquet for all the men of the Parish at Yakima Hotel.

In 1924 the church was extended eastward twenty feet and the parish hall was built, joining the church and the old Rectory-Parish House. Other improvements included a new heating plant, new pews, and new wiring. By December 1924 the stone and timber porch was completed, designed by Harold Whitehouse after the entry to Stoke Poges, Buckinghamshire, England, where Thomas Gray in 1750 wrote "Elegy in a Country Churchyard". In 1954 the church was lengthened thirty feet to its present 108 foot length, increasing the seating capacity to 250 persons, adhering to the original design and using native rock from Garretson's Grade. The church building was placed on the Washington State Historic Register in 1977, and is in regular use today.

82. Yakima church, 1925 postcard

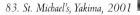

83. St. Michael's, Yakima, 2001

Grace Church

Ellensburg, Washington

The first record of activity of the Episcopal Church in the Kittitas Valley followed the appointment of the Rev. Lemuel Wells as missionary at Walla Walla in 1871. The Rev. Wells visited the few settlers in the valley while making trips on horseback between Walla Walla and Tacoma. In 1885 the Rev. Reuben Nevius became missionary minister to Yakima and Ellensburg. The first regular Episcopal service took place in July of 1888. Nevius conducted services intermittently in Yakima, Ellensburg and Roslyn. In 1888 Bishop Paddock granted mission status to Ellensburg, and the name Grace Church was chosen. Ellensburg services were held in the "Honolulu Block" at Fourth and Pearl and in the Lloyd Theater at Fourth and Pine. Nevius also held services in the Methodist, Baptist, and Christian Churches. Finally they were regularly held in the G.A.R. Hall.

On March 19, 1889, the first women's guild was organized. That year the guild raised enough funds to purchase a lot at Fourth and Sprague for $400 with the thought of building a church. The guild also purchased a lectern and an altar, and when Nevius left in 1890, had an $81 balance in their fund. The parish hall was apparently built in 1890. For the next three years the congregation struggled without a vicar, but Wells, upon becoming Bishop of Spokane, appointed a new clergyman, Rev. D. G. McKinnon. At this time two services were held in Ellensburg twice each month. When Ellensburg and Yakima were no longer served by the same vicar, Ellensburg had regular services, with Roslyn having one service a month. Under the Rev. Mr. Easton a missionary society was formed, and a Church Building Fund started.

A cornerstone was finally laid on August 14, 1897, the new minister, Rev. Andreas Bard, having raised enough money to build. Funds were contributed by the Church Guild of Chicago, a class of young boys in Westchester, Pennsylvania, and locally. This building served Grace Church until it was razed in 1964, having been sold along with the parish hall and rectory to Safeway. At that time a new church building costing $160,000 was started, being completed in 1969.

84. Grace Church, Ellensburg

St. David's Church

Hoquiam, Washington

The Protestant Episcopal Church of Hoquiam began with the missionary efforts of the late 1800s. In 1889, the Rt. Rev. John Adams Paddock visited Grays Harbor with Rev. Dr. R. D. Nevius. Dr. Nevius had visited the area previously and was now prepared to take charge of this new mission field, serving Elma, Montesano, Aberdeen and Hoquiam.

The first services were conducted in a hall used as a skating rink. One morning Dr. Nevius was busily sweeping the floor in preparation for service when a Welsh sailor took the broom and finished the task saying in explanation, "That's no sort of work for you to be doing, Father." The sailor's kindness was rewarded when Dr. Nevius named the new mission St. David's after the patron saint of Wales.

In 1890, Dr. Nevius obtained a home in Hoquiam and reserved a room for the Mission Chapel. In 1892, he moved on, and the Rev. John Henry Forrest-Bell arrived.

In 1893, the city of Hoquiam was badly in need of a hospital. In April if 1893 the diocese purchased the Murphy-Cagley Building at 401 9th Street, on the corner of Ninth and J. for $5,000. In September of that year, with assistance from Fr. Bell and the people of Hoquiam, St. David's Hospital was opened. A chapel was located on the ground floor in a former retail space. They carried a $3,000 mortgage. An article in *The Coast*, "How a Western City Grows" p. 217, of 1903, stated "St. David's Hospital, operated under the auspices of the Episcopal Church, is an excellent institution. It has been established 9 years and has 24 beds. Mrs. N. St. M. Rilky is matron and is assisted by competent trained nurses.

The mission was served by several clergy from 1895 to 1905. In 1904 St. David's Hospital closed in order not to compete with the newly formed Hoquiam General Hospital, and plans to build a church in Hoquiam were renewed.

The hospital building remained the property of the Church Charity Association until 1913, when it was sold to Carl and Mary Lund for $7,000. From the time the hospital closed the upper floors of the three-story building became the Queen Lodging House, run in 1908 by Mrs. Mary Lund (furnished rooms were 50 cents and 75 cents). By 1945 it was the Queen Hotel, run by Mrs. Erika Kylke, and, in 1964, the Queen Apartments, mostly vacant, managed by Amdahl Manford. The main floor had housed the early St. David's chapel. It remained vacant after the new church was built until the sale of the building. In 1922 it housed Byron & Backman Soft Drinks (this was during prohibition), and by 1956, it was occupied by The Corner Cigar Store Tavern, which remained until closing for demolition by 1965. Hoquiam's first hospital and St. David's chapel fell to the wrecking ball of progress in an urban renewal project.

In April of 1906 the present church building was completed. When the new church was built, it was decided to give it a new name, and so the congregation went by the name of Holy Trinity Episcopal

Church. Mr. F. H. Heath of Tacoma was engaged as architect and the building contract was awarded to Mr. Fred Knack. Attached to the Church was a Guild hall, the entire structure costing over $6,000. The first service was held there on Easter Sunday, 1906. The church was regularly served by a succession of rectors, but a hiatus in 1912 and 1913 brought back Dr. Nevius, who officiated at the baptism of Keldon Adams, grandson of Mr. and Mrs. W. L. Adams, on Easter Day, March 23 1913, less than six months before his death.

In the 1920s, Dean George G. Ware became rector, and it was during his time that the rest of the block was given and Ware Hall erected and used for the Church School. In 1941 extensive repairs were made to the church buildings.

The church acquired a number of beautiful stained glass windows over the years. Some were made from stained glass collected from bombed churches in England by Rev. Elvin Toll, rector from 1953 to 1959. The Christ window was given by Mr. George Pauze in 1965.

However, over the years the congregation dwindled and had a quick succession of rectors. Finally the diocese decided that the congregation could not support itself, and the building was in need of expensive repairs. The church building was deconsecrated on June 30, 1991. The stained glass windows, pews and other woodwork were removed. The Christ window is now on display in the chancel of St. Andrew's Church in Aberdeen. The building was sold to Gordon and Dian Marchant, who opened an antique shop in it in 1992. It is now occupied by Child Like Faith Child Care.

85. Holy Trinity Church Hoquiam, circa 1906

86. St. David's Church & Hospital

87. Holy Trinity Hoquiam, 2000

88. Holy Trinity, Hoquiam, 2000

89. Holy Trinity, Hoquiam, 2000

90. Holy Trinity, Hoquiam window, now in St. Andrew's, Aberdeen

St. Andrew's Church

Aberdeen, Washington

The first Episcopal church in Aberdeen was organized in 1890 by the Rev. Reuben D. Nevius. Mission status was given in May, 1890, by the first bishop of the Washington Territory, John A. Paddock. Bishop Paddock conducted the service at the Presbyterian Church at Wishkah and I streets. Maude Perry Douglas recalled in 1942:

"Won't you, in fancy, go back to a Spring evening long ago in Aberdeen and accompany a father and mother who, with their young daughter, were on their way to attend their first Episcopal service after arriving in town?

"Their route down Wishkah Street was on a board sidewalk raised high over a swampy expanse dotted by bunch grass and the small Spruce trees of the salt marsh thru which the tide ebbed and flowed twice daily.

"Bishop John A. Paddock of revered memory conducted this service in the little white Presbyterian Church at Wishkah and I Streets. It was a notable evening in that it marked the beginning of the Church in Aberdeen."

Shortly after Bishop Paddock's visit a Woman's Guild was organized, and church services began to be held in a vacant store building and in Kroehler's Hall on Heron Street, conducted by Rev. R. D. Nevius. The first confirmation class was conducted by Nevius, and held in the old Methodist Church on First and F Streets. The church women raised money by holding fairs, dinners, luncheons, dances and amateur theatricals. They also sold ice cream at regular sales (there being no supply of it otherwise in town).

Two lots were deeded to the church in June of 1892, donated by Samuel Benn and wife. They later donated four more lots in two different blocks.

The Rev. John Henry Forrest-Bell became the first vicar of St. Andrew's in August of 1891. A rectory was built at Third and I, which still stands. Services were held in it's large living room, the altar being in the bay window. On a large stump in the front was hung the Church bell, a gift from the Rector and Vestry of Trinity Church, Seattle. In 1895 the first church building was built at 1st and "G" Streets. The property was a gift from the Samuel Benn family. It was built under the plans and direction of the Rev. L. W. Applegate. When it was consecrated on May 5, 1895, Bishop Barker called it "the best of our Mission churches."

The October 1892 issue of the *Washington Churchman* had the following article:

"The Rev. John Morris, of Grand Mound,

91. First St. Andrew's Church, Aberdeen c. 1895

who is an architect of great ability, a Fellow of the Royal Institute of British Architects, and a friend of the late Sir Gilbert Scott, the great gothic architect of England, has placed this Jurisdiction under obligation by generously giving complete plans for the church. Those who are competent to judge (amongst them one of our well-known architects on the Sound who casually saw the plans) speak very highly of the design, which is wonderfully effective for the estimated cost. The huge square tower, nearly 50 feet high and 24 feet square, rising out of the crossing of nave and transepts, and this topped by a spire rising to the height of 96 feet, will be very effective, especially as the bench on which the church will stand is quite 20 feet above the general level of the city. Another pretty feature is the octagonal baptistry near the main entrance, which is also finished with a spire. Ample room is provided within the triple chancel arches, the chancel proper being 24 feet deep and 20 feet wide. The altar will look very dignified, raised seven steps above the nave, especially when seen from the west end of the church, 80 feet away.

St. Andrews was a mission until 1908 when it gained parish status. The first church being outgrown, the present church was started in 1913 at a cost of $8,000, on the site of the first one. It was dedicated on January 4, 1914 by Bishop Keator, and consecrated in 1918. Shortly after completion the Parish Hall was added. During the rectorship of Rev. Lawrence, about 1961, the church was completely renovated and its garden completed. In addition the property at 408 E. First was acquired and the house there removed. Architects Robert Street and Roy Lundgren worked on the plans to add a wing to create a church cloister.

92. St. Andrews, Aberdeen

93. St. Andrew's Church, Aberdeen, 2000

94. St. Andrew's Church, Aberdeen, 2000

St. Mark's Church

Ocosta, Washington

St. Mark's Church in Ocosta was built in 1892. The lots were acquired in October of 1891 as a gift of George Filley and wife. Nevius recorded the deed on November 16th. By May of 1892, Nevius was living there, probably to oversee the construction. The Ocosta Pioneer reported on the benediction ceremony there on August 31, 1892. "...The Rev. Mr. Bell in a few well chosen remarks alluded to the great work in church building which Dr. Nevius, the veteran missionary, has accomplished, he having built during the past seventeen years the total number of twenty churches in Washington and Oregon. He voiced the feelings of the citizens in expressing his regret that through illness the doctor was unable to be present.

"The church, which is a pretty one, consists of nave with open timber roof and a spacious apsidal chancel. The windows are a striking feature in the design, being of refoil shape and placed close up to the eaves and glazed in rolled cathedral glass, leaded. The three chancel windows are more elaborate, the centre one containing a floriated cross and the alpha and omega in colors. The one to the right contains the I.H.S., the other the Chi Rho, or symbols of our Lord.

"Plenty of space is allowed for the choir, and the altar is approached by four steps.

"We understand that Miss Emily Paddock, the Bishop's sister, has given new furniture for the chancel, and that as soon as a turret is erected a bell, given by a friend in the East, will be hung.

"The interior finishing of the church will be dimension cedar shingles, oiled, and it will accommodate about 120 people.

"St. Mark's Church in Ocosta has the distinction of being the most western Episcopal church in the United States."

In his address to the Convocation of 1895 Bishop Barker reported, "The Ocosta Church, begun long ago under the charge of Rev. Dr. Nevius, has been completed. Here the interior is ceiled or lined with native cedar shingles, the exposed surface of each shingle being planed and varnished. The effect when the lamps are lit is most beautiful, as each shingle reflects back for many gleams of light." In 1892 Ocosta had been made the Pacific Ocean terminus for the Northern Pacific Railroad, and its hopes of becoming a seaport of some consequence seemed about to be realized. Five years later the town was dead! The rapid rise and abrupt collapse of this community in southwestern Washington is typical of numerous boom towns in the West, many of which went through a cycle of "boom and bust" in their early days. On the day the plat was opened for sale, approximately 300 lots were sold for a total of $100,000.

The nationwide depression of 1893 was a major fac-

95. St. Mark's, Ocosta

tor in the decline of Ocosta. The Northern Pacific Railroad, hard hit by this depression, was reluctant to maintain its road to Ocosta, especially after several crippling storms hit the Grays Harbor area. The railroad strike of 1894 was another factor. Citizens in Aberdeen built a railroad branch into that city and turned it over to the Railroad on June 1, 1895. With the new railroad line, Ocosta began to fail quickly. The state bank at Ocosta closed its doors on June 11, 1895. Businesses failed, speculators withdrew, and money became even more scarce. By the early 1900s lots which had sold for thousands of dollars during Ocosta's boom years were selling for $30 each. Ocosta remained an incorporated city until November 25, 1932. As the buildings decayed and crumbled, the soil and the sea reclaimed its own. All that remains today is the memory and the unforgettable name "Ocosta-by-the-Sea." [102]

Today most of the streets of Ocosta are no longer visible. This is true of Sixth and Columbia Streets, where the church stood. The congregation deeded the church to the Diocese in 1925. It is assumed that the church decayed and fell down sometime after that, as in 1989 the church allowed the property to go to the County for taxes (although some might question it's taxable nature). The building was already gone when Ethel Hagen moved there in 1936. It now stands a vacant lot on a bluff overlooking the bay. Traces can still be found of ivy and flowers which must have once graced it's gardens.

St. John's Church

South Bend, Washington

St. John's South Bend, was organized on September 28. 1890 by a group of Episcopalians that petitioned Dr. Reuben Nevius, General Missionary of the Church, requesting that a mission be organized. Thereafter, Dr. Nevius held services at South Bend on the first Sunday of each month. Early services were held in Holcomb's Hall, the upper story of a South Bend Land Company building. The Catholics met there at 10 am, the Episcopalians at 5 PM, and the Baptists at 7:30.

At the same time, a women's guild was organized "with 15 faithful workers who sponsored a supper of oysters, tongue, ham, chicken salad and cakes. Over $100 was raised to purchase an organ."

A movement was started to build a church in 1912, and dedicated by the Rt. Rev. Frederic W. Keator on March 20, 1914. Hard-working guild members sponsored benefits, raising funds and paying off the mortgage in 1921. A $4,000 renovation was done in 1959, and a second in 1982, adding colored glass windows and refurbishing the guild hall. The plans for the church were drawn up by the priest in charge, Rev. A. M. Frost, which show a complete modern church, of gothic design, cruciform in shape, 54 feet from east to west by 36 feet, having two spacious choir rooms, and two rooms for the incumbent, on the same level as the nave of the church, while below was a hall or guild room of the same dimensions as the church itself; added to which was a kitchen completely fitted with all that a parochial kitchen needed, with a woodshed adjoining. On the other side of the parish hall were two other rooms, one for the heating plant and the other to be used as a store room. The church cost about $2500.00 to construct.

The church struggled at times and prospered at times over the years. In 1966 it was combined with St. Peter's, Seaview, into Pacific County Mission, served by one vicar.

The church building has only required two renovations, both due to it's hillside location and the damage of water to the pilings. In 1959 and again in 1982 the foundation was reinforced. In the latter improvement the guild hall and kitchen were also refurbished.

96. St. John's Church, South Bend, circa 1910

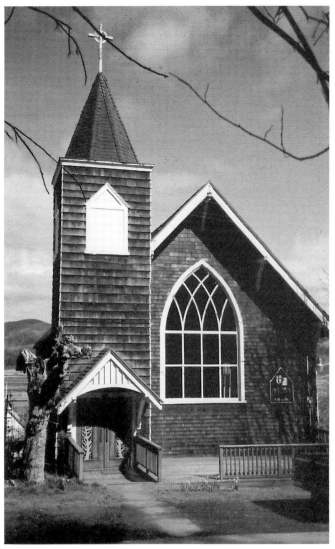

97. St. John's Church, South Bend, 2000

98. St. John's Church, South Bend, 2000

99. St. John's Church, South Bend, 2000

St. Luke's Church

Elma, Washington

The earliest recorded Anglican service in Elma was conducted in the Holliday family's home in 1885 by Dr. Nevius. Organized Anglicanism came to Elma ten years later. In 1895 and 1896, the Rev. L. W. Applegate, missionary for the Aberdeen congregation, traveled to Elma regularly to conduct services there an in nearby Porter. The Rt. Rev. William Morris Barker confirmed 17 communicants on his two visits to Elma in 1895 and 1896. The little frame church was built in 1910 and consecrated in October, 1911, by Bishop Frederic William Keator. At this time the Elma mission was separated from the similar mission in nearby Montesano, the county seat. In the *Olympia Diocese* of October 15, 1913, it stated that the church was closed for the month of August, but the Sunday school was conducted regularly. "The church has suffered from removals, but a small band of faithful communicants remain and they hope to take up the work with renewed vigor in the Autumn."

100. St. John's Church, Elma C. M. Moore photo, 2000

St. Mark's Church

Montesano, Washington

The ministry of the church in Gray's Harbor County was begun in the 1880's by the Rev. Reuben D. Nevius and other circuit riding clergy. The first organized congregation in the East County appears to have been around 1895 in Porter, six miles south of Elma. Lots were deeded to the church, and a building was built there, but the congregation was short lived.

In July of 1885 Rev. Lemuel Wells and Dr. Nevius conducted Episcopal services in Montesano in Mount Zion Congregational Church. After a visit in the spring of 1886, Montesano petitioned the bishop to establish an organized mission. There were five communicants at that time. Bishop Paddock visited Montesano for the first time in August of 1886, and on August 29th met in the afternoon at the Baptist church and confirmed two candidates, Dr. and Mrs. Story and baptized their daughter Eugenie. Nevius had preceded him and given them instruction the week prior. Under Dr. Nevius, services were held in a public hall at the Methodist Episcopal church quite frequently, and a little brown house provided by Dr. Story, by then the church warden. In September of 1886 Dr. Nevius was appointed delegate to the national convention. He traveled east for an extended visit, and upon his return went to Yakima and Ellensburg. The mission at Montesano was announced at the May, 1888 Convocation. Nevius returned to the Gray's Harbor area in June of 1890. Nevius reported that the Women's Guild had purchased two lots in Montesano for $650 on January 7th, 1894. Services were held at the Rink, and at the Methodist church. In 1890 Nevius reported that it was impossible to build a church as the road to their lots had not been graded. In 1891 he reported that the two lots were paid for and partially cleared.

Upon the appointment of Rev. George Buzzelle in 1908, work began again on a church building.

101. St. Mark's Church Montesano, 2000

Services were held at the Odd Fellows Hall. The Women's Guild was revitalized under the leadership of Mrs. A. D. Bishop, and the present church building was begun. The Women's Guild held their first meeting at the church on April 28, 1909. On December 17, 1911, a beautiful brass cross was given in memory of Mrs. Martha S. Sherman. Two brass alms basins were presented by the Sunday School and the Girls' Guild. St. Mark's original building remains with expansions being added in the 1940s and 1950s. Calder Hall was built in 1943 during a remodeling. Services were held during the '30s in the evenings, with the rector of Holy Trinity in Hoquiam coming to lead them. During the war years services were held by lay readers.

Christic Church

Blaine, Washington

Christ Episcopal Church, Blaine, had its beginnings in 1889 when services were held in members' homes. The building had evidently been built in 1875, possibly by another denomination (25th anniversary celebrated in 1900). In 1894 Nevius reported that it was supplied with new prayer books and hymnals. Nevius wrote the following historic note:

"Rev. R. D. Nevius, D.D. took chg. being also chaplain of the Blaine sch'l Apr. 1st, 1894, holding services twice on Sunday and daily in Lent and on all Holy Days with celebrations until Sept. 1st, 1896 when the school having failed he was called to open the mission at Juneau, Alaska. Services were maintained by lay reader Mr. Carl Stevens and afterward by E. P. Young until the fall of 1888 [sic 1898]. After this at long intervals by Rev. R. D. Nevius On the 18th day of 1900. Rt. Rev. Wm. M. Barker D.D. being Bishop of Olympia on or about Nov. 20th, 1903. The Fourth house [Fourth and D] was sold with a view of building a church with the proceeds of the sale and as the rainy season had begun it was thought but to defer the building of the church to the spring of next year and to cease holding services in the meantime except as the Bishop might supply services from time to time."

In 1904, the old church and rectory were sold, and a small wooden church with green, gold and purple leaded glass windows was built on the corner of 4th and Boblett. The Willing Workers, a women's guild, bought the church furniture which was made by a local cabinet maker out of curly maple. Nevius donated a curled maple alms basin which he made. The first pastor was Rev. William Bell, followed by Peter Hyland in 1891. Nevius is listed as rector from 1894-95 and 1900-1902.

The church was built under the direct supervision of Rev. C. I. Grimes, superintendent of home missions. The size of the grounds is 75 feet by 110 feet. The old rectory sale brought $800, and the people, primarily the Women's Guild, raised the balance totaling $3,000. The interior is finished with native wood of gothic design, the panel work beaded plain finish, while the cross beams and massive frame work, together with the pews are tinged with light green and with the leaded stained glass from Czechoslovakia, the elegant designed altar and other furniture, made with curly maple, the whole floor covered with carpet gives a beautiful effect. All furniture and wood work are home manufacture, being made in Blaine.[103]

The church stands today much as it did in 1904. A parish hall was added in the 50's, and porches and ramps have been added. In the sanctuary the choir stalls have been removed, and the wood floors have been exposed. The original furnishings are still in use, and the church has a wonderful feeling of it's origins and the long use that has given it a patina of Christian life. The sign on the church reads Christ Episcopal Church (Anglican) to denote that about half the congregation comes from across the border in Canada.

102. Christ Church, Blaine, 2000

103. Christ Church interior, Blaine, 2000

104. Christ Church, Blaine, 1947

Holy Trinity Church

Juneau, Alaska

R. D. Nevius went as a missionary to Juneau arriving by September of 1895. Bishop Barker had sent Rev. George Buzzelle of Tacoma there, where he held Trinity Sunday services on June 9, 1895, in the Log Cabin church. In his remembrances, Buzzelle stated: "The year the General Convention met in Minneapolis, I was sent to Alaska by the Board of Missions, to spy out the land. At the time the only mission, I think, was Chapman's, at Anvik....I visited south eastern Alaska, and delved as thoroughly as possible into conditions. I held service at Juneau, Douglas, and Sitka. At the latter place I met a number of the naval force then stationed in the north. Some of the officers were very familiar with the people and conditions farther north. My report was made, and the G. C. decided to undertake work there, and elected Bishop Rowe. While there the citizens of Juneau wanted me to stay and carry on a work, offering to build me a church and pay me far more than I was getting in Washington. I refused,

105. Holy Trinity Church, circa 1903

and through my efforts Dr. Nevius was sent to them. Bishop Rowe secured funds for the church at Juneau in the east, thus relieving the people of the joy of doing for themselves."

As a result of Bishop Barker's interest and Buzzelle's enthusiasm, Nevius was sent there as a missionary. He gathered several families for services, organized a Sunday School, and ladies guild. His first services were held in the Presbyterian Log Cabin church on September 8, 1895. By then a ladies Guild had already organized. He may have purchased the lots on which the new church was built. In December the Women's Guild held a bazaar to raise money for furnishing the church.

The December 14 issue of the *Searchlight* noted that construction would soon begin with occupancy scheduled for around March 1st. The church was constructed shortly after he left, and is probably constructed with a design provided by Nevius, since it resembles his other churches. Nevius conducted regular services at 11 a.m. on Sunday mornings at the Log Cabin church, and at 7:30 p.m. in the Mission Chapel. Starting on October 13 he added an early service at 8 a.m. except on the first Sunday of the month, and a 7:30 p.m. service on Tuesdays at Douglas Island in Bear's Nest hall. St. Luke's on Douglas Island was organized shortly after Trinity in Juneau. Several fairs and bazaars were held to raise funds for the new church. At Christmas Nevius gave a magic lantern show for the children illustrating the birth and life of Christ.

106 Holy Trinity, interior. Winter and Pond, Alaska State Library/PCA 87-1127

Nevius must have worn himself out at Christmas, as the paper announced on January 11th that he had recovered from his recent illness enough to hold regular services again. The last service announced as conducted by Nevius was on March 22, 1896. Peter Trimble Rowe, the first Bishop of Alaska, arrived in March of 1896, and Nevius was back in Washington by April. Rev. Henry Beer, a friend of Rowe's who arrived with him, supervised the building's construction, which began in May, and served as the first rector. The church was completed enough for services to be held by July of 1896. Stained glass windows were installed in 1902, and a church organ was dedicated on Trinity Sunday of 1903. In 1910 Mrs. Frances C. Davis, a well known Alaskan artist, painted and donated scenes of Jesus' life that are in the chancel near the altar. The church became the Cathedral of Alaska and served as such until 1944. The church is still in use today.

107. Holy Trinity Church, circa 1950

St. Luke's Church

Douglas Island, Alaska

Douglas Island was named by Capt. George Vancouver for John Douglas, Bishop of Salisbury. Gold was discovered on the island in the 1880s and by 1910 the population was 1722 people. Through a series of fires and mining disasters the population had dwindled to 522 by 1939. Apparently a church was built on the island, as a stained glass window still exists. When the bridge was built from the island to Juneau in 1935, the two congregations combined. One of the stained glass windows from this church is presently in use in another church on the island. Nevius held regular services on the island and the congregation was started shortly after that of Trinity Church in Juneau.

108. Presbyterian Log Church, circa 1895

Trinity Church

Seattle, Washington

Trinity Parish is the Mother Church and the oldest of the Episcopal parishes and missions in Seattle. The first service was held on August 13, 1865, when the city was a hamlet of 250 persons. The service was conducted by the Rev. Peter Edward Hyland, Rector of St. John's, Olympia, at the Methodist Church. The church was organized on the following day, and services were held at the United States Hotel and Plummer's Hall.

At the corner of Third and Jefferson, in January of 1871, Bishop Morris consecrated the first church building, a 24 by 48 foot frame structure. In 1878 the first vestry called the Rev. George Herbert Watson to be rector. He arrived in the autumn and served until his death in 1896. During his rectorate, a vigorous ministry by women which continues today, began and the Chapel of the Good Shepherd in North Seattle, the first of many missions, was established. The *Washington Churchman* was first published, and Grace Hospital was built. The first church was destroyed in the fire of 1889, and the present church building, at Eighth and James was erected in 1891.

When Dean Watson passed away in June of 1896, Rev. Reuben D. Nevius preached the memorial sermon on June 21. Nevius was then rector at Holy Communion Church in Tacoma. He took on the coverage of Trinity Church for the next six months until a new rector arrived. The *Washington Churchman* on September 20, 1896, reported that he would officiate at all regular services in Trinity Church.

Rev. Herbert H. Gowan became the second rector of Trinity in 1897, serving until 1914. The present church dates from the rebuilding of 1904, after a disastrous fire which burned most of the downtown business district. The stone walls were all that remained, and are part of the church today.

109. Trinity Church, Seattle, 1900. MSCUA University of Washington Libraries. neg.no.

110 Trinity Church, Seattle interior postcard, 1909

111. Trinity Church, Seattle, 2000

Church of the Holy Communion

Tacoma, Washington

On Whitsunday 1886 there was begun a new mission on "E" Street near 19th Street, which was known as St. John's Church. It was an offshoot of St. Luke's Church, which was then located at South 6th and Broadway, and the rector was Rev. Lemuel H. Wells. Mr. Wells looked after this new mission until other arrangements were made for ministering to the new flock.

On December 14th, 1887, the name of the parish was changed to The Church of the Holy Communion (after Church of the Holy Communion, New York City, of which the Rev. Henry Mottet, brother of Mr. Frederick Mottet, was rector). For many years the parish was the recipient of much kindness from the "mother church." A small building on one lot on South E street between Seventeenth and Nineteenth streets, which had been used for the mission, was the first church building. In 1888 the first rector, Rev. Robert S. Carlin, was called, who also acted as chaplain of Washington College, the denominational institution which was endowed by C. B. Wright. Later the college was sold to the school board and the endowment and proceeds of the property transferred to Annie Wright Seminary.

When Dr. William J. Jefferis became pastor of the church, in 1892, the property on E street was exchanged for three lots where the church was relocated. The parish was incorporated on November 2nd, 1892. A new church was built at the corner of South 14th and I Streets, which was to serve until a structure of a more permanent character would take its place. $500 of the money which built the church was contributed by members of the New York Church of the Holy Communion, and the rest was contributed by the members of the parish. In 1913 Mr. & Mrs. Fred Mottet presented the parish with two lots immediately south of the three lots purchased in 1893, for the purpose of erecting a Memorial Parish House. On October 30th, 1921, the cornerstone was laid for the new parish house, by the Bishop the Right Reverend F. W. Keator, D. D. and the building was occupied in January 1922.

Nevius was listed as rector of the church from 1897 to 1901. The old church had been a temporary structure, and in 1922 it was determined that it had to be torn down. In 1923 the Nevius Memorial Guild Room was erected for use of the Young People and other parish activities. A new church building was proposed in 1926, and dedicated in 1929. The church was closed in 1976. The church and parish hall were deeded to Hilltop Community Day Care Center on August 9, 1977, a gift of the diocese according to the current director. The old Parish House is used to this day by the school, and the 1929 church stands abandoned and boarded up.

St. John the Divine Church

Buckley, Washington

With the completion of the railroad over the Cascade Mountains in 1888, Buckley's rapid growth began. Most of the pioneer citizens arrived in 1888 and 1889. Shingle mills and lumber mills sprang up. The town voted to incorporate June 6, 1890. Incorporation brought rapid strides in municipal improvements. Stumps were removed from Main Street and it was graded and planked for nearly a half mile. The post office was established in 1888, the Buckley Banner began publishing in January of 1889, and Buckley State Bank opened in 1891. Two years later, the president and cashier absconded with all of the money. In 1891 a new school was built after the third election to fund it. Fire was a real and constant threat. In May of 1892, Buckley experienced the destruction of its business district by fire. A bond for a water works passed in 1893. The missionary congregation acquired Lot 3, Block 17, D. S. Morris's Second Addition to Buckley, by deed on November 15, 1895. Nevius was listed as missionary to St. Paul's, Buckley, from 1898 to 1900. Although diocese reports consistently refer to the Buckley church as St. Paul's Mission, the local paper clearly calls it St. John the Divine.

The congregation built under Rev. Buzzelle held various bazaars and activities to raise funds to build a church. "On Monday, January 6, 1896 (the Feast of Epiphany) the new church building dedicated to St. John the Divine, was opened for Divine service. The service consisting of evening prayer and sermon commenced about 8 o'clock. A congregation of nearly two hundred assembled to take part at the opening service. The service was conducted by the Rev. Geo. Buzzelle, who in addition to being rector of Grace church of Tacoma and Secretary of Convocation for this jurisdiction is also the general missionary for Pierce and King counties." ..."The church building is a very neat edifice of the Gothic order, erected on a lot situated at the corner of Main and A streets. The dimensions of this building are as follows: sanctuary, 12x12; chancel, 8x20; nave 43x20; porch, 6/8; vestry, 14x12. The roof is an open timbered one and presents quite a dignified appearance. The building is constructed entirely of wood and the contractor, Mr. C. C. Doud, is to be congratulated in having carried out his work in a most efficient manner. The altar and lectern which were donated are the work of Mr. C.C. Doud and are good specimens of church furniture."[104]

Nevius retained close ties with the church after he left for Blaine in the fall of 1900. When the high school burned in 1909 several churches came to the rescue. The 8th grade and high school were held at St. John the Divine for the balance of the school year. Nevius conducted the services at the church on July 13, 1913, just five months prior to his death. His obituary, published on December 19, 1913, stated, "He was quite a familiar figure in Buckley, having held services here many times and was often the guest of Mr. & Mrs. H. D. Taylor."

The congregation apparently waned during the twenties, and in June of 1932 the Diocese deeded the church building to Maranatha Mission of the Apostolic Gospel. Maranatha Mission sold the property to Harold A. Parkinson in August of 1938. The price was $800.00, and one assumes that by that time the church building was gone, or in such disrepair as to be of little value. The lot now belongs to the Town of Buckley, and the city hall is on the adjacent two lots.

St. Peter's Chapel

Tacoma, Washington

An article in the Tacoma paper in 1907 reads as follows:

...Erected in 1874, St. Peter's Church is the oldest in Tacoma, and the organization is the oldest in the city. Trials and seasons of adversity have tested the strength of the little congregation which almost weekly gathered at Sunday morning worship.... Solidly built, in those early days when the pioneers stood the heavy boards on end and cleated the cracks, modern structural methods being too elaborate, the building presents few indications of decay. It will stand with few repairs for many years. And the bell tower may also stand, if plans now being considered prove feasible. It is planned to erect a tower around the old trunk, and at the same elevation and in the same place where it hung before, to set the bell again.

Ivy has entwined itself lovingly around the stump and trailed over the little structure. Not content with stretching its branches and tentacles, almost tenderly, it seems, around the two, it has forced its way through cracks in the wall and is growing within the house of worship. No cut decorations of green things or evergreens are needed at Christmas time in this little church. The ivy has twined itself around braces and delicately stretched along beams and rafters until the interior presents a more than noteworthy appearance. Not alone is the church old, the ivy also is old, it having been planted at the base of the now famous bell tower within a short time after the building was erected. It came from St. Peter's church, Philadelphia, after which the Tacoma church was named.

The interior of this little church, though plain, is attractive. The place is neat, the furnishings are of a good order, and the services are conducted in a way to attract the interest of those who attend. Visitors to Tacoma hear of this old church and journey to see it. Postcards bearing its picture have been printed and scattered broadcast over the country. That it is the most historic church in Western Washington there is little doubt. Built at Old Town, when Tacoma, and the former place for that matter, had only a very few houses, the church organization has endured.

Not alone is the church itself a pioneer, but the rector, Rev. R. D. Nevius, has also spent a large part of his long and eventful life in the West, especially the Northwest, and came to Portland from the East about the time St. Peter's was erected. More than 80 years of age, Rev. Nevius is still active and goes about his duties as head of the little church in a way which would put many a younger man to wondering whence came such unusual vitality, Rev. Nevius had spent fifty years in the ministry of the gospel when he took the local church after having retired from active work. But he couldn't stay retired, and finding the church without a pastor, took charge, and has been holding meetings since.

St. Peter's church was established in the year 1873 by the Rt. Rev. B. W. Morris, bishop of the territory which now comprises, after several divisions, the diocese of Oregon and the missionary diocese districts of Olympia, Spokane and Eastern Oregon—each with its own bishop.

In August, 1873, Bishop Morris was with his family in camp on American lake for his summer vacation. George E. Atkinson, who was then superintendent of the Hanson mill, which at that time was with its officers and operatives all there was of Tacoma, and who was a devoted churchman from Nova Scotia, secured from Bishop Morris a Sunday visit and prepared to hold a service in the school house that day.

The service was largely attended and at its close a movement was made to establish a mission at that place. Contributions were immediately offered for building a church and a sufficient sum was raised for the purpose. Captain Edward S. Smith offered a site for the church.

Except along the beach, the land was a vast forest. The chosen site for the church was occupied chiefly by an immense fir tree—the removal of which was the first problem in the process of building. The happy thought occurred to the bishop to utilize the stump of the tree for a bell tower and thus avoid the expense of moving it. It was cut off at a height of 48 feet and the top was prepared as a seat for the bell. The ground was cleared and the building of the church was begun. In two weeks the Rev. Charles R. Bonnell, the first rector, was on the ground and services were begun which, with some interruptions and many changes, have been maintained to this day.

The bell was presented by St. Peter's church, Philadelphia, of which Rev. Bonnell had been rector at the time when he offered himself for missionary work in the diocese to which his old and valued friend had been appointed. The ivy which soon grew to wholly cover tower and bell-cot, also came from St. Peter's church. It was planted and cared for by Mrs. Walters, who is the only resident survivor of the first members of the church (About 1907).

At the 1874 Convocation, Bishop Morris reported on visiting Tacoma, that "Here we found the newest church, with the oldest tower in this Missionary Jurisdiction. This tower is also the highest we have, except perhaps that of Trinity Church, Portland. This church had ground broken, its corner "log" laid, its last nail driven, and services begun, all in the incredible space of twenty days after the terminus [of the Northern Pacific Railroad] was located. Bishop Morris has built this church in fifteen days. It did not cost more than $500 in all. It is churchly in style, capable of seating 120 persons, and has its fine tower painted too. This latter cost nothing. It is a fine fir tree situated at the south west corner of the church and arises more than 70 feet. Here also there is a rectory, erected for the most part by the hands of the clergyman (Bonnell). It consists of a study, a bedroom and kitchen. Here the clergyman and his wife dwell, contented. Its rough board walls, its lowly roof, and the articles of furniture, indicative of taste and refinement, the pictures and the books are in strange contrast...."

...In 1905, the parish being vacant, the Rev. R. D. Nevius, a retired clergyman, resident, and serving in the diocese above mentioned since 1872, undertook to hold at least Sunday morning services, with holy eucharists, as priest in charge. Last January Mr. Burroughs, secretary to Bishop Keater, was appointed to assist in charge of the work of the parish, which Dr. Nevius did not feel able to undertake, since which time the parish has taken on a new life. Evening and weekday services are maintained. The usual guilds for work have been organized, and the attendance has greatly increased, with promise of a healthy and rapid growth...." The church stands today in much the same condition it was in Nevius's day.

112. St. Peter's Church, Tacoma, postcard circa 1890

113. St. Peter's Church, Tacoma, 2000

114. St. Peter's Church, Tacoma, 1908

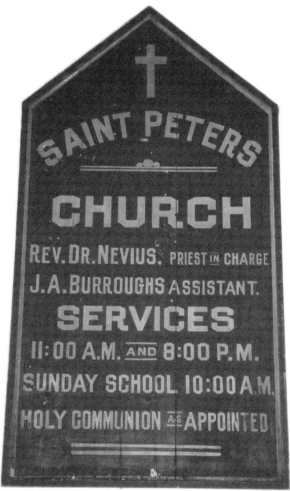

115. St. Peter's Church Tacoma

CHAPTER 3

The Churchman as Naturalist

Throughout his life Nevius held a fascination for botany that was at a professional level. He had five plants named after him, and studiously collected plant specimens from everywhere he traveled, often sending the ones he couldn't identify to his friend Prof. Asa Gray at Harvard University. Rev. J. Neilson Barry wrote in 1953 to Mr. Howard Atwood, Huntington Library:

"He was like an imaginary fictional story-book character, and truly Ubiquitous. Apparently he was everywhere at the same time, with building churches as his everyday job. Few towns do not have a church that he had built: and usually he was the first to start a mission in that town. If he had not been real it would have been like a mythical Paul Bunyan.

"He was much interested in scientific matters, and especially in anatoms [diatoms]... He most eagerly exulted in mud, which he examined with his pocket microscope for anatoms. At such infrequent intervals when he was not holding services or building churches he gave magic lantern lectures on anatoms. Everybody liked him so much that they attended. He was enthusiastic about anatoms, an A-Number-One expert. Building churches which 'stayed put' was his Vocation. Anatoms was his Avocation. He probably dreamed of them at night, and meditated on them when awake."

From the beginning of his career Nevius was a teacher. He began in Ovid when he was 20, in 1847. He taught school in Michigan in 1849. In 1850 he took his brother John's teaching job in Columbus, Georgia, so that John could attend seminary. When Nevius went to Alabama in 1853, he was associated with Christ Church, Wetumpka, and taught at the Episcopal High School in Montgomery. When Nevius resigned his position at St. David's Church, Dallas County, Alabama, in 1855, one of the reasons was the heavy burden of teaching school and leading his parish. When then went to Tuscaloosa, he taught in the parish school, and taught in Mrs. Tuomey's School for Girls. In Oil City, Pennsylvania, there was also a parish school where Nevius must have taught. It was common in those days for a rector to supplement his income with a teaching position. While in Portland, Nevius probably taught at the Bishop Scott Grammar School and/or St. Helen's Hall. During his Eastern Oregon Nevius likely taught an occasional class, but he traveled frequently. Wells had a school for girls in Walla Walla, and a Parish school was in place at Baker City by 1876, when the regular instructor was Dr. P. D. Rothwell.

When Nevius started the church in Spokane Falls, funds were raised for a chapel and school house combined. Nevius named the school the Rodney Morris School for Girls and Boys, in honor of a deceased son of Bishop Morris. In 1883 Nevius was among the speakers at the cornerstone laying ceremony for Annie Wright Seminary for girls in Tacoma. In 1884 Nevius was listed as the botany teacher there. A school for boys was soon built there also. In 1894 Nevius was assigned to Blaine, Washington, and was also put in charge of the school there, which had just begun. In addition to his formal teaching, Nevius was constantly prepared to do so informally. He carried a small microscope in his pocket, and often gave lessons to the children of his hosts as he traveled his missionary routes.

Nevius had a life-long interest in botany which followed him wherever he traveled. He may have developed this during his studies at school. When he taught in Michigan he developed it further, as he later related to Dr. Gray. In Alabama it was undoubtedly stimulated in his close association with Dr. Tuomey. While Tuomey (whose daughter Nevius married after his death) was a geologist, he had an interest in collecting plant material on his hikes through unexplored territory around Tuscaloosa. Nevius, at this time, entered into a correspondence with Dr. Gray of the botany department of Harvard which lasted from 1858 until his death in 1888. Early on he seems to have wanted to identify almost any plant material which was unfamiliar to him, from shrubs to mosses and sedums. He was equally as prepared to give a scientific lecture as to preach. In later life he seemed to specialize in diatoms, microscopic plants which lived along the shores in tide pools and among algae. His knowledge and interest as well as his discoveries became well known throughout the country and even the world in his day.

The study of Botany was at an all time high in popularity in Nevius's time. The period from 1730 to 1840 had been a period of intense intellectual ferment and productivity in botanical history. In 1753 Linnaeus published his *Species Platarum*, establishing new classifications and nomenclature upon which modern botany is based. The Royal Botanic Gardens at Kew were established in 1759, for which many collection excursions were made in future years. Explorers began to collect plant specimens from around the world, including Joseph Banks, who collected on a trip with Capt. James Cook upon which they "discovered" Australia. The Far East became a source of new plant material. The first Harvard Botanic Garden was established in 1801. In 1804 the Lewis and Clark Expedition began. Prior to taking the trip Lewis spent nine months in Philadelphia studying botany under Benjamin Smith Barton. In the same year England's Horticultural Society was formed. In 1823 David Douglas was sent by the Royal Horticultural Society to collect new fruit tree and vegetable varieties in the U.S. In 1825 he arrived at the mouth of the Columbia River, returning to England in 1827. He again visited the West in 1829, and died while collecting in Hawaii after falling into a pit trap containing a wild bull. Douglas introduced over 200 species to cultivation in Great Britain. In 1830 John James Audubon published his *The Birds of America* in London, popularizing natural history, and stimulating the style of having botanical and natural history prints as a standard decoration in Victorian homes.

In 1850 President Millard Fillmore invited Andrew Jackson Downing to design an arboretum and pleasure ground for the Capitol at the Washington Mall. The opening of Japan in 1854 brought a flurry of discovery to the Western world. A Protestant missionary, S. Wells Williams, sent dried specimens to his boyhood friend, the Harvard botanist Asa Gray. In 1858 Charles Darwin first presented his ideas on natural selection before the Linnean Society in London. In 1859 Dr. Asa Gray published his idea that the north American and Eurasian floras had at one time been homogeneous. He proposed that they had been separated through Pleistocene glaciation and evolution (a new concept he had learned through his correspondence with Darwin). That year Darwin published *On the Origin of Species by Means of Natural Selection*, and Gray became his leading advocate in U.S. debates. During this time there was great effort put into developing better strains of agricultural plants.[105]

Nevius was certainly in the forefront of botanical discovery in America during his time. The availability of published works served to stimulate this hobby for many collectors and students. Publications such as the *American Monthly Microscopic Journal* brought news of new discoveries to its subscribers, including Nevius. Mass publication of books made botany available to students in the fledgling schools of the expanding civilized American world. Nevius was always looking for the latest textbooks for his students—things that were not available only a generation earlier. He gave books on botany as prizes for student accomplishment. This chapter follows Nevius's involvement in the botanical world of his day, the plants named for him, and his correspondence with Dr. Asa Gray of Harvard University.

1. Plants Named After Nevius

NEVIUSIA ALABAMENSIS—snow wreath (1858, published 1859) A member of the rose family native to the southeastern United States.

SEDUM NEVII—(1858, published 1859) A sedum native to the southeastern United States.

MNIUM NEVII—(published 1873) A moss native to the Pacific Northwest.

RACOMITRIUM (OR GRIMMIA) NEVII—(published 1873) A moss native to the Pacific Northwest.

CHAENACTIS NEVII—Nevius's chaenactis (1876, published 1883) A member of the sunflower family native to Oregon's John Day Valley, now endangered.

ALLIUM NEVII—(published 1879) A wild onion now known as *Allium douglassii* var. *nevii*, collected at Hood River, Oregon.

ᔥ Neviusia Alabamensis (collected 1858, described 1859)

ROSE FAMILY (ROSACEA)

COMMON NAME: SNOW WREATH

John Kunkel Small, *Flora of the Southeastern United States* (New York: privately published, 1903), p. 524:
NEVIUSIA—A. Gray.

"Shrus [sic, shrub?], with spreading terete branches. Leaves alternate: blades membranous, simple, doubly serrate: stiples slender. Flowers perfect, white, solitary or in open clusters. Hypanthium bractless, flattish. Sepals 5, petal-like, imbricated, spreading, incised-serrate, persisitent. Petals wanting. Stamens numerous, persisitent, in several series: filaments glabrous. Pistils 204, sessile. Style nearly terminal, stigmatose on the inner side. Ovules solitary in each cavity, pendulous. Achenes drupe-like, with a tiny fleshy epicarp and a crustaceous endocarp."

I. Neviusia Alabamensis A. Gray. A branching shrub 6-15 dm. [sic, cm.] tall, with minutely pubescent young foliage. Leaves numerous; blades ovate to ovate-lanceolate, 2-7 cm. long, acute or acuminate, doubly serrate, rounded or subcordate at the base, sparingly pubescent on both sides or glabrous

116. Neviusia Alabamensis

117. Neviusia Alabamensis—drawing

in age; petioles 3-8 mm. long: sepals leafe-like, obovate or oblong-cuneate, 8-12 mm. long, sharply ser-rate above the middle: petal wanting: filiform-clavate, longer than the sepals.

On cliffs, near Tuscaloosa and on Sand Mountain, Alabama. Summer."

Prof. Chambers in a letter to David Powers of July 20, 1987, indicated that the specimen in the Oregon State University herbarium came from Conway County, Arkansas.

Listed as endangered in *Endangered and Threatened Plants of the U.S.*, Smithsonian Institution, 1978.

❧ Allium nevii (described 1879, now *Allium douglasii* var. *nevii*)

LILY (ONION) FAMILY

COMMON NAME: NEVIUS' ONION

Marion Ownbey, *Vascular Plants of the Pacific Northwest*, Nov. 1, 1969, p. 747 lists three varieties of *Allium douglasii*, which was first named in 1839. The other two varieties come from eastern Washington.

Sereno Watson, *Proceedings of the American Academy* v. 14, (1879), p. 231:

"28. A. Nevii. Bulb-coats white or reddish, thin, with compressed transversely oblong reticulation (as in *A. tribracteatum*), the cell-outline not all sinuous: scape slender, 6 or 8 inches high: pedicles rather few, slender, 4 to 6 inches long: perianth-segments light rose-color, lanceolate, acuminate, 3 inches long, scarcely exceeding the stamens and style: cells of the ovary with a thick short crest on each side near the summit.—Oregon (Hood River; Rev. R. D. Nevius)."

Morton Eaton Peck, *A Manual of the Higher Plants of Oregon* (second edition, Portland, Oregon: Binfords & Mort, 1961), pp. 210-211: (Note: the Herbarium of Dr. & Mrs. Peck was at Willamette University at this time, and was later loaned to Oregon State College for lack of room.)

"A. Nevii Wats. Nevius's Onion. Bulb ovoid, 1-1.5 cm. long, the outermost coat purplish, the first inner clearly reticulate, the meshes transversely oblong, or sometimes in part nearly square; leaves about 2 mm. wide, mostly shorter than the scape, often withering before flowering time; scape slender, 1.5-2 dm. high, nearly terete or slightly flattened; bracts 2; umbel many-flowered, the pedicels 8-12 mm. long; perianth rose-color, 6-7 mm. long, the segments lance-ovate, acuminate, thin, somewhat gibbous at base, stamens about equaling the perianth; ovary minutely 6-crested.— Moist clayey soil, northern Ore. east of the Cascades, to Wash. and Idaho.

೫ Chaenactis nevii (collected 1876—described 1883)

SUNFLOWER FAMILY (COMPOSITAE, NOW ASTERACEA)

COMMON NAMES: JOHN DAY CHAENACTIS, NEVIUS' CHAENACTIS

Leroy Abrams and Roxana Stenchfield Ferris, *Illustrated Flora of the Pacific States* (Stanford, California: Stanford University Press, 1960) pp. 241-242:

"Chaenactis nevii [e in nevii is umlauted: "neevii"] A. Gray..

Chaenactis nevii A. Gray, Proc. Amer. Adad. 19:30. 1883.

"Glandular puberulent annual often red-stemmed, 10-25 cm. high, simple or branching from the base and at the midstem with ascending branches, glandular-puberulent, densely so below the heads and slightly arachnoid-villous. Lower leaves at flowering time 4.5 cm. long or less including the petiolar base, pinnately divided nearly to the midrib with 3-5 widely spreading, linear, obtuse lobes, these 5-10 mm. long; upper leaves reduced above in length and often linear on unbranched plants, all leaves sparsely glandular-puberulent to glabrate; heads bright yellow, terminating the branches, the outer flowers regular but larger than the inner, the peduncles 1-6 cm. long; involucres 6-7 mm. high; phyllaries linear-lanceolate, glandular-puberulent with occasional cobwebby hairs, thin, the midrib becoming somewhat prominent in age; achenes blunt, spreading hairs; pappus of 10 vestigial plaeae.

"Barren dry slopes in heavy clay soil, Arid Transition Zone; Wheeler and Grant Counties, Oregon. Type locality: Idaho; probably an error in the collecting data, as the species seems to be limited to the John Day Basin, Oregon. April-May. Nevius' Chaenactis."

Prof. Chambers explained that the dates and locations in Hitchcock *et. al.* mean that the plant was first collected in 1876 but not described by Gray until 1883, by which time the specimen through mislabeling or other error was noted as coming from Idaho. He confirmed that Chaenactis nevii grows only in the John Day basin and that it is one of two wild plants in that vicinity with yellow flowers in late spring.

೫ Grimmia ne[e]vii (described 1873, now *Rhacomitrium aciculare*)

SYNONIMOUS WITH: RHACOMITRIUM ACICULARE (1819)

DICRANUM ACICULARE (1801)

TRICHOSTOMUM ACICULARE (1805)

GRIMMIA ACICULARIS (1849)

R[H]ACOMITRIUM N[E]EVII

MOSS DIVISION (BRYOPHYTA)

Elva Lawton, *Moss Flora of the Pacific Northwest* (Nichinan, Miyazaki, Japan: Hattori Botanical Laboratory, 1971), pp. 141-142:

"Rhacomitrium aciculare (Hedw.) Brid., Musc. Rec. Suppl.

4: 80. 1819.

"*Dicranum aciculare* Hedw., Spec. Musc. 135. 1801.

"*Trichostrmum aciculare* (Hedw.) P. Beauv., Prodr. 90. 1805.

"*Grimmia acicularis* (Hedw.) C. Muell., Syn. I: 801. 1849.

"*Grimmia neevii* C. Muell. Flora 56: 483. 1873.

"Plants in tufts or mats, green to dark green or nearly black when old. Stems 2-5 cm. long or sometimes longer, often branched. Leaves more or less imbricate when dry, spreading when moist, 1.6-3.6 by 0.9-1 mm., oblong or oblong-lanceolate to lingulate, the apex usually broad and rounded, sometimes with a very short point; margins unistratose, recurved to above the middle, usually coarsely toothed at the apex, rarely entire or nearly so; costa ending before the apex, of 2 or 3 layers of cells at the base, rarely thicker, the cells of the ventral layer often larger; cells with thick sinuose walls, the upper cells short, often nearly isodiametric, with several small papillae per cell, becoming elongate at the middle of the leaf; basal cells long and narrow with very thick sinuose walls; a few alar cells differentiated.

"Diocious, male and female plants similar; perigonial bracts to 1.5 mm. long; perichaetial bracts 1.6-3.2 mm. long, the costa long or short, the lamina cells with walls only slightly sinuose. Seta 8-15 mm. long, smooth or somewhat wrinkled when dry; operculum to 1.3 mm. long; annulus of about 3 rows of cells; peristome teeth divided nearly to the base, 0.4-0.5 mm. long, spinosepapillose. Spores minutely papillose, 15-19 u. Clayptra entire or often split at the base, smooth below and rough at the apex. N=12, 13.

"On stones in or near streams, rarely on wood, from sea level to about 2000 m. British Columbia, Washington, Oregon, Idaho, Montana; Alaska, California; Michigan, Ontario; Newfoundland, Nova Scotia, Quebec, New England to Georgia.

"*Illustrations*. Pl. 74, figs 1-9; B. S. G., Bryol. Eur. Pl. 262. 1845.

"*Exsiccati*. Allen, Mosses Cascade Mts. 30; Holz., Musci Acro. Bor. -Amer. 238."

Karl Mu[e]ller, "*Sechs neue Laubmoose Nordamerika's* [Six New North American Leaved Mosses]." *Flora: Algemeine Botanische Zeitschrift*, vol 56 (1873), p. 481: "I. *Mnium (Eumnium) Neevii* C. Mu[e]ller.... Patria Oregon, Portland, vere 1873: Rever. Dr. Neevius; mis. C. Mohr 1873 ex Mobile Alabamae [Native place, Portland, Oregon, truly 1873: Rev. Dr. Nevius; sent by C. Mohr 1873 from Mobile, Alabamae]."

❧ Mnium ne[e]vii (described 1873, now *Plagiomnium venustum*)
Synonymous with: Mnium venustum (1856)

Plagiomnium venustum

Moss division (Bryophyta)

Elva Lawton, *Moss flora of the Pacific Northwest* (Nichinan, Miyazaki, Japan: Hattori Botanical Laboratory, 1971), P. 198:

"Plagiomnium venustum (Mitt.) Koponen, Ann. Bot.　　　Fenn. 5: 146. 1968.

Mnium venustum Mitt., Jour. Bot. & Kew Misc. 8: 231. 1856.

"*Mnium neevii* [sic] C. Muell., Flora 56: 481. 1873.

"Plants green to yellow-green, tufted or growing with other mosses. Stems green to brownish, erect, 2-4 cm high, matted with brown rhizoids below, not stoloniferous. Leaves spreading when moist, strongly contorted when dry, 3-5 by 2-3 mm, obovate, slightly decurrent, shortly acuminate, the apex abruptly narrowed to a sharp point; margins toothed nearly to the base, the teeth sharp, of 1-2 cells; costa percurrent to excurrent; median leaf cells 25-42 u̲, the walls thick and with strong corner thickenings, not pitted; marginal cells long and narrow in 4-5 rows.

"Synoicous. Seta yellow above, reddish brown below, 3-4 cm long, 1-4 per perichaetium. Capsule horizontal to pendent, yellow with a conspicuous dark neck and a dark ring around the mouth, the urn cylindric, 3-4.5 mm long; exothecial cells isodiametric to slightly elongate, the walls somewhat thickened in the corners, the mouth bordered by several rows of smaller, quadrate, darker cells; neck cells short, irregular, yellow-brown, the walls very thick, stomata cryptopore, guard cells partly exposed; operculum conic; annulus of 2 rows of cells; peristome teeth yellow, papillose, the lamellae porminent; endostome yellow-brown, papillose, the basal membrane nearly half the height of the peristome, segments strongly keeled with broad openings, cilia 2-3, long, slightly nodose. Spores 34-40 *u*. N=12.

"On soil, rotten logs, and tree trunks in the woods, from the lowlands to about 1200 m, endemic to western North America. British Columbia, Washington, Oregon, Idaho, Montana; Alaska, California.

"*Illustrations.* Pl. 108, figs. 1-9 [of Lawton]; Sull., Icones Musc. Suppl. Pl. 36. 1874.

"*Exsiccati.* Allen, Mosses Cascade Mts. 64; Holz., Musci Acro. Bor.-Amer. 120."

Karl Mu[e]ller, "Sechs neue Laubmoose Nordamerika's [Six New North American Leaved Mosses.]," *Flora: Algemeine Botanische Zeitschrift*, Vol 56 (1873), P. 483; "5. *Grimmia (Dryptodon Neevii* C. Mu[e]ll.... Patria, Portland, Oregon, vere 1873: Rever. Dr. Neevius legit. C. Mohr ex Mobile Alabamae visit [Native place, Portland, Oregon, truly 1873: Rev. Dr. Nevius collected it, C. Mohr of Mobile Alabama sent it]."

✍ Sedum nevii (collected 1858, described 1859, now usually *Sedum glaucophyllum*)

Orpine family (Crassulaceae)

Albert E. Radford, Harry E. Ahles and C. Ritchie Bell, *Manual of the Vascular Flora of the Carolinas* (Chapel Hill: University of North Carolina Press, ca. 1970), p. 514:

"S. nevii Gray. Similar to no. 5 [S. ternatum Michaux][106] leaves alternate, narrow spatulate on the sterile shoots and linear on the flowering stems. (n=6) May-June; June-July. On limestone or shale, rare, Rockingham and Surry Cos., N. C. [Va., Ala., W.Va.] *S. glaucophyllum* R. T. Claussen—F.

Per telephone conversation with Dr. Kenton Chambers, Professor of Botany and Curator of Oregon State University Herbarium, on July 17, 1987: Some authorities consider Sedum nevii to be synonymous with Sedum glaucophyllum ("waxy white powder leaved"), others consider the two to be separate species. The *Manual of the Vascular Flora of the Carolinas* lists S. nevii separately as a species found in areas of the Carolinas, Georgia and Alabama, and is more recently published (1971) than *Gray's Manual of Botany* (Eighth Edition, 1950) which lists S. nevii as synonymous with S. glaucophyllum.

Gray's Manual of Botany (Eighth Edition, 1950)

" S. glaoucophyllum…Alternate and spirally arranged glaucous leaves; protrate sterile decumbent shoots 0.5-5 cm. long, with a dense terminal rosette; the rosette-leaves obovate—to oblong-spatulate and only 4-16 mm. long and 2-7 mm. broad; flowering stems erect, with 30-50 flat oblanceolate spreading leaves; cyme with 3-several branches and few or no narrow bracts; sepals pale, narrowly lanceolate, 2.5-4.5 mm. long; petals white, lance-acuminate, 4-8 mm. long. (S. Nevii of ed. 7, not Gray)—Damp, chiefly calcareous, rock, Va. and W. Va. May-Aug."

"Sedum nevii, Gray.—Stems low, three to five inches, ascending; leaves alternate, scattered linear-clavate, obtuse; flowers sessile, scattered along the widely spreading or recurved branches of the simple cyme; bracts linear, longer than flowers; sepals linear-lanceolate, acutish, as long as the lanceolate white petals; stamens eight, shorter than the petals; anthers purplish-brown; carpels tapering into the short, subulate style.[107]

"Our present species is one of the handsomest of American kinds. It has not long been known, having been discovered within the past twenty years [1878] by Dr. R. D. Nevius, a clergyman of Alabama, on rocky cliffs near Tuscaloosa in that State. The botany of the South has not yet been well worked up, and zealous collectors are continually finding new species which have wholly escaped the notice of others before them, or new locations for some that have been supposed rare.

"In Nevii the specific appellation is of course derived from the name of the discoverer of the plant, Dr. Nevius, and we may therefore give for its common name "Nevius' Stone-Crop."[108]

118. Sedum nevii—botanical print

2. PLANTS ASSOCIATED WITH NEVIUS

☙ Croomia

FAMILY STMONACEAE ENGLER IN ENGLER & PRANTL 1887 NOM. CONSERV., THE STEMONA FAMILY.

Arthur Cronquist, *An Integrated System of Classification of Flowering Plants* (New York: Columbia University Press, 1981) p. 1224:

The Stemona family are "Erect herbs or herbaceous vines or low shrubs from tuberous roots or creeping rhizomes, commonly produced lactone alkaloids of a unique type, at least sometimes saponiferous [contains a fat which may be made into soap]...

[p. 1225] "The family Stemonaceae consists of 3 genera and about 30 species..., [the genera *Croomia* containing 3]. Except for one species of Croomia that is native to southeastern United States, all species of Stemonaceae are confined to eastern Asia, Malesia, and northern Australia."

3. CORRESPONDENCE WITH HARVARD UNIVERSITY AND OTHER ARTICLES.

The following are letters written by Nevius to Prof. Gray and others at Harvard concerning his botany interests:

1858: May 11
Rev. R. D. Nevius:
    "Tuscaloosa May 11, 1858.
"Prof. Gray
    "Dear Sir:
    "I take the liberty of sending you a plant that I have been unable to determine. I cannot think it undetermined as it is not rare though not common.
    "I found the specimens which I sent last year before I procured your valuable manual and have not been able to procure a specimen for analysis since. Although I cannot think it unknown to you I will take the liberty to affix a description then made.
    " I send also a Sedum which is undetermined in your manual unless it may be called S. pulchellum from which it differs in color and in that it has *very rarely* thin spikes. It is from the same locality as the other. I should not think it worth troubling you with this were I not sending the other.
    " I have the satisfaction of believing it will reach you quite fresh as now after three weeks it is yet blooming though in press.
    "Please do me the favor to give me the names of these two plants and enclose and direct as by the accompanying envelope.

                  "Very Respectfully
                  "Your obedient Servant
                  "R. D. Nevius

"SHRUB 2-5 FT. HIGH

"LEAVES THINLY PUB. WITH OPPRESSED HAIRS ABOVE AND ON VEINS BELOW, PETIOLATE OVATE, ACCUMINATE CRENOTE BENTATE, STIPULATE, PETIOLES ⅛ INCH LONG.

"CALYX MONOSEPALOUS 5 PARTED, DEFLEXED, GREEN, FOLIACEOUS, CILLIATE DENTATE.

"PETALS. NONE.

"STAMENS 00. HYPOGENOUS ⅔ AS LONG AS CALYX, CONSPICUOUS

"ANTHERS TWO LOBED.

"CAPSULES [?] 2, DISTINCT.

"STYLES 2 NEARLY AS LONG AS STAMENS.

"FLOWERS AXILLARY AND TERMINATE ON PEDUNCLES NEARLY AS LEAVES, SOMETIMES 2-4 CROWDED ON THE SUMMIT OF THE SHORT LEAFY BRANCHES.

"GROWS IN THICKETS ON ROCKY CLIFFS IN RICH SOIL."

1858: May 29

Rev. R. D. Nevius:

"Christ Church Rectory

"Tuskaloosa May 29, 1858.

"Prof. Asa Gray:

"Dear Sir

"Your very kind and pleasing answer to my letter of the 11th inst waited my return from Huntsville several days. I hasten to tell you of my very agreeable surprise at finding that I had made a discovery and to thank you for the kind notice you have taken of the same.

"Had I not distrusted my own analysis of the plant, attributing my failure in it, to <u>ignorance</u>, I should have sent it a <u>year ago</u>. Since then I have learned something more of the study of your excellent books, Systematic & Structure Botany, and the Manual &c for which in an humble way, as a [illegible], I thank you in the name of the lovers of the herbal craft.

"Failing in my analysis I submitted the plant to Dr. Garland of the University who agreed with me in thinking it a new species under Spirea. Of a new Genus we did not dream.

"I regret that I did not correct a mistake that was manifest to us in comparing an analysis of the dried specimen with my old analysis of a year ago. I meant to correct it but forgot it after the specimen was prepared for the mail. The Stamens are manifestly <u>not hypogenous.</u> I meant to say and should have said had I not thought it all unnecessary to send you any description that the absence of a Corolla was our great hindrance in our analysis. I am satisfied that *there is none* as I have seen the plant in all stages of flowering. I should say that I was told in the neighbourhood where it grew that it was an <u>Evergreen</u> which I can hardly believe. Its locality is 9 miles away and I have not been able to determine this point but will watch it this winter.

"I shall be very glad to see your published account of the plant which will I suppose be found in the American Journal of Science and nothing will give me greater pleasure than to correspond with you if you will do me the favor to help me in my study regarding those plants with which I have found difficulty.

"Regarding the Sedum. I am satisfied it is not S. Pul= [Sedum pulchellum] as I found a Sedum in the Cumberland Mountains on my way to Huntsville, which answered to S. Pul except that the leaves are closely sessile and complexiant. Sedum Sparsiflorum [?] I cannot compare it with as I have not Torrey & Gray Flora North America.

"I found many new and interesting plants on my way to Huntsville over the Cum. Mts. but have not yet been able to study them up. I was much surprised to find Frasera Carlinensis which I had only seen in Michigan long ago in my first studies of the science.

"Two years ago [1856] I began with Prof. Tuomey to make a register of the Flora of this neighbourhood, but before we had taken our first ramble together He was lost to me and to the Scientific world by death. Since then I have pursued the study alone with many regrets for his loss both as a friend and a teacher. In these studies I have collected 3 or 4 hundred plants and now have a large number upon my shelf of 'Innominatae.' Of these I think some may be new and many imperfectly and incorrectly placed. Nothing would give me greater pleasure than to subject them to your criticism on opportunity. In my rambles one of your old pupils W. S. Wyman late of Montgomery, and now Prof. of Latin lang' in our University is my frequent companion and an enthusiastic lover of the Science of Botany. With him I found this Spring a plant (enclosed) upon the rocky moraye [?"moraine"?] of our river which we could not correctly place. It seems to be a Phacelia bipinnatifia, or Eutoca parviflora except for 5 sinuses in the corella tube about midway, very much as in Kalmia Colifolia. I send you part of the only plant we found. I have found also a Cosmanthus [Phocelia], whether Furshii [Purshii] or fimbriata I can scarcely tell in my confusion between Gray, Wood, Darby, and Elliott. It seems however to be P. fim'. I send a specimen of this also.

"Croomia is abundant here and I will take pleasure in sending you specimens with fruit if I am not too late. And my dear Sir let me add, I shall esteem myself fortunate in being able to do you any service and you may command me in every respect in which I may be able to aid you in your invaluable researches. I will send you the specimens you desire as soon as I can go for them and prepare them for the mail.

"I am dear Sir

"Very truly your obliged

"and humble servant

"R. D. Nevius

"Please do me the favor to tell me if other volumes of your Genera &c may be expected soon. I have by me now the two volumes published from the University library, and should like much to get them all as they come out.

1858: June 21

Rev. R. D. Nevius:

"Christ Church Rectory

"Tuscaloosa June 21, 1858

"Prof. Asa Gray

"Dr. Sir

"Immediately on receiving your kind note of the 8th inst (for which with your generous offer of assistance in my study and your valuable Flo' N. A. [Flora of North America] I thank you most sincerely. I arranged an excursion to the locality of the <u>new unknown</u> and procured the specimens herewith enclosed. I send them immediately as the carpels are not fully perfected and would wither in drying. I hope they will reach you in good order. I send also a specimen of the wood. The shrub has the general habit of growth of the Philadelphus and resembles it very much except in foliage. In the thickets where many twigs grow from the same root, one twig is gracefully bent over another toward the sunny side of the cliff forming a dense mass of foliage almost impervious to the sunlight. The shrub is a very beauty and well worth cultivation.

"In every instance I noticed that the fruiting carpels which are very few as you will see in proportion to the flowers. One carpel was perfected to the obliteration of the others which are truly as you said mostly four. (They are very minute in the flower hence my mistake in my first examination.) I will not occupy space in detailing my examination of the fruit, as I doubt not it is sufficiently advanced to afford you a satisfactory examination though it will be somewhat wilted.

"I will still watch the ripening fruit and send it to you when perfected.

"If the plant proves to be a new Genus it would be gratifying to me and to my friends and associates in the study, Prof. Wyman & Dr. Mallet of the University (I hope you know the latter gentleman also, at least by reputation) to be permitted to name the Genus in complement to our old and lamented friend Prof. Tuomey—<u>Tuomeya.</u>—

"I have no doubt the plant was known to him as he had studied the flora of this neighborhood very thoroughly, and that his sudden death cut short in this instance, and in many others, a further investigation. Please inform me if this name will be agreeable to you. I will leave it to you, if you please, the rite and form of baptisation [sic] and the pleasure (as it will be such I doubt not) of introducing it formally into the family of known plants and of making it known to science.

"The Sedum has cast its seed and has withered. It has scarcely any roots, and its name signifies it barely sits upon the rocks. I have been almost too late for the seed. I send you however some chaff with a few seeds, from which I have no doubt you can secure living specimens next year. I send also a few sprigs of the least dry plants and a few living roots.

"Croomia is abundant, the locality is large. I found it Saturday 6 miles away from this place, where it was first discovered. I do not doubt it can be found anywhere on the river for miles above and perhaps below Tuscaloosa. The fruit is not yet mature. I send some in its present state. I will send you another box, with Croomia and *Tuomeya* (?) [sic] as soon as the pods are repinned [sic, ripened?]. I am daily working up my Innominate, as I get another chance at them. I do not think them of sufficient importance to justify my giving you trouble with them. I thank you however very heartily for your permission to do so. It is possible that I may visit my home this summer. If so I will give myself the pleasure of bringing them to you myself. You kindly propose indemnifying me for my expenditure in P. O. stamps. Permit me to say dear Sir that aside from the pleasure and advantage of a correspondence with you I esteem it a great privilege to contribute in any way to your success in collecting the Flora of our country. And I beg you will permit me to send you what I choose at my own cost.

"I heard of your new work now in press, 'How Plants Grow' some time since and it was so perfectly the thing I wanted—; judging from your excellent chapters on that subject in Shuck' & Spt[?] Bot'—that

I immediately ordered 20 copies as soon as issued, for distribution among my little (*and big*) friends.

"You had the kindness to ask if I could get the Flora of N. Amer if left for me at Ivison & Phinneys. I answer with great pleasure yes, and I shall ever be obliged. I will direct Mr. Daniel Dana, of whom I order all my books to call and get it for me and send it with some books I am now about to order.

"I meant to have said above that I beg you will give the Tuomeya (if I may so call it) its *specific* name. If you wish a descriptive name its beauty and the peculiarity of its habitat will readily suggest one.

"I beg you will do me the favor to write me soon letting me know if this plant does establish a new Genera, and if you concur with me in the choice of a name, for really my interest in it and my desire to call it by its own name and to communicate my designed compliments to Mrs. Tuomey will hardly break delay.

"I am dear Sir

"With every sentiment or regard

"Very truly yr obt Servt

"R. D. Nevius"

1858: July 12

Rev. R. D. Nevius:

    "Tuskaloosa

    "July 12" 1858.

"Prof Asa Gray

    "Dear Sir

"Your kind letter of June is before me, and [I] hasten to thank you for your promptness in writing as well as for cordial agreement with me in naming the *New Genus*. Your disposition to do me the unmerited honor of giving my name was pleasing to me, but far less so than my ability to honor the name of a most excellent and deserving man—my friend—in such an enduring monument, but [?] lead [?] us to the name.

"Shall it be written Tuomeya or Tuomaea? I think the former with the accent thus [:] Two'-mey-a. The name, you know, is Tuomey—Toomey. If written Tuomaea, the long diphthong at [?] [illegible] is more likely to divert the accent from the first syllable than if written with the termination *eya*. I suppose it makes but little difference which termination is used, and *eya* is more true to the name. The name is Irish. Prof. T was himself from Ireland.

"As to the Sedum. I really hope it is now that I may by your favor enter by enrollment, in a more modest way than you at first designed, the honorable and gentle guild of *Botanists*.

"I think however that you have mistaken my name as indeed all people do to whom I do not particularly say it is <u>Nevius</u> not <u>Nevins</u>. My name you will see is already latinized. Perhaps so long ago as when written Naevius by Horace. If so, though I may not claim with modesty a descent so remote, I may with reasonable pride see my name (through your works) incidentally mentioned like his upon a 'monument more lasting than brass.'

"I went out yesterday for the fruit which you desire. Croomia is not yet perfected. I have several specimens in press for you and will send you one by this or the next mail, as you desire, though the plate in the Genra is as perfect as it is beautiful. I will also send a fine specimen of Tuomeya, as you may want it for the same purpose.

"The fruiting plants of Croomia are not more than 5 percent. I fear I cannot procure many seeds. I will however send all I can get. Tuomeya is on this side of the river in only one insignificant locality. I found not one perfected seed but many good specimens which as they retain the persistent stamens are almost as desirable as specimens dried in the Spring. I am satisfied that it has no corolla as indeed I think you will be when you note again the insertions of the Stamens upon the calyx. Dr. Mallet who saw the plants which I found a year ago is of the same opinion. I have not the slightest recollection of a bud. We looked for some to settle the question of the corolla but found none on the specimens from which we worked. I wish Mr. Sprague, to whom I beg to be commended, success in his restorations.

"I will gladly do for you and Dr. Lindley all I can in making a collection of our Orchids. There are but few here, only a few species under Plantanthera, Spiranthes and Coralloriga. Cypripediums are said to be in the neighborhood, but I have not yet found any.

"Very truly your obt Servant R. D. Nevius"

1858: LATE SUMMER
Nevius visited Ovid, New York. See above and below.

1858: October 18
Rev. R. D. Nevius:
  "Tuskaloosa
  Oct. 18, 1858.
"Prof Asa Gray
  "Dear Sir
  "I found it impossible to visit Boston on my last visit home, and to my greatest regret, was disappointed in my expectation of seeing you. I did not, as I intended, send you my plants, because I found by study with a couple of very good botanists in my native town that it was probable I had nothing valuable to you.

  "I am obliged to you for two letters I received from you, one in N. Y. and one at Ovid, and I beg you will now keep the promise made in them and advise me of the progress of Tuomeya etc. I am very glad the Croomia reached you in good condition. I hope you will be able to make something of them. I have a few more seeds of Tuomeya which I will send enclosed and I have also some seeds of Nelumbium lutem [a water lily] which I will gladly send you if they will be of any service to you.

  "I made good use of the few plants I took on with me. I got by exchange nearly 600 determined specimens, among them a good collection of mosses and ferns and a large and almost full suit of Carices [pl. of Carex, a large genus of grassy-looking plants; a sedge]. I shall still keep up my Studies and will gladly serve you in any way.

  "And continue to write as occasion serves to.

"Dear Sir your obliged
"and obedient Servant
"R. D. Nevius

"Can you tell me where I can get the names of the b[o]rders[?] printed as labels for my Herbarium? Can you tell me also where I can get the best and cheapest paper for the same and at what price?

"Please let me have your answer as soon as convenient as I have an order pending at one of our home manufactories.

"I shall never get through writing I fear.

"I should not forget to say that I brought home your 'Flora of North America,' for which I thank you most heartily. As also for your late book 'Botany for Beginners.' I do not doubt it will be a book for the times and I hope it will prove a profitable one to you and find large sales."

1858: November 15

Rev. R. D. Nevius:
"Tuscaloosa
"Nov. 15" 1858.
    "Prof Asa Gray.
    "You may know how greatly I have been disappointed by being anticipated by Prof. Harvey in choice of a name for my new Genus, when I say that the discovery itself scarcely gave me more pleasure than the opportunity it afforded for honoring the name of my deceased friend.

    "Prof Harveys compliment has given me great pleasure, yet I cannot help wishing that he had been a few months later in publishing his book.

    "I do not see what can be done but to accept your kind proposition to give the Genus the less honorable name Nevia, except it would be proper to call it Toomara and trust to the usual note to designate the person. I can hardly hope however that you will think this proper. I will leave the whole matter entirely in your hands, and beg you will be godfather to the new Genus.

    "I only fear that it will be found in some less known book, that I have been superseded in this discovery. I do not however know of any new work lately issued, or about to be issued, except a new edition of Woods Botany. I wish I had specimens to send to him and Darby, but I must wait until Spring.

    "I am delighted with your Botany for Beginners and although I have my class (I am instructing a class in the School of Mrs. Tuomey) pretty well on in the 'Manual' and do not need a more elementary book now, I shall order some for prizes, and gift books. Many girls will study it when they have left school, who will not study the Manual.

    "I have never studied the Carex at all, but with the advantage of the determined species I have procured by exchange I hope I may be able to find the one you want. In the meantime I will watch the Croomia.

    "I must say that I find the New Genus makes excellent pipe stems. I will tell you how I found out. A friend of mine brought me from Florida a pipe stem of a superior quality. I noticed one day, that it closely, yet not exactly, resembled the New Genus, and on examination of the wood under the microscope, I am convinced, that if it is not the same plant, it is the same Genus, and equally good for the purpose above mentioned. If you are a smoker I shall be glad to send you one. In Florida it is known as Indian Red, though the name is a misnomer.

"Again thanking you for your distinguished kindness

"I am dear Sir
"Your obedient Servant
"R. D. Nevius"

1859: February 21

Rev. R. D. Nevius:
"Tuscaloosa
    "February 21" 1859.
"Prof Asa Gray
    "Dear Sir
    "I have just received with great pleasure a sheet containing your article upon the New Genus—Neviusia, and a few days before a sheet came to me by your kindness containing your notice of Henrys Nerris[?] & c. I am greatly obliged to you for both and take pleasure in again expressing my obligations and my thanks for your favor and kindness shown in the matter of <u>Neviusia</u>—both in bringing it out and in keeping me appraised of its progress.
    "Your kind notice of my first intention in giving it a name, and your pleasing tribute to Prof. Tuomey has been particularly gratifying to me. Your article is quite an imposing one and it surprised me by its ful[l]ness. I am glad to know that there is an importance in its discovery, aside from the discovery itself, in its bearing upon the affinities of other genera.
    "This Spring is now fast opening. I am every day expecting to see the Claytonias [spring beauty], Sanguinarias [blood root], and Saxifrages (our first flowers) with the violets, in bloom. My correspondence with you has given me new zeal in the study of plants, especially as it has taught me how very little I know, and what progress I can yet make.
    "Neviusia will be in bloom in two weeks, and I shall make a large collection of specimens for distribution and exchange. I will furnish you with as many as you wish.
    "I hope you will tell me in your answer to this letter if I may yet confidently send specimens to my friends. I do not know if you designed to send a plate of it in the sheet which I have received. No plate came with it. I suppose it is not yet published. I look for it with great interest.
    "I shall keep a sharp lookout for Croomia, but fear I shall be unable to discover germinating seeds in the right stage for determining the quarstis vexata[?].
    "Will you tell me how I can procure a copy of the Published Memoirs of the Acad. S. which contains your article upon Neviusia? I have learned that the publications of the Society are not sent to our University.

"Please commend me in all things in which I can serve you.
"Very truly your obliged
"And obt Servant
"R. D. Nevius"

1859: PUBLISHED AFTER FEBRUARY 21

Prof Asa Gray:

"Neviusia, a New Genus of Rosceae.

   "By Asa Gray, M. D.

   "A Specimen of the plant which forms the subject of this communication was sent to me, in May last, by the discoverer, the Rev. R. D. Nevius, of Tuscaloosa, Alabama. A specimen of a *Sedum*, also apparently undescribed, was communicated at the same time. The two plants were detected by Mr. Nevius in the spring of 1857, along cliffs in the vicinity of Tuscaloosa.

   "The *Sedum*—a small, white-flowered species, with short and nearly terete leaves, which may be named Sedum Nevii—cannot be adequately characterized until better specimens shall be obtained.

   "The other plant—a shrub, with the habit of *Spiraea*—was at once seen to be a new type. As the discovery of a shrub of a new genus within the United States east of the Mississippi is an uncommon event, and as this plant presents some points of peculiar interest, I take this opportunity to indicate its characters and affinities.

   "Mr. Nevius, upon being informed of the interest of his discovery, proposed to dedicate the genus to the memory of our lamented friend, the late Professor Tuomey, who, when suddenly removed from the scene of his scientific labors, was officially and most efficiently prosecuting his researches into the geology and the whole natural history of the State of Alabama. So that this elegant shrub, peculiar to the district of his residence, was appropriately chosen by his near friend and associate to commemorate his scientific labors and deck his early tomb. But the publication of the third part of the *Nereis Boreali-Americana* (since the present communication was made to the Academy) shows that the name of *Tuomeya* is preoccupied, Dr. Harvey having dedicated to Professor Tuomey's memory a curious fluviatile Alga discovered by the latter in Alabama, as well as by the late Professor Bailey in Virginia.

   "I may now, therefore, be permitted to name the present genus in honor of the discoverer. His name, however, is so nearly like that of the celebrated Roman poet, for whom (I presume) the learned Swedish mycologist has named his genus *Naevia*, that I must needs Latinize it in an unclassical, but not wholly unprecedented manner, as follows: —

   "NEVIUSIA, Nov. Gen. ROSACEARUM.

      [There follows a description of the plant in Latin.]

      "N. Alabamensis.—In praeruptis ambrosias prop Tuscaloosam Alabama, obi legit *Dom. R. D. Nevius....*" [The text of the article is accompanied by a plate labeled "NEVIUSIA ALABAMENSIS."

      Memoirs of the American Academy of Arts and Sciences, New Series vol. 6 part 2 (1858), pp. 373-377. The common name for the plant is "Snow Wreath."

1873: MARCH 13 (OR 15)

Rev. R. D. Nevius:
"Portland, Oregon
    "March 13[?], 1873
"Dr. Asa Gray.
    "My dear Sir.
    "Have you published or are you about to publish a Text Book of Botany which will include our plants
of the Pacific Slope? We have nothing but your two volumes of the Flora of North America, that is of
service to us. Perhaps you have published ad[d]itonal Volumes.—It is long since I have done anything in
botany save with the mosses. But there are so many new plants here and so many interested persons Continually applying to me that I find my old love for the Phaenogams returning upon me. And so I find
myself turning to you in my difficulties as I used to do.—By the way, how does Neviusia thrive in Cambridge? Has it come to you from any other quarter than Tuskaloosa? Can you not have a few roots sent
me by Mail, yet this spring?
    "I enclose a beautiful little plant which I gathered without examination while traveling, as the first that
I had seen. It proves to be an enduring puzzle of the botanical Students here. And at the request of a
friend I put in my envelope a fresh specimen of another.
    "The flower of the first reminds me in its general appearance of Elephantopus. Prof. Wood when
here referred it to Roscoe. The petals seemed to me to be distinct and clawed. They are deeply and narrowly cleft through the whole limb: of the five lobes the middle are much the largest and longest.—Note
the singular pubescence of the whole plant.—
    "The second plant is thought to be in Verbenacea. It may be found any time during the winter after
a few warm days.
    "My object in writing is to learn if as we hope you are to help us in our need by supplying text books.
The need is unusual [?] here, and the author who will first supply it will secure large sales. I hope for the
works sake, and for your sake, that the Book will bear your so well known and honored name.
                                                            "I remain, Very truly
                                                        "Your Old Correspondent
                                                                    "And friend
                                                                "R. D. Nevius"

1876: MAY 4

Rev. R. D. Nevius:
"Baker City Or
    "May 4" 1876.
"Dr. Asa Gray
    "I should be very glad to have your Revision of genus Penthstemon. I have a large number of species
and find difficulty with them. I will be extremely obliged for any other revisions which you may send me.
    "I find your Lupines, Another, and Potential so great a help, that I cannot resist the temptation to ask

for more.

"I send my photograph for which I have waited long. It happened to me to get the best likeness ever taken of me, at a canvas tent in the mountains, and I have waited to secure a print from the same negative.

"I am about to take a long tour alone in my buggy 300 miles to the Dalles—and back again, all by a mountain road. What would not many of your poor fellows who grind the brick pavements give for such a holiday! I have a plan to go from here to Boise City Idaho, i.e. 250 [sic, 150] miles east and from thence through several mining camps not visited before, to the Dalles 300 miles west [from the mining camps or from Baker City], and then home [to Baker City] again. I shall have a friend with me. We shall be on the road for three months, and leaving our buggy at the Dalles, shall go by river to Portland and thence to Seattle for the meeting of our Convocation.

"Many of your and my friends who must have a summer vacation, must pay hundreds of dollars for pleasures less than this. And this comes to me incidental to a work that is itself a pleasure.

"again and again I wish for a companion on my journeys who could inform me on questions that occur at every hour as I pass over this wonderful old, old world with all its old glacial and volcanic scars. And it would be an untold delight to take you with me for such a tour in such a season as this. Pardon me for permitting my fancy to run away with. I mean this as a suggestion and an invitation to you or to any of your friends who would be glad to have such an opportunity for scientific study as does not easily or cheaply happen to those who depend upon public conveyances.

"Thanking you again for your many favors and for the opportunity of looking you in the face."

"Very truly yours
"R. D. Nevius"

1880 Summer

Mr. Sereno Watson, botanist from Harvard and colleague of Asa Gray, visited the Pacific Northwest. Nevius seems to have met Watson at Colville, but not to have traveled with him (see March 14, 1887, below).

1885: May

Microscopical Journal:

"Notes.

—Mr. R. D. Nevis [sic], of Olympia, Washington Territory, has sent us some beautiful specimens of a marine plant covered with diatoms. One specimen is thickly spread with *Arachnoidiscus,* and the other has the same diatom and many others, including *Isthmian* and *Tracer-[p. 98]Tim.* Readers who desire some of this material for mounting would do well to send a good preparation of some kind to Mr. Nevis as an exchange."

American Monthly Microscopical Journal
May 1885, pp. 97-98.

1885: November 16

Rev. R. D. Nevius:
[Letter to Harvard University]
"Olympia W. T.
"Nov. 16" 1885
"My Dear Sir:

"I have a letter today from Dr. Lathrop, St. Pauls School, Walla Walla , for whom I procured a Botany California two years ago, to ask if I can get him another at the same price $8.00. Can it be done? If so please order the two volumes sent and expect the money for the same immediately from him. Address H. D. Lathrop D. D., Walla .

"I shall await the announcement of the publication of the promised book on Wood Mosses of N. A. It may have been issued and that the announcement has escaped my notice. If so please have the book sent to me at once. I enclose a stamped envelope.

"I have a puzzle or two to refer to you for an early answer. Will you please give me the names of the enclosed? [Over?] are two others [mailers?] I refer to Dr. Gray glad to find an excuse for writing to him at this time when all are congratulating him and none more heartily than I.

"Very truly yours,
"R. D. Nevius"

1885: November 18

Rev. R. D. Nevius:
"Olympia Washton Ter.
"Nov 18" 1885
"My dear Doctor Gray

"May I claim a place among the friends who will crowd around you to-day for congratulations?

"There are many of us who have never seen your face who must nevertheless feel well acquainted with you because of the freedom with which you have permitted them to approach you for personal assistance by letter in their otherwise unaided studies.

"I hope you will permit me to say that your kindly service to me since the time, and at the time when you helped me to come into the brotherhood of botanists with a new genus in my hand has wrought in me an affection which claims a place among your friends more favored in that only that they have had more frequent and more familiar intercourse with you.

"Let me come to you as of old once more with a Specimen in my hands and a desire for assistance.

"I confess it a scheme not unworthy I hope, for securing a note from you. Yet I am not without a hope of giving you pleasure.

"The enclosed fronds which I have never but once seen growing were found by me in a shallow basaltic dish or basin near Spokane Falls. It grows in a floating tangle and expands laterally and rectangularly from fissures in the edge of the fronds which separate, surface from surface. I suppose it is rooted, yet because of its fragile character I could not determine this as a fact. I should be very glad to know something about this if you can spare the time.

"I have to day been mounting some peristomes, and some diatoms in situ, which latter are very fine, and the former may be of interest to your friends if not to you. I have spent part of the day in mounting these for you. If you will accept them it will give me pleasure. Should they be such an old story to you as to add only duplicates to your cabinet of slides, it will please me if you will give them to any of your Correspondents to whom they will give pleasure. I am afraid I cannot send them until the cement stiffens a little, and I shall hold my letter from the mail until I can send the package with it. Hoping that your friends and the public whom you have so long served by your published books may Congratulate you on many happy birthdays [Dr. Gray's 75th].

"I am dear honored Sir

"Very truly yours
"R. D. Nevius"

1885: DECEMBER 16

Rev. R. D. Nevius:
[Letter to Harvard University]
    "Olympia, W. T.
    "Dec. 16" 1885
"Dear Mr. Watson

"I send a package of slides to day. I could not get them ready before because the cement was too green to clean even imperfectly, and I fear that when they arrive it will not do to handle the mounts for some time.

"I have never seen any peristomes mounted save my own. They may be common however, and not new to you. They will reach you in time to let me add to your Christmas joy by this acceptance of my most kind and affectionate regards.

"I send a postal card to pay for the Mosses of N. A. and thank you for your many favors.

"Very truly yours
"R. D. Nevius"

1887[?]: MARCH 14

Rev. R. D. Nevius:
    "North Yakima, W. T.
    "March 14" 87[?]
Dear Mr. Watson:

"I am thankful that you keep me in mind as witness to see now and then your valued revisions of which I have a good many. I have found them so valuable that I find I must have the Bot. of N. America, and beg you to have it sent to me with the bill.

"I am residing here permanently, it is hoped, at the last church which I have built, though I am engaged in building another at Ellensburgh.

"I wish I had known of your passing in 1880 when I had such a run[?] to overtake you from Coem[?] or Allen to Colville. I would have asked to be your companion. I cannot see why I did not think to go a days ride with you at least.

"Do you know of any one engaged in making a good School of Botany of Or or Wash?

"My address will remain as above for some time, as I have made this my central station and have built me a small cottage here.

"I wish you and any of yours could drop in on me any day and claim hospitality and best service from.

"Very truly yours
"R. D. Nevius"

1889: April 2

Rev. R. D. Nevius:
"North Yakima Wash.
"Apr 2d 89
"Mr. Sereno Watson
"Dear Sir,
"Pending the issue of Synoptic Flora N. A. Vol I, part I (one) and Vol 2 part 2 which all of us are eagerly expecting I would be very greatly obliged if you could send me any revisions of Genera which you can spare me other than those Dr. Gray and you have kindly sent me heretofore. Meantime please tell me the name of the enclosed. I take it to be Tacinium[?] spinescens, but I have not a description of it. Bot. Cal. and in Contributions etc March 1889[-?] only refer to it. I give on another page the Revisions which I now have. I understand that Mr. Lewis Henderson formerly of Portland Or, now of Olympia Wash is preparing a School of Botany of Oregon and Washington but the work goes slowly as he is now absorbed in real estate speculations—with his brother he is booming a town near Tacoma called Puget. There is such a tide of immigration that all towns in the State are booming and additions to additions are stimulating men women and children to speculations and all are "getting in on bed rock" ie. purchasing from original owners and doubling their money in a few months and sometimes in a few days or weeks.

"Very truly yours
"R. D. Nevius

[separate sheet]
[fragment from another letter?]
"I have Vol. 1st Flora N. Amer. 1838-40 given me by Dr. Gray, also part II which is now replaced by the Synoptical Flora.

"What chance is there that Vol. 1st will be republished and revised?

"I shall write today thanking the Secretary of the Smithsonian and ask for _____[-?] 1st part of Bibliographical Index which the preface to the Synoptical Flora informs me is issued.

"I have not yet been in the mountains. I propose to go this Summer to Lake Chelan and may go towards the Penticton mountains [i.e. east of Cascades and then north into the Okenogan Range on the Washington-B.C. border].

"Ellensburgh has had a <u>boom</u> and has grown out of all reason. There are many "gurrs"[?] & [?] "randy"[?] fellows there yet.

"I wish you could have remembered the name of the man, I should like to identify him.

"It is a good botanical field even if you take only plants found in the very streets of the town.

"Enclosed is one which I took last spring from the street and was unable to study it having no botany with me. Prof. Henderson had a look at it and found it a puzzle. I shall look for it now as it comes into season. Meanwhile I would like a report on it from you.

"Very truly yours
"R. D. Nevius

1891: MAY 12

Rev. R. D. Nevius:
    "Tacoma Washington. May 12" 1891
"To the Curator of
"Botanical Gardens
"Cambridge Mass
    "Dear Sir
    "Though it is late for packages of such by mail I will be greatly obliged if you will send a labeled package of <u>Nevuisia Alabamensis</u> to
        Mrs. S. K. White
        Anne Wright Seminary
        Tacoma, Wash
    and will favor me with notice of its dispatching at <u>Hoquiam, Wash.</u>
    I send stamps for postage. Should be glad to know it blooms well for you,—in loose rich soil it should give you long plumes of bloom on its virgin shoots.

"Very truly yours
"R. D. Nevius"

Notes on the Habitat of Diatoms (in Puget Sound) was an article written by Nevius and published in Vol. 15, 1894, pp. 270-271 of the *American Monthly Microscopical Journal.*

"The collector may think himself fortunate if he finds any locality or discovers any habit of growth of these lovely things which will enable him to secure them specifically separate or nearly so and already cleaned by processes of nature.

"I will give some notes of what have been to me lucky 'finds,' hoping to provoke from others reports of similar good fortune.

"Zostera Marina and another species which we have on Puget sound, Z. oregana, have been to me treasures in this respect. The plant is found everywhere floating its long ribbon-like fronds upon the surface at low tide, and always in the tangle of sea-weed which is rolled by the tide and wind on the shores. Arachnoidicus Ehr. often studs this frond thickly. It may be felt by the hand as the frond passes through the fingers as one almost involuntarily reaches for it as he passes over the ground which it frequents and it may be seen glittering on the frond which it often encrusts when the sun has dried the tangle on the beach.

"Isthmia nervosa loves the same habitat, and it laces the surface and fringes the edges of the frond with its zigzag chains.

"This plant is also often gray with encrusted Coconeis scuntellum, and others of the same genus or is frosted with Nitschia or Synedra.

"On other sea weeds I have found Triceratium arcticum in patches, woven and interlaced, chain on chain.

"An inexhaustible and clean find of Atthya decora rewarded by curiosity in noticing that the surf along the Pacific shore was fairly yellow with some floating substance. This I have seen twice for a week at a time in midsummer.

"The bronzed film that shines upon the surface of the mud flats is full of interest because it seems composed of diatoms in mass, pleurosigma mostly with occasional Surirella gemma, all far more beautiful when found than they are after being cleaned for mounting. The writer would be glad to know how to separate and clean them in any quantity proportionate to their numbers as found.

"Notes of personal observation might be drawn out to great length and if from dilligent and careful collectors would be full of interest. I have in these here given only spoken of some of my most lucky finds. I should be glad if others would do the same. Nevius (1894) 270-271.

In a letter from Rev. J. Neilson Barry written in 1953, he tells the following story:

"Once he planned giving two lectures, with magic lantern slides of anatoms [sic. diatoms] in one town. He knew too much to condense an A. B. C. summary in only one hour, so he divided [it] into two one-hour lectures. However—probably to joyous delight of otherwise eagerly impatient enthusiasts for one-hour preliminary instruction on diatoms, a very violent snowstorm and high wind, accompanied with zero weather, happened to come at the same time as his first lecture. He never broke an engagement, or ever was late for an appointment. Yet not even his proverbial strength was sufficient to enable him to wade through the snowdrifts and stand up against the wind. He was compelled to hire a cab, and somehow the driver managed to get the horses through the storm so that Dr. Nevius arrived on time. He was never late for anything—certainly not when giving a lecture on anatoms [sic. diatoms]. However for some inexplicable cause only one enthusiast for anatoms braved the blizzard. Yet Dr. Nevius always held services however few might attend, and felt that such eagerness to learn of anatoms [sic. diatoms] richly deserved reward, so he gave the full hour, with magic lantern slides as though the hall were over-crowded.

"The solitary audience sat by the stove and replenished the fuel to keep the stove red-hot, without the slightest evidence of impatience throughout the hour. Dr. Nevius then stated, that since the first preliminary lecture was introductory to the second, that he would gladly give the second and complementary lecture, if the one-man audience should so desire.

"He replied that he was perfectly willing to remain as long as Dr. Nevius might desire to keep on lecturing. He was the cab-driver by the warm stove, being paid for the time, and would stay as long as Dr. Nevius might wish. That was the only time that Dr. Nevius did not give the second part and that cab-driver never did hear the second part.

"The moral of this is not to be a cab-driver if you want more than the preliminary lecture on anatoms [sic. diatoms].

Asa Gray (1810-1888) is well known as the "Father of American Botany," and champion of Charles Darwin. He joined the Harvard faculty in 1842 as the first Fisher Professor of Natural History. At that time there was no herbarium, no library, and only a small greenhouse and garden. Gray consistently spent his money on the cultivation of his library and herbarium, which soon filled his home. In 1864 he offered his collection to the university under the condition that they build a building to house them. That year they built a small brick building and moved the collections there.

119 Dr. Asa Gray, circa 1865. Photo courtesy of the Library of the Gray Herbarium, Harvard University, Cambridge, Massachusetts, USA.

120. Dr. Asa Gray, circa 1888. Photo courtesy of the Library of the Gray Herbarium, Harvard University, Cambridge, Massachusetts, USA.

CHAPTER 4

UNDER NORTHWEST EPISCOPATES

Morris, Paddock, Barker, Wells

Dr. Nevius was ordained a deacon by Rt. Rev. Stephen Elliott, first Bishop of Georgia, in Savannah. He first served under Rt. Rev. Nicholas H. Cobbs, Bishop of Alabama, who ordained him has a priest, then Rt. Rev. Richard Hooker Wilmer, his successor. He served under Bishop Potter of Pennsylvania for a short time, and then returned to Alabama and Bishop Wilmer. From there Nevius accepted a call to Oregon under Rt. Rev. Benjamin Wistar Morris, whom he served until 1880, when the jurisdictions of Oregon and Washington were separated. He then served under Rt. Rev. John Adams Paddock from 1880 until 1894, first as Bishop of Washington, and when the state was divided into east and west, as Bishop of Olympia. The Rt. Rev. William Morris Barker succeeded Paddock in 1894, and served until 1901. In 1901 the Rt. Rev. Frederick William Keater was elected Bishop of the Diocese of Olympia, and served until 1924, as the last bishop under which Nevius served. There were two other bishops with whom Nevius is said to have had close contact, Rt. Rev. Thomas Fielding Scott, whom he is said to have met in 1853 before Scott became Bishop of Oregon in 1854, and Rt. Rev. Peter Trimble Rowe, whom Nevius was there to greet upon his arrival in Alaska in 1896. Nevius also traveled with and served under Bishop Daniel Sylvester Tuttle from Salt Lake City, whose jurisdiction included Idaho, and who agreed to have Nevius help with missionary work there.

Last but not least is Bishop Lemuel Wells, who served as the first bishop of the Jurisdiction of Spokane from 1892 until 1915. Nevius never served directly under Wells, but their careers coincided so often in the development of the church in Washington, and they worked so closely together at many times, that I have included him. When Nevius first arrived in Baker City in 1873, Wells was the rector at Walla Walla, Washington Territory, the only other Episcopal parish then in existence east of the Cascades in Oregon or Washington. Nevius and Wells worked together in both Oregon and Washington, with Wells starting the church at Pendleton, and Nevius starting the church at Weston, as well as their both working in Southeastern Washington. At times it is difficult to tell which of them got there first or had the most influence on the beginnings of the church. Wells then went to St. Luke's Church in

Tacoma in 1882, and remained there until he became bishop. Nevius was to join him in western Washington in 1883, serving first St. John's Church in Olympia. Until Wells went to Spokane (a congregation founded by Nevius) in 1892, they must have met often. Nevius spent his last sixteen years in Tacoma, a city where Wells was popular and had made his mark on the church, and to which Wells himself retired in 1915, three years after Nevius's death.

There is no question that Nevius had a driving force for his faith, and that his great desire was to open up new territory and to be a missionary for his church. He could not have accomplished nearly as much without the support of his bishops. I have selected the bishops with whom he worked most closely to highlight in this work, Morris, who sent him on his first mission, and who joined him in his work whenever he could; Paddock, who continued to encourage him, and supported him in every way; Barker, who sent him on new missions, even to Alaska, at an age when many would have said he had finished his active life (he was 65 when Barker arrived); and Wells, who was alongside him through much of his missionary work. Nevius had a close but cordial relationship with each of them, and made long trips with them as they toured their dioceses.

RT. REV. BENJAMIN WISTAR MORRIS, D.D.

Bishop of Oregon & Washington Jurisdiction, 1868-1880
Bishop of Oregon Jurisdiction, 1880-1889
Bishop of Oregon Diocese, 1889-1906

Morris was born in Wellsborough, Tioga County, Pennsylvania, on May 30, 1819. He was the son of a prominent doctor, Samuel Wells Morris. He graduated from General Theological Seminary in New York in 1846, and became a deacon that same year. He was ordained a priest on April 27, 1847. He was rector of St. Mattehw's, Sunbury, Pennsylvania, for four years, then St. David's, Manayunk, Philadelphia for six years. He then became assistant rector of St. Luke's, Germantown, Philadelphia, and remained there until his elevation to the Episcopate. He received the degree of STD from Columbia University and the University of Pennsylvania in 1868. Morris was consecrated Missionary Bishop of Oregon and Washington Territory on December 3, 1868. In 1880 his jurisdiction was divided, and Washington Territory was assigned a new bishop.

In October, 1867, Rev. Benjamin Henry Pad-

121. B. W. Morris, circa 1880

dock of Detroit, Michigan, had been elected Missionary Bishop, but declined to serve. Morris was elected in his stead, and was consecrated in St. Luke's Church, Philadelphia, on December 3, 1868, and arrived in Oregon on June 2, 1869. Bishop Scott had built a residence, church, and schools in a downtown location with his own funds. One of Morris's first challenges was to raise $5,000 to purchase the property. In the winter of 1870-71 he enlarged St. Helen's Hall and completed a Grammar School building.

On February 18, 1871, he laid the cornerstone for St. Andrew's Chapel in Kalama, Washington Territory. In April of 1871 he visited Rev. Wells at Walla Walla, and visited Lewiston and the surrounding area. In June of that year he traveled to Seattle and Port Townsend. On August 31, 1871, he laid the cornerstone for St. Luke's Church in Vancouver, Washington Territory. In September of 1871 he traveled east to Baltimore for the General Convention. While in the east for six months he conducted an extensive campaign to raise funds for missionary work in the Northwest. Churches were built at Corvallis, Astoria, Eugene City, Seattle, Kalama, Vancouver, and a church and school at Walla Walla. In 1873 he visited Lewiston, Dayton, and Waitsburg. In addition visiting, Weston, La Grande, Union, Sparta, Baker City, Eldorado, and the Cove. In May of 1873 he organized St. Peter's Church in La Grande. He then held services at Pendleton before taking a boat from Umatilla back to Portland. He had been gone over five weeks and traveled over a thousand miles. In June he went to Oakland and Roseburg, returning to Portland, from whence he went to Seattle in July. He then visited Port Townsend, Port Ludlow, Olympia, and Tacoma. He established St. Peter's Church in Tacoma, where the Rev. Charles R. Bonnell was the first rector.

In his August 28, 1873, address to the annual Convocation, he stated:

"Baker City seems destined to become the largest town in that part of the State [Eastern Oregon]; and yet there is not in this place, nor in the surrounding country, a Protestant Church building of any name or character. Feeling the great importance of immediately occupying this portion of the field, while still there, I wrote to the Rev. Dr. Nevius, who was about to relinquish the Rectorship of Trinity Church, Portland, proposing that he should spend the next three months, at least, in this region, and report to this Convocation the results of his labours."

Morris traveled to Eastern Oregon in the fall of 1873, visiting all the areas where missions were starting. He traveled by stagecoach when possible, with the ride from Union to Baker City taking five to six hours, and one from La Grande to Walla Walla taking fifteen and one-half hours. On Sunday, November 23rd, he too a 9 PM stagecoach from Walla Walla to Wallula, reaching it at 5 am on Monday "with only one upset, and no serious damage."

On Thursday, May 14, 1874, Morris laid the cornerstone of The Good Samaritan Hospital and Orphanage in Portland. Among the clergy in attendance was Rev. R. D. Nevius. In the fall of 1874 the

Bishop again traveled to Eastern Oregon. In a report in the *Oregon Churchman* it stated, "by reason of a change in the arrangements of the mail stage, the Bishop was compelled to cross the mountains from Canyon City to the mouth of John Day River—125 miles—on horseback. This was a fatiguing journey of three days, much of the way over a very rough trail, but it enabled him to reach home only 24 hours after his appointed time....

Morris seems to have taken a special interest in architecture. His son, New York architect Benjamin Wistar Morris III, FAIA (1870-1944) designed buildings for a number of distinguished clients and contributed to the design of the celebrated Cunard liner Queen Mary. The elder Morris made frequent references to architecture in his writing and speaking, and from his praises of "proper" and "churchlike" architecture, seems to have been influenced by the ecclesio-theological seminary in New York City in the mid-1840s.

Like his predecessor, Morris faced formidable challenges. The remoteness of his jurisdiction from the eastern states as well as the vastness of distances within it, negotiable at first only by water or horseback, fostered a sense of isolation. The itinerant nature of the population, many of them drawn to the region by strikes of silver and gold, contributed to a sense of impermanence. The want of established institutions to supply basic needs such as education and medical care contributed to loneliness and discouragement. Clergymen, especially clergymen with families, were difficult to recruit and retain. Prices for goods and services, when available and often of unreliable quality, were much higher than in New England or the South. Money was always short. Funds for almost everything had to be raised elsewhere—Morris spent nearly a third of his time on missionary lecture circuit in the East, based with his family at Philadelphia. But Morris was equal to the task and a successful fund-raiser. He initiated over thirty church, parsonage, school and hospital building projects within five years of his arrival.

Morris continued to lead his diocese even in his old age. Part of his funding came from the national Missionary Society until the Diocese of Oregon was formed. Then all support came from within the diocese with special gifts from supporters in the East. From 1869 (when he came to Oregon, June 2) up to 1893 (when Morris was then 74 years old, and urging his Diocesan Convention for Episcopal assistance—really a successor—so that he might step down without burdening the Diocese any further with his advancing years and declining strength, the "graf line" of Bishop Morris' vigor, purpose, and vision might be thought of as a steadily rise "line" of achievement and popular support and esteem. But after the year 1893 the "graf line" turns downward. The year 1893 or so was the high point. From 1893 to 1906 (and Morris' death) Morris' life in Oregon was one of decline and disarray—though with no lack of earnest devotion and sincere

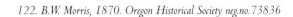

122. B.W. Morris, 1870. Oregon Historical Society neg. no. 73836

commitment on Morris' part. In 1894 the diocese called a coadjutor Bishop, but the candidate declined. The diocese from that time on found itself unable to support an assistant or to support a retired bishop, so Morris struggled on.

In 1901 the General Convention of the Episcopal Church met for the very first time in the West. It met at San Francisco, California. Bishop Morris, then 82, was asked by the Presiding Bishop (Bishop Thomas March Clark) to be the honored preacher at its great opening services. Bishop Wm. Lawrence in his auto-biography, *Memories of a Happy Life*, in the chapter on the Church Pension Fund, mentions this particular situation as a matter of "my own personal education toward the crying necessity of a Church Pension Fund." ..."Here was Bishop Morris, who, in the years of his strength had built up a noble missionary work, now preached the General Convention Sermon... which was really that of a man in feeble old age; and on inquiry I learned that his great Oregon work *was crumbling under him!*"....

123 B.W. Morris, circa 1905

Finally after eleven years of this "crumbling" situation, at the Diocesan Convention in Portland in June, 1905—with Bishop Morris now 86 years old—and with Morris' strength and vigor becoming so feeble that he was having to ask Bishop Lemuel Wells (Spokane), and Bishop Keating (Olympia) to do most of his Episcopal work—Morris put the whole matter of Episcopal assistance and succession finally and bluntly up to this Convention. His proposals were—with his own Episcopal salary six months in arrears—that a new Bishop be elected and receive the entire salary, occupy the Bishop's residence in Portland, and find a small house for Morris and his wife to live out their lives "in seclusion and poverty."

Morris died on Palm Sunday, April 8, 1906, at the age of 86.

JOHN ADAMS PADDOCK, S. T. D.

Bishop of Washington 1880-1892
Bishop of Olympia 1892—1894

Paddock was the first Protestant Episcopal bishop of the missionary diocese of Washington. He was born in Norwich, Connecticut on January 19, 1825. He was the eldest son of Seth B. Paddock and Emily (Flagg) Paddock. His father was for many years rector of Christ Church, Norwich, and his brother, Benjamin Henry Paddock, was the fourth Episcopal bishop of Massachusetts. He was graduated from Trinity College, Hartford, in 1845, and from New York general theological seminary (P.E.), in 1849. He became rector of the Episcopal church in Stratford, where he served from the date of his ordination until 1855, a period of six years. He then became rector of St. Peter's, Brooklyn, New York, where he remained for twenty-five years, his services as rector terminating with his elevation to the epis-

124. J.A. Paddock

copate. He was a member of the standing committee of the diocese of Long Island from the time of its organization, and a member of several important committees or boards connected with church work. The degree of S. T. D. was conferred upon him by Trinity college in 1860. In 1880 he was elected missionary bishop of the then Washington Territory, and received his consecration to his new office December 15th of that year. He preached his first sermon in the new diocese and administered Holy Communion Easter Sunday, 1881, at St. Luke's Church in Vancouver. The following Sunday he officiated at Trinity Church, Seattle. He had planned to be in Olympia the following Sunday but was called back to Portland by the sudden death of his wife.

With stoical courage, Bishop Paddock immediately resumed his interrupted itinerary and the following Sunday held services at St. John's Church in Olympia. His labors as a bishop met with marked success. Among other things accomplished during his bishopric were the erection of a church hospital in Tacoma (Fannie Paddock Memorial Hospital, named after his wife) costing $60,000, and an endowment of $100,000 secured for it. He also established church schools in various parts of the diocese, including Annie Wright Seminary for girls in Tacoma. Among his published works are" "*History of Christ Church, Stratford, Conn.*" (1854), *The Modern Manifestations of Superstition and Skepticism,* (1870), and various sermons, addresses, etc. He died in Santa Barbara, California, on March 4, 1894, and was buried in Vancouver, B.C.

William Morris Barker
Bishop of Olympia 1894—1901

Barker was born at Towanda, Bradford County, Pennsylvania, on May 12, 1854, son of George R. and Anna Ellis (Morris) Barker. His father, a native of Pennsylvania, was the preceptor of the classical school of Germantown, Pennsylvania. He was graduated at the University of Pennsylvania in 1873, and completed his course at the Berkeley Divinity School in 1879. The following two years were spent in Portland, Oregon, as junior master in the Bishop Scott Grammar School. His uncle, Benjamin Wistar Morris, was then Bishop of Oregon and Washington Territory. He was admitted to the diaconate by Bishop Williams in Middletown, Connecticut, on June 4, 1879, after which he served as curate of St. John's Church, Troy, New York. In 1880 he was ordained to the priesthood by Bishop Donne, serving for a time as curate of St. John's of Washington, D.C. and subsequently as rector of St. Paul's. In 1887 he became rector of St. Luke's, Baltimore, Maryland, remaining two years, at the end of which he assumed charge of St. Paul's in Duluth, Minnesota, officiating at the same time as president of St. Luke's Hospital. The degree of D.D. was conferred on him at Seabury Divinity School, Faribault, Minnesota, in 1893, and on January 25 of the same year he was consecrated to the missionary episcopate of Colorado by Bishops Morris (his uncle), Spaulding, McLaren, Gilbert and Nicholson. He served in his mission field over a year when, at a meeting of the house of bishops held in New York in 1894, an order was passed by which Bishop Barker was directed to exercise episcopal functions in the missionary district of Olympia (comprising the western portion of the State of Washington). He entered into this new field with vigor, and developed its church activities and charities in an unexampled manner. On July 13, 1893, he was married to Laura Pindell, daughter of General John Adair, of Astoria, Oregon, and had one child. Bishop Barker died February 21, 1901.

125. W. M. Barker

RT. REV. LEMUEL HENRY WELLS, S.T.D., D.D., D.C.L., L.L.D.
Bishop of Spokane, 1892-1915

Wells was the first Bishop of Spokane, having had the eastern portion of the state separated from the Diocese of Olympia the year he took office. He was born in the old Manor House, Yonkers, N. Y., on December 3, 1841, son of Horace Demming and Mary Smith (Barker) Wells. His earliest American ancestor was Gov. Thomas Wells of Connecticut. The civil war found him a student at Trinity College, Hartford, which he left in 1861, to enter the military service. He recruited part of a company and went to the front as a second lieutenant of the 32nd Wisconsin infantry, after three years being discharged for disability, as first lieutenant. He then entered the junior class at Hobart College, Geneva, N. Y., where he was graduated in 1864.

He took a full course at the Berkeley Divinity School, and was graduated there in 1869. Shortly after graduation he married Elizabeth Folger, niece and adopted daughter of Charles J. Folger, Secretary of War. After spending a year in Europe, he was ordained priest, and became assistant at Trinity Church, New Haven, Connecticut. A year later his wife died, and he entered the missionary field. He went west on one of the first trains across the continent. From San Francisco he took a steamer up the coast to Portland, and then a steamer to the Cascades, forged the Cascades on a narrow gauge railroad, and took another steamer to The Dalles, then a narrow gauge railroad for six miles, and a boat to Wallula, then

126 L H. Wells

a stage for twenty miles to Walla Walla. At Walla Walla the young idealist accepted only the voluntary offerings of the pioneer cattlemen, golddiggers and ranchers of that rough pioneer period, living in shacks and holding services in saloons and dance halls, his income averaging $430 per year. For ten years he was missionary in Walla Walla, Washington, and surrounding country, and established St. Paul's School for girls.

After residing in the East for eighteen months at Willimantic, Connecticut, he, in 1882, became rector of St. Luke's Church, Tacoma, and afterwards built Trinity Church and became its rector. Mrs. Wells was at that time made the first principal of the newly built Annie Wright Seminary. In October, 1892, the general convention of the Protestant Episcopal Church at Baltimore elected him missionary bishop of Spokane, which at first embraced eastern Washington, and afterward also northern Idaho. He was consecrated at Trinity Church, New Haven, Connecticut, on December 16, 1892. In 1892, while rector at Tacoma, he was honored by Hobart College with the degree of D.D. He was married June 17, 1880, at Walla Walla, to Henrietta B., daughter of William Garretson, a senator of Tioga, Pennsylvania. They had a daughter, Mary G., who was born in 1883 and died in 1887.

His second wife was the principal of the school he founded in Walla Walla at the time of their marriage. They attended the Lambeth Conference of 1900 in England, and the bishop dined and lunched with Queen Victoria. His wife died on March 2, 1903. In 1915 he resigned first having traveled East. He married Mrs. Jane T. Sheldon Smith, of Geneva, New York, a friend from college days, and returned to Spokane by way of the Panama Canal. They moved to Tacoma, where they rented a large house. They helped start St. Marks Church there, and supplied the plans. Wells resigned as rector in 1923. They spent a year in Hawaii, witnessing the overthrow of the monarchy there. They traveled to Alaska and British Columbia, and enjoyed their retirement. On March 29, 1922, his third wife died.

He continued to be active in retirement, helping local churches when needed. He sold his large home and moved to a rented cottage and lived with his brother, James. When he was eighty-seven, he and his brother moved to the Frank Tobey Jones Home for old people. During this time he supplied the parish for St. Luke's in 1926 while they were in the process of uniting with Christ Church. After that he helped out at St. Andrews, Tacoma, from 1928 to 1932. His brother died in late 1929. While of somewhat small of stature, Bishop Wells possessed a vivid personality and a rich and powerful voice. In 1931 he published his biography, "A Pioneer Missionary." In 1935 he became senior bishop of the Episcopal Church both in age and date of consecration, as well as senior bishop of the Anglican Communion in age. Wells died on March 27, 1936, at the age of 94.

FOOTNOTES

[1] Helen Sanford Coan Nevius, *The Life of John Livingston Nevius* (New York: Fleming H. Revell Co., 1895), p. 17. Mrs. Nevius reported a family tradition that the name originally had been Neve and that they were French Huguenots who had "scattered" to Belgium, Holland and Great Britain, where the name survived as Neave (pp. 18-19). A family biographer noted that the Dutch name had been Neeff, and that American descendants went by Nevius, Nevyus, Neafie, Neefus, Neafus, Nefie, Nafey, Naphey, Nafis, Naphis, "etc." (A. Van Doren Honeyman *Johannes Nevius and his Descendants;* Plainfield, N.J.: Honeyman & Company 1900; p. 17). The name is pronounced "KNEE-vious."

[2] John was left in the care of his paternal grandparents, where he was "chiefly in the care" of his aunt Ellen Nevius. Helen Nevius, *op. cit.,* p. 28. Another aunt, Gertrude Nevius, married a missionary to Africa about 1849. *Ibid.,* p. 53.

[3] Mary P. Van Loan (Administrative Assistant, Union College), letter to Howland Atwood (Huntington Library), April 21, 1953. Helen Coan suggests that the Nevius brothers prepared themselves to teach.

[4] John wrote his mother, "My time in New York passed very pleasantly. I found Reub as I told you in my last letter...." Helen Nevius, *op. cit.,* p. 49.

[5] The 1850 U.S. Census of Michigan lists an "R. D. Nevins" (noting that spelling is uncertain)" in Marshall, a small town near Battle Creek. Nevius's sister-in-law mentioned visiting a sister, Mrs. A. D. Schuyler, in Marshall in 1881. Helen Nevius, *op. cit.,* p. 393. She also observed that it was common for "enterprising Northerners to seek their fortunes at the South" before the "great Rebellion." *Ibid.,* p. 48.

[6]

[7] *Ibid.,* p. 60

[8] *Ibid.,* p. 59. It is not clear whether this occurred in New York or Michigan.

[9] *Ibid.,* p. 64. About this time an aunt, Gertrude Nevius (their father's sister), married the Rev. Jacob Best, a missionary to Africa. *Ibid.,* p. 53.

[10] The *Journal of the Annual Convention of the Diocese of Georgia, 1852* notes that Bishop Stephen Elliott had received Nevius "as a candidate for Orders, by transfer from the Diocese of Michigan," indicating that Nevius had committed himself to orders before he went to Georgia. The Rev. Robert L. Miller, Registrar of the Episcopal Diocese of Michigan, reported to David Powers in a letter of October 22, 1987, that he was able to find no mention of Nevius in Diocesan records.

[11] Bishop's Address, *Journal* of the Diocese of Georgia, 1853.

[12] *Journal of the Proceedings of the Twenty-Second Annual Convention of the Protestant Episcopal Church, in the Diocese of Alabama, 1853,* pp. 22, 27.

[13] *Journal* of the Diocese of Alabama, 1854, p. 14. Liberty Hill, Dallas County, was about twenty miles west of Selma. It no longer exists, nor does St. David's Church. Civil War-era maps place Liberty Hill in the general vicinity of modern Safford. According to Mr. Curtis Baker, a civil engineer retired from the Oregon State Parks and Recreation Division, who was reared in the Safford area, the site of Liberty Hill is .4 mile from Highway 5 on the road that branches westerly three miles north of Safford.

[14] Rev. DuBose Murphy, Christ Episcopal Church, Tuscaloosa, Alabama, letter to Howland Atwood, Huntington Library, November 14, 1952. In an earlier letter dated November 4, Murphy mentioned that he was Associate Editor of the *Historical Magazine* of the Episcopal Church.

[15] *Journal* of the Diocese of Alabama, 1855, pp. 17-18. Nevius also commented on the "moral worth and deep-toned piety" of Capt. James Ellerbe, an area pioneer who had come from St. David's Church, Cheraw, South Carolina," and a leading parishioner of St. David's, Liberty Hill, who had recently died. Curtis Baker (cited above) observes that the Safford area was largely settled "in the eighteen 'teens" by people from northeast South Carolina. The route of migration was by sea to Mobile and then up the Alabama River. The Ellerbe place was about a half mile east of Liberty Hill.

Bishop Cobbs had visited St. David's Church in March, 1855, and reported that he had confirmed "one white person and ten colored persons." "It is truly refreshing to the heart of the Christian Minister," he said, "to go into this Parish, and to witness the interest manifested by the Negroes in the services of the Church." *Ibid.,* p. 24

16 Athens, which no longer exists, was about two miles south-southeast of Liberty Hill. The plans for the new church "prospectively called St. Mary's" in the "lower part of Dallas County" seem not to have been carried through after Nevius left.

17 Right Rev. Walter C. Whitaker, *History of the Protestant Episcopal Church in Alabama, 1763-1898*, p. 134.

18 *Journal* of 1855, *op. cit.*, pp. 17-18.

19 Nevius had been granted $70.00 the previous year. Whitaker, *op. cit.*, pp. 96-97.

20 By comparison, workmen at Fort Hoskins in Oregon (where prices tended to be generally higher than in the East) were paid as follows in September, 1856: carpenters, $4.60/day; "hurriers and scurriers," $2.40/day; packers $50-75.00/month; teamsters, $50/month; guides "cutting trail & road from Depot to the Post," $5/day. Fort Hoskins Letter Post Returns, Sept., 1856. A Union Army private was paid $13/month during most of the Civil War. *Revised Regulation for the Army of the United States, 1861* (Philadelphia, 1861), p. 526. Taken from *All Quiet on the Yamhill; the Civil War in Oregon*, ed. Gunter Barth (Eugene: University of Oregon Books, 1959).

21 Whitaker, *op. cit.*

22 Whitaker, *op. cit.*, pp. 8, 66, 71, 135. Whitaker observed that a parochial school led to a schedule of daily services, and that Christ Church, Tuscaloosa, was one of three parishes in the state that did so at this time. In a letter to Howland Atwood dated June 20, 1953, the Rev. DuBose Murphy, rector of Christ Church, Tuscaloosa, noted that the chapel had been built in 1852 (rather than 1854 as Whitaker stated) because the church gallery wouldn't hold all the Negro communicants. He said that the chapel "fell into disuse" and burned "about 1860." This date must be too early because it would have been during Nevius's tenure and the loss of interest seems inconsistent with other details of his life. Murphy added that the gallery was removed from Christ Church in a remodeling of 1882.

23 In a letter of May 29, 1858, to Prof. Asa Gray at Harvard University, Nevius mentioned that he had only seen a certain plant "in Michigan long ago in my first studies of the science (of botany)."

24 R. D. Nevius (anonymously), "Biographical Notice of Prof. M. Tuomey, A.M.," *Alabama Educational Journal*, Vol. I, No. 4 (January, 1859), p. 116.

25 R. D. Nevius, May 29, 1858, *op. cit.*

26 R. D. Nevius, January, 1859, *op. cit.*

27 Nevius may have written at the suggestion of W. S. Wyman who, as he explained in his letter to Gray of May 29, 1858, had been a "pupil" of Gray's. Nevius explained that Wyman was "late of Montgomery" (where presumably he and Nevius had met), that Wyman was Professor of Latin at the University of Alabama, and that in his "rambles" Wyman was his "frequent companion and an enthusiastic lover of the Science of Botany."

28 David Powers was indebted to Prof. Kenton Chambers of Oregon State University for this observation.

29 Some of these, such as Gray's Manual of Botany, continue in revised editions to be standard works of reference to the present day. Gray Herbarium at Harvard is named for Asa Gray.

30 Because cursive u and n are easily confused, Nevius's name was often mistaken. It frequently is found as "R. D. Nevins."

31 "I will gladly do for you and Dr. Lindley all I can in making a collection of our Orchids."

32 Nevius mentioned in his letter to Gray of June 21, 1858, "It is possible that I may visit my home this summer," and that if he did he would deliver some specimens to Gray in person. On October 18 he said "I found it impossible to visit Boston on my last visit home, and to my regret, was disappointed in my expectation of seeing you."

33 A large genus of sedges.

34 The third part of *Nereis Boreali-Americana*. This was explained by Asa Gray in his article, "NEVEUSIA, a New Genus of Rosceae," *Memoirs of the American Academy of Arts and Sciences*, New Series Vol. 6, part 2 (1858), pp. 373-377.

35 Mrs. Toumey had opened the school in 1857 after her husband's death. The 1859 catalogue for "Mrs. Tuomey's Home School for Young Ladies" lists a faculty of seven including "Rev. R. D. Nevius, Biblical Studies." It reported that the school would be "reopened for its third year" on October 1, 1859, for the year lasting through the last Friday of June, 1860. Nevius mentioned the school in his parochial report published in the 1860 *Journal* of the Diocese of Alabama: "Among the communicants reported...are six young ladies belonging to 'Mrs. Tuomey's Home

School.' This School is a true nursery for the Church, in principle and practice, and the Rector is glad to say that this portion of his charge has always been one most pleasant in labor and profitable in results." In her reply written in the margins of a letter from Howland Atwood of February 7, 1953, Miss Clara Vewer of Tuscaloosa noted that the building "with six lovely Ionic columns" had once had a "lovely and elaborate garden." She reported it was still standing and "used as a Doctor's Clinic." "During the War," she added, "ladies are said to have met at the school to roll bandages and do other work for the Confederacy."

36 Nevius noted that the Florida plant was called Indian Reed, "though that name is a misnomer."

37 Gray, *op. cit.* Nevius thanked Gray for a "sheet containing your article," apparently a proof, on February 21.

38 Some authorities consider Sedum nevii to be synonymous with Sedum glaucophyllum ("waxy white powder leafed"), others consider the two to be separate species. The *Manual of the Vascular Flora of the Carolinas* lists S. nevii separately as a species found in areas of the Carolinas, Georgia and Alabama, and is more recently published (1971) than *Gray's Manual of Botany* (Eighth Edition, 1950) which lists S. nevii as synonymous with S. glaucophyllum.

39 The common name is Snow wreath.

40 Nevius to Gray, February 21, 1859.

41 Eugene A. Smith, "Sketch of the Life of Michael Tuomey," *American Geologist*, V, XX (October, 1897), pp. 206-212: "Practically all that is known concerning the early life of Prof. Tuomey, has been brought together by Rev. R. D. Nevius...in an article published soon after Prof. Tuomey's death in the Alabama Education Journal." Smith may have got this information from "the only surviving member of Prof. Tuomey's family" whom he gave as Mrs. Nora T. Maclean of Chattanooga, Tenn. Tuomey's daughter Manora is listed in the 1850 Census of Alabama.

In the article, though Nevius candidly admitted that Tuomey's "deepest, holiest thoughts and feelings were not uttered in words," he held that no one could look upon Tuomey's life without failing "to see in him the working of true Christian principle," and that he had been the "perfection of Christian manhood." In his study of Natural Sciences, Prof. Tuomey had opened the book of Nature with all the reverence with which

he opened his Bible. To him it was the Book of God, filled with inspired and unequivocal revelations of His love to man—abounding in sublime themes suggestive of thought, in a true poetry of simplicity and harmonious adaptation of cause and effect, and a history fresh, after the lapse of untold ages, from the hand of God, and in a law of harmonies and correspondencies worthy of the wisdom of its Divine Maker. And while he regarded this book with all the reverence of a Christian, he studied it with all the ardor of a pupil, whom Nature herself taught; and he loved his teacher with all the devotion of a son."

42 Whitaker, *op. cit.*, p. 168.

43 *Ibid.* Whitaker continued, "That it should have been persevered in despite the disastrous crisis evidently now near at hand is confirmation strong as Holy Writ of the sincerity and unselfishness of those who labored, and of those who permitted and encouraged the work."

44 *Ibid.*, pp. 168-169. These sums, seemingly high for the time, were probably inflated dollars issued under Confederate authority.

45 *Ibid.*, p. 1170. The deaconesses were not actually ordained by the "imposition of hands."

46 For more information on the Civil War in Tuscaloosa see entries under April, 1865 in the Biographical Notes *supra*.

47 Joseph Blount Cheshire, *The Church in the Confederate States* (New York: Longmans, Green and Co., 1912), p. 183.

48 *Journal of the Convention of the Episcopal Diocese of Alabama, 1866.* In a letter to Howland Atwood of May 6, 1953, Mrs. Edith Christiansen of St. John's Episcopal Church, Mobile, Alabama, noted that Nevius conducted two funerals and a wedding there in November 1865, and a baptism in January 1866.

49 In a letter to Howland Atwood of October 30, 1953, the Rev. J. Neilson Barry of Portland commented that Nevius "often mentioned Tuscaloosa."

50 After a rest at home, John Nevius attended conferences and lectured in Presbyterian circles. In November 1867 the Episcopal and Presbyterian churches held their respective national conventions simultaneously in Philadelphia, exchanging "fraternal and ministerial courtesies." John Nevius attended the Presbyterian convention. The Neviuses returned to China late in 1868. Helen Nevius, *op. cit., pp. 260-274.*

51 Eastman family records note that William Lyman Eastman married Augusta Nash on June 6, 1866, which could have been an occasion for the family reunion. Half-brother Benjamin Nevius Eastman's wife Cornilia Post Eastman died in Ovid, New York, on March 23, 1866, and half-sister Hannah Eastman Birge died in Ovid on July 10, 1866.

52 Paul Hannaford, Christ Episcopal Church, Oil City, Pennsylvania, letter to Rev. Albert E. Allen, Hood River, Oregon, February 16, 1966.

53 *Journal* of the Diocese of Pittsburgh, 1867, p. 54.

54 R. D. Nevius, entry signed and dated February 1, 1868, *Parish Register,* Christ Episcopal Church, Oil City, Pennsylvania.

55 *Ibid..*

56 Letter from Paul Hannaford, Rector, Christ Episcopal Church, Oil City, Pennsylvania, to Rev. Albert E. Allen, February 16, 1966. Mr. Hannaford also noted that the Rouseville mission was "dissolved after about 10 year of existence."

57 *Ibid.*

58 *Journal* of the Diocese of Pittsburgh, 1867, p. 54.

59 A romance may explain why Nevius resigned his position at Tuscaloosa. Conflicting dates are given for the marriage. Van Doren Honeyman, *Johannes Nevius and His Descendants* (Plainfield, N. J.: Honeyman & Company, 1900), p. 584, gives the wedding date as July 11, 1868, and states, "No children." Birth dates of deceased children are given in other cases. This source contains errors, such as the dates of Nevius's ordinations as deacon and priest and the dates of his wife's birth and death.

60 Honeyman, *op. cit.* states that Margaret Tuomey was born in "1842 or '43." The records of St. John's Church, Mobile, Alabama (see below) state that she was twenty-nine when she died in October, 1870, suggesting a birth date of 1841 or 1842. The 1850 U.S. Census of Alabama lists Margaret as "age 12," suggesting a birth date of 1837 or 1838, but this may have confused Margaret with her sister Manora, listed as "age 7," suggesting a birth date of 1842 or 1843.

61 John Nevius Eastman, *op. cit.*

62 *Journal* of the Diocese of Alabama, 1869, pp. 10-11.

63 *Journal* of the Diocese of Alabama, 1870, p. 33.

64 Rose K. Belk, Reference Librarian, College of William and Mary, letter to Howland Atwood, March 26, 1953. It was an honorary degree, one of 13 conferred in that year, 7 on Episcopal clergymen..

65 Edith Christiansen, Secretary, St. John's Episcopal Church, Mobile, Alabama, letter to Howland Atwood, May 6, 1953.

66 *Ibid.* also *Journal* of the Diocese of Alabama, 1871, p. 65: "He [Nevius] would also gratefully record the kind attentions and official services of his brethren, the Parochial Clergy of the city, during his own illness at that time."

In a letter to Howland Atwood dated October 30, 1953, historian and retired Episcopal clergyman, J. Neilson Barry, reported "gossip" that Nevius's wife had been ill, of "smallpox" he thought. Barry had known Nevius, though not well, and admired him. He reported this tradition as follows: "The doctor had ordered either (1) to give medicine at certain hours (2) or else if she were asleep not to awaken her. I do not know which it was. Whatever it may have been, Dr. Nevius disobeyed. Either he awoke her to give her medicine, or else he did not disturb her sleep and awaken her to give medicine. My impression is that he did not have the heart to disturb her when asleep. Whichever it was he disobeyed the doctor, and Dr. Nevius blamed himself because she died. Really probably nothing to do with it. The GOSSIP is that, in remorse he dedicated himself to missionary work...."

67 Robert Gable letter of March 16, 1984 with unidentified newspaper clipping enclosed.

68 *Oregonian,* April 29, 1872.

69 *Journal,* District of Olympia, 1902.

70 *Oregon Churchman,* March 15, 1873.

71 *Oregon Churchman,* Morris, September 1, 1873.

72 *Oregon Churchman,* December 1, 1873.

73 *Oregon Churchman,* June 15, 1874

74 *Oregon Churchman,* October 15, 1874.

75 *Ibid.* July 15, 1875. The source for this design seems to have been George E. Woodward, *Woodward's Country Homes* (New York: George E. Woodward Co., 1865), "Design No. 9—Rural Church." Nevius's description of the Union church paraphrases the description of the Lake George , New York, church "designed by the Rev. Dr. Cressy" which is described in Woodward's text.

76 Historical notes by Nevius written in the Parish Registers.

[77] *Oregon Churchman*, February 10, 1876.

[78] Letter from Hollis G. Bedell, Gray Herbarium Archives, Harvard University to David Powers, February 23, 1989: "In response to your letter asking about photographs of Reuben Nevius, we do [have] a photograph in our collection. I believe the photo we have is the one mentioned in Nevius's letter to Asa Gray because the back of the photograph has the following written in Nevius's hand: 'Eastern Oregon Mission, May 4 '76'.... It is mounted in Mrs. Gray's autograph album.

[79] Telephone conversation between David Powers and Prof. Kenton Chambers, Oregon State University, July 17, 1987.

[80] *Oregon Churchman*, Morris, September 7, 1876. Olive Creek Diggings was about four miles from the present site of Granite, according to Rob Moffatt of the Water Resources Division, U. S. Geological Survey office in Salem, in a telephone conversation of September 25, 1987, with David Powers.

[81] *Columbia Churchman*, May 15, 1882.

[82] Memoirs of Rev. Lemuel H. Wells, 1914.

[83] Letter Jessett to Powers, December 29 1980.

[84] Rev. Thomas Jessett (1940).

[85] *Journal*, Jurisdiction of Washington, 1887.

[86] *Ibid.*, 1889.

[87] *Yakima Republic*, October 19, 1957.

[88] Jesset 1940, pp. 40-41

[89] *Oregon Churchman*, April, 1893.

[90] Thomas E. Jessett, *Pioneering in Gods Country* (Tacoma, WA: The Church Lantern Press, 1953) p. 31.

[91] *Washington Churchman*, December 1893-January 1894

[92] *Ibid.*, February-March 1894.

[93] *Ibid.*, R.D. Nevius, November 1894.

[94] *Journal*, District of Olympia, 1904.

[95] Copy of article from a church publication among Atwood notes. Jan. 1914, p. 37.

[96] Unidentified newspaper clipping, September 1908, "St. Peter's has Unique Bell Tower..."

[97] Rev. J. Neilson Barry, March 5, 1908.

[98] *Yakima Republic*, Relander, 1960.

[99] Tacoma *Ledger*, December 18 1913

[100] James H. Ackland, *Medieval Structures—The Gothic Vault* (University of Toronto Press, 1972)

[101] Centennial publication of St. Michael's, 1985.

[102] *Pacific Northwest Quarterly*, January 1963, article by Gerald Dale Bogar

[103] *Homeseekers*, 1909 edition of Blaine newspaper.

[104] *Buckley Banner*, Friday, January 10, 1896.

[105] Plant Trivia Timeline, The Huntington Botanical Gardens, www.huntington.org/BotanicalDiv/Timeline.html.

[106] "*S. ternatum* Michaux. Procumbent, mat-forming, perennial, flowering stems erect, very rarely granular-pubescent, 5-15 cm tall, each stem terminated with 3 (rarely 2 or 4) helicoid cymes. Leaves entire, dark green, tapered to peltate petioles. Leaves of sterile shoots in whorls of 3, elliptic to spatualate rounded, 0.7-3cm long, 0.3-2 cm wide, apex truncate or rarely emarginate; on flowering stems, the lowest whorled, the upper alternate, oblanceolate to narrowly spatulate. Flowers perfect, each subtended by a leafy bract. Sepals 5, green; petals 5, horizontally spreading, white, 6-8 mm long, acute or almost acuminate; pistils 5, separate to base. Follicles horizontally spreading, 7-8 mm long, aristate. Seeds dark brown, ellipsoid, 0.7-0.9 mm long. (n=8, 12, 16, 24) April-June; May-July. Rich, often rocky woods; locally throughout pied. and mts. of N.C. and adjacent S. C. [Va., Ga., Tenn., Ky., W. Va.]."

[107] Chapman's *Flora of the Southern United States*. See also Gray's *Manual of the Botany of the Northern United States.*

[108] Thomas Meehan, *Native Flowers and Ferns of the United States*, L. Prang and Company, Boston, 1878.

MODELS
Constructed by David W. Powers, III

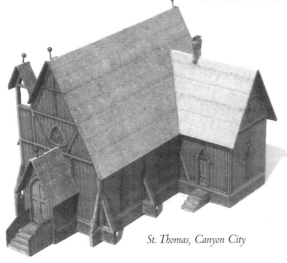

St. Thomas, Canyon City

Ascension Church, Cove

Rectory at Ascention Church, Cove

St. Paul's, The Dalles

St. John's, Union

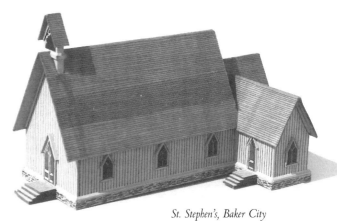

St. Stephen's, Baker City

ILLUSTRATIONS:

1. Nevius, April, 1876. Cover. Sent by Nevius to Dr. Asa Gray, Harvard University, from Baker City, Oregon on May 4, 1976. From the Library of The Gray Herbarium, Harvard.

2. David W. Powers III, Oregon Department of Transportation photo, circa 1981

3. Christ Episcopal Church, Savannah, Georgia, where Nevius was ordained a Deacon in 1853.

4. Eastman and Nevius Brothers taken circa 1866. Standing, (L) Reuben Denton Nevius (Nov. 26, 1827 - Dec. 14, 1913); (R) John Livingston Nevius, (Mar. 4, 1929 - Oct. 19, 1893); Seated (L) Clinton D. Eastman (Sept. 15, 1846 - Apr. 12, 1901); Benjamin Nevius Eastman (Jan 28, 1840 - June 22, 1892); William Lyman Eastman (Apr. 22, 1842 - Nov. 16, 1902), Ovid, New York, 1867. Eastman Family Collection.

5. Margaret "Minnie" Mercer Tuomey Nevius circa 1868. Eastman Family Collection.

6. Reuben D. Nevius, 1872, age 45. Batchel & Stolte Photo, Portland, Oregon. Oregon Historical Society Collection. Neg. 74144.

7. Reuben D. Nevius, circa 1875, age 47, Eastman Family Collection.

8. Reuben D. Nevius, circa 1876, age 48. (sent May 4, 1976) Gray Herbarium, Harvard University. (same as photo #1)

9. Reuben D. Nevius, circa 1883, age 55. Eastman Family Collection.

10. Postcard, Annie Wright Seminary, Tacoma, Washington built 1884. Original owned by Greg Nelson.

11. Mary Denton Nevius Eastman and her son Reuben Denton Nevius, age 59. Ovid, New York, 1887. Eastman Family Collection.

12. R. D. Nevius, age 65 and John L. Nevius, age 63, Chefoo, China. 1893. Eastman Family Collection.

13. R. D. Nevius, age circa 70, possibly with William West. Taken in Chehalis circa 1898. Eastman Family Collection.

14. R. D. Nevius, age about 77, circa 1905. Oregon Historical Society Collection. Neg. 74142.

15. R. D. Nevius taken Nov. 27, 1907, 80th birthday. Diocese of Olympia Collection.

16. Postcard, Fanny [sic] Paddock Hospital, Tacoma, Washington. circa 1908.

17. R. D. Nevius circa 1908, age 81. Episcopal Diocese of Eastern Oregon - Ascension Summer School.

18. R. D. Nevius and friend. Nov. 26. 1910, age 83. Given to David Powers by Jean S. Eastman.

19. R. D. Nevius, Nov. 26, 1910, age 83. University of Oregon Archives, Special Collections.

20. R. D. Nevius in garden circa 1913, age 85. Oregon Historical Society Collection. Neg. 74143.

21. R. D. Nevius circa 1912-13, age 85. Episcopal Diocese of Eastern Oregon - Ascension Summer School.

22. First building of Trinity Church, Portland, consecrated Sept. 21, 1854, northwest corner of Oak and 2nd. Architects: Carson & Barton. Oregon Historical Society Collection. Neg. 60578, file 1773.

23. Second building of Trinity Church, Portland, constructed 1872, consecrated August 31, 1873, southwest Oak and 5th. Architect A. H. Jordan, contractor L. Thurkelsen. Oregon Historical Society Collection, Neg. 30212 or 26851, file 1773.

24. St. Peter's Church, La Grande, circa 1924, before moving to Cove in 1927. Source unknown.

25. St. Peter's Church, La Grande, woodcut, published in *Home and Abroad* (New York), Jan. 15, 1875.

26. St. John's Church, Union, woodcut, published in *Home and Abroad* (New York), Jan. 15, 1875.

27. St. John's Church, Union, early 1875, photo on which woodcut was based, source unknown.

28. St. John's Church, Union, before 1928, source unknown.

27. St. John's Church, Union, after move to Cove in 1928, source unknown.

29. St. John's Church, Union, August 1993, photo by David W. Powers III.

31. St. Stephen's Church, Baker City, woodcut, published in *Home and Abroad* (New York), Jan 15, 1875.

32. St. Stephen's Church, Baker City, c. 1993, photo by David W. Powers III.

33. St. Stephen's Church, Baker City, c. 1993, interior (chancel) photo by David W. Powers III.

34. St. Stephen's Church, Baker City, Nov. 1981, interior, photo by David W. Powers III.

35. Ascension Church, Cove, c. 1876 - 1878, source unknown.

36. Ascension Church, Cove, c. 1890, source unknown.

37. Ascension Church, Cove, summer, 1884, source unknown.

38. Ascension Church, Cove, c. 1993, photo by David W. Powers III.

39. Ascension Church, Cove, side view, c. 1993, photo by David W. Powers III.

40. Interior, Ascension Church, Cove, August 2001, Photo by Gregoty L. Nelson.

41. St. Paul's Church, The Dalles, c. 1876, source unknown.

42. St. Paul's Church, The Dalles, c. 1900, source unknown.

43. St. Paul's Church, The Dalles, late 1890s, Gladys Seufert Collection.

44. St. Paul's Church, The Dalles, 1928, source unknown.

45. Old St. Paul's Church, The Dalles, Dec. 24, 1990, photo by David W. Powers III.

46. St. Paul's Church, The Dalles, alms basin, August, 1983, photo by David W. Powers III.

47. Old St. Paul's Church, The Dalles, September, 1990, photo by David W. Powers III.

48. Altar, St. Paul's Church, The Dalles, August, 1983, photo by David W. Powers III.

49. Old St. Paul's Church, The Dalles, August, 2001, photo by Gregory L. Nelson

50. Old St. Paul's Church, The Dalles, August, 1999, photo by Gregory L. Nelson.

51. Old St. Paul's Church, The Dalles, August, 1999, photo by Gregory L. Nelson

52. Old St. Paul's Church, The Dalles, November, 1990, photo by David W. Powers III.

53. Church of the Redeemer, Pendleton, c. 1880s, Oregon Historical Society, Neg. 53445.

54. St. James Church, Milton-Freewater, August 2001, Photo by Gregory L. Nelson.

55. All Saints Church, Weston, rectory, August, 1983, photo by David W. Powers III.

56. All Saints Church, Weston, now St. James' Church, Milton-Freewater, August, 1983, photo by David W. Powers III.

57. Wells (in honor of Lemuel H. Wells) window, St. James Church, Milton-Freewater, August, 1983, photo by David W. Powers III.

58. St. Thomas' Church, Canyon City, 1908, R. D. Nevius left, Bishop Robert Lewis Paddock (first bishop of Missionary District of Eastern Oregon), right, source unknown.

59. St. Thomas' Church, Canyon City, August, 1983, photo by David W. Powers III.

60. St. Thomas' Church, Canyon City, August, 1983, photo by David W. Powers III.

61. Church of the Nativity, Lewiston, c. 1890, courtesy Lewiston Morning Tribune.

62. Church of the Nativity, Lewiston, c. 1950, courtesy Lewiston Morning Tribune.

63. Church of the Nativity, Lewiston, Idaho, August 2001, Photo by Gregory L. Nelson.

64. St. Luke's Church, Coeur d'Alene, sketch, courtesy of the church.

65. St. Luke's Church, Coeur d'Alene, c. 1892.

66. All Saints Cathedral, Spokane, c. 1905. Courtesy Diocese of Spokane

67. All Saints, Spokane, interior. Courtesy Diocese of Spokane

68. Grace Church, Dayton, August 2001, Photo by Gregory L. Nelson

69. Church of the Good Samaritan, Colfax, c. 1895, Washington State University Library

70. St. Matthew's Church, Sprague, circa 1890, Courtesy of the Diocese of Spokane.

71. St. Matthew's Church, Sprague, interior, Christmas 1887. Courtesy of the Diocese of Spokane.

72. St. Peter's, Pomeroy, August 2001, Photo by Gregory L. Nelson

73. St. John's Church, Olympia, 1939. Washington State Historical Society photo.

74. St. John's Church, Olumpia, c. 1990, interior, photo by David W. Powers III.

75. St. John's Church, Olympia, 2000, Photo by Gregory L. Nelson

76. Church of the Epiphany, Chehalis, Washington. Photo taken June 30/July 1, 1886 at Convocation of Jurisdiction of Washington in conjunction with consecration of the church. Man in center right of lady is Bishop James A. Paddock, and on left of lady is Rev. Nevius. Lewis County Historical Museum photo.

77. Postcard, Church of the Epiphany, Chehalis, Washington, circa 1910, original owned by Greg Nelson.

78. St. Paul's Church, Whatcom (Bellingham) c. 1884, collection of St. Paul's Church.

79. St. Paul's Church, Whatcom (Bellingham), circa 1944, collection of St. Paul's Church.

80. St. Paul's Church, Whatcom (Bellingham), circa 1944 church and rectory, Diocese of Olympia collection.

81. Old St. Paul's Church, 2000, photo by Gregory L. Nelson.

82. St. Michael's Church, Yakima, 1925, postcard.

83. St. Michael's Church, Yakima, August 2001, photo by Gregory L. Nelson.

84. Grace Episcopal Church, Ellensburg, c. 1940.

85. Holy Trinity Church, Hoquiam (successor to St. David's), c. 1910. Polson Museum photo.

86. St. David's Hospital, Hoquiam, 1964 (sold 1913). Polson Museum photo.

87. Holy Trinity Church, Hoquiam (sold 1991), March 21, 2000, photo by Greg Nelson.

88. Holy Trinity Church, Hoquiam, (sold 1991), March 21, 2000, photo by Greg Nelson.

89. Holy Trinity Church, Hoquiam, (sold 1991), March 21, 2000, photo by Greg Nelson.

90. Holy Trinity Church, Hoquiam, Christ window, now installed in St. Andrew's Church, Aberdeen. March 22, 2000, photo by Greg Nelson.

91. St. Andrew's Church, Aberdeen, first church (1895-1914). Diocese of Olympia photo.

92. St. Andrew's Church, Aberdeen, March 22, 2000, interior, photo by Greg Nelson.

93. St. Andrew's Church, Aberdeen, March 22, 2000, photo by Greg Nelson.

94. St. Andrew's Church, Aberdeen, second church, (built 1913/14) March 22, 2000, photo by Greg Nelson.

95. St. Mark's Church, Ocosta, interior view. Collection of Gerald D. Bogar.

96. St. John's Church, South Bend, c. 1910. Diocese of Olympia photo.

97. St. John's Church, South Bend, March 21, 2000, photo by Greg Nelson.

98. St. John's Church, South Bend, March 21, 2000, photo by Greg Nelson.

99. St. John's Church, South Bend, March 21, 2000, photo by Greg Nelson.

100. St. Luke's Church, Elma, March 20, 2000, photo by Greg Nelson.

101. St. Mark's Church, Montesano, March 20, 2000, photo by Greg Nelson.

102. St. Mark's Church, Montesano, March 20, 2000, photo by Greg Nelson.

103. Christ Church, Blaine, interior, 2000, photo by Greg Nelson.

104. Christ Church, Blaine, 1947. Diocese of Olympia photo.

105. Holy Trinity Church, Juneau, circa 1903. W. H. Case, Holy Trinity Archives photo.

106. Holy Trinity Church, Juneau, circa 1900 interior view, Winter and Pond, Alaska State Library PCA87-1127.

107. Holy Trinity Church, Juneau, circa 1950, Holy Trinity Archives photo.

108. Presbyterian Log Church, Juneau, Alaska. Postcard owned by Gregory L. Nelson.

109. Trinity Church, Seattle c. 1900. University of Washington, Archives, Warner Env. No. 47.

110. Postcard, Trinity Church, Seattle, interior, 1909, owned by Greg Nelson.

111. Trinity Church, Seattle, 2000, photo by Greg Nelson.

112. Postcard, St. Peter's Church, Tacoma, circa 1890, owned by Greg Nelson.

113. Postcard, St. Peter's Church, Tacoma, 1908, owned by Greg Nelson.

114. St. Peter's Church, Tacoma, 2000, photo by Greg Nelson.

115. St. Peter's Church, Tacoma, 2000, sign mounted inside porch, photo by Greg Nelson.

116. Neviusia alabamensis.

117. Neviusia alabamensis. From: A. Gray. *Neviusia*, a new genus of Rosacea. Mem. Am. Acad. Arts Sci. II. 6: pl. 30. 1858.

118. Sedum Nevii, L. Prang & Co, Boston, original plate from *The Native Flowers and Ferns of the United States* by Thomas Meehan pub. 1878. Property of Greg Nelson.

119. Dr. Asa Gray, 1865, probably Gray Herbarium, Harvard University.

120. Dr. Asa Gray, circa 1889, probably Gray Herbarium, Harvard University.

121. Rt. Rev. Benj. Wistar Morris, circa 1880, source unknown.

122. Rt. Rev. Benj. Wistar Morris, circa 1870, Oregon Historical Society Neg. No. 73836, file 1773.

123. Rt. Rev. Benj. Wistar Morris, circa 1905, source unknown.

124. Rt. Rev. John Adams Paddock, circa 1890, Diocese of Olympia collection.

125. Rt. Rev. William Morris Barker, circa 1900, Diocese of Olympia collection.

126. Rt. Rev. Lemuel Henry Wells, circa 1930, Diocese of Olympia collection.

A

Abrams, Leroy and Ferris, Roxana Stinchfield. *Illustrated Flora of the Pacific States,* Vol. IV (Stanford, California: Stanford University Press, 1960.

Allen, Rev. Albert

Anon. "Note." *American Monthly Microscopic Journal,* May, 1885.

Anon. "Two of Oregon's Foremost Commonwealth Builders: Judge Reuben Patrick Boise and Professor Thomas Condon." *Oregon Historical Quarterly,* Vol VIII No. 2 (June, 1907), 201-218.

Appleton's Cyclopaedia of American Biography, Ed. James Grant Wilson and John Fiske. New York: D. Appleton and Company, 1888, 1889.

Atwood, Howland. Biographic data about the Rev. Reuben Denton Nevius, D.D. Contributed to Bailey Hortorium, Cornell University, 1959.

B

Baker City (Oregon) *Bedrock Democrat,* 1873: Nov. 19, Nov. 26. 1874: Aug, 19, Dec. 2, Dec. 30. 1875: Jan. 6, June 2, June 23.

Beck, Robert C. *Highlights of a Century.* Walla Walla, Washington: St. Paul's Episcopal Church, 1964.

Black, Helen. *St. Thomas' Centennial.* Canyon City, Oregon: St. Thomas's Episcopal Church, n.d. [1976].

Boren, Charles P. and Thomas W. Campbell. *Episcopal Church of the Nativity, Lewiston, Idaho, 1873-1973.* n.d. [1973]

Bradford, Albert E., Ahles, Harry E. and Bell, C. Ritchie. *Manual of the Vascular Flora of the Carolinas.* Chapel Hill: University of North Carolina Press, ca. 1960.

Buckley Banner, Buckley, WA., various issues including Jan 10, 1896.

C

Chapman's *Portrait and Biographical Record of Portland and Vicinity, Oregon.* Chicago: Chapman Publishing Company, 1903.

Cheshire, Joseph Blount (Rt. Rev., D.D.). *The Church in the Confederate States.* New York: Longmans, Green and Co., 1912.

"The City of Spokane Falls and its Tributary Resources." Issued by the Northwestern Industrial Exposition, Spokane Falls, Washington (October 1 - November 1, 1890. Buffalo: Matthews, Northup & Co., 1890.

Clark, 1975: see Deady (1975).

Clark, Kenneth. *The Gothic Revival: An Essay in the History of Taste.* New York: Harper & Row, 1962.

Clark, Robert D. *The Odyssey of Thomas Condon.* Portland: Oregon Historical Society Press, 1989.

Cole, Lynn (Treasurer, Episcopal Church of the Epiphany, Chehalis, Washington). Letter to David Powers, June 19, 1989.

Columbia Churchman. See Oregon Churchman.

Congregational Convention (a.k.a. Albany Convention, Congregational Churches in the U.S. General Convention). *A Book of Plans for Churches and Parsonages.* New York: Daniel Burgess & Co., 1853, 1854. (Reprinted with the introductory chapters deleted by Geo. F. Woodward under the title *Rural Church Architecture* between 1868 and 1870, and again with revisions in 1876.

Corning, Howard McKinley (ed.) *Dictionary of Oregon History.* Portland: Binfords & Mort, 1956.

Cronquist, Arthur. *An Integrated System of Classification of Flowering Plants.* New York: Columbia University Press, 1981.

D

D.A.B. See *Dictionary of American Biography.*

Deady, Matthew P. (ed. Clark, Malcolm, Jr.). *Pharisee Among Philistines: the Diary of Judge Matthew P. Deady 1871-1892.* Portland: Oregon Historical Society, 1975.

Debus, Allen (ed.) *World Who's Who in Science.* Chicago: Marquis-Who's Who, 1968.

Dictionary of American Biography. Ed. Dumas Malone. New York: Charles Scribner's Sons, 1934.

Downing, Andrew Jackson. *The Architecture of Country Houses.* New York: Dover Publications, 1969 (orig. pub. New York: D. Appleton & Co., 1850)

Downing, Andrew Jackson. *Cottage Residences, Rural Architecture, & Landscape Gardening.* Watkins Glen, N.Y.: American Life Foundation, 1967 (orig. pub. 1842).

Dupree, A. Hunter. *Asa Gray.* Cambridge Mass.: Harvard University Press, 1959.

E

Eastman, John Nevius (Ovid, New York). Letter to Howland Atwood (Huntington Library, San Marino, California).

Eastman, Jean S. (Ovid, New York). Letters to David Powers July 10, 1989; October 23, 1989; May 7, 1990.

Edwards, Rev. Jonathan. *History of Spokane County.* 1900.

Evans, John W., Director of Libraries, Eastern Oregon State College. Letter to David Powers, July 14, 1983.

G

Gamble, Robert S., Architectural Historian, Alabama Historical Commission. Letter to David Powers, February 22, 1984.

Gamble, Robert S., Architectural Historian, Alabama Historical Commission. Letter to David Powers, March 16, 1984.

Gilbert, Frank T. *Historic Sketches of Walla Walla, Whitman, Columbia and Garfield Counties, Washington Territory, and Umatilla County, Oregon.* Portland: A. G. Walling, 1982.

Gray, Asa (ed. Fernald, Merritt Lyndon) *Gray's Manual of Botany, Eighth Edition.* New York: American Book Company, 1950.

H

Harris, Bruce. *The Wasco County History Book.* The Dalles, Oregon: Bruce Harris, 1983.

Hawkins, William John III. "Warren Heywood Williams: Architect (1844-1888)," *Portland Friends of Cast-Iron Architecture Newsletter* No. 17, December 1980.

Hawkins, William John III. "E. M. Burton: Architect (1817-1887)," *Portland Friends of Cast-Iron Architecture Newsletter* No. 19, April, 1982.

Hemenway, Ansel F. "Botanists of the Oregon Country." *Oregon Historical Quarterly,* Vol. V No. 3 (September, 1904), 207-214.

"Historic St. James Church, Milton-Freewater, Oregon; Centennial Celebration, 1875 - 1975." N.d. [1975].

Home and Abroad, New York: Board of Missions [a.k.a. Domestic and Foreign Missionary Society] of the Protestant Episcopal Church in the U.S.A. Dec. 15, 1874; Jan. 15, 1875; Feb. 15, 1875.

Honeyman, A. Van Doren. *Johannes Nevius and His Descendants A. D. 1627-1900.* Plainfield, N.J.: Honeyman & Co., 1900.

Hyslop, Robert B. *Spokane's Building Blocks.* Spokane, Washington 1983.

I

Irwin, Leonard Bertram. *Pacific Railways and Nationalism in the Canadian-American Northwest 1845 - 1873.* New York: Greenwood Press, 1986.

J

Jessett, Thomas E. "The Episcopate of John Adams Paddock, First Bishop of Washington (State)." Pamphlet, reprinted from the *Historical Magazine of the Protestant Episcopal Church,* Vol. XVIII (1949), pp. 282-310.

Jessett, Rev. Canon Thomas E., Historiographer, Episcopal Diocese of Olympia. Letter to David Powers, December 29, 1980.

Jessett, Rev. Thomas Edwin, M.A. "St. John's Church of Olympia (1853 - 1941): A Brief History Compiled Upon the Occasion of the Parochial Diamond Jubilee." Olympia, Washington: St. John's Episcopal Church, 1941.

Jessett, [Rev.] Thomas E. "Thomas Fielding Scott: Bishop of Oregon." *Oregon Historical Quarterly*, March 1954 (reprinted in booklet form).

Jessett, Thomas E., Historiographer, *Pioneering God's Country, The History of the Diocese of Olympia 1853 - 1967.* The Diocese of Olympia Press, Seattle, Washington, 1967.

K

Kowsky, Francis R. "The Architecture of Frederick C. Withers (1828 - 1901)." *Journal of the Society of Architectural Historians*, Vol. XXXV No. 2 (May, 1976), p. 83.

Kowsky, Francis R. *The Architecture of Frederick Clarke Withers and the Progress of the Gothic Revival in America after 1850.* Middletown, Connecticut: Wesleyan University Press, 1980.

Krier, Jean. *One Hundred Years of Community: St. Paul's Episcopal Church and The Dalles, Oregon.* The Dalles Optimist Printers, n.d. [1975].

Kuykendall, Judge E. V. *History of Garfield County (Washington).* 1984.

L

Lange, Erwin F. "Pioneer Botanists of the Pacific Northwest." *Oregon Historical Quarterly,* Vol. LVII No. 2. (June, 1956), pp. 108-124.

Lawton, Elva. *Moss Flora of the Pacific Northwest,* Nichinan, Miyazaki, Japan: Hattori Botanical Laboratory, 1971.

Lewis & Dryden's Marine History of the Pacific Northwest, Ed. E. W. Wright. Portland: Lewis & Dryden Printing Co., 1895.

Lloyd's Clerical Directory, 1911. Chicago: 1911.

Loth, Calder, and Julius Trousdale Sadler, Jr. *The Only Proper Style: Gothic Architecture in America.* Boston: New York Graphic Society, 1975.

Lyman, W. H., *An Illustrated History of Walla Walla County, State of Washington.* Loc. unknown: W. H. Lever, 1901.

M

MacColl, E. Kimbark. *The Shaping of a City: Business and Politics in Portland, Oregon 1885 - 1915.* Portland: The Georgian Press, 1976.

MacKintosh, Mrs. R. G., Member, St. Michael's Altar Guild. Draft nomination of St. Michael's Episcopal Church, Yakima, Washington, to National Register of Historic Places.

McArthur, Lewis L. *Oregon Geographic Names* (Fifth Edition). Portland: Oregon Historical Society Western Imprints, 1982.

McCormick's Portland Directory, 1872.

The H. W. McCurdy Marine History of the Pacific Northwest. Ed. Gordon Newell. Seattle: Superior Publishing Co., 1966.

McLean, Isabel C. *The Church of the Holy Trinity, Juneau, Alaska: A Short History 1897-1977.* Monograph; Holy Trinity Episcopal Church, Juneau, Alaska, 1977.

Minutes of Vestry Meetings, St. Paul's Church, August 11, 1887 to Nov. 28, 1899, incl. Handwritten journal contained among the parish records of St. Paul's Church, The Dalles.

Morris, Benjamin Wistar. "Oregon and Washington Mission." *Home and Abroad,* December 15, 1874; January 15, 1875, and February 15, 1875.

Mueller, Karl (a.k.a. Mueller, C.). "Sechs neue Laubmoose Nordamerika's [Six New North American Leaved Mosses]." *Flora: Algemeine Botanische Zeitschrift* (Regensberg, Germany), 56: 31 (November 1, 1873) pp. 481, 483-484.

N

Nevius, Helen S. Coan. *The Life of John Livingston Nevius,* New York: Fleming H. Revell Co., 1895.

Nevius, Reuben Denton (anonymously). "Biographical Notice of Prof. M. Tuomey, A.M." *Alabama Educational Journal,* Vol. I No. 4 (January, 1859), pp. 111-119.

Nevius, Reuben Denton (La Grande). Letter to Judge Matthew P. Deady (Portland), November 24, 1873. Deady file, Manuscript Collection, Oregon Historical Society.

Nevius, Reuben Denton (Baker City). Letter to Judge Matthew P. Deady (Portland), February, 1874. Deady file, Manuscript Collection, Oregon Historical Society.

Nevius, Reuben Denton (Spokane Falls). Letter to Judge Matthew P. Deady (Portland), December 20, 1880. Deady file, Manuscript Collection, Oregon Historical Society.

Nevius, Reuben Denton. "Notes on the Habitat of Diatoms." *American Monthly Microscopical Journal,* September, 1894.

Nevius, Rev. R. D. "Saint Michael's Parish, North Yakima, District of Spokane Washington," Parish Register, Vol. I ("Church and Clergyman's Record Book"), St. Michael's Episcopal Church, Yakima, Washington, historical entries seemingly made in 1910.

New York Times, December 16, 1913, p. 11.

O

Olympia, Episcopal Diocese of. *More Than 100 Years of Ministry: The Episcopal Church in Western Washington.* Seattle, Episcopal Diocese of Olympia, 1989.

Oregon Churchman, various issues. Published by the Episcopal Church in Portland from 1862 with occasional interruptions, sometimes appearing under the titles *Columbia Churchman* and *Oregon and Washington Churchman.* Held by Oregon Historical Society.

Oregon and Washington Churchman. See Oregon Churchman.

Oregon Historical Society. *OHS Scrapbook 44.*

Oregonian. See Portland Oregonian.

P

Peck, Morton Eaton. *A Manual of the Higher Plants in Oregon,* second edition. Portland, Oregon: Binfords & Mort, 1961.

Perkins, Rev. Louis L. *Benjamin Wistar Morris, Bishop of Oregon 1868-1906, An Exploratory Biography,* Privately reproduced, 1977.

Perkins, Rev. Louis L. *The Centennial Story of St. Peter's Episcopal Church, LaGrande, Oregon as of December 1978.*

Perkins, Rev. Louis L. *A Pictorial Story of the Ascension Episcopal Church School for Girls in 1884, One Hundred Years Ago, and the Beginning of Ascension Episcopal Church Summer Schools in 1924, Sixty Years Ago.* Cove, Oregon, 1983.

Perkins, Louis L. "Samuel Gautier French: 1838-1882." *Historical Magazine of the Protestant Episcopal Church* (Vol. XLII), March, 1973.

"PFCIA." See Portland Friends of Cast Iron Architecture.

Pierson, William H., Jr. *American Building and Their Architects: Vol II, Technology and the Picturesque, the Corporate and the Early Gothic Styles.* New York: Doubleday & Co., 1978.

Pigion, Rev. E. W. Additions to entries of Rev. R. D. Nevius, "Saint Michael's Parish, North Yakima, District of Spokane Washington," Parish Register, Vol. I ("Church and Clergyman's Record Book"), St. Michael's Episcopal Church, Yakima, Washington, historical entries seemingly made on two occasions in 1904 and 1909.

Portland *Oregonian* (a.k.a. Daily Oregonian). 1872: Mar. 27; Apr. 29, 30; May 1; Oct. 24, 25. 1873: Feb. 27. 1909: Oct. 16.

Powers, David. Notes on telephone conversation with Bea Edmundson, Baker, December 24, 1980.

Powers, David. Notes on telephone conversations with the Revs. Dick Toll, Seattle, and Thomas Jessett, DesMoines, Washington, December 26, 1980.

Powers, David. Notes on telephone conversation with the Rev. Albert Allen, Portland, September 28, 1983.

Powers, David W., III. "Albert H. Jordan (ca. 1820-1872): Architecture in Michigan, California, Oregon and Washington." Paper presented to the Northern Pacific Coast Chapter, Society of Architectural Historians, San Jose, California, November 9, 1985.

Protestant Episcopal Church in the U.S.A., Oregon Diocese. "Records of Eastern

Oregon Diocese." Oregon State Library Microfilm 11, Item 116.

Pugin, Augustus Northmore Welby. *The True Principles of Pointed or Christian Architecture.* London: John Weale, 1841.

Q

R

Rand, Helen B. *One Hundred Years of St. Stephen's Episcopal Church, Baker, Oregon; 1873 - 1973.* Baker: Hudson Printing Co., n.d. [1973].

Records of Eastern Oregon District [or Diocese], Protestant Episcopal Church in the U.S.A. Micro-filmed from materials loaned by Rev. Albert E. Allen, June 1856. Oregon State Library Microfilm 11, item 116 (17 reels condensed to 13 reels). These reels contain copies of a variety of materials, including Parish Registers, vestry and guild meeting minutes, miscellaneous correspondence, and notes made by the Rev. J. Neilson Barry between about 1908 and 1910, probably on the occasion of the creation of the Missionary District of Eastern Oregon from the eastern portion of the Diocese of Oregon

Relander, Click. "Little Stone Church's Anniversary Recalls Old Days." Yakima (Washington) *Republic* October 26, 1960. A reorganized version of this story appeared in the Yakima *Herald* of October 27.

Roslyn Community Study. Spawn of Coal Dust - History of Roslyn. 1955

Roth, Mrs. C. L. "Interesting Facts of the Early History of St. Paul's...." *Olympia Churchman*, October, 1927 (Taken from Bellingham *Herald*, February 22, 1925).

Rural Church Architecture. Ed. George Evertson Woodward. New York: Geo. El Wood-ward, between 1868 and 1870.

S

"St. Michael's Church: Centennial Celebration of the Episcopal Church in Yakima, Washington, 1885 - 1985." Yakima, Washington: St. Michael's Episcopal Church, 1985.

Sanborn Fire Insurance Maps:
    Baker City, Oregon, December 1895.
        Held by Baker Public Library.
    Baker City, Oregon, August 1903.
        Held by Baker Pubuc Library.

Schreiner, Charles F. *A History of the Bishops of the Diocese of Olympia, The Episcopal Church in Western Washington,* Puyallup: Valley Press, 1986.

Small, John Kunkel. *Flora of the Southeastern United States* (New York: privately published, 1903).

Smalley, Eugene V. *History of the Northern Pacific Railroad.* G. P. Putnam's Sons, 1883.

Smith, Rev. O. D. "Epiphany Parish History." Chehalis, Washington *Lewis County Advocate,* 1933: Nov. 3, Nov. 10, Nov. 17; Nov. 24.

Sprague, Lamont Edwall...1881 - 1984. Fairfield, Washington, 1982.

Stafleu, Frans A. and Richard S. Cowan. *Taxonomic Literature,* second edition. Utrecht: Bohn, Scheltema & Holkema (Dr. W. Junk b.v.), 1981.

Stanton, Phoebe B. *The Gothic Revival and American Church Architecture.* Baltimore: Johns Hopkins Press, 1968.

Stevens, D. H. *Oregon Papers Nos. VII to XVII.* Portland: A. G. Walling, (Issued as a supplement to the *Portland Evening Telegram*) n.d., 1882.

T

Turrill, Rev. W. B. "History of St. Paul's Parish, Bellingham." Typescript, n.d. (Inter-nal evidence dates the document at 1923). Archives, Episcopal Diocese of Olympia, Seattle. Hand amendments to original, apparently in Turrill's hand, are shown in brackets.

U

United States Government. *Census of Michigan* 1850.

United States Government *Census of New York* 1850.

United States Government *Census of Eastern Oregon, Union County,* 1870.

Upjohn, Everard M. *Richard Upjohn, Architect and Churchman.* New York: Columbia University Press, 1939.

V

Van Loan, Mary P., Administrative Assistant, Union College. Letter to Howland Atwood, Huntington Library, April 21, 1953.

Vaughan, Margot, Director, Cowlitz County Historical Museum. Letter to David Powers, July 31, 1984.

W

Walla Walla (Washington) *Statesman.* March 22, 1873.

Watson, Sereno. ("*A[llium] nevii,*") *Proceedings of the American Academy,* v. 14 (1879), p. 231.

Wells, Rt. Rev. Lemuel H., D. D. Body of article entitled "Episcopalians Build Here First Stone Church in State of Washington." Undated clipping (prob. from an issue of the Yakima *Republic*), files of Yakima Valley Museum, 1914.

Wells, The Rt. Rev. Lemuel H., S.T.D., D.D., D.C.L., L.L.D., *A Pioneer Missionary,* Seattle: Progressive Printing Co., 1932.

West, William. A History of the Church of the Epiphany, Chehalis, Washington, dated September 18, 1909. Typescript from original in Vol 1, Parish Record of the Episcopal Church of the Epiphany.

Whitaker, Walter C. (Bp.) *History of the Protestant Episcopal Church in Alabama 1763 - 1898.*

Who Was Who in America. Vol 2. Chicago: A. N. Marquis Co., 1950.

Who Was Who In America, Historical Volume, 1607 - 1898. Chicago: A. N. Marquis Co., 1967.

Withers, Frederick Clarke. *Church Architecture.* New York: A. J. Bicknell & Co., 1873.

Whithey, Henry F., A.I.A. and Whithey, Elsie Rathburn. *Biographical Dictionary of American Architects (Deceased).* Los Angeles: Hennessey & Ingalls, 1970.

Wood, Charles R. *The Northern Pacific: Main Street of the Northwest.* New York: Bonanza, 1968.

Woodward, George Evertson. *Rural Church Architecture, New and Revised Edition.* New York: Geo. E. Woodward & Co. 1876.

Woodward, George Evertson. *Woodward's Architecture with Hints and Notes on Building, and a Price Catalogue of all Books on Architecture....* New York: Geo. E. Woodward, 1870.

Woodward, George Evertson. *Woodward's Country Homes.* New York: Geo. E. Wood-ward, 1865.

World Who's Who in Science. See Debus.

X

Y

Yakima (Washington) *Republic:* March 22, 1907; October 19, 1957; October 26, 1960.

Yakima (Washington) *Herald,* October 27, 1960.

Yakima Valley Museum. File Notes on St. Michael's Episcopal Church compiled in preparation for printing "Yakima: A Centennial Perspective 1885 - 1985."

Z

General Reference

Fletcher, Sir Banister. *A History of Architecture.* Eighteenth Edition, ed. J. C. Palmes. New York: Charles Scribers's Sons, 1975.

Harris, Cyril M. (ed.). *Historic Architecture Sourcebook.* New York: McGraw-Hill, 1977.

Hitchcock, Henry-Russell. *American Architectural Books.* Minneapolis: University of Minnesota Press, 1962.

The International Atlas. Chicago, New York and San Francisco: Rand McNally, 1969.

Biographic Notes
(Chronology)

The Rev. Reuben Denton Nevius, D.D.
November 26, 1827 - December 14, 1913
David W. Powers III originally written July 1990

with additions by Gregory L. Nelson

"Ovid, New York

"Jan. 10, 1953

"Howland Atwood

"Huntington Library

"San Marino, California

"Dear Sir:

"A letter, which you sent to the Ovid School, has been called to my attention.

"Reuben Denton Nevius's mother was my grandmother. (She was married to Chester Eastman, my grandfather, in 1832). I now live in the house where she died and where Reuben visited.

"Reuben was born Nov. 26, 1827. He was the son of Benjamin Nevius and Mary Denton. He married Minnie Tuomey July 31, 1867. She was a Southern lady. They had twins who died. She died shortly afterward with yellow fever. Reuben was a missionary in Tacoma, Washington for a long time, and in Alaska for some time. After he died in 1913, his body was cremated and sent to Ovid. I placed his ashes on his mother's grave as he had requested. He had a brother, John Nevius, who was a missionary in Chefoo, China for over forty years.

"The enclosed snapshot is the latest one sent by him. (Reuben is on the left).

"I hope that this may be of help to you in compiling the biography.

"Very truly yours

"John Nevius Eastman"

— Early life —
1827: November 26

Born: Ovid, Seneca County, New York

From Helen S. Coan Nevius, *The Life of John Livingston Nevius* (New York: Fleming H. Revell Co., 1895):

The Nevius family was of Dutch descent, the first American ancestor, Johannes Nevius having emigrated to New Amsterdam from Zoelen before 1652. He was elected city "schepen" in 1654 (p. 17).

"There is a tradition that the Nevius family was of French Huguenot extraction, and that about the time of the Revocation of the Edict of Nantes they were scattered in many directions, some going to Belgium and Holland, and others to Great Britain, where the name survives as Neave, while in France it is still Neve. It is not known when its Latinized form—Nevius—became common. The legend that the Latin poet Cn. Naevius was the first progenitor of the family, though not impossible, is only conjecture." (pp. 18-19)

"Peter P. Nevius, of the fifth generation from Johannes, was the great-grandfather of John Livingston [and Reuben Denton]. He died in 1815.... His son, John P..., married Gertrude Hageman. They had eight children. When the eldest of these, Benjamin Hageman—born in 1803—was fifteen years of age, the family removed to what is known as the "Lake Country" of western New York, where the purchased

a large farm between two villages—Ovid and Lodi—in Seneca County. In 1826 Benjamin Nevius married Mary Denton, who still lives (1895), at the age of nearly ninety. On their marriage they went at once to a cottage on the estate, where they remained until he had built a fine, large house a short distance from the homestead. Their two sons, Reuben and John, were born while they lived in the little cottage, which nestled down behind an orchard. [The orchard seems to have been an important part of the farm - it is mentioned several times.] Close by it was a remarkable spring of purest water, and on every side were fields and meadows, with Seneca Lake gleaming through the trees, about two miles distant." (p. 19)

[1827 - 1829]
[Reuben was born November 26, 1927.] "John was born March 4, 1829." (p. 20)

"[Benjamin Nevius] had strong and radical views on some of the burning questions of the day, and, had he lived long, might have been noted as a social reformer. The temperance movement was then just being inaugurated, and he threw himself into it heart and soul."—Couldn't get help for a barn-raising without the customary abundance of liquor, but Mary cooked delicious meals which saved the day. (pp. 20-22)

[1830]
The family moved into the new house that Benjamin built near his father's house in the spring of 1830. (p. 26)

"As it was the custom in those days to take very small children to church, John and Reuben attended [the Presbyterian Church] regularly, the former, no doubt, carried in his father's arms." (p. 24)

Benjamin Nevius died of a fall in August/September 1830 when Reuben was not yet three and "John was only eighteen months old." (p. 24) [A stone for Benjamin H. Nevius in the Ovid cemetery gives his dates as June 29, 1802 - October 10, 1830. See Purdy, July 3, 1953.]

[1832]
John Livingston Nevius (written reminiscences):

"In the course of a few years [in 1832, see John Eastman, Jan. 10, 1953] came a faithful husband [to our mother] and to us a kind father [Chester Eastman]. With him my mother and my brother Reuben went to spend a year in New England and I was left in the care of my grandparents." (p. 27)

"If I remember right, I was rather wilful [sic] and envious and Reub and I were always fighting." (p. 29)

"I was often serious. I had very strong religious convictions before I was six years old." (p. 29)

[1833]

Chester Eastman bought the farm where Jean S. and Earnest Eastman still live (July 1990), a grandson of William Lyman Eastman per letter from Jean Eastman July 19, 1990.

Half-sister Mary Eastman (first) born: Ovid N.Y. January 22, 1833; d. Ovid, N.Y. June 1, 1835 (age 2 yrs. 4 mos.).

[1835]

Half sister Hannah Eastman born: Ovid N.Y. January 9, 1835; m. Dr. David Warner Birge (b. Manchester, Conn. Dec. 6, 1822; d. 1901) November 5, 1856; d. Ovid, N.Y. July 10, 1866 (age 31 yrs. 5 mos.).

Half-sister Mary Eastman (first) died: Ovid N.Y. June 1, 1835. (age 2 yrs. 4 mos.).

[1836]

1836: December 2

Half-brother Benjamin N. Eastman (first) born: Ovid N.Y. December 2, 1836; d. Ovid N.Y. February 9, 1840 (age 3 yrs. 3 mos.).

[1838]

"When I was nine years old [1838] it was determined to send Reuben [nearly 12] and me to the academy in Ovid village.... Sometimes Reuben and I would ride on horseback, but we always quarreled about which should ride before.... [I can remember Mother saying,] 'Children, see that ye fall not out by the way!'... In the winter we drove to school." (pp. 30-31)

"The Presbyterian church of Ovid village was a large and, for the times, an imposing edifice.... Its acoustic effects, by some happy accident, were excellent.... In the absence of any town hall or lecture-room, the Presbyterian church was used once a year for what was called the 'exhibition' of the academy. Here the two boys, Reuben and John, made their first appearance as 'public speakers'.... (p. 23)

[1839]

1839: February 1, 17

Half-brother William C. Eastman born, died: b. Ovid, N.Y. February 1, 1839; d. Ovid, N.Y. February 17, 1839 (age 16 days).

[1840]

Half-brother Benjamin Nevius Eastman (second) born: Ovid, N.Y. January 28, 1840; m. Cornilia Post (b. vicinity Ovid, N.Y. April 16, 1844; d. March 23, 1866) November 26, 1863; d. (Syracuse, N.Y.?) June 22, 1892 (age 52 yrs. 5 mos.).

Half-brother Benjamin N. Eastman (first) died: b. Ovid, N.Y. December 2, 1836; d. Ovid, N.Y. February 9, 1840 (age 3 yrs. 5 mos.)

[1842]

1842: April 22

Half-brother William Lyman Eastman born: Ovid, N.Y. April 22, 1842; m. Augusta Nash (b. Hadley, Mass. September 1, 1842; d. Ovid, N.Y. April 30, 1912) June 6, 1866; d. Ovid, N.Y.(?), November 16, 1902 (age 60 yrs. 7 mos.)

[ca. 1843]

"It was about this time [when John was 'about 13 or 14,' i.e. ca. 1843] that my grandfather connected himself with the Dutch Reformed Church.... He was very soon chosen an 'elder.'" (p. 33)

[1844]

1844: June 30

Half-sister Mary Denton Eastman (second) born: Ovid, N.Y. June 30, 1844; m.

James Harris (b. vicinity Ovid, N.Y.; d. Cleveland, Ohio) 1867; d. Cleveland, Ohio, March 4, 1937 (age 92 yrs. 8 mos.)

[1845]

John was ready to enter college as a sophomore before he was 16. (p. 35)

Reuben and John entered Union College, Schenectady, about September 1, 1845. (p. 36) The two brothers joined the Kappa Alpha Society. (p. 37)

Texas became the 28th state on December 29, 1845.

[1846]

Half-brother Clinton Denton Eastman born: Ovid, N.Y. September 15, 1846; d. Ovid, N.Y. April 12, 1901 (age 54 yrs. 7 mos.)

"When the time for the first college vacation approached, it was decided that Reuben and John should spend it with friends in Massachusetts, it being thought well that they should see more of the world and have the advantage of travel.... (p. 38)

John taught school near Ovid in the autumn of 1846 and early winter of 1847. (p. 40)

Iowa became the 29th state, December 28, 1946.

[1847]

In May of 1847 John, back at Union College, wrote home "again" referring to the fruit trees, "expressing regret at hearing that his 'grafts' were not doing well," and suggesting that "if straw had been put around the peach trees it might have been better." He went again this year to spend the autumn vacation in Massachusetts. (p. 40)

———

1847: November 26. Reuben Nevius's 20th birthday.

Reuben was "taking his turn in school-teaching" in December of 1847. (pp. 40-41)

[1848]

Gold discovered in California by James W. Marshall on property of Johann Augustus Sutter January 24, 1848.

Reuben was home in January, 1848 and then back at Union College in the spring. (p. 42)

Reuben and John graduated from Union College in 1848. (p. 43)*

*This is confirmed in a letter dated April 21, 1953 to Howland Atwood from Union College, which also noted that the degrees conferred were A. B. (Artium Baccalaureus, Bachelor of Arts) degrees. Some sources erroneously give the date of graduation as 1849.

Wisconsin became the 30th state May 29, 1848.

[1849]

"It was a common thing in those days—some years before the great Rebellion—for enterprising Northerners to seek their fortunes at the South.... It was not strange that John, being obliged to make his own way in the world, and being still too young to fix upon his profession, should decide to try the experiment of finding employment where so many others had done well." (pp. 48-49)

———

1849: mid-October

John embarked for Georgia from New York. He wrote, "My time in New York passed very pleasantly. I found Reub, as I told you in my last letter, and later on a college friend, and Mr. D..... and family were very kind to us both." (p. 50)

John sailed from New York for Georgia in late October, 1849 on the steamship "Cherokee." (p. 50) He arrived at Savannah November 3 and then walked across the state to Columbus. (pp. 52-53)

John recorded in his journal that in early December, "What was my surprise to receive a visit from Judge S____ and Mr. B_____, who offered me Mr. B_____'s school—the one I liked best of any I have seen in Georgia. This was unexpected, but gratifying. A few days afterward I was called upon by Mr. S_____ J_____, a patron of the school and an influential man, who wished me to give the situation up, simply because I was a Northerner. The excitement throughout the State is very strong, arising from the difficulty in choosing a Speaker in the House of Representatives. I told him I did not consider my being a Northerner a reasonable objection, and if my friends were still willing I should hold to my agreement. Since my recovery [from a fever] I have been almost unaccountably successful in getting pupils. I shall at least have a 'tolerable' school; maybe a successful one...." (p. 59)

About this time Reuben's and John's aunt Gertrude Nevius married Rev. Jacob Best, "a missionary in Africa." (p. 53)

Mary Denton (Nevius) Eastman, according to various scattered references, was very pious. She hoped that her sons would enter the ministry. In November, 1849 John wrote his mother from Columbus that "you may be surprised to hear that ever since last spring my mind has been much engaged with thoughts of religion." (p. 56) He was desirous of connecting himself with the Presbyterian church [in Columbus}, "but it was in an 'unsettled state.'" Then in late December visiting Presbyterian clergymen held a series of services and John "presented" himself "before the session." "I was received after a short examination," he said. By mid-February he said he "seemed to be living in another world." (p. 60)

[1850]

About this time, "Reuben Nevius united with the Episcopal Church, and it was inevitable that the views of the two brothers should from this time occasionally clash. They wrote with unrestrained freedom, and their letters show that in one or two instances they slightly wounded each other's feelings. Very soon, however, they 'agreed to differ'.... The letters which follow illustrate this.

——

"COLUMBUS, GA.,
"March 6, 1850.
"DEAR BROTHER [Reuben]: You ask me if I think it essential that a person be able to date with precision the time of his conversion. I should say not.... (pp.61-62)

——

"COLUMBUS, April 20, 1850.
"...And now, Reub, about Presbyterianism. I have more and more reason every day to thank God that I am a Presbyterian. Let me recommend to you, if you ever come across it, 'Miller on Presbyterianism'.... Many of my views, particularly on the subject of election, have become much clearer, both to the eye of reason and of faith. I regard the doctrine of election, together with the character of God exhibited in it, the crowning glory of our religion.... (p. 62)

——

"Columbus, May 4, 1850.
"....And now, dear brother, for a little talk. I am thankful we have this privilege.... My conscience acquits me of uncharitableness to other denominations. Particularly do I have a tender feeling for the Episcopal Church, on account of its members whom I love, and whose piety I respect and admire. But you spoke of spiritual difficulties.... We know there is no intermediate link to unite us to God....

"But, dear brother, you say you are sorry to see in me the remains of early prejudice.... I thank you for your frankness.... I do not profess to know very thoroughly the points of disputation between Episcopalians and Presbyterians, although I have of late read not a little. The result of my investigation is this: I have found the Presbyterian Church to meet in every respect my wants. I have not found a doctrine in it which is not fully supported by Scripture, and which does not meet with the full and hearty concurrence of my reason. I am persuaded that, in regard to its form of worship and church government, 'the church to which I belong is of devine appointment.' I think everything goes to show that the Jewish church, as well as the early Christian church, had a 'republican form of government,' and that there is but one order of gospel 'ministers' spoken of in the New Testament. Besides, I can see no argument, either scriptural or per se, for so exclusive use of written forms of prayer,

and I cannot but see many objections. There are other things in the Episcopal Church to which I cannot assent, of which I could not speak without going into detail. Besides, when I look at the characters of the different churches and ask myself which will best promote my growth in grace; when I apply the gospel test, 'By their fruits ye shall know them'; when I look abroad for indications of zeal in Christ's cause and for the promotion of his kingdom, I can never think of changing my church for any other. With this view, I feel it my duty and privilege to labor in and for the Presbyterian Church. At the same time I rejoice that we differ so little in essentials; and I pray that our churches may never separate us in affection.

"And now, dear brother, I have been very plain with you. I wish you always to write in the same manner to me. I will only add that I have not the least doubt of the sincerity of your motives. I rejoice in the belief that we are both traveling to the same heavenly home....

"I have just received a letter from Mother, and she seems to be enjoying almost a heaven on earth in the realization of the answer to her prayers in the conversion of her sons. Let us pray much for her and for each other.... (pp. 62-64)

——

1850: November 23
"In the month of November, 1850, John had the happiness of welcoming his brother to his Southern home, which was to become Reuben's for many years. In his journal he wrote:

"November 25, 1850. After so long a time of expectancy Reuben arrived on the 23rd. At night we drove in a 'rockaway' to get his luggage, and it seemed like old times. Such a quantity of news! We have hardly had time to eat or sleep. I am glad we are here alone, where we can have all the house to ourselves. How charming were the little remembrances from home! Reuben and I have run races and jumped together, and find that we stand nearly on the same footing that we used to.... (p. 66)

"....John, in the autumn of 1850, decided to begin at once his studies for entering the ministry of the Presbyterian Church.... Having decided to be a minister, he had then to take into consideration the question of the theological seminary in which to pursue his studies; and this involved what 'school' of theology he should embrace. His parents belonged to the so-called New School branch of the Presbyterian Church, and their preferences were naturally in favor of Union Seminary in New York City. It was in part owing to the influence of his friends in Columbus that he determined to go to Princeton, N.J., a strongly pronounced Old School institution."* (p. 67)

*Clark (1989) 63-64: "[A] Plan of Union ... had been adopted in 1801 to aid the Presbyterians and Congregationalists in evangelizing western New York and the Ohio River valley, where great numbers of people, belonging to both denominations, had begun to move. The two churches, both Calvinistic, held the same, or similar doctrinal views, both insisted upon an educated ministry, and both suffered a lack of ministers for the new field. They decided to act together to avoid conflict and increase their effectiveness. The plan encouraged the organization of only one church in a community that might adhere to either denomination. Ministers, too, might serve congregations of either denomination and hold membership and the right to appeal or address grievances either to the presbytery or to the nongoverning association of the congregation, or to a council representing both denominations. Ministers moved freely across denominational lines, chiefly Congregationalists to the Presbyterian church.*The Congregationalists and doctrinally more liberal and evangelical ministers in the Presbyterian church, the revivalist party, who came to be called New School, endorsed the plan with enthusiasm. The conservatives, later known as Old School, looked upon the practices of revivalism with some doubt, and on the invasion of Congregational ministers and doctrines with concern. The strictly Calvinistic Old School emphasized the sovereignty of God and the powerlessness of man to act on his own behalf, even in search of salvation. The New School, rooted in the gospel of revivalism, emphasized the individual's freedom and responsibility to act for himself in seeking salvation. Both insisted upon the sovereignty of God in determining who was, indeed, saved or not saved; the individual, at best, could only 'hopefully' believe that he had been converted."* Clark (1989) 72: "The New School Presbyterians, meeting in General Assembly in 1850, restated their opposition to slavery and asserted that 'holding our fellow-men in bondage ... is an offense against God and the Church; but added the disclaimer, 'unless necessitated by the civil laws.'"

*Clark's footnotes give his sources.

———

"John left Columbus early in December of 1850." (p. 68)

Dictionary of American Biography:

John Livingston Nevius: "With his brother Reuben he attended Ovid Academy and then entered Union College. Upon graduating in 1848, he yielded to the lure of new country and went south to Georgia. There he taught school for a year with a considerable measure of success. From his intimate letters to his brother Reuben it is evident that the conversion was the result not of sudden influences from without but of months of inner questioning.... In 1853 he had received appointment from the Presbyterian Board as missionary to China....* He was ordained May 23, 1853, and "in June married Helen Sanford Coan, a school friend of Ovid Academy days. Then in September they sailed by way of the Cape of good Hope for China.

"Their first years in China were full of uncertainties. The climate of Ningpo, to which they had been assigned, is notoriously difficult. Mrs. Nevius' health failed, and in 1857 she had to return to the United States for a period.... He and his wife were pioneers in a mission station in Hangchow in 1859, but had to withdraw because of political unrest. They then spent several months in Japan, and on their return to China proceeded north to aid in the establishment of a mission in Shantung province.

"There Nevius toiled with characteristic energy for more than thirty years. His evangelistic zeal prepared the way for many local churches, the work in each locality being delegated as far as possible to native residents. He kept up a steady output of written material both in Chinese and in English.... A lasting benefit to China's material well-being resulted from his experiments in acclimatizing Western fruits and vegetables.... Study of the 'Nevius method' became a part of the preparation of missionary candidates.... His life ended peacefully at his desk after daily prayers in 'San-lou,' the house which he had himself erected on a hill overlooking the Chinese city of Chefoo.

"*[The chief source of information is *The Life of John Livingston Nevius* (1895), by his wife, Helen S.C. Nevius....]"

Dictionary of American Biography (Vol. XIII), 1934, p. 444.

— Michigan—

1849?-1850:

"During the years 1850 to 1852, possibly as early as 1848, he taught school in Michigan."*

Howland Atwood in letter to various locations in Michigan, all dated January 25, 1954. No affirmative responses were received.

Atwood's notes do not indicate where he got the information that Nevius taught school in Michigan. Apparently his dates were incorrect because Nevius's brother John noted that Reuben was in New York in October, 1849 and then in Georgia in November, 1850. Yet Nevius himself mentioned that he was in Michigan (see May 29, 1858 below). The 1850 Census of Michigan (p. 271) lists a "Nevins, R. D." [*spelling unsure] in Marshall, Calhoun Co. (about 10 miles e.s.e. of Battle Creek). Helen S.C. Nevuis (1895) mentioned visiting a sister, Mrs. A. D. Schuyler, in Marshall, Michigan in 1881 (p. 393). The only "Nevius" listed in the 1850 Census of New York was John M., Lodi (near Ovid), Seneca Co., apparently not Nevius's brother John L. who was in Georgia at the time. No "Nevins, R——" is listed in the New York Census for that year.

In addition Nevius had two aunts, sisters of his father, who emigrated to Michigan, near the Detroit area. Ellen Stothoff Nevius, who married John Cutler Emery, died in Northville, Wayne County, in 1884, and Ann F. Nevius, who married Peter Donaldson in Ovid in 1836, died in Detroit in 1875. It is possible that he may have visited them while in Michigan.

FamilySearch records, LDS Library

Ca. 1850:

Rev. R. D. Nevius (writing in 1858):

"I was much surprised to find Frasera Carolininsis [in Alabama] which I had only seen in Michigan long ago in my first studies of the science [of botany]. Nevius (May 29, 1858), see below.

California became the 31st state September 9, 1850.

— Georgia —

1850: November 23

Nevius arrived in Columbus, Georgia. See above. It seems that his purpose in coming was to take over his brother John's school, as John was leaving to enter theological seminary at Princeton.

[1852]

1852: before May 6

Bishop Elliott:*

[Address to Annual Convention, May 6, 1852]: "I have received Mr. Nevins [sic, Nevius] as a candidate for Orders, by transfer from the Diocese of Michigan, and he is now our only candidate...."

Journal, Diocese of Georgia, 1852

*Rt. Rev. Stephen Elliott, Bishop of Georgia

———

1852:

"Accepted as candidate for Deacon's Orders in Diocese of Georgia...." Allen, 1974

1852: November 26

Nevius's twenty-fifth birthday.

[1853]

1853: early January

[From the report of the Standing Committee dated May 6, 1853]: "They have signed the testimonials of Reuben D. Nevius, a candidate for Deacon's Orders."

Journal, Diocese of Georgia, 1853

———

1853: January 9

Bishop Elliott:

[Address to Annual Convention, meeting at Christ Church, Savannah]: "On Saturday, the 8th of January [1853], I examined Mr. Nevius for Deacon's Orders, and Mr. Gallagher, of the Diocese of North Carolina, for Priest's Orders, and on Sunday, the 9th, I ordained Mr. Gallagher, at the request of the Standing Committee of North Carolina, to the Holy Order of Priests, and Mr. Nevius to the Holy Order of Deacons. I regret to state that I was unable to retain Mr. Nevius in the Diocese. He was at once transferred to the Diocese of Alabama."

Journal, Diocese of Alabama, 1853

———

1853: January

"...Ordained deacon Jan. 1853 and went to Alabama—there met Thos. Fielding Scott, later Bishop of Oregon." Allen 1974

— Wetumpka, Alabama —

Christ Church

1853: February

"Was received into the Diocese of Alabama from the Diocese of Georgia as a Deacon early in 1853; evidently he was ordained Deacon in Georgia. Assumed charge of Christ Church, Wetumpka*, Alabama, in February, 1853, 'in connection with the Episcopal High School in Montgomery' Alabama.

Journal, 1853, p. 22 and 27"

Attachment to a letter from Rev. DuBose Murphy, Christ Episcopal Church, Tuscaloosa, Alabama to Howland Atwood, November 14, 1952. In this letter Murphy observed: "From the statement about his connection with the High School in Montgomery (a few miles from Wetumpka) and from one brief comment in his final parish report (in the Journal of 1855) to the effect that he was in close touch with 'Mrs. Tuomey's School for Girls' in Tuscaloosa,** I infer that he was interested in teaching, as were many clergymen in that period. But neither of these schools survived more than a year or two, and I do not think that any of their records are now available."

** This "brief comment" is not included in a reconstruction of the May 15, 1855 report given below.

———

1853: May 23
Brother John Livingston Nevius ordained Presbyterian minister by the Presbytery of New Brunswick.
Dictionary of American Biography, 1934, p. 444.

———

1853: June 15
Brother John married Helen Coan. John b. Ovid, N.Y. March 4, 1829; d. Chefoo, China October 19, 1893 (age 64 yrs. 6 mos.).

— LIBERTY HILL (DALLAS COUNTY) ALABAMA —
St. David's Church
(Mission Station, Athens)
(St. Mary's Mission Station, lower Dallas County)

———

1853: November 23
"Moved to St. David's Church, Dallas County,* Alabama and began ministry there Nov. 23 1853."
Attachment to a letter from Rev. DuBose Murphy, Christ Episcopal Church, Tuscaloosa, Alabama to Howland Atwood, November 14, 1952.
*St. David's Church was at Liberty Hill in Dallas County. See note to May 15, 1855 below. From a comparison of modern maps to the *Official Atlas of the Civil War* (New York: Thomas Yoseloff, 1958), plate 148, Liberty Hill, Dallas County, was at or very near to the site of present Safford.
"The Diocesan Missionary Society.... Manifestly the Bishop's apportionment to individuals was not overlarge. In 1853 the Rev. J. W. Mitchell, then assisting Bishop Cobbs, in St. John's Church Montgomery, and in connection with this work doing good service in the mission field of the county, received from the Society fifty dollars; the same amount was given to Rev. T. A. Morris, working in Jackson County; and the largest beneficiary, the Rev. R. D. Nevius, then a deacon officiating in St. David's Church, Dallas County, received only seventy dollars."
Whitaker (1898) 96-97

[1854]

1854: May 11-14 (Prob. May 14)*
Bishop Cobbs:**
"May 11, 12, 13 and 14. - Attended the Annual Convention of the Diocese in Carlowville [Alabama]. Whilst I could not but regret to see so small a number in the members in attendance, it was a great satisfaction to witness the kind and fraternal spirit which prevailed. The Rev. R. D. Nevius and the Rev. S. U. Smith were admitted to the Priesthood. The Sermon was preached by the Rev. J. M. Banister, and the Candidates were presented by the Rev. A. J. Massey."
"Bishop's Address," *Journal of the proceedings of the twenty-fourth annual convention of the Protestant Episcopal Church, in the Diocese of Alabama, 1855* (Mobile: Farrow, Stokes & Dennett, 1855) p. 23
*Rev. DuBose Murphy, Christ Episcopal Church, Tuscaloosa, Alabama in an attachment to a letter to Howland Atwood, November 14, 1952, "... the Ordination probably was on the 14th...."
** Rt. Rev. Nicholas H. Cobbs, Bishop of Alabama.

[1855]

1855: October 4
Bishop Cobbs:
"Oct. 4 - Went to Selma and ordained F.A.P. Barnard a deacon. The Sermon was

preached by the Rev. W. H. Platt, and the Candidate was presented by the Rev. R. D. Nevius."
"Bishop's Address" *Journal of the proceedings of the twenty-fourth annual convention of the Protestant Episcopal Church, in the Diocese of Alabama, 1855* (Mobile: Farrow, Stokes & Dennett, 1855) p. 23

———

1855: March 13
Bishop Cobbs:
"March 13 - Preached in St. David's, Dallas County, administered the Communion, and confirmed one white person and ten colored persons. It is truly refreshing to the heart of the Christian Minister to go into this Parish, and to witness the interest manifested by the Negroes in the services of the Church."
"Bishop's Address" *Journal of the proceedings of the twenty-fourth annual convention of the Protestant Episcopal Church, in the Diocese of Alabama, 1855* (Mobile: Farrow, Stokes & Dennett, 1855) p. 24.

———

1855: May 11
"Mr. Lay, of the first Committee, presented the following list of persons wishing to become members of the Society [for the Relief of Disabled Clergymen, and the Widows and Orphans of Deceased Clergymen of the Protestant Episcopal Church, in the Diocese of Alabama].... Rev. R. D. Nevius...."
Journal of the proceedings of the twenty-fourth annual convention of the Protestant Episcopal Church, in the Diocese of Alabama, 1855 (Mobile: Farrow, Stokes & Dennett, 1855) p. 40.

———

1855: May 15
Rev. R. D. Nevius:
[Annual report to the Diocese of Alabama]
"[Heading:] St. David's Church, Dallas County. - Rev. R. D. Nevius, Rector.
"Baptisms - White, infants   3
            Colored, Adults 7, infants 10   Total 17
"Confirmations, - White 1, colored 10   "   11
"Marriages - Colored   1
"Deaths - White   3
"Communicants - White, at last report, 13,
                died 1, present number   14
            Colored, at last report 5, present
                number   27
"Sunday Schools - Teachers 6, Scholars,
            Colored 100   Total 106
"Communion offerings $73.00
"Collections - Diocesan Missions   23.30
            Domestic   "   13.00
            Foreign   "   19.00
            For Church purposes
                generally   74.50
"Time spent in the Parish in the performance of its regular duties, since last report, twelve months.
"Besides this report, the Rector would add that services have been held (with occasional omissions from absence) in St. David's Church, on Sunday morning, for the whites, and in the evening for the slaves. Also, in Athens,* at night, during the last three months. Besides the services mentioned for the slaves, they have been instructed, during the most of the year, in a Sunday School, held in the evening after the sermon. In her sacraments, as well as worship, a growing interest and attachment for the Church is marked by full and punctual attendance.
"In Athens, also, I have been met by good and encouraging congregations. I have also, frequently visited the lower part of Dallas county,** where an interesting field of labor is daily opening. Here a Parish (prospectively called St. Mary's) will very soon be organized, and a neat country Church erected from an ample subscription already raised. This Parish will probably unite with St. David's in calling a Minister.
"Finding that the duties of my school, added to those of my Parish, overtasked my strength, I have resigned my situation, to take effect on 15th of May inst.

"In leaving this field of labor, I shall carry with me happy remembrances of a kind, zealous, and refined people, and a rich harvest of experiences and profit drawn mostly from my connection with the slave population.

"It is fitting here that due tribute should be paid to the moral worth and deep-toned piety of one who, from its beginning, was the Senior Warden of St. David's Parish, and long a prominent and influential member of this Convention— Capt. James Ellerby;*** who, upon the 6th of October, 1854, perfected his conflict as a true soldier of the Cross, in a Christian's victory over death.

"He brought the Christian zeal, and the sound intelligent judgement which made him a prominent member of St. David's Church, Cheraw, South Carolina,**** to our infant Diocese, and for years, even until his strength failed him, he was prominently known among her counselors.

"Among the first to welcome our beloved Bishop to his Diocese, he ever had a strong arm and a generous heart for the support of the Episcopate and every other noble institution. And he has gone to his rest with the hoary honors of a Christian old age upon his head."

Journal of the proceedings of the twenty-fourth annual convention of the Protestant Episcopal Church, in the Diocese of Alabama, 1855 (Mobile: Farrow, Stokes & Dennett, 1855) pp. 17-18. A list of clergy in attendance of p. 3 lists Nevius from St. David's Church, Dallas County with the following footnote: "Since accepted a call to Christ Church, Tuskaloosa."

*"Athens" could not have been modern-day Athens, Ala. in the extreme north of the state, roughly 160 miles from Liberty Hill, Dallas Co. (see below). Civil War-era maps suggest that no railroad connected the two at the time, and even if rail connections were available, "at night" suggests a more immediate vicinity to Dallas County.****

Curt Baker (see ** below) notes that the area around Carlowville is called "lower" Dallas County today. Because this area is twenty miles distant and because there was already an Episcopal church in Carlowville (see May 11, 1854 above), it seems more likely that Nevius was referring to an area on the same side of the Alabama River as Liberty Hill - perhaps in the vicinity of modern Five Points or Crumpton.

From a letter from State of Alabama Department of Archives and History to Howland Atwood, Huntington Library, March 10, 1953: "We think that you are mistaken about Dr. Nevius teaching in Alabama, or rather in Montgomery. As you will notice in his resignation at St. David's, he states that he is teaching there. We think that St. David's must have been at Liberty Hill, Dallas County, Ala., as it was there that Capt. James Ellerbe lived....* We find in the Tuscaloosa Independent Monitor, January 29, 1859, a copy of his sketch of his father-in-law, Michael Tuomey. It states that it is taken from the Alabama Educational Journal. We do not have the January 1859 copy of this letter."

****According to Mr. Curtis Baker, a staff engineer (now retired) with the Parks and Recreation Division, Oregon Department of Transportation, the site known today as Liberty Hill is approximately .4 mile from Highway 5 on a road which branches westerly three miles north of Safford. The Ellerbe place was just east of this junction. The site of the former town of Athens is about two miles south-southeast of Liberty Hill, or about 1 1/4 miles north of modern Safford. It is about 1/2 mile east of Highway 5 on an old road that crosses the highway 1.4 miles north of Safford. This old road appears on Civil War-era maps as the route westerly from Orrville via Liberty Hill to McKinley, Antioch and Linden.

Mr. Baker was born and reared in Dallas County. At my [David Powers's] request he checked the location of Liberty Hill and Athens during a visit with Alabama relatives in the summer of 1986. His information came from John Givham and Murphy Price, life-long residents of the area, and Robert Caine, a ninth generation resident. Mr. Baker observed that the area was settled "in the eighteen'teens," largely by people from northeastern South Carolina (where Cheraw is located) who voyaged around the Florida peninsula and then up the Alabama River. The vicinity "beat" or voting district is still known as Liberty Hill Beat.

DWP 7-7-87
____

1853-55:

"The Right Reverend Walter C. Whitaker, in his History of the Protestant Episcopal Church in Alabama, 1763-1898, mentions Mr. Nevius several times but makes no mention of his having built any churches. In addition to his pastorate at Christ Church, Tuscaloosa, Nevius is also referred to as 'officiating deacon' at St. David's, Dallas County, in 1857. This church is long gone, but had been built in 1844—well before Nevius came. Likewise, the church in Tuscaloosa was a new-classical-style [sic] building dating from 1829.

"Nevius took an interest in 'Christianizing' the slaves in his parish, according to Whitaker. And I've heard that a chapel was built in Tuscaloosa for black Episcopalians—possibly during Nevius's time. But evidently there is no record of its appearance."

Letter from Robert Gamble, Alabama Historical Commission to David Powers, February 22, 1984.

— Tuscaloosa, Alabama —

Christ Church
(St. Philip's Chapel, Tuscaloosa)
1855: ca. June 1
Nevius became Rector of Christ Church, Tuscaloosa, Alabama.

"Negro communicants formed a considerable portion of the congregation at Tuscaloosa, where they worshipped in a chapel built for their own use."

Christ Church parish, Tuscaloosa, built a chapel for its negro congregation about 1854."

From a letter to Howland Atwood from Rev. DuBose Murphy dated June 20, 1953: There was a separate building, St. Philip's Chapel, for the Negro communicants in Tuscaloosa; but Whitaker's dates are confused. The chapel was built because the gallery in Christ Church was not large enough to accommodate the Negroes who attended. The chapel was definitely not the gallery in the church. The chapel was built in 1852, and fell into disuse and was destroyed by fire about 1860. The gallery was removed when Christ Church was re-modeled in 1882."

"The ministerial salary, not over-large in prospect, was oftentimes even smaller in realization. Not a few of the clergy were compelled to eke out their salary by adding school-teaching to their clerical duties. Some of the clergy must have welcomed a bright Sunday morning and a large congregation with somewhat more than spiritual joy, for their whole support came from the unpledged Sunday offerings of the congregation."

Christ Church, Tuscaloosa, was never without its parish school. The operators of these schools brought about more frequent services throughout the diocese. It was a short step from brief devotional exercises in the schoolhouse to public prayer in the church or chapel, and this step at least three congregations had taken by 1854,— Montgomery, Tuscaloosa, and Marion. Daily morning prayer was said in these parishes." Whitaker (1898)

"Dr. Nevius' predecessor was, it seems, a bit erratic in some difficulty arising out of the Church school in which Johnson had an active part. Gradually the turbulence of the situation intensified and in June, 1854 'the vestry requested Rev. Johnson to resign the rectorship of the parish.' He flatly refused. 'The vestry promptly dismissed him, and, after one disorderly public service at which Mr. Johnson aired his personal grievances from the Chancel floor, he was immediately rebuked by several prominent parishioners, and the church doors were nailed up against him.' He attempted to establish a church of his own not too far distant from Tuscaloosa with a few parishioners who followed him, but his efforts were not long lasting.

Whitaker (1898) (after Atwood)

[1856]

1856: November 5
Half-sister Hannah Eastman married Dr. David Warner Birge.
1856: December 14
Helen S. Coan Nevius sailed from China in the clipper ship *Wild Pigeon* for a visit to the United States. She returned to China from New York on March 19, 1858.
Nevius (1895)

1857: March 30

Prof. Michael Tuomey died.*

*The census of 1850 for Tuscaloosa County, Alabama lists "Professor Michael Tuomey, age 46, Born in Ireland; Sara [wife], age 35, Born in [Mer.?] [sic]; *Margaret, age 12, Born in Alabama* [ca. 1838]; Manora, age 7, born in Virginia."

Tuomey was a professor of Mineralogy and Geology and was involved in the geological survey of Alabama. An article in the Gainesville, Alabama *Independent* noted that he had been "State Geologist" in South Carolina and Alabama, and that he died March 30, 1857, "of an affection of the heart and lungs, aged 51 years."

Eugene A. Smith, "Sketch of the Life of Michael Tuomey," *American Geologist*, Vol. XX (October, 1897), pp. 206-212, commented, "Practically all that is known concerning the early life of Prof. Tuomey, has been brought together by Rev. R. D. Nevius, of Tacoma, Washington, in an article published soon after Prof. Tuomey's death in the Alabama Educational Journal. ...[A] daughter, Minnie, was married after the death of her father, to the Rev. R. D. Nevius, the pastor of Christ Church in Tuscaloosa, now of Tacoma, Washington."

An article entitled "Biographical Notice of Prof. M. Tuomey, A.M." appeared in the *Alabama Educational Journal*, Vol. 1, No. 4 (January, 1859) pp. 111-119 [see below]. Authorship for the article is given simply as "for the Educational Journal."

1857[?]: May

"In the 26th Annual Convention [of the Protestant Episcopal Church of the Diocese of Alabama, of May 1857(?)] we find Rev. R. D. Nevius at Christ Episcopal Church at Tuscaloosa where he remained until he left the state [in 1865 or 1866, see below].*

From a transcript attached to a letter from State of Alabama Department of Archives and History to Howland Atwood, Huntington Library, March 10, 1953.

1857: November 26

Nevius's thirtieth birthday.

[1858]

1858: March 19

Helen S. Coan Nevius returned to China from New York. She had left China to visit the United States on December 14, 1856.

Nevius (1895)

————

1858: May 11

Minnesota became the 32nd state.

————

1858: May 11

Rev. R. D. Nevius

Tuscaloosa May 11, 1858.

"Prof. Gray

"Dear Sir:

"I take the liberty of sending you a plant that I have been unable to determine. I cannot think it undetermined as it is not rare though not common.

"I found the specimens which I sent last year before I procured your valuable manual and have not been able to procure a specimen for analysis since. Although I cannot think it unknown to you I will take the liberty to affix a description then made.

"I send also a Sedum which is undetermined in your manual unless it may be called S. puchellum form which it differs in color and in that it has *very rarely* thin spikes. It is from the same locality as the other. I should not think it worth troubling you with this were I not sending the other.

"I have the satisfaction of believing it will reach you quite fresh as now after three weeks it is yet blooming though in press.

"Please do me the favor to give me the names of these two plants and enclose and direct as by the accompanying envelope.

"Very Respectfully

"Your obedient Servant

"R. D. Nevius

"Shrub 2 - 5 ft. high

"Leaves thinly pub. with oppressed hairs above and on veins below, petiolate ovate, accuminate crenate dentate, *Stipulate*, petioles 1/8 inch long

"Calyx monosepalous 5 parted, deflexed, green,* foliaceous, ciliate dentate.

"Petals. none

"Stamens 00. hypogenous 2/3 as long as calyx conspicuous.

"Anthers two lobed

"Capsules[?] 2, distinct

"Styles 2 nearly as long as stamens.

"Flowers axillary and terminate on peduncles nearly as leaves. Sometimes 2 - 4 crowded on the summit of the short leafy branches.

"Grows in thickets on rocky cliffs in rich soil."

*Inserted, perhaps not in Nevius's hand.

1858: May 29

Rev. R. D. Nevius:

"Christ Church Rectory

"Tuscaloosa May 29, 1858

"Prof. Asa Gray:

"Dear Sir

"Your very kind and pleasing answer to my letter of the 11th inst. waited my return from Huntsville several days. I hasten to tell you of my very agreeable surprise at finding that I had made a discovery and to thank you for the kind notice you have taken of the same.

"Had I not distrusted my own analysis of the plant, attributing my failure in it, to ignorance, I should have sent it a year ago. Since then I have learned something more of the study of your excellent books, Systematic & Structure Botany, and the Manual &c for which in a humble way, as a [illegible], I thank you in the name of the lovers of the herbal craft.

"Failing in my analysis I submitted the plant to Dr. Garland of the University who agreed with me in thinking it a new species under Spirea. Of a new Genus we did not dream.

"I regret that I did not correct a mistake that was manifest to us in comparing an analysis of the dried specimen with my old analysis of a year ago. I meant to correct it but forgot it after the specimen was prepared for the mail. The Stamens are manifestly not hypogenous. I meant to say and should have said had I not thought it all unnecessary to send you any description that the absence of a Corolla was our great hindrance in our analysis. I am satisfied that there is none as I have seen the plant in all stages of flowering. I should say that I was told in the neighbourhood where it grew that it was an Evergreen which I can hardly believe. Its locality is 9 miles away and I have not been able to determine this point but will watch it this winter.

"I shall be very glad to see your published account of the plant which will I suppose be found in the American Journal of Science and nothing will give me greater pleasure than to correspond with you if you will do me the favor to help me in my study regarding those plants with which I have found difficulty.

"Regarding the Sedum. I am satisfied it is not S. Pul= [Sedum pulchellum] as I found a Sedum in the Cumberland Mountains on my way to Huntsville, which answered to S. Pul except that the leaves are closely sessile and complexiant. Sedum Sparsiflorum[?] I cannot compare it with as I have not Torrey & Gray Flora North America.

"I found many new and interesting plants on my way to Huntsville over the Com. Mts. but have not yet been able to study them up. I was much surprised to find Frasera Carolinensis which I had only seen in Michigan long ago in my first studies of the science.

"Two years ago [1856] I began with Prof. Tuomey to make a register of the Flora of this neighbourhood, but before we had taken our first ramble together He was lost to me and to the Scientific world by death. Since then I have pursued the study alone with many regrets for his loss both as a friend and a teacher. In these studies I have collected 3 or 4 hundred plants and now have a large number upon my shelf of 'Innominateae.' Of these I think some may be new and many imperfectly and incorrectly placed. Nothing would give me greater pleasure than to subject them to your criticism on opportunity. In my rambles one of your old pupils W. S. Wyman late of Montgomery, and now Prof. of Latin lang' in our University is my frequent companion and an enthusiastic lover of the Science of botany. With him I found this Spring a plant (enclosed) upon the rocky moraye [? "moraine"?] of our river which we could not correctly place. It seems to be a Phacelia bipinnatifia, or Eutoca parviflora except for 5 sinuses in the corella tube about midway, very much as in Kalmia Colifolia. I send you part of the only plant we found. I have found also a Cosmanthus [Phocelia], whether Furshii [Purshii] or Cosmanthus [Phocelia], whether Furshii [Purshii] or fimbriata I can scarcely tell in my confusion between Gray, Wood, Darby and Elliott. It seems however to be P. fim'. I send a specimen of this also.

Croomia* is abundant here and I will take pleasure in sending you specimens with fruit if I am not too late. And my dear Sir let me add, I shall esteem myself fortunate in being able to do you any service and you may command me in every respect in which I may be able to aid you in your invaluable researches. I will send you the specimens you desire as soon as I can go for them and prepare them for the mail.

"I am dear Sir
"Very truly your obliged
"and humble servant
"R. D. Nevius

"Please do me the favor to tell me if other volumes of your Genera &c may be expected soon. I have by me now the two volumes published from the University library, and should like much to get them all as they come out.

"N"

*Croomia is a genus of the family Stemonaceae, "erect herbs or herbaceous vines or low shrubs from tuberous roots or creeping rhiszomes, commonly producing lactone alkaloids of a unique type...." There are three genera of stemonaceae with three species in the genus Croomia. "Except for one species of *Croomia* that is native to southeastern United States, all species of Stemonaceae are confined to eastern Asia, Malaysia, and northern Australia."

――――

1858: June 21
Rev. R. D. Nevius:

"Christ Church Rectory
"Tuscaloosa June 21, 1858.
"Prof. Asa Gray
"Dr. Sir
"Immediately on receiving your kind note of the 8th inst (for which with your generous offer of assistance in my study and your valuable Flo' N. A. [Flora of North America] I thank you most sincerely. I arranged an excursion to the locality of the new unknown and procured the specimens herewith enclosed. I send them immediately as the carpels are not fully perfected and would wither in drying. I hope they will reach you in good order. I send also a specimen of the wood. The shrub has the general habit of growth of the Philadelphus and resembles it very much except in foliage. In the thickets where many twigs grow from the same root, one twig is gracefully bent over another toward the sunny side of the cliff forming a dense mass of foliage almost impervious to the sunlight. The shrub is a very beauty and well worth cultivation.*

"In every instance I noticed that the fruiting carpels which are very few as you will see in proportion to the flowers. One carpel was perfected to the obliteration of the others which are truly as you said mostly four. (They are very minute in the flower hence my mistake in my first examination.) I will not occupy space in detailing my examination of the fruit, as I doubt not it is sufficiently advanced to afford you a satisfactory examination though it will be somewhat wilted.

"I will still watch the ripening fruit and send it to you when perfected.

"If the plant proves to be a new Genus it would be gratifying to me and to my friends and associates in the study, Prof. Wyman & Dr. Mallet of the University (I hope you know the latter gentleman also, at least by reputation) to be permitted to name the Genus in complement to our old lamented friend Prof. Tuomey — Tuomeya.—

"I have not doubt the plant was known to him as he had studied the flora of this neighborhood very thoroughly, and that his sudden death cut short in this instance,

and in many others, a further investigation Please inform me if this name will be agreeable to you. I will leave it to you, if you please, the rite and form of baptisation [sic] and the pleasure (as it will be such I doubt not] of introducing it formally into the family of known plants and of making it known to science.

"The Sedum has cast its seed and has withered. It has scarcely any roots, as its name signifies it barely sits upon the rocks. I have been almost too late for the seed. I send you however some chaff with a few seeds, from which I have no doubt you can secure living specimens next year. I send also a few sprigs of the least dry plants and a few living roots.

"Croomia is abundant, the locality is large. I found it Saturday 6 miles away from this place, where it was first discovered. I do not doubt it can be found anywhere on the river for miles above and perhaps below Tuskaloosa. The fruit is not yet mature. I send some in its present state. I will send you another box, with Croomia and Tuomeya (?) [sic] as soon as the pods are repinned [sic, ripened?]. I am daily working up my Innominate, as I get another chance at them. I do not think them of sufficient importance to justify my giving you trouble with them. I thank you however very heartily for your permission to do so. It is possible that I may visit my home this summer, if so I will give myself the pleasure of bringing them to you myself. You kindly propose indemnifying me for my expenditure in P.O. stamps. Permit me to say dear Sir that aside from the pleasure and advantage of a correspondence with you I esteem it a great privilege to contribute in any way to your success in collecting the Flora of our country. And I beg you will permit me to send you what I choose at my own cost.

"I heard of your new work now in press, 'How Plants Grow' some time since and it was so perfectly the thing I wanted—; judging from your excellent chapters on that subject in Shuck' & Spt[?] Bot'- that I immediately ordered 20 copies as soon as issued, for distribution among my little (and big) friends.

"You had the kindness to ask if I could get the Flora of N. Amer if left for me at Ivison & Phinneys.** I answer with great pleasure yes, and I shall ever be obliged. I will direct Mr. Daniel Dana, of whom I order all my books to call and get it for me and send it with some books I am now about to order.

"I meant to have said above that I beg you will give the Tuomeya (if I may so call it) its specific name. If you wish a descriptive name its beauty and the peculiarity of its habitat will readily suggest one.

"I beg you will do me the favor to write me soon letting me know if this plant does establish a new Genera, and if you concur with me in the choice of a name, for really my interest in it and my desire to call it by its own name and to communicate my designed compliments to Mrs. Tuomey will hardly break delay.

"I am dear Sir
"With every sentiment of regard
"Very truly yr obt Servt
"R. D. Nevius

*According to an obituary in the *New York Times* (December 16, 1913), "Neviusia Alabamensil" [sic, Alabamensis] became a popular hothouse plant in England. See also Oregon Historical Society Scrapbook 44, p. 74. The common name for the plant is "Snow Wreath."

**Publishers "active in the textbook field." Asa Gray "gradually shifted his books" to them after Putnam's financial difficulties of 1854. Dupree, 1959, p. 203.

――――

1858: July 12
Rev. R. D. Nevius:

"Tuscaloosa
"July 12" 1858
"Prof Asa Gray
"Dear Sir
"Your kind letter of June is before me and [I] hasten to thank you for your promptness in writing as well as for cordial agreement with me in naming the New Genus. Your disposition to do me the unmerited honor of giving it my name was pleasing to me, but far less so than my ability to honor the name of a most excellent and deserving man - my friend - in such an enduring monument, but [?] lead[?] us to the name.

"Shall it be written Tuomeya or Tuomaea? I think the former with the accent thus[:] Tuo'-mey-a. The name, you now is Tuomey - Toomey. If written Tuomaea, the long diphthong at[?] [illegible] is more likely to divert the accent from the first syllable than if written with the termination eya. I suppose it makes but little difference which termination is used, and eya is more true to the name. The name is Irish. Prof T was himself from Ireland.

"As to the Sedum. I really hope it is new that I may by your favor enter by enrollment, in a more modest way than you at first designed, the honorable and gentle guild of Botanists.

"I think however that you have mistaken my name, as indeed all people do to whom I do not particularly say it is Nevius not Nevins. My name you will see is already latinized. Perhaps so long ago as when written Naevius by Horace. If so, though I may not claim with modesty a descent so remote, I may with reasonable pride see my name (through your works) incidentally mentioned like his upon a 'monument more lasting than brass.'

" I went out yesterday for the fruit which you desire. Croomia is not yet perfected. I have several specimens in press for you and will send you one by this or the next mail, as you desire, though the plate in the Genera is as perfect as it is beautiful. I will also send a fine specimen of Tuomeya, as you may want it for the same purpose.

"The fruiting plants of Croomia are not more than 5 per cent. I fear I cannot procure many seeds. I will however send all I can get. Tuomeya is on this side of the river in only one insignificant locality. I found not one perfected seed but many good specimens which as they retain the persistent stamens are almost as desirable as specimens dried in the Spring. I am satisfied that it has no corolla as indeed I think you will be when you note again the insertions of the Stamens upon the calyx. Dr. Mallet who saw the plants which I found a year ago is of the same opinion. I have not the slightest recollection of a bud. We looked for some to settle the question of the corolla but found none on the specimens from which we worked. I wish Mr. Sprague, to whom I beg to be commended, success in his restorations.

"I will gladly do for you and Dr. Lindley all I can in making a collection of our Orchids. There are but few here, only a few species under Plantanthera, Spiranthes and Coralloriga. Cypripediums are said to be in the neighborhood, but I have not yet found any.

"Very truly your obt Servant R. D. Nevius"

———

1858: late summer
Nevius visited Ovid, New York. See above and below.

———

1858: October 18
Rev. R. D. Nevius:
"Tuscaloosa
"Oct. 18, 1858.
"Prof Asa Gray
"Dear Sir
"I found it impossible to visit Boston on my last visit home, and to my great regret, was disappointed in my expectation of seeing you. I did not, as I intended, send you my plants, because I found by study with a couple of very good botanists in my native town that it was probable I had nothing valuable to you.

"I am obliged to you for two letters I received from you, one in N. Y. and one at Ovid and I beg, you will now keep the promise made in them and advise me of the progress of Tuomey etc. I am very glad the Croomia reached you in good condition. I hope you will be able to make something of them. I have a few more seeds of Tuomeya which I will send enclosed and I have also some seeds of Nelumbium luteum [a water lily] which I will gladly send you if they will be of any service to you.

"I made good use of the few plants I took on with me. I got by exchange nearly 600 determined specimens, among them a good collection of mosses and ferns and a large and almost full suit of Carices [pl. of Carex, a large genus of grassy-looking plants; a sedge]. I shall still keep up my Studies and will gladly serve you in any way.

"In the meantime accept my thanks for your favor in introducing Tuomeya to the world.

"And continue to write as occasion serves to.

"Dear Sir your obliged
"and obedient Servant
"R. D. Nevius
"Can you tell me where I can get the names of the b[o]rders[?]* printed as labels for my Herbarium? Can you tell me also where I can get the best and cheapest paper for the same and at what price?

"Please let me have your answer as soon as convenient as I have an order pending at one of our home manufactories.

"I shall never get through writing I fear.

"I should not forget to say that I brought home your 'Flora of North America,' for which I thank you most heartily. As also for your late book 'Botany for Beginners.' I do not doubt it will be a book for the times and I hope it will prove a profitable one to you and find large sales."

*The entire letter seems to have been written in haste, as by one clearing his desk after a period of absence.

———

1858: November 15
Rev. R. D. Nevius
"Tuscaloosa
"Nov. 15" 1858
"Prof Asa Gray.
"You may know how greatly I have been disappointed by being anticipated by Prof. Harvey in choice of a name for my new Genus, when I say that the discovery itself scarcely gave me more pleasure than the opportunity if afforded for honoring the name of my deceased friend.

"Prof Harveys compliment has given me great pleasure, yet I cannot help wishing that he had been a few months later in publishing his book.

"I do not see what can be done but to accept your kind proposition to give the Genus the less honorable name Vevia, except it would be proper to call it Toomara and trust to the usual note to designate the person. I can hardly hope however that you will think this proper. I will leave the whole matter entirely in your hands, and beg you will be godfather to the new Genus.

"I only fear that it will be found in some less known book, that I have been superseded in this discovery. I do not however know of any new work lately issued, or about to be issued, except a new edition of Woods Botany. I wish I had specimens to send to him and Darby, but I must wait until Spring.

"I am delighted with your Botany for Beginners and although I have my class (I am instructing a class in the School of Mrs. Tuomey) pretty well on in the 'Manual' and do not need a more elementary book now, I shall order some for prizes, and for gift books. Many girls will study it when they have left school, who will not study the Manual.

"I have never studied the Carex at all, but with the advantage of the determined species I have procured by exchange I hope I may be able to find the one you want. In the meantime I will watch the Croomia.

"I must say that I find the New Genus makes excellent pipe stems. I will tell you how I found it out. A friend of mine brought me from Florida a pipe stem of a superior quality. I noticed one day, that it closely, yet not exactly, resembled the New Genus, and on examination of the wood under the microscope, I am convinced, that if it is not the same plant, it is the same Genus, and equally good for the purpose above mentioned. If you are a smoker I shall be glad to send you one. In Florida it is known as Indian Reed, though the name is a misnomer.

"Again thanking you for your distinguished kindness
"I am Dear Sir
"Your obedient Servant
"R. D. Nevius"

[1859]

1859: January
Nevius's article on Prof. Michael Tuomey appeared in the *Alabama Educational Journal*, Vol. I, No. 4 (January, 1859), pp. 111-119. The author is listed simply as "For the Educational Journal."

"Biographical Notice of Prof. M. Tuomey, A.M."

[Beginning at p. 111] Nevius noted that Tuomey was born "in Ireland, in the city of Cork, on St. Michael's day [September 29], 1805." He was educated at home and at his grandmother's in the [112] country. From her he learned a love of Nature and much about the science of Botany. Another relative instructed him in mathematics. At seventeen he joined a friend teaching school in Yorkshire, England. [113] This lasted only a few months, however, and at an uncertain date Tuomey migrated to Philadelphia with letters of introduction. After several months he "purchased unoccupied land in a remote county of Pennsylvania" and with a partner began farming "with a swelling of pride and self-gratulation into possession of an estate far more troublesome than lucrative." Disenchanted with the rudeness of frontier life, he abandoned his share of the farm to his partner. Then for several years he was engaged as a private tutor by a family in Maryland. While there he met [114] Miss Sarah E. Handy, whom he married later in 1837.

"In the meantime, being anxious to pursue his scientific studies, he went to Troy, N.Y., and graduated in the Rensselaer Institute." After graduating he was engaged in building a railroad (at which time he was married), but the "great monetary crash" in 1838 ended the road building. He taught school for eighteen months and then he and his wife "established a flourishing and lucrative seminary in Petersburgh, Va." While there he assembled "large collections in Geology, Mineralogy and Paleontology" and "entered into correspondence with Agassiz.*

Tuomey corresponded with others as well, including Jas. Hall, State Geologist of New York, Prof. Bache, Superintendent of the Coast Survey, Prof. Dana of Yale College, and Dr. Gibbs of Charleston; "also with many foreign scientific men" including Prof. Hervy of Dublin who named a new genus of algae *Tuomeya* after him. He discovered a valuable bed of "infusorial earth"** (described in a paper published in Silliman's Journal) near Petersburgh, and through Edmund Riffin of the department of Chemical and Practical Agriculture was recommended to Gov. Hammond of South Carolina as State Geologist in 1844. [116] He contributed to publication of "Fossils of South Carolina."

In 1847 he was appointed chair of Geology, Mineralogy and Agricultural Chemistry at University of Alabama, again recommended by Ruffin, and in 1848 was appointed State Geologist as well (without extra pay) by the Governor. In 1849 he gave up his chair at the University to conduct the survey for two years, and then went back to the University [in 1851?] to organize and publish his findings. Before completing this task he became ill and "at length" died March 30 [1857]. [117] "His disease was extremely painful, and his mind seemed inactive under it...."

Though Nevius candidly admitted that Tuomey's "deepest, holiest thoughts and feelings were not uttered in words," he thought that no one could look upon Tuomey's life without failing "to see in him the working of true Christian principle," and that he had been "the perfection of Christian manhood." "In his study of Natural Sciences, Prof. Tuomey opened the book of Nature with all the reverence with which he opened his Bible. To him it was the Book of God, filled with inspired and unequivocal revelations of His love to man—abounding in sublime themes suggestive of thought, in a true poetry of simplicity and harmonious adaptation of cause and effect, in a history fresh, after the lapse of untold ages, from the hand of God, and in a law of harmonies and correspondences worthy of the wisdom of its Divine Maker. And while he regarded this book with all the reverence of a Christian, he studied it with all the ardor of a pupil, whom Nature herself taught; and he loved his teacher with all the devotion of a son."

"In social life, Prof. Tuomey was what all pure minded and true men, who are learned, are—a very agreeable person. To a refined taste in nature, in arts, and in the proprieties of life, he added a rich and sparkling humor, and a wit both subjectively and objectively operative. [118] He was a man of great information, as might be expected on one who read so much, and possessed such a habit of close and quick observation; and his memory was stored with instructive facts and amusing anecdotes. All these qualities, joined to the manners of a finished gentleman of the old school, and a manly, dignified presence, made him a most agreeable companion."

*Louis Agassiz (1807-73). Swiss born, becoming professor of natural history at University of Neuchatel, 1832, which he made a center for scientific study, migrating to the U.S. in 1846 and teaching at Harvard from 1848; strongly influencing a generation of scientists.

** Infusoria (found in infusions of decaying animal or vegetable matter) are a class of protozoa, minute organisms similar to diatoms. Diatomaceous earth, the fossil remains of diatoms, a microscopic class of algae, is useful for sound and heat insulation, in making explosives, and for filters and abrasives.

——

1859: February 14
Oregon became the 33rd state.

——

1859: February 21

"Tuscaloosa
"February 21" 1859

"Prof Asa Gray
"Dear Sir
"I have just received with great pleasure a sheet containing your article upon the New Genus—Neviusia, and a few days before a sheet came to me by your kindness containing your notice of Henrys Nerris[?] &c. I am greatly obliged to you for both and take pleasure in again expressing my obligations and my thanks for your favor and kindness shown in the matter of Neviusia—both in bringing it out and in keeping me appraised of its progress.

"Your kind notice of my first intention in giving it a name, and your pleasing tribute to Prof. Tuomey has been particularly gratifying to me. Your article is quite an imposing one and it surprised me by its ful[l]ness. I am glad to know that there is an importance in its discovery, aside from the discovery itself, in its bearing upon the affinities of other genera.

"The Spring is now fast opening. I am every day expecting to see the Claytonias [spring beauty], Sanguinarias [blood root], and Saxifranges (our first flowers) with the violets, in bloom. My correspondence with you has given me new zeal in the study of plants, especially as it has taught me how very little I know, and what progress I can yet make.

"Neviusia will be in bloom in two weeks, and I shall make a large collection of specimens for distribution and exchange. I will furnish you with as many as you wish.

"I hope you will tell me in your answer to this letter if I may yet confidently send specimens to my friends. I do not know if you designed to send a plate of it in the sheet which I have received. No plate came with it. I suppose it is not yet published. I look for it with great interest.

"I shall keep a sharp look-out for Croomia, but fear I shall be unable to discover germinating seeds in the right stage for determining the quarstis vexata[?].

"Will you tell me how I can procure a copy of the Published Memoirs of the Acad. S. which contains your article upon Neviusia? I have learned that the publications of the Society are not sent to our University.

"Please command me in all things in which I can serve you.
"Very truly your obliged
"and obt Servant
"R. D. Nevius"

——

1859: published after February 21
Prof. Asa Gray:
"NEVIUSIA, a New Genus of Rosceae.
"By ASA GRAY, M. D.

—————

"(Communicated to the Academy, August 12, 1858.)

—————

"A Specimen of the plant which forms the subject of this communication was sent to me, in May last, by the discoverer, the Rev. R. D. Nevius, of Tuscaloosa, Alabama. A specimen of a *Sedum* also apparently undescribed, was communicated at the same time. The two plants were detected by Mr. Nevius in the spring of 1857, along cliffs in the vicinity of Tuscaloosa.

"The *Sedum*—a small, white-flowered species, with short and nearly terete leaves, which may be named Sedum Nevii—cannot be adequately characterized until better specimens shall be obtained.

"The other plant—a shrub, with the habit of *Spiraea*—was at once seen to be a new type. As the discovery of a shrub of a new genus within the United States east of the Mississippi is an uncommon event, and as this plant presents some points of peculiar interest, I take this opportunity to indicate its characters and affinities.

"Mr. Nevius, upon being informed of the interest of his discovery, proposed to dedicate the genus to the memory of our lamented friend, the late Professor Tuomey, who, when suddenly removed from the scene of his scientific labors, was officially and most efficiently prosecuting his researches into the geology and the whole natural history of the State of Alabama. So that this elegant shrub, peculiar to the district of his residence, was appropriately chosen by his near friend and associate to commemorate his scientific labors and deck his early tomb. But the publication of the third part of the *Nereis Boreali-Americana* (since the present communication was made to the Academy) shows that the name of *Tuomeya* is preoccupied, Dr. Harvey having dedicated to Professor Tuomey's memory a curious fluviatile Alga discovered by the latter in Alabama, as well as by the late Professor Bailey in Virginia.

"I may now, therefore, be permitted to name the present genus in honor of the discoverer. His name, however, is so nearly like that of the celebrated Roman poet, for whom (I presume) the learned Swedish mycologist has named his genus *Naevia*, that I must needs Latinize it in an unclassical, but not wholly unprecedented manner, as follows:—

"NEVIUSIA, Nov. Gen. Rosacearum.

[There follows a description of the plant in Latin.]

"N. ALABAMENSIS.—In praeruptis umbrosis prope Tuscaloosam Alabamae, ubi legit *Dom. R. D. Nevius*...." [The text of the article is accompanied by a plate labeled "NEVIUSIA ALABAMENSIS."*

Memoirs of the American Academy of Arts and Sciences, New Series vol. 6 part 2 (1858), pp. 373-377.

*According to an obituary in the *New York Times* (December 16, 1913), "Neviusia Alabamensil" [sic, Alabamensis] became a popular hothouse plant in England. See also Oregon Historical Society Scrapbook 44, p. 74. The common name for the plant is "Snow Wreath."

[1860]

1860: May
Rev. R. D. Nevius:
[From a report to the Annual Convention:]
"Among the communicants reported are five young men in the University of Alabama, and six young ladies belonging to 'Mrs. Tuomey's Home School.' This School is a true nursery for the Church, in principle and practice, and the Rector is glad to say that this portion of his charge has always been one most pleasant in labor and profitable results."
Journal, Diocese of Alabama, 1860, p. 26.

[1861]

1861: January 29
Kansas became the 34th state.

———

1861: April 12
Southern forces opened fire on Ft. Sumpter, South Carolina, beginning the Civil War.

[1862]

1862: March 9
Battle of the USS *Monitor* and CSS *Virginia* (former USS Merrimac) at Hampton Roads, Virginia.

———

1862: November 26
Nevius's thirty-fifth birthday.

[1863]

1863: January 1
President Lincoln issued the Emancipation Proclamation.
1863: June 10
West Virginia became the 35th state.

———

1863: November 26
Half-brother Benjamin Nevius Eastman married Cornilia Post: Benjamin Nevius Eastman b. Ovid, N.Y. January 28, 1840; m. Cornilia Post (b. vicinity Ovid, N.Y., April 16, 1844; d. March 23, 1866) November 26, 1863; d. (Syracuse N.Y.?) June 22, 1892 (age 52 yrs. 5 mos.).

[1864]

[From a history of the Episcopal Church in Alabama, 1898]:
"In 1864 the Bishop [Wilmer] himself confirmed twenty-one Negro adults in Tuscaloosa, where the Rev. R. D. Nevius was interesting himself deeply in the Christianization of the slaves. That such work as this should have been conducted amidst the horrors of a war of which the Negro was the immediate occasion is remarkable. That it should have been persevered in despite the disastrous crisis evidently now near at hand is confirmation strong as Holy Writ of the sincerity and unselfishness of those who labored, and of those who permitted and encouraged the work.

"As the war progressed a new sphere of beneficence opened to the Church. An unusual number of orphans were the fruit of the battle-field, and many of these orphans were left entirely destitute. To many the Church became a veritable nursing-mother. St. John's, Montgomery, was the first parish to undertake the systematic care of orphans. Its 'Bishop Cobbs Orphans Home' was in active operation throughout the entire conflict, and when the Federal troops occupied the city the commanding officer, ascertaining that the Home was named after his old minister in Cincinnati, detailed a special guard and furnished the Home with a month's supply of provisions.

"The Bishop having commended this parish's benevolence to the diocese as worthy of imitation, the Council of 1864 passed a series of resolutions calling on every parish to establish within its boundaries a similar institution. This was a rather more sweeping expression of opinion than the Bishop either expected or desired; for while he believed that a single large institution was less desirable than several small ones he perceived, plainly enough, that it was not practicable, nor desirable, to establish a Church Home for Orphans in every parish. Therefore as the evolution of the scheme had been left to him, he settled upon Mobile and Tuscaloosa as the places where the orphans might most easily be collected. These places, in addition to Montgomery's existing Home, would suffice for the present.

"The attempt at Mobile was ill-timed and unsuccessful. The expense in Confederate money would have been enormous. The city was momentarily threatened by the enemy. Men were in no mood to hear of the planting of another institution, so straitened were they to obtain the necessities of existence, so doubtful of the morrow. The Churchmen of the place, with whom the Bishop held preliminary consultation, emphatically discountenanced even a tentative canvass for subscriptions, and the Bishop reluctantly retired from the field.*

"More successful was the attempt at Tuscaloosa. Here the rector [Nevius] and the vestry were deeply interested, heartily seconded the Bishop's efforts, and gave more than eight thousand dollars. All the parishes in that section of the state were appealed to for help, and all responded most liberally. In a short time $50,000 had been secured. With $30,000 of this a building lot and garden were bought and a dwelling and school-house built. $10,000 was set aside for investment in real estate with a view to endowment, and the remainder was reserved for current expenses. (pp. 168-169)

"During the first few months of its existence only 8 orphans were received in the Home, but in conjunction with the Home a parochial school of 50 pupils was conducted. The immediate charge of this work was committed to 3 deaconesses whom Bishop Wilmer set apart by prayer, but without imposition of hands, in

Christ Church, Tuscaloosa, on December 20, 1864." (p. 170)

Rt. Rev. Walter C. Whitaker, *History of the Protestant Episcopal Church in Alabama. 1763-1898* [?], pp. 168-170.

*Footnote in original "Convention Address for 1865, p. 11."

1864: October 31

Nevada became the 36th state.

1864: December 20

Three Deaconesses were "set apart by prayer" at Christ Church, Tuscaloosa. See Whitaker (1898) above.

[1865]

1865: April 4

"On the third of April, 1865, news came that Croxton's Brigade was quite near, and a guard of citizens was stationed to guard the bridge. Assistance was asked from the cadets [at University of Alabama] and my grandfather [President Basil Manly] said that he himself with the cadets would take charge the next night. Alas! The next night was too late. That very night, about twelve o'clock , the family was awakened by a loud knocking at the front door. Going down, grandfather was met with, 'The Yankees are crossing the bridge!'

"Hurrying over to The University, he gave the command to sound the long roll. In a minute the whole corps of cadets was drawn up ready for action. Under the command of Captain Murfee, they marched at a double-quick toward town. On reaching the girls' college, they could see flashes and hear the shots of the battle then going on between the two skirmish lines about the brow of the hill. The battalion then moved as fast as it could run into a position in the rear of the skirmish line. Captain Murfee gave the command to his platoon to lie down and cautioned them to fire at the flashes of the enemy's guns. Though the enemy were veterans armed with Spencer magazine carbines, while the cadets had never been under fire before and were armed with muzzle-loading Springfield rifles, the enemy soon fell back across the bridge, having suffered some loss, while the cadets had but three wounded.

"Grandfather, fully realizing that if he permitted that handful of boys, few of them of age, to be butchered by the Yankee brigade, he would be execrated by every mother in the State of Alabama, ordered the cadets to retreat, much to the disgust and chagrin of those fiery rebel youths. On reaching the University, they were told to get together only what could be carried in their knapsacks. Again they were mustered and marched down the Huntsville road. It was farewell forever to dear Old University."

Account appearing in the 1906 *Corolla*, campus newspaper.

———

1865: April 4

"Frances Louisa Garland, wife of President Landon C. Garland, saved the home [President's Mansion] from destruction by Union soldiers in 1865. When she saw flames in the direction of the campus, she ran from the Bryce home [Dr. & Mrs. Bryce, where Nevius stayed on his visits in 1888 and again in 1912] where the family had taken refuge and demanded the soldiers put out the fire in the parlor.

"A Mansion in Dixie", history of the University of Alabama, www.sa.ua.edu/osm/corolla

———

1865 April 9

General Robert E. Lee's surrender at Appomattox.

———

1865: April

"During the Civil War, Tuscaloosa was not directly affected until early in 1865. In April of that year, the Federal forces occupied Tuscaloosa and burned the University of Alabama — then only two buildings; but they moved on in a few days. So, in all probability, Dr. Nevius went on about his normal duties without being much disturbed by the war. The University is about a mile and a half from the Church."

Letter from Rev. DuBose Murphy, Christ Episcopal Church, Tuscaloosa, Alabama, to Howland Atwood, Huntington Library, November 4, 1952.

———

1865: April 14

President Lincoln assassinated at Ford's Theater in Washington, D.C.

———

1865: April 15

John Livingston Nevius and Helen S. Coan Nevius arrived in the United States from China the same morning that President Lincoln died. They remained in this country until November, 1868.

Nevius (1895) incorrectly gave the date as "about" April 19.

———

1865: November

Nevius conducted two funerals and one marriage at St. John's Church, Mobile, Alabama. See Christensen (May 6, 1853) below.

———

1865: May 29

President Johnson issued his "Reconstruction Proclamation," granting amnesty to Confederates who took the oath of allegiance. Provisional governments organized in the rebellious states, which were required to amend their constitutions, abolish slavery and repudiate state war debt.

———

1865: December 31?

"On the list of clergy in the 1866 *Journal*,* the words 'on duty abroad' appear after his (Nevius's) name. His successor took charge of Christ Church (Tuscaloosa, Alabama) on February 2, 1866. From the notation on the portrait, I infer that he probably resigned as of Dec. 31, 1865."

"Journal, 1866 p. 7."

Attachment to a letter from Rev. DuBose Murphy, Christ Episcopal Church, Tuscaloosa, Alabama to Howland Atwood, November 14, 1952.

*Probably reported in May, the usual month for annual convocations of the Diocese of Alabama at that time.

[1866]

"On Duty Abroad"
Visit to Ovid

———

1866: January

Nevius conducted a baptism service at St. John's Church, Mobile, Alabama. See Christensen (May 6, 1953) below.

———

1866: February 2

Nevius's replacement took charge at Christ Church, Tuscaloosa.

———

1866: March 23

Half-brother Benjamin Nevius Eastman's wife Cornilia died.

———

1866: April 9

Civil Rights Act passed by Congress.

———

1866: June 6

Half-brother William Lyman Eastman married Augusta Nash.

———

1866: June 13

14th Amendment passed by Congress, defining national citizenship and guaranteeing equal protection of citizens under federal law. Ratification announced July 28, 1868.

———

1866: July 10

Half-sister Hannah Eastman Birge died in Ovid N.Y.: b. Ovid, N.Y. January 9, 1835; m. Dr. David Warner Birge (b. Manchester, Conn. Dec. 6, 1822; d. 1901) November 5, 1856; d. Ovid, N.Y. July 10, 1866 (age 31 yrs. 5 mos.)

— Oil City, Pennsylvania —

Christ Church
(St. John's Church, Rouseville)

1866: August 8

Nevius was given a call from Christ Church Parish, Oil City, Pennsylvania.* He moved there shortly thereafter and remained for "two years and six months" until February 1, 1869. See Nevius (February 1, 1869) below.

*Oil City, about fifty miles south of Erie in northwestern Pennsylvania, is less than 200 miles from Ovid. N.Y.

———

1866: October 21
Bishop of Pittsburgh:

"October 21st. The Twenty-first Sunday after Trinity was given to Oil City and Rouseville. In each town there was a flourishing church congregation. Christ Church, Oil City, and St. John's Church in Rouseville, worshipping in public Halls, under the energetic and effective ministry of their first Rector, then recently settled among them, the Rev. R. D. Nevius.

"In the morning I preached in Oil City — confirmed five and addressed them.

"In the afternoon and again in the evening, I preached in Rouseville; at the latter service confirming four persons and addressing them. In both of these places the work has gone on thoroughly and successfully; and the Offertory has been relied on for the payment of the minister's salary. The population there, and in all such towns and districts, must be in great measure uncertain and varying. This current year [1867] having been one of unusual depression in business, has not given the Church enterprise anywhere there the anticipated scope and help. But faith and energy have kept the work vigorous. A promising parochial school has been begun in Oil City; and if the same pastoral care be continued, I have full assurance as to the future of the congregations in both towns."

Journal, Diocese of Pittsburgh, 1867, p. 54.

———

1866: late [?]

"He [Nevius] was given a 'Letter Di[s]missory' to the Diocese of Pittsburgh by the Bishop of Alabama (Wilmer) late in 1866 or early in 1867. From then on, his name is not mentioned and his activities are not of record here.

"*Journal,* 1867, p. 12"

Attachment to a letter from Rev. DuBose Murphy, Christ Episcopal Church, Tuscaloosa, Alabama to Howland Atwood, November 14, 1952.

———

1866: late [?] [before May 5, 1867]

"In the 1867 Convention of the Diocese of Alabama, a letter dismissory to R. D. Nevius, to the Diocese of Pittsburgh. Page 12, May 5."

From a transcript attached to a letter from State of Alabama Department of Archives and History to Howland Atwood, Huntington Library, March 10, 1953.

[1867]

1867: March 1
Nebraska became the 37th state.

———

1867: March 2

First Reconstruction Act passed by Congress, dividing the South into 5 military districts, subject to martial law. Supplemented by acts of March 23 and July 19, beginning a decade of liberal reconstruction policies in the South.

———

1867: (n.d.)

Half-sister Mary Denton Eastman married James Harris: Mary Denton Eastman b. Ovid, N.Y. June 30, 1844; m. James Harris (b. vicinity Ovid, N.Y.; d. Cleveland, Ohio) 1867; d. Cleveland, Ohio, March 4, 1937 (age 92 yrs. 8 mos.).

———

1867: July 31 (or 1868: July 11)

"He married Minnie Tuomey" July 31, 1867.** She was a Southern Lady."

Letter from John Nevius Eastman to Howland Atwood, Jan. 10, 1953 (see below)

*See information from Census of 1850 at March 30, 1857 above.

**Honeyman, *Johannes Nevius and His Descendants,* 1895, gives the date of marriage as July 11, 1868. Honeyman's entry for Nevius (p. 584) contains many errors.

———

1867; November 5-9

The Episcopal and Presbyterian Churches both held national conventions in Philadelphia. Helen S. C. Nevius noted that John Livingston Nevius attended the Presbyterian convention and that the conventions "exchanged fraternal and ministerial courtesies," but makes no mention of Reuben Nevius.

Nevius (1895) p. 267

———

1867: November 26
Nevius's fortieth birthday
Photograph*

*Letter from Rev. Paul Hannaford, Christ Episcopal Church, Oil City, Pa. to Rev. Albert E. Allen, Hood River, Oregon, February 16, 1966:

...Enclosed you will find copies of two pages from our 75th Anniversary booklet which have a picture and information about Dr. Nevius. Though he was first Rector, it cannot be said he was the founder of the parish since the records indicate that a Dr. Purdon had been sent as a missionary in 1862 to the oil country by Bishop Potter of Pittsburgh. But Dr. Nevius also served the congregation of nearby Rouseville, which was dissolved after about 10 years of existence.

You will also find enclosed a copy of a letter sent by the Vestry extending a call to the Reverend Mr. Nevius. A typed copy of an item in the minutes of the Vestry is also enclosed, showing that one vestryman resigned when the first Rector's salary was decreased!

While we have a picture of Dr. Nevius, we do not have a picture of the church building during his time here since none existed. He had church services in several buildings which no longer stand. Enclosed are several photographs of Dr. Nevius....

———

1867: December 4

The Patrons of Husbandry, popularly called the Grangers, a secret association devoted to the promotion of agricultural interests, was organized in Washington, D.C.

[1868]

1868: February 24 - May 26

Congress passed bill to impeach President Johnson. Impeachment trial began March 4.

———

1868: June 22-25

By passage of the Omnibus Act, Congress readmitted Alabama, Florida, Georgia, Louisiana, North Carolina, and South Carolina to the Union. Mississippi, Texas and Virginia readmitted by 1870; Georgia reoccupied by Federal forces after admission in 1870.

———

1868: July 11 [?]

Honeyman gives this date for the marriage to Margaret Tuomey. See July 31, 1867 above.

———

1868: July 28

Ratification of the 14th Amendment, defining national citizenship and guaranteeing equal protection of citizens under federal law, announced. Passed by Congress June 13, 1866.

———

1868: ca. November 1

John Livingston Nevius and Helen S. Coan Nevius sailed from New York aboard the Steamer *Arizona* "about" November 1, bound for Aspenwall [273], where they took a train across the Isthmus of Panama, and sailed for China aboard the steamer *China* from San Francisco on December 3, 1868 [274].

Nevius (1895) pp. as cited.

——

1868: November 3

Election day. Ulysses S. Grant elected President by narrow popular margin, blacks casting the deciding votes.

[1869]

1869: February 1

Rev. R. D. Nevius (Parish Register):

"In August 8, 1866 the parish [Christ Church, Oil City] uniting with Churchmen afterwards organizing the parish of St. John's, Rouseville, extended a call to the Rev. R. D. Nevius of the Diocese of Alabama, who accepted the call with a canonical transfer to the Diocese of Pittsburgh, and immediately entered upon his duties as Rector. Services were held for about six months in Bascom['s Hall with good congregations, when the congregation removed to Excelsior Hall, which was occupied until Christmas, 1868, when a hall being fitted up in the Mercantile buildings[,] the congregation removed to it.

"In the Diocesan Convention of 1867, the parish with a perfected charter was admitted into union with the Diocese under the name of Christ Church Parish, Oil City,— By the recommendation of the Rector, who advised that the Church should be organized as a Free Church, the Offertory was adopted from the beginning, and was mainly relied upon for his support. The Vestry, however, guaranteed him a stipulated salary of $1200.

"The original call was, at the request of the rector, made for six months only. At the expiration of which period, another Call for one year was made on the same terms and accepted. In February, the rector who had always expressed his preference for the Free Church System, without pledges or subscriptions, accepted another Call for one year, the Vestry pledging him the amount of their individual subscriptions, $600, to be paid *through the Offertory* weekly, monthly or quarterly, the margin of the excess of the offering being relied upon for the rest of his support. He pledging himself and the Vestry that no subscription would be resorted to make up any deficiency. The Ladies Auxiliary Society meantime undertook (and with success) to meet all the contingent expenses of the parish. The result of this scheme was perfectly satisfactory to the rector. The Church as kept free from debt, the support of the rector was not felt as a burden upon the parish, and the parish was self sustaining from the first.

"In Feb. 1869 the rector, after two years and six months incumbency, having received a call to St. John's Church, Mobile, gave up the charge of the parish. William H. Colling and Mr. A. W. Myers being wardens and Mr. Benjamin F. Bundred being secretary.

"The present incumbent, who is the writer of this sketch, at the close of his ministry in this parish, is glad to be able to state that from the beginning the parish has been virtually and pronouncedly a Free Church, though without any formal declaration of the Vestry, no constitution and by-laws fixing this character upon the Church has been urged by him, because he wished the parish and vestry to be assured of success after a reasonable trial of the wisdom and the policy of the scheme. He prays that by the grace of God the parish may under this system remain as heretofore self sustaining and in perfect harmony, and that the ministration of those who follow him in his holy office may be abundantly blessed to the Glory of God in the establishing of His Holy Church and the saving of souls.

"Feb. 1st, 1869

"R. D. Nevius"

Parish Register, Christ Church, Oil City, Pa.

— Mobile, Alabama —

St. John's Church
1869: February

(1870: October 17)

"[From a Parish history}: 'On December 9th, 1868, the names of the Revs. J. H. Tichnor, S. C. Harris, E. G. Perryman, Horace Stringfellow and R. D. Nevius were voted on by ballot. On the 3rd ballot Rev. R. D. Nevius received 4 votes, was duly elected and immediately notified by the Secretary of the Vestry. After some little correspondence about the state of the Parish and kindred matters, Mr. Nevius accepted the call January 11th, 1869,* and arrived in February of that year, remaining as rector until February 1872, just three years.'

"During this time he baptized 216, presented 111 for confirmation, married 61, and buried 120. The records show that on Oct. 17, 1870 Margaret Mercer Nevius, age 29, wife of Rector, died during a yellow fever epidemic and was buried Oct. 18 by the Rev. T. A. Massey, D.D. Rev. Nevius also had yellow fever at this time.

"I also found in the records that in Nov. 1865 he had 2 funerals and 1 marriage, and in Jan. 1866 he held a Baptism service...."

Letter of Edith Christiansen, Secretary, St. John's Episcopal Church, Mobile, Alabama, to "Huntington Library," May 6, 1953.

*Atwood observed in his draft typescript that Nevius was particularly pleased to receive this call because his wife was expecting and naturally wanted to be near her mother.

——

1869: February 21

Bishop Wilmer (diary):

"Feb. 21, 1869. Preached in St. John's Church, Mobile. This occasion was made particularly interesting from the fact that the Rev. R. D. Nevius, who in former years had been so closely identified with the Diocese, officiated for the first time as Rector of the Church. He will be warmly welcomed into the Diocese of Alabama by his numerous friends among the clergy and laity."

Journal, Diocese of Alabama, 1869, pp. 10-11.

——

1869: February 26

Congress proposed the 15th Amendment, forbidding any state from depriving a citizen of his vote because of race, color or previous condition of servitude. Ratification proclamation March 30, 1870.

——

1869: September 24

"Black Friday," on which Secretary of the Treasury George S. Boutwell, with President Grant's approval, ordered sale of $4 million in gold, bringing the price down from 162 to 135 and ruining many speculators, including Jay Gould and James Fisk, though they had induced Grant's brother-in-law to lobby the President against the sale. This followed the "currency issue": on March 18 Congress passed the Public Credit Act, providing for payment of government obligations in gold.

——

1869: October 3

Bishop Wilmer:

"Oct. 3, 1869. Visited, in company with the Rev. Dr.* Nevius, a mission station on West Fowl River; confirming nine persons and celebrating the Holy Communion. We worshipped in a mere shell of an abandoned tenement at the time of my visitation, but since that time a Church has been erected upon the shores of the River, and is now awaiting consecration. The Mission is under the charge of the Rev. Dr. Nevius, who has in many ways aided the people in their pious endeavors by building a Church for the worship of God."

Journal, Diocese of Alabama, 1870, p. 33. "I might add that the Mission of West Fowl River evidently did not flourish, or else Dr. Nevius' successor at St. John did not follow up after his work there; at any rate it is not mentioned in the Reports after 1872." Letter from Rev. DuBose Murphy, Christ Episcopal Church, Tuscaloosa, Alabama to Howland Atwood, February 17, 1953.

*This was written after the visit, and after Nevius received his Doctor of Divinity degree in February, 1870 (see below). The annual meeting of the Convention was usually held in May.

1870: February 22

"Excerpt from Faculty Minutes, College of William and Mary, Feb. 28, 1870....

"The following degrees were conferred, to take effect the 22nd day of February, 1870:

"Degree of Doctor of Divinity on the...Rev. R. D. Nevins [sic], Rector of St. John's Church in Mobile, Ala.'

"(Signed) Benj. S. Ewell

"President"

Letter from Rose K. Belk, Reference Librarian, College of William and Mary, Williamsburg, Virginia, to Howland Atwood, Huntington Library, San Marino, California, March 26, 1953

———.

1870: March 30

Adoption of the 15th Amendment, forbidding any state from depriving a citizen of his vote because of race, color or previous condition of servitude, proclaimed. Proposed February 26, 1868.

———

1870: October 17

Margaret (Minnie) Nevius died.

———

1870: October 18

Margaret Nevius buried. Reuben Nevius ill.

See Edith Christiansen, May 6, 1953 below.

———

1870: October 17-18

"He married Minnie Tuomey July 31, 1867. She was a southern lady. They had twins who died. She died shortly after with yellow fever."

Letter from John Nevius Eastman, Ovid, New York to Howland Atwood, Jan 10, 1953 (see below).

———

1870: October 18

"Huntington Library

"San Mateo 15,

"California

May 7, 1953

"City Clerk

"Mobile, Alabama

"Dear Sir:

"Can you find a record of the marriage of Reuben Denton Nevius to Margaret Mercer (Minnie) Tuomey on either July 31, 1867 or July 11, 1868?

"Are there birth records of their twin sons about 1870, also their death records at about the same time? Is the death of Mrs. Nevius on Oct. 22 1870 [sic] on record? Is the death of her mother, Sarah E. (Handy) Tuomey on record?

"I will greatly appreciate any information you can send me.

"Sincerely,

"Howland Atwood.

[Typed at bottom:]

"In Mobile County the birth records begin in 1871 and death records in 1843. The death of *Margaret Nevius* is recorded here on October 18, 1870, we found no record of the others....

[stamped] "BOARD OF HEALTH
MOBILE, ALA."

[1871]

1871: April 19

Mr. Robert Gamble, 1984:

"It is by no means certain, but I *may* have another possibility of a Nevius church for you..., St. John's Church, Ashville, in St. Clair County, Alabama.... Built in 1860,* St. John's was moved some forty miles southwest of its original location to Elyton (forerunner of present Birmingham) in 1870....** As you can see, the structure lacks the more rigorously Gothic Revival lines of the Upjohn-type wooded churches built in Alabama.... The whole sense of proportion is less taut. Could this have been a Nevius effort at Gothicism...?

"Unfortunately, little is currently known about the short-lived parish at Ashville.... It seems logical that Mr. Nevius would've played a seminal role, since Ashville could've easily been on his missionary route from Tuscaloosa. And even had Mr. Nevius not been directly involved with the founding of the Ashville church, he could have perhaps furnished a plan."

Gamble letter, March 16, 1984

*From an unidentified newspaper clipping enclosed with Gamble's letter: "The Episcopalians had a church in Ashville for ten years. In 1860, a plot of ground was deeded to the Right Reverend A. H. Cobb, Bishop of the Diocese of ...Alabama. On this property St. John's was built, a beautiful little building of board and batten, painted grey, Gothic in style and cruciform in shape. The chancel was in the north and the entrance in the south. There were thirteen stained glass windows. The Reverend Morris was rector. After the Civil War there were not enough members to support the church and the doors were closed. Occasionally a rector would come up from Mobile for a special service.... In 1870 the building was sold.... It was carefully dismantled, loaded on ox wagons, and laboriously transported to Elyton, a distance of fifty miles. Then it was painstakingly rebuilt and the cornerstone was laid on April 19, 1871." [The side walls of this church (though in shadow) appear from the photograph to have an external post-and-beam frame and small buttresses, and a window in the shape of a "spherical triangle," like those at Union, The Dalles and Canyon City was set in the liturgical west end.]

** History of St. John's Parish, Elyton, Alabama; Proj. 3971, May 24, 1938: "The Rev. R. D. Nevius of Tuscaloosa" visited Elyton April 9-12, 1859; "preached four times," May, 1859; visited September 7, 1862; and "spent two Sabbaths and preached four times" around September 2, 1863.

———

1871: May 12

Journal, Diocese of Alabama, 1871, p. 65:

"In Dr. Nevius' report as Rector of St. John's Parish, Mobile, for the year ending May 12, 1871, he makes acknowledgments to the churches in Montgomery and Selma for sending relief (a cash offering, evidently) 'during the prevalence of the yellow fever' in the summer of 1870. "He would also gratefully record the kind attentions and official services of his brethren, the Parochial Clergy of the city, during his own illness at that time."

Letter from Rev. DuBose Murphy, Christ Episcopal Church, Tuscaloosa, Alabama to Howland Atwood, February 17, 1953.

———

1871: December 26

Judge Matthew P. Deady:

"Tuesday [December 26 was] Cold and snowy.... In the evening vestry [of Trinity Church] met at our house. Discussed the question of calling Dr. Nevius of Mobile, Alabama, in accordance with the Bishop's suggestion, or calling Mr. Burton.* Conclusion that the subject be tabled until the Bishop's return [from the East]. At my suggestion made up a purse for Mr. Burton of $75 to put upon the Christmas tree at Trinity on Thursday...."   Deady, December 27, 1871

*The Rev. George Burton, of whom Deady was fond, taught at the Bishop Scott Grammar School and was conducting services at Trinity Church until a permanent rector could be found. (Burton was also a teacher of Deady's children, who attended the school.)

[1872]

1872: January 29 (Monday)

Judge Matthew P. Deady:

"Sent telegram to Mr. George R. Barker at Germantown Pa for Dr. Nevius of Mobile containing a call to the Rectorship of Trinity parish, in pursuance of vote of the vestry on Saturday evening."

Deady, January 29, 1872

1872: February 10 (Saturday)
Judge Matthew P. Deady

...A vestry meeting at my chambers, no one present, but Brooke, Lewis, Glisan, and myself. Mr. Jordan attended with his plans and specifications for the new church. We examined them and gave him directions to obtain bids for the work.

Deady, February 10, 1872

————

1872: February 22 (Thursday)
Judge Matthew P. Deady:

"I got a telegram in the evening of that date from Dr. Nevius in Mobile Alabama, which I interpreted as an acceptance of the call to the Rectorship of Trinity Parish. Operator promised to repeat it for me and get more correct or unambiguous. Have not heard from it yet...."

Deady, February 22, 1872

————

1872: February
Nevius left Mobile, Alabama. See February, 1869 (Christensen, May 6, 1953) above.

————

1872: March 11 (Monday)
Judge Matthew P. Deady:

"Got letter from Dr. Nevius .... Nevius wanted a telegram consenting to his remaining in his present Parish until Easter morning—April 1. Spoke to Brooke & Hamilton* about it and they said yes...."

Deady, March 11, 1872

*Members of the vestry of Trinity Church. See also November 30, 1872.

————

1872: March 12 (Tuesday)

"Sent Telegram to Dr. Nevius, Mobile, as requested in his letter.

Deady, March 12, 1872

————

1872: March 15 (Friday)
Judge Matthew P. Deady:

"Mailed letter to Dr. Nevius, at Ovid, N.Y. containing 1st of Exchange on A E & C E Tilton N. Y. for $215.63 currency...."

Deady, March 15, 1872

————

1872: March 24 (Sunday)
Judge Matthew P. Deady

"...Vestry meeting last night. Agreed to build church and accept bid of Therkelsen for $17,455 it being understood that he will subscribe $445. Lewis subscribed $100 for his godson Henderson B. Deady. Nice thing, wasn't it?

Deady, March 24, 1872

— Portland, Oregon —

1866-1872:

"After the Civil War he went to Oil City, Pa., as rector of Christ Church, but in 1870 returned to Alabama, where he was rector of St. John's Church, Mobile, two years. Then he came to Portland, to become rector of Trinity Church."

Oregon Churchman, January, 1914

————

1872: April 25
Cornerstone laid for new Trinity Church, Portland.

————

1872: April 27
Portland Oregonian

"City.

"Passengers.—The steamer Ajax sailed from San Francisco to Portland on Saturday [April 27]. She brings a cargo of freight and the following passengers:

"Capt. J. C. Ainsworth...., Rev. Dr. Devins [sic]...."

Oregonian, April 29, 1872

————

1872: April 30
Portland Oregonian:

"Ajax will be due here this evening."

"Local Brevities" Oregonian, Apr. 30, 1872

————

1872: May 1
Oregon Churchman:

"Filling up the Ranks.— We are glad to record another and most important addition to our clerical force. Trinity, Portland, which is facile princeps among our parishes, has been for a year without a Rector. Several months since the vestry invited the Rev. R. D. Nevius, D.D., of Mobile, Alabama, to be their Rector. The invitation was accepted, and May the first set as the time for the Rector's arrival. The Doctor arrived by the last trip of the steamer Ajax [on the evening of April 30], and has already set energetically to work.

"Trinity parish has a noble work and bright future before her. The Doctor brings to his work thorough preparation and large experience. Under him we look that 'glorious things may be spoken' of this out-post of 'the city of God.'"

Oregon Churchman, May 15, 1872

————

1872: May 1 (Wednesday)
Judge Matthew P. Deady:

"Dr. Nevius called on me during the day. Makes a good impression."

Deady, May 1, 1872

————

1872: May 2 (Thursday)
Judge Matthew P. Deady:

"Dined at Brookes with the Rev[erends] Burton & Nevius. Good plain dinner. Elegant silver service. Dr. Nevius entertaining. Vestry meeting in the evening. Ordered the stained glass windows from Powell & Sons, London, for the new Church, on my motion.... Passed a resolution of thanks to Mr. Burton...."

Deady, May 5, 1872

————

1872: May 5 (Sunday)
Judge Matthew P. Deady

"Attended S[unday] S[chool] and church at Trinity Dr. Nevius officiated for the first time, except at evening prayer on Friday before. Sermon in the morning on the Holy Communion, only fair. In the evening on the church of the living God, very good. Both extempore, though the latter sounded as if it was memorized...."*

*See September 21, 1872, below.

Deady, Mary 5, 1872

————

1872: May 19 (Sunday)
Judge Matthew P. Deady

"Attended...at Trinity as usual. I don't think Dr Nevius has the gift of order or organization very largely developed, from what I saw of him in S S [Sunday School]."

Deady May 19, 1872

————

1872: May 26 (Sunday)
Judge Matthew P. Deady

"Attended...Trinity. Went with wife to [St. Stephen's] Chapel in the afternoon. On the way said to Mrs. Russel[l]*—You have a fine choral service here—'not me' says she, 'I have nothing to do with it. I consider it an abomination as I do this,' pointing her hands upward in imitation of Dr. Nevius elevation of the alms basin with the offering at Trinity. I told her that I thought she was thin-skinned."

*Edwin Russell (1830-92), branch manager of the Bank of British Columbia, town proprietor and industrialist, played a considerable part in Portland financial circles until an unwise investment ruined him. He disappears from the diary post 1878. His wife, Albina Page Russell (d. 1918) gave her name to the community of Albina." [McArthur, p. 8, notes that Albina was named by Russell for Albina V. Page,

20

wife of William W. Page. MacColl, p. 127, agrees with McArthur and provides additional detail about Page and Russell.

Clark, 1975, xxvii

———

1872: June 18 (Tuesday)
Judge Matthew P. Deady
"Today attended examination at the Grammar School and took lunch there. Edward* done well.... Dr. Nevius delivered an address at the close of the exercise.** Did not hear it all because Mrs. D became faint and [we] had to go out...."
Deady, June 18, 1872
*The eldest of Deady's three sons.
**For the text of this address, see *Oregon Churchman*, July 1, 1872.

———

1872: June 22
Journal, District of Olympia, 1902:
Nevius was officially connected with the Jurisdiction of Oregon and Washington Territory.

———

1872: July 9 (Tuesday)
"[Mrs. Deady and their son Edward were away.] Called in the evening at The Hall [St. Helen's Hall]. Met Miss Lydia [Rodney]* and had a book chat with her.... During the evening Bonnell** and Nevius came in, also Mrs M[orris] when the conversation became more general, but not more interesting. Neither B or N but particularly the latter interest me in conversation. Now I like to talk with Burton or Laing dearly well. There is some food in it. The truth is I am not interested in mere scientists, particularly the petty microscopic ones.***"
*"The Rodney Sisters, Bishop Morris' sisters-in-law, came to Oregon in 1869 to operate the diocesan girl's school, St. Helen's Hall. Mary Burton Rodney (1833-96), the eldest, served as school principal until her death. Lydia (1836-1910), the judge's special friend, was vice-principal and taught literature and history [two of Deady's favorite subjects]. Clementine (1842-1909), who developed oddities as the years progressed, as teacher of music. For all the obvious reasons, Deady's relations with Mary and Clem were never close." Clark, Ed. Deady, 1975, p. xxvii
**The Rev. C. R. Bonnell transferred from Salem to St. David's Church, East Portland, on July 1, 1872. While there her "contracted for the erection of a study or library, which may make a part of the future Rectory" [*Oregon Churchman*, November 1, 1872]. Bonnell went to Tacoma in 1873, arriving about July 29. A clergyman who seems to have had a specific interest in natural history was the Rev. A. S. Nicholson. Nicholson came from the Diocese of California in 1867 and took charge of St. Luke's Church, Vancouver, where he remained through the early 1870s (and possibly longer). In 1871 Bishop Morris noted, "A cabinet of minerals has been purchased of the Rev. Mr. Nicholson [for Bishop Scott Grammar School], at a cost much less than its value...." [*Oregon Churchman*, September 1871].
***Judge Deady had the following comments to make about the Rev. Thomas Condon, pioneer geologist:
January 31, 1871 (Tuesday): "....This evening I attended lecture on geology of Columbia River basin by Rev. [Thomas] Condon under auspices of Y M C A at Philharmonic Hall. Took the boys and Alice. A large audience and an interesting lecture. Mr. Condon is an enthusiast and although a Congregational Minister before he became a Geologist, and still is, I think that in a case of conflict between the Gospel of Christ and the Gospel of Rocks the latter would carry the day with him."
March 15, 1871 (Wednesday): "Last night attended Mr. Condon's lecture on the Geology of Oregon at Philharmonic Hall. The lecturer is a Congregational preacher but I think the Geologist is getting the upper hand of the divine, so that 'Christ and him crucified' is entirely subordinate to 'The Rocks and Them Stratified.' At the beginning he protested that geology was something certain and not 'conjectural' but his lecture was for the most part a tissue of conjectures some of which could not urge the ground of probable cause for their existence."
March 14, 1873 (Friday): "...Attended Condon's lecture on Ancient Oregon. He maintained that when Europe was a mere Archipelago and Asia was not that central Oregon was occupied by the Horse, Camel & Sea—this in the beginning of the miocene period."
February 10, 11874 (Tuesday): "...Heard Condons lecture on differences between Geology and Christianity. His Geology has overgrown his Christianity. A little man, and an enthusiast about his hobby in too deep water."

———

1872: July 10 (Tuesday)
Judge Matthew P. Deady
"Attended morning prayer and Litany at 9 oclock at Trinity. After service as I was going out Mary Ogden undertook to have me stand as Godfather for a child that she had brought in to be baptized. She said Dr. N insisted on a G[od] F[ather] but she didn't think there was any use of it. I forbore to ask her if that was the reason she solicited me, but told her I had not time."
Deady, July 10, 1872

———

1872: July 16 (Tuesday)
Judge Matthew P. Deady
"Attended funeral of Ollie Fs baby — Henry Ellison F. Funeral service read by Dr. Nevius. Rode to the Graveyard with N[evius]...."
Deady, July 16, 1872

———

1872: July 19 (Friday)
Judge Matthew P. Deady
"...Attended services at Trinity this evening. Went and returned with Mrs. B[rooke]. Took a short and unintentional nap during the Drs lecture...."
Deady July 19, 1872

———

1872: August 9 (Friday)
Judge Matthew P. Deady
Got up at 4 A M to see the spire of Trinity church raised. Saw it nearly into place, when I left on *Dixie Thompson* to go to Astoria. Departed at 6 oclock.
Deady August 9, 1872

———

1872: August 30-31 (Fri-Sat)
Twentieth Annual Convocation of the Missionary Jurisdiction of Oregon and Washington, Trinity Church, Portland.
Rev. R. D. Nevius:
"Parochial Reports.
"Report of Trinity Church, Portland, Oregon for the year ending August 31st, 1872.
"The Rev. R. D. Nevius, D.D., Rector.
"Baptisms—Adult, 1; Infant, 7; Total, 8.
"Confirmations, 7.
"Communicants added, 12. Present number, 107.
"[Sunday] School Teachers, 9. Pupils 64.
"Marriages, 1. Burials, 6.
"Number of public services on Sundays, 105; other days, 91.
"Average attendance, 100.
"Collections and contributions—For Salary, $2,598.00; Domestic Missions, $194.10; Foreign Missions, $52.00; Diocesan Purposes, $75.00; Parochial Purposes, $9,936.90; Grammar School Endowment Fund, $184.80; Miscellaneous, $75.00. Total $13,115.80.
"The above report contains a summary of official acts and offerings while the parish was in charge of the Rev. George Burton, as well as those during the incumbency of the present Rector. To the Rev. Mr. Burton the congregation is indebted for faithful and valued services, until the 1st of May.
"Only offerings in church and money actually disbursed by the Treasurer, to date, are reported. The large subscription to the building fund of the new church, to the Endowment Fund of the Bishop Scott Grammar School, and to the fund for the additional building for the same are not included."
Journal, Jurisdiction of Oregon and Washington, 1872.
1872: September 21 (Saturday)

Judge Matthew P. Deady

"Attended morning prayers and Communion at Trinity. Ember season and St. Matthew's Day, my patron saint. Dr. Nevius preached a written sermon and a very good one. Ought to write oftener and not extemporize so much. Laziness. A bird that can sing and won't ought to be made to...."

Deady, September 21, 1872

———

1872: September 29 (Sunday)

Judge Matthew P. Deady

"Attended S S and church at Trinity as usual.... Dr. Nevius preached a rather interesting sermon on the subject of Angels in the morning, the day being the Feast of St. Michael and All Angels. His usual mysticism was rather in place. The Bishop preached a plain practical ethical sermon on the same subject in the evening."

Deady, Sept. 29, 1872

———

1872: October 3 (Thursday)

Judge Matthew P. Deady:

"Went to state Fair in morning train. On the cars met Mrs. Stratton, Mr. Corbett and Dr Nevius. Good company.... In the evening, canvassed some of the members on my bill to buy my reports and the act for the incorporation of Episcopal parishes and Bishops."

Deady, October 3, 1872

———

1872: October 27 (Sunday)

Judge Matthew P. Deady:

"Attended S S and morning service at Trinity. Dr. Nevius preached upon [Albert H.] Jordan's death and done it poorly."

Deady, October 27, 1872

———

1872: October 31 (Thursday, Hallowe'en)

Judge Matthew P. Deady:

"In evening attended church Bazaar at Trinity. Dr. Nevius went home with Miss L[ydia] before the lights were put out, which caused some remarks."

Deady, October 27, 1872

———

1872: November 5

Election day. Grant re-elected President.

1872: November 5 (Tuesday)

Judge Matthew P. Deady

"Attended vestry meeting in the evening at Nevius. Poor fellow, he don't amount to much as a leader and controller."

Deady, November 1, 1872

———

1872: November 15 (Friday)

Judge Matthew P. Deady

"Attended evening prayer at Trinity. Dr. Nevius prolonged the hour by a dull desultory purposeless preach about the Bible."

Deady, November 15, 1972

———

1872: November 24 (Sunday)

Judge Matthew P. Deady

"Attended...Trinity in morning and evening. Nevius long winded and desultory in the pulpit in the morning. Subject—'they gathered up the fragments,' etc. from the gospel for the day—25 Sunday after Trinity.* Bishop p[r]eached in the evening, from the words of the Evangelist, 'and Christ was then about 30 years of age.' Without going out of sight of this apparently unfruitful subject, he gave us an interesting discourse. I walked home, to the Hall, with Miss Lydia...."

Deady, November 24, 1872

*John VI, 5-14

———

1872: November 30 (Saturday)

Judge Matthew P. Deady

"Had informal meeting of vestrymen—Lewis, Brooke, McCracken, Flanders, Wilson and self—at my rooms in the evening. The general opinion that the Rector [Nevius] was so far a failure, and probably would continue to be. McCracken authorized to communicate to him the impression of the vestry."

Deady, December 1, 1872

———

1872: December 1 (Sunday)

Judge Matthew P. Deady

"Attended church.... The Dr [Nevius] a little better than usual...."

Deady, December 1, 1872

———

1872: December 3 (Wednesday)

Judge Matthew P. Deady

"On Tuesday evening [December 3] had vestry meeting at my chambers. Dr. Nevius sent in his resignation to take effect on July 1. Accepted unanimously and voted to pay him usual stipend until that time. Settled with contractor Therkelsen and passed a complimentary resolution.

Deady, December 4, 1872

———

1872: December 11 (Wednesday)

Judge Matthew P. Deady

"In the evening attended Church Baza[a]r at Trinity. Met Miss L[ydia Rodney]. A little icy—on account I suppose of Dr Nevius. However she thawed out a little before the evening was over. A stupid affair."

Deady, December 11, 1872

———

1872: December 17 (Tuesday)

Judge Matthew P. Deady

"In the evening wife and Alice and I attended marriage of Hewett & Piper at Trinity Church. Went in carriage and sat with guests of family. Dr Nevius performed the ceremony without a bob or a blunder and the Bishop added his blessing...."

Deady, December 17, 1872

———

1872: December 25 (Wednesday, Christmas)

Judge Matthew P. Deady

"Attended S S service at Trinity at ½ past 9 oclock. Scarcely anyone present. Dr Nevius made a little talky-talk—nothing in it...."

Deady, December 25, 1872

[1873]

1873: January 6 (Monday, Epiphany)

Judge Matthew P. Deady

"Attended church at 11 oclock at Trinity. Dr Nevius preached an Epiphany sermon, which did not shed much light on the subject. The Misses Rodney sang a beautiful 'Te Deum.'"

Deady, January 6, 1873

———

1873: January 19 (Sunday)

Judge Matthew P. Deady

"Attended—Trinity as usual. Mr. Burton preached for us in the evening. The people appeared to be delighted with him. Walked home from church in the evening with Miss Lydia [Rodney]."

Deady, January 19, 1873

———

1873: January 24 (Friday)

Judge Matthew P. Deady

"Attended church in the evening and Dr. Nevius delivered a pettifogging, sophistical lecture on the miracle of turning water into wine which he attempted to pervert into a justification of his smoking and drinking.* I was disgusted with his disingenuousness."

Deady, January 24, 1873

*Deady drank moderately but did not smoke. From his *Diary*, February 22, 1873: This day five years ago I was crossing the Columbia river bar and made up my mind to quit Smoking and have not made a puff since.... And now that I am quit of both chewing and smoking, I would not be the slave to tobacco again, that I once was, for anything."

———

1873: January 29 (Wednesday)
Judge Matthew P. Deady:
"Vestry meeting in the evening in my rooms. Called Mr. Burton unanimously as soon as Dr. Nevius goes away."

Deady, January 29, 1873

———

1873: February 4 (Tuesday)
Judge Matthew P. Deady:
"Attended vestry meeting in the evening at my chambers. Question discussed, How to get rid of Dr Nevius by the first of April so as to have Burton consecrate the church."*

"Trinity Church was not consecrated until August 31, 1873. Deady described the occasion in his *Diary* on that date. On March 4, Deady mentioned that the vestry "Sent word to the Bishop that church could not be ready for consecration." It seems the vestry saw Nevius's presence as an impediment to raising sufficient funds to pay construction debts, necessary before the church could be consecrated.

———

1873: February 12
Congress passed the Coinage Act of 1873, demonetizing silver and making gold the sole monitory standard. Advocates of the act feared that an increased supply, resulting from discoveries of silver in the West, would feed inflation.

———

1873: February 14 (Friday, St. Valentine's Day)
"St Valentines day, is a day of fragments and fussing after the party. Attended church in the evening. To my surprise Mr. Burton officiated and preached. Nevius away...."*

Deady, February 14, 1873

*It is not clear where Nevius went See   November 1, 1873 below.

———

1873: March 13 (or 15)
Rev. R. D. Nevius

"Portland, Oregon"
March 13 [?], 1873

"Dr. Asa Gray.

"My dear Sir;
                    "Have you published or are you about to publish a Text Book of Botany which will include our plants of the Pacific Slope? We have nothing but your two volumes of the Flora of North America, that is of service to us. Perhaps you have published ad[d]itional Volumes.— It is long since I have done anything in botany save with the mosses.* But there are so many new plants here and so many interesting persons Continually applying to me that I find my old love for the Phaenogams** returning upon me. And so I find myself turning to you in my difficulties as I used to do.— By the way, how does Neviusia thrive in Cambridge? Has it come to you from any other quarter than Tuscaloosa? Can you not have a few roots sent me by Mail, yet this spring?

"I enclose a beautiful little plant which I gathered without examination while traveling, as the first that I have seen. It proves to be an enduring puzzle of the botanical Students here. And at the request of a friend I put in my envelope a fresh specimen of another.

"The flower of the first reminds me in its general appearance to Elephantopus. Prof. Wood when here*** referred to Rosaceae. The petals seemed to me to be distinct and clawed. They are deeply and narrowly cleft through the whole limb: of the five lobes the middle are much largest and longest.— Note the singular pubescence of the whole plant.—

"The second plant is thought to be in Verbenaceae. It may be found any time

during the winter after a few warm days.

"My object in writing is to learn if as we hope you are to help us in our need by supplying text books. The need is unusual[?] here, and the author who will first supply it will secure large sales. I hope for the works sake, and for your sake, that the Book will bear your so well known and honored name.

"I remain, Very truly
"Your Old Correspondent
"And friend,
"R. D. Nevius"

*See November 1, 1873, below.
**phaenogam = phaenerogam: "flowering plant" (*Oxford Universal Dictionary*, 1955)
***"Professor A. Wood made important collections on his journey from San Diego through Oregon in 1866."
Hemenway (1904) 212.

———

1873: March 15
Oregon Churchman:
"Trinity Church.— The Rev. Dr. Nevius has resigned the Rectorship of Trinity Church, Portland, to take effect on the 1st of July, and the Rev. George Burton of the Bishop Scott Grammar School has been elected in his stead."

Oregon Churchman
March 15, 1873

———

1873: April 15
Salem *Oregon Statesman*:
"Hard Times.
The general complaint throughout the State, by merchants, farmers, and everybody is about the dull times and the scarcity of money. The merchant rushes around to the working man with his "little bill," the working man to his employer, who in turn hunts up the merchant, who has been unable to collect on account of dull times. So there it hangs. The bright sunshine, it is hoped, will thaw out some of the "pocket bound" mineral of the speculator. Meanwhile the debtor and creditor will "wait for the turn of the tide."

———

1873: May 4 (Sunday)
Judge Matthew P. Deady
"Trinity as usual. Nevius two long tedious sermons."

———

1873: May 13
Bishop Morris was in Baker City on this date. He wrote to Nevius about this time, suggesting that Nevius spend the next three months, until Convocation, in eastern Oregon.*
*See also June 9 and August 27, 1873.

— Eastern Oregon —

(St. Peter's Church, La Grande)
(St. Stephen's Church, Baker City)
(St. John's Church, Union)
(Ascension Church, Cove)
(St. Paul's Church, The Dalles)
(St. Thomas' Church, Canyon City)

———

1873: June 7
Nevius officially began working in Eastern Oregon. See Parochial Report for La Grande, September 28, 1873, below.

———

1873: June 8 (Sunday)
Judge Matthew P. Deady:
"Attended S S and services as usual. Nevius preached a sermon on the Trinity and

done admirably. The subject suits him. $93 taken up at the offering to assist the Mission at La Grande that he [is] going to make for the next three months. He came home to lunch with me, and we had a pleasant last hour together. This is his last Sunday in the Parish."

Deady, June 8, 1873

_____

1873: June 9
Oregon Churchman:

"The Congregation of Trinity Church contributed $90.00 on Sunday morning [June 8] toward the support of missionary work in Eastern Oregon. Dr. Nevius left Portland on Monday morning last [June 9], to take charge of this work until the meeting of the Annual Convocation in September [August 27]. He is to officiate at La Grande on the 15th, and Baker City on the 22nd. We trust our brother will meet with good success in his Mission, and bring us the report of a successful and abiding work."

Oregon Churchman
June 15, 1873

_____

1873: August 15 (Friday)
Judge Matthew P. Deady

" L[ydia] and I walked on beach to Tillamook Head. ...Conversation about Dr N[evius]. L having her face averted missed seeing the sturgeon leap.

Deady, August 15, 1873

_____

1873: August 28-30 (Thurs. eve-Sat)
Twenty-first Annual Convocation of the Missionary Jurisdiction of Oregon and Washington, Trinity Church, Portland.

Bishop Morris's annual Convocation address:
"Eastern Oregon.

"Baker City seems destined to become the largest town in that part of the State; and yet there is not in this place, nor in the surrounding country, a Protestant Church building of any name or character. Feeling the great importance of immediately occupying this portion of the field, while still there,* I wrote to the Rev. Dr. Nevius, who was about to relinquish the Rectorship of Trinity Church, Portland, proposing that he should spend the next three months, at least, in this region, and report to this Convocation the results of his labours. He gave a prompt and willing reply, and entered as soon as practicable on the work. I make the following extracts from his report:

"'Nothing has gone wrong, and the work is full of promise. In every one of the four stations [La Grande, Union, Cove and Baker], if a church building could be put under way, many, seeing a sure prospect of continuance of services, would flock to the Church. There are so many sad and even vile reactions against excessive sectism, which has swept the country, and the Church is looked to as a refuge. Yet men in their ignorance of her are not sure she will float. To them she only as yet looks as if she might, and they are only half disposed to try her. Only knowledge is wanting, and the grace of God, to show men their need of salvation.' The present condition and prospect of our work in the Grande Ronde and Powder River Valleys furnishes an illustration of the good results to be obtained from an aggressive missionary policy.... [We] have one organized Parish (at La Grande), waiting only for the architect's plan to build their church, and the prospect of good congregations in two other places."

Morris, *Oregon Churchman*
September 1, 1873

*In Baker City, Tuesday, May 13; or in Eastern Oregon April 21-May 23.
"Parochial Reports....

"Report Of St. Peter's Church, La Grande, Oregon, For The Year Ending August 28, 1873.

"The Rev. R. D. Nevius, D.D., Missionary.

"Baptisms—Adult, 16; Infant, 21. Total 37

"Confirmations, 31

"Communicants added, 47. Present number, 47.

"Burials, 1.

"No. of Public Services on Sunday, 15. Other days, 4.

"No. of Families connected with the Congregation, 31.

"Collections and Contributions, as follows: Domestic Missions, $21.45.

"St. Peter's Parish, Union County, embraces, at present, three stations: La Grande, the Cove, and Union. The last two of which are about equal in the number of Church folks, and in promise of future growth. There are four Church families in the Cove, and three in Union. The mission of the Church is received with much favor, and a cheap Church could be built in each place. Services are held in school houses.

"At La Grande the Church is much stronger; its early growth was almost unprecedented, and was full of promise. Faithfulness and zeal still characterize the larger class, confirmed by the Bishop, in May, and the few older members also. They are eagerly waiting for the plans of the new Church, which ere long this, they hoped to have far advanced to completion. I have been employed in this Mission since June 7th.

"Nearly all of the baptisms and all the Confirmations reported are the results of occasional* Missionary visits, by Rev. Mr. Wells, and the Bishop, in the Spring of this year."
*"occasionally" in original

"Report Of The Rev. R. D. Nevius, D.D., For The Mission At Baker City, For The Year Ending August 24, 1873.

"The Rev. R. D. Nevius, D.D., Missionary.

"Baptisms—Adult, 2; Infant 1. Total, 3.

"Confirmations, 1.

"Communicants added, —, Present number, 4.

"Burials, 2.

"No. of Public Services on Sundays, 5. Other days, 4

"No. of Families connected with the Congregation, 4.

"Average attendance, 25.

"Collections and Contributions, as follows: —Domestic Missions, $12.75.

"My time has been occupied since June 7th, serving the stations of St. Peter's Parish, Union County, and the Mission established there by the bishop in this place in May. The promise of good results to follow faithful Church work in this place is encouraging. The people are ready to begin building a church as soon as plans can be secured. In neither of the four points [La Grande, Union, Cove, and Baker City] now occupied by the Church in three valleys, is there a church edifice occupied at present for public worship. The people are everywhere eager to see churches built, and will do something towards their erection. It is doubtful, however, if anything can be done before spring, the season is now so far advanced."

Journal, Jurisdiction of Oregon and Washington, 1873.

_____

1873: Late August/Early September
Rev. R. D. Nevius

"La Grande.— Dr. Nevius writes to the Bishop that the people of La Grande are eager to get their church building up and enclosed this fall.... The ground is already staked out.... The Dr. adds: 'Should we go on this way you will be more likely called to consecrate in November than to lay the corner stone."

Oregon Churchman
September 15, 1873

_____

1873: September 18
"Failure of Jay Cook & Co., a powerful banking house, precipitated a fall off in security prices, starting the Panic of 1873. "Unbridled railroad speculation, notably in the field of construction, combined with overexpansion in industry, agriculture, and commerce weakened the U.S. financial structure, further shaken by the contraction of European demand for U.S. farm products after 1871." — Encyclopedia of American History, 1976.

Smalley (1883) 198-199:

"The financial panic of 1873 destroyed the banking house of Jay Cooke & Co., and severely crippled the Northern Pacific Railroad Company. It was the most serious disaster to the business and industry of the United States that had occurred since the crisis of 1837. ... All at once, with no other warning than a little stringency in the money market, an extraordinary panic began in New York. It commenced on the 18th of September, with the failure of the New York house of Jay Cooke & Co., followed immediately be the suspension of the Philadelphia house and of the First National Bank of Washington. It lasted about a month, and in that short space of less than thirty days it prostrated thousands of [p. 199:] commercial establishments, stopped the wages of hundreds of thousands of laborers, and spread gloom and terror over the entire land."

1873: November 1

Two mosses, *Mnium (Eunnium) Neevii* [p. 481] and *Grimmia (Dryptodon) Neevii* [pp. 483-484] were named for Nevius by Karl Muller in the November 1, 1873 issue of Flora, a German periodical. These had been sent to Muller by Charles Mohr, a German-born and educated pharmacist and botanist living in Mobile, Alabama. The article "Sechs neue Laubmoose Nordamerika's [Six New North American Mosses], described two mosses collected by "J. Boll" of Dallas County, Texas in 1870, two from "Rever. Dr. R. Neevius" of "Portland, Oregon," which had been sent to Mohr in 1873 (suggesting they could have been collected during Nevius's unexplained absence from Portland in February), a moss which had been collected by Mohr in Louisiana the previous December and one that had been collected by Mohr on the West Fowl River in 1871 and sent to Muller, apparently along with those of Nevius and perhaps those of Boll as well, in 1873.
Muller (1873) 481-484.

1873:
November 8. Cornerstone of St. Peter's Church, La Grande laid.
November 17. Cornerstone for unnamed church at Baker City laid.
November 18. Cornerstone of St. John's Church, Union laid.
November 19. Cornerstone for unnamed church at Cove laid.

——

1873: November 24
Rev. R. D. Nevius

"La Grande
"Nov 24 1873

"Hon. M. P. Deady
"Dear Sir,
"The Bishop brought me from you 'Four Phases of Morals,' for which at my first opportunity of writing, I hasten to thank you. A New Book here among the mountains where one almost forgets that there are [n]either new books nor thinking men, is a great pleasure to me.— No greater however than the assurance that you remember my inclination, and care to furnish me with what, save for thoughtful friends, I should greatly lack. I have not yet had time to see of what quality it is. To follow the Bishop in a months visitation, and to go around him like a revolving satellite a half dozen times a day, gives little time for anything else. I write from the Cove, where we have only a semi weekly mail or I should have written three days ago.

"Nowhere could finer weather be found than that we have had all along. No rain yet to speak of. The mountains have been three times covered with snow, but none has fallen in the valley—good New York October weather has prevailed. Today promises to be the best of the Season, and we shall have more such, possibly until Christmas.

"You will hear of our work here from the Bishop and the Oregon Churchman.
"Please give kind regards to all your family and still keep me kindly in mind.
"Very truly yours
"R. D. Nevius."
OHS Manuscript Collection, Deady file.

——

1873: November 26 (Nevius's 46th birthday)
Baker City *Bedrock Democrat:*
"Episcopal Church Grounds.—The work now going on upon the grounds of the Episcopal Church gives that part of our city a lively appearance. Monday of last week the Bishop laid the Corner Stone, and now workmen are engaged upon the foundation of the Church, the enclosing fence and a small house which Dr. Nevius is putting up for an office or study, and which will be the vestry room of the future Church. These grounds occupy four lots on the east side of the square south of that occupied by the Roman Catholic Church, two of which were given by Dr. Boyd, and two were purchased from him. The contract for the new Church will be given out as soon as a plan shall have been adopted, and such work as may be done in shop will go on this winter preparatory to work on the grounds in the Spring. We understand that Bishop Morris left La Grande on Thursday for Walla Walla, after laying corner stones for churches in Union and at Forest Cove. These make four Church buildings begun in this Valley and Grand Ronde at this visitation.... The Episcopal Church leaves good work behind it wherever it goes, whether it builds in wood and stone or in Christian character, and we are glad to see it entering upon permanent possession in our midst."
Baker City *Bedrock Democrat*
November 26, 1873

——

1873: Late
Oregon Churchman, Baker City *Herald:*
"Owing to the closing of the Columbia River, our advices from Baker Co. are quite out of date, but we find in the Baker City Herald, the following items which will be of interest:

"The Rev. Dr. Nevius of the Episcopal Church, preached a very appropriate Thanksgiving sermon at the Court House on Thanksgiving eve. This gentleman is an earnest, zealous Christian worker, and is doing much good in this community.

"We are requested to say that of the four lots on which a Corner Stone was laid last week [on November 17] for an Episcopal church, two were presented by Dr. Boyd. The site for the church is upon the east side of the square in front of the Roman Catholic church. Dr. Boyd seems disposed to have all the churches near himself.

"Bishop Morris left Grande Ronde on Thursday [November 20] for Walla Walla. On this visitation he inaugerated [sic] work for four churches which will be completed in the spring...."
Oregon Churchman
January 15, 1874

[1874]

1874:
Barbed wire first marketed by Joseph F. Glidden.

——

1874: January
Rev. R. D. Nevius:
"We learn from the Baker City papers* that the Rev. Dr. Nevius has completed the vestry-room of the church, and that he is occupying it as a study and rectory. The Dr. is prosecuting his work with much energy and spirit, and writes of his prospects in a very encouraging way. He says in a private letter: 'I spent last Sunday in the country, between here and Sparta, holding service in Sparta the Friday night before. These services in the country school houses do much good. All the people "turn out," and are usually favourably impressed by the Church's ways, and her manner of presenting truth. The people are demonstrative. The results of work appear and bring much encouragement to the missionary. After my first service at Sparta "the boys" met together, and sent me a respectful message, by the proprietor of the stage route, that I was hereafter free to the road and the town, and asking me to come again. My ride home, on horseback, in the teeth of a strong cold wind. Afterward in the stage, it was not very cold, but the wind was very fierce. That night the mercury fell to 10 deg., but the cold did not pierce as much as in Portland at the freezing point. There was no wind, the sky was clear and the atmosphere dry. I worked most of the day at my house, without an overcoat, and people went about the streets in ordinary dress. Now there is snow on the ground, nine inches. Yesterday, while it was falling, I worked all day, enclosing the foundation blocks of the vestry-room, and making a wood cellar. The nails frosted at the touch of my wet gloves and

stuck to my hands, yet I was not cold all day. All this is to show that winter on the mountains is not what it is on the plains or coast.'"

Oregon Churchman
February 1, 1874

* No mention was made of the building of the vestry room or church in the *Bedrock Democrat* in issues of November 1873 through February 1874, other than that cited above. It may be that the reference cited by the *Oregon Churchman* was contained in the Baker City *Weekly Herald*, of which no known copies survive for late 1873 and early 1874.

———

1874: late February
Rev. R. D. Nevius:

"Baker City, Or
February [n.d.]

"My Dear Judge

"I am very sorry to see the attacks made upon you by the Bulletin and not only so because of the malice that inspires them but for the [word scratched out] publicity which is given them by the curious and idle <u>men</u>, those newspaper gossips, than whom the lepers[?] were not more unclean. The evils of the gossip of the fireside or of the tea table or of idlers dry good box, worse than either, are not comparable to those which the art of printing has made possible.

"My impulse to write to you at this time comes from remembering a text of Scripture which came to me, and ever comes when I read or think of you as thus assailed. It is this 'He that departeth from inquiry maketh himself a prey.' The saddest of all is that we have come to such condition in society and civil government as makes such a text [generally applicable, crossed out] find an illustration in our times and in our country.*

"I beg to assure you of the respect and
"Esteem of

"Very truly yours
"R. D. Nevius"

———

1874: March 2
Judge Matthew P. Deady:
William H. Effinger of Trinity Church, Portland, made a special offering of $400, $200 of which was designated "to Nevius' mission."

Deady, March 2, 1874

1874: early March
Oregon Churchman:

"Baker City.

"Dr. Nevius writes very encouragingly concerning his work in Eastern Oregon. At Baker City the plan prepared by messrs. Krumbein & Gilbert, of Portland, has been adopted, and the contract for building the church has been let. The congregation is steadily increasing, more people are taking part in the services, and many are seeking to know more of the Church. The Sunday afternoon catechisings are well attended and the people are beginning to see the excellency of a system which does not content itself simply with preaching, but is also an educator, recognizing its relation to the children, and rightly estimating the position of Baptism in Christian culture. There can be no more important work in which to bend our best energies than this...."

Prob. Morris, *Oregon Churchman*
March 12, 1874

———

1874: June 3
Rev. R. D. Nevius:

"Between the Mountains

"We are accustomed to speak of all that region of our State beyond the Cascades as 'East of the Mountains.' There is one very large scope of country, however, that would be much more correctly called 'between the mountains,' lying, as it does, between the Cascades and the Blue Mountains, and in the valleys of the Des Chutes and John Day Rivers.

Occupying so large a field as the whole of Oregon and Washington Territory, our small missionary force has never, till this season, been able to enter this part of the field, and the first services of our Church ever held in any part of it, away from the Dalles, were by the Rev. Dr. Nevius, at Canyon City, on the last Sunday of May, on his return from a recent visit to Portland. He met with a most hearty welcome, from the people at the Dalles and Canyon City, and sends to the Bishop the following account of his services:

Canyon City, June 3.

"Dear Bishop:—On my way home from Portland, at a service held in the Dalles, three persons, adults, were baptized, and an interesting class of six persons await the coming of the Bishop for confirmation. Services at this place have been very unfrequent supplied by the clergy, who, in passing through, are compelled to stay over night. Should all the clergy who travel on this line remember that there is a little band of Church people at this point, and announce their coming, services could be more frequently supplied to a congregation which will highly value the favor.

"At Canyon City I was encouraged by most courteous reception and entertainment personally, and by large and interested congregations. Some English families, with memories from childhood of the Mother Church, were almost the only ones to whom the services were familiar, yet the hearty interest in a series of services lasting four days was exceptional, the congregations increasing from the first to the last. Five children were baptized, and an interesting class for confirmation will await the visitation of the Bishop.

"As many more children are promised for baptism, and many persons express great interest in the services of the Church, recognizing a vast difference between them and those they have hitherto been accustomed to. John Day Valley is a more important field for us to work in than Grand Rhonde was a year ago, and the whole country is more accessible to us. The Dalles and this place, with John Day Valley, would be a good field for another missionary.

"From Canyon City, where my horse was awaiting me, I went on to Baker City, <u>via</u> Eldorado, a mining town, within my own missionary field, where the Bishop, with Mr. Wells, held a service last summer. Well would it be if the Church would give us six more missionaries to put into the *saddle*, to carry a knowledge of her blessed ways to all the distant valleys and mountain regions of this wide missionary field. The Bishop and Mr. Wells have arranged for a missionary excursion into Northern Idaho in the month of July, which will carry the ministrations of the Church where they have hitherto been unknown, and possibly open another field for her services.'"

Oregon Churchman
June 15, 1874

———

1874: July-August
Bishop Morris:

"Eastern Oregon and Washington.— Bishop Morris returned late on Friday, the 7th of August, from his missionary journey in the Eastern and North Eastern parts of his jurisdiction. He was absent from home nearly six weeks, and made a journey of over a thousand miles.... He went into Northern Idaho, accompanied by the Rev. Mr. Wells.... Taking leave of the Rev. Mr. Wells at Pendleton he crossed the Blue mountains into Grande Ronde [sic] valley, where he was met, at La Grande, by the Rev. Dr. Nevius. Dr. Nevius' mission embraces the whole of Union and Baker counties, and indeed is now extended into Grant county. The Bishop held services at La Grande, Cove, Union, Baker City, Mormon Basin, Eldorado and Canyon City, all within the field of Dr. Nevius' labors....

"The Church buildings at La Grande, Union and Baker City are progressing steadily, though not with the rapidity what we sometimes see on this side of the mountains. At the Cove the work has been delayed from a necessary change in the architect's plan, the first plan being entirely too elaborate and costly. Our work in all that region is gaining strength and has much promise in it. In Dr. Nevius' mission sixty-nine persons have been confirmed within the past eighteen months, and three church buildings are well under way.

"It was an encouragement and comfort to find the missionary at Baker City so nicely fixed in his vestry room, with the church lots fenced and trees planted,* the stone foundation of the church and chancel built, the lumber for the building all on the ground and *all paid for.*** The carpenter work is now going on, and there is a good hope of the church being ready for use by Christmas. At La Grande the church building is more advanced, and by this time is under roof and enclosed. At Union the foundation is built, the lumber on the ground and the carpenter work under way. It is confidently believed that another season will see these churches, together with the one at the Cove, all completed, and continued growth in our work.

"From Baker City the Bishop and Dr. Nevius crossed the mountains to Canyon City, a distance of about 100 miles, holding services on the way at Mormon Basin and Eldorado. Saturday and Sunday, the 1st and 2nd of August, were spent in Canyon City, where there is much promise for the growth and usefulness of the Church. Three services were held, with large and interested congregations. At a very interesting service in the afternoon Dr. Nevius baptized four adults and five children, and in the evening ten persons were confirmed. Two of the persons baptized and confirmed came a distance of 34 miles, evincing in every way their earnestness and sincerity.

"The services and teaching of the Church have made a deep impression in this community, and a capable and earnest Missionary placed there at once would soon built up a good congregation at Canyon City, and establish the Church for all time. By reason of a change in the arrangements of the mail stage, the Bishop was compelled to cross the mountains from Canyon City to the mouth of John Day River—125 miles—on horseback. This was a fatiguing journey of three days, much of the way over a very rough trail, but it enabled him to reach home only 24 hours after his appointed time.... With Eastern Oregon, Washington Territory and Idaho, united in one Diocese, under its own Bishop, as surely it should be, new life and strength would be given to the Church in all that wide region."

Morris *Oregon Churchman*
August 15, 1874

*From Bishop Morris's annual Convocation Address of August 27 (*Oregon Churchman*, September 15, 1874): "At Baker City, four lots have been fenced and planted with trees; the stone foundations of the church are finished, a large vestry-room has been built, which is now doing good service as a Prophet's Chamber,*** the lumber is on the ground, with all things paid for, and the carpenters at work on the building."

**From the Parish Register of St. Stephen's, Baker: "The contract for building was given to Messrs. Low & Crabel. By them the lumber was laid on the ground but Dr. Nevius failing in collecting a sufficient amount for the second payment, Messrs. Low & Crabel threw up the contract on the condition that the money for the lumber should be furnished them. This was done."

***The term "Prophet's Chamber" seems to have been a good-humored reference to II Kings 4.10, wherein is related that a lady of the city of Shunem asked her husband to build a small room high on the roof or wall, and furnish it with a bed, a table, a chair and a lamp for the prophet Elisha to use when he was in town. [II Kings 4.(9) And she said unto her husband, Behold now, I perceive that this is an holy man of God, which passeth by us continually. (10) Let us make a little chamber, I pray thee, on the wall; and let us set for him there a bed, and a table, and a stool, and a candlestick; and it shall be, when he cometh to us, that he shall turn in thither. KJV (Revised, Authorized 1882).]

———

1874: August 28-29 (Fri-Sat)
Twenty-second Annual Convocation of the Missionary Jurisdiction of Oregon and Washington, Trinity Church, Portland.

"The Bishop's Address....

"Church Building.

"I have laid the corner-stones of five churches, and broken ground for the erection of three others, within the last year. These are at La Grande, Cove, Union, and Baker City, in Eastern Oregon, St. James' Church, at McMinnville; Trinity Mission, Watson's Addition, Portland; the Chapel of the Holy Innocents, Upper Astoria; and St. Peter's Church, Tacoma. The Chapel of Trinity Mission is entirely completed.... That of the Holy Innocents is so far completed as to be ready for use....

"St. Peter's, La Grande, and St. James' McMinnville, both now roofed and en-closed, will probably be [the next to be] finished in advance of any others. At Baker City, four lots have been fenced and planted with trees; the stone foundations of the church and chancel are finished; a large vestry-room has been built, which is now doing good service as a 'Prophet's Chamber;' the lumber is on the ground, with all things paid for, and the carpenters at work on the building.

"At the Cove, the church has been put under contract, and the work is now under way. At Union, the foundation is built, the lumber on hand, and the carpenter work going on. It should be borne in mind that in that part of the State, where lumber and labor of all kinds are scarce and costly, church building is a much slower and more expensive work than with us, and that much time and patience are required to complete our designs.

"St. John's Church, Union, is a 'memorial' of the Rev. G. W. Natt, an able and devoted clergyman of the Diocese of Pennsylvania, whose family and friends have sought to connect his name and memory in this way with a missionary work in which he would gladly and thankfully have spent his life. I could ask no better thing for the Bishop and Clergy of this diocese than that they should be animated with such a zeal as was his; nor for their people than that they should live and labor in the same lofty spirit of self-consecration which has sought and secured the erection of this missionary church. This has not been accomplished by the easy diversion of superfluous means from some purpose of self-indulgence, taste, or fancy, but by positive and severe self-denial, in the very likeness of her who of 'her penury cast in all the living that she had.' Did the same spirit animate all our people, those to whom God has given unstinted abundance, as well as those who have but the 'two mites' to return, missionary chapels would spring up in every village and hamlet, grand cathedrals would lift up their spires and send out the sweet music of their chimes over every centre of population and wealth; hospitals, asylums, and schools would open their doors all over the land; and the soothing sanctifying influences of our holy religion would go out to all abodes of vice, and to all broken and desolate hearts. There have been men in our day and generation, who, out of the abundant means with which God was blessing them, made it a rule to build a missionary church every year, single handed and alone. And if we may not expect many such noble examples, there are still multitudes of men who might do this *once in a lifetime!*

"When one beholds the many private homes of elegance and splendor—the very palaces for which our country is becoming noted—the thought will suggest itself, how easy might enough been spared here or there to build one church, to the honor of God. If this had been done, maybe in some cases the day of disaster had been averted, and the auctioneer's cry had never been heard in those grand halls and chambers. Maybe the rich man's sun had set with a brighter hope for the broken hearts that now can only say of all earthly splendor, "Miserable comforters are ye all.'"

"Missionary Appointments.

"The system of missionary appointments for vacant parishes and Missionary stations has been continued much as in past years. By the services of the Bishop, the Rev. J. R. W. Sellwood, and frequent 'details' of the settled Clergy, many points have been reached, monthly or bi-monthly, that could be served in no other way. Such services have been given to Roseburg, Oakland, Junction City, Monroe, Albany, Kalama, Olympia and Seattle, and occasionally at other points...."

"Parochial Reports...

"Report of Eastern Oregon Mission.

"The Rev. R. D. Nevius, D.D., Missionary

"The services of the Mission have been given regularly, each month, to the four places reported below. In these, besides the Sunday service, daily services during Lent were held, ten days in each place. Besides these, services have been given in each of the six places more than once, and in five once.

"Canyon City has been visited twice; the last time in company with the Bishop.

"Baptisms—Adults, 4; Infants, 10, Total 14

"Confirmations, 10.

"The Dalles has been visited three times, in passing to and from Portland. At this place services by myself, previous to this convention year. In this place I have had...

*Baptisms—Adults, 5; Total, 5

*Confirmations, 6

———

"Report of St. Peter's Church, La Grande, Oregon, for the year ending August 31, 1874.

"The Rev. R. D. Nevius, D. D. , Missionary.

"Baptisms—Adults, 2; Infant, 3, Total 5.

"Confirmations, 5

"Communicants added, 5. Removed S. Present number, 34.

"Collections and contributions, as follows: Diocesan Mission, $67.00. Parochial purposes, $800.00; Miscellaneous, $18.00. Total, $882.00.

"The church building is now nearly completed. The seats and other furniture have yet to be made. The means for doing this is in hand, and the church will be occupied some time in October. The money expended upon the church, to advance it to its present condition, has been raised within the Parish. Services are still held in the Methodist Church.

———

"Report of ———— Church, Cove, Oregon, for the year ending August 31, 1874.

"The Rev. R. D. Nevius, D. D., Missionary.

"Baptisms—Adult, 4; Infant, . Total, 4.

"Confirmations, 4.

"Communicants added, 3. Present number, 7.

"Number of Public Services on Sundays, 22. On   other days, 14.

"Number of Families connected with the   Congregation, 4.

"Average attendance, 50.

"Collections and Contributions, as follows: Diocesan Mission, $113.00. Total, $113.00.

"The church building is under contract, and it is hoped that it may be occupied by Christmas. Services are still held in the school house.

———

"Report of St. John's Church, Union, Oregon for the year ending August 31, 1874.

"The Rev. R. D. Nevius, D.D., Missionary.

"Confirmations, 2. [No baptisms listed.]

"Communicants added, 2. By transfer 2. Present number, 8.

"Number of Public Services on Sundays, 18. On other days, 14.

"Number of Families connected with the Congregation, 6.

"Collections and Contributions as follows: Domestic Missions, $15.75; Parochial Purposes $449.00; Miscellaneous, $2.50. Total, $467.25.

"The church at this place is rapidly going on to completion. The amount already expended upon the church is $832.00 - $449 of which has been raised in the Parish.

———

"Report of ———— Church, Baker City, Oregon, for the year ending August 31, 1874.

"The Rev. R. D. Nevius, D.D., Missionary.

"Baptisms—Adult, 4; Infant, 23. Total 27.

"Confirmations, 11.

"Communicants added, 12. Present number, 15.

"Average attendance at Catechising, 14.

"Marriages, 1. Burials, . [blank space]

"Number of Public Services on Sundays, 33. On other days, 27.

"Average attendance, 40.

"Collections and Contributions, as follows: Domestic Missions, Mite Chests, $4.60. Diocesan Missions, $140.00. Parochial Purposes, $888.50. Miscellaneous, $11.00. Total, $1,033.10.

"Services are held in the court house. Work is going on upon the nave of the Church, which will be completed on or before Christmas, but without furniture.

"The vestry room, 12 x 20, is already built and is occupied by the Missionary in charge.

"There has been, already, expended upon the Vestry room, the enclosed four lots, the Church foundations and the lumber, all of which is on the ground and paid for, the sum of $1,088.50. This does not include the purchasing of two of the lots by two friends of the Church, for $150.00. Of the former sum, $706.00 has been raised within the Mission, $198.00 of which was contributed by the Women's Guild."

Journal, Jurisdiction of Oregon and Washington, 1874.

1874: August 30

Judge Matthew P. Deady:

At the Annual Convocation a collection was taken for "building of two churches in Dr. Nevius Mission east of the mountains. Gave $2 1/2.... Rev. Nevius and [Rev. J. E.] Hammond to dinner."

Deady, August 30, 1874

———

1874: September 3

Judge Matthew P. Deady:

Deady called at St. Helen's Hall. Lydia Rodney was there, and "looked resplendent in white. Dr Nevius there. Mrs. D. insists that L likes the Dr and dresses herself for him. I am inclined to differ...."

Deady, September 3, 1874

———

1874: December 2

The Baker City *Weekly Herald* carried a full page article on Schiemann's discovery of Troy.

———

1874: December 15

Oregon Churchman:

Woodcut engraving:

"Dr. Nevius writes to the Bishop under date of December 15 [1874], 'We shall have service here [in Baker City] on St. Stephen's Day [December 26], going into the church on the bare floor, everything extemporized save the stove and lamps. If you do not give us another name I shall call the church "St. Stephen."'

Oregon Churchman

March 2, 1876**

*Rev. Octavius Parker, 1882-1884: "In November the Corner Stone was laid on one of four lots which were given as follows - two by Dr. Boyd the owner of the town site and one by Mr. A. H. [Asa?] Brown and Mr. James W. Virtue - the former two were valued at $50 each and the latter at $75 each. These lots were enclosed together with a fifth lot which was promised by Dr. Boyd to the Masonic Fraternity but was not conveyed to them at the time of Rev. Dr. Nevius' removal to another mission., 1879 (Oct.). On these lots a one roomed house was first erected for a residence for the missionary, which should be the vestry room of the future church. The building of the house and fence was not from the funds raised for the Church building. The contract for building was given to Messrs. Low and Crabel.... The plan for the Church, which was substantially that of St. Johns Church Union, was at the advice of the Bishop changed and a plan was adapted which was supposed to be cheaper. The contract was given to Messrs. Clement & Manning. The Church was built chiefly during the absence of the Missionary and mistakes were made in choosing and placing the roof timbers. When too late the roof was found to be too weak to be self supporting and much to the regret of the missionary the church generally was but a pittiable [sic] piece of work.

**This issue of the *Oregon Churchman* contained a "cut" of the church and a brief history of the Baker congregation to that date.

[1875]

1875: February

Rev. R. D. Nevius:

"Eastern Oregon.

"The pleasant weather which may be always expected here in February, and an excellent line of Stages kept upon the road from Baker City to Canyon City by the enterprise of Messrs. Greer and Kellogg, made a visit to Canyon possible during the winter. This unlooked for opportunity was gladly embraced. And my unexpected and unannounced visit seemed to give great pleasure and to produce good results.

"On my last visit in November, I advised that a Sunday School should be kept up to meet the Church's obligation to her baptized children in the absence of the minister in charge. I appointed a Superintendent from among the male Communicants of the Church, gave general directions, and ordered a sufficient number of books and children's papers to begin on. Meantime I had not heard in general terms of a work which on my arrival showed itself exceptional and exemplary to an extent that will justify mention in the <u>Oregon Churchman</u>.

"In my previous visits I have been more than usually careful to illustrate the relation of Childhood to Christ through the Church and the responsibility of the Church to her baptized little children, and also the effectiveness of her system of instruction by the sequence of Festival and Fast.

"It therefore gave me great pleasure to find that the Sunday School had been made, in the consciousness of teachers and children, subservient to the public catechisings of the Minister, and that the children looked forward to Catechizing with pleasure, and were conscious that the Sunday School was within the Church, rather than just upon its margins.

"It was a pretty thing to see all the children of the Sunday School, large or small, baptized and unbaptized, come forward promptly, and stand in a double row,—the little ones in the inner circle and the larger ones behind,—and though reverent, wholly free from embarrassment, give well coined and thoughtful answers. It was especially gratifying to be able to baptize on the next Sunday before catechizing, five of those who had not before approached Christ in that holy sacrament.

"On my next visit I am quite sure that almost the whole if not the whole of the Class will thus recognize baptism as the initial point of the Church's Culture of the Christian life.

"It was scarcely a less pleasure to learn that the members of the Church met with the children on last Christmas Day, for a special service when the Superintendent read from the Gospel the story of the Nativity, and with the children said the Creed, and suitable prayers, and sang Christmas Hymns, according to a schedule of service which I had sent them. At night the children had their Christmas Tree and to each a little unexpected gift was given from me, and to all a general message sent by mail.

"I should fail to present this narrative of growth and development of Christian life in its full light as an example, did I not say that our first service was held there less than a year ago, and that at that time not a single communicant of our Church was found where now there are 13 communicants, four of whom are men. And 26 other, baptized children and adults, and 5 candidates awaiting confirmation.

"Within that time only four Clerical visits, including that of the Bishop and that of Mr. Sellwood have been made. Nor for the sake of example should I omit to say that such a success is hardly attainable unless a person may be found who being able to attract children is able to play the organ, to sing and to instruct in singing, and who at the same time is willing to be directed, and is so happily constituted by nature or so cultured by grace that a desire to illustrate ones own ability may be forgotten in the paramount desire of being of service to others.

"Parents who give their children a thorough musical education scarcely know how great a power they are putting in their hands for doing good. And thousands of cultural men and women fall short of a great mission by regarding powers which may be consecrated to God's Service, only as social accomplishments.

R. D. Nevius"

Nevius, *Oregon Churchman*

March 15, 1875

——

1875: Spring
Photograph:
The files of the Oregon Historical Society contain a small card-mounted photograph measuring 2 9/16" wide by 4 1/8" high (negative #48335), showing St. John's Church, Union, nearing completion. The following in Nevius's hand, is inscribed on the reverse side:

Horizon line is
faintly marked. It
is a mountain ridge
bare, save with scattered
fir forests near the

summit. It is one
mile away, intervening
country flat fenced
fields.
Fill angle of tower
marked (a) with
battened boards
like front of Church.
Fill windows or
not as you please.
Take the painter
and scaffolding
down.

These instructions were for the engraver who was to make a woodcut or steel engraving from the photograph. The engraver filled in the windows and took the "painter and scaffolding down," but did not fill in the "angle of the tower" or indicate the background scenery. This view was subsequently published in *Home and Abroad*, January 15, 1875.

——

1875: March 30-April 5
Rev. R. D. Nevius:
"Grande Ronde.

"Correspondence of the Churchman.

Mr. Editor: You have asked me to give an account of my Easter Services in this Mission. Story! I have none to tell, Sir, but only to mention, for record on the pages of the *Oregon Churchman*, that Easter Services were held this year for the first time [on April 5] in St. John's Church, Union. They were preceded by daily Services during Holy Week, and with these services seemed effectively to illustrate the value of the Church as a teacher, by the sequence of concentrated lessons. It was all novel to many if not to all, and was, I believe profitable to a few. Only two incidents occur to me as worthy of mention. While waiting for the congregation, I spoke to those present of some of the features of joy which the Church elsewhere presented, and while I was speaking of flower-decked altars when nature's Easter was coincident with that of the Church, most unexpectedly two neat vases were brought in containing each a beautiful tulip, and were timidly presented for the altar, as if, perchance, I might not like it.

"In the afternoon, was Catechizing, of course. A Sunday-school was organized and placed in charge of the Women's Guild. After Catechizing, questions from the older persons, according to a plan adopted of which I have told you before. Two of the questions were characteristic of the plan, which as you will see gives an opportunity for enquiry at the moment regarding matters suggested by the Festivals of the Church. Two questions were good and thoughtful ones, though they were timidly given as main fear that they were not pertinent, and they gave me excellent themes for short lectures; first, upon one of the most beautiful and perhaps the oldest of nature's symbols of the resurrection. And again upon the never too well learned connection of our Christian Feast of Easter with the venerable Passover of the Older Church.

"The first question was, 'Please tell us something about *Easter Eggs*,' and the second, 'When I was a child I used to hear Easter called "Paus" (Pasch.) 'What does it mean?'

"Long years hence when the congregation of St. John's shall gather at the sound of a bell in a church completed in seats, chancel furniture, vested altar, organ and furnace, this record in old files of the *Oregon Churchman* may remind them of the dilatory congregation, the painful temporary benches, the bare cold floor, the halting hymn and the smoking stove, and they will wonder how, with so many hindrances to devotion, our first Easter Service could have been so bright and pleasant."

Oregon Churchman

April 15, 1875

——

1875: June 26-July 8
Oregon Churchman (prob. R. D. Nevius)
"Eastern Oregon Etc.

"Mr. Editor:—Bishop Morris started on his annual visitation to Eastern Oregon on Saturday, the 26th. - ultimo [of June]. This visitation is to extend as far as Lewiston in Bishop Tuttle's jurisdiction, and will include all the churches and mission stations east of the Cascades. He spent Sunday [June 27] at

The Dalles

Where he baptized one child. The church building at this place is in progress. The foundations are built, the lumber is on hand seasoning and the Church will be completed during the summer or early fall. Three days staging brought the Bishop to

Canyon City

At which place he was met by Rev. Dr. Nevius. Services were held on Thursday night [July 1] and Sunday morning [July 4]. One person was baptized and three persons were confirmed. Steps were taken preparatory to building a Church. Further action was deferred until Dr. Nevius' next visit in August when the work will be pushed forward. Sunday afternoon [July 4] the Bishop rode with Dr. Nevius to

Prairie City

And held service. One adult and four infants were baptized, and two persons were confirmed. On Monday [July 5] the Bishop pushed on by stage, two days, to Baker City [arriving on Wednesday, July 7?], intending to visit the Churches in Grande Ronde and return to meet Bishop Tuttle at Baker City on the 13th inst., and with him to visit the Churches and missions as far as Walla Walla; and to consecrate two churches [at Union and La Grande] and lay two Corner-stones [at Pendleton and Weston]. Of this you will hear in due time.

"In addition to what is said above, the *Bed Rock Democrat* of Baker City has the following notice of the Bishop's appointments:

"Bishop Morris will make a visitation to St. Stephen's church, in this place, on Monday and Tuesday, the 12th and 13th of July. Services Monday at 8 P.M., Tuesday 11 A.M. and 8 P.M. Bishop Tuttle, of Salt Lake City, will join Bishop Morris on Tuesday, and will be present at the services at night and will preach. Bishop Tuttle will accompany Bishop Morris on his visitation to churches in Grande Ronde valley, and Walla Walla, for the purpose of acquainting himself with the condition and prospects of the Church in Eastern Oregon and Washington Territory, which, it is hoped may some day be united to a part of his own jurisdiction in the formation of a new missionary Diocese.

"Pendleton.

"The *Tribune* of this place says:

"Work on the Episcopal church was commenced last Monday by the contractors. They intend to go right along with it."

Prob. R. D. Nevius, *Oregon Churchman*

July 15, 1875

———

1875: July 8-15

Oregon Churchman: (Prob. R. D. Nevius)

"Eastern Oregon Etc.

"Correspondence of the Churchman.

"Episcopal Visitation.

"From Canyon City the Bishop went by stage, Monday July 12 and 13, [sic July 5 and 6] to Baker City, 100 miles, where he had a rest of one day [Wednesday, July 7] without public service. After examining the affairs of the churches in this place and Union he determined, with his wonted indomitable energy, and his true brotherhood with his clergy in their cares, to lift the debt on St. John's Church, Union, that it might be consecrated. So the short time intervening before the arrival of Bishop Tuttle being sufficient for a hasty run through the Grande Ronde Mission, this double work was undertaken. Arrangements were made for the consecration of St. Peter's La Grande. The debt of St. John's was lifted. The church now building at the Cove was visited. The usual Sunday Services [July 11] with Confirmations (3 persons) were held at St. John's, Union, and thence back to Baker City.

"On Monday night [July 12], service. Thursday morning, [sic, Tuesday morning, July 13] service and confirmation, one person. Tuesday night, service with Bishop Tuttle who had arrived in the meantime [as scheduled on July 13]; and on Wednesday [July 14] the two Bishops drove to Union, 36 miles, in time for the Consecration Of St. John's Memorial Church.

"This church is a memorial to the Rev. Geo. Natt. Its erection was made possible by the donation of $500 by Mrs. Natt, from whom it has also received many valuable gifts, devotions from her own self denial and the love of old friends and parishioners of her husband. Chancel carpets, Altar and Lectern covers, Bible and Prayer Books, for Chancel, a Communion Service, Alms Basin and Font, make this beautiful church complete for Divine service.

Other generous offerings chiefly from Portland have helped to speed the work. The church is a novel in construction and appearance [emphasis added], and is thought to be a model for a cheap church when labor and material can be had at moderately low prices. The church has cost about $2000. It is believed that the same building could be erected in Portland for $1200 or $1400. It is admirably built, Mr. Samuel Sisson the contractor having wrought upon it with unusual care and faithfulness under many difficulties and perplexities. It is built of undressed 1¼ in. plank placed on the inside of the buttressed frame with open timbered roof. The roof is of dressed tongued and grooved sheeting, supported by heavy truss timbers and chamfered. The framing timbers are beautifully related to each other; they are dressed and chamfered.* A wood cut of the church may be seen in *Home and Abroad* for February, 1875.** [We hope to favor our readers with a cut of the building, in a few weeks.—Publisher.]

"The Consecration Services were very interesting. The congregation was large. Bishop Morris preached the sermon. Offerings for the work of the mission were made.

"After service the Bishops rode to the Cove by moonlight for rest, and after inspection of work upon the church now in progress of erection at that place, rode, on Thursday morning [July 15], to La Grande, where, at 5 o'clock P.M. they consecrated the second church of the Grande Ronde Mission.

"St. Peter's Church La Grande.

"This church was undertaken under an impulse created by the generous donation of $500 by a lady of the Diocese of Western New York. A large number of Church people in this congregation made the services at this place more hearty and satisfying than that at Union. Indeed, it was hardly possible to realize that such a service could be held in a country opened to Church work scarcely more than three years ago.

"The services were divided between the two Bishops, Dr. Nevius, and Rev. Mr. Kaye. Bishop Tuttle preached the sermon. The singing was very hearty, and the responses equally so. The Altar and Chancel were very beautifully and tastefully decorated with a profusion of growing greenhouse plants in pots and baskets.

"Offerings were made for the work of the Mission. St. Peter's Church, though less churchlike than St. John's, Union, is still very neat and beautiful, and its consecration was a delight to a congregation which has laboured for its erection with great harmony and persistency of effort. All the money for its erection and furnishing save the donation of $500 spoken of above was raised within the parish, the ladies of the congregation having raised over seven hundred dollars of the amount...."

Oregon Churchman

July 22, 1875

*The source for the design seems to have been George E. Woodward, *Woodward's Country Homes* (New York: George E. Woodward Co., 1865), "Design No. 9.—Rural Church," pp. 53-57. Nevius's description of the Union church paraphrases the description of the Lake George, New York, church "designed by the Rev. Dr. Cressy" which is described in Woodward's text. See also the reference to chamfered timbers for the preceding design for a "Farm Cottage," p. 52.

** The view was published in the January 15, 1875 issue of *Home and Abroad*. See Spring, 1874 above.

———

1875: summer

Bishop Morris:

"Help For Our Missionaries.—We find the following appeal [indicating that Nevius had received a buggy] in the *Philadelphia Register*, and reprint it with the hope that it may fall under the eye of some 'liberal soul' among our readers. In doing this, it might not be amiss to say that the wants of one of the Missionaries, for whom the Bishop wrote at first, have been supplied through the liberality of a member of Trinity Church, Portland,* but that both a horse and buggy are now needed for the

Walla Walla Mission.

Another Trial.—*Messrs. Editors:* While in the City of Philadelphia, last winter, I made an appeal to your readers for the means to purchase two buggies for the use of our Missionaries in Eastern Oregon. When I saw the costly and magnificent carriages, of every form and description, in which our city brethren take their drives of business or pleasure, I thought I might prevail upon some of them to contribute $400 to furnish two cheap buggies for Missionary use in this district. It seemed I was mistaken. All I got was a contribution of $125 from a brother Clergyman, who wanted to do what he could to lighten the labors of those toiling Missionaries. 'It is the poor man alone that hears the poor man's moan.' This we know is not always the case, but it was so here. This poor man had no carriage of his own, but was willing to do what he could to help his poor brother to one.

I have just returned from a visit to the Walla Walla Associate Mission, and find my fellow missionaries there enduring such unnecessary hardship, for want of a small carriage, that I am compelled to try again, ask your readers a second time if they will not of their abundance furnish me with $150 or $200, for the purpose of relieving the hardships of these Missionaries. They occupy a field larger than an Eastern State, and are required to make long and toilsome rides on horseback under a scorching sun, in order to carry the ministrations of the Church to the scattered sheep, for whom the Good Shepherd gave His life. I do not seek for them the cushions and easy springs that are to be seen in your streets and parks, but I *do* want to save them the extreme fatigue and exposure they now endure, and ask your readers to have the goodness to help me in this undertaking. Do I ask in vain?

Very truly yours,

B. Wistar Morris."

Morris, *Oregon Churchman*

October 7, 1875

*Nevius referred to "a 700 mile buggy ride in the adjacent column, "Eastern Oregon Mission," *Oregon Churchman,* October 7, 1875, and mentioned leaving his horse at Canyon City June 3, 1874.

————

1875: September 28

Rev. R. D. Nevius

"Eastern Oregon Mission.

"[Correspondence of Churchman.]

"La Grande, Sept. 28, 1875.

"The arrival of the Rev. Mr. Kaye as associate in this Mission has given opportunity to the Missionary in charge to make a prolonged tour over ground hitherto only exceptionally visited. Starting from La Grande seven weeks ago [ca. August 10], he spent three weeks in John Day Valley and in the mines on the head of its northern tributaries. Three weeks more were given to the Dalles, where the pretty church, begun three months ago, was near its completion. He has now returned, and after a 700 mile buggy ride, to the full services and churchly companionship of a town where, only three years ago, the Church was hardly known.

"It is difficult to realize the fact that after rough work for a time long enough to get well used to it, he may find both clerical and churchly sentiment, and three completed churches, almost in sight of each other, on ground which so short a time ago was itself wild, unbroken soil for the Church.

"The 'Wayside Home' is very dear to the wandering Missionary, and all the more so, if having once been familiar with it in its rough hewn state, he may come to it again after a prolonged absence, to find that it has taken on the features of a well ordered house.

"At the close of the Conventional year, it will be well to give a general view of the Missions, which it is feared will be too long for a report to Convocation and for printing in the Journal.

"St. Peter's Church, La Grande,

was first occupied for divine service in November, lst year, and was consecrated on the 15th of July, by the Right Rev. B. W. Morris, D.D., assisted by the Right Rev. D. S. Tuttle, D.D., of Idaho. It gratefully acknowledges God's favor in the gift of $500, by Mrs. Peter Porter, of Niagara Falls, N.Y., by which it was encouraged to begin a work which has resulted in building up a strong and growing parish. The church,

though furnished with the least of the things necessary for public worship, is yet greatly in need.

"St. Stephen's Church,

Baker City, is completed to an extent which give us for occupancy and public worship. It awaits consecration until it may be free from debt. This church is situated in the largest and most important town in Eastern Oregon. A resident clergyman is greatly needed here. Nothing would be more gratifying to your Missionary than to be able to secure a man for this place.

"John Day Mission

should be a separate one, and should have the constant services of a Missionary. It is in a fertile and lovely valley, occupied by farms for seventy miles, but quite narrow. In the upper valley are three points opened as stations, where we have church families.

"Canyon City

shows itself to be the first place for a church, by the zeal of its little congregation, and the favor with which the services of your Missionary have been received. The building of a church at this point has been urged by the people themselves, and a subscription has been raised sufficient for building after a very modest manner. The subscription is, however, considering the number of subscribers, the most liberal that has been made in the Mission. The work will, with God's blessing, begin in the Spring.

"Prairie City

is another point where a church is even more needed than Canyon City. The people, however, do not see the need of it yet. Services are well attended, and we have a few names here also.

"School House Station,

nine miles above Prairie City, is an important point, in the best and widest part of the valley. Here was found a father of several families, who, with his children and grandchildren, with the blood of England's Church in their veins, is ready to encourage and sustain the services of England's daughter-church.

"Further down the valley church folks have been found near to School House, where congregations may be gathered.

"The Dalles.

"An interesting congregation has been rapidly gathered at the Dalles. Within the Conventional year a Church building has been begun and is now only waiting for its windows from the East for completion and consecration. This Church has been named St. Paul's Church. It is built like the Church at Union, and is an improvement upon that Church. The plan has been developed with the design of getting the most Church for the least money. It has been much admired.

"Your missionary is glad to record the fact that we have been able to divide the field. The Rev. Geo. T. Kaye, deacon, has been appointed as an associate in the mission. He will reside in Grand Ronde and will keep up services in the three churches that have been built in that valley. He has entered zealously upon the work, and has before him a large prospect of usefulness. His position is a good center for new work. Two more men are needed in this Mission. Baker City desires and needs a man for herself. It is the centre of a large country, surrounded by mines near and far. It is in a large valley, fast filling up with a population which greatly needs the Gospel. It could do much to support a resident clergyman, and we should have a man for the place. At the Dalles, also, your Missionary is called to places both East and West— in Oregon and Washington Territory. Opportunity has not yet been given to visit these points. The work is very great—it is a burden upon the heart. God speed the time when the Church shall wake to a conception of its grand opportunity and responsibility, and give her sons for the work. The efficient work of the Rev. J. W. Sellwood in making a tour of the Mission for your Missionary, at the request of the Bishop, last fall, is thankfully recognized."

Nevius, *Oregon Churchman*

October 7, 1875

————

1875: September 30

Rev. R. D. Nevius, D.D.:

"Report of Eastern Oregon Mission.

31

"The Rev. R. D. Nevius, D.D., Missionary.

"Your Missionary give below a condensed statement of official work, of the growth of the Mission, and of contributions:

———

"Report of St. Peter's Church, La Grande, Oregon, for the year ending September 30, 1875.

"The Rev. R. D. Nevius, D.D., Missionary.

"Baptisms—Adult, 5; Infant, 6. total, 11.

"Confirmations, 7.

"Communicants added, 4. Present number, 38.

"Marriages, 1; Burials, 1.

"[Sunday] School Teachers, 6. Pupils, 40.

"Number of Public Services on Sundays, 30; other days, 16. Total, 46.

"Number of families connected with Congregation, 25.

"Individuals, 95.

"Average Attendance, 30.

"Collections and contributions: Erection of Church, $1,800; Parochial Missions, $147.20; Miscellaneous, $20.70. Total, $1,967.90.

———

"Report of St. John's Church, Union, Oregon, for the year ending September 30th, 1875.

"The Rev. Reuben D. Nevius, D.D., Missionary.

"Confirmations, 2.

"Communicants added, 2. Present number, 8.

"[Sunday] School Teachers, 4. Pupils, 14.

"Marriages, 2.

"Number of Public Services on Sundays, 28; other days, 14. Total, 42.

"Number of families connected with Congregation, 6.

"Individuals, 23.

"Average attendance, 50.

"Collections and Contributions: Erection of Church, $660; Parochial Missions, $43.80; Miscellaneous, $21. Total, $724.80.

———

"Report of ———, Cove, Oregon, for the year ending September 30th, 1875.

"The Rev. Reuben D. Nevius, D.D., Missionary.

"Confirmations, 1.

"Communicants, 1. Present number, 9.

"Marriages, 1.

"Number of Public Services on Sundays, 18; other days, 4. Total, 22.

"Number of families connected with Congregation, 3.

"Individuals, 18.

"Average attendance, 25.

"Collections and Contributions: Erection of Church, $2,100; Parochial Missions, $137. Total, $2,237.

———

"Report of St. Stephen's Church, Baker City, Oregon, for the year ending September 30th, 1875.

"The Rev. Reuben D. Nevius, D.D., Missionary.

"Baptisms—Adult, 1; Infant, 14. Total, 15.

"Confirmations, 1.

"Communicants, present number, 14.

"School Teachers, 1. Pupils, 13.

"Burials, 3.

"Number of Public Services on Sundays, 32; other days, 20. Total, 52.

"Number of families connected with Congregation, 13.

"Individuals, 53.

"Average attendance, 25.

"Collections and Contributions: Erection of Church, $1,000; Parochial Missions, $21.50; Miscellaneous, $9. Total, $1030.50.

———

"Report of St. Paul's Church, The Dalles, for the year ending September 30th, 1875.

"The Rev. Reuben D. Nevius, D.D., Missionary.

"Baptisms—Adult, 3; Infant, 7. Total, 10.

"Confirmations, 5.

"Communicants added, 4. Present number, 11.

"School Teachers, 2. Pupils, 14.

"Number of Public Services on Sundays, 12; other days, 5. Total, 17.

"Number of families connected with Congregation, 9.

"Individuals, 29.

"Average attendance, 20.

"Collections and Contributions: Parochial Missions, $27.80.

"Canyon City.—Baptisms—Adult, 5; Infant, 14. Total, 19.

"Confirmations, 3.

"Communicants added, 3. Present number, 13.

"School teachers, 5. Pupils, 40.

"Number of Public Services on Sundays, 8; other days, 5. Total, 13.

"Number of families connected with Congregation, 11.

"Individuals, 46.

"Average attendance, 30.

"Collections and Contributions: Parochial Missions, $61.57; Miscellaneous, $57. Total, $118.57.

"Prairie City,—Baptisms—Adult, 3; Infant 4. Total, 7.

"Confirmations, 2.

"Communicants, present number, 2.

"Number of Public Services on Sundays, 4; other days, 3. Total, 7.

"Number of families connected with Congregation, 4.

"Individuals, 15.

"Average attendance, 35.

"Collections and Contributions; Parochial Missions, $17.25.

*Note.—In the column of Parochial Missions is placed the aggregate of collections for the support of the Missionary [Nevius]. $123.25 were for the support of the Rev. Mr. Kaye; $49 from La Grande, $24.50 from Union, and $50 from the Cove.

"St. John's Church, Union, and St. Peter's Church, La Grande, were consecrated on the 14th and 15th of July last by Bishop Morris, assisted by Bishop Tuttle.

"The Church (as yet unnamed) at the Cove, with parsonage now building on the church lot, will be ready for occupancy this winter.

"St. Stephen's Church, Baker City, must wait for consecration until its debt is paid. St. Paul's Church, The Dalles, is waiting for its windows from the East. On their arrival it may be consecrated.

"A new Church has been undertaken at Canyon City. Provisions will be made at Prairie City to occupy a Granger Hall, now building, by opening a Church, by folding doors, into its large room. A new point for services has been opened in John Day's valley at a school house in a thickly settled farming community.

"Rev. George T. Kaye, Deacon, has been associated with the Missionary in charge of the Mission, and will reside in the Cove, and will sustain services in Grand Ronde Valley and vicinity."

Journal, Jurisdiction of Oregon and Washington, 1875.

———

1875: Fall

Blue Mountain University established in La Grande under the auspices of the Methodist Episcopal Church, with Rev. H. K. Hines as financial agent, and J. L. Carter as acting president.

1875: October 8-9 (Friday-Saturday)

Twenty-third Annual Convocation of the Missionary Jurisdiction of Oregon and Washington, Trinity Church, Portland.

Bishop Morris's annual Convocation address:

"....There are now in this whole missionary district nineteen clergymen, nine of whom are missionaries of your board [of Missions?]. One of these, the Rev. P. E. Hyland, is at Port Townsend, on Puget Sound, W.T., and one, the Rev. A. S.

Nicholson, is at Vancouver, W.T. Three are in the central part of the field in Oregon; the Rev. J. W. Sellwood, at Oregon City; the Rev. R. W. Summers, at McMinnville, and the Rev. T. A. Hyland, at Astoria. Three east of the Cascade mountains; The Rev. Dr. Nevius, the Rev. J. E. Hammond, and the Rev. Geo. P. Kaye, and one, the Rev. J. R. W. Sellwood, is missionary at large....

"Eastern Oregon And Washington Territory.

"In this part of the field our work is somewhat of the character of 'associate missions,' Mr. Hammond being associated with the Rev. Mr. Wells at Walla Walla, and Mr. Kaye with the Rev. Dr. Nevius, in the Grand Ronde and Powder river mission."

Morris, *Oregon Churchman*

October 14, 1875

"From the *Oregonian* of the 8th inst."

———

1875: December 25

Rev. R. D. Nevius

Oregon Churchman, January 6, 1876:

"[Correspondence of the Churchman.]

"The Dalles.

"St. Paul's at the Dalles was opened for Divine Service on Christmas day. I was not apprised* of the possibility of this until it was too late to reach the Dalles before Christmas Eve. I found the Chancel window and the west windows in place, but the side windows were thought to be too large for the openings, and all expectations of being able to hold Christmas Services in church had been given up. However we all went to work on Christmas morning, and the windows were put in place temporarily. The stove and Chancel furniture were brought in, and as the workmen left the church at 11 A.M. a few persons, who had been hastily called, came in and one more new congregational voice was added to that of 'the Church throughout all the world,' in her Christmas joy.**

"The church is more beautiful and complete than I had hoped. The carpenter's work has been done conscientiously. The painting, varnishing and polishing are admirable. In fact both the painter and carpenters seem to have put their hearts into their work and to them it is due that my pet plan for a cheap and tasteful church is now realized beyond my expectation and my hope. The windows also, of stained glass, from Slack and Booth in Orange, N.J. are beautiful. They are not gaudy and glaring. The Chancel window is a memorial of the son of the gentleman whose gift of $500, made the building of the Church possible.*** It is a single window, with an angular head. The lower compartment contains, centrally, an anchor with the symbol of the United States Navy. Above at the right and left are monograms of the Holy Name, the *Chi Rho*, and the *Alpha and Omega*. Below are a third monogram of the Holy Name, the I.H.S. and a symbol of the Trinity. The top bears an open Bible on which is placed the consecrated sword, while the base bears the legend of memorial. 'To the Memory of J. HORACE EATON,' with appropriate dates.

"The west**** window is a gift of a resident of the city. It is a spherical triangle filled with three circular symbols of our Lord, related to the three great doctrines, the Incarnation, the Atonement, and the Resurrection. It is justly much admired. The side windows are of the usual pattern, and are wholly satisfactory.

"The plan of the church is the same as that from which St. John's, Union, was built. In some important respects it is an improvement upon that much admired church, as might be expected, and it is thought to furnish a model for a cheap church which cannot easily be excelled.*****

"Divine Services have been held in the church on all the Festivals following Christmas. And services will be held for several weeks on all Sundays and Festivals, and on other days according to future appointment.

R. D. Nevius"

*Nevius may have been "apprised" by telegraph, which was completed into Baker City in 1875. See Baker City file.

**See "A curious coincidence," December 31, 1900.

***Gen. Joseph Eaton. See "Historical Notes," February 4, 1876. Young Eaton "died at Annapolis just as he was starting school." (Krier, *op.cit.*, p. 21. Hence the window's nautical theme.

****Nevius was referring to the liturgical west end of the church, which in this case faces east. The window was given by "Hon. L. L. McArthur." See Feb. 4, 1876 below.

*****See also September 28, 1875.

[1876]

———

1876: Mid-January

Oregon Churchman (The Dalles *Oregon Tribune*):

"St. Paul's Church, Dalles.

"The *Oregon Tribune*, published at the Dalles, gives the following account of our new church at that place. The Bishop is to spend next Sunday [January 23] at the Dalles and hopes to make arrangements for the early consecration of the church. The comments of the editor of the *Tribune* on the proper use of a church are excellent, and we are glad to repeat them:

"[']The new church edifice just completed, in Dalles city, by the Episcopal denomination is finished, and Rev. Dr. Nevius has held Divine services in it several times within the last fortnight. Whatever may be thought or said of the Episcopal denomination there is one fact which cannot be denied; which is, that their houses of worship are always a credit to their projectors and founders. They may be small, but they are always neat, cozy and inviting, pleasant to the eye—everything appropriate and in order. The new Episcopal church in this city is no exception to this rule. It is not only cozy, neat and tasteful in all its appointments; but in many respects it is beautiful, and reflects much credit on those who planned and those who executed.

"[']We like another thing which is true of the Episcopal denomination; and that is, their houses of worship are never used for secular purposes. When men go to church they go ostensibly to be benefited. They go that their thoughts may be directed to the contemplation of things sacred and holy. This is true of saints and sinners. Associations have much to do in giving tone and direction to our thoughts; hence, if one goes to a church that has recently been used by some festival, or show, or by some mountebank lecturer and spiritualistic performer, it is utterly impossible to prevent the mind from being more or less occupied with what it has witnessed within the walls of the church where these scenes have transpired. A Church which is used for none but sacred purposes, and whose appointments are all neat, and cozy, and pleasant, has a large per cent of the advantage over one of an opposite character.[']"

Oregon Churchman (Dalles *Oregon Tribune*)

January 20, 1876

———

1876: February 4

Rev. R. D. Nevius:

It was customary for clergymen to write brief histories of their pastorates in Parish Registers before departing. Though the first entry at St. Paul's, The Dalles is not signed or initialed, it is in the same hand as the entry initialed "R.D.N." and dated Dec. 31, 1900 (see below). These entries are found on hand-lettered pages 'I'-"III" through page 3 of Volume I of St. Paul's Parish Register:

"Historical Notes

"Satisfactory records of early Clerical Services at The Dalles cannot now easily be made. Partly full records might be made however by refference [sic] to early Journals of Convocation. Residents now present at The Dalles remember visits from Rt. Rev. Thos. F. Scott, DD, Rev. St. Michael Fackler, DD, Dr. McCarty, Rev. Messrs. Stoy and Nicholson.

"Dr. Fackler baptized a child of Hon. J. K. Kelly 1866. Mr. Stoy baptized Dr. Mitchell 1870. Bishop Morris confirmed him May 1871. These are all the official acts which can be remembered at this time. Feb. 4th 1876.

"In 1871 and 1872 Rev. R. D. Nevius, DD, made two visits holding services in the Congregational House of Worship by courtesy of Rev. Thos. Condon the pastor with whom he was to cultivate relations of the most kind and affectionate Nature. No official acts were performed save the holding the usual services.

"During this time also Services were held by Rev. L. H. Wells on his way up and down the river to his parish at Walla Walla. During this time [illegible] before Sep 7th 1873 Services had been held by Rev. Dr. Nevius 4 times by the Bishop Rt. Rev. B. W. Morris DD, once and by Rev. L. H. Wells once and perhaps twice.

"At this time no Communicants of the Church were found, and no persons holding to their Covenant relation to God and the Ch. In 1873 Sept. 7 Dr. Nevius baptized 5 Adult persons holding services in the Congregational Church and spoke confidently of the establishment of more regular services and the ultimate building of a Church around this nucleus of a congregation for whose culture in the Grace of Our Lord Jesus Christ the Church had now become responsible.

"In the Fall of 1874 —$500 having been given to Bishop for the purpose of build[ing] a Church, an application was made for appropriation of this money to the building [of] a Church at the Dalles. To this the Bishop assented on condition that an equal sum should be raised in The Dalles for the purpose and that a building site should be secured for the Church. This was undertaken by Mrs. Geo. H. Knaggs and successfully accomplished by her. The sum of $655 was raised by her solicitation and collected by her. $105 additional was raised by a Strawberry Festival. Meanwhile a Chancel window was given by Gen. Joseph Eaton as a memorial of his son, and a west window was given by Hon. L. L. McArthur.*

"The Corner Stone was laid by Rt. Rev. B W Morris DD on May 28th 1875.

"The deposits in the Corner Stone were

"1st A Copy of the Holy Bible

"2nd A book of Common Prayer

"3rd The Oregon Churchman of May 30th 1875

"4. Dalles Mountaineer May 22nd

"5. Three Portland Dailey [sic]:

The Oregonian The Bulletin The Evening Journal

"The contracts for building the Church unfinished was let to Mr. Charles Kron for $989.

"The Church was first occupied for Divine Service on Christmas Day 1875 and on January 11th The Church including furniture** with Carpet Organ and lamps costing [blank space]*** of this amt. about $800 was yet to be paid. Rev. Dr. Nevius remained two months holding frequent services 63 in all with 57 sermons and lectures.

[R. D. Nevius]

*Per conversation with Lewis L. McArthur, April 13, 1989: L. L. McArthur (1843-1897) (Lewis McArthur's grandfather) was appointed Fifth Circuit Judge in 1870. He married in 1878. Lewis McArthur at first thought that the window might have been a memorial to a son, Alexander Young McArthur (1882-1884), but upon checking dates realized this could not be the case. He suggested that the judge's circuit may have been much the same as Nevius's.

**Krier, op.cit., p. 51: "Mary Varney Lang [mother of Anne Lang] helped Dr. Nevius with the altar for St. Paul's in 1875. She carved the embossed emblems on the front of the altar - fleur d'lis and IHS, made of walnut.... She also made a book rest for the lectern designed by Dr. Nevius, out of walnut with monogrammed emblems cut of veneer satin wood and ebony." The source of the design for the altar is Frederick Clark Wither, *Church Architecture* (New York: A. J. Bicknell & Co., 1873), Fig. 29, p. XVIII. Withers was a prominent and influential architect of the period. See Francis R. Kowsky, "The Architecture of Frederick C. Withers (1828-1901)," *Journal of the Society of Architectural Historians*, XXXV No. 2 (May, 1976), pp. 83 - 88; and Francis R. Kowsky, *The Architecture of Frederick Clarke Withers and the Progress of the Gothic Revival in America after 1850* (Middletown, Conn.: Wesleyan University Press, 1980).

***The church cost about $2,500. See Morris, Feb. 5-6, 1876 below.

———

1876: February 5-6

Bishop Morris:

St. Paul's Church, Dalles:

"The Bishop visited this new and interesting Parish on Saturday and Sunday last [February 5 and 6].... Dr. Nevius has been at the Dalles since the day before Christmas, holding two services on Sunday, and from four to six on week days. The attenness at all these services has been very good, and the people have been faithfully instructed in regard to the doctrines and usages of the church, and the true principles of Christian life. Good seed has been sown, which in due time must bring forth its fruit, not the hasty hotbed fruits that come of excitement and noise, but the gradual constant growth of the divine life in the soul, that time will only ripen and bring forward to perfection. The little church, capable of holding about one hundred persons, is after Trinity Church Portland altogether the most beautiful church we have. For good taste and fitness it seems almost a model, and the congregation justly take much pleasure in it.

"For all that has been accomplished at the Dalles, the excellent site for the Church, the tasteful building, and the better work in the hearts of the people, we are chiefly indebted to God, to the faithful labours of Dr. Nevius, who saw wants and capabilities in the place that others less hopeful had overlooked. Are there not many places in our wide field, where the same good work can be done, and which yet lie fallow and unoccupied? The Church, with all its appointments, stained glass windows, Organ, Carpet and Chancel furniture, cost about $2,500. Of this amount $800 are still to be raised. This it is believed will soon be done. Three hundred dollars of this are already pledged by three names, and others are ready to give, with equal liberality toward the liquidation of this debt. Dr. Nevius will remain one Sunday more at the Dalles, when he will leave for Canyon City, the next nearest point in his field, distant however 280 [sic, 180] miles. To reach there at this season of the year he must make a circuit of nearly 350 miles, and cross the Blue Mountains twice over such roads and in such conveyances, as would terrify the ordinary traveler, but which are trifles to the hardy Oregon Missionary."

Morris, *Oregon Churchman*

February 10, 1876

———

1876: March 22

Rev. R. D. Nevius:

"Eastern Oregon.

"In a letter dated, Prairie City, March 22d 1876, Dr. Nevius writes as follows:

"I am now waiting an opportunity to cross the mountains on my way home, after an absence of three months. Late rains have so softened the deep snow on the divides as to make the passage very difficult. There is still sleighing for 60 of the 90 miles between Canyon and Baker.

"I sent you a brief report of my late visit to the Dalles. My journey to this valley was unusually pleasant for a winter ride of 180 miles. The winter is far the best time for missionary work in interior towns.

"At that time the miners have come in from their mountain camps and the people have little to do.

"My congregations at Canyon City and this place have been large, and largely made up of men. It has been especially so at this place, and a fine looking, and promising company of men they are. At Canyon City two adults were baptized, and both at that place and this, there are several Candidates for Confirmation.

"We have begun work on the Church at Canyon—that is, the lots have been purchased, and the lumber bill has gone to the sawmill. Desirable lots have been given at this place [Prairie City] for a future Church. I do not, however, at present feel encouraged to begin work.

"There is not now, a Protestant house of worship in Grant County. This part of the Eastern Oregon Mission would afford a large and promising field, and a delightful home for a Missionary."

Oregon Churchman

March 31, 1876

———

1876: April 16

Oregon Churchman: (a "Canadian Churchman")*

"Church Work In Oregon

"The following; written by one who signs himself a 'Canadian Churchman,' we find in the *Church Journal*. It is a round-about way of getting news from our 'Missionary Field,' but we are glad to get it in any way.

"Wednesday before Easter [Wed., April 12] I left Baker City, the principal business place in Eastern Oregon, to accompany the Rev. Dr. Nevius to Grande Ronde Valley, a portion of his mission. A day's steady riding on horseback through a beautiful country, brought us to La Grande, a village at the foot of the Blue Mountains. I could but think, as I rode along, what a great difference there is between the work of the Church here and in Canada, my native country. There the Church of England came in last; here the Episcopal Church does pioneer work. I am glad to see this.

"Good Friday services at La Grande were well attended. Here the Rev. Mr. Kaye, who has immediate charge of the three churches in this valley, joined us. After services, our company mounted and trotted across the valley (a distance of fifteen miles) to a beautiful hamlet called, from its position, the Cove. We were taken care of in Mr. French's fine mansion. For the last year there has been a church in course of erection. It was now completed, and was ready for opening on Easter Day [April 16]. It rained on Friday and Saturday, and the snow on the mountains melting rapidly, ran down the valley, flooding a portion of it, rendering it impossible for many people from a distance to come. Easter Sunday was pleasant. What a glorious day for the opening of a Church! You cannot imagine what a church we have here away out in the mountains of Oregon. The chancel window is in three parts, and is a memorial of Mr. and Mrs. French and their son Thomas. The design is not conventional; the figures are perfect; the effect inspiring.

"The congregation listened attentively to the plain Easter truths, told to many of them for the first time. Mrs. Kaye, whose sweet disposition suits the work, was very successful in forming a choir, so that the grand old chants breathed the music of the Church in every word. A few zealous Churchmen joined heartily in the responses; strangers took up the spirit and mingled their prayers and praises. What a joyous day! How pleased some of your New York people would have been, if they could have been present and witnessed the scene—how glad they would be for having helped along such a noble work!

"The Rev. Mr. Kaye's labors here are bringing forth good fruit. He has taken a great burden from the shoulders of Dr. Nevius, whose mission, with this valley left out, is as large as an empire. He has neglected no part of his field, and in three years he has opened *five churches*, and has made arrangements for *building more.*

"I am sure you will be glad to hear that Church work is progressing with such strides. May all Eastern Church people pray for our noble work and self-sacrificing workers. May they give of their abundance to those who toil the Master. May they have confidence in those who are called to this arduous labor."

Oregon Churchman
June 15, 1876

*Could this be the "friend" who was going to accompany Nevius on his summer tour, mentioned by him in his letter to Asa Gray of May 4, 1876?

———

1876: April 16
Rev. R. D. Nevius:
"Eastern Oregon Mission.

"Mr. Editor: Another church has been added to those which already mark almost every town of considerable size in this part of the state. On Easter [April 16] services were held for the first time in the Church of the Ascension at the Cove in Union County. This church was begun about the same time as the church at Union. The work has been delayed for several reasons, now however, this church is more complete than either of the two others of Grand Ronde Valley. Indeed it would be difficult to find any respect in which it is incomplete. It is built after the plan of St. Luke's [St. Paul's], Walla Walla,—the tower and spire excepted; and it is an improvement upon that church in its interior, —the exterior being the same, with the addition of a bell cote. The windows, however, give the interior a beauty which none other of our churches have—not even Trinity Church, Portland. The side windows are of a new pattern, both of quarry and border glass, and are very beautiful. Each light of the triplet is distinct. The central window has two full figures and the others have one each. They are Memorials to Mr. Robert French, Mrs. Helen D. French and Mr. Thomas French, their son. The central light bears the figure of an angel above the clouds in a starry space receiving an aged Saint. Both figures are beautiful and the grouping is very effective. They represent the reception in the clouds by the angelic host, of the faithful dead caught up to be with their Lord in the air. The North light of the triplet bears a figure of Faith and is a memorial to Mrs. Helen D. French. The face and figure are very beautiful. This figure and that of St. John the

Evangelist which fills the South light of the triplet has little of the conventionalism of sacred art and seems to be a novel trenchment [sic, treatment?]. The latter commemorates the character of Mr. Thomas French. There is a square compartment below the figures in each window which is constructed for ventilation.

"The church has all necessary furniture for nave and chancel. All has been simply yet very neatly made by the carpenter from good and tasteful patterns. Taken all together this last new church exceeds all our churches in beauty. The cost is about $3500. Of this amount $1000 was contributed in the east, or procured by the personal influence of members of the family whose name is on the windows. Of this, $285 was contributed by the Church of the Ascension, New York, and $500 is yet needed before the church can be consecrated. The building of this church and the supply of money has been no care or worry to me. Everything has been done by a zealous Churchman by whose good works the faithful dead who are commemorated yet speak.

"At Holy Communion a massive service of Holy vessels was used from which long ago they whose names are recorded in the window over the altar were accustomed to receive Sacramental refreshment. They were given by the church to which the family formerly belonged, and are in part a gift originally, of a grandmother of the son who has been chiefly instrumental in building the church.

"A Bible and Prayer books for the chancel and altar and a font are yet to come from another member of the family.

"The services of Easter day were very inspiring, and apparently effective—the large congregation having never before to the same extent recognized the beauty and glory of the Church. We had formerly worshipped in the rudest of school houses, and had never before had the aid of an organ and a well trained choir, nor the satisfaction of well sustained responses.

"The congregation was large, filling the church, and quite a number of persons from the churches at La Grande and Union were present.

"The Rev. Mr. Kaye resides here and a parsonage is now well under way for him. He has immediate charge of these three churches of this Mission,* and good results are already seen which can be referred alone to the presence of a Clergyman resident with his family in the Valley. Mr. Kaye seems to like this work and has adapted himself to it quite easily, and has before him a good prospect of great results from an effective and prudent ministry.

R. D. Nevius
Oregon Churchman
May 4, 1876

*i.e., Cove, La Grande and Union.

———

1876: May 4
Rev. R. D. Nevius:

"Baker City Or
"May 4, 1876.

"Dr. Asa Gray

"I should be very glad to have your Revisions of genus Penthstemon. I have a large number of species and find difficulty with them. I will be extremely obliged for any other revisions which you may send me.

"I find your Lupinus, Oenothera, and Potentilla so great as help, that I cannot resist the temptation to ask for more.

"I send my photograph* for which I have waited long. It happened to me to get the best likeness ever taken of me, at a canvas tent in the mountains, and I have waited to secure a print from the same negative.

"I am about to take a long tour alone in my buggy 300 miles to the Dalles—and back again, all by a mountain road. What would not many of you poor fellows who grind the brick pavements give for such a holiday! I have a plan to go from here to Boise City Idaho, i.e. 250 [sic, 150] miles east and from thence through several mining camps not visited before, to the Dalles 300 miles west [from the mining camps or from Baker City], and then home [to Baker City] again. I shall have a friend with me. We shall be on the road for three months, and leaving our buggy at the Dalles, shall go by river to Portland and thence to Seattle for the meeting of our Convocation.

"Many of your and my friends who must have a summer vacation, must pay hundreds of dollars for pleasures less than this. And this comes to me incidental to a work that is itself a pleasure.

"Again and again I wish for a companion on my journeys who could inform me on questions that occur at every hour as I pass over this wonderful old, old world with all its old glacial and volcanic scars. And it would be an untold delight to take you with me for such a tour in such a season as this. Pardon me for permitting my fancy to run away with. I mean this as a suggestion and an invitation to you or to any of your friends who would be glad to have such an opportunity for scientific study as does not easily or cheaply happen to those who depend upon public conveyances.

"Thanking you again for your many favors and for the opportunity of looking you in the face."**

"I am
"Very truly yours
"R. D. Nevius"***

*Letter from [Ms.] Hollis G. Bedell, Ph.D., Gray Herbarium Archives, The Botany Libraries, Harvard University, 22 Divine Avenue, Cambridge MA 02138 to David Powers, 23 February, 1989: "In response to your letter asking about photographs of Reuben Nevius, we do [have] a photograph in our collection. I believe the photo we have is the one mentioned in Nevius's letter to Asa Gray because the back of the photograph has the following written in Nevius's hand: "Eastern Oregon Mission, May 4, '76.... It is mounted in Mrs. Gray's autograph album. This set consists of 5 large albums with handwriting samples, and photographs, of numerous prominent biologists, naturalists, collectors, etc. of the last century."

**Nevius implied later in a birthday letter to Gray dated November 18, 1885, that he had never actually met him. Therefore Nevius must have been thanking Gray for a photograph and enclosing one of himself in return.

***The typescript of this letter in Atwood's notes has typed at the head, "Gray Herbarium Library—Gray Autograph Collection." Other letters came from the same source, but were photocopied at the Harvard Library.

_____

1876: May 15
Rev. R. D. Nevius:
"Missionary Correspondence.
                    "The Dalles, May 15, 1876
"Mr. Editor:
"My ride to the Dalles in my own conveyance [buggy]* gave me an opportunity of visiting a little town, Heppner, which is off the line of travel by public conveyance. It is about 60 miles from Pendleton on the best road to the Dalles, and a very good road it is,—up and along high divides between deep-canyoned creeks, where a sparse population find pleasant homes while their cattle, horses and sheep feed upon their thousand hills. Heppner is a small town, on one of these creeks with less than 100 inhabitants. One of my old parishioners from La Grande, now living in Pendleton had preceded me one day and had announced my coming, and had prepared for service in the school house. I found there also a young woman who had lately been baptized and confirmed in Salem. With their aid we had full evening service, chanting all the canticles. All the people of the town were present, and after service there was a general desire that we might often give them a service. No provision is made for any regular religious services here, and this was the first opportunity for public worship for a long time. Along the creek for 15 miles above and 30, perhaps, below, and upon other creeks not far away, there are hundreds of people who have no opportunity for public instruction in religion. They are desirous for it and large congregations would attend well advertised services.

"In the morning as I was leaving, a man made himself known to me as a member of the Church of England; and asked for a prayer book. Everywhere when I meet an Englishman I find a friend in our work. And often-times I feel that I am specially sent to them to keep God's promise made to them in the covenant of Baptism.

"The people are hospitable and cordial, and I shall have many reasons for remembering my visit to Heppner with pleasure. If we had a clergyman stationed at Pendleton he could do good service among the people settled quite thickly along the Umatilla river, and more sparsely along the creeks in this part of Oregon.
                    R. D. Nevius"
                    Oregon Churchman
                    May 18, 1876
*See Bishop Morris's letter to the *Philadelphia Register,* 1875, above.

Chaenactis nevii, a member of the sunflower family that grows only in Oregon's John Day Valley, was transmitted to Asa Gray at Harvard University in 1876, though not published (and named after Nevius) until 1883 [Abrams and Stenchfield (1960) 241-242]. It is one of two yellow windflowers that bloom on clay hillsides in the vicinity of the John Day Fossil Beds in late spring, withering and drying in late summer [telephone conversation with Prof. Kenton Chambers, Oregon State University, July 17, 1987]. As we can see above, Nevius left The Dalles February 4, 1876. On March 22 he was at Prairie City, still waiting to cross the Blue Mountains to Baker City "after an absence of three months." On April 12 he accompanied the "Canadian Churchman" from Baker City to Cove, to hold the first service in the new church there on April 16. Then on May 4 Nevius wrote Asa Gray from Baker City to transmit a photograph of himself taken sometime earlier "at a canvas tent in the mountains," and to thank Gray for "the opportunity of looking you in the face [by photograph]." By May 15 Nevius was at The Dalles, where he had arrived via Heppner. This suggests the following route: Baker City - Boise City - Eastern Oregon mining camps - (on a mountain road to) Canyon City - Heppner - The Dalles, thence to Portland and Seattle to return to Baker City in mid-August in time to accompany the Bishop on a trip back to Canyon City via the "Olive Creek Diggings" (Granite vicinity, see August 1876 below). The route from John Day (Canyon City) to Heppner (via what is now the Fossil Beds) is not a usual one today, but is very plausible. All this suggests that the samples of Chaenactis nevii which were transmitted to Gray in 1876 must have been collected at this time. Nevius first held services in the John Day Valley in late May and early June of 1874 (where his horse was waiting for him after a trip to Portland), and visited again in late June of 1875. He must have become aware of Chaenactis nevii at these times.

It seems that it was about this time or slightly earlier that Nevius met pioneer Botanist William C. Cusick (1842 - 1922), who said in a letter: "I was interested in plants as early in life as I can remember but I had no book on botany till I was 22 years of age [in 1864], a soldier in the U. S. Volunteer Service at Fort Lapwai, Idaho. I sent to a friend in Portland, Ore. and got Gray's Lessons in Botany. This I studied pretty carefully during the winter. In the spring I made a small collection of plant specimens for the herbarium. Later I got others of Dr. Gray's works till I had most of his books. I did little in study and collecting till coming to Eastern Oregon in 1872. I was so fortunate in making the acquaintance of Dr. R. D. Nevius, and in the fall of 1880 Dr. S. Watson spent a few days at my cabin. I got much botanical information from these gentlemen. Later I learned much by correspondence with Dr. Gray.... [fn; W. C. Cusick to W. W. Eggleston, now in New York Botanical Library, Bronx Park, N.Y.]"

Erwin P. Lange, "Pioneer Botanists of the Pacific Northwest," *Oregon Historical Quarterly,* LVII, 2 (June, 1956), p. 117.

_____

1876: June 25-26
Battle of the Little Big Horn fought, Gen. George A. Custer and his troops killed. U.S. troops defeated Sitting Bull and Crazy Horse October 3,1 1876.

_____

1876: July 4
National centennial celebration, exposition in Philadelphia.

_____

1876: August 1
Colorado admitted to the United States.

_____

1876: August
Bishop Morris:
"Eastern Oregon.
"Episcopal Visitation.
"...On Tuesday morning, Aug. 22nd, the Bishop and Dr. Nevius set out from

Baker City for a drive of 90 miles across the Blue Mountains to Canyon City. Not having taken fully into account the roughness of an untried mountain road, night overtook them when they were some sixteen miles short of the hospitable miner's house where they were expected. Nothing was left but to stop at a deserted cabin, in the forest, long inhabited only by the wood rats, and to make themselves as comfortable as they could, with the remains of their lunch for supper, and a miner's board bunk for their bed. Their poor horses fared worse than this, in a hard snow storm which came up during the night, chilling them to their bones. The bright sun of the next morning cheered and inspired man and beast, and by noon the discouraged travelers were comfortably quartered, and most hospitably entertained for the night by a bachelor miner of the 'Olive Creek Diggings.'"

?On Thursday evening [August 24] Canyon City was reached, and in the afternoon the Corner Stone of St. Thomas' Church was duly laid, and addresses made by the Bishop, and the Rev. Dr. Nevius.

"On Sunday morning the Bishop preached and administered the Holy Communion.... The work at Canyon City continues to grow, and there is every encouragement to prosecute it with vigor. It will be an *effort* [emphasis original] to complete the church, but the effort will be made, and the work will be done, in time, by God's blessing.

"The people so far have shewn [sic] a very commendable spirit, and if their means equaled their willingness, the *completed* building would not long be delayed. The collection of over $100 in coin at the laying of the Corner Stone, and $20 at the Sunday Services is a good index of their spirit of liberality...."

Morris, *Oregon Churchman*

September 7, 1876

*Mr. Rob Moffatt of the Water Resources Division, U. S. Geological Survey (Salem, Oregon office) offered the following information about the "Olive Creek Diggings" in a telephone conversation of September 25, 1987: The "Olive Creek Diggings" was a hydraulic or placer mining operation that continued into the 1930s. It was located approximately at lat. 44 degrees 43 minutes 45 seconds North, long. 118 degrees 28 minutes 45 seconds West, or about four air miles ssw of the site of Granite (then known as Independence). The site of the "Diggings" was where the Eureka Mine in Three Cent Gulch appears on the USGS 7.5 min. series Greenhorn quadrangle (1972). (Mr. Moffatt noted that "Robinsonville" on the quad sheet should be "Robisonville," and that the source of his information was a file on Olive Creek at the Oregon Department of Geology and Mineral Industries, Portland office.)

1876: September 6-7 (Friday-Saturday)

Twenty-fourth Annual Convocation of the Missionary Jurisdiction of Oregon and Washington, Trinity Church, Portland.

Bishop Morris's annual Convocation address:

"...New Churches.

"During the year we have occupied five new churches—St. Peter's, Albany; St. Paul's Church, The Dalles; Church of the Redeemer, Pendleton; All Saint's Church, Weston, and the Church of the Ascension, Cove. They are all well designed and church-like buildings, but those of The Dalles and Cove are such in a remarkable degree.

"The only new church begun this year is that of St. Thomas, Canyon City, the corner-stone of which I laid, with the assistance of Rev. Dr. Nevius, on the 26th of August. This, when completed, will be the first and only Protestant church in a wide scope of country four or five times as large as the State of Massachusetts. The Rev. Dr. Nevius has done good work in laying the foundation of the Church in this part of the country. Two congregations have been gathered—one of them at Prairie City, in the valley of the John Day river—and twenty-three persons confirmed. Canyon City is the county seat of Grant county, sustained by mining and agricultural interests, the latter of which are such as to increase year by year. The church building will necessarily be of moderate size, and be plain and simple in the extreme. But even then, in this mountain region, two hundred miles from water navigation, it will cost twice as much as in Portland. The people there have begun this work by a very liberal subscription, and, at the laying of the corner-stone of the church, an offering was made of a hundred dollars in coin. There is no place in the whole mission at the

present time that I am more solicitous to aid than this, and I have ventured to promise two hundred dollars, when the building is roofed in. Would it be in vain to ask some privileged one to give me the means to redeem this promise? If no such help is given, there will be no way to keep my word but by another draft upon the poor, private purse, always lean and thin but now almost entirely empty. At Prairie City, Dr. Nevius has secured the gift of an entire block of ground, the conveyance of which has been made to the Missionary Bishop [Morris], in trust. Here too, we ought to lay the foundation of a church building before another year.

"The work in the Grand Ronde valley, now more immediately in charge of the Rev. Geo. T. Kaye, has been marked by the erection of the beautiful Church of the Ascension, Cove, and a neat and comfortable Rectory close beside it. This Gothic, timber church with bell gable and cross, admirable chancel arrangements and beautiful memorial windows, is largely due to the liberality of Mr. Samuel G. French and members of his family in the East. It occupies a sheltered 'cove' in the bold and beautiful hills that rise up behind it; and standing in its porch one looks out westward over a well tilled and fertile valley of surpassing beauty, where, fourteen years ago, the untaught and savage Indian had undisputed control, and where no white man had dared to plant his home. Now, in the three corners of this valley, barely out of sight of each other, stand three churches, with a rectory beside one of them, and from one to the other our missionary [Kaye] goes with the messages of salvation and the blessed influences of the church of Christ, to mold and train this pioneer people. You think of the contrast that these few years have made, and you bless God that His Church had been able to set up her banners thus early in the history of his country, and you pray that so she may go on until she has occupied the whole land....

"St. Paul's Church, The Dalles.

"I reported at the last Convocation that I had laid the corner stone of this church, and that the building was in progress. It has since been finished, and though small, is a model of beauty and fitness. In the absence of Dr. Nevius, at other points in his mission, services have been kept up in this church by the Bishop and other clergy, twice a month, with very little interruption. The congregation have thus been kept together, and the way prepared for promising pastoral work among them. Dr. Nevius will make it his headquarters for the greatest part of the coming winter. There are at present 15 communicants...."

"Parochial Reports....

"Report of St. Peter's Church, La Grande, for the year ending Sept. 30, 1876

"The Rev. Geo. T. Kaye, Missionary.

"Baptisms—Infant, 4. Total, 4.

"Communicants—Present number, 18.

"Sunday School Teachers, 4; Pupils, 25.

"Marriages, 1. Burials, 2.

"Number of Public Services on Sundays, 29;   other days, 4. Total 33.

"Number of families connected with the   Congregation, 20.

"Average attendance, 23.

"Collections and Contributions: For Salary, $168; Domestic Missions, $9.10; Parochial purposes, $130; Miscellaneous, $6. Total, $313.

["Geo. T. Kaye,

Missionary in Charge.]

———

"Report of St. John's Church, Union, for the year ending Sept. 30, 1876.

"The Rev. Geo. T. Kaye, Missionary.

[1882]

1882:

Smalley (1883) 414:

"The track reached the shore of Lake Pend d'Oreille January 9th, 1882.

"The crossing of Snake River at Ainsworth is at present effected by a transfer boat which carries an entire passenger train. A bridge is in process of construction, however, and will be completed before the high-water season of 1884...."

1882: February

Wood (1968) 28:

"In February, 1882 there had been an unsuccessful attempt in Congress to take away the Northern Pacific land grant because the road had not been completed, and while this bill failed to pass, Villard was well aware that there would be further attempts, and moved to complete the road as quickly as possible. ... During the two years between September 1881 and August 1883, the track gangs averaged a mile and a half per day."

———

1882: March 3, April 1
Columbia Churchman (April 1, 1882)
"Death Of Mr. French....
[Rev. R. D. Nevius:]

"Pertinent to the announcement of the death of Mr. S. G. French and notwithstanding an obituary notice is expected from his latest pastor, a few words from me relative to his connection with the early life of the Church in Grand Ronde valley may not be amiss [sic]. The mission in that valley was formally opened under my pastoral charge, and Mr. French gave it sympathetic support from first to last, in all the struggles which resulted in building the three churches at The Cove, Union, and La Grande.

"Long before this he had sought pastoral care, first in early times from Bishop Scott from whom, with others, [he] secured a visit, (at that time there were three communicants in the valley), and afterwards from Bishop Morris. The first visitation of the latter was preceded by a visit (perhaps two visits), by Rev. Mr. Wells and resulted in the confirmation of 23 persons at La Grande.

"Very soon after, a prolonged visit was made by me to the valley, and ultimately I took charge of the mission, beginning almost immediately to build Churches at the three points above mentioned and at Baker City.

"Mr. French met me at once with liberal and intelligent advice. And from that time largely sustained the mission until his death. His house was always my home when in the vicinity, and often I had recourse to it for refreshment and study when wearied with journeyings or depressed with discomfort and discouragement.

"Mr. French was socially and intellectually a man of refinement, and was singularly free from the temptation which leads so many in a new country to excuse themselves, in lawlessness of life and rudeness of manners. Eminently a business man, he was untiringly active, and very methodical, orderly and exact. He was inflexible in purpose. And to an exceptional extent, independent of popular favor, prejudice or opinion. Pure in life, consistent in action, and restraining even his generous impulses by his notion of justice and prudent foresight for others, it happened to him as it sometimes does, that he had few lovers yet was universally honored, respected, and esteemed. Ascension Church at The Cove will be his fitting memorial. He supplied $1,800 of its cost, ($2,000). He relieved the missionary entirely from care and responsibility in its erection and alone built the parsonage.

"The Chancel window which is one of the finest in all our churches was given by his relatives in New Jersey and commemorates his honored father, mother and brother and now it perpetuates a name which he has made memorable in Oregon as they had before done in another State.

"R. D. Nevius."

———

1882: April 22-26
Rev. R. L. Stevens(?):
"A Missionary Journey In Eastern Oregon.
"To Editor of Columbia Churchman.

"Early this spring Bishop Morris extended an invitation to your correspondent, to accompany him in his visitation to different mission stations scattered over Eastern Oregon. On [Saturday] the 22nd of April, according to agreement, we left Portland for the Dalles by the morning boat. I remained at the Dalles to hold services on Sunday in place of Mr. McEwan, who was sent before to Pendleton, while the Bishop stopped at Umatilla.... "On Monday we proceeded to Walla Walla.... We journeyed from the Dalles to Walla Walla in a sleeping car, occupying the whole night. How suggestive of the growth and development of Oregon is traveling in such a conveyance, and at such a time. It reminds us that night and day there is a con-

tinual stream of humanity pouring into the state and occupying its fertile valleys and hills, that this immigration is made up of individual souls, sheep without a shepherd, for whom Christ died, and whose everlasting salvation depends upon the provision the Church makes for them. What an opportunity for the Church does this formation period afford, and when can the like ever be found again? Should the Church meet these incoming crowds and show her love and care for them and their children, she would win their affection and gratitude. As the country grew she could develope [sic] these powers for good which would bring forth abundant fruit, and all generations would call her blessed. Could it be once realized by those whom God has gifted with means and powers to work in His service, what is hers to be accomplished, there would be no lack of men or money wherewith to carry on Christ's work. If the Church delays to take this work in hand every opposing force will have time to strengthen itself; prejudice and infidelity will do their work; false forms of religion will occupy the ground and the best opportunity we can ever have, lost.

"At Walla Walla, we were met and hospitably entertained by the rector [Lemuel H. Wells].... Here Dr. Nevius joined us, and with Mr. Wells, accompanied us to Weston. As these two brethren could not wait for the [April 26] Wednesday evening service, but were compelled to return to Walla Walla, we parted from them with many regrets....

"From Weston we drove to Pendleton and the County seat of Umatilla County. We were quite surprised at the evidence of rapid growth and prosperity everywhere manifested. There was a stir and life about it which we have seen in no other town of its size yet visited. We have a Church, the inside of which is more attractive than the outward appearance. This is perhaps due to its color; for it has a quaint bell tower and is fairly proportioned. Its color has given it a name among the town people, which we feel some hesitancy in recording; as, however it has probably never been given to any other Church in the world, we will whisper it in print. They call it (*Horrible dictui*) 'The little brown jug.' We hope when they enlarge this Church (and they have raised a considerable sum for this purpose) that they will paint it another color and this name will then sink into oblivion....

"While in Pendleton [April 27 and 28] The Rev. and Mrs. Octavius Parker arrived. They were on their way to Baker City which Mr. Parker has accepted as his field of labor. He remained here and held services on Sunday the 30th.

"At two o'clock Saturday Morning [April 29] we were called to take the stage running daily from Pendleton to La Grande, in Grande Ronde valley. Then began the hardest portion of our trip. The stage was an ordinary farm wagon drawn by six horses. It had but two motions, the one very rapid, the other very slow, according as we were on the plains or climbing hills. Our route lay over the Blue Mts. and through the snow. We carried shovels in case of necessity and they were brought into play in passing around teams blockading our way. After a journey of seventeen hours during which we changed horses four times, we reached La Grande at 8 P.M....."

"From La Grande we drove to the Cove fifteen miles distant. The Church here is a little gem. A gothic structure with stained glass windows, and with all the appointments for service complete excepting lamps or means for lighting. Close by is a pretty parsonage occupied by Mr. Smith.... At the close of the service the Bishop made a touching allusion to Mr. French by whose influence the Church at the Cove was built and sustained during his life, and who in his death has left such noble monuments of his zeal for the Master's service....

"R. L. S."

Columbia Churchman, May 15, 1882
Journal of the Proceedings of the Second Convocation of the Protestant Episcopal church of the Missionary Jurisdiction of Washington, Held in Trinity Church, Seattle, W.T., June 22-25, 1882.

———

June 22 (Thursday):
"The Rev. R. D. Nevius, D.D., Missionary, Spokane Falls and vicinity" was listed among the clergy of the Jurisdiction. Nevius was also listed as one of three Examining Chaplains. His name is not among those who responded to the opening roll call, but there is no record of his coming later and he seems to have been active from the outset.

Nevius was reappointed to the Committee on Christian Education and Literature with the Rev. Ernest E. Wood, Gov. E. P. Ferry, and R. G. O'Brien.

"Afternoon Session....

"The Rev. Dr. Lathrop presented the question 'who is a communicant in the Episcopal Church?' and submitted the following resolution:

Resolved—That the Clergy of this jurisdiction report to the convocation as Communicants only those who have taken the Holy communion during the previous year, except such persons [that] were by unavoidable circumstances prevented from so doing.

"Pending discussion of the motion to adopt the resolution the Convocation took a recess to attend a meeting of the Women's Auxiliary.... After the meeting of the Ladies in Trinity Rectory they adjourned to the Church, where a report of their proceedings was made, and [they] were addressed by Bishop Paddock, Bishop Sillitoe [of New Westminster], and others.

"Evening Session.

"After Evening Prayer the Bishop delivered his Annual Address whereupon on motion that portion of the address relating to the 'Marriage State' was referred to a committee consisting of the Rev. G. H. Watson, the Rev. Dr. Nevius, and A. M. Brooks, Esq.

"On a like motion that portion of the address relating to 'Sunday Observance' [was referred] to a committee....

Bishop's Address:

"... Immediately after the rising of our last Convocation, I proceeded to the eastern part of the Territory, where I spent the greater part of the Autumn and Winter. It is a region, into which emigrants are now rapidly coming; but the number will probably be increased five fold, on the completion of that great railroad, which will lessen the expense and increase the facilities for reaching this rich agricultural section.

"During the months of September and October [1881], I passed three Sundays at Spokane Falls, and have since given another Lord's Day to that place, in addition to services held with the Rev. Dr. Nevius, on week days.... We have at Spokane, a building, in which a school is maintained. I have purchased during the year, at a low rate, additional lots of land, to which it may be advisable at some future time, to remove the Institution. The School Building, at present is used for the Services of the Lord's Day, the Chancel being cut off, during the week, from the main room, by a heavy curtain. The tinting of the walls during the last year, has added to the appearance of the interior of the structure, and friends have placed in the interior of the Chancel, an Episcopal Chair. There is no debt on the property. We have in Spokane, a good foundation for future growth. But circumstances have prevented progress during the year, and I have advised Dr. Nevius to devote more of his time to other important stations growing up in the District.

"He has been in the habit of visiting, occasionally, two of our Military Posts, and, in the latter part of September [1881], I accompanied him to Fort Colville, about ninety miles to the northwest from Spokane.... It is our duty, as well as a privilege, to offer such services as we can, to those stationed for our protection on the frontier, at places, to a great extent, deprived of religious privileges. The visit of the Missionary and the Bishop is always made pleasant by the courtesy of the officers and their families. At Colville, we have a few Communicants; a Sunday School has been maintained; and, at times, one of the officers has led the Church's Service on the Lord's Day.

"Cheney, to the southwest from Spokane, has been visited by me twice. Two lots, eligibly located have been secured; but we have not felt encouraged to go forward as yet, with a Church Building.

"Sprague, another town farther to the south, presents a very encouraging opening. We were the first to move for the erection of a House of God in the place. A 'Shelter' has already been constructed for holding services, and I hope that, before the close of the season, a little Church will be finished, to be added to those which it has been the privilege of Dr. Nevius to see arise in Mission Stations that have been under his care.

"I visited Colfax in October, and met good congregations and some Communicants. The Rev. Mr. Wells and Dr. Nevius have occasionally held services in the town, and a lot has been donated for a Church....

"The care of Idaho rests on Bishop Tuttle; but it requires so long and arduous a journey, and involves so much expense for him to reach the northern portion, that I have consented to render any assistance in my power, by visitation in that region. At Fort Coeur d'Alene I have confirmed two, presented by the Rev. Dr. Nevius; and at Lewiston eight, presented by the rector, the Rev. J. D. McConkey. At the Military Post, we had the first service at the opening of the very near and Churchly Building erected by the Government, for religious and other assemblings....

"I pray you, Brethren of the Clergy, ever to remember the office laid upon each one of us in this Territory, to be a Missionary. It is a noble office, an honorable name to bear. The Son of God incarnate was a Great Missionary to this sinful world.... It is not enough that we minister faithfully to those who come to us in the Church building. Souls are living and dying, bereft of the Church's Ministrations. Our office is to go out into the villages and towns, the 'highways and hedges,' to 'teach and premonish; to feed and provide for the Lord's family; to seek for Christ's sheep that are dispersed abroad, and for His children who are in the midst of this naughty world, that they may be saved, through Christ, forever'....

"Success in our work is closely connected with men's resting from ordinary toil on the Lord's Day. On my first visitations through the Territory, I was greatly pained at the general and open profanation of holy time. The change, this year, has been marked, and pleasing.... Long continued observation shows that, in the long run, more manual labor can be done by those resting one day in seven, than by those taking no rest from moil and soil.

"The mind, too, needs just that change which the right observance of the Lord's Day brings. From violation of the Divine Law often comes nervous prostration and insanity.... It seems to me that it would be a step backward, greatly to the detriment of our commonwealth and our people, if our Legislature ever repeals the law which helps to make Sunday a day of rest. [Gov. Ferry in attendance.]

"There is a crying evil, the abatement of which should have the aid of all lovers of purity, good order and progress. I refer to the very loose views widely prevalent concerning the marriage relation. Marriage is ordained of God. The relation between man and wife is in Scripture likened to that of Christ and the Church. How proper that the ratification of the nuptial bond should be with the blessing of God sought on the union. It is painful to notice, in our secular papers, with how many the idea seems to prevail of marriage as only a civil contract, made before some Justice of the Peace. Beginning the new life, without imploring the Divine blessing, by action that seems to put God out of thought, or to slight His ordinance, the relationship formed is aptly to be held in low esteem, as an affair of convenience; divorce, only allowed by the Law of God for one cause, takes place on the most frivolous pretexts, society becomes demoralized, and looseness and immorality, the sure precursors, as all history shows, of civil decadence and death, are extended far and wide. It may be well that the voice of the Convocation should be heard on this subject.

"... It had been asserted and understood that in the event of any division of the Jurisdiction [of Oregon and Washington] the Episcopal Fund and the Disabled Clergy Fund should be divided, in proportion to the amount contributed by the State or Territory, I ... received from Bishop Morris on the first of last December, $194.33 for the Episcopal Fund of Washington Territory, and $515.67 for the Disabled Clergy Fund. These amounts I deemed it best to leave for the present where they had been deposited and were drawing interest, but would ask of the Convocation the appointment of a Treasurer or Treasurers for these funds. Desiring to have the aid of others in the management of pecuniary trusts, and believing that such an arrangement would be more satisfactory to the church in general, I have associated with me one of our Clergymen and three Laymen, under the General Law of the Territory, a corporation has been formed, bearing the name of 'The Trustees of the Protestant Episcopal Church in Washington Territory.' The Bishop is always to be the President, and any vacancies occurring are to be filled by the Board, on nomination by the Bishop. I have committed to the custody of this Body a number of deeds for lots and other Church property...."

June 23 (Friday):

The committee on the *Columbia Churchman* reported that a gain of 79 subscribers had been made. "More and more clearly are we convinced of the absolute necessity of the paper as a means of information concerning the movements of the Bishops, of a mode of communications between the Bishops and their Jurisdictions, and as a missionary agency among the people." They recommended that "each Parish and Mission — practically subsidize the paper by taking respectively so many copies as shall ensure its sustenance...."

"The Rev. Geo. H. Watson, from the committee to whom was referred that portion of the Bishop's Address relating to 'Family and Social Morals' [divorce], submitted the following which was adopted:

Your committee to whom was referred that portion of the Bishop's Address which related to the alarming progress of loose theory and consequent immoral action as regards the family relations, not withstanding the sacredness of the nuptial tie which the work of God so plainly teaches, beg leave to respectfully report as follows:

1. That the common sentiment of the masses upon this subject is one which threatens unmistakably the very life of the nation.

2. That we can at least, take heart in the fact that, as this Church has a fair amount of influence in the land, so has she placed upon her Statute Book, a clear rebuke to these socialists of the day, in that she refuses to allow any Clergyman ministering at her altars the right 'to solemnize the marriage of any person who has a divorced husband or wife still living, if such husband or wife has been put away for any cause arising after the marriage;' save that the innocent party in the case of adultery is excepted from this rule, also parties divorced seeking to be united again.

3. That as, however, no law is of any moment unless it be carried out in practice, the Clergy of the Church are requested to keep strictly within the rule of the Cannon, and, in the face of unjust criticism to take their place on the side of purity and justice.

4. That ministers should preach judiciously, but plainly for fidelity in the marriage state, and that the Church Press should proclaim widely what the law of Christ and the Church is as regards this matter, so that the sin may not be laid to our Church.

Geo. H. Watson,

R. D. Nevius,

A. M. Brooks.

"The Rev. Dr. Nevius, from the committee on 'Christian Education and Literature,' submitted the following which on motion was adopted:

"The Rev. Dr. Nevius, from the committee on 'Christian Education and Literature believe it to be unnecessary to mention one by one the Educational Institutions already existing in this Jurisdiction. They are the same as existed and were reported by the committee at the last Convocation. Your committee, however, are glad to say that considerable progress has been made in all the schools of the Jurisdiction.... We are pleased to learn that the Rev. Dr. and Mrs. Lathrop, late of California, have been secured as successor to Mr. and Mrs. Wells [at Walla Walla] Progress in this direction shows that the Church is alive to the wants of the time, and it is anxious to provide for the well being both spiritual and intellectual, of the Children permitted to her charge.

As regards literature, your committee are glad to notice that the *Columbia Churchman* is still running a useful career, and hope that this periodical will be supported more liberally than it has been in the past.

R. D. Nevius

E. P. Ferry,

E. E. Wood."

"The President [Bishop Paddock] announced the appointment of the following named persons as the Diocesan Missionary Committee for the ensuing year: Ex-officio Chairman, the bishop, the Rev. Geo. H. Watson, the Rev. Dr. Nevius, the Rev. Dr. Lathrop, the Rev. Ernest E. Wood, J. J. Beeson, R. G. O'Brien, Capt. Edward Hunter, and Dr. F. E. Towne."

On motion the matter of 'Forms of Parochial Reports' was referred to a committee consisting of the Rev. Dr. Nevius, the Rev. A. S. Nicholson, and Gov. E. P. Ferry, with the instructions to report proper forms for use in the Jurisdiction."

"The Diocesan Missionary Committee presented the following, which was on motion adopted....

The committee feel that they must place on record their sorrow at not having with them at this time the respected Treasurer, Mr. Fletcher [Hon. Joseph M.

Fletcher of Vancouver], who was appointed at last Convocation. His lamentable disappearance is known to all, and they feel deeply for his family in the trouble and grief which is now their lot....

The committee feel strongly that in view of the scattered nature of the work in many parts of the Jurisdiction, a traveling Missionary is required as soon as one can be obtained.... It has been suggested that the Diocesan Committee heartily co-operate with the women in this most necessary work, and that they promise to add to the sum already pledged, an amount sufficient to complete the income of a General Missionary.... It is quite evident to all that such a man is required, and that much good can be done by constant traveling from place to place. Therefore it is hoped that the subject in question will immediately occupy the attention of the Diocesan Committee appointed for the coming year.*

... A circular letter, drawn up by the Bishop of Oregon, has been placed before the committee, to see if it might not serve as a model for a similar one to be sent out by our Diocesan. The letter is proposed to be forwarded to any Church person heard of in outlying districts by the neighboring Clergy, notifying such person that the district in which he or she resides is under the charge of such and such a Clergyman. A committee has therefore been appointed to act in this matter, and to prepare a suitable circular letter. ....They are to submit the result to the Bishop. .... There is no doubt that many of our people are lost to the Church, and swept into the different sectarian bodies, through the feeling that the Clergy have no special interest in those outside their own appointed sphere of labor.

Ernest E. Wood."

*The Standing Committee consisted of Revs. A. S. Nicholson and Geo. H. Watson (Clerical) and Hon. E. P. Ferry and Mr. Geo. E. Atkinson (Lay) in the 1882 and 1884 *Journal* (not mentioned in 1883).

June 24 (Saturday)

"The committee to whom was referred the matter of Parochial Reports reported the following form for use in this Jurisdiction.... [See in original.]

"The Registrar [Nevius] made the following report, which was adopted:

The Registrar of the convocation would respectfully report that so far he has secured only an imperfect suite of the Journals of Convocation.

That [of] the History of the Church in the Jurisdiction, Memorial, Anniversary and Historical Addresses by the Clergy, in their Parishes, will afford the best and most reliable information. That these addresses, etc., unfortunately are not always published, and are not accessible to the Registrar. The Registrar would take this opportunity of expressing a desire for a copy of such addresses, or an opportunity of copying such addresses, by the favor of their authors; and also to be informed of the existence of any other interesting historical documents.

The Registrar would recommend that Missionaries would take care to preserve the record of the first action in establishing Missions and Parishes.

All of which is respectfully submitted.

R. D. Nevius."

"Parochial Reports....

"*Report of All Saints Chapel, Spokane Falls for the year ending June 15, 1882.*

"The Rev R. D. Nevius, D.D., Missionary.

"Baptisms, Infant, 6.

"Confirmations, 1.

"Communicants, 6.

"S.S. Teachers, 1; Pupils, 19; Total, 20.

"Burials, 3.

"No. Families, 9.

"Parish School, No. of Children, 22.

"Collections and Contributions—For Salary, $93; Foreign Missions, $3.25; Diocesan Missions, $5.25; Parochial Purposes, $93; Church Building Fund, $5. Total $199.50.

———

"*Report of Fort Coeur d'Alene Mission, for the year ending June 15, 1882.*

"The Rev. R. D. Nevius, D.D., Missionary.

"Has been visited seven times. Services have been held in the very neat Chapel of the Fort, and as at Colville are largely attended by the officers. The number of enlisted men who attend is increasing. Holy Communion is administered at each visit, and the offerings at Services are ordinarily for the support of the Mission.

"Baptisms, Infant, 2.

"Confirmations, 2.

"Communicants, 6.

"Burials, 1.

"Collections and Contributions—For the support of the Missionary, including offerings, $47.50.

——

"*Report of Fort Colville Mission, for the year ending June 15, 1882.*

"The Rev. R. D. Nevius, D.D., Missionary.

"Has been visited five times. At this place a Sunday School has been maintained with much zeal, and has resulted in great good. There is now a resident Chaplain at this Post, and the Sunday School, formerly under the care of *Capt. Edward Hunter*, has passed into the hands of the Chaplain. Services are held in the Chapel of the Post, and Communion is Administered at each visit. There are but four or five families, (Protestants), in the place. These all attend Services, and their children have, I believe without exception, been baptized.

"Communicants, removed, 4; present No., 3.

"Collections and Contributions—For the support of the Missionary, including offerings, $107.

——

"*Report of Sprague Mission, for the year ending June 15, 1882.*

"The Rev. R. D. Nevius, D. D. Missionary.

"Since last Convocation, this town has sprung into existence within the year, and has attained a considerable growth. Regular Services have been maintained here for the past three months. A Church Building has been erected, at the expense of $200, in which Services are now held, and the people interested are zealously increasing a fund for building a Church. Communion has not yet been administered. There are, however,

"Communicants, 7.

"Marriages, 1; Burials, 1.

"Collections and Contributions—For support of the Missionary, $10.

——

"*Report of Cheney Mission, for the year ending June 15, 1882.*

"The Rev. R. D. Nevius, D.D., Missionary

"Baptisms, Infant, 1.

"Burials, 1.

"There are no Communicants at this place, and at present very little interest is shown in the maintaining of our Services. I hope to give more attention to this important point, and that a church will be established here within the coming year.

——

"*Report of Camp Spokane Mission, for the year ending June 15, 1882.*

"The Rev. R. D. Nevius, D.D., Missionary

"At this place few persons are resident, save two officers and the troops of the garrison. I have not yet been able to visit it.

"Communicants, 4.

——

"*Report of Colfax Mission, for the year ending June 15, 1882.*

"The Rev. R. D. Nevius, D.D., Missionary

"I have made several visits during the year to this place, always desiring to give it the attention it deserves. Lately it has been more frequently visited by the Rev. Mr. Wells.

"Communicants, 5.

"Collections and Contributions—For the support of the Missionary, $17.25."

1882: September 21

John Livingston Nevius and Helen S. Coan Nevius left Seneca County, New York "about the middle of the month of August [401]." They "went by the way of San Francisco, crossing the continent for the first time," and sailed for Shanghai in the *City of Tokyo* on September 21 [402]. Mrs. Nevius does not mention if the two brothers were able to meet at this time.

Nevius (1895) pp. as cited.

——

1882: November 26
Nevius's fifty-fifth birthday.

——

1882:
Rt. Rev. Lemuel H. Wells (1914):

"In 1882, at the invitation of Mr. George Booke, Dr. Nevius began a monthly service at the new town of Sprague, mostly a city of tents. The first service has been held in one of the new buildings, which was a saloon, but as some of the congregations were in undue haste to slake their thirst at the conclusion of the service, and the surroundings were not conducive to devotion, they decided to erect a church ready for the next monthly service. At this next service, the Doctor arrived on Friday and found all the material on the ground, but not a stroke had been done upon the structure. So the whole town got out early on Saturday morning with hammers, axes, saws and any tool they happened to have, and by midnight the church was finished and ready for service the next day."

——

1882:
"St. Matthew's Church
"Sprague, Washington
"First Church Built In 1882—Built In A Day
"Mr. George Brooke Instrumental in Getting it Built—Friend of Bishop Paddock of Portland
"From an article by Mrs. B. Gard Ewing

"In 1882 Sprague was designated as the end of a division of the Northern Pacific Railroad, which brought the car-shops there and insured the building up of quite a town. At that time Sprague was a mere hamlet, without school-house or church.

"The Rev. Dr. Nevius was then at Lewiston, in Idaho, 65 miles away, but with characteristic energy he drove to the city in embryo, and celebrated the first religious services of any description ever held there.

"He then determined to build a church, and summoned the people to a council over the matter. It was decided to have a building up and ready for him to use at his coming in the following month. Subscriptions of money, material, and labor were made, but the building was not commenced and the day for service approached. Something must be done! So, on Friday, the Reverend Doctor saw that the materials were all gathered and on the ground, and summoned the whole population to his help. On Saturday morning daylight saw him at the spot, and a great crowd armed with all the saws and hammers in the place rallied about him. A foreman was chosen, and with the Doctor as Director General, they set heartily to work, swarming like bees about the piles of material and over the building. Noon came; the frame was up. Evening; and the building was enclosed. Night came; and still by lanterns and torches they worked on. As the hours advanced, weariness overcame them, and as the building drew near to completion they one-by-one gathered up their tools and departed until, as midnight approached, one figure alone remained hard at work at the peak of the roof, and just as Saturday ended and Sunday began, the last hammer strokes rang upon the midnight air, and cap boards were fastened in place and crowned the finished structure. Dr. Nevius descended, stiff and exhausted, but happy in the completed tabernacle of his God—the church built in a day."

Sprague...., 1982, 45-50.

*Allen, 1974: "Story in Dayton or Sprague, Washington: Went to railroad to get land for church, went to lumber company and scrounged lumber, had it delivered to property, gave them the plans and said, 'I'll be back in six months.' Came back, lumber still sitting on property with no work done. Went out, got a gang of people, built the church in rough form and held services the following day."

[1883]

41

1883: May 29-June 12:

From "Notes of Bishop Paddock's Visitations" (*Columbia Churchman*, June 15, 1883) and Bishop Paddock Annual Convocation Address (*Journal*, Washington, 1883) can be reconstructed the following itinerary:

Tuesday, May 29: Nevius met Bishop Paddock at Rathdrum, Idaho Territory.

Wednesday, May 30: Morning service in Spokane Falls, evening service in Cheney.

Thursday, May 31: Morning service in Cheney, evening service in Sprague.

Friday, June 1-Sunday, June 3: services in   Spokane Falls.

Monday, June 4-Tuesday, June 5: Fort Coeur d'Alene.

Wednesday, June 6: Cheney

Thursday, June 7: morning service in Cheney, evening service in Sprague.

Friday, June 8 (and Saturday, June 9): Walla Walla.

Sunday, June 10: Consecration of St. Peter's Church, Pomeroy.

Monday, June 11: Dayton.

Tuesday, June 12: Waitsburgh.

——

1883: May 29-June 12

Rt. Rev. John Adams Paddock, D.D.

"Notes of Bishop Paddock's Visitations.

"The Bishop, with a grateful heart, reached the Territory, in health and safety, on Tuesday evening, May 29th. The Rev. Dr. Nevius kindly met him at Rathdrum [Idaho], on the Northern Pacific Rail Road, and escorted him to Spokane Falls. Services were held there on Wednesday morning [May 30], on Friday and Saturday evenings [June 1 and 2], and on Sunday morning and evening [June 3], the 2nd Sunday after Trinity. At the last service, one person was confirmed. Cheney was visited on Wednesday evening [June 6] and on the following morning [June 7], the Baptist house of worship being kindly loaned us. At a meeting of a few interested, a beginning was made in subscriptions towards a little church.

"Thursday evening [June 7] was spent at Sprague. Since the previous visitation, a building has been erected at a cost of $400 on one of the Church lots. Some debt yet remains upon it, and the Consecration Service was not used. We believe that the debt will soon be removed, and improvements made on the unfinished structure.

"At the desire of Bishop Tuttle, a visitation was made on Monday, June 4th, and on Tuesday, at Fort Coeur d'Alene, in Idaho. One person was baptized and confirmed. At the celebration of the Holy Communion twelve participated, and it was pleasant to note that about half the number were officers of the Post, and that it is the custom of the commanding officer to read morning prayer in his parlor, with a few assembled, each Sunday.

"A portion of the week was spent by the bishop at Walla Walla, conferring with the Building Committee concerning a new structure to arise for our Church school for girls. At a service in St. Paul's on Friday evening, June 8th, three candidates received the Rite of the Laying on of Hands. It was a joy to find the Rector improved in health.

"The new church erected in Pomeroy was consecrated on the 3rd Sunday after Trinity, June 10th. It is a very neat and becoming structure, highly creditable to the citizens of Pomeroy. It has been erected at an expense of about $2,000, and the whole cost is paid or pledged. It is the first Protestant house of worship in the town. It bears the name of 'St. Peter's Church: the Francis Memorial.' Two former parishioners of the Bishop, in Brooklyn, New York, having given him aid towards its erection, and expressed a desire that the Church should bear this name. Since he received their gift, they have both been called to the Paradise of God. They, being dead, yet speak for Christ.

"In all these visits, the Bishop was favored with the company and assistance of the Rev. Dr. Nevius.

"On Monday, Festival of St. Barnabas, the Bishop held morning and evening Service in the Congregational house of worship in Dayton; and on Tuesday, June 12th, in the Methodist chapel in Waitsburgh."

Columbia Churchman June 15, 1883

——

1883: June 8

Rt. Rev. Benjamin Wistar Morris,

Columbia Churchman, June 15, 1883

From Bishop Morris's annual Convocation Address:

"EXTRACTS FROM [BISHOP'S] ADDRESS..

"PARISHES AND PASTORS....

"The Rev. Dr. Nevius, in the days when the Church was new and unknown in all that mountain region [around John Day], laid good foundations for its future growth. One thing to be seen as worthy of special notice is the style and character of the church buildings designed and erected by him.

"St. John's Church, Union, St. Thomas, Canyon City, and St. Peter's [sic St. Paul's], Dalles, are examples of a very admirable style of architecture, for small wooden churches of moderate cost, and their influence on the state of the people is already observable. In contemplating other new buildings, they will no longer be content with the rude and unseemly structures that have been so common in our country...."

Journal of the Proceedings of the Third Convocation of the Protestant Episcopal Church of the Missionary Jurisdiction of Washington, held in St. Luke's Church, Vancouver, W.T., June 27-30, 1883.

The Rev. R. D. Nevius, D.D., is listed as "Officiating in St. John's Church, Olympia."

June 28, 1883 (Thursday):

Bishop's Address:

"With a glad and grateful heart I greet you, and welcome you to our Annual Conference in the interests of Zion. Since our last meeting I have journeyed more than ten thousand miles....

"We meet in the same Parish where we were welcomed, two years since.... We miss our layman, who then gave us a welcome, and was with us at our Services and other assemblings. Mr. J. M. Fletcher was a man who, with some peculiarities of temperament, was cordial and warm hearted, and a lover of 'Christ and the Church.' Our sympathies are tendered to those who have so severely to suffer for his sudden disappearance from their midst."

"The Presiding Bishop of the Church having expressed an earnest desire that either the Bishop of Oregon or the Bishop of Washington Territory should visit Alaska, and become informed as to any call or opening for missionary work, and Bishop Morris having devolved the duty on me, I left Port Townsend on the 9th day of July, and during an absence of fifteen days, journeyed about two thousand miles, and visited such points as I could reach, in the south-eastern part of that Territory. At five or six places I found settlements, numbering from fifty to three hundred whites, with from fifty to four or five hundred Indians dwelling near the whites. The Presbyterians have established several mission stations, and feel that they are meeting the needs of this part of the field.... While absent on this missionary trip, I officiated on the ship 'Idaho,' and also in the Church at Esquimault, British Columbia."

"Mr. J. H. Forrest Bell, (candidate for Holy Orders transferred to this Jurisdiction by the Bishop of Oregon), has been through the year, doing good work among the Indians, most of the time at Neah Bay."

"The Rev. Dr. Nevius, who has been for several years engaged in active Missionary labor, east of the mountains, expects for a time to take charge of this important Parish [St. John's, Olympia] in the Capital of the Territory. I am happy to think, when no Clergyman can be present, the Church's service is generally read in St. John's, by a layman of the Parish.

"The Rev. Dr. Nevius has held occasional Services at Fort Coeur d'Alene in Idaho, and, at the request of Bishop Tuttle, I visited the Post on the 4th and 5th of this present month, (June, 1883,) [sic] holding two public Services....

"At Spokane Falls, in our Territory, I have aided Dr. Nevius at six Services, during this month of June [1883], and have confirmed one person. The Missionary has been encouraged, of late, by the coming of some Church families into the place, and believes that brighter days are before us in this growing town. After some outlay of funds entrusted to me, I have felt obliged to allow the School begun here by Dr. Nevius to be closed, at least for a time; very few scholars appearing at the opening of the year, and the burdens resting on me in other directions, for educational undertakings, being all that I could venture to assume. Dr. Nevius has held occasional Services in Cheney, and, accompanied by him, I officiated there in the Baptist house of worship, on Wednesday the 30th, and Thursday the 31st of May. After the last Service something was pledged towards the erection of a Church, on land held by us for that purpose.

"Thursday evening [May 31, 1883], I preached in our little Church building in Sprague, Dr. Nevius reading the Service. This is a very plain structure, reared since my last visit to the place, at a cost of about $400. The building is not yet completed, and there is some debt for that done, so the consecration was deferred.

"It was a joy, on the 3rd Sunday after Trinity, June 10th [1883], to consecrate by the name of 'St. Peter's Church—the Frances Memorial,' the building just finished at Pomeroy. It is the first Protestant house of worship in that town, constructed after a plan obtained by the Rev. L. H. Wells, and is an edifice very creditable to those who have united to build it. Two of my former parishioners in Brooklyn, N.Y., (both of whom have since entered Paradise), enabled me to donate $500, and suggested the name. The rest of the expenditure, (the whole cost having been about $2,000), has been met by the people of Pomeroy."

"It is known to you that, the offer of large donations of land and money having been conditionally made to me, I felt it my duty, in the interest of Christian Education, to go to the Atlantic States, seeking aid for the erection of Church Schools in the eastern and western portions of our Territory. Such undertakings always involve a good deal of hard, sometimes unpleasant work. I toiled, day and night, during my absence, but bear grateful testimony to the very kind manner in which I was generally received, and to the warm interest expressed in our undertakings."

"At the session of our Territorial Legislature, in the autumn of 1881, several petitions were presented for the repeal of the law taxing Schools, Hospitals, and Churches. The vote in favor of such repeal, was, if I am rightly informed, unanimous in the upper house, but failed in the other branch of the Legislature. I took some care to inform myself on the question, during my recent visit to the East. An intelligent citizen of Ohio, honored in the State, and active in all good works, informed me that, while he could not speak of our newer Territories, he did not think that a State east of the Mississippi taxed educational, benevolent, and religious institutions; exempting them on the ground that they are established for the general good, yield no pecuniary return to their founders, but, on the contrary, call for continual gifts for their support, and that it is desirable to encourage the erection of buildings which are an honor and credit to a State, and a lasting benefit to any community.

"We will allow that property owned by the Church, or educational and benevolent institutions, if yielding and income not absorbed in the prosecution of their work, may properly be taxed. But we claim that those buildings should be exempted, which yield no pecuniary return to their founders; but on the contrary, call for continuous outlay, which are for the alleviation of suffering, for the promotion of good morals, the dissemination of sound learning, the diminution of pauperism and crime, and so make for the lessening of else necessary taxes. ...What is to be said of a law which almost forces the congregation to decline the most generous gifts, or is, but a tax on their building, laying on them, struggling to sustain a feeble Church, a burden almost too heavy to be borne?" [There follows many reasons for and examples of non-taxation of churches by various domestic and foreign governments.]

June 29, 1883 (Friday):

"The Committee on Christian Education made the following report, which was accepted:

Your Committee on Christian Education would report, that during the past year there has been on the whole very decided progress in this important interest. St. Paul's School, Walla Walla, notwithstanding its change of teachers and the occurrence of incidents calculated to impair its efficiency and diminish its numbers, has had its most successful year. One hundred and six pupils have received instruction, of whom thirty-nine were boarders. It is expected that a new building will be begun this autumn, commodious and elegant, which will, we trust, be ready for occupancy in another year. We place on record our appreciation of the long [illegible] and faithful labors of the Rev. L. H. Wells, and his accomplished wife, for [?] the establishment of this school, and its elevation to its present high standard of efficiency [?].

Your Committee regret to report that from a combination of adverse causes, the Rodney Morris School at Spokane Falls has been suspended since last July [1882]. There is at Spokane Falls a School-house well appointed for a day school, which is also occupied as a Chapel by the congregation of All Saints' Church. Six valuable lots have been purchased for occupancy by the School, upon condition that a building should be erected upon this property within a year. This term expired last October. An extension of time for twelve months has been asked for, and has been kindly granted.

Your Committee hear, with thankfulness to God, of the success of our Diocesan in collecting from friends in the East, $25,000, which secures the munificent endowment of $50,000 for a School for Girls in Tacoma.

R. D. Nevius,
H. D. Lathrop,
A. Walters"

"The Registrar of the Jurisdiction made his report as follows, which was accepted:

The Registrar of the Diocese would respectfully report, that he has incomplete but growing files of the following journals, reviews and papers:

1st. Of the *Oregon Churchman.*
2nd. Of the *Columbia Churchman.*
3rd. Of Almanacs.
4th. Of the *Spirit of Missions.*
5th. Twelve bound volumes of the *Church Review,* 1854 to 1866, with a number of unbound Numbers.
6th. Journals of General Convocation.

All of which are held subject to order of the Convocation, and are stored at the Chapel of All Saints' Church, Spokane Falls. The Registrar will be glad to receive from his brethren the Clergy any Journals of General Convocation, and old Almanacs which contain statistics of the Church; also Church Reviews of the years 1856 to 1880, inclusive. There are also a large number of the Journals of other Dioceses, and miscellaneous pamphlets of various sorts, which are thought worth preservation.

R. D. Nevius, *Registrar."*

"The following were elected Delegates to the General Convention: Clerical—the Rev. Geo. Herbert Watson, alternate the Rev. R. D. Nevius, D.D. Lay—Mr. Geo. Herbert Atkinson....

"The Rev. A. S. Nicholson offered a resolution, which was seconded by Dr. Nevius, and adopted as follows:

Resolved, That on some Sunday before the annual meeting of Convocation offerings shall be made in all the Churches of the Jurisdiction, which shall be applied[?] to paying the traveling expenses of the Clergy attending the same, and that if the aggregate of all offerings, including that where Convocation is held, shall exceed[?] the amount necessary to that end, such excess shall be applied to the diminution of the expenses of printing the Journal of Convocation."

"On motion it was

Resolved, that the thanks of this Convocation be extended to the O. R.& N. Co. and the N.P.R.R. Co., for reduction in fares for the Delegates."

"The following were appointed Examining Chaplains:

The Rev. Geo. H. Watson, the Rev. R. D. Nevius, D.D., and the Rev. H. D. Lathrop, D.D..

"The Diocesan Board of Missions was selected as follows: The Rt. Rev. J. A. Paddock, D.D., Ex-officio President; the Rev. Geo. H. Watson, Chairman; the Rev. H. D. Lathrop, D.D., the Rev. R. D. Nevius, D.D., the Rev. H. S. Bonnell, Secretary; Mr. R. G. O'Brien, Treasurer; Mr. J. J. Beeson, Capt. E. Hunter, and Dr. F. L. Town."

"Parochial Reports....

"Report of All Saints' Church, Spokane Falls, for the year ending June 25, 1883.

"The Rev. R. D. Nevius, D.D., Rector.

"Population, 1,200.

"Baptisms—Adult, 1; Infant, 3; Total, 4.

"Confirmations, 1.

"Communicants, added by confirmation, 1; by transfer, 4.

"Communicants not resident and not otherwise reported, 9.

"Total number of communicants, 15.

"Communion administered, No. of times, 10.

"Sunday School—Pupils, 13.

"Marriages, 1. Burials, 3.

"No. of Families connected with the Congregation, 12.

"Offerings and Contributions—For salary, by offerings at Services, $676.30; Domestic Missions, $2.35; Diocesan Missions, $3.85; Mission to the Jews, $2.75; Episcopal Fund, $3.25; Parochial Purposes, $114.50; Miscellaneous, $.95; Total, $289.

"Value of Church property—Church, $1000; other property, $1800; Total, $2800.

"Among the Communicants reported as non-resident in Spokane are two living at Colfax. This place, very important and promising a year ago, has lost much by removals, and no services have been held there since last fall. The town still retains its importance, and has wholly recovered from the effects of two destructive fires. A large number of new towns are springing up along the Northern Pacific Railroad, and in the Big Bend country, which ought soon to be visited, and in which, no doubt, valuable property can be secured for future Church buildings.

———

"*Report of Coeur d'Alene Mission, for the year ending June 25, 1883.*

"The Rev. R. D. Nevius, D.D., Missionary.

"Population, 200.

"Baptisms—Adult, 1.; Infant, 4; Total, 5.

"Communicants, added by confirmation, 1.

"Total number of communicants, 11.

"Communion administered, No. of times, 4.

"Marriages, 1. Burials, 2.

"No. of Families connected with the Congregation, 9.

"Offerings and Contributions—For salary, by offerings at Services, $60; Domestic Missions, $3.25; Foreign Missions, $3; Diocesan Missions, $5.20; Hospital Work, $4.55; Total, $76.

"Fort Coeur d'Alene has not this year been reported in Idaho, as it should have been done, and is therefore given here. The visits of the Missionary to this post have always been a great pleasure, and he here records his grateful and enduring sense of many favors from all the officers and their families, and especially from the General commanding the post.

"Services have been held at Rathdrum, also in Idaho. This place has a population of 400, and will be a place requiring the attention of the Missionary. It can be served by him while on his way to Fort Coeur d'Alene.

———

"*Report of Cheney Mission, for the year ending June 25, 1883.*

"The Rev. R. D. Nevius, D.D., Missionary.

"Population, 900.

"Total number of Communicants, 2.

"Marriages, 1. Burials, 2.

"No. of Families connected with the Congregation, 3.

"Offerings and Contributions—For salary, by offerings at Services, $7; Miscellaneous, $4; Total, $11.

"Value of Church Property, $200.

"At this point we have land for a Church, and now at last some encouragement for beginning work.

———

"*Report of St. Matthew's Church, Sprague, for the year ending June 27, 1883.*

"The Rev. R. D. Nevius, D.D., Missionary.

"Population, 700.

"Baptisms, Infant, 2.

"Communicants not resident and not otherwise reported, 4.

"Total number of Communicants, 10.

"Communion administered, No. of times, 2.

"Marriages, 1. Burials, 2.

"No. of Families connected with the Congregation, 7.

"Offerings and Contributions—Parochial Purposes, $325.

"Value of Church Property—Church, $500; other property, $300; Total, $800.

———

"*Report of St. Peter's Church, Pomeroy, for the year ending June 25, 1883.*

"The Rev. R. D. Nevius, D.D., Missionary.

"Total number of Communicants, 5.

"Communion administered, No. of times, 1.

"Offerings and Contributions—For salary, by offerings at Services, $6.50; Parochial Purposes, $2,000; Total, $2,006.50.

"This place has been visited only once before the consecration of the Church on the 10th of June. At that time, as the Church was not completed, and the weather was very inclement, no Services were held. The Missionary was glad, however, to organize a Women's Guild. By this agency a considerable sum of money has been raised for the furnishing of the Church. Great credit is due to Mr. C. B. Foote, the Bishop's financial agent, for pushing the work of building the Church to its happy completion. In connection with Services here, Services have been held at Pataha City and Dayton, in both which places Churches might be built if only they could have a resident Missionary."

1883: July 1
Columbia Churchman:
"The Spokane Mission[,]

"With two centers, Spokane Falls and Pomeroy, about 100 miles apart, has now grown to such importance that it must be divided, and supplied by a larger force of clergy.

"There are chapels at Spokane Falls and Sprague, and a church at Pomeroy. The Bishop has secured resident clergy for these two points, with a prospect of putting a third clergyman in the field for undeveloped stations. Rev. Mr. Burnett, soon to arrive from the East, will have charge of Spokane Falls, giving continuous Sunday services at that place, and occasional services at other places on the line of the railroad and at Fort Coeur d'Alene.

"Rev. William Allan Fair, a foreign missionary from Africa, now on a prolonged vacation at home, will have charge of Pomeroy and places adjacent. It is hoped that Rev. Mr. Davis, lately at Port Townsend, will be stationed at Sprague, to minister at that place, Cheney, and other places adjacent which have not been visited. Rev. Dr. Nevius, who has hitherto had charge of the field, will thus be relieved to take charge of some new field as yet untried, until it can be likewise divided and supplied. He goes first to the Yakima country to spy it out, and report to the Bishop, when he will for a time have residence at Olympia, which is now without a rector. One more clergyman is needed to supply this vast field from a center which should be somewhere in the Palouse country, preferably at Colfax. With the large gain to our clerical force in this part of the Territory, the next year will, doubtless, show great gain to the church. Rev. Mr. Fair and Mr. Davis, who may hereafter join him, are men of experience and devotion of life. They are both missionaries from Africa; the former intends at some future time to return to his foreign work; the latter will be detained in America. He is a man of great simplicity of character and earnestness of purpose, and will be especially effective in pastoral work, in which his excellent wife will be an efficient helper."

- Olympia, Washington Territory -

1883: July
Nevius became rector of St. John's Church, Olympia, W. T. in July 1883. He resigned in the fall of 1886, but did not depart until March 2, 1887.
Jessett, Letter to Powers, December 29, 1980.

———

1883: Summer
Rev. R. D. Nevius, D.D. (*Columbia Churchman*, August 15, 1883):
"The Yakima Country.

"'The Yakima Country,' as it will be known to those interested in our Church work, comprises three Yakima valleys, and the Klickitat valley. The upper Yakima valley is called the Kittitass. These four valleys are separated from each other and from the Columbia by narrow basalt ridges, through which the rivers have broken from old world lake basins, by narrow passes or gaps.

44

"Each of these valleys is larger than [the] Grande Ronde or Powder River valleys, which are so well known to us. They are very fertile, and with the exception of the Klickitat, well located [sic], and much more largely occupied than I expected to find them.

"Klickitat valley seems wholly occupied, farm touching farm. The farm homes are surprisingly neat and large. It seems to me the oldest agricultural country that I have visited in either Oregon or Washington. There is, however, only one considerable town, Goldendale, which is about mid-way of the valley on its longer axis, and is situated in the edge of the timber on the road to Yakima. This is an exceptional town; there are no saloons or bars, and no spirituous liquors are allowed to be sold. Prohibition is also the law of the whole country. The people, mostly Methodists, Presbyterians and campbellites,* generally go to church. I found here one Church-woman, in whose house on my return I was most kindly and hospitably entertained. I held service here in the Methodist Church on Tuesday night, and baptized one adult and one infant. The congregation was large, mostly faithful Methodists, all of whom, with their worthy minister, treated me with great courtesy. I learned of one other person, a farmer without a family, living in the neighborhood.

"I will give you names of these persons and others in a note at the close of my letter. Goldendale is 25 miles from the Dalles, by road which in its first half climbs the mountain, with an unsurpassed view backward over the Dalles of the Columbia and Dalles City, with Mount Hood crowning the background on the far horizon, and showing a more imposing height than from any other point known to me.

"Goldendale is 25 miles from the Dalles, and is most easily reached from Columbus, on the Columbia river, from which it is only 12 miles distant. Columbus is a pretty little town, in which I found no members of our Church resident. One person, a bachelor, is employed there temporarily; from him I had a courteous welcome.

"Yakima City is situated in the gap between the two lower Yakima valleys. The nearer one is very large, level and fertile, and is an Indian reservation.

"The other is large, thickly settled, having many old farms, with neat, commodious farm houses, and is abundantly well watered. Into this valley the railroad is now coming, and at Yakima, or some new town very near it, the capitol will be situated when we secure a state government.

"At present Yakima has about 500 inhabitants. There are Congregational and Campbellite Churches here. The former was kindly loaned to us for service. I held four services at this place, celebrated Holy Communion twice (once in private), and baptized one infant. I found here five communicants, and quite a number of persons who seemed on the near margin of the Church. I think a class can be presented for confirmation at the first visit of the Bishop.

"Yakima is about 70 miles from Goldendale, and the drive is a fatiguing one. It is the only town in its very large country, and will some day very soon be a town of the class to which Walla Walla belongs.

"Ellensburg has about 300 inhabitants. It is a very enterprising, busy town, partaking the qualities of a mining as well as an agricultural town. I found no members of our Church, save three or four who have made other connections, but many friends and much encouragement to begin work immediately. There is no church building here. The Methodists have a monthly appointment in the neat and commodious school house.

"Two valuable lots were offered here on condition that we should buy two others at $35 each, and 30 days were given to consider the offer.

"It is very important that this field should be occupied early; and I have given reason to hope that the Bishop will send a man to make our Church people another visit this fall.

"The round trip from the Dalles by stage is about 300 miles, and expenses (stage fares) about $30.

*Disciples of Christ, separated from the Presbyterian Church ca. 1810.

1883: June-September
Rev. Thomas Jessett (1949):

"The Rev. Reuben Denton Nevius, D.D., came from Spokane to Olympia in June, 1883. Dr. Nevius was a man of wide culture, moving eloquence and warm human sympathies. Full of missionary zeal and a great scholar, he was known nationally as a man of science. In Alabama he discovered a beautiful shrub named after

him by Dr. Asa Gray, the 'Nevusia Alabamensis.' Two specimens of this shrub were planted in the jurisdiction [of Washington}, one in the grounds of the first Annie Wright Seminary and the other in the grounds of Trinity Church, Seattle. Both appear to have succumbed to the ravages of time and change. [fn]28

"Dr. Nevius was a great builder of churches, some thirty in all of the states of Washington and Oregon, and he ranged north and south from his parish in Olympia. Two ladies, Mrs. Cora M. Gardner and Mrs. William Powell, residents of Bellingham Bay, petitioned Bishop Paddock for services and the bishop requested Dr. Nevius to visit the towns around that bay. He did so, organized a woman's [sic] guild at Whatcom on September 12, 1883, conducted two services there, a funeral at Bellingham, and secured the services of Mr. J. H. Birckhead as lay reader for a church at Whatcom. Through the courtesy of property owners, lots were donated for a church at Whatcom and a Bellingham. On this trip Dr. Nevius also held services at Anacortes, LaConner, Orcas Island and the San Juan Island. Upon his return to Olympia he urged and secured the appointment of a committee to plan the erection of a new church in that city.[fn] 29"

[fn] "29 *Columbia Churchman*, September 1, 1883 [sic, some events referenced occurred after Sept. 1]."

Thomas E. Jessett, *The Episcopate of John Adams Paddock, First Bishop of Washington (State)* (pamphlet, 1949 [referenced in a letter from Jessett to Howland Atwood, Oct. 13, 1952], "Reprinted from *Historical Magazine of the Protestant Episcopal Church*, Vol. XVIII, pages 282-310"), p. 8.

1883: August 15
William West (1909):

"When the Territory of Washington was set off from the Diocese of Oregon and made into a separate missionary district [in 1880], the Rt. Rev. John Adams Paddock was sent out as its first Missionary Bishop, who brought with him a young deacon, the Rev. Henry S. Bonnell, who was stationed at Tacoma, at that time a mere village. He, hearing that there were two or three Communicants in Lewis County, made a trip to Chehalis in June 1883, but found none, and returned to Tacoma without holding a service.

"Hearing of which I wrote him, requesting him to come and hold services which he did, and gave us week night services which created considerable interest and were well attended. The only place of meeting being the School House, and on the 15th of August 1883 a meeting of the people was held, and a petition was written, asking the Bishop for the services of a Missionary for Lewis County, and the said petition was accompanied by a subscription list aggregating $400.00 for the payment of his salary....

"No missionary could be sent to us at that time and the Rev. Mr. Bonnell continued with his week night services during the summer and autumn."

1883: August 22-23
Columbia Churchman (September 1, 1883):
Subscription price was "$1.50 per Annum, in advance."

———

The cornerstone ceremony for Annie Wright Seminary was reported. "Addresses were ... made by Bp. Paddock, Hon. Elwood Evans, Rev. Dr. Nevius and Gov. Newell. At the conclusion of governor Newell's address, the choir sang the *Gloria in Excelsis*, after which prayer was offered by Bishop Paddock, and the ceremonies were brought to a close by the pronouncing of the benediction by Bishop Morris of Oregon [apparently substituting for the Lord Bishop of Columbia].

———

"Ordination of the Rev. H. S. Bonnell.

———

"A large congregation gathered in St. Luke's Church, Tacoma, ... to witness the solemn and impressive services attending the advancement to the Priesthood of the Rev. H. S. Bonnell. The services commenced at 11 o'clock with a procession of the Clergy, the choir singing the 175th hymn, 'The Son of God Goes Forth to War.'... Then ... Bishop Morris, of Oregon, preached a most able and interesting sermon, the ordination proper was proceeded with, the Rt. Rev. C. H. Badgley, the rev. R. D. Nevius, the Rev. C. H. Badgley, the Rev. G. H. Watson and the Rev. A. S. Nicholson.... The Clergy present and participating besides those mentioned, were

Rev. John Rosenberg, of Portland; Rev. Edward Davis, Oysterville; Rev. M. D. Wilson, Astoria, Oregon."

—

1883: September 7
Wood (1968) 30:

An elaborate "last spike" (which was the first spike that had been driven in Minnesota) ceremony was held at Gold Creek, Montana (between Butte and Missoula) to celebrate completion of the transcontinental line from St. Paul to Portland to Tacoma.

—

1883: October 15
Columbia Churchman:
"Evolution.

"The point that science has existed for the human mind is* a tradition as far back as there is any monument to tell of the human mind; and therefore [the point is] that the human mind did not begin with apelike adaptations, but was endowed by its Creator with an initial scientific impulse to start with."

"It is impossible then for the Great Pyramid to stand anywhere in the line of Evolution[ary] development of the human mind. If it did it must have monumental antecedents, a series of which should be in existence to give evidence of the Evolution; and it should have constructions following it which are in skill and knowledge and advance upon it. Neither of these is so. The Great Pyramid stands at the beginning of human progress, a witness against the current theory of mental evolution."
*"as" in original.

—

1883: November 15
Columbia Churchman:
"Sisterhoods.

"It is less than forty years since Dr. Muhlenberg founded the first Protestant Sisterhood in the United States, that of the Holy Communion in New York. Since then, Sisterhoods have been founded in nearly every diocese of the Church. Ritualism and Evangelicalism have each developed the same fair fruit of Christlike charity. Unhampered by undue restriction in organization, and accorded the liberty of a Catholic Church, distinctive shades of opinion have found full expression in the rules and observances of the various communities. Perhaps they may all be classed under one of two heads: those who place the religious work before the life, and those who place the religious life before the work. With one system, the devotional life is subservient to the routine of duties. The oratory must never have precedence. The work must be done, though the chapel service be neglected. Here we find many a devotional Sisterhood.

"Foremost among the communities under the other system, is that of St. Mary's, New York. With that the higher life is the supreme object, and its perfection is to be attained at any sacrifice.... "'They who lead this life,' says Dr. Dix, 'must have every help which human nature requires for perseverance. An organization, a uniform, a rule, a ritual; a devotional system much more minute than we need in the world; a pastoral supervision much more intimate and searching—these will be found in practices essential to the realization of the idea of an unworldly, sacrificial and devoted life. The oratory, the hours of prayer, the devotional manual, the coarse dress, the minimum of personal expenses, the simple fare, the narrow bed, the severely plain room—all these belong to the life, and will be professed by those who lead it.'

"Under either system, the life of a Sister means work, loss of individualism and obedience to rules—a hard lesson for most American women....—*Kalendar.* (W.N.Y.)

—

1883: November 21
Columbia Churchman (December 1, 1883):
"DIED,
"At the Good Samaritan Hospital [Portland], of typhoid fever, Nov. 21st, 1883, the Rev. George Wells Boyd, aged 36 years...."

—

1883:

Rev. W. B. Turrill, ca. 1923:
"History of St. Paul's Parish, Bellingham.

"The early history of the Church on Bellingham Bay was a checkered one. From 1852 onward various 'booms' were caused there by the discovery of coal near by and of gold in British Columbia, and still more by the strong prospect of the bay becoming the terminus of trans-continental railroads. These 'booms' burst with the usual result of empty buildings and waste [sic] town sites. There are traditions of pioneer missionaries here through all this, but there was no permanent work. By the early 80's [sic] however a fairly stable population had established itself along the north and east sides of the Bay in the three towns of Whatcom, Sehome and Fairhaven. The situation is a very beautiful one. In front lovely wooded islands rise out of the placid waters of Puget Sound, and behind richly timbered lands and fertile soil attract the logger and the farmer. The whole wide-spread picture is enclosed in a magnificent frame formed by three ranges of snow-tipped mountains at visible distances of from thirty to two hundred miles.

"To the town of Whatcom in 1883 came that fine old clergyman, the Rev. Dr. Nevius, and founded a mission of the Church. Largely by the help of a faithful Woman's Guild under the presidenc[ies] of Mrs. W. W. Gardner [and Mrs. William Powell], his successor, the Rev. J. H. Birkhead, built St. Paul's Church in 1884...."

—

1883: December
Rev. R. D. Nevius, D.D.:
"In December [1883] I was appointed to the Mission [at Chehalis] and my work in the Mission for the last eight months has been characterized by unvarying courtesy and kindness on the part of the people generally, by a complete fulfillment of all promises and pledges, and by steady progress, without a shake of opposition or any grind of causeless friction. It has been an unusual experience in a long and varied Missionary career, and deserves this lasting record. Only three families connected with the Church, all of English birth, were among the supporters of the Mission."

—

1883: December 22
William West (1909):
"No missionary could be sent to us [in Chehalis] at that time [in 1883] and the Rev. Mr. Bonnell continued with his week night services during the summer and autumn. However in the month of December, the Rev. Dr. Nevius who was stationed at Olympia, commenced to give us alternate Sunday services, and also through the week, staying a week at each town, and on December 22nd a meeting was held for the purpose of organizing a mission and of which the following minutes are from the record:
"Chehalis, December 22, 1883
"At a meeting called by the Rev. Dr. Nevius, for the purpose of organizing a Protestant Episcopal Church Mission here, William West was elected chairman and William Birmingham Secretary.
"Resolved that we, members and friends of the Protestant Episcopal Church, will now proceed to organize a Mission of said Church at Chehalis and vicinity, according to the form provided in the Journal of Convocation, of the Missionary Jurisdiction of Washington Territory.
"Resolved that the name of said Mission, shall be Chehalis Mission of Lewis County Washington.
"Resolved that an application according to the form provided, be adopted, engrossed by the secretary, and after being signed be sent to Bishop Paddock.
"Resolved that the subscription list made by William West, be made the basis of a monthly pledge to the Board of Missions, and that the Treasurer be authorized to collect the same, and to transmit the amounts collected, together with the amounts of the Sunday offerings, to the Treasurer of the Board of Missions.
"Signed, Wm. Birmingham, Secretary Pro Tem.'
"These proceedings were accepted by the Bishop and the organization ratified by the Bishop appointing William West, Warden and Treasurer of the Mission.

[1884]
1884: January

Wood (1968) 71, 73-74:

Villard's financial interests collapsed and he resigned from the presidency of the NP. His successor, Robert Harris, decided to complete the "branch" across the Cascades to Puget sound.

——

1884: February 16
William West (1909)

"The Rev. Dr. Nevius continued to give services [at Chehalis] on alternate weeks and during the Epiphany season [the six Sundays following January 6], a series of services were held in the school house every night for a week. The school house was crowded at each meeting and great interest manifested....

"The adherents of the Church we so much encouraged by the success of the Epiphany services that on February 16th, 1884 a meeting was called, at which it was decided to build a Church and the following subscription list was drawn up and circulated.

"Chehalis, Lewis County, Washington Territory, February 16th, 1884.

"We the undersigned citizens and residents of Chehalis and vicinity, hereby promise and agree to pay to Wm. Birmingham and Wm. West or their assigns, the sums set opposite our respective names for the purpose of building a Protestant Episcopal Church, in the Town of Chehalis, on a lot donated by Wm. West for that purpose, one half of said amount to become due and payable when the building material is on the ground, and the other half of said sum when the building shall be roofed and enclosed. Said Church to be under the supervision of the Bishop of the Diocese [list of 52 names with amounts ranging from $2 to $200 omitted].

"The amounts pledged were over $900.00 and an acre of land.

——

1884: March 14, 25
Columbia Churchman (April 1884):

"The Death of the Rev. H. S. Bonnell.

"We are pained to announce the death of the Rev. H. S. Bonnell of New Tacoma. Although he died in California, where he had recently gone for his health, his body was brought to Tacoma and buried on the 25th ult. No account of the funeral has reached us as we go to press. Bishop Morris and the Rev. Mr. Nicholson intended to be present at the funeral, and went as far as Kalama, but learned there that they would be too late, returned the same day on the Portland boat.

"The *Tacoma News* says:

"The death of Rev. H. S. Bonnell, Minister of St. Luke's Memorial Church, was a very severe shock to the community, though they had been prepared for it some days by the information that all hopes in his case had fled. His disease might probably be termed quick consumption. The most prominent feature of his complaint before he left Tacoma was a severe bronchial affection, but his countenance plainly exhibited the inroads of a deep-seated disease, which it was hoped a change of climate and relief from his duties for a short time would alleviate, if not entirely remove. The result, however, disappointed these hopes. Mr. Bonnell rapidly declined, until he passed away peacefully on the 14th inst., in the hope of a blessed immortality. His early taking off will be seriously regretted wherever he was known, and nowhere more sincerely than in Tacoma, the seat of his first religious charge, where he was held in esteem not only by his own people, but by members of all denominations of Christians, and others who came in contact with him. While a devoted son of the Episcopal Church, having imbibed much of the excellent spirit and piety for which his instructor and mentor, the Right Rev. Bishop Paddock, is distinguished, he was liberal and catholic in his instincts, and took an earnest part, in association with his brother Clergymen, in measures of moral reform and philanthropic objects. He was the first president of the Tacoma branch of the Young Men's Christian Association, and much of its success in organization was due to his enthusiasm and earnestness in the work. As a pastor he was popular, and his sermons were noted for their spiritual fervor, and displayed the very deep interest he felt in his work. The death of such a man brings a serious loss to any community where his acts and influence may be exerted, but it will fall severely upon his immediate family and upon the venerable Bishop under whose auspices he was trained in the ministry, and came to Tacoma as one of his representatives."

1884: ca. April
[from a history by Jessett]

"The Rev. Dr. Nevius assumed charge of the Church of the Epiphany, Chehalis, after the death [on March 14, 1884] of Mr. [Henry S.] Bonnell."
Jessett (1949) p. 9

——

1884: April 14
Rev. Thomas Jessett (1940):

"A great missionary, the Rev. Reuben Denton Nevius, D.D., became rector of St. John's [Olympia] in July [sic, June] 1883, coming from Portland, Oregon. A builder of churches..., [he] was undoubtedly the moving force behind a motion made at the annual meeting of April 14, 1884, to erect a new church on the property adjoining the rectory...."

——

1884: June 7
William West (1909)

"Plans for the building [at Chehalis] were furnished by Rev. R. D. Nevius and on the 7th day of June 1884 a contract was made with M. T. Moore to build the Church. James T. Berry, P. C. Beaufort, and Wm. West were appointed a building committee and the building was completed during the following September and the first service was held September 14th at which service Bishop Paddock, Dr. Nevius, and Rev. Janvrin Vincent officiated."

——

1884: July 24-28 (Thursday - Monday)
Journal of the Proceedings of the Fourth Convocation of the Protestant Episcopal Church of the Missionary Jurisdiction of Washington, held in Trinity Church, Seattle, W.T.

Thursday, July 24:

"The Rev. R. D. Nevius, D.D., officiating in St. John's Church, Olympia," is listed among the Clergy. Nevius read the opening lines to the opening service at 10 a.m. Thursday. The Rt. Rev. Dr. Hills, Lord Bishop of Columbia was a guest in attendance. Nevius was appointed to the Committee on Christian Education and Literature (with Hon. E. P. Ferry & 2 others).

"The Rev. Dr. Nevius submitted the following, which upon motion was unanimously adopted:

WHEREAS, It has been so ordered by God's providence, that two branches of Christ's Church, both deriving orders and a heritage of truth[?] and traditions from the mother Church of England, which receiving the same from Apostolic men, has handed them down continuously from the beginning—are permitted today happy reunion, and an opportunity for Christian fellowship and Apostolic counsel, by the presence of the Right Rev. George Hills, D.D., Lord Bishop of Columbia, at this Convocation, I therefore move you, Sir, that this Convocation expresses hereby its pleasure at this glad opportunity, and invites Bishop Hills and his Chaplains, and attending Clergy, to seats in this Convocation, and requests his Lordship to sit at the right hand of its President, when it shall please him to be present at its deliberations. [134 words]

"The Bishop appointed the Rev. Dr. Nevius and Hon. E. P. Ferry a Committee to wait upon the Lord Bishop of Columbia, inform him of the action of the Convocation and escort him to a seat therein."

"Bishop Paddock's Address.

... "Henry S. Bonnell, a Presbyter of this Missionary Jurisdiction, ceased from earthly labors and trials, and entered on the rest and bliss of Paradise, on the 14th day of March, A.D. 1884. Many of you knew him, esteemed him, and loved him. I mourn the loss of one dear to me as a 'son in the faith,' and one who had proved himself 'a good Minister of Jesus Christ.' It was my privilege, when in parochial life, to present him for Conformation, and to admit him to the Holy Communion. After due consideration, he acted upon a suggestion which I made, that he might do well to devote himself to the Holy Ministry. Completing a thorough course of preparation, he was ordained to the Diaconate in Brooklyn, Long Island, by Bishop Littlejohn of that Diocese. Then accepting an invitation to become associated with his former Pastor, in this new country, he gave himself heartily and earnestly to the work offered him. Shortly after our last Convocation, in the presence of some of you, he was admitted to the Priesthood, and, when I left him to engage in work devolved on me in the East, I saw nothing to indicate that I should see his face no more on earth. But, disease soon after fastened on him, and never relaxed its grasp. Our gratitude is due to a Clerical Brother and to members of his household in San Mateo, California, friends who did all that Christian love could do, in the weeks of failing strength and gradual decline. Dear Bonnell expressed his desire to be buried in the Territory, among the people to whom he had ministered, and by whom he was tenderly loved; and in Tacoma his remains await the call of that Saviour who is 'the Resurrection and the Life.'"

"To our clerical ranks has returned one well known and honored for faithful labors during a decade, the Rev. L. H. Wells. Having accepted an invitation, last spring, to return from the East to his old field of Missionary labor, he has been officiating in St. Luke's Tacoma, where Bonnell's ministry was passed."

"At New Tacoma, the substantial and beautiful Church known as 'St. Luke's Memorial,' was consecrated on the morning of July [sic, Wednesday, August] 22nd, 1883. For this edifice Mr. Wright has $20,000 or more; the bell was provided by the wish of the daughter to whom the Church is a memorial, and the sweet toned organ is the gift of her sister.

"The same day, in the afternoon I officiated at the laying of a corner stone of the School for Girls known as the 'Annie Wright Seminary.'... Bishop Morris, the Rev. Dr. Nevius, and the Hon. Elwood Evans united with me in addressing those assembled.

"The next morning [Thursday, August 23, 1883], the Rev. Mr. Bonnell was, in St. Luke's, admitted to the Priesthood, the sermon being preached by Bishop Morris.... On Sunday [August 26, 1883], the sixteenth after Trinity, the Rev. Dr. Nevius preached in the newly consecrated Church, in the morning, and the interesting series of Services was closed by a sermon from me in the evening."

"A new Mission, begun at the desire of one or two earnest Laymen, in Lewis County, by the lamented Bonnell, has been successfully carried forward by the Rev. Dr. Nevius, also in charge of St. John's Olympia.... From $900 to $1000 have been subscribed for a Chapel at Chehalis, and the work of building has begun. Dr. Nevius, with his well known Missionary spirit, also cheerfully acceded to my desire, during the last summer, that he should visit the Yakima district, and the towns about Bellingham Bay, and has this spring made a second trip to the latter country. He thinks that laborers should at once be engaged for these districts, and that a Church may soon be built at Whatcom, on Bellingham Bay."

"The Annie Wright Seminary, Tacoma, is now nearly completed, and Mr. Wright will place in the hands of trustees at the East $50,000 pledged for its endowment. The building is the admiration of all who have seen it, for its location, commodiousness, beauty and adaptation for its purposes. It is expected that it will be opened for the reception of pupils on the 4th of September [1884].

"Mr. F. Janvrin Vincent, B.A., of Trinity College, Dublin, expecting to be ordained on next Lord's Day [July 27, 1884], proposes to receive a class of boys, in the small School building belonging to us in Tacoma, and a few lads or young men can have a home in his family."

"I have, my dear fellow workers, reluctantly, but feeling that 'necessity was laid upon me,' spent much time in the East, seeking to interest people in our field, and in that which we are trying to do, and in raising money for our Schools and Churches. Those who have been engaged in such undertakings will bear witness that such work has peculiar trials, and is not long continued, except from a conviction of duty. I hope to be allowed to rest from it for a time, and to devote myself wholly to journeyings and labors among you."

"A zealous Layman in Philadelphia is urging upon the Church the raising of a fund of $1,000,000, during the next three years, by offerings of five dollars each from 200,000 individuals, the amount to be presented at our General Convention in 1886. He is devoting his own time to the prosecution of this good work, and offers to meet necessary expenses, having already donated $1000. He asks the co-operation of Clergy and Laity all over the land. The Rev. Dr. Lathrop, of Walla Walla, has kindly offered to act as Treasurer of any offerings made in the Territory, and to use his personal efforts to obtain subscriptions. I commend the matter to your attention, and shall rejoice in all that may be done among us.

"This autumn, one hundred years will have rolled by since the consecration of the first Bishop of the American Church, Dr. Samuel Seabury, of Connecticut. The Centennial will be marked by special Services in Scotland, in which several of the Bishops of the American Church will participate.

"In many parts of our land, the first Sunday in October will be improved for calling to mind our feeble condition in these United States a century since, and offering thanks for that which God hath wrought. I suggest to my Brethren of the Clergy, the preaching of an historical sermon on that day, which may give to people needed information on our Church history, and animate them to carry forward work for Christ and the Church; and it may be thought wise to make an offering for the increase of the Episcopal Fund.

———

Friday, July 25 (St. James' Day):
"The Rev. Dr. Nevius submitted the following resolution, which was unanimously adopted:

WHEREAS, the occurrence of Centenary of the consecration of the first Bishop for the Church in these United States reminds us of God's good providence in planting on a new continent a branch of His Church, having an original Charter and historic continuity from Apostolic times, therefore be it

RESOLVED, That so much of the Bishop's Address as relates to the commemoration of the Consecration of the Rt. Rev. S. Seabury, Bishop of Connecticut, and first duly consecrated Bishop of the Church in America, meets the hearty approval of the Convocation. And furthermore, that this part of the Bishop's Address be referred to a Committee, who shall take measure to carry out the suggestions of the Bishop, and to secure a general observance of that day throughout his Jurisdiction, and that the Committee report to this Convocation.

"The Bishop appointed the Committee as follows: The Rev. R. D. Nevius, D.D., Mr. Beriah Brown, and William West."

The Rev. George H. Watson, Seattle, chair of the Committee on the *Columbia Churchman*, noting the national church newspapers "now reach us more quickly than before, and can be purchased, in some cases, as cheaply." proposed a recommendation that the *Oregon Churchman* seek to market itself in Utah, Idaho, Montana and British Columbia; which was moved and adopted.

:The Committee on Christian Education [Nevius] made the following report, which was adopted:

That it is with greatest satisfaction that they have learned from the Bishop's Address, and from the Reverend Principal of St. Paul's School, Walla Walla, of the continued and increased prosperity of that institution, and that they hope that measures inaugurated for supplying a proper and commodious domicile for the School may soon be more effective for that end. Meanwhile, the School is more heartily and confidently commended as a Christian Home, and an efficient agent in Christian Education.

That the work committed to our Diocesan, upon the fulfillment of which, as a condition, a magnificent fund for the endowment of a Church School for Girls at Tacoma, has been so effective that a noble building for that purpose has been completed, and that a Principal [Wells] has been secured for the same, who being tried and known by the successful work in St. Paul's School for Girls in Walla Walla, deserves and commands the respect and confidence of the Convocation. And they recommend that this Convocation commend the Anne [sic] Wright Seminary to the confidence of the public; and they wish for the officers and teachers of the same abundant success. The Committee also congratulates the Bishop upon the fortunate issue of his untiring and self sacrificing labor.

That the Rodney Morris School at Spokane Falls has been revived, after a period of inactivity, and that it still promises to secure to the Church a valuable property, and to grow according to the demand for sound Christian Education in that country, gives the Committee particular pleasure.

That the prospect of the early building of a School for Boys at Tacoma, on the same conditions as those which have secured to the Church by the Annie Wright Memorial Seminary for Girls, has been so well furthered by the laborious efforts of our Diocesan, is a matter of profound thankfulness to Almighty God, for the beneficence of the plan, and the gracious promise of its inception.

The Parish Schools are doing unobtrusive and efficient work at Vancouver and Seattle, and a Kindergarten School has been established at Dayton, by Miss Fair, who is welcomed to the Jurisdiction most heartily, with a wish for its most abundant success.

And finally, that by all these means and agencies Christian Education for the children of the Church, and for the public at large, is measurable offered according to the needs of the times, thus early in the history of Washington Territory, and with a cheering prospect of increase of the same in the future, is cause for thanksgiving and congratulation. "The Committee recommended the passage of the following resolution:

RESOLVED, That the Ecclesiastical Authority of the Jurisdiction be requested to prepare a short and simple form of Prayer, which may be used in Church Schools."

"The Rev. Geo. H. Watson, from the Standing Committee of the Diocese, submitted the following report, which on motion was adopted:

"The Standing Committee for the Jurisdiction of Washington would respectfully report that it has examined the testimonials of John Henry Forrest Bell, candidate for Deacon's Orders, desiring to be admitted to the Diaconate only; Frederick Janvrin Vincent, candidate for Priest's Orders, desiring to be admitted to the Diaconate; and the Rev. George Greene, Deacon, desiring to be admitted to the Priesthood, and found the same to be correct, whereupon they have recommended the above named persons to the Bishop for Ordination."

Saturday, July 26:

"The following report of the Diocesan Missionary Committee was approved:

At a meeting of the Diocesan Missionary Committee of the Jurisdiction held in the vestry of Trinity Church, Seattle, July 24th, 1884, there were present the Rt. Rev. Bishop Paddock, presiding, the Rev. Geo. H. Watson, Chairman, the Rev. Dr. Lathrop, the Rev. Dr. Nevius, Messrs. R. G. O'Brien and J. J. Beeson.

The report of Mr. R. G. O'Brien, Treasurer, was read and approved.

On motion of Mr. Beeson the sum of $100 was ordered to be paid to the Bishop, $50 to apply on account of traveling expenses of the Rev. Dr. Lovejoy, and $50 on account of salary of the Rev. W. A. Fair, by him advanced.

Mr. O'Brien presented the following resolution, which was on motion adopted:

RESOLVED, That this Committee recommend to the Convocation that three offerings per year be asked from each Parish and Mission in the Territory for Missionary work in this Jurisdiction.

The Rev. Geo. H. Watson presented the following resolution, which was adopted:

RESOLVED, That this Diocesan Missionary Committee from its own members does hereby constitute two sub-committees, one to be composed of those members of this Committee residing East of the mountains, and the other of those residing West of the mountains. That each of these Committees organize by the election of their proper officers; that three Missionary meetings be held during the year, and that the officers of said sub-committees report their doings, and the amount of funds received, transmitting said funds to the Treasurer of the general Committee on the first days of January and July of each year.

On Friday, July 25th, 1884, the Diocesan Missionary Committee appointed by the Bishop for 1884-5, met in the vestry room of Trinity Church, Seattle. Present, the Bishop, the Rev. Geo. H. Watson, Chairman, the Rev. Drs. Nevius and Lathrop, the Rev. L. H. Wells, Messrs. R. G. O'Brien and Wm. West.

The Rev. L. H. Wells was elected Secretary, and Mr. O'Brien Treasurer.

Two sub-committees were created, with the following officers: East of the Cascade range, the Rev. Dr. Lathrop, Chairman, Mr. Chas. Boyer, Secretary and Treasurer. West of the Cascade range, the Rev. Geo. H. Watson, Chairman, the rev. L. H. Wells, Secretary, and Mr. R. G. O'Brien, Treasurer."

———

"Parochial Reports....

———

Report of St. John's Church, Olympia, for the year ending July 8, 1884.

"The Rev. R. D. Nevius, D.D., Missionary in Charge.

"Baptisms—Adult, 9, infant 17, Total 26.

"Confirmation 9,

"Communicants, added by Conformation, 9; Transfer, 6.

"Communicants not resident and not otherwise reported, 6.

"Total number of Communicants, 49.

"Communion administered, No. of times, 14.

"Marriages, 1: Burials, 6.

"No. of Families connected with the Congregation, 42

"Offerings and Contributions—For salary , by offering at Services [illegible]; Total, $380.70; General Missions, (S. S. Lent offerings [illegible],) $21.56; Diocesan Missions, $3.50; Mission to the Jews, $4.25; Hospital Work, $7.70; Disabled Clergy Fund, $3.50; Parochial Purposes, $353.15; Convocation expenses, $7.00; The Girl's Guild for S. S., $10; Total $790.36

"Of the amount reported above for Parochial purposes, $189 was contributed by the Woman's Guild, which has been continuously and harmoniously active during the year, in providing largely for the expenses of the Church, and in good work in the parish. The Girl's Guild also deserves especial mention, in a record of activity and influence for good. My work in the parish has been much intermitted by necessary absence on Missionary duty. Only half of my time has been employed in Olympia. Arrangements are now being made which look to a supply of continuous services for the next year on Sundays, and the condition of the parish gives cheering signs of increased good work in the coming year. I have to record my sense, my grateful appreciation and many and uniform courtesies and kindnesses."

———

"Report of Chehalis Mission, for the year ending June 24, 1884.

"The Rev. R. D. Nevius, D.D., Missionary.

"Baptisms—Adult, 2; Infant, 2; Total, 4.

"Confirmations, 10.

"Communicants added by Confirmation, 10; Transfer, 5.

"Total number of Communicants, 15.

"Communion administered, No. of times, 2.

"Burials, 2.

"Offerings and Contributions—For salary, by offerings at Services, $208.10; Disabled Clergy Fund, $4.25; Parochial Purposes, $414; Bible and Prayer Book Society, $7; Miscellaneous, $5; Total, $639.35.

"Value of Church Property—Church, $1,000; Other property, $400; Total, $1.400.

"The Mission in Lewis County was prompted by a petition sent up by a Church of England man, asking for the services of a Clergyman, and with it came the unusual accompaniment of a subscription largely signed by residents of this little town of Chehalis, and vicinity, aggregating $400.

"The Rev. Mr. Bonnell made several visits in the Autumn of 1883, on which he made a very favorable impression for the Church, and deservedly won much affectionate regard for himself. In December I was appointed to the Mission and my work in the Mission for the last eight months has been characterized by unvarying courtesy and kindness on the part of the people generally, but a complete fulfillment of all promises and pledges, and by steady progress, without a shake of opposition or any kind of causeless friction. It has been an unusual experience in a long varied Missionary career, and deserves this lasting record. Only three families connected with the Church, all of English birth, were among the supporters of the Mission. The collections for the support of the Mission, and subscriptions for the building of the Church have been so great a demand—I cannot say burden—that none of the canonical collections for objects outside the Mission have been made.

"There is now a neat Church in process of building, which will cost when complete about $1,200, and it is believed that it may be consecrated without debt this fall. A Woman's Guild has been organized with 18 active members, among whom until last Confirmation, there was not a confirmed member of the Church. Services have been held in the Schoolhouse at Chehalis until last week when the new Presbyterian Church was occupied by the courtesy of its Pastor, from whom many kindnesses have been received. Services have been held at Claquato, three miles distant, in a church belonging to the farmers of the vicinity. One of the three Church families spoken of above lives at this place. Another lives 15 miles away. Service has been held near his, this man's residence, once only, in a country Schoolhouse.

Thronged congregations—full houses—have attended the Services in each of these places. The novelty of the Services has largely caused this no doubt, still it is manifest that it is a better Church-going community than is ordinarily found. The valley of the Chehalis river so far as seen, along a line of 15 miles, is very rich and very beautiful. The farms seem like those of older countries, and the farm houses also, the former being mostly level, free from timber—old 'Indian burns'—on rich alluvial bottom lands, Many of them however have been hewed out of the dense tangle of impenetrable swamps which were at the same everywhere in the low lands of this County challenge the patience and endurance of the maker of homes. The beginnings of a work which challenges time, not as the monarch of the forest, but as the life of the race [sic], merits this record of institution.

———

"*Annual Report of Missionary Work in various places not organized as Missions.*

"The Rev. R. D. Nevius, D.D., Missionary.

"Goldendale—Service held, I; Baptized, Adult I, Infant I; No. Communicants, 2; Contributions, $4.50. Field fully preoccupied.

"Yakima City—Services held, 5; Baptized, Infant, 2; Communion administered, I; NO. Communicants, 3; No. Families connected with congregation, 4; Contributions, $9.00.

"Ellensburg—Services held, I; No. Families connected with Congregation, I.

"San Juan Islands—Services held, I; No. Communicants 3; No. Families connected with the Congregation, 4.

"Anacortes—Services held, I; Baptized, Infant, 2; No. Communicants, 4; No. Families connected with the Congregation, 4.

"Orcas Island—Services held, 3; No. Families on the island estimated at 100; Churches, none.

"La Conner—Services held, 2; Baptized, I; Communion administered, I; No. Communicants, 4.

"Whatcom—No. times visited, 5; No. Families connected with Congregation, estimated, 12; No. Communicants, 7; Contributions, Hospital, $3.50; Expenses, $4.00; Miscellaneous, $200; No. members Women's Guild, 12."

———

1884: July

William West (1909):

"Meanwhile the Rev. Dr. Nevius had been doing effective work for the Church, organizing a Woman's Guild of eighteen members (not one of them having any previous knowledge of the Church or her ways). He also baptized 5 and presented 10 for confirmation at the Annual Convocation held in Seattle July 1884 made the following interesting report of his work at this Mission:

"This new and only organized Mission, was received into union with the convocation at our late, very pleasant meeting, and approved on the floor of the house, by representation, two persons representing the Mission, and one its Woman's Guild. This mission has not before been mentioned in any permanent record of Church work, and on this account, and because it presents novel features, which are much to its credit, I think it deserves more than mere mention. This Mission was established at the request of the people before any visit had been made by a missionary.

"Its petition for a Clerical Service, was accompanied by a subscription largely signed, and aggregating four hundred dollars. This was a most novel and even extraordinary thing.

"It has never asked its Bishop to build its Church, and did not wait to begin building until it could know how much money the bishop could give them for this purpose.

"It has kept to the full every pledge made by it, and every promise, both of support and personal labor and care, that grew out of its early zeal. It has met the Missionary at every service with large and often crowded congregations. It has built, or will have built, a neat common building within its first year and will present it for consecration free from debt. During its existence it has with unvarying courtesy, met every personal need of its visiting Clergy, and every suggestion of its Missionary, with ready compliance.

"And from the first, it has had not one shock of opposition, or any jar of needless friction, and thus it has been a continued pleasure to its Missionary.

"It might be inferred from this unstinted praise that there was in Chehalis, the center of the Mission, a large population and a strong Church influence. Chehalis has a population of less than 500 and had only one confirmed member of the church until 3 weeks ago, and but one resident communicant until then. In its Guild of 18 persons, there were only two who had any relation whatever to the Church. One Church family lived at Claquato 3 miles away. Within the Mission, there have been two adult and two infant baptisms, and ten confirmed. An acre of ground has been given for a Church, and we see our way to expending $1200.00 on it. This will make it ready for use—complete.

"The Woman's Guild has undertaken to secure a bell of 400 pounds and will succeed—of the amount raised and to be raised, the Bishop has kindly offered to supply $250.00. It is hoped and intended that the Mission shall never call upon the Missionary Board for support.

"The Missionary in Charge thinks that this record cannot well be surpassed by any small farming town, in which there is no one man, who is, being rich, also willing to build a Church, and maintain services chiefly at his own cost, and this extended record is given, with the hope that such an example, may be for the encouragement and emulation of others.

"R. D. Nevius

"Missionary in Charge"

[Taken from *Columbia Churchman*, August, 1884]

1884: August 13-19

Rt. Rev. John Adams Paddock

Journal, Jurisdiction of Washington, 1885:

"During August [1884], I made a visit with the Rev. Dr. Nevius, who has been a pioneer in so many mission fields, to that sometimes called the Bellingham Bay region. On Wednesday, the 13th, divine service was held in the Baptist house of worship at La Conner; on the morning and evening of the 17th, (10th Sunday after Trinity) in the Congregational meeting house at Whatcom, one adult being baptized by me, and several children by Dr. Nevius; in the afternoon we had the Service, with a sermon, at Bellingham.

"During the days passed at Whatcom, a number of calls were made on residents, and subscriptions were obtained for the erection of a Church.

"On Tuesday, the 19th, Services were held at the house of Mr. Amos Bowman, at Anacortes. At the close we had the pleasure of obtaining from the little congregation six subscribers for our paper, the *Columbia Churchman*."

1884: August

Rev. Thomas Jessett (1949):

"During August, 1884, the bishop visited with Dr. Nevius in the Bellingham Bay region. He officiated at Whatcom, Bellingham, La Conner, and Anacortes. He is also visited Puyallup."

Jessett (1949) p. 9

———

1884: September

Columbia Churchman:

"The Annie Wright Seminary....

"The Tacoma News gives a graphic description of our School for girls at that place. It is styled an 'Educational Palace.'... Mrs. Wells, the principal, has gained great credit for her executive ability and tact in the management of scholars.... Mrs. Wells will be assisted by [a] corps of able teachers and lecturers, the list being as follows....: The Rt. Rev. J. A. Paddock, D.D., Rector; the Rev. Lemuel H. Wells, A.M., Chaplain; Mrs. Lemuel H. Wells, Principal; Miss Annie A. Breck, English and Latin; Miss Stella B. Garreston, vocal and instrumental music; Mrs. A. H. W. Raynor, English and Mathematics; Miss E. Follick[?], drawing and painting; Madame Merkel, French, German and Calisthenics. Lecturers—The Rev. R. D. Nevius, botany; the Rev. L. H. Wells, history."

———

1884: September 10

Rt. Rev. John Adams Paddock

Journal, Jurisdiction of Washington, 1885:

"On Tuesday, the 10th of September [1884], a meeting of the Convocation of Western Washington began in St. John's Church, Olympia, and on Wednesday Mr. John H. Birckhead was ordained to the Diaconate, Dr. Nevius presenting the candidate, and the sermon being preached by the Rev. Mr. Wells."

———

1884: September 10
Rev. Thomas Jessett (1949):
"On September 10, at St. John's Olympia, the bishop ordained John H. Birckhead, the lay reader at Whatcom, to the diaconate. Mr. Birckhead continued work in the Bellingham Bay region.... During the summer of 1884, Mr. Birckhead visited on Orcas Island in the San Juan Straits...."

Jessett (1949) p. 10

———

1884: September 14
William West (1909)
"... The building [at Chehalis] was completed during the following September and the first service was held September 14th [1884] at which service Bishop Paddock, Dr. Nevius, and Rev. Janvrin Vincent officiated.... When the church was completed a considerable sum was still needed to free it from debt, and prevent liens upon it, which condition was made by the Contractor, spending the money for drink that ought to have been used to pay for material and labor. A deficiency of between six and seven hundred dollars remained which was paid by Captain James T. Berry and myself and the Church was opened for public worship free from debt, although not consecrated until June 1886, when the convocation for that year was held in it, and it was named the Church of the Epiphany."

———

1884: September–October
Rt. Rev. John Adams Paddock, D.D.
"Bishop Paddock's Notes of Visitation.
"On Sunday, September 21st, the Bishop read service and preached morning and evening in the Methodist Chapel at Puyallup.
"Leaving Tacoma, accompanied by the Rev. J. H. F. Bell, on the 22nd, Goldendale, in the Klickitat country, was reached on the 24th.... the next day a stage ride of about seventeen miles brought the Missionaries to Yakima. The closing days of the week gave opportunity for making the acquaintance of a number of the residents. On Sunday [September 28], the 16th after Trinity, about sixty assembled in the morning, in the Congregational Church, and the Holy Communion was administered to twelve, one of whom had not enjoyed the privilege of attendance for nine years, and came twenty miles for this service. In the evening a hundred and fifty met in the campbellite House of worship.
"A stage ride of fifty miles on Monday [September 29] brought us to Ellensburgh, in the Kittitas valley, in time to meet a congregation of sixty gathered in one of the rooms of the academy. Returning the next day [Tuesday, September 30] to Yakima, we had the pleasure of meeting a goodly number of ladies in the evening, of organizing a 'Church Aid Association,' and of making arrangements for the opening of a Sunday School.... Another stage ride of fifty miles over another rough and dusty road, brought us on Wednesday to Prosser....
"The number at St. Paul's School, Walla Walla, is diminishing under the pressure of 'hard times,' but we hope and pray that this year may prove a successful one in the blessed influence exerted on the forty or more assembling from day to day....
"October 12th, 18th Sunday after Trinity, the Bishop aided in the services at the institution of the Rev. Geo. W. Foote to the Rectorship of Trinity Church, Portland, and preached in the Church in the evening.
"On Monday evening [October 13] he read service and preached in the Church of the Epiphany, Chehalis. (On another page of the CHURCHMAN appears an account of the opening of this little Church, from the pen of Rev. Dr. Nevius, who has done a good work in this neighborhood and is highly esteemed by those among whom he has ministered.)...
"On Tuesday morning, October 23d, preached and celebrated the Holy Communion at the first service of a convocation called at Trinity Church, Seattle. The clergy and lay delegates, at a business meeting, chose the name of 'The Western

Deanery' for this body composed of clergy and lay delegates from the parishes and missions west of the Cascade Mountains. The Rev. Mr. Watson was appointed Dean, the Rev. Mr. Wells, Secretary, and R. G. O'Brien, Esq., Treasurer. At the service on Thursday evening, after papers read by the Rev. Mr. Watson and the Rev. Dr. Nevius, the Bishop made an address...."

Columbia Churchman, November 1884

———

1884: October 13
Rt. Rev. John Adams Paddock
Journal, Jurisdiction of Washington, 1885:
"...October 13th [1884], I officiated in the Church of the Epiphany, Chehalis. The Mission in Lewis County, of which this is one of the most important stations, has continued to prosper, the Rev. Dr. Nevius and the Rev. Mr. Vincent officiating during the first half, and the Rev. A. L. Parker during the latter part of the conventional year."

———

1884: October 23
Rt. Rev. John Adams Paddock
Journal, Jurisdiction of Washington, 1885:
"A meeting of the Convocation of Western Washington was called at Seattle, on the 23d of October [1884], but the Rev. Dr. Nevius only was able to meet with his brethren resident in that city [i.e., no clerical or lay delegates other than Nevius from elsewhere than Seattle?]. The clergy and lay delegates present resolved to change the organization to the 'Western Deanery of Washington Territory.' The Rev. Mr. Watson was thereupon appointed Dean, the Rev. Mr. Wells [of Tacoma], Secretary, and Mr. R. G. O'Brien, Treasurer."
"The stringency in money matters has prevented the progress which friends of Grace Hospital had hoped for during the year...."

———

1884: Autumn
William West (1909)
"The Rev. Dr. Nevius remained in charge [at Chehalis] until the Autumn of 1884 [sic, February 1, 1885; see below].... During the autumn of 1884, Dr. Nevius was sent elsewhere as general missionary and we were supplied for some time by the Rev. J. Vincent who came from Tacoma each week for Sunday services. On the completion of the church, a Sunday School was organized...."

———

1884: November 4
Election day. Democrat Grover Cleveland elected.

———

1884: November 11
Corning (1956):
The Oregon Railway and Navigation Company and the Oregon Short Line, a subsidiary of the Union Pacific commenced from Granger, Wyoming in 1882, joined at Huntington, Oregon, completing a second transcontinental link to the Pacific Northwest.

———

1884: December 14
Relander (Yakima <u>Republic</u>) 1960:
"[A] social given by the Episcopal Guild was the last event at Yakima City or Old Town, now Union Gap, before North Yakima, now Yakima, was founded in an atmosphere of strained feeling, optimism and misgivings in January, 1885.... The social was on December 14 [1884] in the residence of Mr. and Mrs. George W. Carey in Old Town, with 'a clever company who made the house fly with fun of dance, song, games and very nice supper.'*
*St. Michael's centennial brochure credits the "Washington Farmer" for this quotation.

———

1884:
St. Michael's Church (1985):
"The church congregation was originally organized at Yakima City (Union Gap)

in 1884 by Dr. Nevius who with Bishop James Adams Paddock, first Bishop of Washington Territory, visited the city before the January move to North Yakima. According to the Washington Farmer the activity was 'participated in by a clever company, who made the hours fly with the fun of dance, song, games, and a very nice supper.' Most of the Episcopal congregation in Yakima City participated in moving their homes and businesses to North Yakima where the Northern Pacific Railroad company, in platting and promoting the new city during the extension of their line to Puget Sound, had donated to them two lots at the southeast corner of East Yakima and Naches Avenues. Services in the new city were first held in a small room on the second [sic] floor of a building at North Front and A Streets and at the Moxee schoolhouse."

[1885]

1885: February 1

Rev. R. D. Nevius, D.D.

Journal, Jurisdiction of Washington, 1885:

"Parochial Reports....

"Report of St. John's Church, Olympia, for the year ending June 21st, 1885.

"The Rev. R. D. Nevius, D.D., Rector....

"The Mission at Whatcom and parts adjacent remained under my charge part of the year, and that at Chehalis until February 1st [1885].

"Baptized at Whatcom, Adult, 2; Infant, 12; at Anacortes, Infant, 1; at Winlock, Infant, 4; at Chehalis, Infant, 4; Marriages at Chehalis, 1."

———

1885: early-mid

Rev. Thomas Jessett (1949):

"Three churches were built about this time [mid-1885]: St. John's, Edison; St. Luke's, Whatcom; and Emmanuel, East Sound.... [Emmanuel, East Sound] ...was consecrated by the bishop on the third Sunday in Advent, 1885, as was the first church on Orcas Island.... Early in 1885 the Rev. A. L. Parker assumed charge of the Church of the Epiphany, Chehalis, and in April the mission became a parish with an acre of ground and free from all encumbrances."

Jessett (1949) p. 11

———

1885: March 29

Rt. Rev. John Adams Paddock

Journal, Jurisdiction of Washington, 1885:

"At a visit made to St. John's [Olympia] this spring, (Sunday before Easter [i.e. March 29, 1885],) I confirmed two; and accompanied by Dr. Nevius, held an afternoon Service at Tumwater. Mr. Birckhead, since his ordination, has been zealously at work in the Bellingham Bay region, and a Church at Whatcom has been built, under his supervision, to be consecrated as soon as a small indebtedness shall be removed."

———

1885: April

William West (1909):

"Our first rector in charge of the mission [at Chehalis] was the Rev. A. L. Parker, who held his first service January 25, 1885. A week's mission was held the following April conducted by the Bishop, Rev. R. D. Nevius, J. W. Sellwood, and A. L. Parker at the close of which fifteen persons were confirmed...."

———

1885: May

Microscopic Journal:

"NOTES.

—Mr. R. D. Nevins [sic], of Olympia, Washington Territory, has sent us some beautiful specimens of a marine plant covered with diatoms. One specimen is thickly spread with *Arachnoidiscus*, and the other has the same diatom and many others, including *Isthmia* and *Tricera*-[p. 98:]*tium*. Readers who desire some of this material for mounting would do well to send a good preparation of some kind to Mr. Nevins as an exchange."

American Monthly Microscopical Journal

May 1885, pp. 97-98

———

1885: May/June

Columbia Churchman (June 1885):

"St. John's, Olympia

"A local paper of this place gives an account of a successful fair held by the ladies of the parish for the benefit of the Church. The ladies had been working for some time in manufacturing articles for sale, which, when offered in this way, brought in a handsome sum to the Church. The paper referred to gives the following account of the fair:

"Four booths were arranged around the hall. One of flowers—redolent and gay with the choicest buds of the season—ruled by Miss Lillian Gunn and Mrs. Harry McElroy; one of ladies' fancy work—rich with embroidery and decorated linen—presided over by Miss Addie Wood and Mrs. Tom Ford; another of candy—sweet and tempting with home-made taffy-superintended by the Misses McKinney and Ellis; and the last but not least, the Japanese booth—interesting and amusing with the bric-a-brac and curios of the eastern empire—under the sceptre of Miss Annie Stevens and Mrs. Ross O'Brien. In addition to booths, tables for ice cream service were spread at the south end of the hall, each of which was faithfully attended by a pretty miss in charming costume.

"The center of the hall was taken up with seats for the spectators of the evening's performance, which for the first evening was a light but laughable farce entitled "Boston Dip." with the following cast of character[s]: Moses Mulligrub, Prof. Follensbee; Hannah Mulligrub, Miss Ida McKinney; Annie, Annie Ellis; Kattie, Jennie Moore; Dasher, Chas. Moore; Monsieur the professor, Geo. Williams; Saunder Rids, G. D. O'Brien.

"For the second evening the following musical programme was artistically and creditably rendered:

"1. Piano Solo, Prof. Robers.

"2. Trio, "The Distant Chimes," by Mesdames Percival, Jones and Hicks.

"3. Quartette, "Silent Night," by Messrs   O'Brien, West, Ouilette and Cowles.

"4. Vocal solo, "Where the Daisy Grow," [sic] by Mrs. Jones.

"5. Vocal solo, "Swanee River," by Mrs.   Percival.

"6. Quartette, "After the Battle, Mother," by Messrs O'Brien, West, Ouilette and Cowles.

"7. Vocal solo, ———, by Miss Yantis.

"8. Vocal solo, "The Bridge," by Mrs.   Harrington.

"The hall was crowded both nights. The bazaar is estimated to have net[ted] the good ladies of the Episcopal Church the neat sum of $250."

Journal of the Proceedings of the Fifth Convocation of the Protestant Episcopal Church of the Missionary Jurisdiction of Washington, held in St. Luke's Church, Tacoma, June 24th and 25, 1885:

———

1885: June 24 (Wednesday, St. John Baptist's Day):

The Rev. R. D. Nevius, D.D., Rector of St. John's Church, Olympia is listed in attendance. He was reappointed to the Committee on Christian Education and Literature. "At 10 o'clock A.M. an Ordination Service was held, in the prescribed form, at which the Rev. F. J. Vincent and the Rev. J. H. Birckhead, Deacons, were advanced to the Order of Priests.

Bishop Paddock's Address:

"Beloved In The Lord:

"I welcome you, for the first time in Convocation, to the city [of Tacoma] which, under the force of circumstance, it has seemed best to select for the residence of the Bishop. Those circumstances are, at least partially, known to some of you....

"During August [1884], I made a visit with the Rev. Dr. Nevius, who has been a pioneer in so many mission fields, to that sometimes called the Bellingham Bay region. On Wednesday, the 13th, divine service was held in the Baptist house of worship at LaConnor; on the morning and evening of the 17th, (10th Sunday after Trinity) in the Congregational meeting house at Whatcom, one adult being baptized by me, and several children by Dr. Nevius; in the afternoon we had the Service, with a sermon, at Bellingham.

"During the days passed at Whatcom, a number of calls were made on residents, and subscriptions were obtained for the erection of a Church.

"On Tuesday, the 19th, Services were held at the house of Mrs. Amos Bowman, at Anacortes. At the close we had the pleasure of obtaining from the little congregation six subscribers for our paper, the *Columbia Churchman.*"

"The [Annie Wright] Seminary [in Tacoma] was formally opened...., a religious service being held in the Study Hall, on Tuesday, September 4th, [1884] with addresses from clergymen and laymen, work being begun by teachers and pupils the next morning.

"On Tuesday, the 10th of September [1884], a meeting of the Convocation of Western Washington began in St. John's Church, Olympia, and on Wednesday Mr. John H. Birckhead was ordained to the Diaconate, Dr. Nevius presenting the candidate, and the sermon being preached by the Rev. Mr. Wells.

"At a visit made to St. John's [Olympia] this spring (Sunday before Easter [i.e. March 29, 1885],) I confirmed two; and accompanied by Dr. Nevius, held an afternoon Service at Tumwater. Mr. Birckhead, since his ordination, has been zealously at work in the Bellingham Bay region, and a Church at Whatcom has been built, under his supervision, to be consecrated as soon as a small indebtedness shall be removed.:

"...October 13th [1884], I officiated in the Church of the Epiphany, Chehalis. The Mission in Lewis County, of which this is one of the most important stations, has continued to prosper, the Rev. Dr. Nevius and the Rev. Mr. Vincent officiating during the first half, and the Rev. A. L. Parker during the latter part of the conventional year."

"A meeting of the Convocation of Western Washington was called at Seattle, on the 23d of October [1884], but the Rev. Dr. Nevius only was able to meet with his brethren resident in that city [i.e., no clerical or lay delegates other than Nevius from elsewhere than Seattle?]. The clergy and lay delegates present resolved to change the organization to the 'Western Deanery of Washington Territory.' The Rev. Mr. Watson was thereupon appointed Dean, the Rev. Mr. Wells [of Tacoma], Secretary, and Mr. R. G. O'Brien, Treasurer."

"The stringency in money matters has prevented the progress which friends of Grace Hospital had hoped for during the year...."

"A committee was also appointed last year, looking to 'enlarging the sphere of our paper, *The Columbia Churchman,* by its circulation in contiguous Territories.' Replies have been received by me, to letters addressed to the Bishop of Utah, the Bishop of Montana, and the Lord Bishop of British Columbia, but as they did not consider that anything in this direction can be done at present, it has not been deemed best to put the committee to the expense and trouble of convening. The letters received will be placed in the hands of our regular committee on the *Columbia Churchman.*

"I must say to you, beloved, that the sum granted by the Domestic Missionary Society (whose office is in New York,) is the same per annum as when I first came to you, while new stations are calling, every year for aid. Our work cannot go forward unless some of the clergy and laity, in stations that have received aid, will offer or consent to relinquish the whole or a portion of the stipend, enabling it to be applied for work elsewhere."

———

1885: June 25 (Thursday):

"The Committee on the Incorporation of Parishes made the following report which on motion was adopted:

Your Committee appointed upon the incorporation of Parishes beg respectfully to submit their report as follows:

From information received we believe that the Parish of the Church of the Epiphany, at Chehalis, has been canonically organized, and we recommend that it be admitted to all the rights and privileges of this Convocation.

We also recommend the same action in the case of St. Luke's Parish, Tacoma, which has also been canonically organized.

"The Committee on the *Columbia Churchman* made the following report, which was adopted:

Your Committee on the *Columbia Churchman* would respectfully report that the proposal of last year, looking towards the enlargement of the sphere of our paper by extending its circulation through contiguous Territories, has failed of good result...."

"The Committee on Christian Education and Literature [Nevius chair] reported as follows, with report was on motion adopted:

The Committee on Christian Education and Literature respectfully report—that it seems proper to put on record in the Journal, which largely historizes the progress of the church in this jurisdiction, the fact that the Annie Wright Seminary has passed through a successful year of work. It is peculiarly gratifying to know that the first year of the existence of this institution has, under the admirable management of its Principal and the efficient labors of its Teachers, resulted in a financial success.

"The same can be said of St. Paul's School, Walla Walla, notwithstanding it has in a year of great depression in business labored under the disadvantage of being inadequately housed, and the necessity of competition with other well furnished schools in the country from which it has had its patronage.

The Parish Schools at Seattle, Vancouver, and Dayton, mentioned favorably in the annual report of the Bishop, are doing a good though more unobtrusive work.

It is pleasing to note that a School for boys, of a similar character to the Annie Wright Seminary, is provided for at Tacoma, and that the building has been begun, and that there is a good prospect for the beginning of its work this year.

With respect to Church Literature generally, your committee begs to point out the present difficulty of obtaining books, papers, Catechisms, etc., and the usual lack of knowledge on the part of those in need of the same, both as to the most desirable publisher with whom to deal and as to the best publication dealing with the points at issue. There are, for instance, many catechisms suitable for most classes in our Sunday Schools, yet on examination it will be found that one is preferable to another, for general use in a mixed school, or one where there are few classes, or then again, one is preferable from its Church teaching.

The same is true of all other literature usually required in Sunday School and Parish work. Moreover, by our present method of furnishing literature the highest price is paid for every article.

To remedy, in part, our present condition, it is suggested that it is advisable that a committee of one, acting under the advice of the Bishop, be appointed by convocation, through whom all orders be made for the purchase of literature. Said committee could procure not only more favorable terms than if different parties were to order indiscriminately, but also literature better adapted for the required needs.

If such committee should be appointed it would be desirable for it to publish in the *Columbia Churchman* its ability to meet the object recommended in this report.

"The Rev. A. Parker of Chehalis was appointed as a committee [of one], as recommended by the report.

"The Bishop appointed the following as Missionary Committee for the ensuing year: The Rt. Rev. J. A. Paddock, D.D., ex-officio President; the Rev. Geo. H. Watson, Chairman; the Rev. L. H. Wells, Secretary; Mr. R. G. O'Brien, Treasurer; the Rev. H. D. Lathrop, D.D.; the Rev. R. D. Nevius, D.D.; Messrs. William West, Chas. Boyer, and J. J. Beeson."

"Parochial Reports....

"*Report of St. John's Church, Olympia, for the year ending June 21st, 1885.*

"The Rev. R. D. Nevius, Rector.

"Baptisms—Adult, 3; Infant, 4; Total, 7.

"Confirmations, 2.

"Communicants—Added, 2; Removed, 6; Present No. 51.

"Sunday School—Teachers, 7; Pupils, 53.

"Marriages, 2; Burials, 6.

"No. of Families connected with the Congregation, 73.

"No. of souls connected with the Congregation, 220.

"Collections and Contributions—For Salary, $579; Domestic Missions, $5.50; Sunday School Lenten offerings, General Missions $15; Diocesan Missions, $25.20; Parochial Purposes, $293.50; Episcopal Fund, $5.45; Disabled Clergy

Fund, $5.55; Convocation Expenses, $14.65; Miscellaneous, $18; Total, $966.85.

"The Mission at Whatcom and parts adjacent remained under my charge part of the year, and that at Chehalis until February 1st.

"Baptized at Whatcom, Adult, 2; Infant, 12; at Anacortes, Infant 1; at Winlock, Infant, 4; at Chehalis, Infant, 4; Marriages at Chehalis, 1.

"All of these official acts are reported among those of these stations made by the clergy in Charge of the same."

1885: September 29 (St. Michael and All Angels' Day)

Probable date of formal establishment of mission at Yakima. 25th Anniversary celebrated from this date (see September 29, 1910, below).

1885: September 30

Columbia Churchman (November 1885):

"Sept. 30th, 1885.—The Western Deanery of Washington Territory met at St. Luke's Church, Tacoma.... The Dean, Rev. George H. Watson, in the chair.

"Present, Rev. D. H. Lovejoy [Memorial Hospital, Tacoma], Rev. A. L. Parker [Chehalis], Rev. F. J. Vincent [Tacoma], Rev. L. H. Wells [Tacoma], Rev. J. H. Birckhead [Whatcom/Bellingham].... Treasurer made verbal report through Dr. Nevius....

"Dr. Nevius gave account of his visit in company with Rev. L. H. Wells to Montesano. They had a good congregation. Four persons partook of the Holy Communion. Seven expressed a wish to join the Church. One child was baptized. Two lots were offered if we would build a church. At Elma there was a large congregation. Two children were baptized. Dr. Nevius held an interesting service at Anacortes. Thinks there is not much for us to do there, but there are a few Episcopalians that should be looked after."

———

1885: November 16

Rev. R. D. Nevius

[Letter to Harvard University]

"Olympia, W. T.

"Nov. 16" 1885

"My Dear Sir;

"I have a letter to day from Dr. Lathrop, St. Paul's School, Walla Walla, for whom I procured a Botany California two years ago, to ask if I can get him another at the same price of $8.00. Can it be done? If so, please order the two volumes sent and expect the money for the same immediately from him. Address H. D. Lathrop, D.D., Walla Walla.

"I shall await the announcement of the publication of the promised book on Wood Mosses of N.A. It may have been issued and that the announcement has escaped my notice. If so please have the book sent to me at once. I enclose a stamped envelope.

"I have a puzzle or two to refer to you for an early answer. Will you please give me the names of the enclosed? [Over?] are two others [mailers?] I refer to Dr. Gray glad to find an excuse for writing to him at this time when all are congratulating him and none more heartily than I.

"Very truly yours,
"R. D. Nevius"

———

1885: November 18

Rev. R. D. Nevius:*

"Olympia Washtn Ter.

"Nov. 18" 1885

"My dear Doctor Gray

"May I claim a place among the friends who will crowd around you to-day for congratulations?

There are many of us who have never seen your face because of the freedom with which you have permitted them to approach you for personal assistance by letter in their otherwise unaided studies.

"I hope you will permit me to say that your kindly service to me since the time, and at the time when you helped me to come into the brotherhood of botanists with a new genus in my hand, has wrought in me an affection which claims a place

among your friends more favored in that only that they have had more frequent and more familiar intercourse with you.

"Let me come to you as of old once more with a Specimen in my hands and a desire for assistance.

"I confess it a scheme not unworthy I hope, for securing a note from you. Yet I am not without a hope of giving you pleasure.

"The enclosed fronds which I have never but once seen growing were found by me in a shallow basaltic dish or basin near Spokane Falls. It grows in a floating tangle and expands laterally and rectangularly from fissures in the edge of the fronds which separate, surface from surface. I suppose it is rooted, yet because of its fragile character I could not determine this as a fact. I should be very glad to know something about this if you can spare the time.

"I have to day been mounting some peristomes,** and some diatoms in situ, which latter are very fine, and the former may be of interest to your friends if not to you. I have spent part of the day in mounting these for you. If you will accept them it will give me pleasure. Should they be such an old story to you as to add only duplicates to your cabinet of slides, it will please me if you will give them to any of your correspondents to whom they will give pleasure. I am afraid I cannot send them until the cement stiffens a little, and I shall hold my letter from the mail until I can send the package with it. Hoping that your friends and the public whom you have so long served by your published books may Congratulate you on many happy birthdays.

"I am dear honored Sir
"Very truly yours
"R. D. Nevius."

*On the occasion of Dr. Asa Gray's seventy-fifth birthday. See Dupree (1959) 402.

**In mosses, the fringe of teeth surrounding the orifice of the capsule." WebNCD

———

1885: December 16

Rev. R. D. Nevius:

[Letter to Harvard University]

"Olympia, W. T.

"Dec. 16th." 1885

"Dear Mr. Watson

"I send a package of slides to day. I could not get them ready before because the cement was too green to clean even imperfectly, and I fear that when they arrive it will not do to handle the mounts for some time.

"I have never seen any peristomes mounted save my own. They may be common, however, and not new to you. They will reach you in time to let me add to your Christmas joy by this acceptance of my most kind and affectionate regards.

"I send a postal card to pay for the Mosses of N.A. and thank you for your many favors.

"Very truly yours
"R. D. Nevius"

[1886]

1886: spring

Rev. Thomas Jessett (1949):

"[In his address on July 29, the bishop reported] the removal of the Rev. Mr. Birckhead from Bellingham Bay due to the severe monetary depression, and the abandonment of the church at Kalama due to the removal of population [fn]38 [In 1888 or early 1889] The furnishings from St. Andrew's, Kalama, were taken by the Rev. Dr. Nevius to the Church of the Epiphany, Chehalis, except for the bell which went to All Saints' Church, Spokane Falls. [fn]39"

[fn]"39 *Washington Churchman*, March, 1889"

Jessett (1949) p. 12

1883-1886

[While in Olympia Nevius had founded an "Agassiz Association" to encourage young people to take up the study of Natural History. See October 12, 1952 below.]

———

1886: June 29 - July 1

Journal of the Proceedings of the Sixth Convocation of the Protestant Episcopal Church of the Missionary Jurisdiction of Washington, Held in the Church of the Epiphany, Chehalis, June 30th and July 1st, 1886.

1886: June 29 (Tuesday)

"Preliminary Services.

"On St. Peter's Day, June 29th [1886], the Church of the Epiphany was consecrated by the Right Rev. J. A. Paddock, D.D., the Rev. R. D. Nevius, D.D., preaching the sermon, and Mr. William West reading the instrument of donation."

———

1886: June 30 (Wednesday)

The Rev. R. D. Nevius, D.D. is listed as Rector of St. John's Church, Olympia. He was appointed to the Committee on *The Columbia Churchman* and reappointed to the Committee on Education and Literature.

"The Registrar of the convocation [Nevius] reported as follows:

The Registrar would respectfully report, that he has in hand imperfect files of the *Oregon* and *Columbia Churchman*, running through all the years of its publication; also imperfect files of the Journals of the Jurisdiction of Oregon, and perfect files of those of Washington: of Almanacs and the "Church Review" including bound volumes of the first 14 years; and of the Journals of Conventions and General Conventions, with various miscellaneous in hand.

"R. D. Nevius,
"Registrar."

Bishop Paddock's Address:

"Five years have passed since I first met with you in council. At that time no Church Services had been held in Chehalis. The lamented Bonnell, during his brief earthly ministry, officiated here on a few occasions, and is remembered with affection and regard by those who then united with him in the worship.... Services, continued by the Rev. Dr. Nevius, the Rev. Mr. Vincent, and the Rev. A. L. Parker, have been so blessed, that, with the co-operation of a few faithful, zealous Church men and Church women, the edifice, in which we are assembled, has been built on ground donated, thirty-one have been confirmed, a goodly number have been enrolled as parishioners, forty-six of whom are communicants, and a Sunday School, having on its register the names of six teachers and sixty-two pupils, meets on each Lord's Day."

"Although, my Brethren, it has always and everywhere been true, that 'the cross does not find friends, it makes them,' yet, the trials and discouragements of Bishop, Clergy, and Laity engaged in planting the cross in this new country, are confessedly greater than in some localities. We are, in numbers, but 'a feeble folk,' and we have to contend with indifference, hardness of heart, unbelief in its various forms, sins of every kind openly and boldly committed. Sometimes the Clergyman finds, in his congregation, few, if any, ready to give sympathy, cheer, co-operation. O! what comfort and strength may even one faithful Layman be to his Pastor!"

"At Spokane Falls, the Church building, begun before I was called to charge of the Territory, has been completed, and, during the last year, has been removed to another location, and improved by painting and the addition of a bell-tower with its bell. A Parsonage, so desirable at every station, has been also built and paid for. Through funds entrusted to me, by Churchmen and the East, I was enabled to purchase, some three years since, in this flourishing city, a small plot of land, which has largely risen in value, and may eventually be of service to the Church."

"At Cheney, we have two lots secured, if a building be placed on them, within a limited period. Services are occasionally held in the town, but we are not, as yet encouraged to build."

"At Sprague, a structure, at first so small and plain that the pioneer Missionary [Nevius], under whom the work was begun, only called the building a 'shelter,' has been enlarged, neatly finished, and this Spring, a small, sweet-toned bell has been purchased, and, from its place, calls to the House of God."

"Before my coming to the Territory, a Church was built at Kalama, which place it was then expected, would then be the terminus of the Northern Pacific Railroad. Brethren of the Clergy and I myself have officiated, many times, in this House of

Prayer; but the population has gone, so that I have allowed the chancel furniture and the bell to be placed in other Churches, and am contemplating the removal of the building itself to some locality where it may be used for holy purposes."

"In the region about Gray's Harbor, at Elma, Montesano, Cosmopolis, and Hoquiam, a few Services have been held during the past season; and the Rev. Dr. Nevius, who has broken ground here, as in so many other places, thinks that a Missionary should, at once, become a resident and worker in this field."

"Within the last four years, the Church edifice at Port Townsend, through the efforts of the Rev. J. B. Alexander, has been removed to a more eligible location, secured while Mr. Davis was the Missionary, and the building has been greatly improved in the external and internal appearance."

"At Whatcom, a Church has been built on land donated. The Missionary [Birckhead], while resident at this station, cared also for Sehome and Bellingham, and made some visits to La Conner, and other points. For a time the work at Whatcom gave good promise; but, the population was reduced by the extreme monetary depression, which has been so trying, all over the Territory; and as very little could be done for the support of the Missionary, it was deemed best to remove him to another locality, the Bishop and some of the Clergy occasionally giving a Service at Whatcom and the other stations.

"At East Sound, on Orcas Island, a Mission has been established, and a Church built, Mr. S. R. S. Gray, a candidate for Holy Orders, having labored zealously, the Rev. Mr. Watson [of Seattle], Dean, giving advice and aid."

"St. John's Parish, Olympia, some time since erected a small building, for its Rector's use, on a portion of the Parsonage lot, and has recently, I rejoice to say, accepted plans and secured subscriptions, looking to the immediate erection of a new Church. By the Rector at Olympia, a Service has occasionally been given at Tumwater; and by other Clergymen and by the Bishop in the village of Steillacoom, and at the Asylum for the insane."

"I have also been permitted to erect, in Tacoma, on land donated, the Bishop's House, some offerings having been given me by eastern friends, especially for that purpose; the whole property to belong to the Church, if that yet due shall be paid within five years from the time of the completion of the building. This I shall expect to effect, if God spare my life."

"Immanuel Church, East Sound [Orcas Island], has been consecrated; and yesterday...., the Church of the Epiphany, in which we are now assembled, was in like manner....

"A communication from our Brethren in Oregon will probably come before you, looking to a more general distribution of our paper called *The Columbia Churchman*. I believe that great good may result, if the plan proposed can be adopted and acted on."

"The Rev. A. L. Parker offered the following resolution, which on motion was adopted:

Resolved— That the Convocation of Washington Territory ... having, in view of the paucity of our Clergy, especially throughout the West, requests the General Convention to take measures for the more general revival of the ancient order of Readers, which is being used with good results in many parts of the Anglican Communion.

"The Convocation proceeded to the election of Delegates to the General Convention, with the following results: Clerical—the Rev. R. D. Nevius, D.D., substitute, the Rev. A. S. Nicholson. Lay—Colonel F. E. Trotter."

———

1886: July 1 (Thursday)

"The Rev. A. L. Parker, of the Committee on Church Literature, appointed at last Convocation, reported that:

About one hundred dollars worth of books and Sunday School supplies have been obtained through our agency. Most of the publishers in New York, the young Churchman Company, Milwaukee, and Kensington, London, England, give us a discount of 25 per cent.

"The Committee on *The Columbia Churchman* made a report, which was on motion recommitted."

"The Committee on *The Columbia Churchman* [Parker, chair] presented the following amended report, which was on motion adopted:

Whereas, a proposition has been laid before this Convocation from the Convocation of the Jurisdiction of Oregon, looking towards a combined effort for the better support of *The Columbia Churchman*, based upon an issue of 1500 copies at 50 cents per annum per copy, and a larger distribution, and the payment by this Jurisdiction of $200 towards defraying the same;

It is recommended that a financial agent be chosen by this Convocation, to secure that amount, and that when he shall be able to satisfy the editor that the payment of said sum of $200 is secure, that he may on the part of this Convocation perfect the arrangement proposed.

"The Rev. A. L. Parker was elected as such agent.

"The Committee on Incorporation of Parishes made an amended report, which was adopted, as follows:

Your Committee on the Incorporation of Parishes would respectfully report, that no business coming within its province has been brought before it. They however, announce that the organization of the following Missions has been effected: Immanuel Church, East Sound, Elma, and Montesano."

The Committee on the State of the Church reported....;

At Tacoma a Boy's school has been erected and occupied; giving great promise of usefulness in the future. The Annie Wright Seminary has just closed a prosperous year.

St. Paul's School at Walla Walla is also reported as in flourishing condition. The Parish Schools at Seattle and Vancouver are still maintained, and are means of usefulness in their respective Parishes.

The Hospital in Seattle is nearly completed, and will soon be ready for the care of the sick."

"A meeting of the Western Deanery was held during the Convocation, and the Rev. Geo. H. Watson was elected Dean, and the Rev. L. H. Wells elected Secretary, in place of Rev. Mr. Birckhead, removed to the Eastern Deanery."

——

"Parochial Reports....

"*Report of St. John's Church, Olympia, and Elma and Montesano Missions, for the year ending June 29, 1886.*

"The Rev. R. D. Nevius, D.D., Missionary.

"Baptisms-Adult, 4; Infant, 14; Total, 18.

"Confirmations, 8.

"Communicants—Added 9; removed 6; Present number, 53.

"Sunday School—Teachers, 7; Pupils, 50.

"Burials, 10.

"No. of Families connected with the Congregation, 73.

"No. of souls connected with the Congregation,   220.

"Collections and Contributions—For salary, $608; Domestic Missions, $24.50; Foreign Missions, $4.50; Diocesan Missions, $35; Parochial Purposes, $275.95; Disabled Clergy Fund, $7.50; Convocation Expenses, $10.30; Total $955.75.

"Four visits have been made to the towns on the Lower Chehalis river and Gray's Harbor, the first being made last Summer in company with Rev. L. H. Wells. We held service in the five towns along the line above indicated, and were made to think the field an important and promising one, at Elma and Montesano, each a nucleus of several Church families, and five or six communicants are found in these two towns, though the friends of the Church have only asked the bishop, by a petition, to organize a mission in them, with a resident Missionary. I have been much encouraged by the prospect of the early establishment and growth of a strong center of work in these places with a foresight of extension to the towns further down the river and on the harbor. Two adults and six infants have been baptized at Montesano. Candidates for confirmation in both places await the proposed visit of the Bishop. The baptisms in these places are reported in my statistical report above.

"Communicants at Elma, 5. Communicants at Montesano, 5.

"At Olympia the condition of our church building which—originally an old carpenter shop—was turned into a church building thirty years ago, and has been many times repaired, is such that we have been compelled to move toward the building of a new church. For this the ladies of the Women's Guild have, through long

patience and well directed labor and economy, accumulated about $800; a liberal subscription has been started by the vestry, and beautiful plans have been secured and we hope to begin work immediately."

——

1886: August 7-9
Bishop Paddock's Address
Journal, Jurisdiction of Washington, 1887:

"On Saturday, [August 7, 1886], in Emmanuel Church, East Sound, I admitted to the Diaconate, Sidney Robert Spencer Gray, the Rev. Mr. Watson, Dean of the Western Convocation, preaching the sermon, and the Rev. Dr. Nevius aiding in the Services.

"On the following day [August 8], I baptized several children and adults, confirmed three men presented by the Rev. Mr. Gray, and administered the Holy Communion. Addresses were made by Dr. Nevius and Mr. Watson, as well as myself, and we were favored by the presence of a few lay people from Seattle, who came with their rector to show their interest in this mission work and the missionary.

"On Monday morning [August 9] we united in an open-air Service on Lucia Island, and a short business meeting of the Western Deanery was held."

——

1886: August 22-29
Bishop Paddock's Address
Journal, Jurisdiction of Washington, 1887:

"On Sunday [August 29, 1886] (tenth after Trinity), in the morning, I read Service and preached in the hall of the Grand Army of the Republic at Elma, and in the afternoon at the Baptist house of worship at Montesano, where I also administered the rite of confirmation to two candidates. This was my first visit to this, the Gray's Harbor region, where I hope, ere long, we may have a Missionary at work. The Rev. Dr. Nevius had preceded me, and during the week [August 22-29] before my coming instructed those confirmed."

-Visit East -

1886: August 15
Rev. R. D. Nevius, D.D.
Journal, Jurisdiction of Washington, 1887:

"My official acts up to September 15, 1886, at which time I left Olympia for General Convention, and a prolonged visit East, will be supplied from the Register by the Clerk of the Vestry.

——

1886: August 15
Rev. Thomas Jessett (1940):

"In 1886 Dr. Nevius was elected the delegate to General Convention from the convocation of Washington, and on August 16 [sic 15], he resigned as he did not plan to return west after the meeting of the General Convention in October. The vestry granted him leave of absence and tried to get him to return, but on March 2, 1887, he mailed his resignation from Utica, New York. Shortly afterward he returned [to Washington State]."

Jessett 1940, 35

——

1886: mid-October
Bishop Paddock's Address
Journal, Jurisdiction of Washington, 1887:

"It was a pleasure to me that our Territory was represented in the House of Deputies, the Rev. Dr. Nevius, elected as your delegate, being able to attend through the [mid-October] session."

——

1886: October
Rev. Thomas Jessett (1949):

"The bishop and Dr. Nevius attended the General Convention meeting in October in Chicago, afterward which the bishop visited "in my native place, Norwich, Connecticut.... Also Dr. Nevius remained in the East instead of returning with the bishop, although he still kept his canonical connection with the district, promising to return."

Jessett (1949) pp. 12-13

———

1886: October
Rev. Thomas Jessett (1949):
"In October, 1886, the paper [the *Columbia Churchman*] changed its name to the *Oregon and Washington Churchman* and came under the joint editorship of the Rev. John W. Sellwood of East Portland, Oregon, and the Rev. Mardon D. Wilson, new rector of St. Lukes, Vancouver. [fn]44."
"[fn]44 *Oregon and Washington Churchman*, November, 1886."

———

1886: November
Oregon & Washington Churchman:
"The Rev. R. D. Nevius, D.D., rector of St. Paul's church, Olympia, W. T., is in attendance at the General Convention. We are sorry to say that he does not expect to return at present.
1886: November
"Frequent Visitor"
Oregon and Washington Churchman:
'John Day Valley.....
"This Mission field is feeling the hard times as well as other places."

———

1886:
John Livingston Nevius published *Methods of Mission Work.*
Nevius (1985) 415

———

1886: late
Bishop Paddock's Address
Journal, Jurisdiction of Washington, 1887:
"On the following Sunday [in late 1886], in my native place, Norwich, Conn., [I] preached twice and addressed two Sunday schools; on Tuesday evening following, I spoke to the Ladies' Guild of St. James' Church, New London; the next Lord's Day I was at my former parish Church and Sunday school, St. Peter's, Brooklyn, New York, and at the Church of the Redeemer, Astoria; on the following Tuesday, in Trinity Church, New Haven, I made an address at the anniversary of the Women's Auxiliary of the Diocese of Connecticut. It was refreshing to see the large Church filled to overflowing on the morning, afternoon and evening of the week-day, by hundreds of delegates coming from all parts of the State and by other hundreds of their Church sisters of New Haven. The $700 received through the offertory was divided between the seven Missionary Bishops present; and I also received $50, sent me by a Christian woman for the promotion of our Missionary, Educational or Charitable work. The Good Lord bless and reward all our helpers and co-laborers

[1887]

1870: January
Rt. Rev. B. Wistar Morris
Oregon and Washington Churchman:
"'Tis no easy matter to induce the young clergymen of the east to undertake missionary work in our far off country; and the last place, as I ventured to say in a public missionary address the other—for the 'Western fever' to break out, in a theo-logical seminary. And even when there are hopeful appearances of the 'Infection' and a young student or deacon is 'almost persuaded' to cast in his lot with us, I have known the whole thing dissipated and broken up by so simple a thing as the will or word of a young woman.

1887: January
Rt. Rev. B. Wistar Morris
Oregon and Washington Churchman:
"'Tis no easy matter to induce the young clergymen of the east to undertake missionary work in our far off country; and the last place, as I ventured to say in a

public missionary address the other day—for the 'western fever' to break out, is a theological seminary. And even when there are hopeful appearances of the 'infection' and a young student or deacon is 'almost persuaded' to cast in his lot with us, I have known the whole thing dissipated and broken up by so simple a thing as the will or word of a young woman!"

———

1887: March 2
Rev. Thomas Jessett (1940):
"In 1886 Dr. Nevius was elected the delegate to General Convention from the convocation of Washington, and on August 16, he resigned as he did not plan to return west after the meeting of the General Convention in October. The vestry granted him leave of absence and tried to get him to return, but on March 2, 1887, he mailed his resignation from Utica, New York. Shortly afterward he returned [to Washington Territory]."
Jessett 1940, 35

———

1887: March 13
Rev. R. D. Nevius, D.D.
Journal, Jurisdiction of Washington, 1887:
"On the 13th of March, 1887, my six months leave of absence having expired, I found my duty constraining me to defer my return to W. T., and I accordingly re-signed the charge of St. John's Church, Olympia, thereby surrendering a relation which I had found uniformly a pleasant one." [Jessett erroneously gives a date of March 2 for the resignation in a letter to David Powers, December 29, 1980.]

———

1887: June
Wood (1968) 77:
NPRR line over the Cascades completed via temporary switchbacks over Snoqualmie Pass.

———

1887: June 29 (Wednesday)
Bishop Paddock's Address
Journal, Jurisdiction of Washington, 1887:
"The Rev. Dr. Nevius, who has resigned St. John's Olympia, continues his canoni-cal connection with the Jurisdiction, and writes that he may desire to return in the autumn."

———

1887: June 30 (Thursday):
"The Rev. M. D. Wilson was elected Registrar of the Jurisdiction in the place of the Rev. Dr. Nevius, resigned."
"Parochial Reports....
Report of St. John's Church, Olympia, for the year ending June 27, 1887....
"Report of The Rev. R. D. Nevius, D.D.
"My official acts up to September 15, 1886, at which time I left Olympia for General Convention, and a prolonged visit East, will be supplied from the Register by the Clerk of the Vestry. On the 13th March, 1887, my six months leave of ab-sence having expired, I found my duty constraining me to defer my return to W. T., and I accordingly resigned the charge of St. John's Church, Olympia, thereby surren-dering a relation which I had found uniformly a pleasant one.
"During my absence I have officiated as minister in charge at Trinity Church, Utica, N.Y., for three months, and from Sunday to Sunday in many places , and have often had an opportunity of reporting to Churches from which in the past, assis-tance in our Missionary work has come, the progress of the work which by their aid we have been enable[d] to do. And I have secured from Trinity Church and Calvary Church, Utica, $56 for the building of a Church for Gray's Harbor Mission.
R. D. Nevius, Missionary."
1887:
Wood (1968) 74:
OR&N leased to the Union Pacific.

- North Yakima, Washington Territory -

(St. Michael's Church, Yakima)

(Grace Church, Ellensburg)

———

1887: March

Oregon and Washington Churchman:

"Dr. Nevius' Work in the Far West.

"The untiring and efficient labors of the Rev. R. D. Nevius, D.D., since his arrival here fifteen years ago, in what was then known as the Missionary Jurisdiction of Oregon and Washington Territory, have been potent in founding and building up the Church in the State of Oregon and the adjoining Territories of Washington and Idaho. These labors covered an area of 500 miles from East to West and 250 miles from North to South, a country greater in distance and future than many an Eastern State with its four or five dioceses and justly entitle him to be called the greatest pioneer Missionary of the north-west. He commenced his work on the coast in 1872 as Rector of Trinity Church, Portland, resigned it within a year, and, at the request of Bishop Morris he took charge of the Missionary work in Eastern Oregon, then very sparsely populated, the settlements small and far apart, occupying only the small fertile valleys, whilst over the vast stretches of rolling prairie and rugged mountain, at intervals far apart could be found the isolated home of some adventurous pioneer, and through those vast solitudes roamed the red man in his native freedom. He proceeded at once to the Grande Ronde Valley, and, making his headquarters at La Grande, he opened Mission stations at different points in the valley, gathering congregations and building Churches at La Grande, Union, and The Cove; then turning over his work to a resident Missionary. He worked for some time at The Dalles, holding a series of Mission Services accompanied with faithful work from house to house, gathering by these means a congregation and building a Church, and though so blessed in his labors, yet so exacting was his work elsewhere that he found it impossible to be present at the laying of the corner stone, much to the regret of his Bishop and the earnest band of faithful Christians that he had infused with so much of his zeal and spirit for the work. Next we find him at Baker City four hundred miles east, making that place a centre of operations, traveling great distances to all outlying points, often having to ride on horseback 50, 60 or 70 miles from one appointment to another, visiting isolated families wherever found and building Churches at Baker City, Lewiston* and Canyon City and again giving up his work when well established to a successor. Again forming a new base of operations at Spokane Falls, a point near the line of British Columbia and several hundred miles West and North from Baker City, he there held services and established Mission stations at all available points within reach in Washington and Idaho, building a Church and School at Spokane Falls, a Church at Pomeroy and at Sprague, and, as an instance of his restless energy, holding service in the Church at Sprague on the Sunday following commencement of the building. In 1883 he became Rector of St. John's Church, Olympia, which he held until his return to the East last September [1886], still continuing his Missionary labors and making regular visits during 1884 in the adjoining county of Lewis, holding Mission services at three different points [Bellingham, Chehalis, Whatcom], building a Church at Chehalis, meanwhile organizing a guild of 18 members, not one of them being at that time communicants of the Church, baptizing five and presenting to the Bishop at his first visitation ten candidates for confirmation; all before the completion of the building. There are now within the country about 70 communicants. These Missionary journeys were alternated by trips along Puget Sound, visiting Bellingham, Whatcom, Sehome and La Connor on the mainland and the islands of San Juan, Orcas, and Fidalgo, holding services at all accessible points and building a Church at Whatcom. During the last year of his pastorate at Olympia he made several visits down the Chehalis river and around Gray's harbor, holding services at five different points, finding along the route scattered members of the Church, bringing to them its privileges and consolations, baptizing ten, prepared several candidates for confirmation and established Mission stations at Elma and Montesano. Thus during an earnest self-denying Missionary career of fourteen years, he has been instrumental in extending the Church's lines of occupation to the farthest limits of the continent, reaching the shores of the Pacific and the Islands on its coasts, along the meanderings of its rivers, and now buildings consecrated for Christian worship dot the landscape of its peaceful interior valleys, its wild mountain gorges and bustling railroad towns. Working from four successive centres of operations,** within and around which twelve Churches have been built,*** all of which are now active centres of work for resident Missionaries, he has held regular appointments at 26 other places, in some of which, other Missionaries have since built Churches. In most of these, as well as in many other places, he was the first to proclaim the Gospel of our Lord Jesus Christ, thus shewing that the old Apostolic Church has not lost the vigor of her youth or slighted the commands of her Divine Master, but that as a pioneer, she is still marching in the front of civilization, claiming the earth as the Lord's with the fullness thereof, redeeming the waste places and making the desert to blossom as the rose. May the work in which he under God's blessing has been the approved instrument never cease to shed its blessings in an ever increasing ratio, on all succeeding generations. "LAYMAN"

Oregon and Washington Churchman, March, 1887

*Church of the Nativity. Nevius seems to have established the congregation but not to have built a church building. See October 16, 1879.

**La Grande, The Dalles, Spokane Falls and Olympia.

***La Grande, Union, Cove, The Dalles, Baker City, (Lewiston), Canyon City, Spokane Falls, Pomeroy, Sprague, Chehalis and Whatcom. Nevius founded a congregation but did not build a church at Lewiston. See October 16, 1879.

———

1887:

John Livingston Nevius began to propagate "fruits and vines from abroad" in China.

Nevius (1895) 429

———

1887:

Northern Pacific Railroad completed to Seattle.

———

1887: November 26

Nevius's sixtieth birthday. Of it, John Livingston Nevius wrote to their mother, "I did not forget Reuben's birthday, but thought a great deal of it as marking the three-score epoch, which I too am fast approaching. From this point of view there seems to be not much future left, and I am beginning to make plans for rounding out what remains of life and turning it to the best account."

Nevius (1895) 433

- Visit South (and East") -

1887: December 25 (Christmas)

Oregon and Washington Churchman, February 1888:

"The Rev. R. D. Nevius, D.D. assisted in the services at St. Paul's Church, Chattanooga, Tenn., on Christmas Day, acting as celebrant at the 10 o'clock service, and preaching the sermon in the evening."

[1888]

1888: January 3

Oregon and Washington Churchman, March 1888:

"We take the following from the Tuscaloosa, Ala., Daily Gazette of January 3d:

"The Rev. Reuben D. Nevius, D.D., who was rector of Christ Church Parish, Tuscaloosa, from 1855 to 1866, is in the city, on a visit to old friends. He preached an able sermon Sunday last in the church of which he was formerly rector. Dr. Nevius is now a resident of Olympia, Washington Territory. It has been twenty-two years since he left Tuscaloosa, but he finds hosts of friends here who remember him for his elegant scholarship, his genial manners, his great affability and kindness of heart, his happy turn for making others happy, and his noble work as a christian [sic] minister in Alabama, and who are therefore delighted to take him warmly to their hearts once more. Dr. Nevius is the guest of Dr. and Mrs. Bryce, and will remain here four or five days. Would that Neviusia the beautiful new flower, which he discovered on the banks of the Warrior river, during his residency here, and which was named in honor of its discoverer, could bloom out a New Year's greeting."

1888: January
Oregon and Washington Churchman:
"The Rev. R. D. Nevius, D.D., is general missionary of Washington Territory, and is to be addressed at Olympia, W.T."

———

1888: January 30
Dr. Asa Gray died in Cambridge, Massachusetts, age 77 yrs., 2 mos., 12 days.

———

1888: spring
Rev. Thomas Jessett (1949):
"Dr. Nevius also returned [in 1888] and took up duties as general missionary, covering a goodly portion of the state, with headquarters at Ellensburg and North Yakima.[fn]50."
"[fn]50 *Oregon and Washington Churchman*, various issues, 1887-1888.
Jessett (1949) p. 15

———

1888: April
Oregon and Washington Churchman:
"NOTES.
"Dr. Nevius has accepted the position of general Missionary in the Jurisdiction of Washington Territory, and is for this month engaged in work in Yakima and Ellensburg and parts adjacent. We hope to hear from the Doctor soon."

———

1888:May 27
Wood (1968) 77:
Stampede Tunnel through Snoqualmie Pass opened for through traffic to Puget Sound on NPRR.

———

1888: May, June, Summer
Rev. Thomas Jessett (1940):
[p. 36] "For nearly two years St. John's [Olympia] was without a regular rector.... Efforts toward the building of a new church never ceased and plans were drawn by C. N. Daniels, architect, of Tacoma. In May 1888, calls for bids were printed in the *Washington Standard*, Olympia, the *Post-Intelligencer*, Settle, and the *Morning Oregonian*, Portland, Oregon, and on June 8 these were opened. During the summer the Rev. Horace Hall Buck came from Nevada to be the rector of St. John's and under his leadership construction was begun." See April 22, 1889; October 20, 1889; below.

———

1888: June 30 (Saturday)
Rev. E. W. Pigion (1928, see below at October 30, 1909):
"Dr. Nevius held service [at Yakima] on June 30. Services held in on [sic] first floor of a wooden building on No. 1st St. about where Western Auto Supply Co. is now (1928) no. 110 No. 1st St."
St. Michael's Church (Yakima, 1985):
"In 1888 Dr. Nevius formed a building committee of Colonel William Ferrand Prosser, special agent of the General Land Office for Oregon and Washington who in 1886 was elected Yakima County Auditor; William Steinweg, who came to North Yakima in 1886 to be cashier of the First National Bank of Yakima; and Henry Blatchford Scudder, who arrived in April, 1886, with Mrs. Scudder and their seven children to develop a dairy in the Moxee area.* Plans for the new church, drawn as a gift by Edward Tuckerman Potter, a church architect in New York and of Newport, Rhode Island, were received by Mr. Scudder on June 5, provided for a much larger church, and were to be used in subsequent additions.
"The new church, built of uncut basalt rock hauled from Garretson's Grade ('Painted Rocks') by horse-drawn wagons, is Gothic in style. The structure, seating 125 people, was 45 feet by 25 feet with 12 foot high walls and a high pitched roof. The front gable of the church (west end) was carried up above the planes of the roof in three equal stages of six feet each, was surmounted by a large stone cross, and had three long narrow windows of cathedral glass from Coulter and Sons, Cincinnati."
*Ibid: "The first communion service, later sent to Bishop Rowe in Alaska, was

given by the Rev. Leonard K. Storrs of St. Paul's, Brookline, whom Mr. Scudder had previously served as senior warden." Relander (Yakima *Republic*) 1960: "Alice Scudder was 17 years old the year the building was finished. To her father's home, four miles east of Yakima, Dr. Nevius rode frequently to talk about the building progress with H. B. Scudder."

———

1888: June
Rev. Geo. Herbert Watson
Journal, Jurisdiction of Washington, 1888
(report dated July 5, 1888):
Annual report of the "Western Deanery of Washington":
"Two meetings have been held during the past year: one at Whatcom in August 1887 (while Nevius was East), and the other at Seattle in June just past. The winter meeting appointed for La Conner, was omitted by reason of the clergy being unable to leave their parishes at the designated time.
"The sessions at Whatcom were especially interesting, good congregations being in attendance; the pleasure of the affair being enhanced through the presence of a large Deanery party of ladies and gentlemen who had come by special boat to be present on this occasion.
"This summer trip of the Western Deanery has already become an 'institution in itself,' and it is proposed this year, if a proper craft can be secured, to extend the tour to a week in length, and to hold services at a number of points where the 'Voice of the Church' is seldom heard.
"It is hoped that a still larger number of the Clergy and laity may be included in the purser's list this year, for thus in a pleasant way may practical mission work be accomplished, and the need observed for a more systematic and energetic occupancy of the rapidly growing district of Puget Sound."

———

1888: July
Rev. R. D. Nevius, D.D.,:
"Bishop Paddock.
"Bishop Paddock has started on his journey to attend the Lambeth Council, stronger, and in better health than he had hoped.
"Previous to the annual Convocation, which required from him much labor and care, he made a visitation to the Eastern deanery, visiting all its parishes and missions and preaching once or more in each. Ellensburg, Yakima, Sprague, Spokane, Farmington, Colfax, Pomeroy, Dayton, Waitsburg, Walla Walla, were all visited, and in each place persons were confirmed. In each of these places the Bishop performed all the duties of an Episcopal visitation without omission, and returned home, much to our surprise rather the better for his journey.
"The last few days, before leaving home for England, tried him severely with the many cares incident to preparation for a long absence from home, but he got away on the day appointed stronger and better than any one thought possible. We wish him a safe voyage and increasing strength all his way, until his happy return.
"R.D.N."
Oregon and Washington Churchman, July 1988

———

1888: July
The Oregon and Washington Churchman:
"The Bishop of Oregon has gone to England to attend the Pan-Anglican Council. He will not return to his Jurisdiction probably until November, as he expects to remain in the Eastern States to attend the Missionary Council. Mrs. Morris and Miss Morris accompanied the Bishop, and his sons will join them either in New York or London. We wish them a delightful journey and a safe return in health and prosperity. The Bishop's address during his absence is care of Melville Evans & Co., 75 Lombard St., London, England.
"The Bishop of Washington Territory has also gone to England to attend the Pan Anglican Council. Bishop Paddock also expects to remain some months in the Eastern States to raise money for his work. Miss Paddock and the Bishop's son accompany him. We are glad to say the Bishop seemed in reasonably good health at the time of his departure, and he hopes and expects to return much strengthened both

in body and mind; which expectation we trust may be realized. The Bishop's address during his absence is care of J. S. Morgan & Co., Bankers, 22 Old Broad St., London, England."

———

1888: Late July
Rev. R. D. Nevius, D.D.
Journal, Jurisdiction of Washington, 1889:
"Remarks—St. Michael's Church, Yakima, was begun about July 20 [1888], and was completed for service on Christmas day."

———

1888:
Rev. R. D. Nevius (1904, see below):
"... In Eighteen hundred and eighty eight (1888) the plans for a stone church were approved and the nave was built. It was built of local stone rubble work unfinished work on both in- & exterior. A temporary chancel was built of wood until the original plan of transept should be built.

———

1888:
Yakima *Republic*, October 19, 1957:
"Services were held on the second [sic, first] floor of a building on North Front St. until the present structure was completed in 1888. Heading the drive for this stone church building was the H. B. Scudder family, then recently moved to Yakima from Boston.... The original church was 25 feet wide and 50 feet long.... The building is of native rock from Garretson Grade."

———

1888: November 6
Election day. Democrat Grover Cleveland re-elected.

———

1888: November 15
Relander (Yakima *Republic*) 1960:
"[Alice Scudder] baked her first pan of biscuits on Nov. 15 [1888?] and served them at dinner to Dr. Nevius, who usually brought mail and papers when he rode out on a black horse or came in a carriage with some of the Scudders.... Dr. Nevius was a botanist of ability and gave botany lessons to Alice.... In summer-time road dust was two inches deep.... [Alice Scudder] would pick gooseberries to serve when Dr. Nevius came to dinner. In the winter [the Scudder children] tobogganed on the slope from which sagebrush had just been grubbed.... The Scudder girls were active in the Guild which provided $450 toward the building fund by holding Eggletaires, in which food was prepared with eggs."

———

1888: December 23-28
Rev. E. W. Pigion (1928, see below at October 30, 1909):
"1888. Dr. Nevius came to stay [at Yakima] until Wednesday [December 28, 1888]. Service Sunday Dec. 23 & Christmas Day, Tuesday."

———

1888: December 25 (Christmas)
St. Michael's Church (1895):
"The first services in the new church were held on Christmas Day 1888 when Dr. Nevius used 'God With Us' as his text. The Yakima Herald observed that this joyful feeling of thanksgiving 'effervesced throughout the building. There was a good congregation though the number of persons connected with the mission is comparatively small. On this account, the singing [chanted responses?] which was very good seemed rather thin.' Dr. Nevius reported that the building had cost about $4,000 with $450 provided by the Women's Guild of the mission. About $600 was given by personal (non-resident) friends of the parishioners and of Dr. Nevius, including Rev. Philips Brooks, Rector of Trinity Church, Boston, later Bishop of Massachusetts and writer of the Christmas hymn 'O Little Town of Bethlehem.' $500 was carried as a long term loan from the church building fund, and they hoped to raise $750. The first Communion service, later sent to Bishop Rowe in Alaska, was given by the Rev. Leonard K. Storrs of St. Paul's, Brookline, whom Mr. Scudder had previously served as senior warden. In March 1889 the walls of the church were

planted by the Sunday school children with ivy started from a cutting from the Trinity Church of Boston, Massachusetts."

October, 1888-February, 1889:
Rev. Thomas Jessett (1949):
"The *Oregon and Washington Churchman* suspended publication after its October, 1888 issue. Lack of popular support caused the two bishops to withdraw their subsidies simultaneously and the paper folded. Two months later [December, 1888] the *Washington Churchman* was started by a group of clergy in the state, with the Rev. M. D. Wilson as editor. After one issue it was turned over to the Rev. George Herbert Watson, rector of Trinity Church, Seattle, and the February, 1889 issue was printed there.[fn54"
"[fn] 54 *Washington Churchman*, December, 1888."
Jessett (1949) p. 16

———

1888:
"The completion of the Northern Pacific Railroad across the Cascades made transcontinental travel direct to Puget Sound much easier, and clergy reinforcements arrived all through 1888."
Jessett (1949) p. 16

———

1888: December
The December 1888 issue of the *Washington Churchman* carried a letter from the Rev. Octavius Parker describing his arrival in Alaska and the establishment of his mission there.

[1889]

1888/1889:
Rt. Rev. John A. Paddock, D.D.:
"Permitted in the goodness of God, to return to the Territory with improved health, at the end of the last year, the Bishop, on the first Sunday after Christmas [December 30, 1888] preached morning and evening in All Saints' Church, Spokane Falls, and made an address to the Sunday School. He had the joy of seeing tokens of life and interest manifest on all sides; a new and commodious church building in process of erection, a flourishing boarding and day school in operation under the care of some church ladies, and their brothers, with the aid of the Rector of the Parish, and a valuable lot of land donated for the erection of a school building.

"Some little towns in the region round about Spokane offer fields for missionary labors....
[Monday, Dec. 31 spent at Sprague.]
"At North Yakima, a new stone church, erected under the supervision of the Rev. Dr. Nevius, greeted the Bishop; and, after service and a sermon, the Holy Communion was administered. The building is devoid of ornaments, but with its admirable proportions and neat appearance gives delight to the beholder. Part of a day was spent in visiting the neighboring settlements of Moxee, where it is hoped that a successful mission may be established, an Eastern gentleman offering liberal aid toward sustaining services.
"At Ellensburgh, placed under the care of Dr. Nevius, the way has not seemed to him open as yet for any forward movement."
[Epiphany, Sunday January 6, 1889 spent at Tacoma.]
Oregon Churchman, March, 1889

———

1889: Early January
Rt. Rev. John Adams Paddock
Journal, Jurisdiction of Washington, 1889:
"At North Yakima, it was a joy to officiate in the new church, (St. Michael's), erected during my absence. The building, of rough stone, is unique and quaint. Nothing has been expended for mere ornamentation; but so excellent are the proportions, so correct the lines, that all seeing it are favorably impressed, and feel that the words can here be properly spoken, 'Strength and beauty are His sanctuary.'

"The expenditure has been about $4,000, the two valuable lots, on which the building stands, having been given to the Bishop some years since, for a church building.

"There are now sittings for 125 persons, but that done is designed only to form a portion of the nave of the greater church, which, it is hoped, will eventually be built, and for which the plans are in hand. There is considerable indebtedness for that done, but the missionary and laymen co-operating mean that the debt shall be largely reduced, if not entirely removed, during the year.

"Thus far, I have found much to gladden; but going on at Moxee [Moxee City, near Yakima], nothing had been done, the way seeming to the missionary [Nevius] barred against what we had hoped for; and, in the growing city of Ellensburg, I was saddened by finding that but little church progress had been made. Accompanied by Dr. Nevius, an evening and morning Service were held in the Methodist meeting-house, and one person received the 'laying on of hands.'

"A committee was appointed to co-operate with the missionary, and we hope and expect that another year will tell of advance which will change our sorrow into gladness."

——

1889:
Rev. E. W. Pigion (1928, see below at 1904):
"1889. Bishop Paddock here [at Yakima] Jany 1st. In new Church Jany 6th Epiphany. Easter Day Apr 21. 80 at Church, May 12 Confirmation. Rev. [???] Cheal[?] had service on Sept 13.

——

1889: February
Washington Churchman, February 1889
(R. D. Nevius, D.D.):
"North Yakima – St. Michael's Church
"[The Rev. R. D. Nevius, D.D., Minister in Charge.]
"The editor of the Yakima *Herald* says:

"['] The church is surprisingly attractive considering its simple construction, without ornaments of any kind and the material of which it is built—common field stone[,] the break-down of the basaltic bluff. The stone is used as it came to hand and is uncut throughout, even to the arch stones, which are only chosen for three places and properly laid like all the rest, in mortar, and painted [sic, pointed] deep with dark cement. To our surprise we found the inner wall left as laid up, like the outer. The effect is wholly satisfactory, and all the prettier for its strangeness. The seats and chancel furniture so far as supplied are of choice cedar and oiled.

"['] St. Michael's church, of North Yakima, is Gothic in style, is built of rough stone and is a part of the nave of the greater church, for which we have the plans and which will be built in sections as needed in the future. For this reason the chancel end is built of wood and will be removed as the church is extended.

"[']The building is forty-eight by twenty-five feet, with twelve-foot walls and high-pitched roof. The chancel is eighteen feet wide by sixteen feet deep, including the sanctuary, and is apsidal with three windows, the center of which is a figure of the Crucifixion. The front gable of the front (west end) is carried up above the planes of the roof in three equal stages of six feet each, and is surmounted with a large stone cross, and has three long, narrow windows. The windows are all of cathedral glass, from Coulter & Sons, Cincinnati. The outer wall of the chancel is covered with shingles in chevron on tongue-and-grooved casing, and will wait for its inner wall until the church [congregation] is able to properly complete the same. The roof is supported on heavy trusses, and is open to the peak, and is ceiled under the pur-lines vertically, with narrow tongue-and-grooved fir. The walls are massive, and the church is unique and quaint. In fact, it already looks 100 years old, and when it is covered with ivy, as it is hoped it may soon be, it will stand well for the hoary antiquity of the church, and will present an anomalous appearance in a town not yet five years old, still glittering in fresh brick and new paint.

"[']The building has cost about $4,000, exclusive of its two valuable lots, which were given by the Northern Pacific Railroad Company. Of this amount about $450 was supplied by the Women's guild of the mission. About $600 has been given by the personal friends (non-resident) of the members of the mission and the minister

in charge. Four hundred dollars has been given by non-resident property owners. Five hundred dollars will be carried by the mission on a long loan from our church building fund, seven hundred and fifty dollars, yet due, we hope to raise without intermitting the efforts which have led to results reported above.

"['"] The minister in charge and the building committee (Col. Prosser, Mr. Scudder and Mr. Steinweg) take this opportunity of most heartily and sincerely thanking all friends at home and abroad for their generous assistance in our work. The subscription list and the roll of benefactors will be preserved in the records of the mission. The building committee also gratefully records the generous aid of dear friends in the East who have responded to our call for aid, and without whose co-operation we would have been able to build only a small temporary wooden chapel. The church will be, in our thoughts of it, largely a memorial to private friendships; the names of most of those who are most dear to us being built up enduringly in the church's walls, as also in our hearts.['"']"

——

1889: February
The February, 1889 issue of the *Oregon and Washington Churchman* carried a letter from the Rev. Octavious Parker describing his mission in Alaska.

——

1889: February 27-28
Washington Churchman (March 1889):
Nevius attended the spring meeting of the Western Deanery in Chehalis. The meeting opened at 10:30 Wednesday, February 27 with Morning Prayer, led by Nevius, and Holy Communion. The chair was taken by the Dean, the Rev. G. H. Watson, at the request of the Bishop.

"The Rev. Mr. Wilson gave in the report [sic] of the Committee on the church at Kalama. Dr. Nevius stated that by permission, he, on the completion of the Church at Chehalis, had gone to Kalama and brought the seats, organ, books, etc., to Chehalis.* The Bishop stated that on account of the death of Kalama he had given the Doctor permission to remove furnishings, and that after consulting informally some members of the Standing Committee he had sold the property, the bell being taken to Spokane Falls."*....

*The first service was held in the newly completed Church of the Epiphany, Chehalis, September 14, 1884. Bishop Paddock did not report abandonment of the Kalama church until June 1886. The property was reported sold in March 1889, at which time All Saints' Church, Spokane, was nearing completion. It is unclear exactly when the furniture and the bell were removed from Kalama.

——

1889: March
Washington Churchman
(Rev. R. D. Nevius, D.D.):
"Yakima – St. Michael's Church.
"In charge of the Rev. R. D. Nevius, General Missionary.
"Services morning and evening on Sunday and during Lent; Wednesday and Friday, at 4 p.m.; Good Friday at 11 a.m. and 4 p.m. Confirmation to be late in Lent.
"Services at Ellensburgh on Tuesday evening, at 7:30 o'clock.
"The Sunday school of St. Michael's Church had their pre-Lenten review of memory lessons since Advent, on Shrove Tuesday [March 4], with picture, song and story; Bible narrative, narrative hymns and transparencies of best pictures of the Bible, illustrating at the same time the life of Our Lord, the Creed, and the Christian year. It was very successful as an entertainment, but more to be approved because of the preparation therefor. The missionary has never found anything of the kind stand all tests of value so well as this. All the work comes easily into Sunday school work and abides in the memory, while, at the same time, it is a lesson in good taste. The children sang well and repeated the Bible stories in unison, and answered to the reading of the pictures and the catechisms beautifully.
"The review will be repeated Tuesday and Whit-Sunday, and the regular work of Lent and the Easter season will prepare for it.
"The children of the mission will meet on Thursday to plant the walls of the church with ivy. It may prove to be a day to be remembered. It is proposed to make it a reverent act, hoping to attach the children lovingly to the house of God."

1889: March

St. Michael's Church (Yakima, 1985):

"In March 1889 the walls of the church were planted by the Sunday school children with ivy started from a cutting from the Trinity Church of Boston, Massachusetts."

———

1889: Spring

Rev. Thomas Jessett (1949):

"Financial conditions around Puget Sound improved considerably in the spring of 1889, and the population increased rapidly due to the completion of the Northern Pacific Railroad. Seattle had a population of about 25,000...."

Jessett (1949) p. 17

———

1889[?]: March 14

Rev. R. D. Nevius, D.D.:

"North Yakima, W.T.

"March 14" 89[?]

Dear Mr. Watson:

"I am thankful that you keep me in mind as witness to see now and then your valued revisions of which I have a good many. I have found them so valuable that I find I must have the *Bot. of N. America,* and beg you to have it sent to me with the bill.

"I am residing here permanently, it is hoped, at the last church which I have built, though I am engaged in building another at Ellensburgh.

"I wish I had known of your passing in 1880, when I had such a run[?] to overtake you from Coem[?] or Allen to Colville.* I would have asked to be your companion. I cannot see why I did not think to go a days ride with you at least.

"Do you know of any one engaged in making a good School Botany of Or and Wash?

"My address will remain as above for some time, as I have made this my central station and have built me a small cottage here.

"I wish you and any of yours could drop in on me any day and claim hospitality and best service from.

                    "Very truly yours,
                        "R. D. Nevius"

*Nevius seems to have met Watson at this time. The text may read "from Orin or Arden," both of which are near Colville in Washington's northeast corner. Watson was in the Pacific Northwest in 1880 (see note May, 1876).

———

1889: April, October

Rev. Thomas Jessett (1940):

[p. 36] "At the annual meeting held in Tacoma Hall on April 22, 1889, the borrowing of fifteen hundred dollars [to build St. John's Church, Olympia] was approved and it was secured from the American Church Building Fund Commission. The basement of the Church was built and converted into a chapel and services were held there beginning October 20, 1889.... [p. 37] Work on the Church proper was delayed for about a year...."

———

1889: April 2

Rev. R. D. Nevius:

"North Yakima Wash.

"Apr 2d 89

"Mr. Sereno Watson

            "Dear Sir,

Pending the issue of <u>Synoptic Flora N. A.</u> Vol 1, part 1 (one) and Vol. 2 part 2 which all of us are eagerly expecting I would be very greatly obliged if you could send me any revisions of Genera which you can spare me other than those Dr. Gray and you have kindly sent me heretofore. Meantime please tell me the name of the enclosed. I take it to be Tacinium[?] spinescens, but I have not a description of it. Bot. Cal. and in Contributions etc March 1889[?] only refer to it. I give on another page the Revisions etc which I now have. I understand that Mr. Lewis Henderson*

formerly of Portland Or, now of Olympia Wash is preparing a School Botany of Oregon and Washington but the work goes slowly as he is now absorbed in real estate speculations—with his brother he is <u>booming</u> a town near Tacoma <u>called</u> Puget. There is such a tide of immigration that all towns in the State are booming and additions to <u>additions</u> are stimulating men women and children to speculations and all are "getting in on bed rock" i.e.. purchasing from original owners and doubling their money in a few months and sometimes in a few days or weeks.

            "Very truly yours
                "R. D. Nevius

[separate sheet]

[fragment of another letter?]

"I have Vol. 1st Flora N. Amer. 1838-40 given me by Dr. Gray, also part II which is now replaced by Synoptical Flora.

"What chance is there that Vol. 1st will be republished and revised?

"I shall write today thanking the Secretary of the Smithsonian and ask for _____[?] 1st part of Bibliographical Index which the preface to the Synoptical Flora informs me is issued.

"I have not yet been in the mountains. I propose to go this Summer to Lake Chelan[?] and may go towards the Penticton[?] mountains [i.e. east of Cascades and then north into Okenogan Range on the Washington-B.C. border?].

"Ellensburgh has had a <u>boom</u> and has grown out of all reason. There are many "gurrs"[?] & [?] "randy"[?] fellows there yet.

"I wish you could have remembered the name of the man, I should like to identify him.

"It is a good botanical field even if you take only plants found in the very streets of the town.

"Enclosed is one which I took last spring from the street and was unable to study it having no botany with me. Prof. Henderson had a look at it and found it a puzzle. I shall look for it now as it comes into season. Meanwhile I would like a report on it from you.

            "Very truly yours
                "R. D. Nevius

*"Louis F. Henderson (1854-1942)

"The last of the pioneer botanists to be considered here was Louis F. Henderson [fn: Louis F. Henderson, 'Early Experiences of a Botanist in the Northwest,' manuscript at the University of Oregon Library, Eugene; also Louis F. Henderson, 'Autobiographical Sketch,' *Oregon Journal* (Portland), October 22, 1926.).] a graduate of Cornell University in 1874. From 1877 to 1889 he was a faculty member of the Portland High School. Here he began his travels through the northwest on weekends and summers, and no botanical explorer covered the states of Oregon, Washington and Idaho more thoroughly than this kindly pioneer. For almost sixty years he explored the Northwest on foot, on horseback, by wagon, by boat, by auto, and by train. He corresponded with many botanists on both continents but he met few. Among the western botanists, he know intimately and collected with the Howells* [Thomas (1842-1912) and Joseph], Suksdorf [Wilhelm N. (1950-1932)],* Piper [Charles V. 1867-1926], Gorman [Martin W. (1852-1926), Bolander [?], and Nevius.* He never met Cusick* [see note at May, 1876 above].

"A siege of typhoid in 1889 caused Henderson to leave school work for several years, during which time he lived in Olympia and botanized in all of northwestern Washington. In 1892 he was hired by the State of Washington to prepare a display of flora and forest products of that state for the Chicago World Fair.... From 1893 to 1911 he was professor of botany at the new University of Idaho, and during this time built up a large herbarium and carried on an extensive botanical search of central Idaho for the U. S. Department of Agriculture.... In 1900 Henderson was granted a sabbatical leave and spent a pleasant year at Cornell and Harvard Universities.... He left the University of Idaho in 1911 and retired to the Hood River Valley. In 1924 Henderson accepted the position as curator of the herbarium, University of Oregon...."

Erwin F. Lange, "Pioneer Botanists of the   Pacific Northwest," *Oregon Historical Quarterly,* LVII, 2 (June, 1956), pp.   122-124.

*Corresponded with Asa Gray in the 1870s. Suksdorf, however, came to the

Bingen, Washington area from Iowa and California after 1876. Thomas Howell published the first catalogue of plants of Oregon, Washington and Idaho in 1881. This was a commercial venture, intended for selling collections of pressed specimens, but was the most comprehensive listing yet available [pp. 110-111]. Howell published the first *Flora* of the Northwest in seven parts from 1896 to 1903 (when it was published under one cover), setting the type himself [pp. 111-112].

———

1889: April 14-30
Rev. R. D. Nevius, D.D."
"Yakima – St. Michael's Church.
"The Rev. R. D. Nevius, D.D., Rector.
"The Lenten services, Wednesday and Friday and during Holy week [April 14-20, 1889], were well attended and Easter [April 21] was gladly celebrated in the churches in a memorable way. The congregation was largely made up of strangers, though all of our own people were present who could attend.
"The children's offerings for missions were $4.35.
"A service was held on [Tuesday] the 30th, Inauguration Day, in accordance with the Bishop's pastoral and the special service set forth by him.
"The work at Ellensburgh goes on slowly, but is indeed going on at last. The guild is large and very active. Plans are being considered for a chapel and we expect next month to report the building begun. By a consciously imperfect count the persons, adult, who are know to the missionary as connected with the church—nominal communicants—is 52. The largest number at service at any one time has been 15. Services are held on Wednesday nights in the Methodist church."
Washington Churchman, May 1889

———

1889: June 6
Great fire of Seattle.

———

1889: June 26-28
Journal, Jurisdiction of Washington, 1889
The Rev. R. D. Nevius, D.D. is listed as "Missionary at Yakima." He attended Convocation and was reappointed chair of the Committee on Christian Literature and Education.

———

1889: June 26 (Wednesday)
Bishop Paddock's Address:
Bishop Paddock reported that his trip to England left him with "health improved by rest and change." He reported that he sat on a committee on "The Lord's Day," and that among its findings was, "That the growing laxity in its observance tends to impair its sacred and beneficent character," and "That, especially, the increasing practice, on the part of some of the wealthy and leisurely classes, of making the day a day of secular amusements, is most strongly to be deprecated."
"I declined a number of invitations to preach in England and elsewhere, keeping in mind that I left home partially for that rest and change, which might strengthen me, if so God will, for longer and active work in my Western field. But I felt called to accept the invitation given to preach some sermons in behalf of the 'Venerable Society of the Propagation of the Gospel,' remembering that, as expressed in the preface of the Prayer Book, we, in the early settlement of our country, were indebted to the church of England, acting through her missionary societies, 'for a long continuance of nursing care and protection.'
"I make record also of one Service of special interest, the advancement by me to the priesthood, on July 8 [1888], of the Rev. J. H. Forrest Bell, whom I ordained deacon, some years since, in this Territory. In this Service, held, by invitation, in the Bishop's chapel at Salisbury, English clergymen took part. An address was made by the Lord Bishop, the Rt. Rev. Dr. Wordsworth, and the Rev. E. E. Wood, formerly a missionary among us, presented the candidate. So far as I can learn, this is the first ordination held in England by an American Bishop. Mr. Bell remained abroad for a time, to attend upon an aged and inform mother, but hopes eventually to be again ministering the Gospel on this Western coast."
"When in our Territory, the not uncommon alteration of encouragement and disappointment, of joy and sorrow, awaited me before reaching my home. At Spokane Falls, the new church, commodious and tasteful, was beheld then approaching completion. The cost of it, finished, is from $7,000 to $8,000, and it contains some beautiful gifts 'in memorium' of those 'gone before.'... My heart was gladdened by these and other tokens of church life and growth in this beautiful and prosperous city, where, I trust, there will, ere long, be a call for another parish and church.
"At North Yakima, it was a joy to officiate in the new church {St. Michael's}, erected during my absence. The building, of rough stone, is unique and quaint. Nothing has been expended for mere ornamentation; but so excellent are the proportions , so correct the lines, that all seeing are favorably impressed, and feel that the words can here be properly spoken, 'Strength and beauty are His sanctuary.'
"The expenditure has been about $4,000, the two valuable lots, on which the building stands, having been given to the Bishop some years since, for a church building.
"There are now sittings for 125 persons, but that done is designed only to form a portion of the nave of the greater church, which, it is hoped, will eventually be built, and for which the plans are in hand. There is considerable indebtedness for that done, but the missionary and laymen co-operating mean that the debt shall be largely reduced, if not entirely removed, during the year.
"Thus far, I had found much to gladden; but going on at Moxee [Moxee City, near Yakima], nothing had been done, the way seeming to the missionary [Nevius] barred against what we had hoped for; and, in the growing city of Ellensburg, I was saddened by finding that but little church progress had been made. Accompanied by Dr. Nevius, an evening and morning Service were held in the Methodist meetinghouse, and one person received the 'laying on of hands.'
"A committee was appointed to co-operate with the missionary, and we hope and expect that another year will tell of advance which will change our sorrow into gladness."
"St. John's, Olympia, has now for its rector the Rev. H. H. Buck, formerly of Nevada, where he left a good record. The old church building and site have been sold, and a new edifice has been begun on the lot adjoining the rectory. It having been found that the completion of the building would involve the Parish heavily in debt, the Rector and Vestry have, wisely, as I think, concluded simply to enclose the structure and finish the basement for use, until increased means can be obtained. A small debt, the reduction of which is steadily aimed at, may not be an injury to a parish, but a large debt is likely to have a depressing influence, and to deter strangers from connecting themselves with the church."
"The hearts of all of us were made sad not long since by hearing of the terrible destruction wrought by the flames in Seattle [on June 6, 1889]. And we felt the tenderest sympathy with the rector and members of Trinity church, when we heard that they were obliged to take up the lament of God's people of old, 'Our holy and our beautiful house, where our fathers praised Thee, is burned up with fire.' ...A new and larger edifice should be built. An insurance of $3,500 makes a beginning for a building fund; and the old lots, if sold to be used for business purposes, will bring enough, it is thought, to purchase another site in a more desirable location and to add a considerable amount to the building fund."
"Recently, accompanied by the Rev. Dr. Nevius, I made a visitation through the Gray's Harbor region. Services were held, and visits made from house to house, in Elma, Montesano, Aberdeen and Hoquiam.
"We are encouraged by the outlook in all these places. Land was offered and something pledged for the erection of a church in each little town.
"At one of the stations, a lady generously offered $500 and I believe that if a man, faithful and wise, can be found to act as the missionary in this region, two or three little churches may be erected within the next year or two.
"I have recently had more letters than ever before, from clergymen wishing to come among us. But, our missionary allowance is not increased, and, if we are to go forward and take up new stations, the missionary committee must receive more aid from established parishes, and the stations, which have been aided for some years, must be content with a smaller allowance from the missionary committee."

———

"The Secretary read the Report of the Registrar [The Rev. Mardon D. Wilson]....:

The Registrar desires to report that the money so generously provided for his use by Gov. E. P. Ferry, at the last Convocation, has been entirely used in payment of charges on packages of papers and books from Olympia through The Rev. Nevius, and from New Haven, Conn., and in sending out copies of Journal [of Convocation] of 1888....

Mardon D. Wilson, Registrar.

[As a P.S.] The Registrar would also say to Convocation that a tradition has reached his ears that there is a box of papers, etc., belonging to the Registrar lying somewhere at Spokane Falls; as yet however this is but a tradition.

"The Rev. Dr. Nevius offered the following resolution which on motion was adopted:

Resolved, That a Committee of one be appointed to secure the sending of monies collected for what is known as the Centennial Fund,* to the Treasurer of the Centennial Fund.

"The Rev. Dr. Nevius was appointed as such Committee."

*In his Annual Convocation Address of 1884, Bishop Paddock mentioned a "hundredth anniversary fund" (see above) and that the Rev. H. D. Lathrop, D. D. of Walla Walla had "kindly offered to act as Treasurer of any offerings made in [Washington] Territory." In his Address of 1887 he noted Lathrop had "removed" from the Jurisdiction.

———

1889: June 27 (Thursday)

As Chair of the Committee on Christian Education and Literature, Nevius gave a lengthy report on the development and conditions of the various parochial schools in the Jurisdiction.

"The Rev. J. C. Taylor [of Port Townsend] offered the following, which was unanimously adopted:

Resolved, that the Convocation hears with regret of the retirement of Mrs. Wells from the principalship of the Annie Wright Seminary, and in view of her long and effectual connexion with that institution, that a committee be appointed to draft suitable resolutions and present them.

"The Rev. J. D. Taylor and Dr. Nevius were appointed such committee."

"The committee appointed to report on the retirement of Mrs. Wells from the Annie Wright Seminary, offered the following which was adopted by a rising vote:

WHEREAS, This Convocation has heard through the Committee on Church Education that Mrs. Wells has resigned the principalship of the Annie Wright Seminary, therefore be it

Resolved, in view of her long and effective service for the Church in this jurisdiction through the educative channel, that we hereby express our appreciation of the same, and warmly commend her to the wise and loving care of the Master in the enjoyment of her well earned rest.

"The Rev. Dr. Nevius moved to reconsider the vote by which we elected a Treasurer yesterday [no mention in *Journal;* N. B. Coffman submitted the Treasurer's report which was read by the Secretary of Convocation], and offered the following resolution which was adopted:

Resolved, That this Convocation do now proceed to election of a Treasurer of this Jurisdiction who shall be under bonds, and to whom all the moneys collected for any purpose, or any fund, shall be sent, to be by him transmitted to treasurers of vested funds, or investment or disbursement as directed by this Convocation, and that such Treasurer be required to give bonds to the Bishop of this Jurisdiction in the sum of $5000, and that such Treasurer be required to make a report of all funds received, disbursed and held by him, to each Annual Convocation.

"On motion the Convocation proceeded to election of [a] Treasurer in accordance with [the] foregoing resolution. L. E. Post and Geo. E. Atkinson were placed in nomination. Upon a count of the ballots it was found that L. E. Post had received 12 votes and Geo. E. Atkinson 8 votes, upon which L. E. Post was declared elected Treasurer for the ensuing year."

———

1889: June 28 (Friday)

"The Rev. Dr. Nevius presented the following resolution, which was on motion adopted:

WHEREAS, The indiscriminate taxation of Church property is, in the sense of this Convocation, neither in accordance with justice, nor the dignity and honor of the State, therefore be it

Resolved, That a committee be appointed by the Bishop to act with him in all matters affecting taxation of Church, Schools and Hospital property, whenever necessary. [No report of disposition of the motion.]

———

"Parochial Reports....

"*Report of St. Michael's Church, North Yakima, for the year ending June 26th, 1889.*

"The Rev. R. D. Nevius, D.D., Rector.

"Wardens—Col. Wm F. Prosser

"Congregation—Families, 14. Adults 31;   Children 17, Total, 48.

"Baptisms—Adults 1, Infant 3, Total 4.

"Confirmed, 3.

Communicants—No. last reported 15. Added 3, Present number 19.

"Baptized members 49.

"Marriages, 2.

"Public Services—Sundays 73, Other days 7, Total 80.

"Holy Communion—In Church 10.

"Sunday School—Teachers

"Offerings—Salaries $163.25; Current Expenses $76.25; Improvements $848; From Womens Guild for building and furnishing $350; Disabled Clergy $10.30; Hospital work $3.15; Convocation Fund $3.85; Domestic Missions $3.80; Foreign Missions, $2; Total $1460.50.

"Remarks—St. Michael's Church, Yakima, was begun about July 20, and was completed for service on Christmas day. It has cost $3484.17. Of this about $1200 was raised in Yakima, nearly the same amount was given by personal friends of the Missionary and other members of the Mission. That part of the indebtedness remaining, which is not covered by a loan of $500 from the Church building fund, will, we believe, be paid within the year. The Women's Guild of this Mission contributed nearly $400 to the building and furnishing [of] the Church.

———

"*Report of Grace Church, Ellensburgh, for the year ending June 26, 1889.*

"The Rev. R. D. Nevius, D. D., Rector

"Wardens—Dr. James Smith.

"Congregation—Families 17. Adults 40, Children 33, Total 73.

"Baptisms—Adult 1, Infants 3, Total 4.

"Confirmed, 3.

"Communicants--No. last reported 14, Added 3, Present No. 17.

"Baptized Members, 55.

"Marriages, 1.

"Public Services—Sundays, 14; Other Days, 17; Total 31.

"Holy Communion—in Church, 2.

"Offerings—Current Expenses $63; Total $63.

"Remarks—This mission has, only recently, secured a lot for the Church, by purchase, the first steps necessary for building a Church have been taken. It is confidently hoped that it is entering a new Convocation year with newly awakened zeal and increased ability. Roslyn has been visited and services held twice during the year, and two towns on Gray's Harbor, twice. Communicants—Roslyn 8, Montesano 7, Aberdeen 5, Hoquiam 2, Elma 6, Total 28. Offerings for Diocesan Missions $29.50.

———

1889: September

Rev. R. D. Nevius, D.D.

(*Washington Churchman,* October 1889):

"Gray's Harbor Mission.

"This important and interesting mission was visited last month [September] by me, and in August by Rev. Mr. Buck of Olympia. Everywhere I heard the most flattering reports of Mr. Buck's services, and a desire to have more visits from him.

"The railroad had reached Elma, and that town was feeling the first breath of its boom. There is no fear that the church will lag in its work here for lack of interest or enthusiastic labor. A Guild was informally organized in this place; Mrs. William Haliday, president, Mrs. Carney, secretary, and Mrs. Oscar Wood, treasurer.

"At Montesano lots were chosen and will be purchased, no suitable lots being held by persons able and willing to give them.

"Some new members have come to increase our force here, and more are expected from the immigration which will follow the completion of the line of railroad, which is now a matter of a few weeks at most. A Woman's Guild was formed at this place; Mrs. F. C. Story, president, Mrs. Dr. Molineux, secretary, Mrs. Bignold, treasurer.

"At Aberdeen our working force has been increased by the coming [of] a family, all of whom are skilled in church music. Under the training and lead of one of these the chants and hymns were sung better than I have ever known them to be in any mission before visited. Could such a leader be employed to go around with the missionary the planting and growth of our churches would be much facilitated. The clergyman to whom this mission will be entrusted will be much encouraged at this place by hearty co-operation.

"Hoquiam is growing very rapidly and will be a beautiful and important town, and very soon will be equaled in importance by Gray's Harbor, the new town three miles below. These two towns will be united in one interest by a railroad now almost entirely graded, and by a very lovely drive.

"I was able on this visit to make such subscriptions for the support of the clergyman who shall be sent to this mission as will secure to him from the whole field $1,200 for the first year, without a stipend from the Board. A letter from the Bishop while I was there informed me that he had a letter from a clergyman known to him and the clergy of the Sound, who would take the mission and 'come at once.' On the strength of this I promised the people a missionary almost immediately. On arriving at Tacoma I learned that in another letter just received he had declined to come. It can be imagined with what regret and chagrin I was compelled to write to the expectant people of this important and interesting mission—four churches to be built at once, a fair support independent of the Missionary Board, and a life stimulated to activity by association with active men in stirring time of the sudden opening of a new country to immigration and trade."

———

1889: November 2
North Dakota became the 29th state.
South Dakota became the 40th state.

———

1889: November 8
Montana became the 41st state.

———

1889: November 11
Washington became the 42nd state.

[1890]

1890: March
Rev. R. D. Nevius
(Washington Churchman):
"Letter from The Rev. R. D. Nevius, D.D.
"St. Michael's, Yakima
Rejoices in continued gifts from eastern friends. A contribution from the Sunday school at Longwood, Mass., through the rector, Rev. Mr. Howe, and Miss Scudder, a former teacher in that school, and amounting to $93, will be applied to furnishing clergy stalls, chancel rail, etc. A handsome service of vessels for the altar, five pieces, has been received from Mrs. Amos Laurence, Boston. We hope with the first sign of recurring prosperity, now surely expected, to get at work at our floating debt of $1000 and to lift it."

———

1890: May 15
Rev. R. D. Nevius, D.D.
Journal, Jurisdiction of Washington, 1890:

"Parochial Reports....
"My pastoral relation with this Mission [in Yakima Valley] ceased on the 15th of May."

———

1890: May
Relander (Yakima *Republic*) 1960:
"Dr. Nevius completed his mission work preached a farewell sermon in May, 1890 and moved to Gray's Harbor."

- Gray's Harbor vicinity, Washington -

(Elma)
(St. Andrew's Church, Aberdeen)
(St. David's Church, Hoquiam)
(South Bend)

———

1890: May/June
[Rev. Thomas E. Jessett:]
"Just before the convocation [of June 25-26, 1890] opened Dr. Nevius moved to the Gray's Harbor area, living at Montesano. He reported a small congregation at Elma, with a site for a church; a woman's guild at Montesano, with $500.00 just raised to purchase two lots, but services held in the old Methodist Church 'poorly attended;' at Aberdeen, a woman's guild, two lots, and services in the Presbyterian Church or the opera house; at Hoquiam, a woman's guild, a site and an organ; at South Bend an organized mission.[fn]70"
"[fn]70 *Washington Churchman*, November, 1890."
Jessett (1949) p. 20

———

1890: June 8
Deed recorded by R. D. Nevius, dated April 5th, 1890, from D. W. Fleet and Lillian Fleet to R. D. Nevius for consideration of one dollar, Lot 1, Block 9, Fleet's Addition to the City of Montesano, Chehalis County, Washington.

———

1890:
Rev. Thomas Jessett (1940):
[p. 37] "Work on the Church proper [at Olympia] was delayed for about a year and then, stimulated by a gift of $500.00 from Governor Ferry, work was resumed under the direction of Mr. Henry Lame, and was pushed as rapidly as that excellent craftsman would permit. Only the best lumber was used and workmanship was of the highest order. The cost of the building was $10,361.75. From the old church, the bell, the stained glass window of St. John and St. Mary, and the Bishop's and Rector's chairs (which had come around the Horn in early days) were saved and incorporated into this building. The window had to be sent back to the Lamb's Studio in New York to have additions to the top and side to make it suitable. The women paid for this...."

———

1890: June 25-26
Journal, Jurisdiction of Washington, 1890:
Convocation met at St. John's Church, Olympia (in the basement of the uncompleted church; see Bishop Paddock's address for 1891). The Rev. R. D. Nevius, D.D. is listed as "General Missionary, Montesano." He was not present on the first day but answered to his name at roll call on the second day of Convocation. The Rev. John Dows Hills, St. Luke's Church, Tacoma, was appointed chair of the Committee on Christian Education and Literature. Nevius was not appointed to the committee.

———

1890: June 25 (Wednesday):
Bishop Paddock's Address:
Bishop Paddock noted that he had attended the General Convention of 1889 in New York. "That general council was correctly designated 'The Centennial Convention,' for we went into our House of Bishops, after the opening service in St. George's church, on the actual anniversary of the day (Oct. 2, 1789) when three

bishops first met and organized the upper house of the General Convention; the three, in God's mercy and by His blessing, now increased to more than three score, the clergy in the land, then numbering 190, now exceeding 4000. As you are aware, the chief matter calling attention was action in reference to the 'Book of Common Prayer.' Nine years had elapsed since the movement for revision began, with the avowed purpose of enriching and making more flexible the Prayer Book."

"As usual, when at the East, I devoted the Sundays, during the General Convention, and my time for some weeks after, to presenting the needs and claims of this portion of the missionary field. We have cause to be very grateful for aid extended to us thus far in our history. But I discovered, on the part of some, a feeling that we were becoming sufficiently rich and strong to do more for ourselves, and not continue to be as largely dependent on the East."

"Permitted to return, in the Advent season [Advent Sunday—December 1, 1889], to my special field of labor, I passed my first Sunday with 'All Saints' Church,' Spokane Falls, where I found a good congregation assembled in their new church, and a goodly number of the young gathered in the Sunday School. ... Returning to Spokane Falls, I was present on two or three occasions at the opening services of All Saints' School, where, in a commodious and pleasant building, now completed, a good work is being done."

"A well located lot has been purchased in Colfax, and I trust the next missionary will be permitted to see a church building erected. While there, I had the joy of securing a lot for a church in the neighboring town of Palouse, in which place, it is hoped, we may occasionally hold services, although a church building cannot at present be erected."

"For some time the church at Sprague was closed, but services have, since February last [1890], been regularly maintained by Mr. Watson Somerville, a candidate for Holy Orders.... On my visit, I was pleased to find a neat and comfortable vestry room erected and the exterior and interior of the church improved, chiefly through the zeal and energy of the ladies of the parish...."

"I went to the eastern part of the state this season feeling rather depressed, but I left cheered, and encouraged to believe that a faithful and wise itinerant missionary may there accomplish much during the next year or two. Such a clergyman, as, I trust, is engaged to begin work early in the autumn. At North Yakima I found, on my return from the East, an increased attendance in the neat stone church. At a second visit, six were confirmed.

"At Ellensburgh, the lot offered was not deemed by the missionary suitable, and another was purchased by him. A 'Parish House' has been begun, which is to have the lower floor set apart for services, and the upper part designed for rooms for the clergyman and his family.

"The Rev. Dr. Nevius has recently given up the charge of Yakima and Ellensburgh, and taken up work in the Gray's Harbor district, where already some lots have been offered us, and there is good promise to two or three churches being built within the next year."

"St. Paul's, Whatcom, under Rev. Mr. Hyland, has added to its church property a little parsonage, the cost of which, I am thankful to add, has been entirely met by the parishioners."

"A vigorous and most encouraging beginning has been made in Blaine. Services have been held for some time, with more or less frequency, by Rev. Mr. Bell, of the Diocese of New Westminster."

"Emmanuel Church, East Sound, has added a chancel to the building and suitably enclosed the church grounds."

"The progress made in Tacoma during the past year has been very cheering to me. The congregation and Sunday school at St. Peter's, Old Tacoma, has been increasing under the Rev. T. N. Wilson.... A small but neat rectory has been built under his supervision and entirely paid for. A considerable sum is in hand toward the erection of a new church.

"Trinity Chapel, built under the direction of Rev. Mr. Wells, has been opened for about half a year, with large congregations."

"The Church of the Holy Communion has been without a pastor.... Recently seven thousand dollars have been subscribed toward the erection of a larger edifice."

"On the retirement of Rev. Mr. Wells, St. Luke's called the Rev. John D. Hills,

from Mt. Holly, New Jersey.... The church is full. The fund for a Parish House, begun by Mr. Wells, has increased under his successor until it amounts to $6,000.... Valuable lots have been offered to the Parish for a new church, and a subscription of $10,000 toward the building having been made by two gentlemen from the East, the parishioners have already added to this sum $12,000, and it is expected that a new stone church, to cost $40,000 or more, will be erected the next year, the present church building being allowed to stand on the site where it now stands."

"At our last General Convention Oregon passed from a missionary jurisdiction to that of an independent diocese. This was made possible by having secured a residence for the Bishop and $25,000 for the Episcopal fund, $20,000 having been added to this by our General Missionary Board.

"I have this year been privileged to make the last payment requisite for securing the house and grounds now occupied by me, as the residence for all time of the Bishop of Washington, and a sum equal to that donated to Oregon awaits us from the Missionary Board; whenever we ourselves have raised the sum of $10,000.

"Our Episcopal fund amounts to only about $500, and the annual collection asked of each Parish by Convocation is barely made. I should rejoice if we could obtain gifts, the matter being brought before our people year by year, that would permit us to come before the next General Convention and become an independent diocese.

"Beloved, new towns are springing up over our State, calling for the utmost diligence, zeal and self-denying efforts on the part of Bishop, clergy and laity, to meet the spiritual wants of our increasing population."

———

1890: June 29 (Thursday)

"On the Call of the roll the Rev. R. D. Nevius, D.D., and Mr. Geo. M. Moore, of Seattle, answered to their names."

A resolution was passed calling for the raising of $10,000 within the Jurisdiction for the endowment of the Episcopate, in order that Washington might apply for diocesan status at the General Convention of 1892.

A resolution was passed calling upon the Treasurer of Convocation to be "the legal recipient of all funds within the control of said Convocation, and that the Treasurer of the various funds be requested to hand to the Convocation Treasurer such moneys as shall be in their hands."

A committee was appointed to organize in December 1890 a commemoration of the tenth anniversary of the organization of the Jurisdiction of Washington.

"On motion of the Rev. R. D. Nevius, D.D., seconded by the Rev. A. S. Nicholson, the following resolution was adopted....:

Resolved, That the thanks of the Convocation be expressed to the Rector and Parish of St. John's Church, Olympia, for the courteous and hospitable entertainment and at the same time to congratulate this Parish, one that may be called the mother of Parishes on the Sound, that after many years of depression, on account of giving of her strength to the growth of other Parishes, prosperity has come to her, and especially that she has been able to build to the honor of God a beautiful house of worship in which, as well as in her hospitable homes, she may illustrate the generous hospitality for which she has always been noted.

"After Prayers by the Rev. R. D. Nevius, D.D., and the Benediction by the Bishop, the Convocation adjourned *Sine Die*.

———

"Deanery Reports.

The Western Deanery of Washington....

"I have to report progress this year all along the line. This is owing especially to the immense immigration of churchman to the Puget Sound basin as well as to faithful work among your little band of clergy and the lay helpers, who are not few.

"While we have been able to hold but two meetings of the Deanery—one at Seattle in February last, and the other at Olympia just preceding the Convocation—the application[s] from Blaine, Snohomish, and Centralia to be allowed to organize as Parishes, (not to speak of the new Parish of Trinity, Tacoma), the expressed intention of St. Paul's, Port Townsend, to be henceforth independent of missionary aid, the strong nucleus for a self-supporting Church which exists at Fairhaven, the excellent condition of the Mission Parishes at Whatcom, Old Tacoma and Olympia, and of the unique Island Mission at East Sound, Orcas, the beginning of work in the Gray's Harbor region, the call for aid from South Bend on the Willapa, and the commencement of services at Ballard—all these facts are evidences of that strong current of Apostolic Faith and Fellowship which ... will enable us soon to reap somewhat of the fruit of our labors....

Geo. Herbert Watson,

Dean of Western Washington."

"Parochial Reports....

Report of St. Michael's Church, Yakima, for the year ending June 25th, 1890.

"The Rev. R. D. Nevius, D.D., Rector.

"Baptisms—Infants 6, Total 6.

"Communicants—No. last reported, 19, Added 3, Present Number 23.

"Sunday School—Teachers 4, Pupils 30.

"Marriages—1.

"Burials—1.

"No. of Families connected with the Congregation—13.

"Whole No. of Individuals connected with congregation—53.

"Offerings and Contributions—Salary of Clergyman, $333; General Missions, $13.88; Parochial Purposes, estimate, $300; Total $646.88. Value of Church Property, $5,000; Seating Capacity 150.

"Remarks—St. Michael's rejoices in two valuable gifts during the year. First, a sufficient sum to supply chancel furniture, and second, a large complete communion service for the altar. My pastoral relation with this Mission ceased on the 15th of May. The mission is still without clerical services but is seeking such, and believes itself able, as it is desirous to maintain the same without the aid of Ellensburgh."

———

Report of Grace Church, Ellensburgh, for the year ending June 25th, 1890.

"The Rev. R.D. Nevius, D.D., Rector.

"Baptisms—Infants, 4, Total 4.

"Communicants—No. last reported 17, Added 4, Present Number 21.

"Marriages—1.

"Burials—1.

"No. of Families connected with the Congregation, 16.

"Whole No. of Individuals connected with Congregation, 61.

"Offerings and Contributions—Salary of Clergyman, $193; General Missions, $3.98; Parochial Purposes, $75.90; Church Building fund, $576; Total, $848.88. Value of Church Property, $600.

"Remarks—Services have been held since July 1st [1889] on Sunday morning continuously in connection with afternoon services at Yakima, a rented hall being used for the same. I have felt constrained to change my field of work to Gray's Harbor before the completion of a house of worship for this interesting and important mission. I am glad to report a plan secured and a sufficient subscription to insure the beginning of the work.

———

"*Report of Gray's Harbor Mission, for the year ending June 25th, 1890.*

"The Rev. R.D. Nevius, D.D.

"This Mission has been visited by me two to three times a year for five years, and having promised for so long a time that clerical services would be secured for it, I felt constrained, in the failure to secure a Missionary for it, to take it myself, though my action would leave Yakima and Ellensburgh without a clergyman.

"I had secured sites for churches at Aberdeen and Elma on time conditions, and a site at Hoquiam had been lost by failure to occupy it, but might be recovered by immediate action, and it was necessary that the field should be occupied at once.

"I have now had charge for one month, but am unable to report with precision the strength of the Church in either of the four places now occupied.

"Elma has 3 Communicants.

"Montesano has 4 "

"Aberdeen has 6 "

"Hoquiam has 4 "

"In each place are many friends of the Church from whom it is hoped classes for confirmation may at once be found.

"Women's Guilds have been organized in each place and sites for churches secured. The Woman's Guild at Montesano have purchased two lots for a church of $600 and have raised more than $300 of the purchase price.

"It is greatly hoped that Churches may be built this summer. At present Hoquiam and Aberdeen give largest promise for growth.

"Three other towns in the neighborhood, which are growing at terminal points of railroads now building will claim such attention as may be given. Gray's Harbor City, and Ocosta, on Gray's Harbor, and South Bend on Shoalwater Bay, are claiming attention now. In each of these sites for churches have been promised and will be secured.

"R. D. Nevius, Missionary."

———

1890: July 3

Idaho became the 43rd state.

———

1890: July 10

Wyoming became the 44th state.

———

1890: August/September

Helen S. Coan Nevius:

"At the end of our voyage [from China aboard the steamer <u>Abyssinia</u>] we went down Puget Sound, which surprised us by its beauty, equaling, we thought, the inland sea of Japan. After a week or two in the State of Washington we crossed the continent to Minneapolis. We spent a few weeks with the family of my brother, William V. Coan, in Clinton, Iowa, and in the dear home in Marshall, Mich. , and then returned to Seneca County, New York, where again Mrs. Eastman had the happiness of welcoming back her boy [John Livingston Nevius], whose head was now grayer than her own.... [453]: No mention of R. D. Nevius is made. They remained in the United States until September 18, 1892 [457]. J. L. Nevius worked on his book *Demon Possession* during this visit [454]." His "love of music" is mentioned [455].

Nevius (1895) pp. as cited.

———

1890: September

Washington Churchman:

"South Bend, Pacific county, Washington, has quite a number of church people and persons well affected toward the Church; but up to the present time no service has been held there. A loud call comes from a faithful Churchman of South Bend for a missionary visit from a live clergyman, authorized to set things in order and begin work. Who will go for us?"

———

1890: November

Rev. R. D. Nevius

(Washington Churchman):

"The Rev. R.D. Nevius, D.D.

"Diocesan Missionary for Washington.

"The Gray's Harbor Mission has been remiss (mea culpa), in sending reports. My excuse is that each month I have hoped to send an encouraging report for your next issue. I am able now for the first time to report definitely of all stations in my Mission, that sites for churches have been secured in each, and that building on them cannot be thought of until Spring.

"At Elma,

The first station approached from Olympia, the missionary has from the first had all the encouragement possible. Our force is small but the church folk are loyal, demonstrative of interest and generous of offerings. Communicants, five, services held in Methodist church. Congregation good. Confirmations none. Church site well and centrally located.

"At Montesano,

The Women's Guild has raised $500 for purchase of two lots well and centrally placed. The Bishop has given $100 for the same purpose. Twenty-five dollars is yet due on the lots and [a] $70 assessment for street improvement. Communicants, four.

Services held heretofore in the Rink are now held in the old Methodist church and are poorly attended. Confirmations at late visitation, two. It has been impossible to build a church on account of clearing and grading a road to the grounds which are not yet ready for occupancy, and for want of means.

"At Aberdeen,

For want of [a] suitable place, only week night services have been held., with two Sunday services, and only one celebration. Church lots admirably placed, are being graded (a work not possible until now) at an expense of $300 which has been provided for by the Women's Guild which has been vigorously and harmoniously at work from the beginning of the Mission. The Church has been named St. Andrew's. The coming within the last week of a large family from Kentucky adds six communicants to our number. We have lost three good helpers by removal. Our present number is 14. Services are held on week day nights in the Presbyterian church; on Sundays, in the Opera house.

"At Hoquiam,

It has been impracticable to occupy the generous site secured to us by the Land Company. For the present, services are held in the lower rooms of the house occupied as a parsonage. The Women's Guild have generously helped to fix up the room and have purchased a fine organ. Services are held frequently on Sunday and on Tuesday evenings. Confirmation, one. In all of the places above mentioned it is proposed to begin building in the Spring.

"Southbend,

Has now for the first time been visited. It is from this place that I am writing. I have been delighted and surprised at the manner in which my efforts to open this place as a Mission have been met. I found several men ready to give time, thought, labor and money to the work. Twelve men answered an informal call to meet for conference. A Mission was organized under the name, St. John's, South Bend. Provision was made for its maintenance. A fine site was generously and promptly offered for a Church, and another was secured and another promised for future chapels on the two outer margins of the present town. Services were held on Sunday, with celebration in the morning, at which seven persons received. Registered number of communicants, ten. Twenty-six men signed their names as members of the Church and subscribed to its support. Arrangements were made for services once a month and more frequent services asked for, with a promise to double the subscriptions for two services and to quadruple them for four in each month.

"A committee was formed to solicit subscriptions for a church, and it went immediately to work with good promise.

"Missionary Committee: Mr. L. W. Bristol, Warden; Mr. C. James, Treasurer; Mr. Herbert K. Relf, Secretary.

"A Woman's Guild was organized on Wednesday at the request of the ladies of the Mission: Mrs. L. W. Bristol, President; Mrs. W. H. Bartell, Treasurer; Mrs. J. A. Logan, Secretary.

"The Mission at South Bend is one of exceptional promise from the first. May its future fulfill the presage of its first days.

"South Bend is beautifully situated with picturesque surroundings. It is on deep water and a fine harbor. The Northern Pacific is expending large sums in substantial terminal works in the upper end of the town, and a second road is projected to what is called Sea Haven. Both these roads are to reach us from Chehalis, at which place we have friends interested in the lower town of Sea Haven who will care for our work there in the future with the same prompt and generous common interest shown us by the General Managers of the South Bend Land Company and the Northern Land and Development Company, to both of whom my thanks are due and generously rendered."

———

1890: December

The December 1890 issue of the *Washington Churchman* gave Nevius's address as Montesano.

[1891]

1891: Spring

Rt. Rev. John Adams Paddock

Journal, Jurisdiction of Washington, 1891:

"[In the spring of 1891] I went on to South Bend, one of Dr. Nevius' stations. I spent a Sunday with him there, where the promise seems good. The Missionary accompanied me to his other stations, viz., Hoquiam, Aberdeen, Montesano and Elma, in which places seven were confirmed. The pecuniary support which the missionary hoped to receive at these places has not been realized and no churches have as yet been erected; but the lots have been secured in most of the towns and arrangements made for erecting buildings on two of them [at Aberdeen and South Bend]...."

———

1891: May 12

Rev. R. D. Nevius:

"Olympia [Tacoma], Washington.* May 12" 1891

My Dear Mr. Watson:

"Will you be so kind as to give the enclosed proper direction?

"My present address is Hoquiam Wash, the new center of my work as General Missionary. My work is in towns along the Coast including South Bend, the Pacific Coast terminus of the N.P. Rail Road.

"I have five stations [Aberdeen, Elma, Hoquiam, Montesano and South Bend] and two church buildings [Aberdeen and South Bend] in hand and find no time for botany.

"In Nat. Hist. study diatoms absorb me for now I have large opportunity for collection.

"Very truly yours,
"R. D. Nevius"

*The two letters of May 12, 1891 are written on letterhead which reads:
"General Headquarters
"National Guard of Washington
*
"Adjutant General's Office
"R. G. O'Brien
Brigadier General and Adjutant General"
"Olympia" is crossed out in the letter to "The Curator" and "Tacoma" is written in above.

———

1891: May 12

Rev. R. D. Nevius:

"Tacoma Washington. May 12" 1891

"To the Curator of

"Botanical Gardens

"Cambridge Mass

"Dear Sir

"Though it is late for packages of such by mail I will be greatly obliged if you will send a labeled package of <u>Neviusia Alabamensis</u> to

Mrs. S. K. White*

Annie Wright Seminary

Tacoma, Wash

and will favor me with notice of its dispatching at <u>Hoquiam, Wash.</u> I send stamps for postage. Should be glad to know it blooms well for you,—in loose rich soil it should give you long plumes of bloom on its virgin shoots.

"Very truly yours

"R. D. Nevius"

*Miss Sarah K. White had succeeded Mrs. [Lemuel H.] Wells as principal of Annie Wright Seminary by October, 1889. —Jessett (1949) p. 19.

———

1891: June

The June 1891 issue of the *Washington Churchman* gives Nevius's address as Hoquiam.

Journal, Jurisdiction of Washington, 1891:

Convocation was held at St. Mark's Church, Seattle. Nevius listed only as "General Missionary" (all others noted with station). He was present at opening services, reading the Litany.

―――

1891: June 24 (Wednesday)

Bishop Paddock's Address:

"I have been permitted during the last year, without interruption by protracted sickness, to devote time and strength to the work which God has given me to do among you.... [Paddock reported that] at the Decennial Commemoration, held during this last year, church, school and hospital property increased from a valuation of $62,000 when I came among you, to $550,000 at the expiration of the decade.... During a portion of the fortnight that I have been absent from the state since our last Convocation I was with Bishop Morris and his brethren of the clergy and laity ... in the opening of their new St. Helen's Hall; the other week I was in San Francisco making several addresses at missionary meetings, for which Bishop Nichols sought to gather all the Bishops on this western coast....

"....With advancing years and physical powers diminishing, with stations multiplying, and the strictly episcopal work increasing I have thought that I might profitably to you and to myself call in more largely the aid of clergy approved among you, in supervising and extending our missionary work.... From information gathered by my correspondence and through printed journals, I learn that of sixty-two dioceses and missionary jurisdictions, fifty-nine have presbyters specially designated to oversee and set forward the missionary work.... In most cases the title of dean is given; in some, that of Archdeacon; as to their duties and position, the canon of Connecticut says; 'It shall be the duty of the Archdeacon to take the general oversight of the missionary work in his district and to confer, respecting its plans and details with the Bishop.' The canon of Albany makes it a part of his duty to 'stir up missionary interest and zeal and to urge more liberal offerings for the work of church extension.' ... The Rev. Mr. Seymour, appointed to one of the Archdeaconries in Connecticut, writes thus of the working of the system: 'Naturally, a good deal will depend upon the man who holds the office. Until this year the Archdeacon had very little responsibility and no authority; this year both were given him, without encroaching on the Bishop's prerogative.' 'I do not think,' he adds, 'that the name has helped or hindered; there has been no attempt to use it as a title.' ... I would suggest, then, an addition of four to our present number of Deans and as the assignment of their fields will require the redistricting of the state, I recommend the appointment of a committee of five who may confer on the whole subject and present a report at this Convocation.

"It does not seem, to some among us, clear whether by our Civil and Ecclesiastical Law perpetual deacons engaged in business life, can be eligible to the office of vestrymen, or as to who is entitled to vote at parish elections. In some of our parishes, the privilege of voting is granted to Christian women, in other parishes they are refused. I would recommend the appointment of a committee of three clergymen and two laymen, who may report on these questions."

"There have also been donated in Ledgerwood Park, Spokane, four lots, on one of which I have had the pleasure of laying the corner stone of a chapel, to be known as St. David's; the building estimated to cost about $1,000.... In one of our cities in this state, two lots, given a few years since, are now worth about $50,000. Such facts lay obligations upon all those clergymen living in cities to be active, letting not lethargy or any selfish regard for their own parishes lead them to incur the guilt of keeping back the new church, which will be needed for gathering in the Multitudes soon to be found in the cities of our land; but the new small towns, springing up all over this state, must not be neglected; precious souls are there to be found, and none can tell where or how soon in any one of these places, the population will be largely increased. I am happy to report that many new stations have been taken up the last year, and efforts have been made to establish churches in Fairhaven, Anacortes, Ballard, Blaine, Snohomish, Kent, Elma, Aberdeen, Montesano, Hoquiam, South Bend and Colfax, with occasional services rendered at other new towns; and although in only one of these (Blaine) has a church been built, we trust that another year will see several structures completed in these and other towns."

"Fairhaven gives promise of that rarely seen among us, a parish self-supporting at once without ever receiving missionary aid."

"The Rev. Dr. Nevius resigned the charge of North Yakima and Ellensburgh last fall [sic spring 1890?]. There has seemed but little encouragement to continue services at Ellensburg at present. Two Clergymen have accepted the charge of North Yakima—one afterwards withdrawing his acceptance, the other now asks that he may delay his coming until autumn."

"St. John's, Olympia, in the basement of which we met for convocation last year, has completed its beautiful new church and only awaits the arrival of some articles for furnishing before opening the building for divine services."

"[In the spring of 1891] I went on to South Bend, one of Dr. Nevius' stations. I spent a Sunday with him there, where the promise seems good. The Missionary accompanied me to his other stations, viz., Hoquiam, Aberdeen, Montesano and Elma, in which places seven were confirmed. The pecuniary support which the missionary hoped to receive at these places has not been realized and no churches have as yet been erected; but the lots have been secured in most of the towns and arrangements made for erecting buildings on two of them [at Aberdeen and South Bend....]"

"Proceeding to the north [from Walla Walla], I was met at Colfax by the Rev. J.N.T. Goss, our general missionary in that part of the state, who accompanied me on my visits to his stations [Colfax, Palouse City, Farmington, Oaksdale and Pomeroy].... At Pomeroy is our only church building in this district. I was pleased to find the aspect of things there, in and about the building much improved. Mr. Goss seems well adapted to the work of general missionary, and hopes to erect in his district one or two Church building during the next year."

"Perhaps no city of the state has felt the pecuniary depression more than Spokane.... I have already alluded to laying the corner stone of a chapel in one of the outlying additions, and there is a Sunday school organized in another district.

"In none of our towns has there been more advance visible this year, I think, than in Seattle. Trinity Church has built a Guild House, 30x60 feet, on the site of its proposed new church, in which hall services are held and meetings of the church societies."

"It has been a disappointment and a grief to me that no boarders at our Church schools have come forward for confirmation"

―――

"On motion ... that portion of the Bishop's address relating to the increase of the number of Deans was referred to a special committee of five clergymen. The Bishop named as said committee the Rev. L. H. Wells, Rev. R. D. Nevius, D.D., Rev. V. M. Law, Rev. D. C. Garrett, Rev. B. O. Baker.

"On motion ... that portion of the Bishop's address relating to Perpetual Deacons as Vestrymen, and women voting in parishes, was referred to a committee of two clergymen and three laymen....

"The Committee on Endowment [Revs. Watson, Wilson and Nicholson] presented their report, which was adopted as follows:

The Committee on Endowment appointed by the last Convocation beg leave to report that by reason of the continued depression in financial circles, they have found it inexpedient to push the matter entrusted to them. The Committee however are glad to report that the Bishop has pledged $1000 toward this fund, payable Jan. 1, 1892, and that one small lot has been given as a beginning of the landed endowment.

"The Committee therefore report progress, and desire to be continued for another year with ... changes [in membership], and we further desire to express our firm conviction that we shall be able to accomplish the desired object in time to make our request for admission to the Convention of 1892."

"The Committee on Care of Funds and Valuable Property presented their report....:

...1st. That the Trustees provided for in the Canon of 1888 should be incorporated under the laws of the State of Washington.

2nd. That the same Trustees be charged with the care of the Episcopal Fund, and that such stipulation should be inserted in the Articles of Incorporation.

"The Committee on increasing number of Deaneries made their Report through the Rev. Mr. Wells, as follows:

The Committee appointed to report on so much of the Bishop's address as referred to the division of the Diocese into six or more Deaneries would voice the regret of the whole convocation at the Bishop's expressions of failing strength, and would suggest two ways of meeting the need.

1st.—The appointment of some number of Deans and Deaneries by the Bishop, say seven or eight.

1st.—Spokane Falls.

2nd.—Walla Walla.

3rd.—Vancouver.

4th.—Tacoma.

5th.—Seattle.

6th.—Gray's Harbor.

7th.—Fairhaven.

8th.—Yakima and Ellensburg.

The object of this is through supervision of outlying places and work, which would need the direct work of the clergy we now have, who are largely occupied with their parochial duties.

[2nd.—] Another way to supply this need is to obtain additional Episcopal supervision or the support of a number of general missionaries.

"[The] Committee on right of Perpetual Deacons to seats in vestries and Women voting made their report....:

...They are of opinion that perpetual deacons, not being laymen should not hold office as vestrymen.

That *all* persons [including women] who contribute to the support of parishes should be entitled to vote at parish elections.

June 25 (Thursday):

"The Bishop then announced the committee on State of the Church, Rev. D. C. Garrett, Rev. R. D. Nevius, D.D., Rev. H. H. Buck and Dr. E. C. Story.

"The Convocation resumed consideration of report of the committee on Increase of Deans and Deaneries.

"After discussion had been participated in by Rev. L. H. Wells, Rev. M. D. Wilson, Rev. M. Law, the Bishop, Rev. L. W. Applegate, Mr. Chas. Prosch, Mr. Wm. C. Taylor and Mr. W. R. Bissell, on motion of Rev. L. W. Applegate seconded by Rev. T. N. Wilson [sic] the following resolution was adopted:

Resolved: That the first part of the Report of the Committee on the increase of Deaneries is adopted, requesting the Bishop to call to his assistance such clergymen as he may deem expedient to supervise and care for the outlying districts in their respective localities, operating so much of what is known as 'The Deanery System' as is adapted to the Missionary Jurisdiction of Washington.

"In accordance with this resolution the bishop called to his assistance the Rev. G. H. Watson, of Seattle, Rev. C. B. Crawford, of Spokane, Rev. L. H. Wells, of Tacoma, Rev. M. D. Wilson, of Vancouver, Rev. V. M. Law, of Walla Walla, Rev. L. W. Applegate, of Fairhaven and Rev. R. D. Nevius, D.D., of Gray's Harbor."

"The Rev. V. Marshall made a statement of the condition and prospects of St. Paul's school, Walla Walla. ...The following resolution was moved by the Rev. S.R.S. Gray, seconded by Rev. R. D. Nevius, and adopted:

Resolved, that the clergy and lay members of this Convocation be earnestly requested not only to push the interests of our diocesan schools, but also to use all influences possible to bring the children of the Church within the influences of church schools.

"The Rev. R. D. Nevius, D.D. for the Committee on the State of the Church presented and read the following report:

The Committee on the State of the Church would respectfully report the satisfaction with which they see such an increase of clergy as supplies all our established parishes and every erected mission church, except Chehalis and Yakima, for both which places clergy have been supplied though not yet in residence. New missions have been opened to a larger extent than ever before.

All our church schools are increasing in usefulness and are enlarged to the proportion of opportunity and demand.

This is to be regretted and recorded that all along the line the Church painfully feels the depression in money affairs of the country, to which must be referred cessation of work on some projected lines, and a certain recognized heaviness in carrying the work already undertaken, which encourages to excusing inactivity for the present in expectation of a better time soon to come.

"The Bishop appointed as the Diocesan Missionary Committee the Rev. Geo. H. Watson, Chairman..., Rev. R. D. Nevius...."

"On motion of Rev. R. D. Nevius, D.D., the resolutions appended to report [sic?] were adopted.

"On motion of the Secretary it was resolved that the assessment of 10 cents per communicant reported be levied for this year for convocation expenses.

"It was resolved that one-half the expenses of clergy from east of the mountains be paid by the Treasurer if money be available."

———

"Parochial Reports....

"*Report of St. Andrew's Church, Aberdeen, for the year ending May 31, 1891.*

"The Rev. R. D. Nevius, D.D., Missionary.

"Parochial Statistics—Families and part of Families 17, number of persons 58; Baptisms, infant 1, adult 1, total 2; confirmed 4; burials 1; Communicants, number last reported 6, received from other parishes 16, added by confirmation 4, total gain 20; loss 1, present number of communicants 26; number who have communicated within the year 14; Public Services, Sundays 19, other days 9, total 28; Holy Communion, public 3. Services are supported by subscriptions and by offerings.

"Financial Exhibit—Expenditures, parochial—Salary Clergyman $92.50, current expenses, including other salaries, fuel, etc., $18, other objects within the parish $405, total parochial $515,50.

"Receipts—Offerings at Church services $92.50, all other sources $423, total $515.50. Amount of salary pledged Minister from parish from June 1, 1890, $180.

"Pledges for Clergy support have been made only since June 1st, 1890. A fine site for a Church has been given, with a building condition, and the lots have been cleared and graded, at an expense of $300, by the Women's Guild, which has worked continuously and efficiently during the year. An organ has also been purchased by them. A Chapel will be built during the summer.

———

"*Report of Montesano Mission, for the year ending May 31, 1891.*

"The Rev. R. D. Nevius, D.D., Missionary

"Parochial Statistics—Families and parts of families 7, number of persons 36; Baptisms, infant 1, adult 1, total 2; confirmed 2; Communicants, number last reported 4, added by confirmation 2, otherwise 3, total gain 5; loss by removal 2, present number of communicants 7; number who have communicated within the year 6; Public Services, Sundays 15, holy days 1, other days 4, total 20; Holy Communion, public 3. Services are supported by offerings.

"Financial Exhibit—Expenditures, Parochial—Salary Clergyman $41.25, other objects within the parish $327.25, total parochial $368.50.

"The earnest and persistent effort of the Women's Guild have resulted in paying for two valuable lots, $625, and partially clearing them. No movement yet made for building, but it is hoped that we may undertake a small Chapel this summer.

———

"Parochial Reports....

"*Report of Hoquiam Mission, for the year ending May 31, 1891.*

"The Rev. R.D. Nevius, D.D., Missionary.

"Parochial Statistics—Families and parts of families 14; number of persons 36; Baptisms, infant 1, total 1; confirmed 2, burials 1; Communicants, number last reported 4, added by confirmation 2, added otherwise 8, total gain 10, loss by removal 1, loss otherwise 1, total loss 2; present number of communicants 19; number who have communicated within the year 6; Public Services, Sundays 17; holy days 2, other days 7, total 26. Services are supported by voluntary offerings.

"Financial Exhibit—Expenditures, Parochial—Salary Clergyman $37.50, other objects within the parish $153, total parochial $199.50.

"Receipts—Offerings at Church services $37.50, all other sources $50, total

$87.50 [? sic].

"Services are held in the lower rooms of the Missionary house. We wait for a favorable time to erect a Chapel on lots promised by the Land Company. The Women's Guild have supplied an organ, and have met all other expenses incidental. There is at present no male communicants in the mission, and no Warden has been appointed to take the place of the one removed.

———

"*Report of St. John's Mission, South Bend, for the year ending May 31, 1891.*

"The Rev. R.D. Nevius, D.D., Missionary.

"Parochial Statistics—Families and parts of families 24, number of persons 56; present number of communicants, 17; number who have communicated within the year 14; Public services, Sundays 18; holy Communion, public 4. Services are supported by subscriptions and voluntary offerings.

"Financial Exhibit—Expenditures-Parochial, Salary Clergyman $231.05; current expenses (including other salaries, fuel, etc.,) $63.15, secured by Women's Guild for parochial purposes $473.05, total Parochial $797.25; General—Domestic Missions $3.55; total for all objects $800.80 [numbers total to $770.80].

"Receipts—Offerings at Church Services $90, subscriptions $141 [?], all other sources $413.25, total $797.25 [totals $644.25].

"A fine site for the Church has been given, a deed for which will issue as soon as a building shall be let to contract. This is about to be done.

———

"*Report of Elma Mission, for the year ending May 31, 1891.*

"The Rev. R.D. Nevius, D.D., Missionary.

"Parochial Statistics—Families and parts of families 7; number of persons 22; Communicants, number last reported 3, present number of communicants 6; Public Services, 12; offerings $37.75.

"Services have been held on Sunday Mornings, in the Methodist Church, with good attendance, the evening of the same day being given to Montesano. We have not seen our way towards even beginning to build a Church. A fine site for it is reserved and held for that purpose.

"The hope of building Churches in the weaker stations of my mission, Elma, Montesano, and Hoquiam, during the last year, has not been realized, on account of depression in the money market; and on account of its continuance must still longer be deferred. The best that can be done at present is to hold on at these three places, and wait for better times and more help. Our Church sites are secure as long as the work goes on. With only monthly services, however, little can be done but to keep these places open and our few Church fold and friends hopeful, so that they will not seek other connections. I greatly hope the field may be divided, around the two centers of Aberdeen and South Bend, where Chapels are about to be let to contract. At Ocosta, Gray's Harbor City, and Willapa there are Church folk and some communicants not named in the above reports. In each of these places sites for Churches are reserved, except at Willapa, which I have not yet visited, but deeds will be given only after work has begun. Other towns on Willapa Harbor and Shoalwater Bay will require attention, and may have it from South Bend as a centre.

"R. D. Nevius."

———

1891: June 24-25

Rev. Thomas Jessett (1949):

The convocation of 1891 was held at St. Mark's Church, Seattle, June 24-25. In his address Bishop Paddock asked for greater assistance from clergy "approved" by the convocation to service the multiplying number of mission stations and to extend missionary work. "As a result of this appeal the two convocations of Eastern and Western Washington were divided into eight deaneries, three in eastern Washington and five within the area of the present diocese of Olympia. Appointed to head the sub-divisions on the west side were the Rev. Messrs. M. D. Wilson, R. D. Nevius, Lemuel H. Wells, George H. Watson and L. W. Applegate. They were granted permission to use the title dean."

Jessett (1940) pp. 22-23

———

1891: July 19 (Sunday)

Washington Churchman, August 1891:

"Opening Services At St. John's Church, Olympia.

"One of the most notable events in Olympia's church history was the opening of the upper portion of St. John's Episcopal church on Sunday, July 19th. The church stands a monument to the untiring efforts of the congregation, and especially the ladies, who have labored zealously to raise the funds to push it to completion. That their efforts have been rewarded in presenting to the people of the capital city the most beautiful place of worship that can be boasted of, nobody will question.

"The entire church is covered with a dark red carpet, made in New Haven, and the gift of the Ladies' Guild. The chancel is exquisitely furnished and the interior of the church presents an appearance of comfort, richness and cheerfulness. The edifice has a seating capacity a little in excess of 200, and the seats and balance of the furniture are in solid oak. Each pew is furnished with a book rack and foot rest [sic].

"There are three windows on each side of the church. The middle north window has been contributed by Mrs. S. W. Percival as a memorial to her two infant children. It is of stained glass and represents the Good Shepherd with two lambs. The window was made in England.

"The Chancel Window is of Gothic design, and was in the old church at the corner of Main and Seventh street. It was sent to New York to be enlarged and remodeled. The subject is St. John leading the Virgin from the cross. The handsomest window in the church is the circular window, which is the gift of St. John's workers. It is nine feet in diameter, and was also made in England. The window cost fully $500. The design is a beautiful one, with three worshipping angels for a centre piece and groundwork of palms and lilies.

"Few churches, if any, in Washington, have handsomer chancel furniture. The eagle lectern was contributed by Mrs. Wilkeson, of Tacoma, daughter of Judge Elwood Evans, who formerly resided here. It is admired by everybody.

"The Pulpit Was Made

by Springer, White & Company. It is of octagonal design, exquisitely carved. The baptismal font is of carved oak, and was contributed by the Sunday school of St. Thomas' church, New Haven, Conn. George B. Scammell presented a clergy's stall. A beautiful cross of solid brass bears the following inscription on the base: 'Presented by St. John's church, East Hartford, Conn. St. John's in the East to St. John's in the West.'

"The Organ

was erected by Henry Pilcher's Sons of Kentucky, who have one of the most complete establishments in the country. Placed in position the organ cost $1500. It is called a two manual pipe organ, each manual having a compass of 58 notes. — *Olympia Tribune*...." [Details of the service follow. No mention is made of Nevius attending.]

———

1891: July 19:

Rev. Thomas Jessett (1940):

[p. 39] "The opening of the new house of worship [at Olympia], with the dedication of its memorial windows, pulpit and lectern, on July 19, 1891, was a great occasion. Carpet for the chancel and cushions for the pews were supplied by St. John's Guild. To raise money for these and other projects associated with the new Church, they made sheets and pillow slips and hemmed curtains for the first Olympian Hotel; bound blankets for the National Guard of Washington; had teas and garden parties; gave bazaars and excursions. The work was carried from house to house for the different meetings in a large wicker clothes basket.... In 1891, as a result of the labors for several years of a group known as St. John's Musical Society, a pipe organ was purchased from Pilcher and presented to the church. It cost $1500.00 and Mr. Pilcher himself came West to install it. This organ in its original condition still serves the parish [in 1940]. It is believed to be one of the oldest pipe organs in the Northwest. This Society... gave a series of [p. 40] entertainments presenting such operettas as 'The Chimes of Normandy,' 'The Mikado' and 'Pinafore.' These operettas were given in Seattle and Tacoma as well.... Nearly every one in town, and some young men from Tacoma, who could sing assisted at one or more of the entertainments...."

———

1891: August

The Rev. John N. Forest Bell noted that he relieved Nevius in the Gray's Harbor Mission in August 1891. See Bell, December 1891 below.

———

1891: August

The August 1891 issue of the *Washington Churchman* gives Nevius's address as South Bend.

-Ocosta, Washington -

1891: August

Rev. Thomas Jessett (1949):

"The Rev. J. H. Forrest Bell succeeded Dr. Nevius as missionary in charge of the Gray's Harbor Missions in August 1891. [fn]82. He took up residence at Aberdeen, and also held services at Hoquiam, Montesano and Elma. He also visited South Bend and Ocosta where Dr. Nevius was living."

"[fn]82 Ibid. [*Proceedings of the Twelfth Convocation,* June 22-24 and Sept. 24, 1892], pp. 66-69."

Jessett (1949) p. 23

———

1891: November

The November 1891 issue of the *Washington Churchman* gives Nevius's address as South Bend.

———

1891: December

The December 1891 issue of the *Washington Churchman* gives Nevius's address as Ocosta.

———

1891: December

Rev. John N. Forrest Bell

Washington Churchman, December 1891:

"Gray's Harbor Missions.

"The Rev. John N. Forrest Bell, Missionary.

"St. Andrews — Aberdeen

"Services—Holy Eucharist, first Sunday in the month at 8 a.m. Evensong every Sunday except the second, at 7:30. Fridays at 7:30.

"The Missionary, on succeeding Dr. Nevius in August, fixed his residence here, as being the most promising point in the field. The services have been improved so that we are now able to have them nearly full choral, which meets with general approval. We are fortunate in having a very lively Woman's Guild, which now numbers nearly thirty members. About two months ago the committee called upon the Guild to help with the erection of a rectory. They at once pledged themselves for $260 and afterwards said they would raise $300. Over $100 has been already secured, and they are busy raising the balance and [are] also talking about a bazaar and sale for after Easter. The rectory is quite a handsome little house, and will be occupied before the 10th of the current month. Only two rooms are yet finished and the Guild, who are desirous of completing it soon, will be glad of help, either in cash or furnishings of any kind. The front room has been made especially large in order to accommodate a Sunday School and various classes and meetings. Connected with this is a pleasant and roomy dining room, and in the rear a 'lengthy' kitchen. On the second floor one bed room is completed and the studding up for another and a study. We feel quite proud of our Guild and the house they have been instrumental in erecting so expeditiously. Steps are being taken in order that the much-needed church may be commenced in the early spring. We all feel the great disadvantage of having no 'church home.' The school house where we at present worship, has only one good point—it is central. We are, however, grateful to the directors for its use. Increased services and other causes are helping us, and we hope that a confirmation and instruction class may, in due course, add further to our members.

———

"St. David's — Hoquiam.

"Services—Holy Eucharist, third Sunday after Morning Prayer. Morning Prayer, first third and fifth Sundays at 11 o'clock. Tuesdays, in Advent and Lent at 7:30 p.m.

"With more frequent services greater interest is being manifested, and the Guild, working heartily with the clergyman and committee, make things look brighter for the future. We trust that before a great while we shall be able to erect the church all wish for. All the towns and harbor are suffering from the hard times, and Hoquiam feels the pressure as much as any. The spring will, we hope, make a change for the better. We are fortunate in the meantime, however, in having the use of 'the parsonage' for our services. This house belongs to Dr. Nevius.

———

"Holy Trinity – Montesano.

"Services—Holy Eucharist, third Sundays [sic? see Hoquiam] Morning Prayer, second and fourth Sundays at 11 a.m.

"The Warden, Dr. Story, has very kindly given the use of a cottage for the services, and made such alteration, aided by the Womans' Guild, as to provide a neat little chapel with a room for the clergyman. The guild are working earnestly and successfully, and have just spent over $100 in the purchase of an organ and are now working hard for a sale on December 15. They ever keep before them the erection of a little church on lots they paid $650 for. Their labor will do a great deal to accomplish this.

———

"Elma.

"The handful of people at this point bravely bought an organ a month or so ago and paid a quarter of the costs, I believe, on delivery. They have $150 towards a building fund and a promised lot. They deserve to succeed and also to be helped. Since taking charge of the field, it has been daily becoming more clear that Elma should be attached to another charge, not that it is inaccessible, but because four towns are too many for one man to care for as they ought to be. It is hoped that this may be accomplished in the near future, giving the extra time to the three towns lower down the river [Montesano, Aberdeen and Hoquiam].

"Looking over the whole field, the outlook for the future is promising, though at present, owing to the general dullness of trade, progress is slow and money not easy to raise. Patience is necessary, and all true progress is apt to be slow. In our eagerness for material growth we are too prone to expect more than we have a right to look for, and also apt to forget that above all 'God reigns,' and in His own good time the seed shall yield its increase."

———

First Sunday
8:00 am Aberdeen (Eucharist)
11:00 am Hoquiam (Morning Prayer)
7:30 pm Aberdeen (Evensong)
Thursday (Advent & Lent)
7:30 pm Hoquiam (Evensong)
Friday
7:30 pm Aberdeen (Evensong)
Second Sunday
11:00 am Montesano (Morning Prayer)
Thursday (Advent & Lent)
7:30 pm Hoquiam (Evensong)
Friday
7:30 pm Aberdeen (Evensong)
Third Sunday
11:oo am Hoquiam (Morning Prayer & Eucharist)
7:30 pm Aberdeen (Evensong)
Thursday (Advent & Lent)
7:30 pm Hoquiam (Evensong)
Friday
7:30 pm Aberdeen (Evensong)
Fourth Sunday
11::00 am Montesano (Morning Prayer)
7:30 pm Aberdeen (Evensong)
Thursday (Advent & Lent)
7:30 pm Hoquiam (Evensong)

Friday
7:30 pm Aberdeen (Evensong)
Fifth Sunday
11:00 am Hoquiam (Morning Prayer)
7:30 pm Aberdeen (Evensong)
Thursday (Advent & Lent)
7:30 pm Hoquiam (Evensong)
Friday
7:30 pm Aberdeen (Evensong)

[1892]

1892: April 20
Rev. M. D. Wilson
Journal, Jurisdiction of Washington, 1892:

"The report of the Endowment Committee of the last Convocation [Rev. M. D. Wilson "Chairman and Secretary" in 1891] was read as follows....

"The Committee met again at 107 South G Street, Tacoma, on the evening of April 20, 1892. There were present the Rev. Messrs. Wilson, Watson, Hills and Wells, and Messrs. West, Richards and Seymour (by proxy.)

"The chairman opened the meeting with prayer, and the minutes of previous meetings were read and approved.

"The chairman then stated that final decision was now necessary either to attempt the raising of the Endowment Fund at once or formally to abandon all thought of a Diocese until the General Convention of 1895.

"After preliminary discussion it was moved by the Rev. Mr. Watson and seconded by Mr. West, that the Committee proceed to the trial of raising the amount of $10,000 still needed (namely, $8,400) in the next sixty days, and to accomplish this object that one man employ his whole time during this period in canvassing the Jurisdiction in the interest of the Fund. After a protracted discussion, in which every person present took part, the motion prevailed.

"It was moved, seconded and carried that a committee of two from Tacoma be appointed to wait upon the Rev. H. H. Cole of Tacoma [no parochial affiliation noted in the "List of Clergy" of 1892, not listed in 1891 or 1893, may have been retired from another diocese], on his return to that city, and on behalf of this Committee to urge his acceptance of this work, and, in case of his refusal, that the Chairman, the Rev. Mr. Wilson, be asked to make the canvass. This being carried, the chairman appointed the Rev. Messrs. Hills and Wells as such committee. The Rev. Dr. Nevius [who was either present at the meeting or later] offered to assist in this projected canvass by taking the duties of the Rev. Mr. Wilson, in Vancouver, if he were the canvasser. Meeting adjourned."

———

1892: May
The January 1892 issue of the *Washington Churchman* gives Nevius's address as "Ocosta, etc." "Our last issue accredited to the Rev. L. H. Wells the oversight of the Gray's Harbor Mission. We should have said that the Rev. R. D. Nevius, D.D., was the dean of that district, Mr. Wells' deanery comprising the counties of Pierce, Mason and Thurston." The *Churchman* carried an article urging acceptance of an invitation from Walla Walla for Convocation to meet there, noting that there had been opposition to meeting in a place so remote from the population centers of western Washington.

———

1892: May 17
Rev. M. D. Wilson
Journal, Jurisdiction of Washington, 1892:

"The report of the Endowment Committee of the last Convocation [Rev. M. D. Wilson "Chairman and Secretary" in 1891] was read as follows....

"Under the date of May 17, 1892, the Sub-Committee reported that the Rev. Mr. Cole had declined to undertake the work, and a little later the Rev. Dr. Nevius found himself unable to take the place of the chairman at Vancouver."

———

1892: June 5
Rt. Rev. John Adams Paddock
Journal, Jurisdiction of Washington, 1892:

"One of the finest church, perhaps I may say the finest church building in the Jurisdiction—Trinity Church, Seattle—built at a cost of $25,000 or $30,000, was set apart with a Service of Benediction on Whitsun-Day [June 5, 1892] and the following days.... Whitsun-Monday the Holy Communion was administered at 10:30 A.M.; at 8 P.M., (the anniversary of the great fire of [June 6] 1889, at which time the old church was destroyed,) a service of thanksgiving for the renewal was held, with addresses made by the Rev. Dr. Nevius, the Rev. Mr. Wells, and the Rev. Mr. Wilson."

———

1892: June 22
Half-brother Benjamin Nevius Eastman died: Benjamin Nevius Eastman (half-brother): b. Ovid, N.Y. January 28, 1840; m. Cornilia Post (b. vicinity Ovid, N.Y. April 16, 1844; d. March 23, 1866) November 26, 1863; d. (Syracuse N.Y.?) June 22, 1892 (age 52 yrs. 5 mos.).

———

1892: June 22-24
Journal, Special Session, Jurisdiction of Washington, 1892:

"[There are in eastern Washington] the following towns with populations set opposite their respective names...: Spokane, 30,000; Cheney, 1200...; Palouse City, 1800; Pullman, 2000; Colfax, 2500...; Sprague, 2000...; Ellensburg, 3500...; Dayton, 2000...; North Yakima, 2700...."

———

1892: June 22-24
June 22 (Wednesday)
Journal, Special Session, Jurisdiction of Washington, 1892:

Convocation met in two sessions; June 22-24 at St. Paul's Church, Walla Walla and September 22 at Trinity Church, Seattle. Nevius is listed in charge of St. John's Mission, South Bend and St. Mark's, Ocosta. His name is not among the clergy answering to their names at opening roll call, but he is mentioned in reports of Committee discussions later on the opening day.

Rt. Rev. John Adams Paddock:

"On the 3rd of February [1892], returning from a visit on the mission at East Sound, I fell on a dark landing in Fairhaven, a height of about ten feet, and in a condition of unconsiousness, was carried by the Rev. L. W. Applegate and some of his laymen to the hotel, where I remained for ten days, under the kind care of these friends and members of my family summoned to my aid. At the end of that time I was removed to my home, but for a month was compelled to lie upon my back, in much suffering and weakness. For another month I could move only with the aid of crutches, but by the middle of March I resumed work in a moderate degree, and endeavored first to bring up arrears of correspondence consequent on this long illness.

"It is an impossibility with many to realize the pressure arising from the number of letters *requiring answer*, received by one in the episcopal office. The reply to five or ten each day, and day after day, is comparatively a slight thing, but with prolonged detention from accomplishment of the daily task, the accumulation soon numbers hundreds. Letters of every variety! Letters from a loving mother far away from the wandering son; letters from a perplexed Rector, in reference to matters of doctrine, or the temporalities of his parish; letters from laymen complaining of ministerial acts, inexplicable to *them*; letters from a brother clergyman or his widow, who would safely invest their little savings in Western securities; letters from a missionary, burden[ed] with unforeseen trials incident to illness, and seeking pecuniary relief; letters from Eastern clergymen, who would be told minute details of the work in our Jurisdiction, (but who, after much correspondence, decide at last to devote their abilities to another field); letters of grateful acknowledgment for every sum received and aid of our work, even a 10c. offering from a little child; these and many others, for neglect of which I should be severely and justly censured, to say nothing of circulars, reports, etc., amounting to thousands in the yearly aggregate—these multitudinous letters *must*, unless the law of Christian courtesy is ignored, be duly acknowledged. The correspondence of *every* faithful Bishop, even though he received much aid kindly given by members of his family, makes it obligatory upon him to spend a considerable portion of time at home, and is as essentially a part of his work as is the journeying from place to place, for the 'Laying on of Hands' or other Episcopal duty."

"...Spending the first Sunday after Easter [April 24, 1892] in Spokane..., I visited the new St. David's Chapel, Ledgerwood Park, and made an address. This little stone church, for which four lots were given, was erected at a cost of $1600, and is so planned that the present structure may be converted into the chancel of a large church at any future time. ... Going on to Pullman [in late April, 1892], I was met by the Rev. Mr. Goss, who has charge of this with other mission stations. Under his supervision a church has been erected here, pleasing in its appearance, with accommodations for about 250. This was opened by us for the service of Almighty God, Sunday, May 1st.... We are indebted to the Rev. John Morris, an aged clergyman resident at Grand Mound, near Centralia, in this state, for the excellent plans of this and one or two other church buildings.

"With Mr. Goss, on May 31st [? sic] I visited Pomeroy, held service, preached, and confirmed three. There I was glad to find a new Rectory, nearly completed. I always rejoice to record the erection of such a building. It not only increases the strength of the parish, but it secures a home and additional comfort for the 'Man of God' called to minister in holy things. The third Sunday after Easter, May 8th, I passed in Walla Walla...."

"I now allude briefly to the work of the six months following our last Convocation.

"On the 10th of July [1891] I preached and confirmed a class of six in St. John's Church, Olympia, the service being held in the basement of the new church, then in process of erection.

"September 6th [1891], fifteenth Sunday after Trinity, was spent with the Rev. S.R.S. Gray, at East Sound. While there, I advised with him as to a site for another chapel, which he hopes soon to see built on Orcas Island, and accompanied him to the place where a lot is offered for the purpose....

"September 29th [1891], assisted by the Rev. Mr. Goss, I laid the corner stone of Trinity Chapel, Palouse—a building of 50x25 ft., with basement 30x25 ft. At night, a service was held in the Methodist Chapel, kindly loaned to us, and two men were confirmed.

"October 30th [1891], it was my privilege to assist in the first Church service ever held in the town of Pullman, and with the Rev. Mr. Goss, on the morning of All Saints' Day, I laid the corner stone of a church."

"January 3d, 1892, in St. Michael's Church, North Yakima, I ordained to the Order of Priesthood the Rev. Rufus S. Chase. The candidate was presented and the sermon preached by the Rev. Lemuel H. Wells, of Tacoma. To this mission Mr. Chase has devoted his entire services, it being deemed inexpedient by him, and by others with whom he counseled, to continue work at present in Ellensburg, to which place the Rev. Dr. Nevius, his predecessor, had given a portion of his time. Ill health, I regret to say, has since this address was written, compelled Mr. Chase to return to the East.

"The Rev. Dr. Nevius has within the last year been engaged mostly in missionary work at Ocosta and South Bend, but since the departure of the Rev. H. H. Buck from Olympia, has also taken charge of St. John's Church in that place. At Ocosta, he informs me, a little church will soon be ready for use."

"In Anacortes a plain little church was erected under the supervision of the Rev. Dr. Platt, and opened October 11 [1891]."

"One of the finest church, perhaps I may say the finest church building in the Jurisdiction—Trinity Church, Seattle—built at a cost of $25,000 or $30,000, was set apart with a Service of Benediction on Whitsun-Day [June 5, 1892] and the following days.... Whitsun-Monday the Holy Communion was administered at 10:30 A.M.; at 8 P.M., (the anniversary of the great fire of [June 6] 1889, at which time the old church was destroyed,) a service of thanksgiving for the renewal was held, with addresses made by the Rev. Dr. Nevius, the Rev. Mr. Wells, and the Rev. Mr. Wilson."

"As we thus review the twelve months since we last assembled in convocation, we find the record of advance, in many ways. Eleven new churches, chapels or mission houses have been added to our number. Other buildings are nearly ready for use, and many services have been held in small towns or hamlets hitherto unrelated.... It is pleasing to record here, that in the vast area of the State of Washington, there are not more than five towns numbering 1,000 in population, where we have not a chapel or service held by the missionary regularly. Of these comparatively few towns now unoccupied, at Dayton and Waitsburg, services were held for two more years, but, in the judgment of the Rectors now living near, it is considered inexpedient, with a meager encouragement given, to continue services at present. Some of the churchmen, formerly residents, have removed, and the number now interested and willing to aid, is very small. Occasionally such cases occur, as the result of some indiscretion or unbecoming spirit on the part of a missionary or layman, producing an unfavorable impression and making it wise, if not necessary, to discontinue, for a time, the attempt to establish regular services. Some of the other towns unoccupied are mining camps, with population migratory, reaching a thousand or more for one month and perhaps lessening to five hundred within the next few weeks.

"While it is gratifying that we have been enabled so well to cover the missionary field, yet we have need, my dear brethren, to be constantly on the alert and watchful to improve our opportunities. Many new towns, now small and unimportant, may, with a sudden—often an unexpected—change of affairs in our new country in course of one year, rapidly develop into places of strength and importance."

"As I write these words a message comes to me of the departure from earth of the Rev. E. F. Miles, M. D., who was the first superintendent, and long identified with the work of the Fanny Paddock Hospital. Dr. Miles was a physician of good standing, educated in Dublin, and practicing in New York City. When, in the providence of God, I was called into this Western land, he expressed a desire to come also, and to devote himself to the care of souls, while not entirely relinquishing care of the body. Ordained to the Diaconate by me, the hospital offered opportunity for the work he desired, and to this he gave himself, during most of the remainder of his life. But he also held for some time the Rectorship of St. Peter's Church, Tacoma, and then, being called to the church of the Epiphany, New York City, he was away from us for two or three years. At the end of that time he resumed his care of our hospital, until ill health incapacitated him from duties.

"He was called to enter into the eternal rest before, in earthly years, he had reached three-score. But his work was well done, and we know that his reward is with the Lord in his recompense with his God."

"The changes among our clergy during the past year, by which we have lost—at least for a time—some good and valuable men, have, in almost every instance, been caused by dissatisfaction on the part of a minority of the congregation, which coming to the knowledge of the rector, has occasioned distress and anxiety, and at last resulted in the dissolution of the connection of the pastor and people. My dear brethren of the laity, I would earnestly urge upon you increased affection and gentleness and forbearance towards him who is appointed to minister to you in holy things. No bishop, priest, or deacon is faultless; it is comparatively easy for any one sitting in judgement to be harsh and censorious, and so make heavy and sad hearts. Ever remember, not all have the like gifts from God. One may be blameless in life, ever manifesting the power of the gospel in holy example, ever patient, gentle, loving and constant in labors, and yet he may be wanting in the gift of ready utterance or commanding eloquence. But in the lapse of years, the example of the meek and holy man of God, and such work as he can perform, may win as many souls to Christ and accomplish as much for the cause of his Church, as is effected by another who by the 'gift of tongues' moves audiences to tears, and is honored for his brilliant oratory, but who is at times rash in speech, hasty in temper, offensive in his bearing, and in other ways guilty of a spirit unbecoming a follower of the meek and lowly Saviour. I ask no allowance made for bishop, priest, or deacon who shows himself to be without the spirit of Christ. But for the confessedly true and consistent followers of their Lord and Master, who may be deficient in certain popular gifts, my heart aches when I know that, with advancing years and failing powers, they are harshly spoken against by those not altogether faultless, and virtually dismissed from their position, perhaps cast out to suffer and die, like the brute beast who has toiled in obedient and constant labor till too old and worn to prove profitable, and then turned out on the common to starve. But in the one case, we suppose the beast knows only physical suffering; in the other we are certain of the keen, constant trial to the sensitive, cultured Christian man. May God give us to be gentle with all men, and ever possessed with the spirit to work faithfully, ever remembering that to those 'their reward also is with the Lord, and their recompense with their God.'"

"At our first convocation, August, 1881, the report of a committee presented the value of school property, church buildings, etc., in the jurisdiction, at $37,000, and the number of communicants, 306. We find last year reported 2,262 communicants, with twenty-eight clergy, forty parishes or missions, and property valued at $550,000."

"At the convocation of 1891, a committee was appointed to seek the endowment of the Episcopate of Washington. This committee will present a report, through their chairman. I merely state here that several meetings have, to my knowledge been held, but I understand that, with the unprecedented stringency of money matters, it has not been found possible to raise the full amount necessary to make Washington an independent diocese. I have not felt justified in entering a parish, unsolicited by the Rector, in order to solicit for contributions to this fund, especially as our strongest parishes are burdened with debt. I have rested content with issuing a letter upon the subject and making my own offering in aid of the cause. Should it at last be found impracticable to raise the amount needed, I propose, if agreeable to you, setting before the House of Bishops at the general convention the fact that the jurisdiction of Washington embraces an area equal to that of the dioceses of New Jersey, Connecticut, and Massachusetts and the four dioceses of the state of New York, and though in portions sparsely populated, has been and continues rapidly increasing in population. I would therefore ask the setting apart of the eastern portion of the state as a separate Missionary Jurisdiction and the appointment of another Missionary bishop to serve there."

———

"The Bishop ... called the Rev. Mr. Watson to the chair and retired from the room.

"The report of the Endowment Committee of the last Convocation [orig. Revs. Watson, Wilson and Nicholson in 1890, Wilson "Chairman and Secretary in 1891, see other members below] was read as follows:

"The Endowment Committee of the last Convocation desire to report as follows:

"The Committee met at St. Luke's Parish House, Tacoma, on September 24, 1891, and again at the residence of the Rev. John Dows Hills [St. Luke's, Tacoma] on December 9, 1891. The only results of these meetings were certain articles which have appeared in the *Washington Churchman*, and the general conclusion that it was impossible to do anything in the matter at that time.

"The Committee met again at 107 South G Street, Tacoma, on the evening of April 20, 1892. There were present the Rev. Messrs. Wilson, Watson, Hills and Wells, and Messrs. West, Richards, and Seymour (by proxy).

"The chairman opened the meeting with prayer, and the minutes of previous meetings were read and approved.

"The chairman then stated that final decision was now necessary either to attempt the raising of the Endowment Fund at once or formally to abandon all thought of a Diocese until the General Convention of 1895.

"After preliminary discussion it was moved by the Rev. Mr. Watson and seconded by Mr. West, that the Committee proceed to the trial of raising the amount of $10,000 still needed (namely, $8,400) in the next sixty days, and to accomplish this object that one man employ his whole time during this period in canvassing the Jurisdiction in the interest of the fund. After a protracted discussion, in which every person presented took part, the motion prevailed.

"It was moved, seconded and carried that a committee of two from Tacoma be appointed to wait upon the Rev. H. H. Cole of Tacoma [no parochial affiliation noted in the 'List of Clergy' of 1892, not listed 1891 or 1893], on his return to that city, and on behalf of this Committee to urge his acceptance of this work, and, in case of his refusal, that the Chairman, the Rev. Mr. Wilson, be asked to make the canvass. This being carried, the chairman appointed the Rev. Messrs. Hills and Wells as such committee. The Rev. Dr. Nevius offered to assist in this projected canvass by taking the duties of the Rev. Mr. Wilson, in Vancouver, if he were the canvasser. Meeting adjourned.

"Under the date of May 17, 1892, the Sub-Committee reported that the Rev. Mr. Cole had declined to undertake the work, and a little later the Rev. Dr. Nevius found himself unable to take the place of the chairman at Vancouver. The chairman therefore found himself unable to leave Vancouver until after June 10. About that time the quiet persistent influence of the Rev. Mr. Watson and a letter from the Rev. Dr. Law induced the chairman to go to Seattle on Monday, June 13th....

"Allowing $200 for expenses, we can safely say that the Fund now amounts to $3265.18, of which $1600 is promised on condition the whole amount is raised by September 1, 1892, and $1,555.18 is cash on hand.

"We therefore ask the passage of the following resolution:

Inasmuch as we are confident that the method of applying for admission as one Diocese in the State of Washington is the only method likely to be allowed by the General Convention;

And also in view of the great success that has greeted the efforts thus far set forth; therefore,

Resolved, that the matter be pressed forward to a conclusion at the earliest possible moment, and that when we succeed in raising the necessary $10,000 the Bishop be requested to call a Primary Council for the organization of the Diocese of Washington."

"signed for the Committee,

"Mardon D. Wilson, Chairman."

"...The Rev. Mr. Cole explained that he had not undertaken the work because he could not take the time necessary....

"The following amendment was offered...."

Resolved, That the Bishop and delegates to the General Convention be requested to ask of the House of Clerical and Lay Delegates and the House of Bishops their consent to the setting aside of Eastern Washington as a Missionary Jurisdiction, and if the consent of Bishop Talbot is obtained, that Northern Idaho be added to the Missionary Jurisdiction.

"On motion it was resolved that the whole matter of division or endowment be made the special order for Thursday [June 23]."

In the evening session "Addresses on 'Christian Socialism' were made by Rev. Messrs. Watson, Eubanks, Dickson, Hills and Cole."

June 23 (Thursday)

"The following resolution was offered by Mr. J. Lyon, of Spokane, and duly seconded:

Resolved, That a committee of six be appointed by the Eastern and Western Delegations to endeavor to reconcile the interests of the different portions of the State in regard to a separation in to Diocesan and Missionary Jurisdictions, said committee to report the result of its deliberations at the meeting at 1:30 P.M. today.

"The point of order was raised that there already were before the Conference the resolution and the amendment above mentioned.

"The chair [Watson] decided the point well taken, whereupon the mover of this resolution ... asked for the unanimous consent of the House that this resolution be considered, with the understanding that it was to take the place of both resolution and amendment previously offered.

"This unanimous consent was granted, whereupon the resolution of Mr. Lyon was adopted.

"On motion a recess of three minutes was taken to allow delegations to name their representatives.

"At the expiration of this time the delegation from Eastern Washington reported as their representatives—the Rev. Mr. Goss of Colfax, the Rev. Mr. Hughson of Spokane and Mr. J. F. Boyer of Walla Walla, and the Western Delegation reported as their representatives—the Rev. G. H. Watson of Seattle, the Rev. J. D. Hills of Tacoma and the Rev. M. D. Wilson of Vancouver."

"Report Of The Committee Of Six.

"The Committee of Six, appointed by the Conference, respectfully present the following report:

"The Endowment Committee shall, if possible, push the raising of the necessary ten thousand dollars to an immediate conclusion. If the sum be raised, the Bishop shall be requested to call a Primary Convention during the third week in August. That Convention shall elect Clerical and Lay Deputies to present to the General Convention in October a petition for the admission of the Jurisdiction of Washington as a Diocese, and to the board of Missions for the twenty thousand dollars from the various funds towards the endowment of the episcopate of the said Diocese of Washington.

"The aforesaid Clerical and Lay Deputies of Washington shall be instructed that in case of the admission of the said Diocese, they apply to the same General Convention for the setting aside of such portion of the State of Washington as lies east of the Cascade mountains as a separate Missionary Jurisdiction. ... [Including, if Bishop Talbot of Wyoming and Idaho consents] that portion of the State of Idaho known as the "Panhandle."

"The Committee of Six shall be continued....

"If the state as a whole shall be admitted as a Diocese, and the portion east of the mountains afterwards be set apart as a Missionary Jurisdiction, the income arising from the episcopal fund shall be used *in toto* for the support of the Bishop of Western Washington. *Provided* that at the time of the establishment of the Diocese of Eastern Washington, a division of this fund shall be made exactly proportioned to the amounts raised in the two portions of the state towards the ten thousand dollars necessary....

"It is understood that if the necessary $10,000 be not raised for Washington or Western Washington, the Bishop and delegates to the General Convention be requested to petition that body to divide the present Jurisdiction of Washington into two Missionary Jurisdictions, to be divided by the Cascade Mountains....

"This report was unanimously adopted."

———

"Deanery Reports....

"Gray's Harbor Deanery.

"The Rev. R. D. Nevius, D.D., Dean.

"South Bend should have, as is desired by the people there, a resident clergyman and continuous services immediately. At present, however, I fear the mission could not develop sufficient sustaining force to secure even with aid of a missionary stipend from the Board of Missions, such a man as they desire. Valuable lots are held here under contract to build a Church, and a considerable amount has been paid upon them for taxes in street improvements and for clearing. The people have not yet been able to undertake the work of building.

"Ocosta has a small population, and but few communicants. They have been, however, harmonious and generous in undertaking a work which by many and even by myself, would have been thought impossible. Valuable lots have been given, and a Church building is in progress, and there is fair prospect that it may be completed without any other debt than that of $500 borrowed from the Church Building fund.

"There are no towns in these counties in which services have not been held during the year except those on the Columbia, Ilwaco, Knappton and Skamokawa. I have visited the former and latter, and in Knappton services have been held by Rev. Mr. Short of Astoria, and Lenten offerings have been made, which have been duly accredited to Washington. Services should be held in these places this year. Kalama also is growing in importance, and a missionary could well be placed upon the Columbia river below Vancouver. There have been found in these towns fifteen communicants, and it is probable that with advertised services another visit would develop many more. Thanks are due to Rev. Mr. Short of Oregon, for service and pastoral care in the Washington towns in the vicinity of Astoria."

"Parochial Reports....

Report of St. Mark's Church, Ocosta, for the year ending May 31, 1892.

"The Rev. R. D. Nevius, D.D.

"Edmond Croft, Warden.

"Parochial Statistics—Families and parts of families, 10, number of persons, 37; present number of communicants, 10, number who have communicated within the year 8; Public Services, Sundays 38, holy days 3, other days 2. Total 23 [sic]; Holy Communion, public 7; Sunday School, officers and teachers 4, scholars 16; public catechisings, number of times 3. Seats free and unassigned. Services are supported

by monthly subscription, by weekly envelope system, and by voluntary offerings.

"Financial Exhibit—Expenditures, parochial-Salary of Clergyman $106.30; current expenses, (including other salaries, fuel, etc., $32.50; music $13; other objects within the parish $350; total parochial $501.80; General, domestic missions $2; Church building fund $2; total general $4; total for all objects $505.80.

:Receipts—Offerings at Church Services $58.30; subscriptions and donations $48; total $106.30; value of Church property $1500 [?], amount of mortgage $500. The parish has a house of worship.

———

[From *Journal* of Special Session, September 22, 1892:]

"*Report of St. John's Church, South Bend, for the year ending May 31, 1892.*

"The Rev. R. D. Nevius, D.D., Missionary.

"Parochial Statistics—Families and parts of families, 14; No. persons, 43; baptisms, infants, 3; marriages, 1; No. communicants, 17; No. who have communicated within the year, 12; services, Sundays, 13; Holy Days, 2; total 15; Holy Communion, public, 6. Seats are free and unassigned. Services are supported by annual subscriptions and weekly envelope system and by voluntary offerings.

Financial Exhibit—Expenditures, Parochial—Salary Clergyman $113; Current expenses (including other salaries, fuel, etc.) $47.50; taxes, grading, etc., $300; total parochial $460.60 [sic]; general domestic missions, $2; total general, $2; total for all objects $464.60.

Receipts—Subscriptions and donations $113 [?], total $113 [?], amount of salary pledged minister from other sources, $300; total amount pledged from all sources, $300 [sic]. Four valuable lots are held on condition of building a church thereon. Taxes and improvements have been paid."

1892: ?June

"The State of Washington was divided into the Missionary District of Olympia (Western Washington) and the Missionary District of Spokane (Eastern Washington) in 1892. The Rt. Rev. William Morris Barker [a nephew of Bishop Morris] became the first Bishop of Olympia.... [Actually, he was the first bishop elected to that position, but Paddock was the first Bishop of the Missionary Jurisdiction of Olympia, having named the Diocese after the separation of eastern and western missionary districts.] In June 1893, at a Convocation held in Tacoma, an [p. 41] attempt was made to divide the jurisdiction of Olympia by setting apart all the territory north of Tacoma as the jurisdiction of Seattle."

Jessett (1940), 40-41

———

1892: August 31 (Wednesday)

Ocosta Pioneer, Sept 2, 1892

Washington Churchman, October 1892:

"Benediction of St. Mark's Church.

"The ceremony of the benediction of St. Mark's Episcopal Church of Ocosta, was conducted Wednesday evening of this week by the Rt. Rev. J. A. Paddock, D.D., Bishop of Washington, assisted by the Rev. John H. Forrest-Bell, of Aberdeen. The service consisted of the office for the benediction of a church as authorized by the Bishop of Albany, followed by shortened evensong. An interesting sermon was preached by the Bishop, and the Rev. Mr. Bell in a few well chosen remarks alluded to the great work in church building which Dr. Nevius, the veteran missionary, has accomplished, he having built during the past seventeen years the total number of twenty churches in Washington and Oregon. He voiced the feeling of the citizens in expressing his regret that through illness the doctor was unable to be present..

"Mrs. Forrest-Bell presided at the organ, and the music and singing throughout the services were most excellent and inspiring.

"The church, which is a pretty one, consists of nave with open timber roof and a spacious apsidal chancel. The windows are a striking feature in the design, being of trefoil shape and placed close up to the eaves and glazed in rolled cathedral glass, leaded. The three chancel windows are more elaborate, the central one containing a floriated cross and the alpha and omega in colors. The one to the right contains the I.H.S., the other the Chi Rho, or symbols of our Lord.

"Plenty of space is allowed for the choir, and the altar is approached by four steps.

"We understand that Miss Emily Paddock, the Bishop's sister, has given new furniture for the chancel, and that as soon as a turret is erected a bell, given by a friend in the East, will be hung.

"The interior finishing of the church will be dimension cedar shingles, oiled, and it will accommodate about 120 people.

"St. Mark's Church of Ocosta has the distinction of being the most western Episcopal church in the United States.—*Ocosta Pioneer, Sept. 2, 1892.*"

————

1892: August 30

Rev. Thomas Jessett (1949):

"Bishop Paddock on August 30 [1892] opened the new St. Mark's Church, Ocosta, which had the distinction of being the westernmost church in the United States."

Jessett (1949) p. 25

- Hospitalization, Tacoma -

1892: August - 1893: March

Nevius was hospitalized. See March 31, 1893 below.

————

1892: September 10

Washington Churchman, September 1892:

"The Church Endowment Fund, which has been breasting wind and wave in an adverse sea of financial disquietude, is almost within sight of land, and to the loyal Church people of Washington a cry over the waters is coming; no true heart can let that right and commendable effort to reach a foothold with sister dioceses, go down in sight of its native shores. Mr. Wilson has carried the fund up to $8,000, and somewhere immediately good promises must be made that the additional $2,000 shall be forthcoming. There are ten days, or until the 20th of September, for the necessary pledges to come in, and no time can be lost. It is not a question of who the Bishop shall be or the Assistant, if Bishop Paddock so desires. There are none among the local clergy who aspire to a position so freighted with woe as is the high office of overseer of God's people. The heart of one truly called to such duty must faint under the weight of one drop of the blood of Calvary, and the terrible force of the 'still small voice' would shatter an unworthy ambition. Let that question remain outside of the present emergency, and let a few more Church people who listen to voices that once called to good deeds, hear them again from among the waves of possible failure with their old persuasive accents crying for relief to the race which is 'not to the swift, nor the battle to the strong.'"

————

1892: September 18

John Livingston Nevius and Helen S. Coan Nevius sailed for China from Vancouver B.C. in the *Empress of China*. No mention of R. D. Nevius is made.

Nevius (1895) 457

————

1892: September 22

Journal, Special Session, Jurisdiction of Washington, 1892:

A special session of the Twelfth Convocation of Washington was called on the authority of Bishop Paddock on September 22, 1892 at Trinity Church, Seattle. Nevius is not listed in attendance nor does his name appear in reports or proceedings.

"In place of a sermon, the Rev. M. D. Wilson made a hurried report of his work during the summer in the interest of the Endowment Fund. There had been raised in the jurisdiction in cash $100, in subscriptions $4871, in addition to $1,215 raised in Washington between May 10, 1888, and June 1st, 1892. In addition there has been raised from friends in the East the sum of $1,850, with the further promise from one gentleman in New York of the last $1000. With all this, by the best possible showing , we were still $5,000 short of the necessary $30,000. This amount would have been raised if it had been found possible to secure to the benefit of the Jurisdiction the generous offer made by Mr. Geo. Lewis Gower, of Tacoma. But it was found impossible to sell the property, and therefore we remain a Missionary Jurisdiction for three years longer."

"The Bishop stated that he had inserted in his report to the General Convention

a request that the Jurisdiction be divided and an additional Bishop appointed for Eastern Washington."

"Memorial [to the House of Bishops]

"We would respectfully request that you consent to that portion of the Memorial submitted by Bishop Paddock, in which he advises the separation or division of the Missionary Jurisdiction of Washington, into two Missionary Jurisdictions, the state to be divided longitudinally by the Cascade range...."

"[There are in eastern Washington] the following towns with the population set opposite their respective names...: Spokane, 30,000; Cheney, 1200,,,; Palouse City, 1800; Pullman, 2000; Colfax, 2500...; Sprague, 2000...; Ellensburg, 3500...; Dayton, 2000...; North Yakima, 2700...."

————

1892: September 22 - October

Rev. Thomas Jessett (1949):

"A special session of the convocation of Washington was held in Trinity Church, Seattle, on September 22, 1892, to discuss the establishment of a diocese. Efforts to raise the $30,000.00 necessary had been carried on for several years with only about one-third of the amount in sight. An offer by Trinity Church, Seattle, to transfer itself and property to the diocese for cathedral purposes was rejected. Instead a committee was appointed to draw up a memorial to the General Convention meeting that October, petitioning the House of Bishops to divide the jurisdiction along the range of the Cascade mountains. [fn]91

"Bishop Paddock and the Rev. John Dow Hills attended the General Convention which was held at Baltimore, Maryland. The General Convention approved the division and the Rev. Lemuel H. Wells, rector of Trinity Church, Tacoma, was chosen and consecrated as the Bishop of Spokane, the name given to the eastern half of the state. Rivalry between Seattle and Tacoma probably prevented Bishop Paddock from choosing the name of Tacoma."

"[fn]19 *Ibid.* [*Proceedings of the Twelfth Convocation, op. cit.*], Special Session, pp. 94-108."

Jessett (1949) pp. 25-26

————

1892: October

Washington Churchman, October 1892:

"The Endowment.

"The earnest effort made by a portion of the committee on the Endowment Fund has, so far as any hope of Diocesan independence for another three years is concerned, met with disheartening failure.

"It is, however, only right to say that this defeat was not unexpected by those who worked hard for success.

"The cause of failure that will be openly alleged, *viz.* the prevailing financial stringency, was only one of many reasons for the apathy with which the matter was received on every hand. Individualism, local ambitions, new plans for the management of Church affairs in Washington, fear of losing missionary aid on the part of dependent missions; all these things, with others, contributed to make the effort of the committee null and void from the start.

"In all probability, these very same causes of failure would have militated strongly against unity of action in the proposed new Diocese; and, if this view be correct, better is it by far that we are still left in our period of probation.

"It remains only for the true Churchmen of Washington to deprecate all bitterness, to watch closely that no attempt be successful to bend the Church to the service of two masters, God and Mammon, and to gather together in serried ranks for the future effort to 1895 to obtain then by unity that which was lost in 1892 by disunity."

————

1892: October

Washington Churchman, October 1892:

"S. Andrew's, Aberdeen

"Just about a year ago the rectory was commenced with $5 in hand; so far the building has cost nearly $600, and with the exception of $23 in all paid for. Many kind friends in Tacoma, Seattle and other places have helped in this good work, and only recently the Rev. John H. Forrest-Bell took advantage of a trip over to

Vancouver to raise some funds in Portland among the friends who remembered him in connection with the Good Samaritan Hospital and Trinity Mission (since S. Mark's Church) some twelve years ago. Seventy-eight dollars was the result which is hereby gratefully acknowledged. The rectory is yet almost entirely unfinished internally, but this is to wait for the more important object of building the church. The Rev. John Morris, of Grand Mound, who is an architect of great ability, a Fellow of the Royal Institute of British Architects, and a friend of the late Sir Gilbert Scott, the great gothic architect of England, has placed this [Missionary] Jurisdiction [of Washington] under obligation by generously giving complete plans for the church. Those who are competent to judge amongst them one of our well-known architects on the Sound who casually saw the plans speak very highly of the design, which is wonderfully effective, especially as the bench on which the church will stand is quite 20 feet above the general level of the city. Another pretty feature is the octagonal baptistery near the main entrance, which is also finished with a spire. Ample room is provided within the triple chancel arches, the chancel proper being 24 feet deep and 20 feet wide. The altar will look very dignified, raised seven steps above the nave, especially when seen from the west end of the church, 80 feet away. A loan for the building has been promised by the Building Fund Commission, and other funds promised; $500 in cash is, however, needed before the committee care to begin the building. All hands are busy getting ready for a fair to be opened in Aberdeen December 14th by Governor Ferry. Will not readers of the CHURCHMAN help forward this good work by contributing to the bazaar either in work, material or cash. Many hands make labor light.

"During the illness of Dr. Nevius, Mr. Forrest-Bell visited St. Mark's Church at Ocosta and held service. This the doctor's twentieth church, is quite a gem in its way and when finished, will be one of the neatest of the smaller churches of Washington. Mr. and Mrs. Forrest-Bell have made arrangements to spend several days in each month at their various missions in order to arouse if possible a little more enthusiasm amongst our people."

———

1892: October
The October 1892 edition of the *Washington Churchman* gave Nevius's address as Tacoma.

———

1892: October 21 (Friday)
Washington Churchman, October 1892:
"Friday, October 21st, has been set apart by the civil authority for the celebration of the four hundredth anniversary of the discovery of America. An order of service in many dioceses has been authorized for that day. Service will be held in Trinity Parish Church, Seattle, and in many others in the Jurisdiction of Washington."

———

1892: November 1 (All Saints' Day)
Washington Churchman, October 1892:
"The laying of the corner-stone of the cathedral of St. John the Divine, New York, will occur on All Saints' Day, just after the adjournment of the General Convention. The occasion will be one of import to the entire American Church, for the cathedral will seek to minister to the National Church in the spirit and power of the apostle whose name it bears, upon whose life was the seal of Love."

———

1892: November 8
Election Day. Grover Cleveland re-elected to a third term.

———

1892: November
Washington Churchman, November 1892:
"The Missionary Jurisdiction of Spokane.
"The division of Washington into districts, and the establishment of the new jurisdiction of Spokane, comprising the entire portion of the State east of the Cascade Mountains, marks a new era of Church growth in the Pacific Northwest.
"The election of Dr. Wells of Tacoma as the Missionary Bishop is also both an honor to the coast and an evidence of a growing appreciation of the fact that Western fields need Western men to oversee and cultivate them.

"If further, the report is correct that Western Washington is to be hereafter called the Jurisdiction of Olympia, the indications would seem to be favorable for future sub-divisions and the erection of a number of small dioceses, each with a city as its centre.
"It, however, should be remembered that the smallest diocese here will even then be larger than many Eastern dioceses, in population as well as square miles, if we increase in the next decade with the same rapidity as in the last. In 1880 Washington had a population of only 75,000. The census of 1890 reports 350,000."
The *Churchman* also reported the death of Mrs. Benjamin Harrison.

———

1892: November 26
Nevius's sixty-fifth birthday.

[1893]

1893:
Maude Perry Douglas (1942):
"The year after Bishop Paddock's visit [in April 1892], was held Aberdeen's first Confirmation class [in 1893, date may not be reliable]. The group was prepared by the Rev. Dr. R. D. Nevius and confirmed by Bishop Paddock in the old Methodist Church on the corner of First and F Streets. Four young women comprised this class.... On this visit Bishop Paddock baptized several children, including my little brother, Percy Perry, with his rubber boots on in evident expectation of more water than is commonly used in baptism but really because of the very rainy day.
"In those days money was raised for the Church in the hard way—by church fairs, dinners, strawberry shortcake luncheons, dances and amateur theatricals. There was no good ice cream sold in town then so, about once in so often, the good Church women made some and disposed of it downtown in a vacant store at 10c a dish. Making the custard at home, dragging it down town in a child's wagon, enticing some boys to turn the crank on the large heavy freezer, the poor women cracked ice and stood ankle deep in ice and salt before the product was ready to sell—what a contrast to the present day methods of ice cream making!

- Visit to China -

1893: March 31
Oregon Churchman:
"Gone to China.—The Rev. R. D. Nevius, D.D., formerly rector of Trinity Church, this city [Portland], and for many years a pioneer missionary in Oregon and Washington, left Tacoma for northern China on March 31st, to visit a brother who has been a missionary in that country nearly forty years. He goes to benefit his health, having been an inmate of the Fannie Paddock hospital since last August. Dr. Nevius has many friends in Washington, and, it is through their kindness that he is able to make the trip."

Oregon Churchman
April, 1893

———

1893: April 12
Deed recorded from O. M. Murphey and Mary M. Murphey, Hoquiam, to John A. Paddock, of Tacoma, for $5,000 of Lot 1, Block 50, Town of Hoquiam, dated April 11, 1893. This was for the St. David's chapel and hospital site.

———

1893: May-June
Begin of Panic of 1893. A drain on U.S. gold reserves caused a drop in stocks on the New York Stock Exchange on May 5, and a crash on June 27.

———

1893: April-September
Helen S. Coan Nevius
"In April of this year my husband's brother, Rev. R. D. Nevius, D.D., came to us in extreme ill health from the west [p. 462] coast of the United States, in the hope that a sea-voyage and the change might restore him. This hope was realized, and at the end of five months [September?] he returned to America, and is now compara-

tively well. For more than forty years the brothers had seldom met, and it was a kind of providence which brought them together again in the far-away home of the one, even though the flight of time and different environments had made them as unlike as brothers often are. Still they were alike in many things. Neither had changed at all in, for instance, his love of poetry; and many pleasant evenings were spent listening to 'Dr. Reuben' reading Tennyson or the Brownings, or to 'Dr. John' reading or reciting from Shakespeare or Byron, or his old favorite, 'Gertrude of Wyoming.' 'Dr. Reuben' liked also to interest his plodding brother in the marvels of nature [seen] through the microscope, and to get his assistance in studying the flora or the geology of this new, strange land. Sometimes they would go off boating on the bay, crossing over to the bluffs for a picnic; but such outings were not frequent—time was too precious and work too pressing."

Nevius (1895) 461-62

———

1893: June 21, 22
Journal, Jurisdiction of Olympia
Convocation was held at Trinity Church, Tacoma. Nevius was not in attendance and was listed without cure among the clergy.

———

1893: June 21 (Wednesday)
Bishop Paddock's Address: The Bishop apparently was too ill to assume the chair or read his address, which was read for him. In it he noted his poor health, and acknowledged the assistance of Bishops Wells of Spokane and Sillitoe of New Westminster. The Rev. L. W. Applegate accepted appointment as General Missionary (apparently replacing Nevius). He noted that he had requested the House of Bishops to appoint an Assistant Bishop.

"Two of our brethren of the clergy are not with us to-day. One [Nevius] has gone across the seas for the benefit of his health, and 'one is not,' for God has taken him [Rev. Albert Scott Nicholson, brief obituary follows].

Paddock noted that the revision of the Prayer Book was authorized to be used on and after All Saints Day [November 1] 1892, and that all churches were expected to adhere to it.

"During the session of the General Convention and for a few weeks following I visited a number of Eastern parishes and friends and made known our wants. In response to my appeals, I gratefully received a number of offerings. On Bishop Wells' return from the East, after his consecration, I presented him with one thousand dollars, a portion of the funds I had raised, to be used by him, especially in completing work begun by me, east of the mountains."

"On August 30, 1892, I opened St. Mark's Chapel, Ocosta, erected under the supervision of Rev. Dr. Nevius. The building is sufficiently finished for occupancy, and, when completed, will be attractive and well adapted to its work. Stated week-day services are now held there, by Rev. A. J. Mooney, of Centralia."

"The mission at Blaine has paid the balance due on its combined parish house and rectory.

———

The Rev. Geo. Herbert Watson of the Deanery of Seattle reported the "completion of the Great Northern Railway."

Discussion continued about dividing western Washington into two diocese.

———

1893: June
"In June 1893, at a Convocation held in Tacoma, an attempt was made to divide the jurisdiction of Olympia by setting apart all the territory north of Tacoma as the jurisdiction of Seattle."

Jessett (1940) 40-41

———

1893: July
The July 1893 issue of the *Washington Churchman* gave Nevius's address as "Tacoma."

———

1893: July 12
Washington Churchman, July 1893:

"Proposed Diocese of Seattle.

"A conference of the Protestant Episcopal clergy and laity of the nine northern counties of Western Washington met the twelfth of July at Trinity Church [Seattle] for the purpose of taking steps toward the erection of a new diocese, to be composed of these nine counties.... Clergy: Rev. L. W. Applegate, of Tacoma, Secretary to the Bishop and Dean to the northern convocation; Rev. J. H. Forrest-Bell, Rector of St. Clement's; Rev. James Cheal, in charge of West Seattle and Kent; Rev. J. W. Dickson, in charge of Mount Vernon; Rev. D. C. Garrett, Rector of St. Mark's; Rev. S. R. S. Gray, of East Sound; Rev. P. E. Hyland, in charge, Ballard; Rev. D.L.V. Moffett, Rector of New Whatcom; Rev. C. E. Roberts, in charge of Woodland Park; Rev. George Herbert Watson, Rector Trinity Church.... Rev. George Herbert Watson was elected to the chair and Rev. S.R.S. Gray secretary.

"Dr. Watson stated the object of the meeting and read the resolutions adopted at the annual Convocation ... a couple of weeks ago.... He then stated that the conference had been called by Rev. J. H. Forrest-Bell, with the approval of the Bishop of Olympia, and read the following letter from Bishop Paddock, in response to an invitation to be present:

I have no objection to interpose to the proposed convening by you of clergy and laity, but hardly think it best for me to attend. One difficulty would be that I am not in good health, and it might be very detrimental to me. Rest content with my prayers, and that the Holy Spirit may rest abundantly on you all, enabling you to act wisely and well, and to do that which will rebound to God's honor and glory....

[A memorial petitioning the House of Bishops to set aside a separate missionary jurisdiction consisting of Clallam, Island, Jefferson, King, Kitsap, San Juan, Skagit, Snohomish and Whatcom counties was adopted.]

"A motion was carried that the Chair appoint two other clergymen besides himself as a committee to present the memorial to the House of Bishops, and Dr. Watson stated that it was not certain whether a majority of the Bishops would be in attendance this year at the annual meeting of the General Missionary Council which convenes at San Francisco in October.... It was not certain, therefore, whether the memorial could be laid before the body at that time."

———

1893:
Great Northern Railroad completed to Seattle.
[Speaking of Bishop Paddock:] "During his thirteenth year episcopate [1880-1894] the completion of the transcontinental lines of the Northern Pacific Railroad to Portland in 1883 and to Seattle in 1887 and the Great Northern Railroad to Seattle in 1893 brought a tremendous rush of new settlers. Population increased over 400 per cent in the state as a whole. In western Washington the Gray's Harbor area and the region north of Seattle to the Canadian border were opened up extensively as the lumbering industry developed. Depressions in 1886-87 and 1892-93 failed to stop the advance."

Thomas E. Jessett, *Pioneering God's County* (Tacoma, WA; The Church Lantern Press, 1953), p. 31

———

1893: October 19
Nevius's brother, John Livingston Nevius died in Chefoo, China: John Livingston Nevius (brother), b. Ovid, N.Y. March 4, 1829; m. Helen Coan June 15, 1853; d. Chefoo, China October 19, 1893 (age 64 yrs. 6 mos.).

Nevius (1895) p. 469.

———

1893: November ?
Rev. R. D. Nevius, D.D.
Washington Churchman, December 1893 - January 1894:
"An Interesting Letter from Dr. Nevius.

"*Dear Churchman:*—I am glad to announce my arrival at home after a few months' visit to my brother in China, and I owe to the friends whose kindnesses made the visit possible for me this much—that I should make some of my impressions and observations common to them and myself. Writing for this month's issue, as I should have done for your last [in December 1893] had I not been still quite fatigued and unable at once to do the thousand things presenting themselves to me on my arrival; I must give my letter a sad coloring by announcing the very sudden death of the dear brother whom I visited and whom I left last October apparently in good health. He was known to only a few of those to whom your paper will come. They as well as all your readers who are known to me will be touched with a sympathetic pain for me in my bereavement.

"Rev. John Livingston Nevius, D.D., for forty years a missionary of the Presbyterian Board of Missions, had his residence for the last twenty-five years in Chefoo, the most northern treaty port of China. He had retired from active work in the interior where for fifteen years he had been engaged every year in visiting city and village in long itinerating tours of from three to seven months, preaching and founding missions and centers of Christian work. In his old field of work are now some sixty established missions and parochial organizations served by native preachers and teachers; most of whom came to him sometime during the year for a short or long residence with him for instruction and encouragement. While he was specially engaged in the revision of various translations of the scriptures and in other literary work, I thus became acquainted personally with many of the native Christians and their discouragements and successes, and at the same time I came to know much of the difficulty which meets our missionaries at first in the antipodal character of the language, if I may coin the word. I never before saw how much we are Greeks and Romans in our habit of thought and expressions. Almost all of our idioms are either one or the other or both at once. There is little or no difficulty in translating any Greek or Roman, and I may add, any European tongue into our common speech. The Chinese have a wholly different habit of thought and wholly different idioms, and we find scores of words in our sacred scriptures for which they have no equivalent, so that it is necessary to be either strictly literal or to find the nearest possible equivalent expression. The former which is absolutely necessary in conveying the truth will require study of our idiom to find our the meaning of a phrase, and the latter will hide the truth by softening it down or covering it over with the film of their crude superstitions.

"Since the first protestant missionary [Morrison], the Bible has been partly or wholly translated by many persons, and there is a variant use among the many protestant sects. Four years ago there was a great conference of all protestant missionaries, some 400, of which my brother was a chairman or moderator, and by it a commission was appointed for making a revision and a new translation for common use. It was this work which I saw going on day by day in my brother's house. These difficulties dominated the thought and the conversation of the whole house during all my visit. Take for instance the text, 'In the beginning was the word, and the word was with God and the word was God.' How should it be told in a speech which has no tradition or prophecy of the eternal Logos—no absolute word for God, though there are many half equivalents or wholly misleading terms for that holy name, and no idea whatever of the spiritual relation between God and man. Or take the expression 'Baptized into Christ.' How shall the spiritual union with the mystical body of the Eternal One be shown, where even the words have to be supplied to the language and the poor best effort seemed to be between these two expressions, 'Joined to the body of Christ's people,' or 'Baptized into the true religion.' Such difficulties occurred at every step, and expressed themselves especially in the effort to give with any adequate force the grand, and to us, easily accessible arguments of the Apostles in their Epistles.

"Five months of my absence was spent in perfect rest at Chefoo. I did not go into the interior, but I had a fine opportunity to become acquainted with the missionary work and its trials, dangers and successes.

"Chefoo is one of the stations of that powerful missionary organization known as the 'China Inland Missions,' which has two large and fine schools (boys and girls) for the children of missionaries and foreign residents in China. It also has a sanitarium for the missionaries and two hospitals for natives, all under the superintendency of Dr. Douthwaite—a missionary of beautiful devotion of life and a man of eminence in his profession as a physician. It is also the seat of a strong central mission of the Presbyterian Board and also of the English Mission of the S.P.G.* Society under Bishop Scott (Missioners [sic] Rev. Messrs. Greenwood and Brown.)

"This church which has a hospital and school attached, was the place at which I

often received holy communion, and in it I was glad to be able twice to preach.

"Chefoo is a place of summer resort, having a northern exposure on a beautiful harbor, with a fine beach for sea bathing. Here many missionaries come to recruit their health from the interior and from the hot southern ports, and here also I met some who were returning after a vacation spent at their homes in England, Canada and Australia, and some who were waiting to return home after long service. Here, too, I met with great pleasure, Rev. Mr. Ross and Mr. Douglass, who, with their families, had come down from Manchooria [sic] for their health. It was thus that I met one hundred or more of those who are engaged in the work of foreign missions and heard their story of individual privation and danger (often from bloody and fatal riots and alarms), and their great and encouraging success. Most of these I saw at my brother's house where they were entertained, and from them and from reading many books on China during my enforced rest, I learned much of the interior, which having seen one place well, I was content to see it with the eye of fancy only and not to explore.

"I am glad to say to my many friends to whom I am so much beholden for their ready generous sympathy in my long illness, and although I am advised to have a longer period of rest, I am almost restored to health and have good hopes soon to engage in active work as before.

"R. D. Nevius."

*Society for the Promulgation of the Gospel?

———

1893-1894:

The December 1893-January 1894 issue of the *Washington Churchman* gives Nevius's address as St. John's Mission, South Bend.

[1894]
- Blaine, Washington -

1894: February 1:

A church-sponsored school opened at Blaine, Washington, "only a few days before the building was completely destroyed by fire—and it was necessary to take temporary headquarters." See *Journal*, Olympia, June 27-28, 1894, below.

———

1894: February 20

Deed recorded from John A. Paddock to The Church Charity Association, for $5,000, of Lot 1, Block 59, Town of Hoquiam, being St. David's hospital and chapel.

———

1894: February/March

Washington Churchman, February-March 1894:

"The Rev. Dr. Nevius is at present in charge of the Mission at Blaine and is improved in health. Blaine is an important town on our northern border, and a veteran missionary like Dr. Nevius can accomplish much good for the church in that locality. We have received inquiries concerning the school lately acquired by the church in Blaine and refer inquirers to the Rev. L. W. Applegate of Tacoma."

———

1894: March 4

Washington Churchman, February-March 1894:

"The Bishop of Olympia [John Adams Paddock] was stricken with paralysis at two o'clock on the afternoon of Tuesday, February 27th, at Mirimar, California, and lingered unconscious until Sunday evening, March 4th, at 10 o'clock, when he passed peacefully to his rest.

"In Trinity Church, Santa Barbara, at five o'clock P.M., Tuesday March 6th, Bishop Nichols conducted funeral services, Bishop Leonard of Nevada reading the lesson....

"On Tuesday, March 13th, at nine o'clock in the morning the Bishop of Oregon assisted by the Bishop of New Westminster, B.C., celebrated the Holy Eucharist, and at two o'clock in the afternoon said the Office for the Burial in St. Luke's Church, Tacoma...., the internment being made in the beautiful new cemetery at Edison."

———

1894: March 28

Journal, Jurisdiction of Olympia, 1894:

The Rt. Rev. William M. Barker, Bishop of Western Colorado, received a Commission from the Presiding Bishop to take charge of the Missionary District of Olympia.

———

1894: April 18
Journal, Jurisdiction of Olympia, 1894:
Bishop Barker arrived in Tacoma.

———

1894: late March - early May
"Coxey's Army" of unemployed workers marched on Washington D.C.

———

1894: May 4
Journal, Jurisdiction of Olympia, 1894:
Bishop Barker visited Christ Church, Blaine, making a "short address" in the evening.

———

1894: May 6 (Sunday)
Journal, Jurisdiction of Olympia, 1894:
Bishop Barker confirmed 25 persons in the evening in Blaine.

———

1894: June
Washington Churchman, June 1894:
"The Rev. Dr. Nevius writes that his work as Chaplain of the Blaine school and in the Mission is wholly pleasing to him. He has been able to hold continuous services. His congregations have been large and he has presented a large class for confirmation—twenty-five—four of whom were from [the] Skagit county mission, and all of whom with the class confirmed last year made their first communion at the early celebration on the next morning after the confirmation. He is compelled to take his work slowly and with frequent intervals of rest, and he seems as surprised as he is grateful for the great mercy shown him in being so far restored to health.

———

1894: June 13
Journal, Jurisdiction of Olympia 1894:
Bishop Barker and the Rev. George Herbert Watson attended the funeral of Bishop Sillitoe in New Westminster, B.C.

———

1894: June 27, 28
Journal, Jurisdiction of Olympia 1894:
The Conventional year ended May 31. Convocation met at St. Luke's Church, Tacoma. Nevius was listed as resident at Christ Church, Blaine. "The Rt. Rev. William M. Barker, D.D., Bishop of Western Colorado, [is] in charge of the Missionary District of Olympia by Commission from the Presiding Bishop...." Bishop Morris of Oregon was present as well as the Rt. Rev. Dr. Perrin, Lord Bishop of Columbia. The journal notes that the Rev. S.R.S. Gray, Deacon, C. E. Roberts, Deacon and J. H. Forrest-Bell, Priest, all transferred to the Diocese of Milwaukee in October 1893, and that the Rev. D.L.V. Moffett, Priest, transferred to California in December 1893. These clergymen all had participated in the meeting to form a separate Diocese of Seattle on July 12, 1893.

———

1894: June 27 (Wednesday)
Bishop Barker's Address:
Bishop Barker gave a brief summary of Bishop Paddock's life. "With the permission and approval of Bishop Paddock's family I have determined to take the offering at the Memorial service to-morrow morning as the nucleus of a fund for placing a suitable memorial stone to mark the Bishop's resting place in 'God's Acre.' This fund will be under the control of the Bishop of Olympia and will be allowed to accumulate until enough is secured to defray the expenses of erecting a dignified and simple memorial. Knowing the wishes of the Bishop, his friends will understand that nothing elaborate is contemplated. Should a larger sum than is needed be secured, it will be retained as the nucleus of a fund to provide a suitable chapel for the Annie

Wright Seminary." He also noted the passing of the Bishop of New Westminster, the Rt. Rev. Dr. Sillitoe, attending Sillitoe's funeral in New Westminster on June 13, 1894, and that Sillitoe had been a "long time friend" of Rev. Dr. Watson of Seattle. Barker noted that he had received his commission to Olympia from the Rt. Rev. John Williams, Presiding Bishop, on March 28, 1894, reaching Tacoma on April 18 "by way of Northern Pacific railroad from St. Paul and went directly to the Bishop's house as the guest of Bishop Paddock's daughters."

"The school at Blaine has had a troubled half year. Burned out just when it was started and moved into strange quarters, it has finished its first half year with credit to itself and satisfaction to the pupils and parents. Plans for rebuilding have been prepared and this summer will decide its future and the record of its life will appear from time to time."*

———

Nevius was appointed by Bishop Barker as one of four examining chaplains, one of five Trustees of the Church Charity Association, and one of four members on the committee on the State of the Church.

———

1894: June 28 (Thursday):
The Rt. Rev. Lemuel H. Wells, Bishop of Spokane was present.
"Rev. Dr. Nevius, from the committee on State of the Church, submitted the report of the committee, which was read and accepted...."
Bishop Barker appointed Nevius chair of a committee of three on Bishop Paddock's memorial (see Bishop's address, above).
No parochial reports were included in the journal.
*Report of "The Blaine School;" "The Association was induced last fall to accept the gift of a valuable property in Blaine for the purpose of establishing an inexpensive Church school for the sons and daughters of farmers, mechanics, and others unable to bear the expenses of school already established. There are examples of such schools in Wilder, Minn., and Kearney, Neb., that are wielding a wide influence for the Church. Preparation were being made to open the school on February 1st—only a few days before the building was completely destroyed by fire—and it was necessary to find temporary quarters.

"The school opened as advertised, with three excellent teachers, who in one-half year have built a reputation for the school throughout the northern part of the state. There were during the term 56 pupils in attendance. Robert C Applegate, M.A., a graduate of Columbia college, New York, and with experience as an educator, is the Principal.

"There has been considerable delay in adjusting the insurance upon the building; but the amount of $7,500 is expected in a few days, and all preparations have been made to erect a new building for occupancy in the fall....
"Chas. McCutcheon,
Secretary."

———

1894: August
Washington Churchman, August 1894:
"The Blaine School.

"This institution is located at Blaine, Whatcom county, on the border line of British Columbia, and is just entering on its second year. Its place in Christian education is unique. It undertakes to occupy a field not heretofore cultivated. It can best explain its work by illustration. The church in Minnesota has her excellent school for both boys and girls at Faribault, and yet a school similar to the Blaine [school] was established in the farming regions to the west to gather in both boys and girls of farmers and mechanics, and give them a good English education. The school in three years grew from 30 to 400 pupils. In Nebraska, with her excellent schools in Omaha, the same movement has been made at Kearney, with good results. There are thousands of children who will never enter any save the district school, unless there is some institution brought to their notice, where with very little expense they can get just the advantages they need to fit them for their place among the toiling masses.

"The school at Blaine, therefore, gives particular attention to a thorough English education—a grounding of pupils in principles—a knowledge of what they need to know for every day business. The teachers are among the best. The surroundings are refined and cultivated. The school fits for college if desired; but its aim is that already described.

"The one exception it makes to its general plan is in the musical department. It might almost be said that it has as an annex a *music school*, and pupils are admitted for music alone. The lady in charge of this department is a person of rare talent, and is apt to teach.

"The characteristic features of this school are very concisely told in a circular that has just been issued. We quote from it as follows:

"Co-Education.

"We believe that a school is an enlarged home. Boys and girls, young ladies and gentlemen, should be able to study and recite together, and in common enjoy the drawing room and play grounds. Under proper restrictions and a firm and wise government this is possible. We surround students with refining influences, and we want no pupil who is not susceptible to them, or who would willfully abuse them.

"Co-Operation.

"We educate *for* life, not *away* from it. Work is honorable, and the masses must always work. We educate the pupils in self-dependence, and fit them to perform their respective duties in their own households in a few years hence. Each pupil devotes not to exceed one hour a day in the duties of the home, the boys outside about the premises, the girls indoors in dining room, kitchen and dormitory. This is one of the most important branches of education, to which this institution gives the most careful attention.

"Elective Course.

"This is a department school of the highest order. Our teachers are all specialists in their respective departments.

"Pupils may take any course they desire. English and classical, music—vocal and instrumental, drawing and painting, stenography and typewriting, business."

"The principal of the school is Robert C. Applegate, M.A., a graduate of Columbia college, New York.

"The institution was very unfortunate in the loss by fire of its school building last winter. The school is in temporary quarters while the new building, now under process of construction, is completed. We give herewith a picture of the building. It is admirably adapted to its work, and the seven acres of land about it will give ample room for recreation grounds.

"The second school year will begin on September 5th, and its regular terms are one hundred and sixty dollars a year. The principal will be pleased to give further particulars to those who desire them."

———

1894: September
Rev. R. D. Nevius:
"Notes on the Habitat of Diatoms.
"By R. D. Nevins [sic],
"Blaine, Wash.
"The collector may think himself fortunate if he finds any locality or discovers any habit of growth of these lovely things which will enable him to secure them specifically separate or nearly so and already cleaned by processes of nature.

"I will give some notes of what have been to me lucky 'finds,' hoping to provoke from others reports of similar good fortune.

"Zostera marina and another species which we have on Puget sound, Z. oregana, have been to me treasures in this respect. The plant is found everywhere floating its long ribbon-like fronds upon the surface at low tide, and always in the tangle of seaweed which is rolled by the tide and wind on the shores. Arachnoidiscus Ehr. often studs this frond thickly. It may be felt by the hand as the frond passes through the fingers as one almost involuntarily reaches for it as he passes over the ground which it frequents and it may be seen glittering on the frond which it often encrusts when the sun has dried the tangle on the beach.

"Isthmia nervosa loves the same habitat, and it laces the surface and fringes the edges of the frond with its zigzag chains.

"This plant is also often gray with encrusted Coconeis scutellum, and others of the same genus or is frosted with Nitschia or Synedra.

"On other sea weeds I have found Triceratium arcticum in patches, woven and

interlaced, chain on chain.

"An inexhaustible and clean find of Atthya decora rewarded by curiosity in noticing that the surf along the Pacific shore was fairly yellow with some floating substance. This I have seen twice for a week at a time in midsummer.

"The bronzed film that shines upon the surface of the mud flats is full of interest because it seems composed of diatoms in mass, pleurosigma mostly with occasional Surirella gemma, all far more beautiful when found than they are after being cleaned for mounting. The writer would be glad to know how to separate and clean them in any quantity proportionate to their number as found.

"Notes of personal observation might be drawn out to great length and if from diligent and careful collectors, would be full of interest. I have in these here given only spoken of some of my most lucky finds. I should be glad if others would do the same."

Nevius (1894) 270-271.

Nevius published an article entitled "Notes on the Habitat of Diatoms (in Puget Sound)" in the *American Monthly Microscopical Journal*, vol. 15, 1894, pp. 270-271. See February 18, 1953, below.

———

1894: October 17
Washington Churchman, October 1894:
"The New Bishop.
"It is with great pleasure that we announce the election by the House of Bishops on St. Luke's Day, October 17th, of the Rt. Rev. William Morris Barker D.D., as the bishop of the missionary jurisdiction of Olympia."

———

1894: November
Rev. R. D. Nevius, D.D.
Washington Churchman, November 1894:
"Blaine.
"We are just now rejoicing in the introduction of the new prayer books and hymnals. The church is fully supplied with both, and the choir, with the hymn[al]s with tunes—Tucker's. After a very careful review of our competent organist, Mrs. Davenport, (who, being in charge of the musical department of the Blaine School, gives her valuable and appreciated services to the church;) we are, though, without a critical comparison with the other musical editions, more than pleased and satisfied with our choice. So far, we have found all our old favorites though not always set to the hymns to which we have been accustomed to use them, and we have already found many new hymns and tunes which we have learned to love. We wish the book had not been made so bulky by the printing of so many alternate tunes, and there is quite a number which I think I should never wish to use. I like the clean open page for the use of the choir, but I shall hope for a cheaper and smaller edition which might be expected to come into use in the congregation.

"R.D.N."

———

1894: December 14
Bishop Barker's Address
Journal, Jurisdiction of Olympia 1895:
Bishop Barker visited Blaine the evening of December 14, 1894, where he "confirmed 2 and preached."

[1895]

1895: February 4 (Saturday)
Alaska Searchlight, Juneau, Alaska p. 4
Local Rays
Shortly before twelve o'clock last Saturday night, flames were seen issuing from the roof of the residence of Dr. H. A. Hofste, on Sixth street. The alarm was quickly rung by the fire bell and both hose companies turned out in good time. Hose company No. 2 was the first at the hydrant at the corner of Seward and Fifth streets and the hose was quickly connected, but its 300 feet of hose was not long enough to reach the burning building so 100 feet from hose-reel No. 2 was coupled

on and in a few minutes a stream was playing upon the flames and the fire was soon under control though it was more than an hour before it was completely extinguished. It was very fortunate that there was but little wind blowing at the time and that all the roofs of the buildings near by were covered by snow. The hose companies worked well and did effective work in keeping the fire from spreading but it gained such headway that it was impossible to save the building, which is completely ruined though walls and roof are still standing. Dr. Hofste went to Sitka several weeks ago and Mrs. Hofste joined him there on the last steamer, and during their absence the house has been closed. From the appearance of the fire there is but little doubt that it originated from the stove or pipe, as when first discovered the flames were pouring out of the terra cotta chimney. It is supposed that some one must have started a fire in the house for the purpose of drying it out and preventing dampness, and that the fire started in this way.

Nothing was saved and Dr. and Mrs. Hofste lost all their clothing and household effects. The building and most of the furniture was the property of J. Montgomery Davis, whose loss will be about $900.00.

———

1895: February 7

Deed recorded in Chehalis County, Washington, dated January 16, 1895, from R. D. Nevius, of Blaine, Washington, to The Trustees of the Protestant Episcopal Church in Washington Territory (now State), a corporation of Tacoma, conveying Lot 1, Block 9, Fleet's Addition to the City of Montesano, Chehalis County, Washington.

———

1895: mid-February

Rev. Mark Jukes

Washington Churchman, April 1895:

"New Whatcom, Wash., April 14, 1895.

..."Shortly before the middle of February we had the pleasure of welcoming the clergy of Skagit, San Juan, and Whatcom counties. The opening Sermon was preached by Dr. Nevius."

———

1895: April

Prob. Rev. R. D. Nevius, D.D.

Washington Churchman, April 1895:

"Christ Church, Blaine.

"The Lenten season began with daily services and sermons in which the Missionary was aided, for the first week, by Rev. Mark Jukes of Whatcom, who preached at every service and it is believed greatly to edification.

"Daily evening prayer with a short sermon followed until Holy Week when early celebration except on Good Friday and Easter even, and evening service with sermon brought us to a happy Easter. Easter offerings in the church and in the Sunday school amounted to $17.72. Baptisms on Easter even, 4 (one adult,) previously in Lent, 2 adults."

———

1895: April 23

Rev. L. W. Applegate

Washington Churchman, May 1895:

"Grays Harbor Missions.

"The following letter from the Rev. L. W. Applegate was received too late for publication in our April issue.... We are glad to see that the good work done by the Rev. Dr. Nevius and the Rev. J. H. Forrest-Bell is not to be lose....

"Hoquiam, Wash., April 23, 1895. "

"Rev. Geo. H. Watson, D.D.

"*My Dear Brother*.... The new church in Aberdeen is completed, and is a gem, and is to be consecrated May 5th. This has given the Aberdeen people new courage.... In Montesano we have moved three times into larger quarters, and Mr. Oxnam has done an excellent work there. A new church, for which they have raised nearly enough money already, will be begun within the next two weeks. ... The church at Ocosta has been completed very tastily, and the whole town is proud of it. At Elma we are buying the Baptist church, and shall fix it up as soon as the deeds are deliv-

ered. At Hoquiam the chapel has been changed to a larger store building in the hospital property, and has been nicely fitted up for services, and pews provided."

———

1895: May 13 (Saturday)

Alaska Searchlight, Juneau, p. 7

Mr. and Mrs. J. Montgomery Davis have generously offered to donate to the Episcopal board of missions, New York city, for building a church the lot on Sixth street where the cottage occupied by Dr. Hofste was burned last January. The site is a very good one and it is hoped that Juneau may soon have a new church.

———

1895: June 8 (Saturday)

Alaska Searchlight, Juneau

Sunday Services (p. 7)

Episcopalian—Rev. George Buzelle, Log Cabin church, 11 a.m. Morning prayer, sermon and Holy Communion. Court house, 8 p.m., evening service and sermon.

Local Rays (p. 8)

Rev. George Busselle will hold services at the Log Cabin church Sunday forenoon at 11 o'clock; at the Court house Sunday evening at 8 o'clock, and at the Treadwell boarding house in Douglas island at 8 o'clock Monday evening.

Local Rays (p. 8)

The steamer Willapa arrived from Sound ports last Monday night having made the trip in less than five days. It brought 250 tons of freight for Juneau. The cabin passengers were: N. L. Osborne, W. F. Morley, Miss Louise Evans, Rev. Geo. Buzzelle, P. J. Moran, G. P. Runmeolin, W. F. Woodward, John Salbur, Geo. Cox, W. P. Warnsle, Geo. Fillhouer, E. Maystron, D. Matheson, Wm. Essener, R. K Hooer. Eleven steerage.

Local Rays (p. 10)

Rev. George Buzzelle, an Episcopalian clergyman of Tacoma, arrived on the Willapa. Mr. Buzzelle will visit Sitka on the next Topeka and return home on the same steamer.

———

1895: June 15 (Saturday)

Alaska Searchlight, Juneau

Local Rays (p. 6)

Last Sunday the services held at the Log Cabin church and at the court house by Rev. George Buzzelle, were largely attended. Mr. Buzzelle is an eloquent preacher who is thoroughly conversant with western life. He expressed much gratification at the reception he had met with in Alaska and said that he felt sure some steps would soon be taken to organize an Episcopal church here. After the evening services many remained to talk over the plan of organizing a society and all seemed to favor it. Monday evening services were held at the Treadwell boarding house and Tuesday evening at Kane's hall in Douglas city.

———

1895: June 21 (Saturday)

Alaska Searchlight, Juneau

Births (p. 6)

Thursday, June 27, to Mr. and Mrs. J. Montgomery Davis, a daughter.

1895: June 26, 27

Journal, Jurisdiction of Olympia, 1895:

Convocation met at St. Mark's Church, Seattle on June 26 and Trinity Church, June 27. Nevius is listed as resident at Christ Church, Blaine, as one of four Examining Chaplains and one of five Trustees of the Church Charity Association. He was present at Convocation (see below). At opening session he was appointed to a committee of two on credentials of lay delegates.

———

1895: June 27 (Thursday)

Bishop Barker's Address:

In his annual Convocation address Bishop Barker noted that he had spent September and October 1894 in western Colorado, and that the Presiding Bishop had "found it impossible to obtain a Meeting of the House of Bishops in June, 1894, to take action on the vacancy caused by the death of Bishop Paddock and the

Meeting was summoned for October 17 in New York at the Church Mission House." He noted his plans to go East from January to April 1895 "for the purpose of securing additional funds for maintaining our work." "Western Colorado was placed in my charge by a Commission from the Presiding Bishop until Easter Monday, April 15, 1895, when it passed by a similar Commission to Bishop Leonard of Nevada and Utah.... I shall never forget my experience in that most interesting country, with its mining camps, its agricultural towns on the various irrigating ditches, its 'cattle country' with the haze of the Utah mountains in the distance, the peaks and pinnacles and cathedral-like spires of the rockies behind and about us and the glorious unclouded blue above us.... The general Railroad strike prevented my going to Western Colorado for July and August [1894, from Portland] to fill visitation appointments there. ... I then started [after September 5, 1894] for Western Colorado to make a complete visitation there. From Western Colorado I went to Boston to conduct a 'Quiet Day' in Emmanuel Church, October 15, for the Massachusetts Branch of the Woman's Auxiliary. I was in New York at the time of the Meeting of the House of Bishops, October 17 and 18 [1894]" Barker was in Portland November 4 and Tacoma by November 18. He visited Blaine the evening of December 14, "confirmed 2 and preached."

Barker was in Ocosta May 3, 1895 and in Aberdeen Sunday, May 5. "Aberdeen, 11 a.m., consecrated the new St. Andrew's Church, one of the most beautiful Churches in the West." Elaborating, May 5 [1895] I consecrated the beautiful new St. Andrew's Church, Aberdeen. Long ago an effort was made to secure funds for this Church, but the actual building was given up for a time. Many gifts were made, old resources turned into cash and a down-town site procured and there was built what is today the best of our Mission Churches. Dignified, simple, substantial, it is an honor to the Church and to the city. Three native woods are used in the interior; fir for the wainscoting, cedar for the walls, and then a frieze of two feet in width of spruce. The roof timbers show and the entire finish is in wood.

"The Ocosta Church, begun long ago under the charge of Rev. Dr. Nevius, has been completed. Here the interior is ceiled or lined with native cedar shingles, the exposed surface of each shingle being planed and varnished. The effect when the lamps are lit is most beautiful, as each shingle reflects back in many gleams of light."

"Southern Alaska has come to the front lately from a commercial point of view. People are going there in large numbers to make homes or establish themselves in business. The General Board of Missions, desiring full information of the life in this far-away and yet near country and of the immediate needs and possibilities of Church work, requested me to send some clergymen there to make a full report to them in writing. Rev. Mr. Buzzelle started at once at my invitation has just returned from his trip and his interesting statement will soon be sent to New York."

"I am convinced, after a careful examination of the work, that a better plan than the deanery system [inaugurated in 1884 and enlarged in 1891] can be put into action. I do not think that it is wise for us to employ machinery, titles, organizations or unnecessary complicated methods in carrying on simple work. It is impossible for us to have a deanery system that is of any binding force on any one in a Missionary Jurisdiction, for a Missionary Jurisdiction is not empowered to formulate law. I therefore recommend that a resolution be offered which shall do away with a piece of machinery which the present bishop does not feel the need of and which is of no binding force on anyone connected with the Jurisdiction. With the growth of the work, the Bishop will probably, within a year or two, need to appoint a General Missionary to aid him in the duty of caring for and directing all Mission work done in the Jurisdiction."

Barker also recommended that and illustrated quarterly be published in lieu of the monthly *Washington Churchman*, and that the Jurisdiction be named "Western Washington" rather than "Olympia."

***

Convocation resolved upon publication of the quarterly paper. "On motion of the Rev. Dr. Nevius it was resolved that the Bishop, in case a satisfactory apportionment of the funds between the Jurisdictions of Spokane and Olympia be not made before August 1st, 1895, associate with himself two clerical or lay assessors to act with a like committee of the Jurisdiction of Spokane for that purpose and report to the next Convocation.

"On motion of Rev. Dr. Babbitt it was resolved that on or before August 1st, 1895, the system of the Jurisdiction of Olympia know and described as the 'deanery system' be abolished in all its features and traces from the said Jurisdiction, the same being done in accordance with the suggestion made by the Bishop in his address to the convocation of 1895."

"On motion of Rev. Dr. Nevius it was resolved that this Convocation values highly the opportunity of attending the meeting of the Woman's Auxiliary of Olympia on the first day of its meeting [Wednesday, June 26, 1895] and to catch something of the enthusiasm of that splendid organization, which it is glad to recognize as the better half of the body corporate of the Church of this Jurisdiction.

——

1895: August 3 (Saturday)
Alaska Searchlight, Juneau

Rev. George Buzzelle, of Tacoma, the first clergyman to hold Episcopalian services in this part of Alaska, has not forgotten his promises to do all he could toward securing the organization of a church in Juneau. In a letter to Judge Bugbee received by the last mail he writes that Bishop Barker will undoubtedly send a minister here temporarily by the next steamer, a man of much learning and intelligence and an old-timer in the missionary field. Mr. Buzzelle's report on Alaska accompanied by a warm letter from the bishop recommending its adoption has been forwarded to the New York Board of Missions but no action can be taken on it at present as this board is not in session during the warm weather and will not meet until the latter part of next month.

——

1895: August 24
Alaska Searchlight, Juneau
Local Rays (p. 7)

The ladies of the Episcopal church guild wish to announce that they will give a social on Tuesday evening next at 8 o'clock in the court house. The public are cordially invited to attend. An extensive assortment of aprons for ladies and children will be offered for sale. Admission, including refreshments, fifty cents.

——

1895: August 31 (Saturday)
Alaska Searchlight, Juneau
Local Rays (p. 4)

The sociable given by the ladies guild of the Episcopal church at the courthouse last Tuesday evening proved a very pleasant affair in spite of the weather. The principal feature of the evening's entertainment was the music furnished by a quartet composed of Mrs. H. W. Mellen, Mrs. W. B. Hoggatt, Edward Haley and A. W. Corbus, two playing guitars and two banjos. The sale of some very pretty aprons materially increased the receipts, which netted $65 for the building fund. After refreshments were served, the dancers enjoyed themselves until midnight brought an end to what we trust is the beginning of a series of delightful entertainments.

——

1895: January-October:

The issues of the *Washington Churchman* through October 1895 give Nevius's address as Blaine, Washington. The *Churchman* seems to have been issued late in the month because it often contains items with dates through the middle of the month.

- Juneau, Alaska -
1895: September 7 (Saturday)
Alaska Searchlight, Juneau
Episcopal Church (p. 5)

A meeting of the members and friends of the Protestant Episcopal church in the United States of America, will be called for 2 p.m. at the Log Cabin church on Monday next to organize a mission [Quoad parish], by the nomination for appointment by the bishop, of a warden, a secretary, and a treasurer, for the year. At the same time a financial committee will be elected to solicit funds for the building of a church. All persons interested are earnestly requested to attend this important meeting. Notice of services next Sunday in another column.

Church Services (p. 6)

Episcopal church Rev. Dr. Nevius, rector. Services every Sunday at 11 a.m. in the Log Cabin church, and at 7:30 p.m. in the mission chapel.

Local Rays (p. 8)

Rev. Dr. Nevius has come to the city under special commission of Bishop Barker of the diocese of Olympia, to open and take charge of a mission of the Episcopal church in this place. Services will be held in the Log Cabin church at 11 a.m. next Sunday and in the court house at 8 p.m. Appointments for the future in Juneau and on Douglas island will be made at the time of the meetings announced above.

——

1895: September 21 (Saturday)

Alaska Searchlight, Juneau

Local Rays (p. 4)

The ladies' guild of the Episcopal church gave a most enjoyable social at the court house last Wednesday evening. There was a good attendance present all of whom had a pleasant time. Dancing was the chief feature of the evening's entertainment. The net receipts were $23.50, which amount will be expended in the purchase of material for making useful and fancy articles for a fair, which will be held during Christmas holidays.

Church Services (p. 5)

Episcopal Church. Dr. Nevius, rector—Services every Sunday at 11 a.m. in the Log Cabin church, and at 7:30 p.m. in the Mission chapel.

Local Rays (p. 8)

A meeting to take into consideration proposals for site, plans and building of an Episcopal church and for the maintenance of its services, will be held next Monday evening at the Log Cabin church.

——

1895: September 28

Alaska Searchlight, Juneau

At a meeting held at the Log Cabin church last Monday evening to take into consideration proposals for sites and plans for building an Episcopal church here it was decided to erect a church building as soon as funds could be raised for that purpose. Mr. and Mrs. J. Montgomery Davis' generous offer of the lot on Sixth street where the dwelling occupied by Dr. Hofste was burned last winter was discussed. This site is an excellent one but some thought it would be better to purchase a lot nearer the center of town. The vote resulted in a decision to purchase a down-town lot if a suitable one could be obtained at a reasonable figure. The matter of raising subscriptions was left to the finance committee. If our citizens give liberally Juneau will have a church to be proud of. (p. 4)

Church Services (p. 5)

Episcopal church. Rev. Dr. Nevius, rector—Services every Sunday at 11 a.m. in the Log Cabin church, and at 7:30 p.m. in the Mission chapel.

——

1895: October 5

Alaska Searchlight, Juneau

Local Rays (p. 4)

The finance committee of Trinity church are meeting with good success in their laudable efforts to raise money for the erection of a church building here. Over $900 has already been subscribed and there are several persons yet to be seen who will doubtless contribute liberally. The plans of the building show a very neat and pleasing structure which can be erected for a modest sum of $1200. It was voted to buy a lot downtown but this matter will be reconsidered when the finance committee makes their report and the church will doubtless be built upon the Sixth street lot which Mr. and Mrs. J. Montgomery Davis have so kindly offered to donate.

Local Rays (p. 4)

Another of the pleasant socials of the Episcopal church guild occurred at the court house on Tuesday evening last and was very well attended; considering the inclement weather. About 9 o'clock the guest began to arrive and at 10 o'clock the room was well filled with Juneau's best people, all eager for the enjoyment that always attends these receptions. The Music was furnished by G. W. Creese and Mrs. Wm. Huson, with Mr. Mathew, of Portland, as prompter. All enjoyed themselves to the full limit. The receipts of the evening were $25. Refreshments were served at

12 o'clock after which the dancing continued and it was 2 o'clock when the orchestra played "Home Sweet Home." It is probable that another reception will be given in the near future.

Local Rays (p. 5)

The success of the lunch served at the Trinity church social Tuesday night is largely due to the skill of Mrs. M. B. Archer, of Douglas.

Local Rays (p. 5)

The ladies' guild of Trinity church will hold a bazaar the last of November or in December for the purpose of raising money for the building fund. The new hall which is to be built at the People's wharf has been engaged for it. The ladies are hard at work and with the assistance of our townspeople will make it a great success.

Church Services (p. 6)

Trinity church, Rev. Dr. Nevius, rector—Sunday at 11 a.m. in the Log Cabin church, and at 7:30 p.m. in the Mission chapel. Early celebration 8 a.m. at Log Cabin church except on the first Sunday in the month, when it will be at 11 o'clock service.

Episcopal church service at Douglas island on Tuesday night, in Bear's Nest hall, at 7:30 o'clock. R. D. Nevius missionary in charge.

Local Rays (p. 7)

The coming social events—Trinity church bazaar and Hose Co. No. 2 dance—Don't miss either of them.

——

1895: October 19, 1895 (Saturday)

Alaska Searchlight, Juneau

Church Services (p. 6)

Trinity church, Rev. Dr. Nevius, rector—Sunday at 11 a.m. in the Log Cabin church, and at 7:30 p.m. in the Mission chapel. Early celebration 8 a.m. at Log Cabin church except on the first Sunday in the month, when it will be at the 11 o'clock service.

Episcopal church service at Douglas island on Tuesday night, in Bear's Nest hall, at 7:30 o'clock. R. D. Nevius missionary in charge.

The ladies' guild of Trinity church will give another of their enjoyable socials at the court house next Wednesday evening which the public are cordially invited to attend. Besides a pleasant social and a fine supper there will be good music in attendance and allow all who delight in dancing will have ample opportunity to indulge in this favorite pastime. Tickets for gentleman and lady, including supper, only $1.25.

——

1895: October 26 (Saturday)

Alaska Searchlight, Juneau

Local Rays (p. 5)

The ladies' guild of Trinity church gave an enjoyable social at the court house last Wednesday evening. The attendance was not large owing to the wind and rain, which seems to be the fated accompaniment of every entertainment the ladies assay, but all who braved the elements report a very pleasant time. The music and dancing were the chief features of the evening. The lunch was most delicately prepared and daintily served. About forty persons were in attendance and the receipts some $20.00.

Local Rays (p. 6)

The building fund of Trinity church has not been growing very rapidly of late. The finance committee meet to-night at Dr. Bentley's office.

Church Services (p. 6)

Trinity church, Rev. Dr. Nevius, rector — Sunday at 11 a.m. in the Log Cabin church, and at 7:30 p.m. in the Mission chapel. Early celebration 8 a.m. at Log Cabin church except on the first Sunday in the month, when it will be at the 11 o'clock service.

Episcopal church service at Douglas island on Tuesday night, in Bear's Nest hall, at 7:30 o'clock. R. D. Nevius missionary in charge.

Local Rays (p. 8)

The bazaar to be given by the ladies' guild will be opened the week before Christmas in the new hall at the People's wharf. The ladies' guild of Trinity church meets every Friday evening, with Mrs. S. D. Wallace at her residence on Harrison and Fifth streets.

1895: November

The November 1895 issue of the *Washington Churchman* gives Nevius's address as Juneau, Alaska. This address continues through the April 1896 issue.

1895: November 2 (Saturday)
Church Services (p. 5)

Trinity church, Rev. R. D. Nevius, rector—Sunday at 11 a.m. in the Log Cabin church, and at 7:30 p.m. in the Mission chapel. Early celebration 8 a.m. at Log Cabin church except on the first Sunday in the month, when it will be at the 11 o'clock service.

Episcopal church service at Douglas island on Tuesday night, in Bear's Nest hall, at 7:30 o'clock. R. D. Nevius missionary in charge.

Local Rays (p. 7)

Trinity church society has purchased a lot on Gold street opposite the residence of Karl Koehler from the heirs of the Reed estate for $375. As soon as the sale has been confirmed the erection of a church building will be begun. The location is a good one and will doubtless prove satisfactory to all.

1895: November 9 (Saturday)
Alaska Searchlight, Juneau
To the Public (p. 4)

The ladies' guild of Trinity church will hold a bazaar on Wednesday and Thursday evenings, December 4 and 5, at the new hall at the People's wharf, for the purpose of raising money for the building fund. All are cordially invited to attend and to contribute liberally as possible toward this laudable undertaking. Donations of every kind of useful or fancy articles for sale will be very gladly received. They can be sent to any member of the guild at any time. Gifts from any of our storekeepers will be greatly appreciated. They will be disposed of by lot and care will be taken to make each of these a valuable advertisement for the donor. Articles for decorating the hall and refreshments for the tables will prove most welcome. Out of your abundance give liberally and help along this good work.

Committee

Church Services (p. 6)

Trinity church, Rev. Dr. Nevius, rector—Sunday at 11 a.m. in the Log Cabin church, and at 7:30 p.m. in the Mission chapel. Early celebration 8 a.m. at Log Cabin church except on the first Sunday in the month, when it will be at the 11 o'clock service.

Episcopal church service at Douglas island on Tuesday night, in Bear's Nest hall, at 7:30 o'clock. R. D. Nevius missionary in charge.

Local Rays (p. 8)

The executors of the estate of W. F. Reed filed their final account in the probate court, Tuesday, and a decree was made setting apart the property to Mrs. Mary F. Redmond, of Franklin, Tenn., a sister of the deceased.

Local Rays (p. 8)

Judge Bugbee is making several handsome little sketches for the bazaar to be held by the ladies' guild.

1895: November 23 (Saturday)
Alaska Searchlight, Juneau

The fair to be given by the ladies' guild of Trinity Church will open in the new hall on the People's wharf next Wednesday afternoon and continue until Thursday evening. This will be a fine opportunity to buy souvenirs to send away to your friends for Christmas presents. Everyone should attend and assist the ladies in this laudable enterprise. The proceeds of the fair will go to furnish the new church to be built on Gold street. (p. 3)

Local Rays (p. 5)

Do not fail to attend the fair given by the ladies' guild of Trinity church, December 4 and 5, in the new hall on the People's wharf.

Church Services (p. 8)

Trinity church, Rev. Dr. Nevius, rector—Sunday at 11 a.m. in the Log Cabin

church, and at 7:30 p.m. in the Mission chapel. Early celebration 8 a.m. at Log Cabin church except on the first Sunday in the month, when it will be at the 11 o'clock service.

Episcopal church service at Douglas island on Tuesday night, in Bear's Nest hall, at 7:30 o'clock. R. D. Nevius missionary in charge.

1895: December 7 (Saturday)
Alaska Searchlight, Juneau
Local Rays (p. 8)

The ladies' guild of the Trinity church opened their bazaar last evening at the new hall on the People's wharf. The decorations were very handsome and a large variety of useful and beautiful articles were offered for sale in tasteful booths. Dancing commenced shortly after ten o'clock. The attendance was large and every one expressed pleased surprise at the brilliant success of the affair. The ladies deserve great praise. Everyone should attend this evening. It is the only proper thing to do.

1895: December 14, 1895 (Saturday)
Alaska Searchlight, Juneau
Bazaar a Success (p. 8)

The bazaar given by the ladies' guild of Trinity Church closed last Saturday evening and the ladies scored a signal success. Skillful hands transformed the hall into a bower of beauty. Prettily decorated booths were arranged around the hall, where works of art, needle work, confections and refreshments were offered for sale. The art booth was perhaps most generally admired; here were pretty pictures in oil and water colors besides a choice collection of Alaskan photos. Mrs. J. P. Whitney and Mrs. H. W. Mellen were in charge and proved themselves Capable salesladies. The booth containing fancy needle work was another chief attraction and Mesdames C. D. Taylor and J. J. Rutledge found many purchasers among the admiring throng. Some of the needle work was exquisitely done. Mrs. A. C. Van Doran assisted by Miss Fitzgerald presided over the fish pond where some of the prizes captured caused no small amount of merriment. Mrs. R. I. Bently and Mrs. John Timmins offered many useful articles to tempt that class of buyers who always want to be sure they are getting value received when they spend their money. Besides usefulness their comforters, laundry-bags, aprons and sofa pillows were very handsome. Miss Mary Ebersole presided over the booth where a large assortment of French candies proved too tempting for most people to resist. Mrs. John McLoughlin sold the toys and pretty little Christmas gifts for the little folks. Mrs. S. C. Leonhardt in the charmingly quaint costume of Japan served tea in prettily decorated cups. The many attractive wares in the Japanese booth and its bright decorations made it one of the features of the fair. The refreshment tables, loaded with delicacies and some of the more substantial articles of food were in charge of a skilled caterer, Mrs. M. B. Archer, who served her patrons with the finest of coffee and real cream. The drawing of the prizes resulted as follows: Silk crazy quilt—Judge Bugbee; Mount Shasta, an oil painting by Mrs. J. Montgomery Davis—F. C. Hammond; water color sketch by Judge Bugbee—Frank W. Young; Silk umbrella—Mrs. F. D. Nowell; Pansies, an oil painting by Mrs. J. P. Whitney—Mrs. R. I. Bentley; sofa pillow— Mrs. C. H. Pearce; Quilt—Mrs. R. I. Bentley; sofa pillow—Mrs. Yager; gold ring set with opal and rubies—Fred D. Nowell; doily—Mrs. McGlew; lamp shade— R. J. Hiltz.

There was dancing both evenings which was heartily enjoyed by many of those present. The attendance was large, proving the public interest taken in the work. The receipts were nearly $400 and after paying all expenses some $280 remain in the treasury which will be expended in furnishing the new church. Besides the money derived from the sale of articles donated, the ladies realized $2 from the phonograph, and $15 from the kinetoscope, this sum being one half the receipts of the first evening and all of those of the second; $5 from Y. Kawakami, which was more than twenty per cent of the sales of the Japanese Bazaar, while Winter & Pond generously donated the entire amount received from the sale of the photos. These were the only concessions granted and they paid well.

Local Rays (p. 9)

Work on Trinity church will soon commence and the building is expected to be ready for occupancy about March 1.

Local Rays (p. 9)

Rev. Dr. Nevius is arranging a Christmas entertainment for the young people of the Episcopal and Presbyterian churches. Magic lantern pictures illustrating the birth and life of the Savior will be the principal feature.

Local Rays (p. 10)

The consecration of Alaska's new bishop, Rt. Rev. Peter Trimble Rowe, took place at St. George's church, New York city, November 30. The occasion was one long to be remembered. There was scarcely standing room when Bishop Doane of Albany, consecrator, assisted by Bishop Potter, of New York, and Bishop Davies, of Michigan, began the services. The following Bishops were present: Starkey of Newark, Walker of North Dakota, Whittaker, of Pennsylvania, Brooke of Oklahoma, Leonard of Nevada, Brewer of Montana, and Wells of Spokane.

Church Services (p. 10)

Trinity church, Rev. Dr. Nevius, rector— Sunday at 11 a.m. in the Log Cabin church, and at 7:30 p.m. in the Mission chapel. Early celebration 8 a.m. at Log Cabin church except on the first Sunday in the month, when it will be at 11 o'clock service.

Episcopal church service at Douglas island on Tuesday night, in Bear's Nest hall, at 7:30 o'clock. R. D. Nevius missionary in charge.

———

1895: December 21 (Saturday)

Alaska Searchlight, Juneau

To the people of Alaska Christmas brings joyous festivities the same as to those resident in more populous parts of our country. Our people feel the sweet solemnity of the season as do those who dwell neath the sacred shadows of taller spires. Our children hail the coming of Santa Claus with just the same enthusiasm as does merry childhood in the happiest homes in Christendom. The services and festivals of the week here will be as follows: Trinity church, Episcopalian, Rev. Dr. Nevius pastor. Christmas day, early celebration 9 a.m. Morning service, sermon and celebration at 11 a.m.; Log Cabin Church.

Christmas eve, 8 p.m. the children of Trinity church and the members of the Presbyterian Sunday school will have a combined carol service at the Presbyterian mission church. The story of the Nativity will be presented in pictures, song and story. The festival is given for the children and the teachers of the Sunday school. Every child in town who cares to come will be welcome and each will receive a token of the thoughtfulness of the ladies who have it in charge.

———

1895: December 28 (Saturday)

Alaska Searchlight, Juneau

Christmas Festivities (p. 20)

Trinity Church.

The entertainment given on Christmas eve for the children of the Episcopal and Presbyterian churches drew a large audience. The story of the Nativity in picture, story and song was full of interest to all. The stereopticon worked well and the slides were works of art. Rev. Dr. Nevius explained the pictures and his explanations were interspersed with appropriate songs. At the close of the entertainment all received bags of candy, nuts and fruit.

Church Services (p. 20)

Trinity church, Rev. Dr. Nevius, rector—Sunday at 11 a.m. in the Log Cabin church, and at 7:30 p.m. in the Mission chapel. Early celebration 8 a.m. at Log Cabin church except on the first Sunday in the month, when it will be at the 11 o'clock service.

Episcopal church service at Douglas island on Tuesday night, in Bear's Nest hall, at 7:30 o'clock. R. D. Nevius missionary in charge.

[1896]

1896: January 4
Utah became the 45th state.

1896: January 11 (Saturday)

Alaska Searchlight, Juneau

Local Rays (p. 12)

Rev. Dr. Nevius has so far recovered from his recent illness as to be able to hold services again to-morrow.

———

1896: January 18

Alaska Searchlight, Juneau

Church Services (p. 8)

Trinity church, Rev. Dr. Nevius, rector—Sunday at 11 a.m. in the Log Cabin church, and at 7:30 p.m. in the Mission chapel. Early celebration 8 a.m. at Log Cabin church except on the first Sunday in the month, when it will be at the 11 o'clock service.

Alaska's First Episcopal Bishop (p. 9)

The Rev. Peter Trimble Rowe, M.A., missionary bishop-elect of Alaska, was born in Toronto, Canada, November 20, 1856. His collegiate education was pursued at Trinity university, Toronto, from which source he received the degree of G.A. in 1878, and M.A. in 1880; both in course. Was ordained deacon November 3rd, 1878, and priest November 14th, 1880, both by the Rt. Rev. F. D. Fauquier, D.D., D. C. L., bishop of Algoma. He was stationed after his ordination, among the Ojibeway Indians at Garden River, Ontario, in the diocese of Algoma, then almost the frontier and had charge of the Indian and white missions along the north shore of Lake Huron, including the islands of St. Joseph and Cockburn. On June 1, 1881, he married Lora H. Carry, daughter of the late Rev. Dr. John Carry. He was received into the American church by Bishop Harris of Michigan, in July, 1882, and placed in charge of the mission of St. James, Sault Ste. Marie and of other missionary work in Chippewa county, and has since continued at the same port. At the time of his election to the episcopate he was a member of the Standing Committee of the Missionary District of Northern Michigan, and also an Examining Chaplain. Was elected Missionary Bishop of Alaska by the General Convention of 1895. His consecration took place in St. George's Church, New York City, on St. Andrew's Day, November 20, 1895. Mr. Rowe will be the first Bishop of this communion in Alaska, a former election by the House of Bishops having proved invalid by a technicality.

Rev. Mr. Beer of Redwing, Minn., has been selected as rector of Trinity church and will arrive here with Bishop Rowe.

———

1896: January 25 (Saturday)

Alaska Searchlight, Juneau

Church Services (p. 9)

Trinity church, Rev. Dr. Nevius, rector—Sunday at 11 a.m. in the Log Cabin church, and at 7:30 p.m. in the Mission chapel. Early celebration 8 a.m. at Log Cabin church except on the first Sunday in the month, when it will be at the 11 o'clock service.

Local Rays (p. 11)

The Episcopal diocese of Alaska of which Rt. Rev. P. T. Rowe has been elected missionary bishop comprises the following churches: Juneau, Trinity church, Rev. R. D. Nevius, soon to be succeeded by Rev. Henry Beers; Anvik, mission in charge of Rev. John W. Chapman, 4 infant baptisms, 3 marriages and 36 pupils reported for 1895; Fort Adams mission, Rev. J. L. Prevost, 1284 baptized members and 50 communicants; Point Hope mission, E. H. Edson, 84 pupils.

———

1896: February 1 (Saturday)

Alaska Searchlight, Juneau

Church Services (p. 8)

Trinity church, Rev. Dr. Nevius, rector—Sunday at 11 a.m. in the Log Cabin church, and at 7:30 p.m. in the Mission chapel. Early celebration 8 a.m. at Log Cabin church except on the first Sunday in the month, when it will be at the 11 o'clock service.

Rev. Dr. Nevius Lecture (p. 11)

Last Monday night Dr. Nevius delivered at the Presbyterian church, under the auspices of the Midwinter club, a most interesting lecture entitled "Observations in Japan and China." The audience was large and appreciative and the evening a most enjoyable one. The reverend gentleman's remarks were based upon his personal observations of the countries referred to, made during a recent tour, and were illustrated by lantern slides exhibiting various scenes of interest which were commented upon and explained in pleasant conversational style that encharmed the interest of the audience to the very close. Many of our citizens, by reason of business engagements attending the departure of the mail steamer, were prevented from attending the entertainment, and a general desire has been expressed that the lecture be repeated. In response to a written request the lecturer has consented to deliver other and different observations illustrated in a similar manner at the same place on Monday evening next.

Dr. Nevius during his five months stay in Juneau has made many warm friends outside his parish, and as the period for which he was appointed to this mission has expired, undoubtedly many people will avail themselves of this privilege of seeing and hearing the refined and scholarly gentleman. There is an especial fitness in making this coming entertainment a somewhat substantial testimonial of the regard of our people and with this end in view the gentlemen who have the management of it have wisely fixed upon a moderate charge for admission and placed tickets upon sale at the various prominent stores of the town. We need not say that we trust that as Juneau is lacking in intellectual pleasures our people may not miss the opportunity now offered to enjoy one of such high character and to attest their appreciation of whatever is refining and instructive as well as entertaining.

Local Rays (p. 12)

Sunday afternoon a fire started in the Log Cabin church and had it not been for its timely discovery the building would soon have been in ashes. Some wood piled close to the red hot stove fell over upon it and quickly ignited. Fortunately it was discovered and extinguished before any damage was done.

———

1896: February 8 (Saturday)

Alaska Searchlight, Juneau

Church Services (p. 9)

Trinity church, Rev. Dr. Nevius, rector—Sunday at 11 a.m. in the Log Cabin church, and at 7:30 p.m. in the Mission chapel. Early celebration 8 a.m. at Log Cabin church except on the first Sunday in the month, when it will be at the 11 o'clock service.

Local Rays (p. 10)

Rev. R. D. Nevius may be sent to Sitka to organize a mission of the Episcopal church there. Dr. Nevius has a grand record as a missionary and has been instrumental in the founding of many missions on the Pacific coast. He has made many warm friends in Juneau who earnestly hope that he will remain in Alaska.

———

1896: February 15 (Saturday)

Alaska Searchlight, Juneau

Church Services (p. 8)

Trinity church, Rev. Dr. Nevius, rector—Sunday at 11 a.m. in the Log Cabin church, and at 7:30 p.m. in the Mission chapel. Early celebration 8 a.m. at Log Cabin church except on the first Sunday in the month, when it will be at the 11 o'clock service.

———

1896: February 22 (Saturday)

Alaska Searchlight, Juneau

Church Services (p. 8)

Trinity church, Rev. Dr. Nevius, rector—Sunday at 11 a.m. in the Log Cabin church, and at 7:30 p.m. in the Mission chapel. Early celebration 8 a.m. at Log Cabin church except on the first Sunday in the month, when it will be at the 11 o'clock service.

Local Rays (p. 12)

During Lent services will be held at the Log Cabin church every morning at 11 o'clock, conducted by Rev. Dr. Nevius until the arrival of Bishop Rowe, when other arrangements will probably be made.

———

1896: February 29 (Saturday)

Alaska Searchlight, Juneau

Church Services (p. 9)

Trinity church, Rev. Dr. Nevius, rector—Sunday at 11 a.m. in the Log Cabin church, and at 7:30 p.m. in the Mission chapel. Early celebration 8 a.m. at Log Cabin church except on the first Sunday in the month, when it will be at the 11 o'clock service.

———

1896: March 7 (Saturday)

Alaska Searchlight, Juneau

Church Services (p. 8)

Trinity church, Rev. Dr. Nevius, rector—Sunday at 11 a.m.. in the Log Cabin church, and at 7:30 p.m. in the Mission chapel. Early celebration 8 a.m. at Log Cabin church except on the first Sunday in the month, when it will be at the 11 o'clock service.

———

1896: March 21 (Saturday)

Church Services (p. 8)

Trinity church, Rev. Dr. Nevius, rector—Sunday at 11 a.m. in the Log Cabin church, and at 7:30 p.m. in the Mission chapel. Early celebration 8 a.m. at Log Cabin church except on the first Sunday in the month, when it will be at the 11 o'clock service.

———

1896: March-April

Washington Churchman, April 1896:

"The Alaska Mission.

"The following clipping is from *Boston Ideas:*

"Mr. C. D. Emmons left Port Townsend, Wash. March 28, on the steamer Alki, to join Rt. Rev. Peter Trimble Rowe as assistant on his trip from Juneau, Alaska, over the mountain ranges at Dyea to the headwaters of the Yukon. They will build their own boat, saw their own lumber, and afterward row 2600 miles to reach the Yukon's mouth, landing at St. Michael's then taking a steamer of the Alaska Commercial company's line to Ounalaska. Thence they will proceed to Cook's Inlet, where they will remain six weeks, then going on to Sitka, where the Bishop will establish his headquarters, being the first Episcopal Bishop assigned permanently to the new territory. Mr. Emmons has had six years' experience in these northern regions, and will make the Bishop a most able assistant. We are informed that the residents of Washington Territory and vicinity are Alaska—crazy, and that thousands leave for there every week."

"The Mr. Emmons referred to is a Seattle churchman, and will, doubtless, make the Bishop a pleasant companion on the Yukon trip. We would suggest to our contemporary at 'The Hub' that Washington has been a State for some years.

"In a late letter form Bishop Rowe, he refers to the collie dog 'Fosco,' presented to him by Mrs. Griffin, of Trinity Parish, Seattle.

"A strong friendship has sprung up between the Bishop and his dog, which will doubtless be fully cemented during the long journey to the Yukon.

"After partaking of Seattle dainties, 'Fosco' seemed to have a little trouble with the Juneau bill of fare. Possibly the charge of $1 a meal was too much for him. But the bishop was of the opinion that before he was through with the 4000-mile trip he would probably be ready to eat almost anything.

"Meanwhile we wish the prelate, Mr. Emmons, and 'Fosco' good luck and a safe return to headquarters.

———

1896: March 29 (Saturday)

Local Rays (p. 1)

Bishop Rowe will preach the morning sermon at the Log Cabin church to-morrow, and Rev. Henry Beer will fill the pulpit at the Mission chapel in the evening.

Church Services (p. 8)

Trinity church, Rev. Henry Beer, rector—Sunday at 11 a.m. in the Log Cabin church, and at 7:30 p.m. in the Mission chapel. Early celebration 8 a.m. at Log Cabin church except on the first Sunday in the month, when it will be at the 11 o'clock service.

Local Rays (p. 9)

The steamer Topeka arrived in port Monday last at 7 p.m. with a full cargo of freight and the following list of passengers: F. D. Farrer, Edwin Farrer, W. A. Barrows, I. M. Turner, A. L. Maldon, Dr. H. S. Wyman, Mulberry, C. L. Watson, Sam'l Halton, Mrs. E. Graison, F. E. Smith, Mrs. R. Jacobs, H. Beer, P. S. Rowe, J. R. Wilson, C. M. Crawford, Mrs. L. Rubach, J. King, Chas. Knight, A. I. Thompson, R. W. Thompson, A. Mosier, R. S. Kinwood, W. A. Sherman, John Y. Ostrander, Geo. W. Vogel, N. T. Collet, Peter Peternoff, C. Flemming, Mrs. C. Sickman, Geo. A. Carpenter, Mrs. A. C. VanDoeren, Miss A. Brown, Mrs. Brown, Ed Burke, T. N. M. Bain and wife, J. P. Jorgenson, Ed. Decker, Henry Gelcher, A. McClain, J. D. Tackerburg, H. J. Singleton, E. Singleton, Mrs. D. O'Neil, Miss L. Cordswell, G. L. Echlin, J. A. Stewart, J. F. Keck, C. J. Pound, C. A. Renstrom, P. Black, E. T. Tunker, S. F. Horkins, E. D. Smith, Jno Silva, Joaquin Dwinis, M. Vieva, A. Williamson, H. W. Girdwood, L. F. Arthur, C. Shea, Antone Rabbett, Joe Mews, W. H. Pore, M. Fitzgerald, H. P. Morton, J. C. Berry and wife, Fred Berry, L. Grakke, E. Sweeny, P. McBeth, B. Beecher, F. Rafouny, Mrs. H. D. Townsend, Miss Coery, Geo. Miller, L. Goldie, Mrs. W. B. Clark, Mary Anderson, Dr. J. P. Sweeny, Jno Lave, J. C. Stephens, J. H. Langford, Moses Goldsmith. And 104 steerage.

An Alaskan Missionary (p. 10)

Mid-Lent Sunday was of more than usual interest, owing to the presence in the chancel of Trinity Parish church of the Rev. Henry Beer, chaplain to the bishop of Alaska.

The reverend gentleman is slightly past middle age, but of fine physique, calculated to withstand any hardships which he may be called upon to endure in the far north. He is an old-time friend of the Right Rev. Dr. Rowe, who, as soon as he was elected bishop, chose him as his chaplain and confidential secretary. After an experience of missionary work in Minnesota and North Dakota, Mr. Beer still remains as enthusiastic as ever, and seems only anxious for new fields to conquer.

After the usual morning service, the chaplain chose for his text these words from the Apostle's creed: "I believe in the communion of saints." The preacher took a practical view of his text, maintaining that a saint in the ordinary biblical acceptation, is a believer who has pledged himself to a holy cause, and has promised, therefore, to be holy, and that the word "communion" may fairly be taken to imply the communicating by one Christian of some gift which he possesses to another who has it not.

"Looked at in this light," said Mr. Beer, "the article of the creed may be regarded as asserting that we believe in missions, and that we are ready to obey the command of the Divine Master, 'Freely ye have receive, freely give.'"

The speaker referred to the opportunity now opening in Alaska for the religious fold in Seattle to care for those who are now pressing forward to the mountains and valleys of the far north in their eager search for gold.

"Men are so apt to degenerate when they get beyond the bounds of civilization," said he, "that they need a church to hold them in check. They fall by the way, too, and need the hospital to care for them in sickness, and to demonstrate the charity which is the very heart of christianity.

"We cannot all be missionaries; but, as in the late civil war, the men and women at home wept for, prayed for, worked for the 'boys in blue' at the front; so may the church have in mind those who are willing to carry the standard of the cross to the Alaskan wilderness."

In closing, the preacher, in answer to the complaint that times are hard, portrayed in eloquent language the picture of Jesus sitting over against the treasury in the temple, watching as the people made their offerings, and commending above all the others the widow who cast in but a mite.

"The sermon left a pleasant impression on the hearers, who will henceforth take a deeper personal interest in the Alaskan work since they have had the pleasure of meeting and hearing the bishop and his chaplain.— P. I. March, 16.

Local Rays (p. 11)

Bishop P. S. Rowe, accompanied by Rev. Henry Beer, arrived on the Topeka

Monday. A reception was tendered these gentlemen on Tuesday evening in the rooms of the Juneau Board of Trade, in the Ajsit block.

———

1896: April

Washington Churchman, April 1896:

"The Rev. Dr. Nevius has returned from Juneau, Alaska, and resumed work in the jurisdiction.

———

1895-1896:

Isabel McLean (1977) I-4:

"... The City of Juneau developed from the mining camp which sprang up in 1880 following the discovery of gold in the hills on both sides of Gastineau Channel. ... The remarkable Presbyterian missionary, Dr. Sheldon Jackson, assumed the post of education agent, but recognizing the impossibility of discharging his duties alone Dr. Jackson turned to the missionary board[s] of other churches for assistance. In this way an informal agreement was worked out in the hope of bringing teachers for the Natives to most of the huge areas, without overlapping the denominations. Because of the work of the missionaries of the Church of England, the Natives of the whole interior area were left to the Episcopalians.

"With missionaries already stationed in widely separated places, the Missionary District of Alaska was constituted in 1892 and a Bishop for Alaska was elected in 1895.... Peter Trimble Rowe (1856-1943), the first Bishop of Alaska, was born, educated, and ordained in Canada. He came to the United States in 1882.... Bishop Rowe headed north to his district [at the age of 40] in 1896 and continued in the field until his death in 1942.

"Arriving in Juneau aboard the steamer 'City of Topeka' in March of 1896, Bishop Rowe was accompanied by the Rev. Henry Beer from Michigan, who would stay in Juneau. ... Bishop Rowe and Mr. Beer were not totally unexpected when they arrived in Juneau. The previous year the Rev. R. D. Nevins [sic] had been sent by the Bishop of Olympia temporarily. He had gathered several families for services, organized Sunday School classes, and a ladies guild. It was these first services conducted by the Rev. Dr. Nevins [sic] in the Presbyterian log cabin church on Trinity Sunday [sic, June 9, Nevius not yet in Alaska] in 1895 which suggested the name for the new congregation.

"Bishop Rowe wrote:

The present population is about 1800 whites with some hundreds of Natives. Saloons, variety shows are very numerous and alarmingly active and seductive. Mr. Beer and I lodge together in one small room, cold and bare, and are obliged to skirmish around for meals. While for a place to do our writing, we are obliged to resort to use the small quarters 'formerly?' occupied by the Rev. Dr. Nevins [sic] and which belong to the Presbyterians. Our mission here is to the white. It is the only mission to the white population in this part of Alaska. A citizen of this place with no partiality for us or for our work said in reference to it that, 'The Episcopal Church deserves all respect for having spirit enough to undertake missionary work here among the white population.' We have 24 communicants to care for. I must say that we shall be obliged to build, and that, as soon as possible.

"Leaving Mr. Beer in Juneau, the Bishop then made his way north to visit the missions, first stopping in Sitka, where he had decided to build his residence.

"Mr. Beer set to work to build a church and rectory. Lots 8 and 9, Block 15, were purchased for $375. Contracts were let to begin work on the buildings. The trustees of the church, who contracted with builder George E. James, including R. D. Bently, J. J. Rutlege, C. D. Taylor, and Montgomery Davis. The rectory was quickly finished and Mrs. Beer arrived with the Rowe family on their way to Sitka. The new house faced Gold Street behind the church, and cost $1,400. ... There was a social at the rectory May 19, 1896, to welcome Mrs. Beer. Mr. Beer and a few volunteers then assisted Mr. James with the building of the church according to plans furnished by Bishop Rowe. Labor costs were $700. Including the materials, the total was $2,600 for the church. As there was no kiln to dry the spruce lumber commonly used, high quality fir was imported from Tacoma....

"Bishop Rowe meanwhile had landed at Dyea, hired a helper and packed over the Chilkoot Pass. He whipsawed lumber, built a boat, and made the long trip down the

Yukon to Forty Mile and to Circle. [He returned by way of St. Michael in October.]"

———

1896: April 4 (Saturday)
Alaska Searchlight, Juneau
Local Rays (p. 9)
Episcopal services will be held in the court house on Sunday morning next and the evening services will be held in the Mission church as usual.

———

1896: April 18 (Saturday)
Alaska Searchlight Juneau
Local Rays (p. 8)
Bishop P.T. Rowe, will leave in a few days for the Westward on his first annual tour of inspection of the diocese of Alaska. Bishop Rowe will be absent several months and will visit the famous Yukon country before his return.
Church Services (p. 8)
Trinity church, Rev. Henry Beer, rector—Sunday at 11 a.m. in the Log Cabin church, and at 7:30 p.m. in the Mission chapel. Early celebration 8 a.m. at Log Cabin church except on the first Sunday in the month, when it will be at the 11 o'clock service.

———

1896: April 25 (Saturday)
Alaska Searchlight, Juneau
Local Rays (p. 9)
The ladies' guild to the Episcopal church will give a dance at the court house, Thursday evening, April 30. Tickets and refreshments $1.

———

1896: May 9 (Saturday)
Alaska Searchlight, Juneau
Local Rays (p. 7)
The Episcopal rectory is now very rapidly approaching completion and will soon be quite an ornament to our city. This house is one of the best residences in Juneau, and Mr. James is to be congratulated on the style and finish of the structure. It must be remembered that this addition to our town has been built from outside money entirely, and may be looked upon as a present to Juneau. When the church, which it is proposed to build immediately, shall have been erected, the corner of Gold and Third streets will look very much better than the mud and stumps that have hitherto prevailed there.
Local Rays (p. 9)
The services of the Episcopal church on Sunday will be held in the court house instead of the Log Cabin church and Mission church as was announced. Services commence at the hours stated from the pulpit, namely 8 a.m., and 8 p.m.
Local Rays (p. 10)
The erection of the new Episcopal Church on Gold Street will begin in a few days.

———

1896: July 25 (Saturday)
Alaska Searchlight, Juneau
An Invitation (p. 8)
To The Public: —the new Episcopal Church on Gold Street, which is to be known as Holy Trinity Church, is now so far completed that it is being used for services on Sundays. Stoves, seats and other necessary articles of furniture have been put in the church, and the rector wishes the people of Juneau to bear in mind that it will be open to all every Sunday at 11 a.m. and 8 p.m. The seats are free and it is earnestly desired that worshipers may crowd the "courts of the Lord's house: every Lord's day. This beautiful building has been erected at considerable expense for the benefit of the people of Juneau, and only by attending its services can that benefit be attained. We are bidden to keep the seventh day holy and it has always been recognized that the practical way to do this is to assemble for worship during at least a portion of the day, and spend the time in prayer and praise and learning about holy things. Let us take advantage, then, of the opportunities while we may. Yours

truly,

Henry Beer, Rector.

-Tacoma, Washington -

1896: June 13
Washington Churchman, July 1896:
"At sunset on Saturday, June 13 [1896], there passed to Paradise the soul of the faithful Priest who had 'served God's altar' in Trinity Parish Church for nearly eighteen years [Rev. George D. Watson]."

———

1896: June 21
Rev. R. D. Nevius, D.D.
Washington Churchman, July 1896:
"Memorial Sermon.
Preached By The Rev. R. D. Nevius, D.D., In Trinity Parish Church, Seattle, Sunday, June 21, 1896.
"The words of my text are found in the second verse of the fourth chapter of St. Paul's first Epistle to the Corinthians:
"'Moreover it is required in stewards that a man be found faithful.'
"Every man's consciousness of himself and every man's character, as it comes before us when his name is mentioned, has a certain shape, a certain color,— definite, distinct and emphasized, —and this to the extent to which the man is a man.
"St. Paul's consciousness of himself, as we find it expressed in all his epistles, is as of one faithful to a trust, a steward of something that had been committed to him. This something, so committed, made him responsible, under that committal, not simply for the holding of it and the keeping of it, but for its transmission also. Everywhere in all the epistles you find these words, 'faith,' 'faithfulness,' faithful.' He thanks Jesus Christ our Lord, for that he has enabled him being counted faithful, putting him into the ministry [sic]. This is the initial of consciousness in the mind of the Apostle. It was not of himself; he had been enabled from without himself. And it was with thankfulness that he had been counted faithful; and faithful, as to a trust he meant to be all his life; faithful before God, before man, before his own consciousness of himself. This was a great thing a controlling purpose of St. Paul, and this consciousness and this purpose shaped and colored all his life.
"Accordingly, as he was approaching the end of his life's work, and looking back over the sphere on which his activities had been exercised, with a humble thought of what God had enabled him to be and to do, he spoke, as if in a song of triumph: 'I have finished my course. I have kept the faith. Henceforth there is laid up for me a crown of righteousness, which the Lord, the righteous judge, shall give me at that day. ['] I have kept the Faith.' That is the work which crowns his life at its ending, and the song is as if one should humbly yet rejoicingly crown himself before his approving God.
"Now, the something committed and so kept, the Faith, was to him not to be perceived as by our bodily senses of sight and touch, nor as something offered to the larger power and sense of the mind, our reason. Eye hath not seen, neither hath the ear heard, nor can it enter into the heart of man to conceive the things of God. The faith is revealed to faith, a faculty which we may call the larger sense of the sprit, the large, full faculty of a man's whole nature, that, in the use of which he may say no 'I know' merely, but, with a larger reach toward that which is told us, 'I believe.'
"It is well for us to distinguish between these two faculties, these powers of reach, which are but measures of environment. Reason, by which we may reach to the comprehension of the Universe of God; and Faith, by which we may go, with a larger reach, into the illimitable, outlying sphere of what God may reveal to us, His own things which we may not know unless He tells us.
"The mind of man is indeed the measure of the universe of God; not by inclusion or any embrace of contact, but as with a unit of measure which may be laid upon what part of it we may touch as we grow to it. Just so the spirit of man, in which God hath made him kin to Himself, is the measure of the things of God, the invisible things, as St. Paul calls them, which eye cannot see, the ear hear, nor the heart of man conceive.
"In the one category, we may use the associated words, reason, comprehension,

knowledge; in the others, the as logically associated words, faith, apprehension, belief.

"Now the things of God are expressed to us in brief formulas which are called the Catholic Creeds. They conserve to us the great things which are outside the reach of all our powers except faith. They conserve to us the great things which are outside the reach of all our powers except faith. They are The Faith, which St. Paul rejoiced to keep. The holding of these gives a man a certain vantage and security against the difficulties and trials that come of doubt, which characterizes the whole process of growth. The process is as that of one who drives a straight furrow from a given point of departure. They give us the initial point and the straight beginnings of our lines through a period during which our collaborators spoke who spake as they were moved by the Holy Ghost. We get our line of direction by looking backward. We correct our conclusions by referring back to that which must be kept. And in the process we are always forming opinions which must be referred to it; they are not to be kept except as they conform to it.

Our holding of opinions today may be, must be, larger, fuller, more confident, than that we give to probabilities, until they are tested by that which can not be changed, by that which must be kept.

"Our opinions today may be, must be, larger, fuller, more confident, than those held yesterday. Tomorrow they may reach to a larger and higher plane of the truth. The narrow man is he who holds his opinions as if they were articles of a creed.

Very much is heard nowadays and very much of praise is spoken of a certain sort of broadness which is but an acceptance of opinions more or less probable, as if they were to be kept as of the Faith. It is but narrowness if one draws his circle from some distant and variable point as a center. It may be that his center is far out on the horizon of furtherest reach, but it is not concentric, and is not therefore harmonious, it stands not included and is not broad but narrow. Broadness is required of a man who measures the things of God. But he can be broad in every direction and harmoniously so only with the symmetry of a circle, within which all advance and all growth is concentric. The creeds are to a man as a centre, on which placing himself, he may sweep with his powers any circle possible to him, as with a pair of compasses, the movable foot will sweep a true curve only when the other is firmly held in place. With some such spirit as is suggested by such a parable, the true man will go forth, seeking to grow with a growth which may honor Him who made man in is own image. Such a man drifts not. He is a ship that swings with the changing tide or the buffeting wind, concentrically true to its fixed anchor and always with its bow towards the force which it resists.

"I think of him whom today we honor before God, whose memory we cherish, and in the thought of whom, as having finished his course, we are worshipping today, as one who did not drift. I can conceive of him as consciously taking from the end of his course upon the sphere of his earthly labors, and rejoicing with St. Paul in that, in intention and in fact, within the limits of his nature, he had kept the Faith. He conceived largely of the responsibility which was laid upon him with his commission. And they who knew him best will always think of him as having ever before his mind and heart the words of our text:—'Moreover it is required of stewards that a man be found faithful.'

"You, who are faithful parishioners of this Trinity Church, in which he has for so many years been your instructor, have grown after the manner of his manhood. Not his memory alone but very much of his life will remain with you, in that which you have absorbed from him by contact of sympathetic natures. The character of a man after a long pastorage will always inhere upon his parish. And long after his memory shall pass away with those who were his contemporaries, this Church will bear the impress of his character.

"For us today, this beautiful Church, which will witness to his churchly, cultivated taste, the things of the Church in ritual and all Godly ways, and the reverent and worthy services in which he has today been commemorated and for which this Church is known, will not be drifting things of a day. They will live with the things for which they stand, the fixed things of God.

"Firmly, strongly, and I might say, masterfully, he lived as we all live, on various planes. But on each he had a center of growth and exercise. Personally, as a Churchman, this center was a Faith, committed and to be transmitted. Officially, as a Minister, it was his beloved parish, for which he wrought untiringly, with complete ab-

sorption and manly self-denial. And as a man and a citizen, it was the town in which he lived, whose prosperity he sought with diligence and pride. These things I mention are small things beside that of which I began to speak to you, but they show the symmetry of his character and they mark him before us with a mark which shall endure and which we shall be glad to remember.

"Let us cherish with firmness and fixedness what we regard as important things; let us illustrate with that firmness and fixedness the elasticity with which one may reach toward the furthest possible growth who does not forget the Divine relation, and one of the lessons of his life will remain with us in its entirety, and so may God be praised for the example of his saints who have finished their course in faith, who rest from their labors."

——

1896: June 24, 25
Journal, Jurisdiction of Olympia, 1896:
Convocation met at Trinity Church, Tacoma, Wednesday June 24 and St. Luke's Church, Tacoma, Thursday, June 25. Nevius was appointed to a committee of two on the Credentials of Lay Delegates. He was reappointed as one of three Examining Chaplains.

——

1896: June 25 (Thursday)
"On motion of the Rev. Dr. Nevius, it was resolved that the visiting Clergy be invited to seats in the Convocation. There were present under this resolution the Rev. H. Chetwood and M. D. Wilson of the Diocese of California."

"On reassembling [at 1:30] the Bishop read his Address."

"On motion of the Rev. Dr. Nevius, the Chair appointed Rev. R. D. Nevius, Mr. Walter Turrell and Mr. Fred. R. Rowell a Committee to nominate Trustees for 'The Episcopal Church in Western Washington.'"

The "minutes" of the Clergy assembled at the funeral of the Rev. George Herbert Watson, D.D., apparently drafted by Nevius (first of three signers), were adopted by the Convocation, as follows:

We, who have been appointed to speak for the clergy of this Missionary Jurisdiction of Olympia, now bereaved by the sudden and lamented death of one of our oldest and most respected Clergymen, would most affectionately express what we believe to be a universal sentiment of loving and honorable regard for the memory of our departed brother, the Rev. George H. Watson, D.D., late Rector of Trinity Church, Seattle. And we would also give expression to the high regard in which he has always been held for his manly and sturdy character as a Christian, a Churchman and a friend. Even more tenderly if possible would we speak of our loving sympathy with Mrs. Watson in a sorrow which we feel is too great, as well as too sacred, for the intrusion of any other than brotherly and reverent feeling of which we would assure her and with which we have approached the honorable duty to which we have been assigned.

The Clergy of the Missionary Jurisdiction of Olympia.
Committee: R. D. Nevius, D.D.,
            Peter E. Hyland,
            James Cheal."

"A Committee having been appointed to prepare a message of congratulation to the Bishop of Oregon on the fiftieth anniversary of his Ordination to the Diaconate, the following resolution, offered by the Rev. Dr. Nevius, was unanimously adopted by a rising vote:

WHEREAS it has come to the knowledge of this Convocation that the venerable and beloved Bishop of Oregon, once our own Bishop during the period when this vast territory, now twice divided and three times increased, was known as the Missionary Jurisdiction of Oregon and Washington, has approached his fiftieth year of laborious, successful and honored Ministry, and

WHEREAS the Anniversary of his Ordination to the Diaconate will, on Sunday next, be celebrated in Portland by his friends and neighbors,

Resolved, That we do hereby entreat our honored Bishop Barker, who may be present on that happy occasion, to convey to our still dear Bishop Morris our loving congratulations, for that he has been spared through so many years of active and successful labor to a promise of yet more fruitful and even more honored years, and we would have our beloved Bishop, on whose kinship to Bishop Morris we fain would be also kin, to wish for him a continuance of Divine favor in the bestowal of health and strength until the latest day of his life.

For the Committee of the Missionary Jurisdiction of Olympia.

R. D. Nevius,

Chairman of Committee."

———

1896: August 16

Gold discovered on Bonanza Creek, near Dawson, Canada, starting the Klondike gold rush.

———

1896: September

The September 1896 issue of the *Washington Churchman* gives Nevius's address as Tacoma.

———

1896: September 20

Washington Churchman, September 1896:

"On Sunday, September 20, Dr. Nevius will officiate at all the regular services in Trinity Church [Seattle].

———

1896: October

Washington Churchman, October 1896:

"Tacoma.

"The Parish of the Holy Communion has once more resumed its work. Daily service is held at 5 p.m., except Friday, when at Evening Prayer, 7:30 p.m., Dr. Nevius is giving an interesting series of instructions on Church music. This Parish is now under the spiritual charge of the Bishop, who has made it the centre of Associate Mission Work. The Clergy are the Archdeacon, Rev. L. W. Applegate; the Rev. Edw. R. Davis; and the Rev. R. D. Nevius, D.D. The Mission House is at 1218 South I street, where Rev. Mr. Davis and several lay helpers reside."

———

1896: November 3

Election day. Republican William McKinley elected President.

[1897]

1897: June 15 (Tuesday)

Journal, Jurisdiction of Olympia 1897:

Convocation was held at St. Luke's Church, Tacoma. Nevius was listed in charge of the Church of the Holy Communion, Tacoma, but his address is given (as of November 1, 1897) as Fannie C. Paddock Hospital. Nevius was present, was reappointed one of the three Examining Chaplains, and was appointed chair and one of three members of a committee on Church Literature. Nevius moved that "Those Clergymen engaged in active work in this Jurisdiction, but not canonically entitled to seats in this Convocation, be admitted to seats and take part in discussions if they desire." "It was moved by Rev. Dr. Nevius that certain parts of the Bishop's Address containing recommendations be re-read paragraph by paragraph. Carried. The first paragraph referred to 'Sunday School Instruction.' The Rev. Dr. Nevius moved that a Committee be formed, of which the Bishop shall be Chairman, with two such persons as he may associate with him, to suggest topics and outlines with reference to Scripture and standard theological books. Carried."

———

1897: November 26

Nevius's seventieth birthday.

[1898]

1898: February 15

U.S.S. *Maine* sunk in Havana Harbor, beginning the Spanish-American War, which was concluded by the Treaty of Paris, December 10.

———

1898: April (Easter - April 10, 1898)

Rev. E. W. Pigion (1928):

"Church [at Yakima] consecrated April 1898."

———

1898: June 22 (Wednesday)

Journal, Jurisdiction of Olympia, 1898-1899:

Convocation met at St. Mark's Church, Seattle. Nevius's address, given as of "June 1st, 1900," was Fannie C. Paddock Hospital, Tacoma. He was listed as pastor at the Church of the Holy Communion, Tacoma and St. Paul's mission, Buckley, and as first of four Examining Chaplains. No list of clergy present was given, only that "18 Clerical and 16 Lay Delegates were found to be present." The minutes note that "Visiting Clergy were on motion invited to seats with the Convocation." No mention of Nevius was made. [No Bishop's Address?]

[1899]

1899: October 11 (Wednesday)

Journal, Jurisdiction of Olympia, 1898-99:

Convocation met at Trinity Church, Tacoma. Nevius's address, given as of "June 1st, 1900" was Fannie C. Paddock Hospital, Tacoma. He was listed as clergyman in charge at the Church of the Holy Communion, Tacoma and St. Paul's mission, Buckley, and as first of four Examining Chaplains. He was appointed chair of the three-member Committee on Church Literature. Nevius was present. "The Bishop having declared a quorum present, the Rev. Dr. Nevius moved that the courtesy of the floor of the Convocation be extended [to] the Clergy present not canonically resident within the Jurisdiction and to the laity present. This was seconded and carried unanimously." [Bishop's Address.] "At the conclusion of the Bishop's Address the Report of the Committee on Missionary Progress [Revs. Llwyd, Rowell, Redfield & Bader] was read by the Rev. H. L. Bader, as follows: '...In closing this report we desire to call the attention of the Convocation to this field [of Missions], believing that the time has now come when a more strenuous effort should be made in this direction. Money is necessary for this work, but more than all we need men. How shall they be obtained.... We are nevertheless of the opinion that no subject has a greater demand upon your time than the subject of Missions, and we believe it would be wise for the Convocation to devote a considerable portion of its time to a discussion of this subject.' A lengthy discussion ensued, in the course of which the Bishop gave a very clear description of the Missionary field in the Jurisdiction. The following speakers also took part: The Revs. R. D. Nevius, H. L. Badger, C. McLean, J. P. D. Llwyd, H. H. Gowen, and Messrs. Rowell and Harris."

"Moved by Dr. Nevius, seconded and carried, that the Secretary [the Rev. H. H. Gowen] be authorized to print 500 copies of the Journal for 1898 and 1899, and that an assessment of 5 cents per communicant [the usual rate] be made for the necessary expense and for other expenses of the Convocation."

[1900]

1900: June 1

Journal, Jurisdiction of Olympia, 1898-99:

Nevius's address, given as of "June 1st, 1900," was Fannie C. Paddock Hospital, Tacoma. He was listed as pastor at the Church of the Holy Communion, Tacoma and St. Paul's mission, Buckley.

———

1900: June 7

Nevius's mother died in Ovid, N.Y.: Mary Denton Nevius (mother), b. September 11, 1805; m. Benjamin Hageman Nevius 1826; m. Chester D. Eastman (b. 1794, d. 1879) 1832; d. Ovid, N.Y. June 7, 1900 (age 94 yrs. 9 mos.).

———

1900: October 9, 10 (Tuesday, Wednesday)

Journal, Jurisdiction of Olympia, 1900:

Convocation met at Trinity Church, Seattle. Nevius was listed as first of four Examining Chaplains. In his address the morning of Wednesday, October 10, Bishop Barker noted, "We must guard against 'parochialism,' which , by a false proportion destroys one's perspective. Each clergyman must of necessity be much engrossed with the details of his own Parish or Mission, but there is a wider horizon than the bounds of one's own immediate work. In a very real sense we are all charged with the duty of advancing the general interests of the Church in this Western field. We must all work together. We must all give courtesy, generosity, [and] loyalty to leader and comrade. No army can hope to win victories if comrades fault the honest work of comrades. Leadership is absolutely impossible without a generous, loyal willingness to share in plans and methods of work. I plead for breadth of view, acceptance of common responsibility, [and] generous aid for advance work." He also advocated a "Quiet Day" for the clergy immediately before Lent. "What a blessing it would bring into our lives, to spend at least one whole day together, under some spiritual leadership. Common thoughts, common praise and prayer,; united presence at a Celebration of the Holy Communion. What a help it would be to us all."

Nevius was appointed a member to the Committee on "Quiet Day" chaired by Llwyd, which reported, "The committee requests the Bishop to suggest the name of some trained [?] and devout clergyman of the Church who is fitted in his judgement for such work; and it further suggests that the Quiet Day should not be given for the clergy alone, but also for the laity of the jurisdiction who may desire to attend." A motion to do so was adopted.

———

1900: November 6

Election day. Republican William McKinley (assassinated September 6, 1901) re-elected.

- Blaine, Washington -

1900: December 31

Rev. R. D. Nevius, D.D.:

The following is inscribed on pages 2 and 3 of Volume I of the Parish Register of St. Paul's Church. The hand is that of Nevius, though in a stiffer, less fluid style than earlier notations. Some or all of the margin notations, which are in the same hand, may have been added subsequently:

[In margin:] [illegible] Altar ornaments The Red

The red Altar cloth with the linen with white embroidery was given through Miss Mary Austin and was made by Altar Society of St. Marks Philadelphia

[In margin:] Green

The green Altar cloth was bought of Lamb by the Guild of this[?] Parish

[In margin:] Altar cross

The Altar cross was given by Mrs. Alice Sheldon in memory of her husband Charles L. Sheldon

[In margin:] Cadllb[e?][r?]bra [sic, "Candelabra"]

Were given by Mrs. Sheldon in memory of her sisters Anna and Eva Schenck

[In margin:] Brass altar desk

was given by Rev. Mr. and Mrs. Sutcliffe

[In margin:] Stoles

The red and green stoles given by the S.S. class of Miss Ann[e] Lang aided by the Davenport ["Society," crossed out] fund.

[In margin:] White altar Cloth

was given by the Davenport fund

[In margin:] Alms basin

The curled maple alms basin was made by Rev. R. Nevius. It was the first one used by the mission and was carried for years[?] by the first boy baptized. The only male member of the church [added in an unidentified hand, "(Leslie Knaggs)"]

[In margin:] Enlargement of Church

The Church was enlarged during the winter of 1900 under the direction of Mr. J. C. Crandall [sic, C. J. Crandall], and was advised and undertaken by the Guild. The nave was extended to the front by the addition of ["14," crossed out] 16 ft and the tower was built.

The church was opened for services on Sunday, the [illegible, "belate"?] of Christmas day by Rt. Rev. B. W. Morris, D.D., attended by Rev. R. D. Nevius, D.D. - under the direction of whom - the latter - the mission was opened and the Church planned and built. It was the 25th anniversary of its first use for divine services [that it was] reopened after this enlargement. On the occasion the sermon was preached by Rev. Dr. Nevius. The Bishop [Morris] was the celebrant at the Holy Eucharist.

R.D.N.

Dec. 31, 1900

[1901]

1901: February 21

Jessett (1953) p. 37:

Bishop Barker died at age 46, of a heart condition.

———

1901: April 12

Half-brother Clinton Denton Eastman died in Ovid, N.Y.: Clinton D. Eastman (half-brother): b. Ovid, N.Y., September 15, 1846; d. Ovid, N.Y. April 12, 1901 (age 54 yrs. 7 mos.).

———

1901: April 26 (Friday)

Journal, Jurisdiction of Olympia, 1901:

Bishop Wells: "On Friday, the 26th [of April], I visited Christ Church, Blaine, preached and confirmed eight persons. Dr. Nevius is not only ministering to his people in the ordinary way, but is also bringing in the young people, through the study of Nature, to the worship of Nature's God."

1901: May 21 (Thursday)

Journal, Special Session, Jurisdiction of Olympia, 1900:

A special session of Convocation met at St. Luke's Church, Tacoma. Nevius was listed (as of September 12, 1901) as residing at Blaine. He was listed as first of four Examining Chaplains. Convocation "put on record its sense of the loss sustained by the premature removal of Bishop Barker...." On motion it was resolved that Dr. Nevius be requested to edit the resolutions passed by the different parishes and missions of the Jurisdiction and have them bound and engrossed." Lemuel H. Wells was listed as "Bishop in Charge."

———

1901: September 6

President McKinley assassinated at Buffalo, N.Y. He died September 14.

———

1901: September 10 (Wednesday)

Journal, Jurisdiction of Olympia, 1901

Convocation met at St. Luke's Church, Tacoma. Nevius was reappointed first of four Examining Chaplains. In this address, Bishop Wells noted, "In taking up the work laid down by your Bishop [Barker], I was deeply impressed with the remarkable condition in which he left his affairs. Everything is attended to up to the very day of his death. His accounts and papers were all in perfect order. Nothing appears to have been left until tomorrow and all things indicate that he gave his attention to every minute detail of the institutions and business matters of his Jurisdiction. His exactness and prompt business methods have made the task of taking up his work far more light and pleasant. I am convinced that his painstaking and loving care for all the persons and interests of the district, patient and unremitting though they were, were almost as little appreciated as the Providence of our Devine Father who rests not day and night in scattering the sunbeams and distilling the dew and providing for the spiritual and material needs of His children. I have learned at his feet a lesson of patient [illegible] and wise forethought that I trust will hereafter bear fruit in the administration of my office. When Bishop Barker took charge of the Jurisdiction, it was in confusion and embittered by strife as well as burdened [?] by debt and involved in law suits, but he left a district at peace [?] with itself and with its finances wonderfully improved."

———

1901: September 14

President McKinley died after being shot September 6. Theodore Roosevelt took the oath of office.

———

1901: October 19

Rt. Rev. Frederic W. Keator, D.D.

Journal, Jurisdiction of Olympia, 1902:

"I was elected Bishop of Olympia at the General Convention meeting in San

Francisco on October 19th, 1901, and was consecrated under the same title in St. John's Church, Dubuque, Iowa, on Wednesday, January 8th, 1902, by the Bishops of Chicago, South Dakota, Minnesota, the Bishop Coadjutor of Nebraska, the Bishop Coadjutor of Chicago, and the Bishops of Milwaukee, Michigan City and Quincy. As soon as the work of packing up and removal could be accomplished, I came out to my new work and entered upon its great responsibilities. I arrived in Tacoma on Saturday, January 25th, 1902."

[Between the 1901 and 1902 Convocations, the term "Missionary Jurisdiction" was changed to "Missionary District."]

[1902]

1902: January 8, January 25
Rt. Rev. Frederic W. Keator, D.D.
Journal, District of Olympia, 1902:

"I was elected Bishop of Olympia at the General Convention meeting in San Francisco on October 19th, 1901, and was consecrated under the same title in St. John's Church, Dubuque, Iowa, on Wednesday, January 8th, 1902, by the Bishops of Chicago, South Dakota, Minnesota, the Bishop Coadjutor of Nebraska, the Bishop Coadjutor of Chicago, and the Bishops of Milwaukee, Michigan City and Quincy. As soon as the work of packing up and removal could be accomplished, I came out to my new work and entered upon its great responsibilities. I arrived in Tacoma on Saturday, January 25th, 1902."

———

1902: March 19 (Wednesday)
Rt. Rev. Frederic W. Keator, D.D.
Journal, District of Olympia, 1902:

"Wednesday, March 19, in Christ Church, [Blaine] I assisted Dr. Nevius at Evening Prayer, and preached the sermon. After the service I met the people of the mission informally."

———

1902: July 18 (Friday)
Rt. Rev. Frederic W. Keater, D.D.
Journal, District of Olympia, 1902:

"Friday, July 18, in Christ Church, Blaine, I assisted the Rev. Dr. Nevius at Evening Prayer, and preached."

———

1902: September 24 (Wednesday)
Journal, District of Olympia, 1902:

Convocation met at St. Clement's Church, Seattle. Nevius's address was given as Blaine. He was present and was listed as one of four Examining Chaplains, and was appointed chair of the Committee on Christian Education (with three others).

Bishop Keator's Address: Bishop Keator reported that Bishop Lemuel H. Wells of Spokane had been in charge of the District of Olympia "from the date of the last [special] convocation until the date of my taking charge January [25] last."

"The cost of maintaining the work of our missions as I find it is in round numbers $3,500 per annum. Of this amount $1,500 is appropriated by the General Board of Missions, leaving a balance of about $2,000 to be provided from other sources, chiefly, as has been the case from 'specials' [?] in answer to appeals made by the Bishop by letters or by personal visitation among friends in the East."

"And I must say, in all frankness, that the one thing now lacking in this District above all others is Unity. It would scarcely be an exaggeration to say that all our parishes and missions are as separate as if they belonged to different districts instead of one and the same district."

———

1902: November 16
Half-brother William Lyman Eastman died: William Lyman Eastman (half-brother): b. Ovid, N.Y. April 22, 1842; m. Augusta Nash (b. Hadley, Mass. September 1, 1842; d. Ovid, N.Y. April 30, 1912) June 6, 1866; d. Ovid, N.Y. (?), November 16, 1902 (age 60 yrs. 7 mos.).

———

1902: November 26

Nevius's seventy-fifth birthday.

[1903]

1903: May 27 (Wednesday)
Journal, District of Olympia, 1903:

Convocation met at St. Luke's Church, Tacoma. Nevius was present. The Journals of 1903 and 1904, bound together, listed the cure of Blaine as vacant. Parochial statistics show activity at Blaine for the 1903 Convocational year. Nevius was reappointed as chair of the Committee on Christian Education. Bishop Keator, though he mentioned the comings and goings of several clergymen in his address, did not mention Nevius's or his whereabouts. He noted, "The Rev. Henry L. Badger, for many years among the most faithful and devoted priests of this District, has been obliged to resign the charge of St. John's, Olympia, by reason of the continued ill health of Mrs. Badger, who requires a different climate." In connection with the subject of special services, I have to mention the Conference of Church Workers, concluding with a Quiet Day for the Clergy, which was held in Trinity and St. Mark's Church, Seattle, in the week before Lent."

"On motion of Rev. R. D. Nevius, D.D., the following resolution was adopted: 'The Convocation has heard with deep regret that our clerical brother, Rev. H. L. Badger, finds it necessary to remove from this District to some place with a climate more favorable for the health of his beloved wife. This convocation desires to express to our brother, Rev. H. L. Badger, its profound sorrow both for his removal and for the cause which has made it necessary, and we would assure our brother whose work and helpful comradeship in this District has won all our hearts of the high esteem and affection in which he is held in the District of Olympia.'"

———

1903: July 14 (Tuesday)
Journal, District of Olympia, 1904:
Bishop Keator was in Blaine. He gave a sermon at Evening Prayer.

———

1903: September 19 (Saturday)
Journal, District of Olympia, 1904:

Bishop Keator "Gave consent to the sale of the parish house at Blaine."

———

1903: September 25 (Friday)
Journal, District of Olympia, 1904:
Bishop Keator noted "At Blaine. Conferred with the church committee on plans for the new church."

———

1903: December 16 (Wednesday)
Journal, District of Olympia, 1904:
Bishop Keator noted, "Conference with the church committee in Blaine regarding the building of the new church."

- Retirement -

St. Peter's Church
Chaplain, Fannie Paddock Hospital
1903:

"In the fiftieth year of his ministry, at the age of seventy-six, he retired from this arduous [missionary] service and became priest in charge of old St. Peter's Church, Tacoma."*

[copy of article from a church publication, approx 6½x8½", among Atwood notes] Jan., 1914, p. 37.

*The fiftieth anniversary of Nevius's ordination as Deacon was January 9, 1903. He turned 76 November 26, 1903.

[1904]

1904: May 31 - June 1
Journal, District of Olympia, 1904:

Convocation was held at Trinity Church, Tacoma. Nevius was in attendance. There were no Parochial Statistics for Blaine in the 1904 Journal. In his address, Bishop Keator noted, "At Blaine the old church house and lots have been sold, and a new church erected on lots well located, at a cost of $1,800, with an indebtedness of $500, which it is expected will promptly be taken care of." "St. David's Hospital, Hoquiam, has been closed. Owing to the erection of a new General Hospital in that city and the threatened [illegible] petition, it was deemed best to sell the good will for a satisfactory sum offered and retire. The building is still owned by the Church Charity Association and is rented so that it is bringing in an income."

——

1904:

U. S. construction of the Panama Canal (opened 1914) began.

——

1904:

Ansel F. Heminway:

Heminway mentioned "Mr. R. D. Nevius, of The Dalles" in an article, "Botanists of the Oregon Country," published in the September, 1904 *Oregon Historical Quarterly.*

Heminway (1904) 212.

——

1904: November 8

Election day. President Roosevelt (Republican) elected in his own right.

[1905]

1905:

"In 1905, the parish being vacant, the Rev. R. D. Nevius, a retired clergyman, resident, and serving the diocese since 1872, undertook to hold at least Sunday morning services, with Holy Eucharists, as priest in charge [of old St. Peter's, Tacoma]. Last January [1908?], Mr. Burrows joined him.

Presumed local church history.

——

1905: May 23-24 (Tuesday-Wednesday)

Journal, District of Olympia, 1905:

Convocation was held at Epiphany Church, Chehalis. Nevius was present. He was listed in charge of St. Peter's Church, Tacoma, and first of four Examining Chaplains. The Disabled Clergy Fund was merged with the General Fund.

[1906]

1906: April 8

Benjamin Wistar Morris died in Portland, age 86.

——

1906: May 29-30

Journal, District of Olympia, 1906:

Convocation was held at St. Luke's Church, Tacoma. Nevius was present, and was reappointed an Examining Chaplain. In his address, Bishop Keator noted, "It is fitting that this Convocation should take appropriate action [to?] the memory of Bishop Morris, and I have requested Dr. Nevius, [a long-time?] friend and for a time the close companion of him, to prepare at the proper time a resolution which I am sure you will be glad to adopt."

The Bishop's House at Tacoma was sold for $18,000.

"The following resolution, proposed by the Rev. R. D. Nevius, and seconded by the Rev. J. P. D. Llwyd, was passed unanimously by a rising vote:—

Whereas, the late Bishop of Oregon, the Rt. Rev. Benjamin Wistar Morris, D.D., one time Missionary Bishop of this Northwestern part of the United States, of which this District of Olympia was for more than ten years an integral portion, has, after a long life of arduous, [illegible] labor, been called to the joy of his Lord;

Therefore this Convocation of the Diocese [sic] of Olympia desires to put on record its loving recognition of his wise and arduous service in the planting and nourishing of the Church in this part of the Lord's vineyard [?].

It would also record its loving memory of his virtues, his wise administration of

his holy office and his worth and example as a man.

And we would respectfully give expression to our heartfelt sympathy with the Diocese of Oregon, now deprived of his invaluable fatherly counsel, and with his bereaved and revered family, with whom we would rejoice for his good example and for the new and further testimony to the comforting word, "The memory of the just and blessed."

——

?1906: September 29

Rev. R. D. Nevius (September 29, 1910):

"The Harvest Festival and the Anniversary of the Parish [St. Michael's Church, Yakima], 21st birthday, was observed [in 1906?] with much enthusiasm, the Rev. R. D. Nevius D.D. the founder of the parish being present in the Chancel and the preacher for the day.

[1907]

1907: June 3-4

Journal, District of Olympia, 1907:

Convocation met in St. Paul's Church, Bellingham. Nevius was listed as "Priest in charge St. Peter's, Tacoma," and first of four Examining Chaplains. Bishop Keator: "At the last Convocation I reported the sale of the old Bishop's house property in Tacoma. This year I have to report the purchase of a new and beautiful site for a new Bishop's house on Yakima Avenue, Tacoma. The preparation of plans is now in the hands of the architects."

——

1907: March 13 - November 4

Slide into the Panic of 1907.

——

1907: November 16

Oklahoma became the 46th state.

——

1907: November 26

Nevius's eightieth birthday.

c. 1907

Rev. Albert E. Allen (September 19, 1969):

"9/19/69

"Notes taken of Conversation w/Mrs. Quinn Trott Neal - Trott

"Grandfather Trott came to Wa Terr. Willapa Bay, Seah[aven?] 1st Epis. service held Trott dining room Seahaven on piling.

"Story [?] on him: 1893: - 1904-05 Moved to Tacoma. Rector of C[hurch] of Holy Communion [at Tacoma] - Trott sisters sang in choir.

"1907 Mrs. Neal moved to Tacoma.

Dr. Nevius in charge of St. Peter's Old Town (Tacoma). 1st Sunday she was taken to see Dr. Nev. She was quite taken aback at small church informality: Dr. Nevius said 'Charles will you take up [the] collection?" - Mrs. Neal knew him well. He would take her to beach where he would gather samples of water to study diatoms.

" - He often visited at Seahaven. Wild cattle would rub against piling. One time Dr. Nevius thought there was an earthquake.

"- Mince meat. - 3 shots of liquor by Aunts. Dr. Nevius thought it was the best ever.

"- Very friendly w/Thomas Fletcher Botanist at Tacoma Hi.

"- Came to dinner often.

"- Would throw rocks @ Fr. Grimes[?] (in fun).

"-Very descriptive of Bp. K[e]ator.

"Lived in upstairs room across from Fannie Paddock Hosp. She (Mrs. Neal) took candy & cookies at Christmas - He gave her a very beautiful copy of Spencer's Fairie Queen. He inscribed it 'to Quinn Trott from her first lover R.D.N.' - Then he said 'Some day someone is going to ask you who is R. D. N.!'

"Tide flats to dig for diatoms - called himself a 'diatomainiac!'

"Invited himself to dinner (felt himself one of the family.) Regularly!

"At H[oly] C[ommunion] he lost his upper plate [-] fell but it didn't faze him a bit - put them back & went right on.

"- He was remarkably spry - in his late eighties."

Rev. Albert E. Allen, "Notes taken of conversation with Mrs. Quinn Trott Neal," September 19, 1969.

[1908]

1908: March 5
Rev. J. Neilson Barry:

"The cornerstone of a Parish House to be called 'Nevius Hall' was laid by Rt. Rev. Robt. L. Paddock [at Baker City]."

Barry, *Records*.

——

1908: May 13
White House Conservation Conference held.

——

1908: May 18-19
Journal, District of Olympia, 1908:

Convocation met in St. Luke's Church, Vancouver. Nevius was listed as "Priest in charge St. Peter's, Tacoma." and first of four Examining Chaplains. Nevius was elected one of four clerical delegates to the Eighth Missionary Council, and was re-appointed an Examining Chaplain. Nevius's stipend for the year was $225. The Bishop's salary was $1500, the Rev. George Buzzelle, General Missionary's was $925.

——

1908: July
Journal, District of Olympia, 1909:

Bishop Keator attended the Lambeth Conference in London.

——

1908: September

The Missionary District of Eastern Oregon was separated from the Diocese of Oregon in actions taken on June 14 and October 14, 1907. The first Convocation of the new Missionary District was held in Pendleton in September, 1908. Nevius attended.

——

1908: October 6
R. D. Nevius, D.D. to Augusta Eastman:

Found the church {St. Thomas, Canyon City?} in perfect condition after 3 [could be 4 or 9] years. Service today. Made an address. Reception last night. Made speech and in fine weather. Enjoying my hearty welcome everywhere. R.D.N.

——

1908: November 3
Election day. Republican William H. Taft elected.

[1909]

1909: March
Oregon Churchman:

"A Pioneer Missionary

"Of the eleven Church buildings in Eastern Oregon, six are the result of the labors and consecrated efforts of Rev. R. D. Nevius, D.D., who in 1873 resigned the rectorship of Trinity Church, Portland, Oregon, in order to give himself as a pioneer missionary, seeking the places where no other missionary of the Church had been before, and working under the direction of the Bishop to start missions and build churches in new fields wherever the possibilities of future development justified it. He was the first resident clergyman of the Church in Eastern Oregon, starting on June 7, 1873, in the Grande Ronde Valley, where the churches at La Grande, the Cove and Union are evidences of his self-sacrificing labors. Crossing into the Powder River Valley, he gathered the congregation and built the Church at Baker City, and with that as a center, extended his ministry into the John Day River Valley and built the church at Canyon City, besides preaching at Connor Creek, Granite Creek, Heppner, Humboldt Basin, Lostine, Malheur (Eldorado), Mormon Basin, Sparta,

North Powder, Rye Valley, Prairie City and many other points. During this same period he built the Church at The Dalles, residing there for several weeks at a time in ministering to the people.

"Although a native of New York State, his early ministry was spent in the South. He was ordained deacon at Savannah by Bishop Steven Elliott in 1853, and had charge of a plantation church at Liberty Hill, Alabama. After his ordination to the priesthood by Bishop Cobbs, in 1854, he became rector of Christ Church, Tuscaloosa, Alabama, where he remained for eleven years, being there during the stirring times of the Civil War.

"Then going to Pennsylvania, he established the first Church mission in Oil City, and built the church at Rouseville.

"Returning to Alabama, he became rector of St. John's Parish, Mobile, from which he was called to Trinity Church, Portland in 1872.

"Since leaving Eastern Oregon in October, 1879, the same consecrated zeal has shown itself in his work in building churches at Spokane, Pomeroy, Sprague and Yakima, in Eastern Washington; and on Puget Sound at Chehalis, and Whatcom; while he started the work which resulted in the building of churches by his successors at Lewiston, Idaho; Ellensburg and East Sound, in Washington, and Juneau in Alaska.

"Upon his completing the fiftieth year of his ministry, he retired from responsible work, although he is still as young in mind and as interested in all that affects the Church as he was half a century ago, and although 81 years old, drove by stage across the Blue Mountains last summer to revisit the scene of his former labors. He is now resident at Tacoma, being priest in charge of old St. Peter's Church, whose famous steeple is the oldest in the United States." *Oregon Churchman*, March, 1909, p. 32

1909: May 7
Rand (1974) 16:

Nevius Hall in Baker City was "first used on May 7." Nevius attended the dedication.

——

1909: June 3
Journal, District of Olympia, 1909:

Convocation met in St. Luke's Church, Tacoma. Nevius was present and was listed in charge of St. Peter's, Tacoma (as of May 1, 1909), and first of four Examining Chaplains, to which post he was reappointed.

——

1909: July 12
Congress proposed the 16th Amendment, enabling the income tax. Declared adopted February 25, 1913.

——

1909:
Elisabeth L. Lang (1917):

"The Dalles, Oregon. November 19, 1917

"Prof. Albert R. Sweetser,

"Eugene, Oregon....

"When Nevius Hall, at Baker, was dedicated the Doctor wrote a very complete sketch of his life. It was read and then given into the keeping of Bishop Paddock. My sister and I wish very much for a copy of it and I will try to get it from the Bishop that you may have a copy also.

——

1909:
Rev. J. Neilson Barry (October 30, 1953):

"Mr. Howland Atwood

"San Marino,

"California....

"Dear Mr. Atwood:

"Although as Registrar for ten years of the District of Spokane and for five years of the District of Eastern Oregon I had occasion to record some data of earlier times with records of Dr. Nevius, it had only to do with such limited records.

"However having heard so much of him, I named Nevius Hall, in Baker, to insure commemoration....

"Unless, possibly, for some statistics, I had no occasion to write him, and did not meet him until Nevius Hall was dedicated [on May 7(?), 1909], when he talked more of his beloved anatoms than of early times out here, with some anecdotes of other people."

———

ca. 1909:

Rev. J. Neilson Barry (July 17, 1955):

"Dr Nevius [had] left the Spokane region when I first went there in 1895.... He had been away from eastern Oregon for many years prior to my going there in 1907.... He had his hobby, scientific—apparently of ANATOMS, and was enthusiastic. I have heard him lecture, with magic lantern slides. He had no vestige of the orator. He knew what he had to say, and what it was about, and said it understandably, and then stopped.... He was a really GOOD man, and his presence and influence promoted righteousness in others.... Everywhere I went people always talked of him with esteem and affection.... As a conversationalist, he always had something worth-while to say and had a keen sense of humor and was good at causing visualizing of the 'picture.' I presume his sermons were like that—omitting the humor. I always enjoyed listening to him talk.... He had a very large library, and when he moved, or something that caused him to dispose of it, instead of selling it he gave it away. Anybody who wanted anything might take it, and the clergymen 'skinned' [sic] it of religious and theological books.

"I named the Parish House of St. Stephen's parish at Baker, Oregon NEVIUS HALL in his honor. Our parochial Boy's Athletic Club adopted the name NEVIUS BOYS' CLUB. He donated the remnant of his books to that club.

"About three or four large boxes arrived by freight. I do not think the clergymen had left even one book that one of those boys would even open. Yet if opened, would have read a page of it.

"It would have required many shelves, and there was no space for them and no money to construct them, and no one would have contributed a cent. It was like a gift of the proverbial white elephant.

"The Librarian of the Public Library balked. The Library was willing to accept a gift of such books as might be suitable, but only on condition that they could only take what they wanted.

"I had no place to store the huge cases, great big wooden boxes three to four feet. I had a baggage wagon take them to the Library where they were put in a room.

"Dr. Nevius wanted a particular book and I had to go through all of the three or four boxes. It seemed interminable. It was not there. One of the clergymen probably had taken it.

"Later he wanted another. And I had to wade through them all again but it was not there. It was a relief when I went back to Washington D.C. Many dreary hours of that sort of thing, twice, was sufficient.

"Subsequently Dr. Nevius went to Baker [in 1909?], expecting to find his gift to the Boys' Club on shelves at Nevius Hall. He was grievously disappointed. He went to the Library.

"They had stipulated that they would not keep such as they wanted by themselves, but would distribute to whatever classification they belonged. Such as they had selected were scattered. Probably the rest destroyed. He was much chagrined, and probably blamed me. Yet they were totally inappropriate for an athletic club...."

[1910]

1910: May 24

Journal, District of Olympia, 1910:

Convocation met at St. Mark's Church, Seattle. Nevius was present and was listed as priest in charge, St. Peter's, Tacoma (as of May 24, 1910). He was again appointed first of four Examining Chaplains. Nevius's Missionary Stipend was $150. In his address, Bishop Keator noted the passing of the Rev. Peter Hyland:

The Rev. Peter Hyland came first to this Northwest country in 1858, and to what is now the District of Olympia in 1865, and from that year until 1871 he was in charge of St. John's Church, Olympia. In 1871 he was removed to Ontario, but came again to this Coast in [illegible]. During the early days of his work here he

served as General Missionary in many places in this Puget Sound country. In [illegible, that he?] was among the first of the pioneer clergy of the Church in the Pacific Northwest. Many places, including Olympia, Blaine, Ballard, Bellingham and Seattle, knew of his faithful work, and wherever he was known he was loved. When I knew him, after my coming to this District, he was in failing strength, but so far as he was able to do so, he willingly gave all that he could to the services of the Church. Latterly, he was associated with St. Mark's Parish, Seattle. He was called to rest on November 29, 1909, and it was my privilege, assisted by the clergy of Seattle, to perform the [last?] service on earth for this faithful Missionary and Minister of [illegible, God?].

Bishop Keator gave a brief history of the Missionary District of Olympia, named "after the capital of the State," noting that the Territory of Washington consisted of 7 congregations, 9 clergy and 212 communicants with property valued at [illegible] when it was separated from Oregon in 1880. In 1892, when eastern and western Washington were separated, there were 28 congregations, 20 clergy, [illegible] communicants, and property valued at $250,000.* At the present time (1910) there were 50 congregations, 5500 communicants, 35 clergy and property valued at $750,000. Then Keator outlined the steps necessary to become a self-supporting diocese, which elected its own bishop and voted (four clergymen and four laymen as opposed to one clergyman and one layman, both nonvoting) at General Convention. This required and endowment fund of $50,000 "for the support of the Episcopate." $18,000 needed yet to be raised.

"On motion ... it was resolved that a committee be appointed to draft suitable resolutions upon the death of the Rev. Allen Patterson, the Rev. Peter Edward Hyland and the Rev. Henry L. Badger of Pomona, Cal., sometime rector of St. John's Church, Olympia. The Bishop appointed as the committee; Rev. R. D. Nevius, D.D. and the Rev. F. T. Webb, S.T.D."

"Resolutions On TheDeath Of The Rev. Peter Edward Hyland, and The Rev. Allan Patterson.

The District of Olympia is called to mourn the loss by death of two of its canonically resident Clergy, and of one who though no longer resident here, is still gratefully remembered by all who knew him. One of them spent a long life in active missionary and parochial work, leaving behind him many memorials of successful labor, and an enduring record of a most kindly nature among his contemporary pioneers, few of whom remain to testify his worth. Another has been called away almost in the bloom of his youth.

The Rev. Peter Edward Hyland was one of the four clergy who followed Bishop Scott who came as the first Bishop of the Pacific Northwest in 1854, and his ministry extended through the time of the formation of five dioceses and missionary districts out of the territory over which Bishop Scott had jurisdiction.

Mr. Hyland came to what is now the District of Olympia in 1865. In that year he took charge of St. John's, Olympia and remained there until 1871 when he removed to Ontario, Canada. In [illegible] he returned to the coast, and at different times had charge of the work at Bellingham, Blaine [and] Ballard and as general missionary to other points. In 1905 he retired from active work on account of advancing years. He continued however to assist[?] in the services at St. Mark's, Seattle, as his strength permitted. He died at his home in Seattle, November 29, 1909. Mr. Hyland will long be affectionately remembered by all who knew him, for his faithfulness and devotion as a Minister of God.

The Rev. Allan Patterson came to the work of the Ministry from business life. After careful preparation for his new work under the painstaking tutelage of the Rector of Trinity Parish [Rev. H. H. Gowen], he also had charge of the work at St. Andrew's Mission, Seattle. In both parish and mission he greatly endeared himself to all who knew him, and the success which he was making in his work gave promise of even greater success in days to come. He was looking forward to advancement to the Priesthood within a few weeks, when the summons came suddenly, July 28, 1909, bidding him "come up higher."

The Rev. Henry L. Badger who for ten years was canonically resident and labored in the District of Olympia will be remembered by both the clergy and laity who knew him as faithful and [illegible] in service, wise in council, gentle in manners and much beloved. On account of the ill health of his wife he was obliged to give up his work here, and remove to California. His death occurred December 20, 1909.

R. D. Nevius

Frederick T. Webb

*In his Annual Address of 1892, Bishop Paddock noted that in 1881 there were 306 communicants and church property was valued at $37,000. "We find last year reported 2,262 communicants, with twenty-eight clergy, forty parishes or missions, and property valued at $550,000."

———

1910: September 14 (Washington)

Journal, Special Convocation, District of Olympia, 1910:

A Special Convocation was held at St. Mark's Church, Seattle, 'for the purpose of organization as a diocese and the transaction of its[?] business as properly pertains thereto." Nevius was present, and listed "in charge of St. Peter's Mission, Tacoma." A motion passed to submit an application for admission as a diocese to the General Convention to be held in Cincinnati in October 1910. Nevius was elected fourth alternate Clerical Deputy to the Convention."

———

1910: September 29 (St. Michael's Day)

Relander (Yakima *Republic*) 1960:

"In September, 1910, he [Dr. Nevius] came from retirement to return to Yakima and preach the 25th anniversary sermon...."

———

1910: prob. September 29 (St. Michael's Day)

Parish Register, St. Michael's Church, Yakima

Rev. R. D. Nevius:

[Unsigned yet in Nevius's hand, the following appears on "Historic Notes" pages of the "Church And Clergyman's Record Book," Parish Record Vol. I, St. Michael's Episcopal Church, Yakima. A break in the hand and format suggests that it was written in at least two sittings. While the first part could have been written as early as 1904, it is here assumed that the entire account was written when Nevius is known to have been in Yakima for an historic occasion in 1910.]

"Saint Michael's Parish, North Yakima, District of Spokane Washington

Rev. R(euben)* D. Nevius, D.D., 1885.

*1885** The work was begun in the year eighteen hundred and eighty-five by the Rev. R. D. Nevius, D.D.

*1888** in Eighteen hundred and eighty eight (1888) the plans for a stone church were approved and the nave was built. It was built of local stone rubble work unfinished work on both in- & exterior. A temporary chancel was built of wood until the original plan of transept should be built.

[Nevius left a space of about an in inch and a half between his entries, seemingly so that others could fit in parts of the history he did not know. In 1928 the Rev. E. W. Pigion (there 1923-1944) added the material shown here inset in brackets.]

[*1888. Dr. Nevius came to stay until Wednesday [December 28, 1888]. Service Sunday Dec. 23 & Christmas Day, Tuesday [Added, above] Dr. Nevius held services on June 30. Services held in on [sic] first floor of a wooden building on No 1st St, about where Western Auto Supply Co is now (1928) no. 110 No. 1st St.*]

[*1889. Bishop Paddock here Jany 1st. In new Church Jany 6th Epiphany. Easter Day Apr 21. 80 at Church, May 12 Confirmation. Rev. [???] Cheal[?] had service on Sept. 13]

*1891 Rev. Rufus S. Chase. 1891-92

"In September 1891 Rev. Rufus S. Chase came from the East and took up the work, continuing until June 1892. [In Pigion's hand: "Ordained by Bp. Wells Jany 3-1892 in St. Michael's."]

*1893 Rev. [blank] MacKennon

"Assumed charge in June and continued in the parish but a short time.

*1894 Rev. Alfred H. Brown 1894-5

"Assumed charge in November 1894 and remained but about seven months leaving in June (16) 1895.

*1896 Rev. Hamilton M. Bartlett 1896-1904

"Assumed the burdens of an unpaid Church debt [added above: in October (1), leaving a comfortable Eastern parish in the suburbs of Wilmington Delaware and

during the following year the debt was paid off. In 1898 the lot was paid for on which the rectory stands and plans for the rectory were prepared, and in 1899 work was begun on the same. It was contracted for and cost [blank]. [In Pigion's hand: Church consecrated April 1898"]

"In 1900 the rectory was finished, one of the best buildings in Yakima, built of the same native [blank] stone of which the Church had been constructed.

*1904 Rev. Henry Clinton Collins, M.D. 1904***

Dr. Henry Clinton Collins, sometime Missionary of the church in China, assumed charge of the work on Sunday April tenth nineteen hundred and four having been called from a mission work in Salmon Idaho, where he built up the work known as Church of the Redeemer. Dr. Collins accepted the parish of The Dalles, Oregon in Lent 1905.

[Here a change of Nevius's hand, including possibly the last sentence above, and a change in format indicate a break in the writing of this account. It is possible that the above portion could have been written as early as 1904.]

*1905 Ven. Maurice J. Bywater, Archdeacon of Colorado was called to the parish in July 1905 and arrived in North Yakima on Thursday Sept. 28th 1905. A largely attended reception was given at the house of the Junior Warden, Mr. Alex Miller, in the Evening of the same day in honor of the new Rector and his wife.

"The first service held was the celebration of the Holy Communion on the Feast of St. Michael and All Angels Sept 29th at which service four persons Communicated with the new rector and his family.

"This month a new furnace was installed in the Church and paid for by the Woman's Guild, costing about $350.00.

"On Easter 1906 [sic, 1907****] was installed and consecrated for use a beautiful hand carved Altar of quartered oak in dull wax finish and credence table to match the altar. These were the gift of St. Agnes' Guild.

"On the patronal day of the parish St. Michael and All Angels Sep 29th 1907 was installed the heating plant of the rectory at a cost of $800.00 which was borne by the young ladies of St. Margaret's Guild. The Harvest Festival and the Anniversary of the Parish, 21st birthday, was observed [in 1906?] with much enthusiasm, the Rev. R. D. Nevius D.D. the founder of the parish being present in the Chancel and the preacher for the day.

"On Easter 1907 Mrs. James M. Thompson presented the Font Cover in memory of her mother Mrs. Julia Spaulding Reynolds. The ladies of the Guild presented the Rector and Mrs. Bywater with silver ware and [a] box of gold coin.

"On New Year's day [added: 1909] the Guild and Choir presented the Rector and Mrs. Bywater with several beautiful presents including a silk umbrella with [new page. "1908-1909" above] gold mounted handle.

"On being offered the Archdeaconry of the Yakima Valley by Bishop Wells on August 12th whilst officiating in Trinity Parish Church Seattle Rev. Mr. Bywater resigned the parish on Oct 22nd 1909 to take effect Oct 31st 1909. The Bishop was invited by the Rector and Vestry to meet with them on Oct 30th to place in nomination a successor to the Rector, who returns to the same kind of work from which he came and prays that the prayers of the faithful will be offered for his success in the larger field which is so ripe for the Harvest....

*Added, as if a doodle.

**Margin dates, in Nevius's hand, seem to have been added as an afterthought.

***In Pigion's hand: "at Crescent, Oregon -'35' Crescent is a small roadside community about sixty miles south of Bend.

****See Yakima *Ledger*, March 22, 1907, above. Easter was on March 31 in 1907 and April 15 in 1906. Other of Nevius's dates may be incorrect.

———

1910: October

The Diocese of Olympia was created by the General Convention of the Protestant Episcopal Church, assembled at Cincinnati, Ohio.

———

1910: December

Rev. R. D. Nevius, D.D.:

On reverse of a photograph of Nevius and an unidentified woman dated in Nevius's hand, "Nov. 26th 1910.:

"My dear Augusta*

"Christmas time gives me no time for letters but I want to assure[?] you of loving[?] wishes[?] this day and I want to let you see me as I was on my birthday [November 26] with my charming friend who gave a birthday dinner for me.

"I am very anxious to hear from you as soon as you know the result of your late[?] recourse to the surgeon[?]. I think of you daily with prayerful anxiety let me be in your thoughts today. I am without any change in condition.

"As ever loving yrs.

"R.D.N."

*Augusta Nash Eastman was the wife of half-brother William Lyman Eastman. He died in 1902, she in 1912.

[1911]

1911: May 30-31 (Tuesday-Wednesday)
Journal, Diocese of Olympia 1911:

The First Annual *Convention* met at St. Paul's Church, Seattle. Nevius was present. He was listed as first of four Examining Chaplains, was reappointed, and was listed in charge of St. Peter's, Tacoma. His Missionary Stipend was $160. The question of the name of the Diocese was raised. In his address Bishop Keator observed that it might be wise to "employ to advantage the ancient Deanery system, properly adapted[?] to meet present day needs."

"The Rt. Rev. Chairman called for the business of the hour: The report[?] of the Committee on the Change of Name of the Diocese.

"The committee to which was referred the question of the change of name of this Diocese, respectfully report as follows: After careful consideration of the reasons for the several names mentioned—Olympia, Puget Sound and Tacoma—it seems best to this committee to recommend that, inasmuch as Tacoma has always been, and still is, the see city, Tacoma be the name of the Diocese. [Signed by Frederick T. Webb, Willis H. Stone, F. K. Howard, H. O. Wilkinson, H. F. Garretson.]

"The name recommended by the committee was not accepted by the [illegible] and on motion it was resolved that the name as provided in [illegible] constitution remain unchanged for the time being."

———

1911:
The Conquest of the Continent, by Hugh Latimer Burleson, published by Domestic and Foreign Missionary Society has the following article on pages 156 & 157:

"Another honored name is that of the Rev. Dr. Nevius who, in 1873, resigned the rectorship of Trinity Church, Portland, the largest parish in Oregon, in order to give himself to the work of a pioneer missionary. In places where no other missionary of the Church had ever gone he worked for forty years, opening new fields wherever the opportunity presented itself. He was the first Church clergyman to reside beyond the mountains in the present district of Eastern Oregon. Six of the first eleven churches were built by him. In 1879 he passed over into Washington and did a like work there, where six other churches and many missions begun by him bear testimony to his zeal for the extension of the Kingdom. In the fiftieth year of his ministry he retired from active missionary work and became, curiously enough, the priest in charge of old St. Peter' Church with its fir tree belltower, built by his faithful predecessor fifty years before."

[1912]

1912: January 6
New Mexico became the 47th state.

———

1912: February 14
Arizona became the 48th state.

———

1912: March 31
Tuscaloosa News, p. 5
"The friends of Dr. R. D. Nevius, former rector of Christ church parish, who is

expecting to visit Tuscaloosa this spring, will be interested to know that he has stopped in Los Angeles, where he has met an old school friend, Ex-Senator Cole of California. They were boys together in Ovid, N.Y. in 1840, and have not met before in 72 years."

"Senator Cole invited his schoolboy friend to his Colegrove home."

"As soon as Dr. Nevius gets through his Los Angeles visit, he will come to Tuscaloosa to visit his friends here."

"Dr. Nevius is 85 years old and Senator Cole is nearly 90."

———

1912: April 14-15
HMS *Titanic* struck an iceburg, sinking with more than 1,500 persons lost.

———

1912: April 19
Tuscaloosa News, p. 3
"Dr. R. D. Nevius will leave tomorrow for Mobile where he will be the guest of friends for a few days. He was the rector there after leaving Tuscaloosa and has old friends living in the city. He will return here to spend a week with Mrs. Bryce after his visit to Mobile."

———

1912: April 22
Half-brother William Lyman Eastman's wife Augusta died in Ovid, N.Y.: William Lyman Eastman (half-brother): b. Ovid, N.Y. April 22, 1842; m. Augusta Nash (b. Hadley, Mass. September 1, 1842; d. Ovid, N.Y. April 30, 1912) June 6, 1866; d. Ovid, N.Y.(?), November 16, 1902 (age 60 yrs. 7 mos.).

———

1912: April 28
Tuscaloosa News p. 5
"Rev. R. D. Nevius will preach at Christ church at the eleven o'clock service this morning. The reverend clergyman will leave Tuscaloosa this week to continue his travels and visit other friends."

———

1912: May 1
Tuscaloosa News, p. 3
"Dr. R. D. Nevius left this morning to begin his journey home in [sic] Tacoma, Washington. He will stop in Birmingham for a few days to see his nephew, Mr. McLean, grandson of Dr. Michael Tuomey, Alabama's distinguished early geologist [and father-in-law of Nevius] and will also stop in Chattanooga for a visit to his sister-in-law, Mrs. McLean, who was Miss Nora Tuomey."

"While the guest of Mrs. Bryce, his friends have enjoyed his genial and delightful company on many occasions, and his return to the scenes of his early manhood has been a great pleasure to his companions and former pupils of those early days."

———

1912: May
Oregon Churchman:
"CHURCHES IN EASTERN OREGON.

———

"Easter Day [April 7,] 1912, marks an event of importance for Eastern Oregon, as on that day the first service was held in the Church of the Holy Apostles, Prairie City, the first church erected since the creation of the district in 1907.

"This is the fifteenth church to be erected in the eastern part of the State, the others being:

"(1) St. Peter's, La Grande (1874), under charge of Rev. R. D. Nevius, D.D. It was consecrated July 15, 1875. In 1887 it was moved from the old town to its present location, and a chancel added in 1889, Rev. R. W. Powell being in charge.

"(2) St. John's Memorial Church, Union, was built under the direction of the Rev. Dr. Nevius in 1875 and was consecrated July 14th of that year.

"(3) St. Stephen's Church, Baker, was erected in 1875 by Rev. Dr. Nevius, and extensive improvements were made in 1889 through the efforts of Rev. J.N.T. Goss. It was consecrated Sept. 4, 1889.

"(4) St. Paul's Church, The Dalles, was built in 1875 by Rev. Dr. Nevius, who held the first service on Christmas day of that year. It was consecrated November

23, 1879. In 1889 it was improved and enlarged, Rev. Joseph DeForest being in charge.

"(5) The first Church at Pendleton was built in 1876, under the direction of the present Bishop of Spokane, Rt. Rev. L. H. Wells, D.D. It was named the Church of the Redeemer, but was popularly called 'The Little Brown Jug.'

"(6) All Saints, Weston (1876), was also built by the present Bishop of Spokane, and was consecrated August 1, 1877.

"(7) The Church of the Ascension, Cove, was erected in 1876 by Rev. R. D. Nevius, D.D., assisted by Rev. George T. Kaye. It was consecrated July 25, 1877. the chancel was enlarged in 1897, Rev. Henry Harris being in charge.

"(8) St. Thomas' Church, Canyon City, was built in 1877 by Rev. Dr. Nevius, and was consecrated June 20, 1889.

"(9) Through the efforts of Rev. W. E. Potwine, St. John's Church, Adams, was erected and was consecrated September 24, 1884. It was subsequently sold to the Methodists.

"(10) In 1898 the small, modern church at Pendleton was replaced by the present stone edifice, Rev. W. E. Potwine being rector. It was consecrated June 4, 1899.

"(11) All Saints' Church, Heppner, was erected by Rev. W. E. Potwine and was consecrated May 13, 1900. It was destroyed by a cloudburst June 14, 1903.

"(12) All Saints' Memorial Church was then erected at Heppner, Rev. Mr. Potwine being in charge, and it was consecrated April 10, 1904.

"(13) St. Mark's Church, Hood River, was built in 1903 through the efforts of Rev. Clarence H. Lake, and was consecrated Jan 10, 1904."

(14) St. Paul's Church, Sumpter, was built in 1904, Rev. J. M. Goodheart being in charge."

Oregon Churchman[?}, May [?], 1912[?]

——

1912: May 28-29 (Tuesday-Wednesday)
Journal, Diocese of Olympia, 1912:
Convocation met at St. Luke's Church, Tacoma. Nevius was listed as first of four Examining Chaplains, and was listed as "Priest in Charge" of St. Peter's, Tacoma, but the Journal notes under Parochial Reports, "No report for 1912." Bishop Keator reported that three deaneries had been created, at Whatcom, Seattle and Chehalis.

——

1912/1913:
"Dr. Nevius was here [at University of Alabama] for a brief visit in 1912 or 1913, but I saw him only a little while, and neglected to get more details about his work around here. I do not know that he ever published anything, in botanical literature at least."
Letter from Rowland M. Harper, Geographer, University of Alabama, to Howland Atwood, Huntington Library, August 22, 1952.

——

1912: November 5
Election Day. Democrat Woodrow Wilson elected.

——

1912: November 26
Nevius's eighty-fifth birthday.

[1913]

1913: February 16
The 16th Amendment, authorizing the income tax (proposed July 12, 1909), was declared adopted.

——

1913: April 1
Deed recorded from Church Charity Association to The Diocese of Olympia of Lot 1 and the Northeasterly half of Lot 2, Block 59, Town (now City) of Hoquiam, for one dollar, dated October 1, 1912. This was St. David's hospital property.

——

1913: May 27-28
Journal, Diocese of Olympia, 1913:

Convocation met at St. John's Church, Olympia. Nevius was listed as first of four Examining Chaplains, but St. Peter's Church, Tacoma, was listed in the care of L. G. Drake, a Lay-Reader. Nevius's name was listed among the Non-Parochial clergy, and he was present at convocation.

——

1913: December 14 (Third Sunday in Advent)
Nevius died suddenly while at the home of Howard Taylor at Eagle Gorge near Tacoma. Taylor was Speaker of the House of Representatives for the Washington Legislature. See December 15, 1913, below.

- Posthumous -

1913: December 15
Oregon Daily Journal (Portland):
:The News of Sunday....
"Reuben D. Nevius, D.D., founder of more than 30 Episcopal churches in the Pacific Northwest, died in Tacoma, aged 86."
Oregon Daily Journal (Portland)
December 15, p. 15

——

1913: December 15
Portland *Oregonian*
"REUBEN D. NEVIUS DIES

"Church Founder and Botanist Passes in Tacoma Aged 86.

"Tacoma, Dec. 14—Reuben D. Nevius, D.D., who founded more than 30 Episcopal Churches in the Pacific Northwest, died in this city today at the age of 86.

"He came to the Coast 41 years ago and settled at Portland as rector of Trinity Church, later becoming general missionary for Oregon, Washington, and Idaho. He was a botanist whose work was recognized throughout the world and a plant named in his honor, the 'Neviusia Alabamaensis' is grown extensively in the conservatories of England."
Portland *Oregonian*
December 14, 1915, p. 1
Also, OHS Scrapbook 44, p. 74

——

1913: December 15
Tacoma *Ledger:*
[Photograph]
"Rev. Reuben Denton Nevius, D.D., aged 86, for years pastor of St. Peter's church, botanist and scientist of international fame, died of heart trouble yesterday afternoon in the home of Howard Taylor, speaker of the state Senate [sic*, at Eagle Gorge.

"In the annals of church history of the Northwest, Dr. Nevius occupied a prominent position. He was founder of more than 30 Episcopal churches, among them being those at Spokane, Sprague, Pendleton [sic], La Grande and South Bend.

"As a botanist his efforts were recognized by the world's greatest scientists, and a plant which he discovered was named in his honor, the 'Neviusis Alabamaensis [sic],' and is now grown in all the larger conservatories of England.

"Dr. Nevius was born in Ovid, N.Y., and entered in to the ministry at an early age. He was married in Alabama, but lost his wife and two children a few years later during an epidemic of yellow fever. He moved to the coast 41 years ago and settled in Portland, where he was rector for a number of years of Trinity church of that city.

"He became general missionary under Bishop Morris of Oregon, and it was during this missionary work through Oregon, Washington and Idaho that he founded the numerous Episcopal churches.

"From the missionary field he accepted the pastorate of St. Peter's church, Tacoma, and after a number of years of faithful service there, he became pastor of the Episcopal church in Blaine. For several years he was chaplain of the Fannie Paddock hospital.

"For the last five years Dr. Nevius lived quietly in Tacoma without any active charge, and for the last ten months of his life his sight failed rapidly, so that he was almost totally blind at the time of his death.

"Funeral services will be held from Trinity Church, Tacoma,** Wednesday [December 17] morning at 11:00. Bishop F. W. Keator and Rev. Charles Y. Grimes officiating. The body will lie in state at the church for two hours preceding the funeral."

[A large two column picture accompanies the article.]

Tacoma *Ledger* December 15, 1913 (from a typescript provided by Washington State Historical Society in Atwood notes).

* Howard Taylor was Speaker of the House in the Washington State Legislature in 1913. He became President *pro tem*, of the Senate in 1919.

** Now Christ Church, Tacoma.

———

1913: December 16
New York Times:
"The Rev. Reuben D. Nevius
"TACOMA, Wash., Dec. 15—The Rev. Reuben D. Nevius, one of the most widely known clergymen of the West, who established more than thirty Episcopal churches and chapels in the Pacific Northwest, died here yesterday, aged 86 years. He was an authority on some forms of plant life, and a plant named in his honor, 'Neviusia Alabamaensii,' is grown extensively in England."
New York Times, December 16, 1913, p. 11

———

1913: December 17 (Wednesday)
Nevius's funeral was held at Trinity Church, Tacoma. See above and below.

———

1913: December 18
La Grande *Evening Observer:*
"TALENTED MAN PASSES AWAY
"HAD LONG AND USEFUL CAREER AS DIVINE.
"Labored in the Grande Ronde Valley For Many Years.
"The many friends of the Reverend Reuben D. Nevius, D.D., in this vicinity, were shocked to learn of his sudden death, on Monday [sic, Sunday] last, while visiting a friend at Eagle Gorge, Tacoma, Wash. He had attained the ripe age of 86 years and was apparently in good health until the last. He was a remarkable man of great intellectual attainments and in earlier life was a botanist and scientist of repute. We have been furnished with the following sketch of his ministerial career.

"Of the eleven church buildings in eastern Oregon, six are the result of the labors and consecrated efforts of Rev. R. D. Nevius, D.D., who in 1873 resigned the rectorship of Trinity church, Portland, Oregon, in order to give himself as a pioneer missionary, seeking the places where no other missionary of the church had been before, and working under the direction of the bishop to start missions and build churches in new fields wherever the possibilities of future development justified it. He was the first resident clergyman of the church in eastern Oregon, starting on June 7, 1873, in the Grande Ronde valley, where the churches in La Grande, Cove and Union are evidences of his self-sacrificing labors. Crossing into the Powder River Valley, he gathered the congregation and built the church at Baker, and with that as a center, extended his ministry into the John Day river valley and built the church at Canyon City, besides preaching at Connor Creek, Granite Creek, Heppner, Humboldt Basin, Lostine, Malheur (Eldorado), Mormon Basin, Sparta, North Powder, Rye Valley, Prairie City and many other points. During the same period he built the church at The Dalles, residing there for several weeks at a time in ministering to the people. Although a native of New York state, his early ministry was spent in the South. He was ordained a deacon at Savannah by Bishop Steven Elliott in 1853, and had charge of a plantation church at Liberty Hill, Alabama. After his ordination to the priesthood by Bishop Cobbs, in 1854, he became the rector of Christ church, Tuskaloosa [sic], Alabama, where he remained for 11 years, being there during the stirring times of the Civil War. Then going to Pennsylvania, he established the first church mission at Oil City, and built the church at Rouseville.

Returning to Alabama, he became rector of St. John's parish, Mobile, from which he was called to Trinity church, Portland, in 1872. Since leaving eastern Oregon in October, 1879, the same consecrated zeal has shown itself in his work in Sprague, and Yakima, in eastern Washington; and on Puget Sound at Chehalis and Whatcom; while he started the work which resulted in the building of churches by his successors at Lewiston, Idaho; Ellensburg and East Sound, in Washington and Juneau in Alaska. Upon his completing the fiftieth year of his ministry, he resigned from responsible work, although he is [sic, was] still as young in mind and as church [sic].

"As instance of his virility of mind, only last week, the Rev. Upton H. Gibbs received a letter from him enclosing some Mss. [manuscript], asking for his criticism and revision. The doctor wrote, 'I have dictated my thoughts in a compact and merely suggestive way, in a series of what I call theses, mere dogmatic statements, as compact as I could make them and brief. Having now no pulpit of my own I have imagined a congregation made up of my godchildren, young and old, to whom I have preached lying on my couch.'

"Full of years and labors and rich, not in this world's goods, but in the love of his friends and former parishioners, he has now gone to his reward.
"Life's work well done,
"Life's race well run,
"Now cometh rest."
La Grande *Evening Observer*
December 18, 1913

———

1913: December 18
Tacoma *Ledger:*
"With three bishops and nineteen clergymen officiating, the funeral of Rev. R. D. Nevius, the pioneer missionary of the Episcopal church in the district of Oregon, Washington and Alaska, who died Sunday at the age of 86, was held yesterday in Trinity Church." The officiating bishops were Frederic W. Keator of the diocese of Olympia, Lemuel H. Wells, of the diocese of Spokane, and Charles S. Scadding of Oregon.

"The full robed choir of Trinity church sang. The celebration of holy communion was directed in charge of the three bishops and Revs. Charles Y. Grimes of Trinity church, Tacoma,* and H. H. Gowen of Trinity Church Seattle.

"The pall bearers were: Rev. E. M. Rogers, Rev. C. W. DeBois, Rev. Rodney Arney and Rev. Cameron Morrison.

"The only relative of Dr. Nevius present was Charles Dunlap of Puyallup, a cousin. The body was cremated."

[There follows the service detail and names of officiating clergymen and members of the choir.]

Tacoma *Ledger,* December 18, 1913 (from a typescript provided by the Washington State Historical Society in Atwood notes).

*Now Christ Church, Tacoma.

[Baker and The Dalles papers (at UO library, Eugene) checked, December 15-19, 1913. No reference to Nevius found.]

[1914]

1914: January
Seattle Churchman (January 1914):
"Reuben Denton Nevius
"When the history of the Church's work in the Pacific Northwest comes to be written it is certain that a distinguished place must be given to the life and labor of Dr. R. D. Nevius, who passed away from a long earthly ministry at Eagle Gorge on Sunday, Dec. 14. To few have been given to accomplish so much in so many and so varied fields and to hold high to the last the brimming cup of an enthusiasm greater and more precious than that of youth. The deceased priest was born over 86 years ago and was ordained in 1853, by Bishop Elliott of Alabama. After work at Montgomery, Liberty Hill and Mobile, Alabama, and Oil City Pennsylvania, he came to Oregon in 1872, and was in charge of Trinity, Portland. Since then Dr. Nevius has

labored effectively at a large number of missions, including those of La Grande, Baker City, Canyon City, Union, the Dalles and Cove in Oregon, and Lewiston, Spokane, Pomeroy Sprague, Olympia, Chehalis, Whatcom, Yakima, Ellensburg, Hoquiam, Aberdeen, South Bend and Blaine in Washington. He was for a short time missionary at Juneau, Alaska, and in recent years Chaplain of the Fanny Paddock Hospital. It has been stated that in the course of his sixty years' ministry, Dr. Nevius was instrumental in the erection of forty churches and the establishment of thirty missions.

"In addition to his work as a priest of the Church, Dr. Nevius achieved much as a man of science and was recognized as an authority on diatoms. As a botanist his distinction was recognized in the fact that Prof. Asa Gray named after him the newly discovered Neviusia Alabamensis, a fine shrub of which we have one specimen (the only one in Seattle) in the grounds of Trinity Parish Church. The funeral of Dr. Nevius was held in Trinity Church, Tacoma, on Wednesday, Dec. 17, and was attended by Bishops Keator, Wells, and Scadding, and about twenty of the clergy. At the Requiem Celebration of Holy Communion, Bishop Keator was the celebrant. It is hoped that some permanent memorial to Dr. Nevius may be established in the form of a Church Building Fund, the interest of which is to be used for assisting the erection of Mission Churches. Memorial or no memorial, Dr. Nevius will always be regarded as one of the finest types of clergy through whom the Church in the Northwest has been extended. R.L.P.

"The addition may be made to the above notice, that Mr. N. B. Coffman, of Chehalis, Treasurer of the Diocese, has been appointed by the Bishop, Treasurer of the Nevius Memorial Church Building Fund, and will be glad to receive subscriptions."

———

1914: January
Oregon Churchman:
"THE REV. REUBEN D. NEVIUS, D.D.
"Memory of Well Known Clergyman Revered and Treasured.

"Many and eloquent are the tributes paid to the memory of the Rev. Reuben Denton Nevius, D.D., whose death at Tacoma at the age of 86 years removed from the scene of earthly labors a truly historic character in the life of the Church on the Pacific Coast. He was intimately identified with it in the early stages of its growth, and the most eloquent eulogy of him is expressed by the enduring evidences of his faithful, efficient and loving work in his Master's service. He was affectionately known as 'the Nestor of the Clergy of the Pacific Coast.'

"Dr. Nevius graduated from Union College in 1849.* and was ordained deacon in 1853 by Bishop Stephen Elliott, a priest in 1855* by Bishop Cobb. His work was in Alabama until 1856 [sic 1866]. After the Civil War he went to Oil City, Pa., as rector of Christ Church, but in 1870 returned to Alabama, where he was rector of St. John's Church, Mobile, two years. Then he came to Portland, to become rector of Trinity Church. It is stated that he founded more than thirty parishes and missions in Oregon and Washington. He was also in Alaska for some time.

"Bishop Scadding went to Tacoma December 18 to attend the funeral.

"Dr. Nevius will be missed by the multitude of friends of every faith and condition, which he made by the sweetness and the usefulness of his fruitful life."
Oregon Churchman
January, 1914
*Nevius graduated from Union College in 1848 and was ordained a priest in 1854.

———

1914: January
Unidentified publication:
"On the Third Sunday in Advent, December 14, the Rev. Reuben D. Nevius, D.D., died In Tacoma, Washington, at the age of eight-six years. Throughout the West, and elsewhere in the Church where missionary work is known, the name of Dr. Nevius is held in honor. He is one of those who helped to lay the very foundations of the church in the Northwest.

"Ordained deacon by Bishop Stephen Elliott of Georgia, in 1853, he had completed sixty years in holy orders. He was made priest by Bishop Nicholas Hammer

Cobbs, of Alabama, that saint of the southern Church, and for fifteen years as priest and teacher he exercised his ministry in the South. In 1872 he was called to be rector of Trinity Church, Portland, Oregon, the largest parish in the state. It was even then a city of goodly promise set amid beautiful surroundings, and to the priest of forty-five years it offered a healthy sphere of activity as well as a haven of comfort. A life of usefulness and honor might well be expected.

"But this indomitable man was greatly concerned for the sheep who were without a shepherd. He could not forget the desert places beyond the mountains, with their handful of scattered settlers, and so it was that in the middle [of] life he resigned his parish, and for forty years traveled in places where no herald of the Church had ever gone, opening new fields everywhere. He was the first Church clergyman to reside beyond the mountains in the present district of Eastern Oregon. Six of its first eleven churches were built by him. In 1879 he passed over into Washington and did like work there, where six more churches and many mission stations begun by him bear testimony to his zeal in the extension of the Kingdom. He also at one time made a scouting trip to Alaska. In the fiftieth year of his ministry, at the age of seventy-six, he retired from this arduous service and became priest in charge of old St. Peter's Church, Tacoma.

"This little church has one remarkable feature. When built it was a center of lumbering operations. The proprietors of the mill offered the necessary lumber for its construction and the mill men themselves gave labor and money. The church was erected in three days. It had, however, no bell tower, but beside it there stood a noble fir tree; this was cut off thirty [sic, fifty] feet from the ground and a bell placed upon the flat top. When the rings of the tree were counted it was found to be 275 years old. St. Peter's Church, therefore, claims that it has the oldest bell tower in the United States.

"It was in this quiet spot, but still among the scenes of his earlier activity, that the old doctor passed his sunset days, cheered by the honor and regard of those about him. He was a lover of nature and of men. Among other of his interests, he was a botanist of repute, and the plant Neviusia Alabamensis [sic] was named in his honor.

"It was a courageous and vivid life which was lived by this man, and his passing takes away one more of those early pioneers who have stood as striking figures in the history of the Church's progress. It is to lives such as his that the Church owes whatever a stability and power she has in the newer lands of the West.
[copy of article from a church publication, approx. 6 1/2x8 1/2", among Atwood notes] Jan., 1914, pp. 37-38

———

1914: January 6 (Epiphany)
Rand (1974) 22:
Nevius Hall at Baker City burned to the ground.

———

1914: January 6
Deed recorded from The Diocese of Olympia Inc., to Carl Lund and Mary Lund, of Lot 1, Block 59, Town (now City) of Hoquiam, and the northwesterly half of Lot 2, dated December 30, 1913, for $7,000, being the St. David's hospital and chapel property.

———

1914:
Rt. Rev. Lemuel H. Wells
"EPISCOPALIANS BUILT HERE
"FIRST STONE CHURCH IN
"STATE OF WASHINGTON

———

"Bishop L. H. Wells Tells of
"Pioneer Days With Dr.
"Reuben D. Nevius

"Bishop Lemuel H. Wells, who has recently resigned his post as bishop of the Protestant Episcopal Jurisdiction of Spokane [In January 1914], closed his years of faithful, active service in this state by a memorable historical address delivered at All Saints' Cathedral, Spokane.

"In it Bishop Wells, who was a pioneer Tacoman, and whose work in this city is well remembered, told some of the struggles of early church workers in the state of Washington. The address follows:

"I have been asked by your bishop to give an historical address upon the Missionary District of Spokane. As my papers are all packed away for removal, I will have to rely entirely upon my memory, which I trust will prove accurate enough for this purpose.

"In 1871 Bishop Morris, with his residence in Portland, was in charge of Oregon, Washington and Northern Idaho. In that year I was appointed, by him a missionary at Walla Walla; it was then a place of about 1300 inhabitants—the largest city in the state, and the only town of any size in Eastern Washington, indeed, the whole white population east of the Cascades was about 7000, and the Episcopal church had six communicants—one man and five women. Such was the beginning of our work in the District of Spokane.

"Nevius Joins Him

"A few years later [in 1879] the Rev. Reuben D. Nevius, D.D., joined me, making two clergymen of our church in the Inland Empire. He was a great pioneer missionary, traveling far and near with his famous span of horses visiting Eastern Oregon and Idaho; taking along coffee pot and frying pan, his food and blankets, prayer books and hymnals, and some candles to light up the school houses. When meal time came, he cooked and ate; when night came, he slept—sometimes under his buggy or sleigh.

"Dr. Nevius was a great church builder, having erected twenty-five [sic] houses of worship. In those days there were no railroads, few wagon roads, and fewer bridges, as well as a dearth of hotels. Outside of Walla Walla there were not many families, mostly single men living in cabins of one room, with a cook stove, bunk, chair or homemade bench, and a rough table. They were all most hospitable, the families letting you sleep in the bed with the children, and the single men would take you into the bunk with them, or let you spread your blankets on the floor with the other travelers. If the floor was too dirty, then there was a barn or haystack, or the ground under the big sagebrush, which was always available.

"Beginnings in Spokane

"About 1889, when the Northern Pacific railway was building and the city of Spokane had about 600 [?, poss. 650] inhabitants, Dr. Nevius, then living in Lewiston, began holding occasional services here, then moved here and built a little church at the edge of the town, on the corner of Riverside and Lincoln, opposite the present post office. He soon opened a school for boys and girls in the church, and called it the Rodney Morris school. After the first spurt, Spokane did not grow very fast—indeed it seemed to be dying out. Cheney was the largest place and the most promising. Soon our church got into difficulties and languished and Dr. Nevius became discouraged.

"Bishop Paddock, who had become the bishop of the whole state of Washington, sent me up here to investigate whether it would be better to abandon the mission and shut up the church. I reported that I thought Spokane would always have six hundred inhabitants, perhaps more, even if it did not grow like Cheney; that there were some good, earnest people here who were very anxious to have the services of our church, and so I advised that the mission be continued. During this visit, Dr. Nevius said the school should have more land. He took me away into the woods to his [sic, this?] block on the corner of Sprague and Madison as well fitted for the school, because it was away from the allurements of the city and had more trees and less rocks than most places. I obtained from the Northern Pacific railway a contract to sell it to us for $240 for the school, if the building should be put upon it within a year, but to be sure I put into the contract 'For school, religious and benevolent purposes.' On the last day of the year nothing had been done, and we were about to lose the land when the vestry of All Saints' church moved their church (which was also used for the school) upon the land and saved the property. It was deeded to the trustees of the Protestant Episcopal church in Washington, and Bishop Paddock paid the $240.

"When Dr. Nevius moved on to North Yakima [sic, Olympia in June 1883], Bishop Paddock sent the Rev. C. C. Burnett to take his place, who died here; but his widow is still going in and out among us, an honored name in Israel.

"How the Beginnings Were Made

"In 1882, at the invitation of Mr. George Brooke, Dr. Nevius began a monthly service at the new town of Sprague, mostly a city of tents. The first service was held in one of the new buildings, which was a saloon, but as some of the congregation were in undue haste to slake their thirst at the conclusion of the service, and the surroundings were not conducive to devotion, they decided to erect a church ready for the next monthly service. At this next service, the Doctor arrived on Friday and found all the material on the ground, but not a stroke had been done upon the structure. So the whole town got out early on Saturday morning with hammers, axes, saws and any tool they happened to have, and by midnight the church was finished and ready for service the next day.

"When Dr. Nevius moved on to Yakima [sic. Olympia in June 1883], Mr. and Mrs. Brooke kept up the services between them and for years shared between them the duties and emoluments of sexton, Sunday school teacher, superintendent, treasurer, warden and lay reader.

"In 1893 [sic, 1885], when the Northern Pacific was built through, a town was started at North Yakima, and Dr. Nevius moved there, having previously held some services. In a short time he had collected a congregation, and built a pretty little stone church, designed by Mr. Stone [sic. Edward Tuckerman Potter], the great church architect of Boston [sic, Schenectady, N.Y.]. This was the first brick or stone church erected, I believe, in the state of Washington. From North Yakima Dr. Nevius went over to Bellingham, and the greatest missionary we have had was lost to this section.

"Acts of the Apostles

"I have thus written the early history of our church in the district of Spokane as a kind of Acts of the Apostles. For, as St. Paul was everywhere outside of Judea found first preaching the gospel and establishing the church, so Dr. Nevius, as soon as a town was started, was first on the ground holding services, obtaining a lot, and building a church.

"I remember how we heard that a town called Dayton had been started about thirty miles from Walla Walla; so we mounted our horses and rode up there. We found a large acreage surveyed, and laid out in city lots, but only one house, and the proprietor explained with some emotion that owing to the dearth of inhabitants, the city would be postponed for a year. He generously gave us a lot for a church, but it is still outside the center of population. Dr. Nevius pushed on thirty miles farther to Pomeroy, where there was a young town, and there he gathered a congregation and built a church.

"After Dr. Nevius left this district several excellent clergymen came[?] and ... [missing].

"Then and Now

"When Bishop Paddock broke down in 1892 relief was given him by dividing the state, creating the District of Spokane and electing me Bishop.

"On taking charge I found about 500 communicants, four clergymen, two parishes (All Saints, Spokane; St. Paul's, Walla Walla), ten missions, nine church buildings (no rectories or parish houses), two schools (one of them closed, the other leased).

"I found property valued at about $170,000, with an indebtedness of about $40,000. The four clergymen were the Rev. L. M. Lane, rector of All Saints, Spokane; Dr. Law, rector at Walla Walla; Mr. Collier, missionary, and Rev. J.N.T. Goss, missionary of the rest of the district south of Spokane. The Rev. Rufus Chase had just left North Yakima. Two army chaplains were at Fort Walla Walla and Old Fort Spokane.

"When I gave up the reins to my successor last January, the district had: 3042 communicants, five parishes, 42 missions, 18 active clergy, 38 church buildings, five parish houses, three schools in active operation, one hospital with 100 beds, one church home for children. The property is valued at about $900,000; endowments in bonds, etc., $25,000; indebtedness, about $100,000.

"I am sorry to leave this indebtedness to my successor. I had hoped to clear it off and have all our institutions endowed, at least moderately, thus leaving him free to inaugurate his own plans without inheriting a burden.

"When I was consecrated, Bishop Morris, who was the preacher, told this incident. He told how Bishop Horatio Potter of New York with much impressiveness said to him: 'The mistake of my episcopate has been that I have not founded institutions.' Turning to me Bishop Morris said, 'My brother, the advice of a great Bishop of New York is well worth your consideration.' I have tried to follow this advice and I thank God for the institutions he has enabled me to start and carry on thus far, even though they represent much toil and self-denial and have not yet grown into all I hoped and prayed they would become. When ... [missing]."

———

1914: May 20
Journal, Diocese of Olympia, 1914:
Convocation met at St. Mark's Church, Seattle.
Rev. Frederic T. Webb, Secretary (of Convention):

"An expression of gratitude for the long years of service of the Rev. Reuben Denton Nevius, Doctor in Divinity, venerable and beloved, whose name for many years has stood first in place and in honor on our Clergy list, was called to his reward December 14th, 1913. Certainly it was not without significance that this date coincided with the Third Sunday in Advent, when the work of the Christian Ministry is the appointed subject of prayer and praise in all the Churches; for who of us who knew dear Dr. Nevius, can but realize how splendidly exemplified in his life and work were the words found in the Epistle appointed for the day,* setting forth the mark of the good steward of the mysteries of God—'that a man be found faithful.'

"Dr. Nevius came to the Northwest in 1872, when he was called to be Rector of Trinity Church, Portland, Oregon. In the following year when Bishop Morris, who was then Bishop of the Church in that large field which now embraces the Dioceses of Oregon and Olympia, besides the Missionary Districts of Idaho, Spokane and Eastern Oregon—wanted a General Missionary to minister to the widely scattered congregations, Dr. Nevius quickly and gladly gave up his parish that he might take up this work; and to that work he gave himself unstinted devotion and self-sacrifice. For forty years his life, with all his rare powers of mind and heart, was given to Missionary work; and if the results of his labors were to be left out, the history of the Church in the Northwest would have to be rewritten. In what is now the Diocese of Olympia, he labored in Olympia, Chehalis, Aberdeen, Hoquiam, Ocosta, South Bend, Buckley, Whatcom, (now Bellingham), Blaine and Tacoma. In many of these places the church buildings which he built still stand as monuments to his untiring zeal and devotion. In recent years, when failing physical strength had unfitted him for the continuous care of a mission, I have found it hard to say him Nay when he has pleaded with me to let him take up the work in some place and build one more Church. When denied this privilege, he was, nevertheless, always ready to go wherever he might be sent for a single service, and even after his eyesight had so failed that he could no longer read the services in the Prayer Book, he found some one to read them to him over and over again until he could say them from memory, in order that he might be useful. While his physical powers waned with increasing years, his spiritual strength was unabated even to the moment when the call came which summoned him to the clearer vision of the Lord whom he loved and whom he had served so faithfully and well. With us through so many years, we miss him today, but who shall say he is not with us still? Who shall say that his prayers no longer go up with our blessing upon and His guidance of this Diocese which he loved so well."

Bishop Keator noted that he had attended the General Convention of 1913 in New York, which among other actions:

"Resolved, That the Church should work toward the adoption of one Pension System covering the entire territory of the Church and the entire scope of pension activity and operating under definite and known rules.

"Resolved, That the Pension System of the Church should be so constructed as to take cognizance of the problems of accrued liabilities.

"Resolved, That the contributions and the continuing liabilities should be actuarially calculated so as to balance.

"Resolved, That the assessments to support the continuing liabilities should be adjusted upon the principle of an actuarial relation between the liabilities and the benefits.

"Resolved. That the principle of distribution should be so arranged that the maximum pension should not exceed $2000 per annum, and that the minimum

limit should be $600 per annum.

"Resolved. That the Joint Commission on the support of the Clergy be continued, with power to become a corporation, and to take such other steps as may be necessary to put into operation these pension principles, it being understood, however, that until they can be successfully established, the Church should continue to support the existing incorporated agencies."

Keator continued, "The subject of an adequate Pension System for the Clergy, and those dependent upon them, it goes without saying, is a very large and a very intricate subject which I may not venture to discuss at length, at the expense of your time and patience. Suffice it to say, that it is a subject which for a long time increasingly has lain upon the mind and conscience of the whole Church, as well as the separate parts of it. It is a subject to which it now appears, the church has decided to face and to face squarely, with the determination, if possible, to find some satisfactory solution. It is a subject certainly, in which every clergyman, old and young, in this Diocese, is vitally concerned. A subject, no less, in which the whole Diocese, Laymen as well as Clergymen, ought to be interested.

"As aiding to the realization of how very practical and timely the present consideration of this subject is, I may remind you first of the very inadequate Disabled Clergy Fund of this Diocese, the principal of which has been seriously impaired within the past few years by reason of the necessary care of two of our aged clergy; and second, of the fact, as shown by the official statement of the General Clergy Relief Fund which shows that during the past year there has been appropriated from this fund to five beneficiaries in this Diocese, the sum of $1000, while 13 out of 52 Parishes and Missions have contributed to the fund $1991.61, leaving a deficit, to anything but a credit of this Diocese, of $800.39.

"The truth which is demonstrated, not only in our experience, but in the experience of the whole Church, is that a pension system which has to depend upon general and indefinite appeals is not only inadequate, but doomed sooner or later to utter failure. I am spared the necessity of speaking further on this subject, at the present time, and you of listening to me, for the reason that a carefully prepared discussion of the subject, by Mr. Moneel Sayre, an expert Actuary, has been sent for distribution at this Convention.

"What action is asked of us today will be seen in letter from the Bishop of Massachusetts, who, a leader in many things, if *facile princeps* in this, and has put the whole Church in his debt by reason of his devotion to the cause.

"In short we are not asked to commit ourselves to any policy, not even to the principle itself, but to appoint a committee—strong, efficient and hopeful, who shall make a study of the proposed system, with such help as they will readily receive from the promoters of the plan and report to our next Convention the results of their study, and the details of the plan so far as it will affect us, upon all which we may then take such action as may seem not only best but feasible."

"The House of Churchwomen

"The history of the movement leading up to this organization in this Diocese is brief but important. It began in the first convention of the Diocese [in 1911] after its admission into union with the General Convention in October 1910. Our Convention met in May, 1911, in St. Paul's Church, Seattle, and we were engaged in the preparation and first adoption of our Constitution. It happened that during this session I was called away for a short time to attend an important matter which had suddenly arisen, and on my return I learned that a motion had been made and tentatively adopted by the Convention by virtue of which women were made eligible for election on vestries in the Parishes of this Diocese.** It was evidently based upon the very laudable feeling that since in all our Church work our good Church women are always so active and so efficient it was no more than right that they should be officially recognized and given a voice and a hand in the management of the same token in the affairs of the Diocese also. It was a feeling in which every true man could not but share. At the same time the action taken was short-sighted, as sober second thought clearly showed, not because of its effect upon the women, but rather because of its effect upon the men. For the almost certain result would have been that the men in their generosity would have been altogether likely to say that since the good women are so interested and so efficient[,] why not let them do it all. In other words, and in short, the chances were that we should have the women bearing the whole burden of church work while the men were permitted to side-step and go free. When this issue was fairly presented, the men of the Convention realized that it meant unfairness rather than fairness to the women, and the result was that they reconsidered their action, and in its stead the following found its way into our Constitution and was finally adopted as Article IV, Section 7: 'Provision may be made by Canon for a House of Churchwomen to meet in the same week with the Convention, with power, subject at all times to the constitution and Canons of the Diocese, to legislate for the conduct of women's work in the Church, and to act in an advisory capacity upon such other matters as the convention may from time to time submit to it for its opinion.' Subsequently, and at our last Convention in 1913, a Canon was adopted by virtue of which our first House of Churchwomen has been called to meet at this time. Unfortunately it now appears that the Canon adopted in the rush of business last year failed to make proper provision for some of the essentials of organization, such, e.g., as the number necessary to constitute a quorum, the officers of the organization, etc., and it will be necessary to adopt at this time—and I understand the Chancellor of the Diocese at the proper time will propose—certain amendments to the Canon to cure these defects. This will not, however, prevent the organization at this time, I take it, and we shall hope to launch today, the new House with many hopes for its future usefulness and helpfulness.

"Many have been the questions which have come to us concerning it and I am bound to add not a few criticisms. [']Now that you have got it, what do you propose to do with it?['] This has been the chief question. And to it I can only answer, 'Wait and See.'... We shall have the example of the House of Churchwomen of California to help us as our guide....

"One of the criticisms which I have heard is, as to the effect of this organization upon the Woman's Auxiliary of the Diocese, but with all respect I feel sure that there need be no conflict between the two. The Auxiliary has to do chiefly with the work of the General Board of Missions. The House of Churchwomen will have to do chiefly with the work of the Diocese...."

"One has recently written, 'There is a kind of music popular with uncritical audiences and with people who know no better, which answers to the name of Ragtime. It is the music of those who do not know good music, or who have not the moral force to demand it.' But as he goes on to say, 'The spirit of ragtime is not confined to music,' for there is a ragtime business, ragtime politics, ragtime society, ragtime literature, and even ragtime religion. Surely it is the mission of the Church of Christ, teaching the old Faith, proclaiming the whole Gospel, and ministering the Sacraments ordained of Christ himself, to hold up before men the true values and help them realize the same.*

"All the problems which confront us, the lack of money, the lack of helpers, the indifference so wide-spread about us, all these are but a challenge to us for more love, more patience, more sincerity, more courage, more zeal."

***

In other business the Convention appropriated $17.42 for a "Memorial notice" of Rev. R. D. Nevius, D. D., to the Churchman Co., New York and $8.40 to The Living Church, Milwaukee. The *Journal* also recorded the establishment of a Nevius Memorial Building Fund, "Account opened March 3rd, 1914." with "Receipts to day" of $72.00, of which $70.00 and being invested and $2.00 remained as a "Balance on hand." The *Journal* also carried the following memorial notice:

Rev. Reuben Denton Nevius, D.D.

The Convention of the Diocese of Olympia, desires to put on record an expression of gratitude to Almighty God for the many and useful years of the life of the Rev. Reuben Denton Nevius, D.D.

Born in Ovid, New York, over eighty-six years ago, the beginning of his ministry was passed in the South, with the chivalrous spirit of whose best people he never ceased to be in sympathy and of which he might to the end of his days be called an honorable exponent. He came to Portland, Oregon in 1872, and was the successful rector of Trinity Church, the important and only parish then in that metropolis, until, Bishop Morris desiring him for the work, he took up the labors of a pioneer missionary. These he carried on with great enthusiasm, because his heart was wholly in his task. In the new Northwest it was a period of unusual opportunity and Dr. Nevius won results that have not often been surpassed in the field of mission-

ary endeavor. He built a large number of Churches and established more than thirty Missions in Oregon, Idaho and Washington, among them many which are now strong, self-supporting parishes.

Dr. Nevius was also distinguished as a botanist, the Neviusia Alabamensis being named after him by Dr. Asa Gray. His joy in plants and trees and in the microscopic forms of life, kept his spirit fresh and buoyant. He lived near nature's heart. He was a rare thinker and his theological conception was clear, positive and wholly in accord with the Catholic faith. His life thus, in a double sense, inwardly in thought and outwardly in converse with nature, was lived near to God.

The friends of his earlier years, those at least who grew old along with him, were the friends of his later years, for he made friends and kept them, and few there are who stood in the center of a wider circle of people, so esteemed and honored and loved for the qualities that make up a true man, a true Christian and a true priest.

He has entered, we believe, into that Presence which nature scarcely concealing, at least in part revealed to him—into the Presence of his Lord, who has for him the crown and the "Well done, good and faithful servant."

The history of the Church in these five Dioceses and Missionary Districts could not be well written without giving large place to his name and work. His memory truly is blessed.

*I Corinthians IV. I. "Let a man so account of us, as of the ministers of Christ and stewards of the mysteries of God. Moreover, it is required in stewards, that a man be found faithful. But with me it is a very small thing that I should be judged of you, or of man's judgement: yea, I judge not mine own self. For I know nothing by myself; yet am I not hereby justified: but He that judgeth me is the Lord. Therefore judge nothing before the time, until the Lord come, who both will bring to light the hidden things of darkness, and will make manifest the counsels of the hearts: and then shall every man have praise of God." [Book of Common Prayer, 1890 ed.]

**The *Journal* for 1911 notes only: "The Bishop having been called away, the Convention was [illegible] on motion of the [Rev. E. V. Shayler, into a committee of [illegible] with the Rev. Dr. Webb as chairman, for the consideration of the [illegible] of the Constitution."

———

1914:
Panama Canal opened.

[1915]

1915: May 15
Journal, Diocese of Olympia, 1915:

The "Annual Report of the Treasurer," May 16, 1914 to May 15, 1915, reported the Nevius Memorial Building Fund had a beginning balance of $172.00. Contributions had been made by Mrs. Kate C. Millett, Chehalis, $200.00; Mrs. E. A. Frost, Chehalis, $40.00; Dr. E. A. Goldsmith, Seattle, $5.00; and Mr. Charles E. Shepard, Seattle, $5.00; as well as a "Canonical offering" by the Church of the Epiphany, Chehalis of $7.85 for a total of $257.85 in contributions. $5.30 had been earned in interest, less $1.29 "paid for earned interest," leaving a "Total of principal and interest invested: of $333.86.

[1917]

1917: November 19
Elisabeth L. Lang:
"The Dalles, Oregon. November 19, 1917
"Prof. Albert R. Sweetser,
        "Eugene, Oregon.
"My dear Professor Sweetser:
"I owe and hereby offer you my sincere apologies for not responding to your letter of October 11th. Upon arrival it was laid aside that I might answer it on a less busy day - which has not yet arrive - meantime, your second letter brings my sin of omission accusingly before me. Please excuse me and lay it in all truth to the Red Cross.
"When the Lang family arrived in The Dalles, in October, 1875, Dr. Nevius was serving as Episcopal missionary throughout Eastern Oregon with headquarters here

and was building St. Paul's Church, in this city. Our friendship with him became very close and was broken only by his death, a few years ago.

"He was a man of delightful personality, of wonderful learning and the wisest botanist I have ever known. He loved the study of plant life above all else. Death had taken his entire family - wife, children, parents, brother and sisters, and apparently filled that terrible void in his life by devotion to the study of growing things. Children always loved him as dearly as he loved them and it was wonderful to find the numberless places in which he had sown the seeds of his craft. I know of many persons whose love of forestry and plants was begun in childhood through the marvels disclosed by Dr. Nevius' microscope. I wish I had the power to describe him to you properly; a gentleman of the highest breeding and refinement; a scholar of the most advanced class, and a most affectionate and kindly teacher of all who came under his ministrations.

"When Nevius Hall, at Baker, was dedicated the Doctor wrote a very complete sketch of his life. It was read and then given into the keeping of Bishop Paddock. My sister and I wish very much for a copy of it and I will try to get it from the Bishop that you may have a copy also.

"A few years before his death Dr. Nevius' Eyesight became much impaired and he began dividing and giving his precious books where he wished them finally to go. I believe his herbariums and various collections went in the same manner but through a clergyman in Tacoma it may be possible to learn positively. I will write to him and let you know of my findings.

"If in any way I can be of service to you in the matter of our dear old friend's history, it will give me pleasure to send you all I possibly can, and I certainly will answer promptly should you call on me in future.

"Sincerely yours,

"Elisabeth L. Lang

[Handwritten postscript at bottom of above typescript, apparently added about 1952:] "This is a copy of a letter sent to the late Prof. Sweetser of the U. of Ore. (Eugene) some years ago. Whether the two starred items [request for copy of Nevius's autobiographic sketch and inquiry of clergyman in Tacoma] were completed, I do not know, but if so, the letters relating to them were not contained in Professor Sweetser's notes relative to Dr. Nevius. (Helen M. Gilkey, O.S.C.)"

[1936]

1936: March 27
Rt. Rev. Lemuel H. Wells died in Tacoma, Wa. age 94.

[1937]

1937: March 4
Half-sister Mary Denton Eastman Harris died in Cleveland, Ohio: Mary Denton Eastman (half-sister); b. Ovid, N.Y. June 30, 1844; m. James Harris (b. vicinity Ovid, N.Y.; d. Cleveland, Ohio) 1867; d. Cleveland, Ohio, March 4, 1937 (age 92 yrs. 8 mos.)

[1939]

1939: September 23
Evening East Oregonian (Pendleton):
"*Church Survives All*
"Episcopal House
At Canyon City
Half Century Old
"Canyon City, Sept. 23—Consecrated to the Lord and baptized in fire is the record of the half century old St. Thomas Episcopal church.

"Erected in 1876 on the ashes of a fire that destroyed Canyon City in the late seventies, the little church went unscathed through the fire that leveled that town in 1898. And, again, on April 19, 1937, when fire for the third time destroyed the business section of that city, this little church held out its restraining hand and the fire stopped—right at its door-sill. It seemingly bears a charmed life.

"Erected Under Nevius

"When eastern Oregon was but a sparsely settled country with Canyon City its most populous center, Doctor R. D. Nevius, then residing in The Dalles, caused the erection of eight Episcopal churches, and among the first was the St. Thomas church at Canyon City—a mission church.

"Built in the true, old style of architecture, with sharp pitched roof and window frames, the church stands on a lot in the center of town donated by W. H. Clark, a prominent miner of the seventies, father of R. A. Clark and Mrs. [illegible] Hicks of Canyon City, and Mrs. Minnie Myrtle Ford[?], now of Portland (who, by the way, was the second white child born in Canyon City).

"The interior of the church was finished in knotty pine[*]. The rafters are of hewn, beveled, crossed timbers, open to the roof. The pews are plank, whip-sawed from the nearby forest. The windows, of diamond shaped stained glass, were shipped by freight wagon. It has an ample vestry and quarters for a rector.

"Most of the present furniture of the chancel was presented in memorial of departed loved ones. The altar was donated in memory of Villa P. Sells and of Johanna Wood Chambers; the election set, in memory of Margaret Wood and Isaiah H. Wood; the candelabra in memory of William Otis Patterson, Mary Blake Patterson, and Mary Zoe Patterson; the cross on the altar in memory of Anna M. Lucas. The collection plate was presented by Lottie Mildred Sollinger, aged 7, and Fay Elizabeth Sollinger, aged 5. The font was presented by Oscar Schmidt.

"Reared in Lusty Era

"When the church first reared its belfry, Canyon City was a wild and wooly mining camp; throbbing with the lust of gold, and the tension of boom town life. It looked down on a straggling street, filled with pack trains, roughly dressed miners, black coated gamblers; upon the violence and lawlessness of a western mining camp. Many killings have taken place almost within the shadow of this histori[c]al little edifice.

"For over fifty years this church, steeped in history, has stood as a monument to the untiring labors of Doctor Nevius, offering its welcoming hand to all seeking spiritual guidance. Many rectors have come and gone, but the little church goes on forever. It is known to every man, woman and child in Grant county, and to many hundreds throughout the state. It is a structure revered and loved by all: a shrine to the clergy of the Episcopal faith. And, like the cabin of Joaquin Miller, which stands on a nearby hillside, one of Oregon's historic structures."

Evening East Oregonian (Pendleton)
September 23, 1939

[1943]

1943:
Rand (1974) 38, 39:
Nevius Hall at Baker refurbished, used by the U.S.O.

[1945]

1945:
Rev. Herbert H. Gowen:
"...There are...those whose work follows so vividly to our own day and who have left so permanent a mark in our missionary structure that they cannot be left unnoticed, ...and have died in within the memory of many of us. The first is Rev. Reuben Denton Nevius, D.D., who, after a sad domestic bereavement, came to us from his native Alabama [sic]. From that day until his death in 1913 at Tacoma at the age of 86, Dr. Nevius was indefatigable in the founding and organizing of missions, all the way from Eastern Washington to the Grays Harbor country, and from Aberdeen northwards to Blaine on the borders of British Columbia. Whatever work he touched he beautified. A man of wide culture, of moving eloquence, and of warm human sympathies, he made his mark wherever he went, not least among the girls of the Annie Wright Seminary. He was notable not only for his missionary zeal and his scholarship, but was also known nationally as a man of science. In Alabama he discovered the beautiful shrub named after him by Dr. Asa Gray, the 'Neviusia Alabamensis.' Two specimens of this shrub were planted in the District, one in the

grounds of the old Annie Wright Seminary and the other in the grounds of Trinity Church, Seattle. Alas, it seems that both have succumbed to the ravages of change. Also to be regretted is the disappearance of the Reuben Denton Nevius Fund which was inaugurated at a meeting following Dr. Nevius' funeral from Trinity Church, Tacoma, in 1913. This fund was intended to assist the foundation of new missions, but only $150 was collected and this was ultimately returned to the parish which had taken most interest in the effort, Epiphany Parish, Chehalis."

Rev. Herbert H. Gowen, D.D> "Some Early Missionaries in our Northwest" (pamphlet, "Published by the Historiographer, Diocese of Olympia, 1945), pp. 12-13.

[1951]

1951:

Journal, Diocese of Olympia, 1951:

"Our small diocesan Loan Fund has been greatly increased by the generous bequest of the late Albert T. Timmerman. $40,000 has so far been distributed to us, and a like amount to the Cathedral; our share has been added to our little Church Assistance Fund, and the whole has been set apart now as 'The Nevius Fund,' to perpetuate the memory of Dr. Nevius, one of our distinguished pioneer missionaries and church builders. This loan fund, which will approximate $60,000 by the end of this year, is administered by the Loan Committee of the Department of Finance. From it loans will be made to our congregations for building purposes, where local resources are not available. They will be interest-bearing loans. Mr. Timmerman's bequest to the Diocese prescribes that this fund be held in trust, the income to go for missionary work in the Diocese. If the principal is to be used for loans, then it is clear that the loans must be carefully and prudently made and that they must earn their fair value. The income will go into the missionary budget. Thus, in effect, every dollar will work twice and so fulfill in double measure the intention of the fund and its donors."

[1952]

1952: May 13
Mrs. Gertrude Dunlap
334 2nd St. S.W.
Puyallup, Wash.
"May 13th, 1952
"Mr. Howard [sic] Atwood.
"Dear Sir. I am very sorry that I can not give you the information you want, regarding Cosin Rubens Papers & other personel [sic] property. at the time Cusin Rubbin, was pastor in one of the Oldest Churches in Tacoma. it was an Old wooden Church with Iva [ivy] vine almost covering it and how he Loved it. Since his Death that building has been Torn down & a new Church Built. Cusin Ruben roomed at a Home across the street from the Fannapadic [Fannie Paddock] Hospital and was Chaplin there. the Name of the Church St. Lukes [sic, St. Peter's] Apiscepol Church. My Husband has been gone 32 years and Cusin Ruben passed before he did. where he roomed it seemed she had charge of all arangements [sic] & his business. we did not know till the day before his Funeral he had passed away. my Husband & I were the only relatives there. I do not know of one of his relatives Living not eny out west. but my Sister in Law a widow of my Husband's Bro. & I don't think she knew eny of the Family as they were of a very small Family. you might get some Information from the Church about Cusin Ruben. I would gladly go look it up but I am so crippled up with Archritas [sic] and am 76 years so don't get around verry much. I am a verry poor writer but you might make this out. Resp. yours Mrs. G. Dunlap"

———

1952: October 13
Prof. Trevor Kincaid
University of Washington
Department of Zoology
Seattle 5
"October 13 - 1952

"Mr. Howland Atwood
"Huntington Library
"San Marino 9
"California
"My dear Mr. Atwood,
"I regret not being able to contribute to your history of the activities of Dr. Nevius in the Northwest. When a boy in Olympia I found he had encouraged there the establishment of an 'Agassiz Association'* for the study of Natural History. It has been disbanded however a number of years previously as these young people grew up and scattered.
"I met Dr. Nevius only once when he was in my office ant the University many years ago. I have been with the University since 1894....
"Nevius did a great deal to encourage young people to take up the study of Natural History, but in a pioneer community this was an uphill proposition.
"Yours sincerely,
"Trevor Kincaid."
*After Jean Lous Rudolphe Agassiz (1807-1873), Swiss-born American naturalist. He taught at Harvard University after 1848 and strongly influenced a generation of American natural scientists.

[1953]

1953: January 7
Harold F. Miller
The Office of the Principal
Ovid Central School
OVID, NEW YORK
"January 7, 1953
"Mr. Howland Atwood
"Huntington Library
"San Marino
"Calif.
"Dear Mr. Atwood,
"I have not been able to find any information about Rev. Nevius in our school records There are two people here in Ovid who know about him and I have turned this over to them. One is Miss Clara R. Purdy, Ovid, N.Y., who will be sending some information to you. The other is John Eastman, Ovid N.Y., who is a relative of Mr. Nevius. Union college is at Schenectady, N. Y.
"I believe that you will be hearing from these people or you may wish to contact them.
"Sincerely yours,
"Harold P. Miller
"Supervising Principal"

———

1953: January 10
John Nevius Eastman:
"Ovid, New York
"Jan. 10, 1953
"Howland Atwood
"Huntington Library
"San Marino, California
"Dear Sir:
"A letter, which you sent to the Ovid School, has been called to my attention.
"Reuben Denton Nevius's mother was my grandmother. (She was married to Chester Eastman, my grandfather, in 1832.) I now live in the house where she died and where Reuben visited.
"Reuben was born Nov. 26, 1827. He was the son of Benjamin Nevius and Mary Denton. He married Minnie Tuomey July 31, 1867. She was a southern lady. They had twins who died. She died shortly afterward with yellow fever. Reuben was a missionary in Tacoma, Washington for a long time, and in Alaska for some time. After he died in 1913, his body was cremated and sent to Ovid. I placed his ashes

on his mother's grave as he had requested. He had a brother, John Nevius, who was a missionary to Chefoo, China for over forty years.

"The enclosed snapshot is the latest one sent by him. (Reuben is on the left.)

"I hope that this may be of help to your in compiling the biography.

"Very truly yours
"John Nevius Eastman"

1953: February 3
Clifford C. Gregg:
Chicago Natural History Museum
Roosevelt Road And Lake Shore Dr.
Chicago 5, Illinois
Office of The Director
3 February, 1953
"Dear Mr. Atwood:

"In response to your letter of the 21st, inquiry had been made here concerning the late Rev. Dr. Reuben Denton Nevius. According to one of his correspondents, Dr. V. A. Latham, 1644 W. Morse Avenue, Chicago, Illinois,* Dr. Nevius maintained no private collection of diatoms; instead, he sent material to other workers in this field. Some of these specimens are in the possession of Dr. Latham; others may be expected to be present in the H. L. Smith collection at Shortridge High School at Indianapolis, Indiana and in the general collections of the Academy of Natural Sciences in Philadelphia and of the New York Botanical Garden....

"Very truly yours,
"Clifford C. Gregg
"Director"

*See March 1, 1953, below.

———

1953: February 18
G. Dallas Hanna:
California Academy Of Sciences
Golden Gate Park
San Francisco 18, California
"February 18, 1953
"Mr. Howland Atwood...

"I find two titles in my bibliography which have bearing on Dr. Nevius' work:
Diatoms from Washington Territory
"American Monthly Microscopic Journal, vo. 6, 1885, pp. 97-98.

"Notes on the Habitat of Diatoms (in Puget Sound) "American Monthly Microscopic Journal,
"vol. 15, 1894, pp. 270-271.
"Sincerely yours,
"G. Dallas Hanna"

———

1953: March 1[?]
Dr. V. A. Latham:
Microscopical Society of Illinois
608 South Dearborn Street
Chicago 5, Illinois
"Mar 1/53.
"Howland Atwood, Esq
"San Marino
"Calif.
"Dear Sir....

"I believe we corresponded in the 1890s. He sent me some small collections fresh from the Pacific Coast to aid in their study for bibliography. Most lived in vials in my N. window for quite some time much to the surprise of our friendly members of the Micro Section of the Academy & State Micro. Soc. Esply[Especially] the Pleurosigma[?] of several species. Fond of hiking & taking Sunday & day school lads & girls similar of [sic] today's Scouts - Using Nature for talks all over, using containers & tools as best he could get or make these[?][.] I sent sketches of small aquaira & easy to make [containers] for living material much to the Enjoyment of the classes. Life [Live?] was [worth] more to him than dead if to be had. He was in Seattle, Tacoma [and] Olympia [which] he said was especially good [for collectioning] then[,] & later in Blaine, Washington Territory. From here he sent a short paper on 'Notes on the habitat of Diatoms' & said how fortunate a worker should be if he finds any localities of habitats of growth of them! And [he] tried to urge others to send reports of the good fortune & stimulate others...

"In a letter he asked 'how to separate & clean diatoms in any quantity proportionate to their number as found?['] He wished others would do the favor to collectors (with reason) of lucky finds, localities, & be willing to Exchange Material for others not so well situated. Especially on the West[?] Coast & so compare the finds. Some forms seem to be only got in certain areas. Where to find - I said Tidal marshes, floating logs to skim the deposits, piers piles, boat bottoms, rocks....

"V. A. Latham"

———

1953: April 10
T. H. Kearney:
[Fragment of letter to "Calif. Acad. of Sciences...."]
"Dear Prof. Steers:...

"In the Botany of California (Vol. 2, p. 559) there is the following note by Sereno Watson (abbreviated):

"Mention should also be made of those whose collections though not made within the State, have been from so near its borders.... While in Oregon very important collections have been made...more recently by Rev. R. D. Nevius of the Dalles and Baker City....

"Sincerely yours,
"T. H. Kearney"

———

1953: April 21
Mary P. Van Loan, Union College:
Wells House
Union College
Schenectady 8, N.Y.
"April 21, 1953
"Mr. Howland Atwood
"Huntington Library
"San Marino 15, Calif.
"Dear Mr. Atwood:
"...A list of the graduates of the class of 1848 is enclosed.
"Sincerely yours,
/S/ Mary P. Van Loan
"(Mrs. c. J. Van Loan, Jr.)
"Administrative Assistant
[Enclosure]
"1848
"Graduates, A. B.
"Note—After occupation of each alumnus, the first place named is that of his residence at entrance; the second, that of his last known residence; the figures following indicate the year of his death....
"Nevius, John L. Missionary, Ovid, Chefoo, China, 93. D.D. Union, 1869; Princeton Theological Seminary, 1853; Missionary in China and Japan, 1854-93.
"Nevius, Reuben D. D.D., Ovid, Tacoma, Wash....
"—from Old Alumni Directory - 1907"

———

1953: April 24
Rev. Arthur Bell:
Reverend Cannon Arthur Bell, D.D.
818 North Fifth
Tacoma 3, Washington
"April 24, 1953
"Mr. Howland Atwood
"Huntington Library

"San Marino, California

"Dear Mr. Atwood:

"Your letter was received regarding Dr. Nevius and I find it rather difficult to get information that you asked; however these facts may be of use to you. The Tacoma Public Library tell me that they have the notice of his death from one of the papers of 1913. They give the different parishes where he worked from 1845-1913. You might write them.

"At the time of his death the only surviving relative was Mrs. T. F. Harris of Cleveland, Ohio to whom his papers and personal effects were probably sent.

"You might apply to the Bishop's Office...and ask them if they have any information. These in a fund known as the Nevius Fund which probably came from his family....

"Sincerely yours,
"Arthur Bell"

———

1953: May 6
Mrs. Edith Christiansen:
St. John's Episcopal Church
P.O. Box 4095
Mobile, Alabama
"May 6, 1953
"Huntington Library
"San Marino, California
"Dear Sir:

"In going through the church records I found very little about Dr. Nevius. From a brief history of the church I copy the following paragraph:

"On December 9th 1868, the names of the Revs. J. H. Tichnor, S. C. Harris, E. G. Perryman, Horace Stringfellow and R. D. Nevius were voted on by ballot. On the 3rd ballot Rev. R. D. Nevius received 4 votes, was duly elected and immediately notified by the Secretary of the Vestry. After some little correspondence about the state of the Parish and kindred matters, Mr. Nevius accepted the call January 11th, 1869, and arrived in February of that year, remaining as rector until February, 1872, just three years.'

"During this time he baptized 216, presented 111 for confirmation, married 61, and buried 120. The records show that on Oct. 17, 1870 Margaret Mercer Nevius, age 29, wife of Rector - died during a Yellow fever epidemic and was buried Oct. 18 by the Rev. T. A. Massey, D.D. Rev. Nevius also had yellow fever at this time.

"I also found in the records that in Nov. 1865 he had 2 funerals and 1 marriage, and in Jan. 1866 he held a Baptismal service.

"I regret that this information was not sent sooner but St. John's was without a rector for a year and I have worked here only a few months.
"Sincerely,
"Mrs. Edith Christiansen
"Sec."

———

1953: May 7
Tacoma General Hospital
The Fannie C. Paddock Memorial
Tacoma 3, Washington
"May 7, 1953
"Mr. Howland Atwood
"Huntington Library
"San Marino, 15, California
"Dear Mr. Atwood:

"I have attempted to discover the whereabouts of Dr. Nevins' [sic] papers, etc., but so far have had no success. Neither can I seem to find anyone who knows what years he was associated with the hospital.

"Our hospital was founded in 1882 at a site removed from where it now exists. I am enclosing a copy of our magazine with a short history of our hospital and photographs of the first and second buildings.

"We have been disassociated from the Episcopal Church since 1912. I would refer you for further information to the Episcopal Bishop of the Diocese of Olympia, Diocesan House, 1551 Tenth Avenue, North, Seattle, 2, Washington.
"Sincerely yours,
"W. J. Dobyns
"Director"

———

1953: May 22
Howland Atwood:
"Huntington Library
"San Marino 15,
"California
"May 22, 1953
"Clerk
"Pierce County Court House
"11th and South G Streets
"Tacoma, Washington
"Dear Sir,

"I am compiling a biography of Rev. Reuben Denton Nevius, D.D., Episcopal clergyman and missionary of the Pacific Northwest, who died in Tacoma, Washington Dec. 14, 1913.

"Do you have any records of Dr. Nevius? I have been trying to locate his papers, and to learn what became of his botanical books, herbarium and diatom collection. I thought perhaps he might have left a will that would give some clues. Do you know of any persons who might have information or other sources of information?

"Do you have any records of Oliver Whitmarsh[?] Bean who died in Tacoma in 1910?

"I will greatly appreciate any information you can send me.
"Sincerely,
"Howland Atwood"
[Reply typed at foot of page:]
"Dear Sir: We do not have the probate records of either of the above named parties on record in this court.
"Robt. L. Dykeman, Clerk"

———

1953: May 28
Tacoma Public Library:
"Tacoma Public Library
"May 28, 1953
"Mr. Howland Atwood
"Huntington Library
"San Marino 15, California
"Dear Mr. Atwood:

"The Tacoma Ledger of December 15, 1913 carries an obituary article plus a portrait of the Rev. R. D. Nevius and Ledger for December 15, 1913, page 7 carries the account of the funeral.... We also located an obituary item in the Tacoma News for December 15, 1913....

"At the time of his death Rev. Nevius lived at 1012 South 4th Street. Upon checking our city directories we find that a C. F. Biglow lived at that address at the time and according to the last telephone directory, just published, still lives there.* Howard D. Taylor at whose home Rev. Nevius died, lived for along time in Seattle. His widow, he married a second time, now lives at 418 Loreta Place, Apt. 316, Seattle, Washington."

"The library has no books written by Rev. Nevius nor are any listed in the Library of Congress catalogue.... One other possible source of information might be the Episcopalian Church, Diocese of Olympia, 1551 10th North, Seattle, Washington....

"Very truly yours,
"Miss Elfriede Gudelius, Head
"History, Travel & Biography"
*See replies below.

———

1953: n.d.

Julia S. Taylor:

"Dear Mr. Atwood -

"I am sorry not to be able to give you the desired information about Dr. Nevius. You see I am the second wife of the late Howard D. Taylor. The Mrs. Taylor to whom you have written passed away some twenty years ago. She has a brother, Paul E. Page of Tacoma, Washington. I do not know the street address, but I am sure he could give you some information as he and Mr. Taylor were associated in business together in Eagle Gorge.

"I do not know the Dr. Nevius was a guest at the Taylor home at the time of his death.

"Sincerely,

"Julia S. Taylor."

———

1953: June 11

Barrycrest

J. Neilson Barry

3852 S. W. Greenleaf Drive

Portland 1, Oregon

"June 11, 1953.

"Mr. Howard Atwood,

"Huntington Library,

"San Marino 15,

"California.

"Dear Mr. Atwood:

"....I was Registrar of the Episcopal Missionary District of Spokane for ten years, and of the Missionary District of Eastern Oregon for five years, and compiled elaborate records, but turned them over to the Church authorities. Such as have not been destroyed probably are not available. However I also had some material pertaining to Dr. Nevius, which I had retained, and sent them to Mr. Allen; who probably is now the most well-informed person for you to communicate.

"I was a clergyman of New York City and obtained permission from my Bishop to go to help in the Missionary Jurisdiction of Spokane in 1895 and volunteered three more times, with aggregate of a quarter of a century in eastern Washington and eastern Oregon. Everywhere I went I heard very much highest praise of good Dr. Nevius and usually found in every town a church that he had built. He seemed to be more than twins, but rather like all twelve Apostles, and as though all of his ministry had been in each town visited. While everybody seemed to have known him and esteemed him, he was everywhere greatly beloved.

"I hardly think that Bishop Paddock would have retained anything pertaining to history or to business until the next day.

"Dr. Nevius donated his library of scientific books to the Nevius Boys Club of St. Stephen's Parish, Baker, Oregon. They were all of the Civil War period, that not one boy of the club would even open to see if there might be any pictures. I managed to persuade the Public Library to accept, but only on conditions, that they might file separately under the various classifications and need not retain what would be of no value. Since all had long been obsolete I doubt whether the Library now has any.*

"When greatly advanced age caused good Dr. Nevius to give up his office-library, he allowed his friends to select all the books they wanted, and then sent what no one wanted to the boys' club, and told me I might have all I wanted. I found two I wanted, and was using one of them today. Twice he asked me to return some special book, and I waded through three large packing boxes of them, examining each. Apparently someone had got the two he wished; since neither was among the books sent. They were like a substantial headache wished in me [sic].

"He was like an imaginary fictional story-book character, and truly UBIQUITOUS. Apparently he was everywhere at the same time, with building churches as his everyday job. Few towns do not have a church that he built: and usually he was the first to start a mission in that town. If he had not been real it would have been like the mythical Paul Bunyan.

"He was much interested in scientific matters, and especially in anatoms. He most eagerly exulted in mud, which he examined with his pocket microscope for anatoms. At such infrequent intervals when he was not holding services or building churches he gave magic lantern lectures on anatoms. Everybody liked him so much that they attended. He was enthusiastic about anatoms, an A-Number-One expert. Building churches which 'stayed put'* was his Vocation. Anatoms was his Avocation. He probably dreamed of them at night, and mediated on them when awake.

"Mr. Allen can give particulars of his biography, and how not even Indians unpleasantly scalping travelers could stop him going through hostile Indian country to hold services....

"Once he planned giving two lectures, with magic lantern slides of anatoms in one town. He knew too much to condense an A.B.C. summary in only one hour, so divided [it] into two one-hour lectures. However —probably to joyous delight of otherwise eagerly impatient enthusiasts for one-hour preliminary instruction on anatoms, a very violent snowstorm and high wind, accompanied with zero weather, happened to come at the same time as his first lecture. He never broke an engagement, or ever was late for an appointment. Yet not even his proverbial strength was sufficient to enable him to wade through the snowdrifts and stand up against the wind. He was compelled to hire a cab, and somehow the driver managed to get the horses through the storm so that Dr. Nevius arrived on time. He was never late for anything—certainly not when giving a lecture on anatoms. However for some inexplicable cause only one enthusiast for anatoms braved the blizzard. Yet Dr. Nevius always held services however few might attend, and felt that such eagerness to learn of anatoms richly deserved reward, so he gave the full hour, with magic lantern slides as through the hall were over-crowded.

"The solitary audience sat by the stove and replenished the fuel to keep the stove red-hot, without the slightest evidence of impatience throughout the hour. Dr. Nevius then stated, that since that first preliminary lecture was introductory to the second, that he would gladly give the second and complementary lecture, if the one-man audience should so desire.

"He replied that he was perfectly willing to remain as long as Dr. Nevius might desire to keep on lecturing. He was the cab-driver by the warm stove, being paid for the time, and would stay as long as Dr. Nevius did not give the second part and that cab-driver never did hear the second part.

"The moral of this is not to be a cab-driver if you want more than the preliminary lecture on anatoms.

"Very sincerely,

"J. Neilson Barry."

[Corrections have been made to obvious typographical errors.]

*"stayed put:" Nevius's expression or Barry's?

*In checking in the library in 2001 I found only one book which may have belonged to Nevius or may have been presented by him. G.N.

Rev. J. Neilson Barry, n.d.:

"Dr. Nevius

"in 1895 I obtained permission from Bishop Potter of New York City to help in the Jurisdiction of Spokane.

"Everywhere I traveled here were warm and friendly remarks about good Doctor Nevius.

"Nearly everywhere there was a church he had erected.

"Apparently he seems always to have been everywhere at the same time—and usually building another church.

"The conventional memorial does not give link-up with normal activities.

"By naming the Parish house at Baker NEVIUS HALL, it insured that his memory would be kept fresh, and his name familiar.

"Nevius Hall has been sold. Another reminder is needed.

———

"Biographers will cite details of his innumerable Church activities. He was an ardent enthusiast for the Church, and an indefatigable worker and traveler. Even when hostile Indians made it unsafe to travel, even for a stagecoach, he still went on his journeys as usual.

"However, probably every man, besides his professional VOCATION has some

AVOCATION for mental relaxation and recreation.

"Dr. Nevius was absorbed in study of anatoms [sic]. He always carried a pocket microscope and delighted in scrutinizing slime of stagnant ponds for anatoms. Such interests the run-of-the-mill, garden-variety of people generally a little less than scientific analysis of Sanskrit grammar. However he made his lantern-slide lectures interesting and understandable—so far as anatoms can be understandable.

"He used to tell this story:

"The complicated matter of anatoms can not be made intelligible in less than two lantern-slide lectures; which were free.

"Since everybody liked him, everyone in a small town attended.

"Unfortunately for a first lecture the night was terrific. It was cold, and violent wind and fine penetrating drifting snow, and pitchy blackness. Not even the energy of Dr. Nevius was adequate to wade through the ever-increasing snow-drifts. Yet he Always Kept An Engagement.

"He had to hire a hack at the livery stable. It had trouble.

"On such a fearful night he had not expected anyone to attend.

"However, to his surprise, one man braved the terrible storm.

"Dr. Nevius felt that anybody who cared enough about anatoms to venture out on such a terrible night richly deserved the lecture. Therefore he gave it all, with his lantern slides, and was pleased that the lone man in his audience, who constantly replenished the stove, did not indicate the slightest sign of impatience.

"When he finished, he explained that this was only the first part and if the man should like, he would give the second part.

"The man replied that he was perfectly willing to remain as long as Dr. Nevius would like. It was warm and comfortable, and the night very horrible outside. He was the driver of the hack...."*

Rev. J. Neilson Barry, "Records"

[Minor changes made to punctuation]

*The account ends with a comma, suggesting it may have been continued on another page. This page only appears in the microfilmed records.

———

1953: June 19
Barrycrest
J. Neilson Barry
3852 Greenleaf Drive
Portland I, Oregon
"June 19, 1953.
"Mr. Howland Atwood,
        "Huntington Library,
            "San Marino 15,
                "California.
"Dear Mr. Atwood:
"I have just run across two photographs of Dr. Nevius, of about 1910. They were used for cuts in the Oregon Churchman of about that date.
"I know that the one with him and Bishop Paddock in front of St. Thomas Church Canyon City was taken about that date. I do not know when the other was taken, yet it is like Dr. Nevius looked at that date....
                "Very sincerely,
                "J. Neilson Barry."

———

1953: June 20
Mrs. C. Biglow:
"Tacoma June 20 1953
"Mr. Howland Atwood
"Dear Sir;
"Receiv[ed] your letter as my husband pass[ed] away at the age of 90 and I doubt if he would know. The doctor [Nevius] was up in years he was pass 84 [or 89] when he died; his wish was to cremate his body and send his ashes east I forgot the city to be layed along side of his mother. I never heard him speak of a sister. I do not remember when he was chaplain in the Fanny Paddock hospital that was a good many years ago & then I did not know the Dr. As far as leaving his estate for a Nevius

Fund, I don't think he had anything to leave. All his books & what belong[ed] to the Dr. was taken care of by some of his friends at the church. The two pastors who were his good friends have pass[ed] away. His picture I think hangs in Annie Wright Seminary, a school for girls in Tacoma. I am sorry I have no address of the Dr's friend or relatives. I am sorry I cannot give you more information about the Dr. Sorry I kept you waiting so long for an answer.
"Sincerely
"Mrs. C. Biglow
"excuse pencil
"writing.
[new page]
"Come to think of it [when] we move[d] in[to] this house [in] 1898 the Dr. I think was living their [sic, there] in Hospital. I know he ate his meals their. In a few years they torn down the old hospital & build a new one which we have now, and a short time afterward, he came to us and rented 2 rooms at $8.00 a month; & stay with us till his pass[ed] away."

———

1953: July 3
Clara R. Purdy:
"Miss Clara R. Purdy
"OVID, NEW YORK
"July 3, '53
"ans
"Dear Mr. Atwood,
"The Nevius book came promptly. I am glad you found something of interest in it.
"My brother copied inscriptions from Ovid cemetery, all he could find.
"Sincerely,
"Clara R Purdy
[enclosure]
Robert J. Purdy
32 Main Street
Ovid, N.Y.
Phone 20R
"Chester Eastman Apr 16, 1794—Mch 13 1879
"Children of Chester and Mary D. Eastman
"Mary 1833-1835
"Benjamin N. 1836-1840
"Hannah Birge 1835-1866
"Clinton D. Eastman July 15 1846 April 12 1901.
"Mary Denton Sept 11 1804 June 7th 1900
"widow of Benjamin H. Nevius
                "and
"Chester Eastman and mother of
"Reuben Nevius D.D.
        "Tacoma, Wash.
"John Nevius D.D.
        "Chefoo, China....
"Benjamin H. Nevius
"June 29th 1802 - October 10th 1830...."

1953: October 30
Barrycrest
J. Neilson Barry
3852 Greenleaf Dr.
Portland I, Oregon
"October 30, 1953
"Mr. Howland Atwood
        "San Marino,
            "California

III

"Dear Mr. Atwood:

"Although as Registrar for ten years of the District of Spokane and for five years of the District of Eastern Oregon I had occasion to record some data of earlier times with records of Dr. Nevius, it had only to do with such limited records.

"However having heard so much of him, I named Nevius Hall, in Baker, to insure commemoration. It was first burned, and after being re-built was sold, and apparently extinguished any memorial or commemoration of him.

"Unless, possibly, for some statistics, I had no occasion to write him, and did not meet him until Nevius Hall was dedicated [on May 7(?), 1909], when he talked more of his beloved anatoms than of early times out here, with some anecdotes of other people.

"The local people knew nothing of his early life.

"He often mentioned Tuscaloosa, Alabama, where, I think, he was stationed during the Civil War, and from there to be Rector of Trinity Church, Portland. I had heard that he was a New Englander, but not ever of his being elsewhere than Tuscaloosa.

[There follows a typescript of Nevius's entry in Lloyd's Clerical Directory, 1911, and an outline of the process to enter Holy Orders.]

"Dr. Nevius often spoke of Tuscaloosa, but it is not listed [in Lloyd's Directory]. My impression was that it was during the Civil War. There is hiatus in the clerical register 1856-1867.

"The GOSSIP I heard, but have nothing except gossip, is that the wife of Dr. Nevius was sick. I think smallpox. The doctor had ordered either (1) To give medicine at certain hours (2) Or else if she were asleep not to awaken her. I do not know which it was. Whatever it may have been, Dr. Nevius disobeyed. Either he awoke her to give medicine, or else he did not disturb her sleep and awaken her to give medicine. My impression is that he did not have the heart to disturb her when asleep. Whichever it was he disobeyed the doctor, and Dr. Nevius blamed himself because she died. Really probably nothing to do with it.

"The Gossip is that, in remorse he dedicated himself to missionary work....

"Bishop Leonidas Polk, Consecrated 1838, became a Confederate General in the Civil War, and created much dissention. It may be that it caused omission in the records, because of not recognizing some formalities. But I know nothing whatever except that Dr. Nevius often mentioned Tuscaloosa, but nowhere else back east. Possibly his being a Northern man in the deep South may have prevented "canonical" residence. He must, undoubtedly have been engaged in some religious activity, yet like my work among prisoners and outcasts not recognized by the Church but merely as "non parochial."

"You may find an interesting story in that hiatus.

"Very sincerely,
"J. Neilson Barry."

[1955]

1955: July 17
Barrycrest
J. Neilson Barry
3852 Greenleaf Dr.
Portland 1, Oregon
"July 17, 1955
"Dear Mr. Atwood:

"Dr. Nevius left the Spokane region when I first went there in 1895, sixty years ago. He had been away from eastern Oregon for many years prior to my going there in 1907. I never heard him preach, nor anyone mentioning the subject.

"He had his hobby, scientific—apparently of ANATOMS, and was enthusiastic. I have hear him lecture, with magic lantern slides. He had no vestige of the orator. He knew what he had to say, and what it was about, and said it understandably, and then stopped.

"The fundamental cardinal rules for a sermon are (1) Have something to say. (2) Say it. (3) Then *STOP*.

"He was a really GOOD man, and his presence and influence promoted righteousness in others. His sermons probably were dry, but sincere, and what he was

INSIDE made them effective, with what he did.

"Everywhere I went people always talked of him with esteem and affection; but never mentioned his preaching.

"As a conversationalist, he always had something worth-while to say and had a keen sense of humor and was good at causing visualizing of the 'picture.' I presume his sermons were like that—omitting the humor. I always enjoyed listening to him talk.

"'A man is known by his friends' is a saying, and probably also may be known by his books. He had a very large library, and when he moved, or something that caused him to dispose of it, instead of selling it he gave it away. Anybody who wanted anything might take it, and the clergymen 'skinned' [sic] it of religious and theological books.

"I named the Parish House of St. Stephen's parish at Baker, Oregon NEVIUS HALL in his honor. Our parochial Boy's Athletic Club adopted the name Nevius Boys' Club. He donated the remnant of his books to that club.

"About three or four large boxes arrived by freight. I do not think the clergymen had left even one book that one of those boys would even open. Yet if opened, would have read a page of it.

"It would have required many shelves, and there was no space for them and no money to construct them, and no one would have contributed a cent. It was like a gift of the proverbial white elephant.

"The Librarian of the Public Library balked. The Library was willing to accept a gift of such books as might be suitable, but only on condition that they could only take what they wanted.

"I had no place to store the huge cases, great big wooden boxes three to four feet. I had a baggage wagon take them to the library where the were put in a room.

"Dr. Nevius wanted a particular book and I had to go through all of the three or four boxes. It seemed interminable. It was not there. One of the clergymen probably had taken it.

"Later he wanted another. And I had to wade through them all again but it was not there. It was a relief when I went back to Washington, D.C. Many dreary hours of that sort of thing, twice, was sufficient.

"Subsequently Dr. Nevius went to Baker [in 1909?], expecting to find his gift to the Boys' Club on shelves at Nevius Hall. He was grievously disappointed. He went to the Library.

"They had stipulated that they would not keep such as they wanted by themselves, but would distribute to whatever classification they belonged. Such as they had selected were scattered. Probably the rest destroyed. He was much chagrined, and probably blamed me. Yet they were totally inappropriate for an athletic club.

"He said I might take as many as I wanted. One I am using frequently. I think I took two others, but have not retained them, but do not remember which they were.

"Most were scientific, of Civil War period; long obsolete.

"His favorite subject was of anatoms. He carried a pocket microscope and delighted in anatoms. His lectures with magic lantern slides were interesting, but I have very vague and indefinite comprehension of anatoms. They are related to algae and diatomaceous earth, and scum on stagnant pools. If he had not been a clergyman, he probably would have been an expert scientist for investigation of the earliest forms of life at the Smithsonian Institution in Washington, D.C.

"Very sincerely,
"J. Neilson Barry."

[1964]

ca. 1964:
Rand (1974) 51:
Nevius Hall at Baker was demolished between 1960 and 1964. The church silver was stolen in 1964.

[1969]

1969: September 19
Rev. Albert E. Allen:

"9/19/69
"Notes taken of Conversation w/ Mrs. Quinn Trott Neal - Trott...." See at ca. 1907 above.

[1980]

1980: December 24

David Powers:

Notes on Telephone conversation with Mrs. Bea Edmundson, Baker 523-5263:

Mrs. Edmundson did not recall any local traditions about the design of St. Stephen's. She suggested that I contact the Rev. Dick Toll, 1130 19th Ave. E., Seattle, 98112 (home: (206) 323-6099, cathedral: (206) 323-0300), because he was very interested in the history of St. Stephen's, and knowledgeable. She said that Helen Rand, author of the centennial history of St. Stephen's, is now in Boise.* She said that "Dr. Evans" (with the school system?) collected old photographs, and that Alice Warner, Secretary of the Baker Historical Society, should have information on old photographs.

David Powers, December 24, 1980

*I spoke to Mrs. Rand later, but she said that her memory was failing her and that she couldn't remember where her information came from.

———

1980: December 26

David Powers:

Notes on Telephone Conversation with Rev. Messrs. Dick Toll and Thomas E. Jessett:

On December 26, 1980, I spoke by telephone with the Rev. Dick Toll in Seattle. He was not familiar with the oral tradition that St. Stephen's, Baker was designed by anyone in particular. He did think there was a tradition that the design of the rose window had been copied from New York or Boston. He mentioned that all the stained glass came from England and was shipped "around the Horn and up the Columbia." He suggested I talk to Canon Tom Jessett, Wesley Gardens Retirement Home, Des Moines, Washington, telephone (206) 824-5000, which I did.

Canon Jessett was very familiar with Nevius, and noted three Nevius churches in Washington:

All Saints, Spokane - now demolished

St. John's, Olympia, now a Baptist church

Good Samaritan, Colfax - burned

All had square towers - especially Colfax, where "the tower was as big as the Church." It had to be removed while Mr. Jessett was rector because "it creaked when the wind blew." He noted that surveyors used this tower for a landmark for miles around. All these churches had nave, choir and chancel separated by steps.

Canon Jessett thought that Nevius "tried to duplicate the design of the church he came from, which was a usual custom then." He had no knowledge of the disposition of Nevus's papers, but suspected that they were lost. He observed that the Diocesan records only go back to 1924. Earlier records are at the Oregon Historical Society in Portland or are lost. A dispute arose when the Diocese moved from Tacoma to Seattle.

David Powers, December 26, 1980

———

1980: December 29

Rev. Thomas E. Jessett:

"Dec. 29, 1980

"Dear Mr. Powers:

"Re: The Rev. Reuben Denton Nevius, D.D.

"Looking [at] my History of St. John's Church of Olympia, which I wrote in 1941, I find that Dr. Nevius became rector of St. John's in July 1883. At the annual meeting on April 14, 1884, the subject of building a church was brought up.

"In the fall of 1886 Dr. Nevius attended the General Convention and sent a letter to the parish resigning, although this was not completed, due to the vestry's effort to get him to return, until March 2, 1887.

"Plans for the new church were drawn by C. N. Daniels of Tacoma, Wash., and

bids were called for in May 1888. From the appearance of the church it was not of Dr. Nevius' idea of a church. That is from the exterior, the interior resembles All Saints Cathedral in Spokane and the Church of the Good Samaritan in Colfax.

"Enclosed here with a reproduction of the church in Colfax which I hope will serve your purpose.

"Sincerely yours,
"Thomas E. Jessett (Rev. Canon)
"Historiographer Diocese of Olympia.

———

1989: June 29

Notes on telephone conversation with Mrs. Jean S. Eastman, Ovid, New York:

Mrs. Eastman and her sister have been compiling family records - she has Eastman and Denton family genealogies.

Denton family records indicate R. Denton Nevius's marriage was July 31, 1867. Clara Purdy died in 1966.

Half-siblings:

	Birth	Death
Hannah Eastman	Jan. 9, 1835	Jul. 10, 1866
Benjamin Eastman*	Jan 28, 1840	Jun 22, 1892
William Lyman Eastman	4/22/42	11/16/02
Mary Denton Eastman**	6/30/44	Mar 4, 1937
Clinton Eastman		Sep 15, 1846
4/12/01		

*Lived at Syracuse N.Y.{?]

**Married James Harris, lived in Pennsylvania and Cleveland, Ohio

———

1989: July 27

During the course of a week at the archives of the Episcopal Diocese of Olympia in Seattle, I learned from Diocesan Treasurer that the Nevius Fund had been depleted by the 1930s. In the late 1940s a gift of about $5,000 restored the fund and then in the 1950s it was combined with two other funds. The worth of this fund at the time was $1,943,804.

———

2000: January 29

Notes on telephone conversation with Mrs. Jean S. Eastman, Ocala, Florida, and Greg Nelson:

She said that the home of Nevius's grandfather, his mother's home, and the farmhouse of his half-brother, where she and her husband now live, are still standing. She has a picture of the home where Nevius visited his mother taken about 1875, with his mother standing in front.